FoxPro 2.5 for Windows:

Developing Full-Scale Applications

by Nelson King

A Subsidiary of
Henry Holt and Co., Inc.

a subsidiary of Henry Holt and Company, Inc.
115 West 18th Street
New York, New York, 10011

First Edition—1993

ISBN 1-55828-261-0

Printed in the United States of America.

10 9 8 7 6 5 4 3 2 1

MIS:Press books are available at special discounts for bulk purchases for sales promotions, premiums, fund-raising, or educational use. Special editions or book excerpts can also be created to specification.

For details contact: Special Sales Director
MIS:Press
a subsidiary of Henry Holt and Company, Inc.
115 West 18th Street
New York, New York 10011

Trademarks

Throughout this book, trademarked names are used. Rather than put a trademark symbol after every occurrence of a trademarked name, we used the names in an editorial fashion only, and to the benefit of the trademark owner, with no intention of infringement of the trademark. Where such designations appear in this book, they have been printed with initial caps.

Dedication

For Vita, Wer hat das Verständnis, and Kevin, who got it all started.

Acknowledgements

Ken Kaufmann and the gang at Nova Technology, Inc. And Mark Cherne and Jim Biggs at Microsoft Corporation.

Table of Contents

Introduction

This is a book for those who want to exploit the power of FoxPro 2.5 for Windows, including those who program and those who don't (yet). The main purpose of the book is to illuminate and help guide someone through the transitions from menu user to complete application builder. This is not an easy progression, but a welcome outcome. There's a near desperate need for efficient ways to create custom business applications, and for people with the skills to make it work. The FoxPro for Windows software development environment provides state-of-the-art data-management and programming tools to accomplish this. But keep in mind that since FoxPro for Windows is rich, complex, and powerful, it has a long learning curve if you are serious about tapping its power.

Does the word serious imply this book is not for beginners? Perhaps. It won't explain every word of jargon, or describe database concepts in great detail. It assumes that you are familiar with the basic mechanics of starting FoxPro for Windows, and using the menus, windows, and other simple procedures.

When you start with FoxPro for Windows, it's all too easy to jump into what seems to be an important component, for example the Screen Builder, without realizing that it has at least two prerequisites for successful use: a solid understanding of database management and of FoxPro programming. The Getting Started tutorials make it seem like using the Screen Builder is a snap. Parts of it are, until you reach something like a *code snippet*. What, you ask, is a code snippet? That's what a lot of professional programmers asked, too, when they first saw code snippets in FoxPro 2.0 for DOS. They were familiar with code fragments, but had no idea what Fox was trying to do with snippets. They learned. You can too, but it's definitely real programming.

This illustrates an important difficulty with learning a complex software development system like FoxPro for Windows. Many of the most important language elements and programming tools have simple uses that are easy enough for beginners, but they also have some extremely complex aspects more suitable for expert use. Unfortunately the reference manuals don't make this distinction. They simply list everything, which leaves you to sort out what to know and what to use. Without experience this is hard to do.

This book tries to help with the sorting process in a number of ways. First, it follows a (hopefully) natural progression. It's organized into four sections in roughly ascending order of expertise and in a pattern often followed by people working their way through FoxPro. Although this book is generally not a tutorial, there's a building-block approach inherent in this progression.

- **Using the System Menu** starts with the menu options to explore basic concepts. It provides an introduction to the roots of database management and the Xbase/FoxPro programming language.
- **Basic Programming** covers the most important commands and functions of the Xbase/FoxPro language in the context of the Command Window and in a simple program file.
- **Building Applications** gets into the more complex aspects of programming—in particular the user interface—and covers the FoxPro power tools.
- **Creating the Complete Application** deals with the issues involved in building a large scale application—security, network operation, data dictionaries, and so forth.

Second, the book emphasizes context, examining major programming and database elements as in this series of questions:

- Why is this here and where did it come from?
- What is it used for?

- What is it *not* used for?
- Are there alternatives?

Third, the book highlights the decision-making process inherent in database management and especially in creating database applications. This is a process that starts with design, goes on to programming, testing, installation, and perhaps even distribution and training. Approaching a database project, even a relatively simple one, has many steps and many things to consider.

Overall, the book is pointed in the direction of those who want to learn FoxPro programming and build their own software applications for Microsoft Windows. You can take this at whatever level you find useful. The goal is to provide some insight, some tips, some tricks, and, above all, a systematic view of what's going on with FoxPro for Windows database management.

There is a great deal of code that is appropriate for personal use. Some of this is in code fragments, example snippets, and miscellaneous functions. The largest portion of code on the accompanying disk is a more or less complete suite of "system maintenance" modules:

- Data Dictionary manager
- Print/output manager
- Security system
- System codes manager

This comprises more than 1 MB of FoxPro for Windows code. Each module is independent and may be plugged into your applications with a minimum of fuss. Most of the Section IV of the book is keyed to this software both to illustrate programming concepts and the approaches to an industrial-strength application. Make good use of the accompanying software on disk to save yourself a lot of keystrokes.

Few things in the world of computers have more facets and complexities than a full-blown data-management system. FoxPro for Windows, being both an end user system, and a complete software-development environment, is bigger than most. And what you see on the surface only hints at the major software issues involved: object oriented programming, client/server databases, user interface design, and application development, to name a few.

FoxPro 2.5 for Windows gives you *the* fastest database engine (the routines that organize and manipulate data) in the microcomputer business. FoxPro has built its reputation on speed. It has been challenged from time to time, but to this day FoxPro maintains an overall performance advantage.

FoxPro for Windows provides several avenues of approach to this engine. The simplest is through the System Menu.ib.ENDDO;. This is a "point-and-shoot" gallery of basic data-management operations like creating a file, indexing, and data entry. The second approach, part of the heritage from the DOS versions, is through the Command Window.ib.ENDDO; where database management commands can be typed and executed directly (providing you know what those commands are). The third approach is to write a program. FoxPro for Windows implements a superset of the Xbase programming language, with over 620 commands, functions, and operators, supported by an array of tools. With FoxPro for Windows it is possible to create small, personalized programs as well as fully professional applications of almost any size and complexity.

Section I

Using the FoxPro System Menu

Like other major-league data managers for Windows, FoxPro provides an interactive user interface. For the majority of people, this means using the standard FoxPro for Windows menu system, shown in Figure I.1.

The standard menu conforms to the conventions of all Microsoft Windows products. If you're at all familiar with using Windows, you should find it easy to maneuver in FoxPro for Windows menus.

NOTE

> This menu can be modified through programming (and often is). For this reason, the standard menu does not include the programs, screens, reports, and so on that you (or somebody) can create and attach to the system menu, or that can be called through the Run menu option.

As you learn to use the menus, you may find them a slightly odd mix, with things like reports buried in the Database option, and deletions in the Record option. In fact the word *database* is no longer used in conjunction with data files, though it persists in the system menu. These incongruities are mostly because the menu options are a blend of the old DOS FoxPro menus and the obligatory Windows approach.

Figure I.1
The Microsoft FoxPro for Windows menu system.

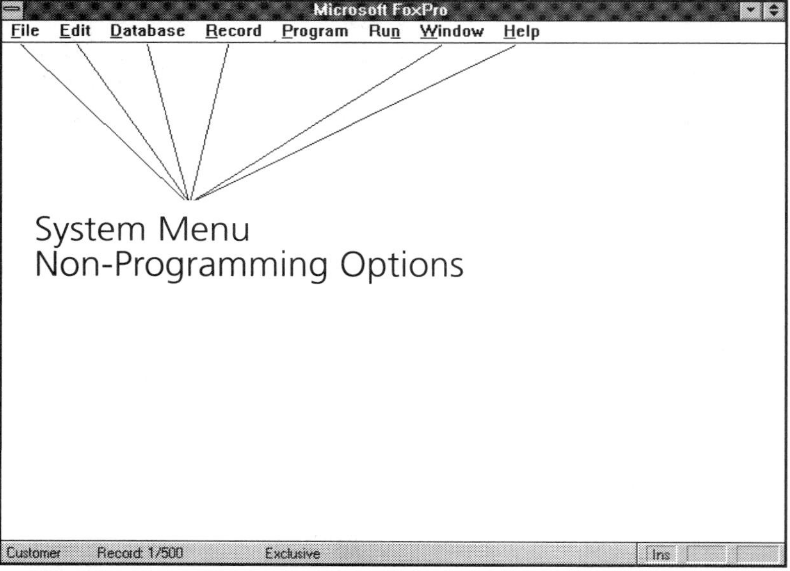

However, the user-friendly approach of a menu system still requires fundamental knowledge of database concepts, while at the same time it often appears to mask the user from those concepts. Much of the time, the system menu assumes you know what you are doing.

Rather than cover the details of how to use the system menu, easily found in the FoxPro for Windows manuals, this section emphasizes the options of the menu system in the context of database management concepts and practice. It treats the FoxPro for Windows menu system as a collection of convenient access points to the workings of database management. Even if you quickly go on to the programming aspects of FoxPro for Windows (Sections II through IV), there are elements of the menu system that continue to be very useful. Most people, including hard core programmers, use a combination of system menu, Command window, and programming to do much of their day-to-day database work.

Before going further, there are a few pieces of terminology and typography to explain.

Table I.1
Common terminology and typography.

Command verbs	Commands, the most basic building block of the Xbase language, are always expressed as verbs, for example, DO, COUNT, and so on. Most of the system menu is composed of command verbs. In this book command verbs are always capitalized.
Command clauses	Many of the command verbs also have additional clauses that modify or augment the action of the verb, such as: COUNT..FOR, BROWSE..FIELDS, and so on. In the system menu, many command clauses appear as push-button options in menu pop-up windows. Note that learning commands also means learning the clauses, which about triples the quantity.
Functions and operators	Functions and operators are the second building blocks of the language. Functions are in form roughly analogous to mathematical functions. They provide ways of extracting information, perform sub-processing, and so on, for example, DATE( ) and SEEK( ). Operators are less conspicuous, but equally important. They include =, +, -, /, *, > and <>.
Menu options	System menu options (the selections you can make in the menus) are capitalized on the first letter.
Sample code	Throughout the book, whenever the user might type something, a standard typewriter style font is used. All sample code is represented this way: `SET ALTERNATE ON`.

Chapter 1
File Organization

The Table Structure Window: Creating a DBF

In the beginning is the data file.

When you jump into FoxPro for Windows to do your first work, the first thing you have to do is create a data file and put some data in it. In many respects the whole point of data management is to get information into some sort of structured format so it can be accessed and manipulated. Even as you progress further and further into programming and application development, you will never be far from the data file—that's what programs like FoxPro for Windows are about. Otherwise, you might be working with Basic or C++. In FoxPro for Windows, as with all other Xbase products, the data file is called a DBF (a *database file*, so named because of the DOS file extension).

The mechanics of creating a DBF are deceptively simple. Activate the System Menu with mouse or keyboard, and select **File, New** (**Alt-F, N**), then select **TABLE/DBF** and press the **New** button, as in Figure 1.1 on the next page.

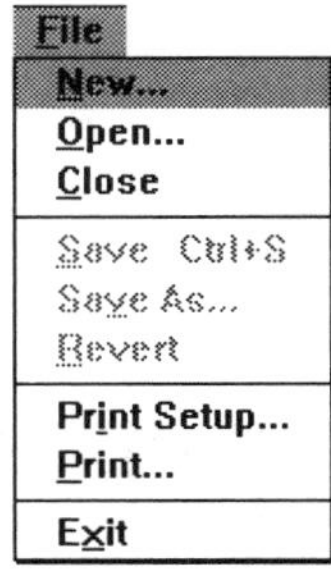

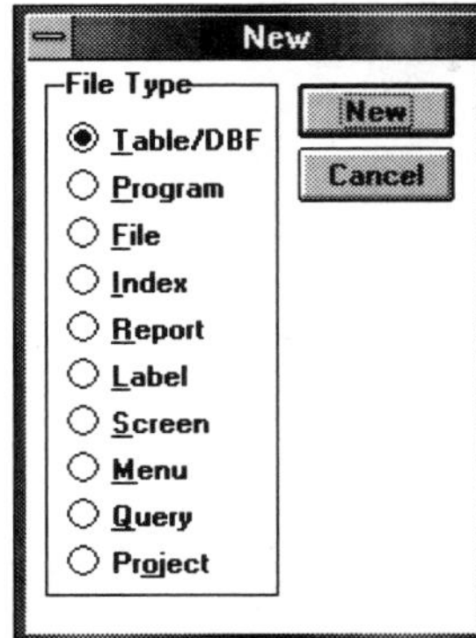

Figure 1.1
The File menu.

Up pops the Table Structure window (Figure 1.3), and you are in business. You need to specify a name for the file and define fields by name, type, and length, and that's it, basically. But yes, there is more to it than that.

It will help down the road to have a little more technical knowledge about the DBF. In fact, if you're inclined to visualize things, a mental "picture" is useful, and looks something like Figure 1.2.

Figure 1.2
The structure of a typical database file.

FILE HEADER

RECORDS	FIELD 1	FIELD 2	FIELD 3	FIELD 4	FIELD 5
1					
2					
3					
4					
5					
6					
7					
8					

The DBF has a beginning , a *header*, a middle, the *data records*, and an end, which is simply where the records stop. The header contains information about the DBF file, including how many records are in the file plus, the names of *fields* in a record and their properties. Following the header are the records (visualized as rows). For example, if the file contains a mailing list, then each record has the information of one mailing address. FoxPro for Windows can theoretically handle up to one billion records in a DBF.

The traditional way to depict files, records, and fields is in a table with rows (records) and columns (fields). The file on a disk doesn't actually look like the diagram, but it does have a similar sequence. In many other database systems and particularly in the Structured Query Language (SQL), the file itself is referred to as a *table*. In FoxPro for Windows, Microsoft is shifting from use of the word file to the word table. It still makes sense to talk about the data physically stored on disk as files, and uses tables to refer to the logical structure of the files.

Working in the Table Structure Window

Fact is, when you look at the Table Structure window, shown in Figure 1.3, you are looking at the most important single screen in FoxPro for Windows. This is where you define the fields for a table and then save the table structure to a DBF file on disk.

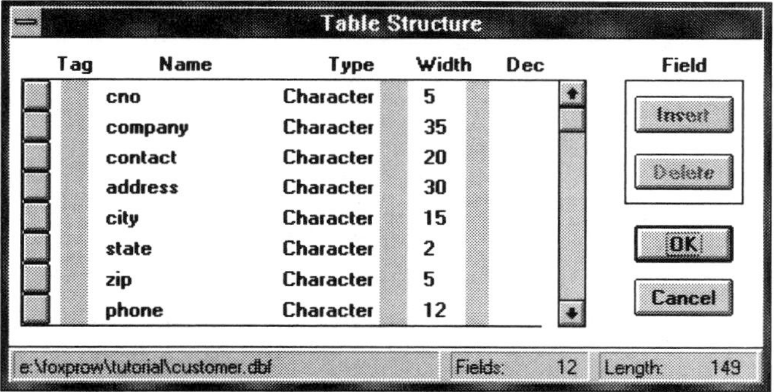

Figure 1.3 *The Table Structure window.*

Naming Data Files

If you only have three files in your database system, it doesn't really matter what you call them. On the other hand, if this is a somewhat larger system with say 100 to 200 files of different kinds, and is being developed or maintained by different people, then file naming is no longer trivial. Plus, since FoxPro for Windows has one foot still in DOS, all file names must conform to the miserable eight-dot-three limitation (<filename>.<extension>). It would be nice to name a file `Cedar Hills accounting payables` file.

But you can't. Instead you might have CHACCPAY.DBF. Everyone gets into the game of making mnemonic file names—names you might possibly remember. So, if it's a game, make some rules (conventions) and stick to them.

For example, because you may still use DOS commands to copy files, design your file names to support the process. The file extensions (.DBF, .CDX, and .FPT) help, but you can also put in something to distinguish files by project or type. For example, use the first two (or three) letters of the file name to represent the project or module. If the project is for lab services, begin all of those files with LS. If all of the files belong to the general ledger module, start them with GL.

```
GLMAIN.DBF |
GLUPDATE.DBF | GLACCTS.DBF
COPY GL*.DBF F:\GL\DBF
```

Common sense should rule. This is only the first of many times where size of project and number of people involved suggest that you establish conventions.

Preparation for Table Design

It's important to understand that in larger professional applications perhaps one-third of the total project time is spent *preparing* to design data tables and enter the field information. That's because each table and field represents a definition of what kind of data is supposed to be captured in a database system. And before you can specify what information should be captured, there usually have to be interviews, analysis, design, and discussion. This process is largely beyond the scope of this book, but it should never be underestimated. It's what's up front that counts. Do your early homework well, and you are much more likely to have a successful project.

The table fields are the most fundamental components of a FoxPro for Windows database system, and shouldn't be taken lightly. Not only is the choice of fields important, but decisions about naming, type, and length have impact on the entire data management and software development process. Most people tend to start with drawing up tentative table structures (the field design) on paper. This is disgraceful (not for the people, but for all Xbase products). Current methods of defining fields inside programs like FoxPro for Windows leave much to be desired. Missing are useful tools, like a way to view the structures of many files at once, or a method for annotating field names and other field information. This is the realm of a data dictionary, which will be explored in Section IV.

Whatever method you evolve to design tables and fields, the point still remains that thought should occur before committing the design to a real file. Not that it's difficult to change a FoxPro for Windows file. It's startlingly easy, at least until the files get filled with data. But as you will see in the discussions about relational data-management systems in this chapter, there is a lot to using the capability of FoxPro for Windows to organize information. Doing it right takes intelligence, diligence, experience, and some luck.

Creating Data Fields

What is a field? In an example using a table that is to contain a mailing list of customers, what would you expect? The customer's name, of course, probably in the form that separates last name and first name (so you can sort and search on the last name). Perhaps the "customer" is a company, then you would need to include company names in the table. Next you would need the customer's address, which has different components like street, city, and zip. Each of these things helps define what is meant by a customer. In your data table, each item will be a field.

The records of a table all have the same fields, visualized as the columns. In FoxPro for Windows there can be up to 255 fields in a table. The data in each column (field) must be of the same type and should be of similar content. For example if you define one field to hold a last name, then that field in every record should contain a person's last name, or else be blank. Each field is given a name (such as `Lastname`) and a few properties, depending on what type of data it is supposed to contain.

Field Names

When you start entering fields into a table, presumably after having done your homework on what fields to include, you need to give each field a name, data type, and width. Over a period of time, and even in a single project, you'll be creating a lot of fields. Without making too much of this, it's good practice to establish a naming convention for fields.

- **Make the fields mnemonic.** That is, they should remind you of what's in the field. Since you are limited to ten characters, this isn't always easy.
- **Use logical and consistent abbreviations**. Suppose you want a field to cover the total cost of goods sold. You could call the field `TCGS`, or `TOTALCOGS`. The first approach takes the first letter of each word. The second attempts to abbreviate while still retaining some meaning. Either way works. Like all programming conventions, there is no one way to do things. Some ways may be better in certain circumstances. The point with conventions is not so much how you do it, but that you do it consistently.
- **Use identical field names in different tables when they mean the same thing**. If you need a last name field in two different tables, call the field `LASTNAME` in both tables. Once upon a time this could cause problems, but today with the consistent use of an alias and the alias operator (for example, `INV.LASTNAME`), overlapping field names are safe. The gains from doing this include easier transfer of data between similar files, easier creation of relations between files, and most importantly it makes it clear that the content of the fields is in fact the same.

Data Types

Data typing is one of the first things in data management that can drive the average user crazy. It may be hard to understand why 5 + 6 = 11 but "5" + "6" = "56". The trick is the 5 and the "5" are different. The former is a number. With numbers you can do math. The latter is a character, just like the letter *b*. You can't do math with characters. The + (plus) sign used in "5"+"6" indicates *concatenation*—joining characters together.

Data types are largely an accommodation to computer limitations. Computers are so literal they have to be told exactly what type of information they are working with. Human beings have accepted the limitations and made useful categorizations out of them. Data types become one element of how a database "models" and captures the information of the real world. This is becoming more and more important as we introduce things like sound, images, and so on into our databases. The data types of fields dictate what we can do with the data. For example, later in this book you'll encounter many functions that are designed to work only with specific data types.

In FoxPro for Windows there are seven data/field types, shown in Table 1.1.

Table 1.1
FoxPro for Windows field types.

Data Type	Total Length of Field	Numeric Precision (decimal places)	Content
Character	1-254		Text (alpha-numeric)
Numeric	1-20	1-16	Simple Numbers
Date	8		All dates
Logical	1		True/false
Float	1-20	1-16	Advanced math, floating point
Memo	10		Free-form text (in DBF)
General	10		OLE data (in DBF)

In practice, the majority of fields are of character type (text). It's very important to remember that characters are not limited to the alphabet—spaces, symbols, and numbers can all be character data. The next most common field is the simple *numeric* type, which is used for almost all business numbers. These two data types cover about 85 percent of all fields.

The other five field types are specialists. The *date* field is one of the strangest, from a purely database management point of view. It appears to the user like 01/01/93, but is stored internally as a number. Whenever you work with a date field or variable, you have to remember it is not made up of characters.

Memo fields and their close cousins the *general* fields are worlds unto themselves. The memo field has historically been the free-form text field of the Xbase language. The data of memo fields is stored in a separate file (with an extension .FPT), and there are no limits to its length or structure, other than available disk space. That's why it became a convenient place to put anything that didn't fit into more standard field types. With FoxPro for Windows the .FPT also becomes the home of the Multimedia Extension—the general field, which can contain graphics, images, music, and more specifically any OLE information from other Windows programs.

The *logical field*, as its name implies, contains a logical value true or false (expressed as .t. or .f.). This field is frequently used in FoxPro to store input from screen check buttons. Finally, the *float field* is a numeric field with a floating decimal point, used mostly for special calculations where the decimal value is not known in advance.

Field Widths

As you quickly find out, every field must have a *width*—the amount of space allocated in the data file for each field in each record. Some widths are automatic by data type—memo (10), general (10), logical (1), and date (8). With character, numeric, and float fields, you must assign the width. With numeric and float fields you also need to indicate the number of decimal places, if any, which also adds to the total width of the field. It used to be conventional wisdom that you *always* sized fields at the minimum to save storage space on disk. The calculation of just how much space is simple:

1. Add up the widths of all the fields to equal the record size in bytes.
2. Multiply the result by the expected number of records.

This calculation is important, but be realistic, disk space is not the problem it was even a few years ago. The standard disk size is now 80MB, and most networks go into the hundreds of megabytes. The most important factor (outside of actual disk space available) is the number of records. If you're going to have one million records, then obviously a "few bytes here and there" can really add up. On the other hand, if you have a relatively small table, say under 5,000 records, it doesn't really matter if you add a few hundred kilobytes to the total.

Leave enough space for character and numeric fields to allow the data to grow, and especially with character fields so that they don't need data to be *truncated*—cut short. Truncation has an important side effect. It usually forces users to find ways of making their data fit, which means they make weird abbreviations that eventually no one understands. Whenever possible, give your fields enough room to cover the data.

Ordering Fields

The Table Structure window has buttons along the left side of the fields that allow you to set the order of fields. (Click and hold on the button with the mouse and then drag the field where you want it.) This can be useful in a couple of ways, keeping the most important fields near the top (since only eight can be displayed at a time), and grouping similar fields together. This is mostly cosmetic, but it helps to look good.

Creating an Index Tag

Before leaving the Table Structure window, there's one last thing to note—the Tag column. By clicking on this space for a field, you signal FoxPro for Windows to create an index tag. The tag is on one field only, in either ascending or descending order. As you'll soon see, this is a relatively limited capability. A complete discussion of indexes and tags follows shortly.

Using the View Window

The View window deserves special attention. Because of its versatility and visual presentation, it's a tool that remains valuable long after menu options have taken a back seat to programming. From this one spot, you can:

- Create, open, and modify data files.
- Define the setup for a table (field display, filters, and so forth.)
- Create and modify complex indexes.
- Open more than one table at a time.
- Set relations between tables.
- Set system configuration parameters.
- Create a "view" of a database system.

A lot of data management can be accomplished in the View window, although, as you can see in Figure 1.5 and Figure 1.6 on the next two pages, it may mean traversing quite a few screens.

Figure 1.5
The View window menu.

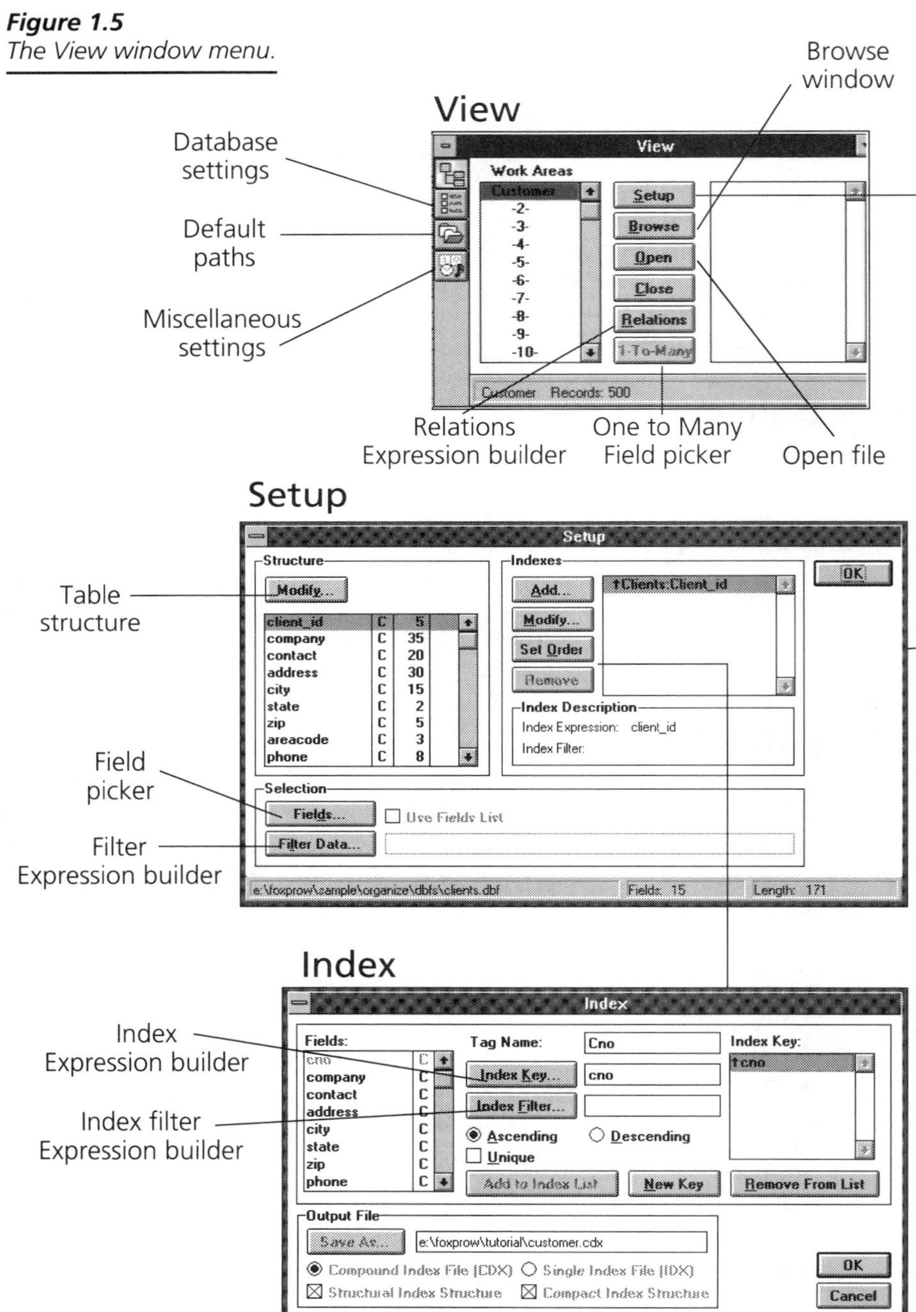

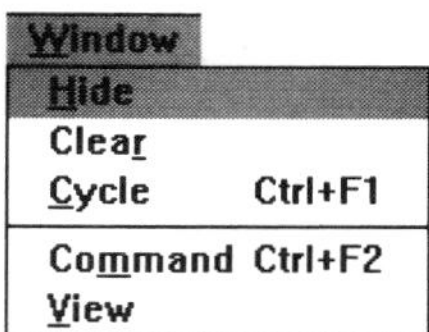

Figure 1.6
The Window menu.

The View window is reached from the system menu options Window, View (**Alt-W,V**). While this screen is hardly a paragon of GUI design, it does provide a relatively compact way of dealing with some complex database setup tasks like setting relations, and indexing. In short, the View window is *the* place where you can complete the job of organizing your data files, and set up a working data management session.

Incidentally, the View window is so named, because you can create what is called in SQL a view. You can open several tables at once, set their order (index), link related files, and set other conditions like fields to be displayed, and selection filters. All of this constitutes a view, which can be saved to disk for later use. Tables, index orders, links...this is a lot of jargon, but it's also the heart of what is very loosely called a *relational database system.*

Is This a *Relational* Database System?

In database management the word "relational" gets kicked around a lot. These days, the majority of data-management software claims to be relational, or at least "SQL compliant." It's difficult to get a fix on just what this means: There is a huge dichotomy between the various real world approaches to a relational system and the academic or theoretic definitions.

It should be noted that Microsoft does refer to FoxPro for Windows as a relational database management system (an RDBMS). What it should say is that FoxPro for Windows has some relational data management properties, such as table-to-table relations. This is not only closer to the truth, but puts the technical issues on the back burner. For most users, even those who program, it's not necessary to deal with all of the ins and outs of a true relational system. Instead, you need to satisfy various practical requirements using (among other things) the relational capabilities available in FoxPro for Windows.

In this context don't confuse the *design* of a relational database system with *setting relations* between tables in FoxPro for Windows. The relational database design is a complete world view of data management, including a mathematical theory and years of research. The latter is a simple mechanism provided by FoxPro for Windows to persistently link related files. These two kinds of relations are not kissing cousins.

Over time you need to develop a strong sense of what a relational system is about, how it is designed and implemented, what it's strengths and weaknesses are, and how to maintain it. A relational system, by almost any definition is above all an approach, or possibly even a mind-set, to organizing information. Your notion of this approach will grow through practice, but let's start with some basics.

In a sense, if not by formal definition, a *database* is a collection of data tables, indexes, and other support files that are considered related by subject matter. There are databases of auto parts, sports records, movies *ad infinitum*. When you set out to create a database project in FoxPro for Windows, whether it involves programming or not, you start with creating the elements of the database system—data files, indexes, and so forth, which may look something like Figure 1.6.

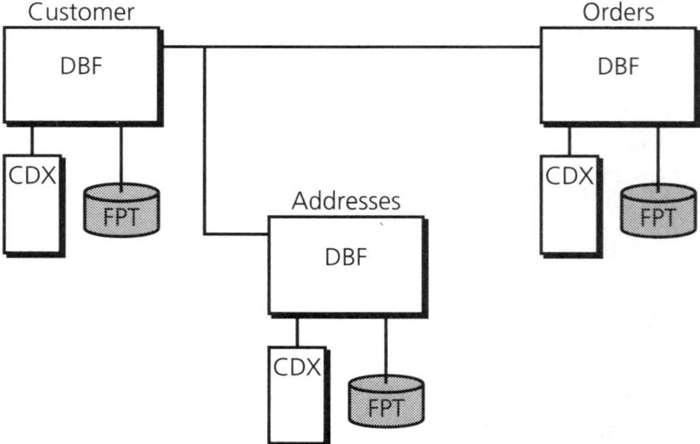

Figure 1.6 *A Fox Pro for Windows relational database system.*

In designing this database of customer information, the address information could have been included in the customer file. But suppose these business customers are likely to have more than one address—perhaps as many as four? In the customer file, you would need repetitive fields, something like city1, city2, city3, and city4 for each possible address. And if a customer has only one address? Then you have three sets of redundant blank address fields wasting space. A Solution? Put the addresses in a separate file, *linked* to the customer by a customer identification number (CUSTOMERID). In the address file the fields cover all of the standard address information (STREET, CITY, STATE, ZIP, PHONE). Each record contains one customer address, only now there is no limit on how many addresses a customer may have. There is also no wasted space.

This is an example of the way you approach information in a relational system, in this case separating repetitive data into another table. It illustrates one of the major elements of a relational system: the ability to break up a complex database into component parts (files), each a self contained unit of logically similar data. And then be able to *relate* these files so that they function as a single database.

There are many formal rules concerning the design of a relational database system, particularly in the choice of data tables and fields. The main process is called *normalization*, in which you segregate data items (fields) into tables. We'll come back to normalization several times in this book, but the topic is so broad, it's highly recommended to pick up a specialized book on the subject.

From time to time, however, the people you work for (clients, employers, yourself) might ask, "Why relational?" Or, more specifically, "I used to keep everything in one file. Now you've spread it all over ten files. What good will that do?" You need to do more than stammer, so here's a thumbnail list of the *positive* reasons for a relationally designed database:

- **Maintainability**. Or, in other words, relational systems tend to be robust. For the most part they are easier to modify and maintain than other systems. By putting differentiable data into separate files, changes in one file don't mess up data in other files.
- **Formal consistency**. The design and implementation of relational systems is guided by a formal theory. This tends to make relational products more standard and comprehensible.
- **The SQL standard**. The Structured Query Language, which is based on the relational database system design, has become a database industry standard for doing all kinds of queries.

Of course there is also a *negative* side to a relational system. It's your discretion about how much you say of this:

- **Performance problems**. The mechanics of linking and doing constant lookups in a number of tables puts a heavy burden on the CPU and disk drives, especially in local area networks. Relational systems, particularly badly designed ones, can be embarrassingly slow.

- **Proliferation of files**. Relational systems tend to sprout data files, index files, other kinds of files like mushrooms after a rain. After a while you've got 300 files in a directory, half of which you have no idea what they do.
- **Data integrity problems**. These systems are very dependent on having good, clean data, especially in primary index fields. Most relational systems handle various kinds of data integrity problems only with a considerable amount of effort on the part of the user or programmer.

The concept of a relational database system, like some other aspects of computing, tends to have staunch followers and an air of near religiosity about its theory and practice. Don't be put off either by the strident and demanding tone of the purists, or the apparent complexity of the basic theory. Relational systems have a very strong place in the world of data management, though they are certainly not the best in every situation.

You will probably find in practice that in the FoxPro for Windows environment, necessity, ingenuity, and the wide range of tools available can lead you far afield from pure relational database management. This hazards a lack of discipline and consistency, which can be bad news in any kind of collective development effort. But you are still free to solve a problem, using whatever it takes.

View Window: Setup

The Setup button of the View Window puts you into the Setup window, shown in Figure 1.7, the master-control screen for data tables.

The Setup Window is largely informational and provides you with a gateway to other windows where you actually do something. There are three main areas represented: Table Structure, Table Indexes, and Table or View Selection. These areas are all accessed via buttons:

- **Structure Modify** puts you into the Table Structure window where you can add or modify fields in a table.
- **Index Add** and **Modify** get you into the Index window to build or change the indexing of a table.
- **Index Set Order** makes any index you've selected the "master" for the table, which sets it's sort order.

Figure 1.7
The Setup window.

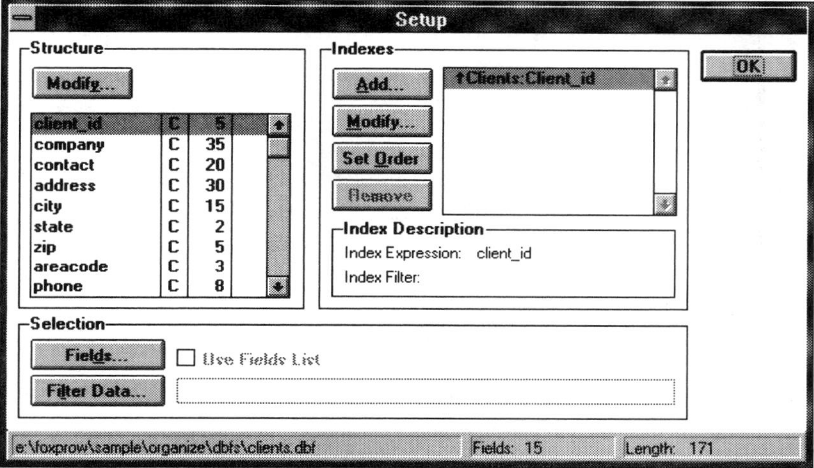

- **Index Remove** deletes an existing index.
- **Selection Fields** allows you to choose which fields will be visible for processing and display (as in a browse).
- **Selection Filter Data** opens a Filter Expression Builder where you can specify what data in a table will be visible for processing or display.

Some of the capabilities of the View window, such as setting filters, field display, and browses, are be covered in other chapters. Here, the focus is on using the View window for table organization, especially indexing.

View Window: Indexing

Once a data file has been created, you will usually add indexes to the table. This can be done in either: the Modify Structure window, or the View window. The View window is by far the most comprehensive and useful of the two. From the Setup window, in the Index section there are two buttons Add and Modify that bring you into the Index window, shown in Figure 1.8.

Figure 1.8
The Index window.

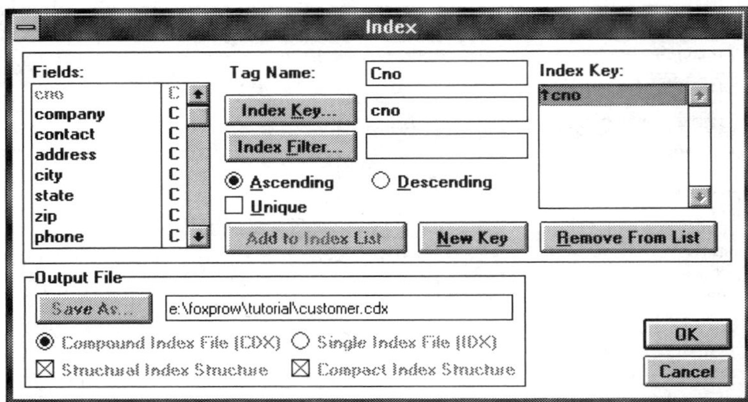

There may appear to be a lot going on in this screen. Relax, 95 percent of the time the only thing you need to do is select the Index Key button, either to create a new index or modify an existing one. But before getting into making indexes, some background is important.

Indexing

Outside of creating the DBF files, indexing is the most important component of file organization in FoxPro for Windows. It's a rare data file that doesn't have one or more indexes. Why? Indexes provide all of the following:

- A "sort" of the file into a specific processing order.
- The ability to do an instantaneous search.
- Support for relational links between files.
- Support for the Rushmore Technology.

NOTE

Why mince words? Indexing is *vital*. Much of the speed and efficiency of the FoxPro system comes from it's exploitation of indexing. It's very important for you to have a strong grasp of indexing, and use the heck out of it.

What is an Index?

Here's an old analogy: A library has a jillion books, stored in a mile of stacks. To find one book you could walk (run?) along the mile, searching until you happen to find the book you want. Hopefully the books are arranged in the stacks by some kind of order, say alphabetically. Then you only need to get to the general location of the book title to home in on the volume you want.

But what if you don't know the title of the book? Let's say you only know the author. Unfortunately it's physically impractical to rearrange all the books alphabetically by author. You don't want to resort to a random search of all the books. Of course, the library has a card catalog. You learned this in grade school. The card catalog lists every book in the library by title, author, and topic. It also provides an exact numbering system that directs you to the location in the stacks where the book is (supposed) to be located.

Like the library of books, a data file can be sorted physically (record-by-record) in some order as in Figure 1.9. But it can only be sorted one way at a time, and to resort anything but a very small file for each change in order is impractical. So, most data management systems use indexes, in much the same way as the card catalog.

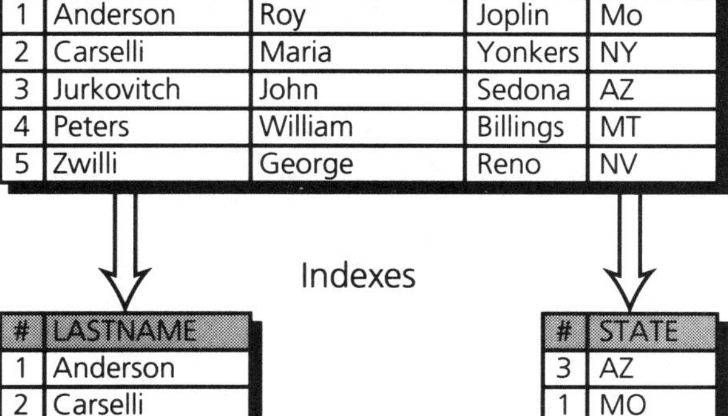

Data Table

#	LASTNAME	FIRSTNAME	CITY	STATE
1	Anderson	Roy	Joplin	Mo
2	Carselli	Maria	Yonkers	NY
3	Jurkovitch	John	Sedona	AZ
4	Peters	William	Billings	MT
5	Zwilli	George	Reno	NV

Indexes

#	LASTNAME
1	Anderson
2	Carselli
3	Jurkovitch
4	Peters
5	Zwilli

#	STATE
3	AZ
1	MO
4	MT
5	NV
2	NY

Figure 1.9 *Data table indexing.*

Like the card catalog, an index to a data file is maintained separately. This way you can have many indexes available. In the FoxPro system, when you index a file, you create a subfile. The actual structure of a FoxPro for Windows index is quite complicated, though essentially it is similar to a data file in that it has a header (containing information about the index), and *node* records that hold the content of the index key and a pointer to either another node or to an actual record in the data file. Each index is itself sorted in some order, for example alphabetically. How it's sorted depends on the data type of the index key.

Index Keys

In FoxPro for Windows the simplest key for an index is a single field. Most of the fields in a data table are candidates to be an index key (except memo and general fields). Using Table 1.2 as a sample, LASTNAME could be a key. Its index would be a sorted list of all of the last names in the table combined with the record number location in the data table. If the key is a character field, then the index is sorted alphabetically. You can specify if you want the order to be ascending (A to Z) or descending (Z to A). Likewise, if the key is a date it can be sorted from most current to oldest, or from oldest to most current.

When you search for a name, "Smith," the lookup routine uses the index LASTNAME and tries to match the contents of its key (which is, of course, last names) with your search name. If a match is found, an associated record number points to the location in the data table where the record for Smith is located.

Table 1.2
A sample table.

Record#	Lastname	Firstname	City	State
1	Brown	John	Bozeman	MT
2	Smith	Pamela	Walker	MN
3	Zybrinski	Leonid	Chicago	IL

The Xbase language, and FoxPro for Windows in particular, are unusually flexible about the construction of index keys. They can be any of the following:

- A single field.
- Two or more fields concatenated.
- One or more fields with FoxPro for Windows functions and operators.
- All of the above, with the addition of user defined functions (UDFs).

In practice the vast majority of indexes are on a single field. This has been accentuated even further by the Rushmore Technology, which can best use single field indexes. On the other hand there are many many cases where specialized indexes are needed to group and look up information.

Choosing Index Keys

When you look at the structure of a data table, how do you know what to index and what keys to use? The truth is, it's hard to anticipate every index. But there are some basic questions, that depend on your estimation of what the users of a table are likely to want.

- What will be the primary key?
- What will be secondary key(s)?
- What are the probable sort orders?
- What keys will be needed for a specialized lookup?
- What keys will be needed for the Rushmore Technology?

Let's apply these questions to the sample in Table 1.3 on the next page.

Table 1.3
A sample data table structure.

Field	Type	Width
CustomerID	C	8
Lastname	C	45
Midname	C	20
Firstname	C	25
Company	C	60
Street	C	50
City	C	30
State	C	2
Zip	C	9
Phonehome	C	14
Phonework	C	14
Spousename	C	25
Firstorder	D	8
Custtype	C	2
Status	C	1

The first two questions are about keys that are more technical in nature. The *primary key* of a table is usually the default sort order and includes the field(s) that uniquely identify each record. A very large percentage of the time the primary key is (or should be) some kind of unique ID, index number, or something similar as in part number or customer ID. The CUSTOMERID field above, for example, is an eight-character number unique to each customer. In FoxPro for Windows a table is not required to have a primary key, but about 98 percent of them do. *Secondary key*(s) are those used by a table as a lookup into other tables. CUSTTYPE above is a field containing a code whose full definition is located in another table. To show that a customer of type BS means Big Spender you would do a lookup (probably into a primary key) of a codes table. Secondary keys are sometimes called *foreign keys*, which reinforces the idea that they point elsewhere for their meaning. Both primary and secondary keys are typically single fields, although there are plenty of exceptions.

Usually, when somebody says "sort order," the thought is for output—a report, display on screen, and so on. It could also apply to a processing order inside of a program. In any case when you look at the structure of a table, think about the ways it is likely to be used in reports, label runs, and the like. If any of the fields, or combinations of the fields, stand out in this respect then they should be made index tags. In the above table, the ZIP and LASTNAME fields are good candidates for setting a sort order.

Finally many tables contain information that is not generic enough to be a primary key, but is used often and in specific ways. For example in the above table, let's say that a constantly used lookup is based on entering a customer's last and first name. This requires a concatenated key of the LASTNAME+FIRSTNAME fields. Expressions like this are entered by selecting the Field Expression button in the Index Window, then using the Index Expression Builder window. (This is four windows down from the View Window, and a pain to get at—one of the reasons many people move on to direct commands in the command window to do this kind of database work.)

It's often easy enough to look at a file structure and pick out the top candidates for an index. Most of the indexes (and keys) will be of the single field variety. This is also the way to prepare for the Rushmore Technology. A word of caution, however. Don't get carried away with making indexes. What FoxPro gives in query speed with indexes, it takes away when adding to or updating a file with many indexes. Every time you add a record, every index must be updated. The overhead for this can be anywhere from considerable to unbelievable—especially on a local area network. This, like so many other decision points in building a database application, requires your good judgment on balancing requirements and constraints.

Sorting Versus Indexing

The data file itself may or may not be sorted. There is an important distinction between sorting and indexing. Sorting *physically* rearranges the records in a data file so that they are in a particular order. Indexing *creates a separate file* that is sorted, but makes no changes in the data file itself. The advantage to this is that the index file is much smaller than the data file, and it is independent. Changes in the index file have no affect on the data file. On the other hand, indexes introduce a number of real-world complications. There are several ways that an index file can be put out of synch with the data file. Most of them are caused by relatively infrequent incidents such as power outages, user reboots, and program crashes. The FoxPro for Windows indexing system is quite robust. But no indexed database system is free of problems, which means that special provision must be made for rebuilding indexes.

Compound Index Files

FoxPro for Windows supports two kinds of index files—standalone index (IDX), and compound index (CDX) as shown in Figure 1.10.

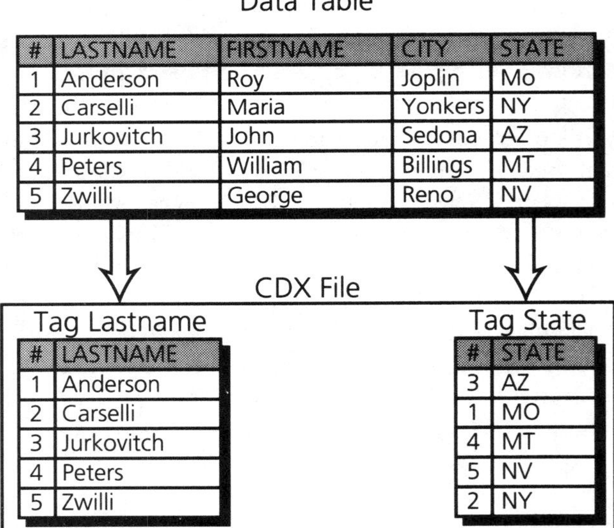

Figure 1.10
The CDX index file.

When a compound index file has the same name as the data file it is also known as a *structural index file*. Other than seeing IDX files in older applications, forget 'em. Since FoxPro for Windows is a new product, forget the past and go exclusively with compound index files . There are at least four good reasons:

- FoxPro for Windows automatically maintains (updates) all indexes in a CDX.
- One file holds all of the indexes for a data table, which uses less DOS file handles.

- There is a performance advantage especially when using Rushmore Technology.
- It's easier to keep track of indexes when they're all in one place.

Working with structural indexes couldn't be much easier. FoxPro for Windows itself assumes you're working with a structural CDX, so whenever you define an index in the View Window it creates a *tag*—the name for an index within a compound index file. If a CDX file doesn't already exist, FoxPro for Windows creates one with the same name as the data file (a structural CDX). The tag is automatically added to the CDX file and is be opened and updated whenever you open the data table.

However, there is one small "gotcha" to using tags in a CDX file. When you open your data table, the CDX is also opened with all of its tags. But no tag is applied to the data table. You have to specify a tag to set the order and become the master index. This is done in the Index window by selecting a tag and clicking on the **Set Order** button (or press **O**). A tiny key icon then appears next to the tag (a nice GUI feedback).

Building an Index Key

For starters, an index key has to be built on fields in a table. This may seem obvious, until later when you may want to index an array—a problem, since indexing is strictly for data tables. To create a new index, begin with entering the index key. In the View window, select the appropriate table. Then select the **Setup** button. From the SETUP window, select **Add** in the index section, which puts you in the Index window. Here you select the **Index Key** button to enter the name of the field, or other expression that will be the key.

Much of the time, this means selecting a field from the field list, and that's that. In this case, the key is the single field, and the tag has the same name as the field.

```
Key: LASTNAME                                    Tag: LASTNAME
```

Concatenated keys are built by using a plus sign to join fields, which can only be used with character fields or fields that have been converted to character.

```
Key: LASTNAME+FIRSTNAME                          Tag: LASTFIRST
```

The native FoxPro functions are often used in keys, for example to convert a noncharacter field, such as date, into character data:

```
Key: LASTNAME+DTOC(FIRSTORDER)          Tag: FIRSTORDER
```

Sometimes to reduce the size of a key, or to standardize the key against future changes in the width of a key field, the TRIM( ) function is used:

```
Key: TRIM(LASTNAME)+TRIM(FIRSTNAME)     Tag: TLASTFIRST
```

In some special cases, you may need to create a function of your own, a User Defined Function or UDF, and use this in the key. You do this when there is no built-in FoxPro for Windows function, or would be too clumsy to use. A simple example would be the situation where you need a lookup based on the mixed case spelling of names (for example, not browning, or BROWNING, but specifically Browning). There is a FoxPro function called PROPER( ) but this function merely capitalizes the first letter of each word. This won't work for some names (like McDonnell). So perhaps you create your own function called NameCap()to do the job, and you put it into the key:

```
Key: NameCap(LASTNAME)                  Tag: CAPLAST
```

The possible combinations for a key are vast. On the other hand, you need to be creative only occasionally. Later in this section a lot more will be covered in using functions, UDFs, and building expressions. As your general knowledge of FoxPro increases, the more you will know about making index keys to fit any situation.

Once you've specified the key, FoxPro for Windows can strut its stuff. It's amazing to see 100,000 records index in a couple of minutes. The speed with which indexes are built tends to encourage their liberal use. With small files, say less than 25,000 records, indexing takes a negligible amount of time. However in larger files, say 100,000 records or more, ten indexes may take a long time, even on very fast equipment.

Unique Indexes

You may have noticed the checkbox in the center of the Index Window: Unique. When you select this option, FoxPro for Windows produces an index that has no duplicate keys. Each entry in the index is unique. It's presence is a reminder of an old problem in data management.

It is often said that one of the big weaknesses of Xbase data management systems is their inability to automatically enforce index uniqueness. While it's not true that all indexes, or even primary keys, must be completely unique, much of the time they do. A little thought would reveal that having one customer with multiple IDs could lead to chaos in accounting, not to mention creating redundant data.

Enforcement of key field uniqueness in FoxPro for Windows is left to programming. However, when you specify that an index be built uniquely, all nonunique entries will be excluded. This doesn't do anything about duplicate keys—like remove them—but for some uses it at least hides duplicates from processing.

NOTE

Incidentally, building a unique index and getting a count of the records included (with SET TALK ON you'll automatically get a count), then subtracting that number from the total number of records in the table should give you the number of duplicates keys. Finding and eradicating them is another matter.

Indexes and Rushmore Technology

With FoxPro for Windows there are two main ways to "search" a data table, sequentially—record-by-record—or via an index. Just like the library analogy, the sequential search can be very time consuming. So most searches are done with an index. Until the advent of the Rushmore Technology, several of the main search commands (LOCATE, LIST, and FOR) worked sequentially and were practically useless in very large tables. The Rushmore Technology changed all that by incorporating indexes into the way these commands execute.

The Rushmore Technology changed a lot of things in FoxPro. It not only became the main claim to fame and the engine behind the SQL/RQBE capability, but also the workhorse behind the scenes. Accordingly, it would seem care and feeding of Rushmore should become a priority. Unfortunately, this is easier said than done. The inner workings of the Rushmore system are patented and have never been published, although some more or less educated guesses have been made. However, in practice it's sometimes difficult to predict what Rushmore will do and what kind of setup it should have.

We do know that Rushmore likes indexes, particularly single field indexes. If it finds these available, it can go to work immediately. Otherwise it may try to create indexes of its own, which in very big files is a problem. The key word for indexes is availability. Rushmore does not like to be forced to use a particular index. If you invoke a Rushmore based command like **BROWSE FOR** with an index tag already open, you may slow it down. The standard wisdom is to **SET ORDER TO** (close all indexes) before using Rushmore. This allows it to make it's own index selections.

Rushmore can use complex indexes (concatenated, with functions, and so on) but this has proven to be a hit-or-miss proposition. The safest bet is to provide all of the appropriate single field indexes on which a table might reasonably be queried. It should be emphasized this does not mean you should index all the fields of a table (called *table inversion*). If certain data is never or rarely queried, then indexes will not only be superfluous, but will also slow down other kinds of processing.

Table Relations

Once the data files have been created and indexes defined, the tables of a database are ready for relations. As pointed out earlier, a relational database uses links between tables to allow distribution of information into many files. These links are created between one table and the index key (typically the primary key) of another table. There are two kinds of links—a *lookup* and a *relation*. The lookup, as its name implies, takes the content of one table (the source or parent table) and searches in an index key of another table (the target or child table) for a match. If the indexed search is successful the data in the target record is available. A relation is a similar matching link, but it does an automatic lookup in the target table every time a source record changes. This is an important distinction. Both methods are based on doing a match from one table into an index key of another table, but the lookup is a one-at-a-time shot and a relation is a persistent link between the two tables. You need to learn how to distinguish between the two, and to learn when to use a lookup and when to set a relation.

In some cases there is no option. The BROWSE is one place where you *must* use relations to display data from other tables. On the other hand certain on-demand operations, such as when the user makes a menu choice or selects an action button, are usually best done with lookups. There are other circumstances, particularly in programming loops, where you need to make careful decisions about repeated lookups vs. a relation. Both techniques are based on indexing and are very fast, but repeating an operation thousands of times in a loop can make a difference. The point is to avoid thinking, "This is a relational database so I should be using only relations." Sometimes there are other more appropriate methods.

Another point worth highlighting is the relative flexibility of establishing a relational link. The only "rule" is that the link be a legitimate and useful index relationship. Figure 1.11 gives some illustrations.

Figure 1.11
Relational link candidates.

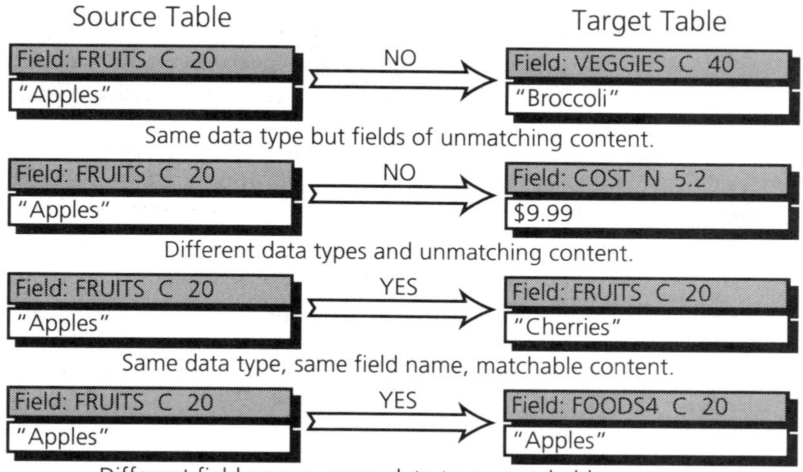

One-to-Many Relations

As a final option for file setup in the View Window, you can choose to make a relation between two tables a *one-to-many relation*. In the language of relational data systems, a one-to-many relation has a special place. It simply means that a single record in a source file (*parent*) is related to many records in the target file (*child*). A customer with many orders is a typical example. There is one entry for each customer in the customer table, but there may be many order records per customer in the order file. In FoxPro for Windows a one-to-many relationship can be established from the View window by selecting the source (parent) table, and then choosing the **1 to Many** button. This brings up the 1-To-Many window, shown in Figure 1.12.

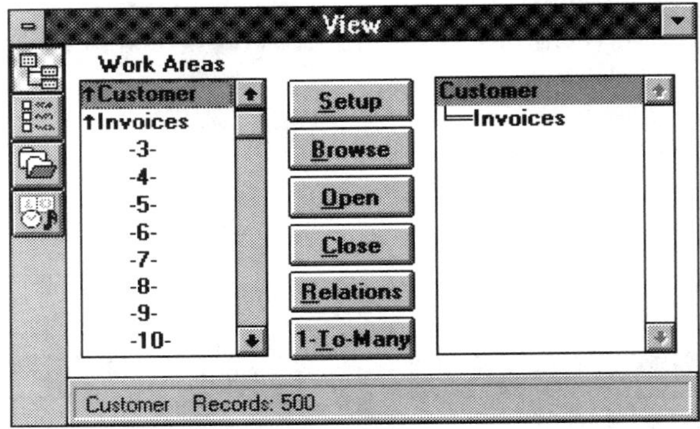

Figure 1.12
The 1-To-Many View window.

The left panel of Figure 1.12 shows a list of candidate tables for the one-to-many relation. Simply clicking on the one(s) you want completes the process. From this point FoxPro for Windows treats a record of the parent table and all of the related records in the child table as one set of records. This is particularly useful in a Browse dialog box, shown in Figure 1.13, since FoxPro will screen the information from the parent record followed by all of the child records, while blanking the redundant data that normally would accompany each of those records.

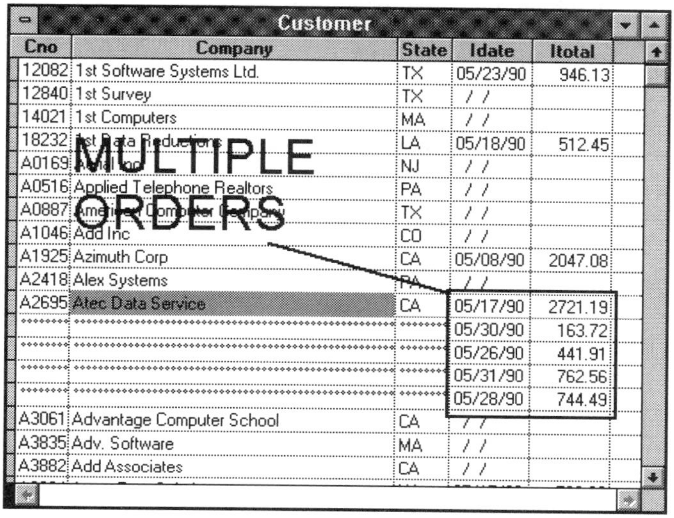

Customer

Cno	Company	State	Idate	Itotal
12082	1st Software Systems Ltd.	TX	05/23/90	946.13
12840	1st Survey	TX	/ /	
14021	1st Computers	MA	/ /	
18232	1st Data Reductions	LA	05/18/90	512.45
A0169	[illegible] Inc	NJ	/ /	
A0516	Applied Telephone Realtors	PA	/ /	
A0887	American Computer Company	TX	/ /	
A1046	Add Inc	CO	/ /	
A1925	Azimuth Corp	CA	05/08/90	2047.08
A2418	Alex Systems	PA	/ /	
A2695	Atec Data Service	CA	05/17/90	2721.19
			05/30/90	163.72
			05/26/90	441.91
			05/31/90	762.56
			05/28/90	744.49
A3061	Advantage Computer School	CA	/ /	
A3835	Adv. Software	MA	/ /	
A3882	Add Associates	CA	/ /	

MULTIPLE ORDERS

Figure 1.13 *The Browse dialog box with a 1-To-Many view.*

Chapter 2
Data Entry and Edit

efore diving into the menu options that make up data entry and edit, it's important to first cover some very basic concepts:

- Variables
- Expressions
- Input: append
- Input: edit
- Editing text
- The Text menu

Variables

You already know about one kind of variable, fields. A field is like a container whose content conforms to a certain definition (such as data type and width), but can also be different from record to record (variable). However, it's not common practice to refer to fields as variables. Variables are more of a mathematical and programming notion, as in the following example.

```
cLastName = "JOHNSON"
```

In the Xbase programming language cLastName becomes a variable by virtue of assigning it the value "JOHNSON". The equal sign in this case means "assign the value to" or "store in" and reads like "Store JOHNSON" in the variable cLastname." In fact there is an alternate way of doing the same thing:

```
STORE "JOHNSON" TO cLastName
```

This actually expresses what is happening better than the equal sign. But it takes more keystrokes, so programmers (being efficiency experts in these matters) don't use STORE very much. A more mathematically traditional variable could be created this way;

```
x = 3
```

A variable that is based on data in a table might look like this:

```
cLastName = LASTNAME
```

In this case LASTNAME is a field. The value stored in the field is transferred to cLastName, so that it now contains "JOHNSON". It's very useful to think of variables as named storage spaces (usually temporary). They hold data that is used by FoxPro for Windows in commands, calculations, and the like.

In programming, variables are ubiquitous. They are used less often when working with the system menu but are still important. For example when doing a count of records in a table, you can have the result stored in a variable. However, the other examples above can't be created without using the Command window, which is ahead just a bit in Chapter 7.

At this point, what's important is to begin understanding the concept of variables, and perhaps visualizing their use. One approach leans on the notion of variables residing in the computer's memory (RAM), hence they are often called *memory variables* to distinguish them from fields. In this context variables can be pictured as if they are in a column of memory locations, as in Table 2.1.

Table 2.1
Variables in RAM.

Memory Location	Variable Name	Data Content
000100	cLastName	JOHNSON
000111	x	3
000116	dToday	11/23/93
000126	is_open	.t.

Each location has one name and one item of content. When a variable is created it's assigned a location in memory and if it contains data, space is opened to store the content. Likewise, when variables are released, the space is removed from memory. Unlike some other programming languages, Xbase takes care of the "bookkeeping" for memory locations and space allocation. All you need to know is what a variable is called, and perhaps what kind of data is in it.

In general the Xbase language is very flexible about variables, some would say impossibly lax. You don't have to declare a variable (that is, name it) before you use it. You don't have to define its data type, since this happens automatically when you assign a value to a variable. And you can change the content at any time with anything. So a variable you have originally given a number…

```
thefirst = 14
thefirst = "Mary"
```

…can turn right around and contain text. As you will see, in programming this can be dangerous.

Constants

Before moving from variables to expressions, a short stop is at the word *constant*. In the programming world this is held to be the opposite (so to speak) of a variable. A number, any number (like the value of pi—3.1416), is a numeric constant. A letter, or word, is a character (or string) constant. You'll see references to constants throughout the FoxPro for Windows manuals. In most cases it means you supply a fixed value, either by programming or by entry of a value. The most common use of a constant is in functions, where you might pass a constant value to one of the parameters, such as in: SUBSTR("Now is the time", 1, 10).

Expressions

If there's any place that separates the data managers from the data manglers, it's the mastery of expressions. Of course, mastery is not easy. But building expressions like the concept of indexing, is fundamental. Expressions are also the basic requirement for all kinds of data queries, and other conditional statements. Therefore, learn expressions, use them, and be fluent with them.

So much for the tough talk. It's just that the concept of data expressions is a major stumbling block for many people. This chapter will do its best to keep the subject clear and move forward with a careful progression. But there's no getting around it, you will need to know not only what

```
"JOHN" $ LASTNAME AND STATE="CA" AND (SALES >= 10,000 OR
GROSSMARG > 5)
```

means, but you will need to be able to create such expressions yourself. If you've done any algebra within recent memory, most of this will be old hat, but the data-management context can make it look quite unfamiliar.

On the road to building expressions, start with a very simple example:

```
SALES + RETURNS > 10,000
```

SALES and RETURNS are both *terms*, in this case fields of a table. A term is a standard concept in mathematics, but not heard so often in data management. It just means that expressions usually contain variables, fields, or constant values (all terms) as part of the expression. These can be spoken of as "terms of an expression," just as they would be in the algebraic sense.

To have anything happen in an expression, you need *operators*. The plus sign (+) and greater than sign (>) in the example are typical operators. As you can see in the list of operators in Table 2.2, some of these are obvious, some unfamiliar but useful, and others arcane.

Table 2.2
Table of Operators.

Operator	Data Types	Description	Example
+	Numeric/float	Addition	`3.56 + 3`
+	Character	Concatenation	`"Ab"+"by"`
+	Date, numeric	Adding days to dates	`DATE()+ 3`
-	Numeric/float	Subtraction	`356 - 3`
-	Character	Trimmed concatenation, blanks are added to end	`"Tom & "-"Jerry "`
-	Date, numeric	Subtract days from dates	`DATE()- 3`
=	Character, float, numeric	Equal to "Ab"2=2DATE() date, memo	`"Ab" = =CTOD("12/1/93")`
==	Character, memo	Equal to and equal in length (exact match)	`"Tom" == "Tom"`

<>, #, !=	Char, float,num, date, memo	Not equal to:
		<> - math style
		!= - "C"language style
		# -dBase style
			`"Ab" <> "Tom"`
			`4 # 3`
			`nType != cType`

>	Char, float, num, date, memo	Greater than	`1000 > 999` `"Jerry" > "Tom"`
>=	Char, float, num, date, memo	Greater than or equal to	`999 >= 999`
<	Char, float, num, date, memo	Less than	`999 < 1000` `"Tom" < "Jerry"`
<=	Char, float, num, date, memo	Less than or equal to	`999 <= 999`
^, **	Numeric, float	Exponentiation	`x^2, x**2`

(continued)

*	Numeric, float	Multiplication	`2*4`
/	Numeric, float	Division	`x/3`
%	Numeric, float	Modulus (remainder)	`2%3`
$	Character, memo	Substring comparison (string contained in)	`"Ab" $ "Abby"`
AND, .AND.	Logical	Logical AND	`AND ("Ab"$"Abby")`
OR, .OR.	Logical	Logical inclusive	`OR ("Ab"$"Abby")`
NOT, .NOT.,!		LogicalLogical	`NOT ("Ab"$"Abby)`

This table is only the basics of the use of operators. Much more is said in the chapters on programming. But to build even the most rudimentary expressions, you need to have an idea of what operators are available.

Expressions

Given the first two building blocks, terms and operators, you're ready to start making expressions. FoxPro for Windows uses four types of expressions: character, numeric, date, and logical, corresponding to the data types. Table 2.3 provides an example of each:

Table 2.3
Data types and their expressions.

Type	Expression
Character	`TRIM(LASTNAME)`
Numeric	`SALES + 10,000`
Date	`DATE()- 30`
Logical	`"Ab" $ "Tintern Abbey"`

In many respects, each expression is a self-contained unit. Everything in it relates to the data type of the expression and what it is supposed to accomplish. In the simple example used at the beginning of this section, SALES+RETURNS is a numeric expression (presuming these are both numeric fields), and the whole thing (SALES+RETURNS < 10,000)is a logical expression because it *evaluates* to true or false depending on the values in SALES and RETURNS.

Functions, along with logical and mathematical expressions, evaluate to something. When an expression is evaluated, it produces a result. A character expression evaluates to characters, a numeric expression to a number, a date expression to a date, and a logical expression to true or false. Table 2.4 provides some examples:

Table 2.4
Data types, their expression, and their evaluation.

Type	Expression	Evaluation
Character	`TRIM(LASTNAME)`	`"Johnson"`
Numeric	`SALES + 10,000`	`25,000`
Date	`DATE()- 30`	`11/01/92`
Logical	`"Ab" $ "Tintern Abbey"`	`.t.`

The actual evaluation of an expression is done by FoxPro for Windows when you execute a menu option containing an expression, enter an expression in the Command window, or run a program containing expressions. Evaluation usually moves from left to right in an expression, but there is such a thing as an order of precedence especially in numeric and logical expressions. This order determines what evaluates first.

Order of precedence is another potentially confusing concept, yet important: It is very easy to make mistakes in "logic" that are really mistakes in the order of precedence. For example:

```
DATE() + OVERDUE / 30
```

This creates a "Data type mismatch" error, because FoxPro for Windows will carry out the division before the addition, and can't divide a date by a number. Put another way, the expression looks like this to FoxPro for Windows:

```
DATE() + OVERDUE
----------------
      30
```

Problems like this can be avoided, not by memorizing the table below, but by learning just three things:

- Evaluation basically flows from left to right.
- Parentheses always control the order of precedence.
- You can check a table of precedence, if need be.

Table 2.5 lists the order of precedence for FoxPro.

Table 2.5
Order of precedence.

1	Expressions enclosed with parentheses
2	Functions
3	Exponentiation
4	Multiplication and division
5	Modulus calculation
6	Addition and subtraction
7	Character string operations
8	Relational operators
9	NOT
10	AND
11	OR

Parentheses control the order of precedence—that is your best tool. The problem expression above is easily fixed:

```
DATE() + ( OVERDUE / 30 )
```

The parenthesis force calculation of OVERDUE/30, which results in a number that can be added to a date.

When you look at one of your expressions, and you're not sure how it will actually evaluate, use parentheses to make it evaluate the way you want it to:

```
STATE = "CA" AND NOT ZIP = "90210" OR ZIP = "90211"
STATE = "CA" AND NOT (ZIP = "90210" OR ZIP = "90211")
```

The first formulation would not include zip 90210, but would include zip 90211. By putting parentheses on the part of the expression after the NOT it makes FoxPro evaluate the entire expression before doing the negation.

Creating complex expressions, especially of the logical variety, is really a matter of practice. The rules above may help, at least you should be aware of them. But they're nothing if not reinforced by making many expressions of your own—making mistakes—and learning from them. As you go along in FoxPro programming, this is an area where experience, and the sensitivity that you can really get it wrong, go hand in hand with building useful expressions.

Pardon the Expression

Now that you've seen some of the jargon of expressions, this is the point to tackle a problem people often have with FoxPro's use of expression terminology. Most people, when they think about the word "expression," either have an image of some text like "See Spot run.", or a mathematical expression like x + y = 24. This is not exactly how the Microsoft manuals use the word. An expression may be any one of three things:

- A constant value, as in the number 24 or the text "Spot runs."
- A variable or field, as in the variable nCount which contains 24, or LASTNAME which contains the value "Johnson".
- A function or another expression that can be evaluated, such as 12+12, or TRIM(LASTNAME).

This is not a very common use of the word expression. People tend to be confused because of their greater familiarity with a mathematical type of expression (that is, one that evaluates to something). Most of the time a constant is called a constant and not an expression. Same goes for variables and functions. Still, throughout the FoxPro manuals you will see things like the following function for swapping one character string for another.

```
CHRTRAN( <expC1>, <expC2>, <expC3> )
```

Each <expC> (which means character expression) can take an expression in Fox's sense of the word. This means you can plug into each <expC> above, a character constant, field, variable, or other expression that evaluates to a character. It's like saying, "This is a slot for data. The only rule is whatever you put into the slot has to be of the specified data type." As a result, this function could look like this:

```
CHRTRAN("See Spot run.",cSpot,TRIM(LASTNAME))
```

This same approach lies behind all of the FoxPro expression types, shown in Table 2.6.

Table 2.6
FoxPro expression types.

<expC>	Character expressions:	
	`"Spot runs"`	text (character strings)
	`cLastname`	variables or fields containing text
	`UPPER("spot")`	functions or other expressions that return character data
<expN>	Numeric expression:	
	`3.1416`	numbers
	`nCount`	variables containing numbers (numeric or float data types)
	`SALECOUNT`	fields containing numbers
	`RECNO()`	functions or other expressions that return numeric data
<expD>	Date expression:	
	`dStartDate`	variables containing dates
	`ENDDATE`	fields containing dates
	`DATE()`	functions or other expressions that return dates
<expL>	Logical expression:	
	`.t./.f.`	logical symbols
	`is_done`	variables and fields containing a logical value
	`FOUND()`	functions or other expressions that return true or false

This book will usually annotate, as appropriate, the FoxPro use of expression with the more mathematical use of expressions (meaning they have terms, operators, and evaluate to something), or with some kind of constant, variable, or field.

Logical Expressions

So far, this chapter has been about the general use of expressions. There is one type, however, that deserves special attention: *logical expressions*. These are also sometimes called conditional expressions because they're so often used to select information from a table based on satisfying a logical condition. In fact, nearly every major table operation command can take a logical expression attached to either a FOR or a WHILE clause.

Table 2.7
Commands with a FOR clause.

AVERAGE	COUNT	JOIN	REPORT
BROWSE	DELETE	LABEL	SCAN
CALCULATE	DISPLAY	LIST	SORT
CHANGE	EDIT	LOCATE	SUM
COPY TO	EXPORT	RECALL	TOTAL
COPY TO	ARRAY	INDEX	REPLACE

The FOR clause causes FoxPro to go to the top of a file and process every record while testing against the logical expression in the clause. If a record evaluates to true, then it is included in the results of the operation, otherwise it is ignored. This can be interpreted as: "Execute this command FOR all records that meet the specified condition." This is an extremely common use in commands like COUNT FOR… and REPLACE FOR….

The WHILE clause is very similar, except that it begins at the current record and runs until the expression is no longer true. It's used most frequently after an indexed search to run through all the records that match the same condition as the search.

Logical expressions in the FOR clause are a prime vehicle for using the ultra fast Rushmore Technology.

Building a Logical Expression

The form of a logical expression is like that of any algebraic relation. There's a left side, and a right side, and in the middle some kind of relational operator (=,==,<,<=,>,>=,<>,$), shown in Table 2.8. This is not to be confused with database relations. In this case it means that the left side *relates* in some way to the right side, and this relation evaluates to either true or false.

Table 2.8
The form and examples of logical expressions.

Left	Operator	Right
Field, Variable, Constant	=,==,<,<=,>,>=,<>,$	Constant, Field, Variable
13	>	4
"CA"	<>	STATE
cSTATE	=	"CA"
SALES	>	10,000

As you might guess, the variations in logical expressions are almost infinite. But most of the time you'll be using them to test for some condition, and depending on whether the result is true or false, some sort of action will occur. That action will help you determine how to build the expression. For example, if you want to delete some old records from a table, then you would use a field (typically a date of entry field or similar) to test if the record is older than say 90 days, and if so, delete it. Your expression might look like this:

```
ENTERDATE + 90 < DATE()
```

Each logical expression in a FOR or WHILE clause needs to make sense within the context of the table being scanned. You wouldn't normally create an expression that doesn't test for some condition in the fields of a table.

While using the system menu, logical expressions are always associated with various commands. However, logical expressions are also used constantly in programming to control loops and conditional structures like IF/THEN. In short in or out of programming, logical expressions are one of the most important elements in FoxPro. The more you can practice creating them, the better. The place to do this is in the System menu is in the Expression Builder screen.

The Expression Builder

The Expression Builder is not to be found as a menu option. It always comes as part of a command option screen like Locate, Index, Replace, usually when you elect to use a FOR clause.

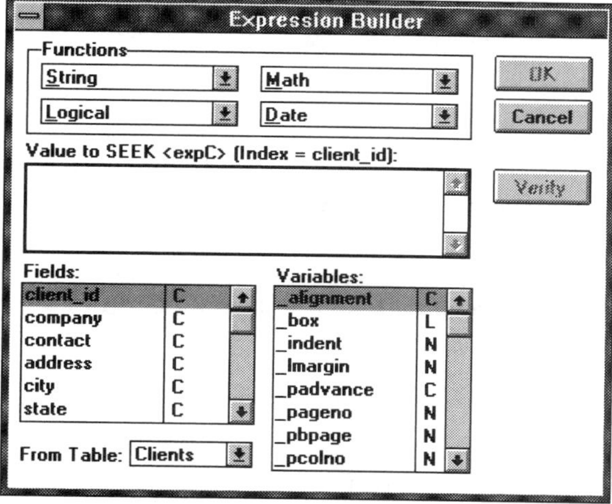

Figure 2.1
The Expression Builder dialog box.

Let's say you've just opened a file called CUSTOMER and selected Record, Replace from the system menu. Your task is to run down the list of customers in the table and replace the contents of the current date field with today's date. However, you want this to happen only for active customers. Active customers are indicated by an "A" in the STATUS field. So you would select the **For** option in the Replace dialog box, and up pops the Expression Builder.

The Expression Builder is intended to *support* building expressions. It is in no way a tutorial, a hand-holding device, or one of Microsoft's "wizards." It presumes that you already have some notion what an expression is (in the FoxPro sense), and in particular that you know the form of a logical expression and how the relational operators work. What it does provide are convenient listings of fields, variables, operators and functions to help you if you forget what's available. The Expression Builder dialog box is always adjusted to the database environment at the time, and to the type of expression that needs to be built. But it's up to you to know how to put the pieces together.

Since the Expression Builder can be included lock, stock, and barrel in applications, you should have knowledge of how it works before you unleash it on some unsuspecting user. Even in the example started above, when you build the FOR expression, you need to know what the STATUS field is, and what it contains so you can enter STATUS = "A". This kind of knowledge about data tables is not always practical for many users.

Compound Expressions

It's a guarantee that at some point you will need to construct logical expressions with more than one simple expression in it—a so-called compound expression. These are constructed of one or more expressions, glued together with the Boolean operators AND, OR, and NOT, and clarified by the liberal use of parentheses. For example, let's look at the compound expression used at the beginning of this chapter:

```
"JOHN" $ LASTNAME AND STATE="CA" AND (SALES >= 10,000 OR
GROSSMARG > 5)
```

In English this could mean, "Select all records of salespeople where John is part of the last name, who live in California, and have sales over $10,000 or else a gross margin higher than 5 percent." As you break down the compound expression it has these simple expressions:

- Character: `"JOHN" $ LASTNAME`
- Character: `STATE = "CA"`
- Numeric: `SALES >= 10,000`

- Numeric: `GROSSMARG > 5`

The overall flow of logic makes three tests (designated by the ANDs), the first two character tests, then either of the two numeric tests (signified by the OR). The parentheses are not required, but they make this expression easier to understand, and in some cases may make a huge difference in the way an expression is evaluated.

Understanding when and how to use AND, OR, and NOT is unfortunately not a good subject for rules of thumb, because there are so many possible variations. There are lots of formal ways to approach Boolean logic, and if you go on to study database administration (or something similar) you will encounter the more precise and mathematical definitions. However, in the less august atmosphere of day-to-day database management, you can usually get by using common sense and the standard English meanings of the three words. "You can go to the movies only if you've done the dishes AND you've got the money." With condition x AND condition y both conditions have to be true. In condition x OR condition y, only one of the conditions needs to be true. "You can eat dessert if you've broken your diet OR you don't care."

It may be helpful to note that 80 percent to 90 percent of all database expressions are made of three or fewer clauses. Don't expend much of your time mastering compound complex expressions unless you are sure that's something you will need. Or unless you make a hobby of it.

Scope

Perhaps you've had some time to explore the Database and Record menu selections. You may have assumed that anything under Database would be active with an entire table, and those under Record with one record at a time. Well, almost. Actually this is a matter of command scope. There are commands under both that act on one record at a time, or on the entire file. In fact almost all can be limited in scope.

In FoxPro, the scope of a command refers to the number of records it will act upon. Scope is an option that is very often grouped with For and While. It too helps select which records a command will affect. In all screens where it appears, you can select the **Scope** button and a dialog box is displayed. Here you can choose from several clauses, as shown in Table 2.9 on the next page.

Table 2.9
Scope clauses.

ALL	The command acts on all records in the table.
NEXT <expN>	The command acts on the next <pick a number> records.
RECORD <expN>	The command acts on a specific record.
REST	The command acts on all records from the current record to the end of the table.

In general, scope clauses are not used very often with the exception of ALL. All of the basic operational commands have a default scope of one record—they act only on the current record. This is a good thing too, for many of these commands can do a lot of damage if unleashed prematurely on the entire table. It's common to practice the setup for some of these commands, either by having them act on a harmless record in the current table, or else on a dummy table. When everything seems to be working turn on the ALL clause and let 'er rip.

As for the other scope clauses, knowing exactly how many records to include in the NEXT is often difficult (and a mistake can be bad news). Working on an exact RECORD is definitely a special case application. REST is occasionally used with indexed searches, where it is known that the rest of the table contains only target records.

Getting Located

Logical expressions and the command scope are two of the more common ways of affecting what records a basic operation command will act upon. Another approach, especially to find and edit a specific record, are the location commands. These are all found in the Record menu: Goto, Locate, and Seek.

There are essentially two different flavors here. The Goto options get you to a specific place in a table—namely a record—if you already know, more or less, where you want to go. When you don't know where something is located, Locate and Seek carries out a search in the table. The word *search* really means "look for a match." In all cases, FoxPro finds something only if the contents of your search expression matches something in the table. Your expression can be something as simple as a character expression—"Jackson"—which you want to match with any Jackson in a last name field of a table. Like all expressions, search expressions can also be very complex, usually with the intention of finding something very specific.

GoTo

Selecting **Goto** brings up the GoTo dialog box, shown in Figure 2.2, with four rather specific options.

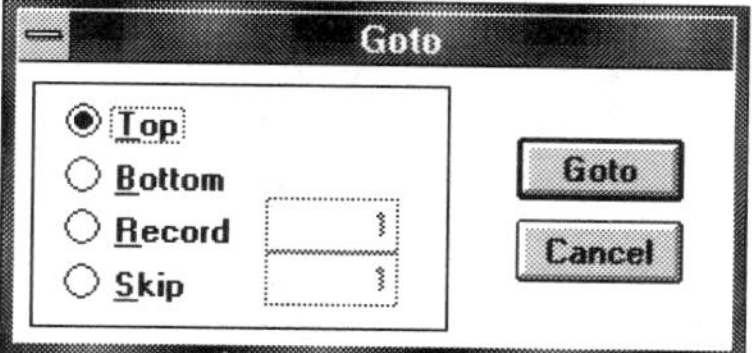

Figure 2.2 *The Goto dialog box.*

Top and Bottom simply put you at the first record of a table, or at the last record of a table. This should not be confused with the terms *beginning of file* (BOF) and *end of file* (EOF), which are actually beyond the first and last records.

The Record option, when checked, allows you to enter a specific record number. This is obviously useful only if you are familiar with the record numbering in a particular table, which is not likely to be all that often.

The last option, Skip, let's you move forward or backward in a table of specified number of records. Entering a positive number will move forward (toward the bottom of the table), a negative number moves backward (toward the top of the table). This can be useful if you are aware of the general layout of the table, so that you know a move of 50 records will put you into a different section, and so on.

All of the Goto options move you very quickly to a specific record, but are generally less useful than opening a Browse window and scrolling through a table—unless the table is large. The more records in a table, the more likely you are to use the Goto and other location commands.

Locate

Locate is the generalist in the FoxPro searching business. When you select it from the Record menu, you'll notice the Locate dialog box is very simple, as in Figure 2.3.

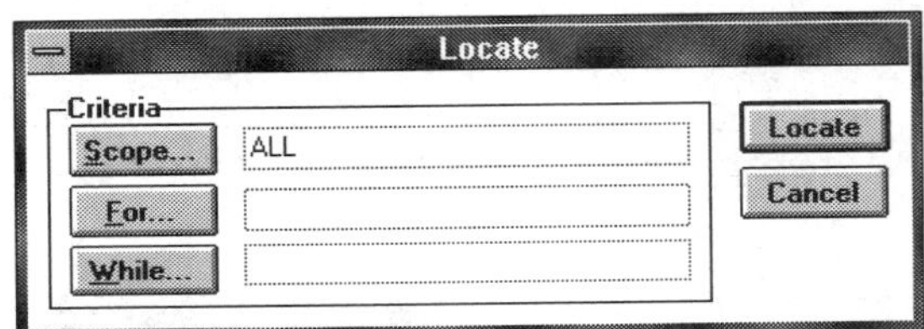

Figure 2.3
The Locate dialog box

It has only Scope, For, and While. For the most part the For clause is the workhorse. Here you specify a logical expression, which must contain one or more fields. (Unlike Seek, Locate makes no assumptions about which fields to search.) Most of the time, when you hit the **Locate** button, FoxPro does one of two things: first it checks if anything in you expression can be linked to an existing index. If so, then all or part of the expression is sent to the Rushmore processor. If not, it traverses the entire table from top to bottom, looking at each record as it goes. This latter process, often called a *sequential search*, is relatively slow. If your table is very large it can take a lot of time (hours even). It was for this reason in the days before Rushmore, that Locate was used sparingly. However, with the possibility that the Rushmore Technology can kick in and boost the speed of a Locate by orders of magnitude, this option is getting far more use.

Locate has another capability, which enhances its use considerably. If it finds any matches, the search stops at that record. By selecting the **Continue** option in the Record menu (which is available only during a Locate search), the search continues until it finds another match, or reaches the bottom of the table. In this way, Locate can "hop" from match to match, even if they are spread out through the table.

Seek

Seek is one of the key commands in you arsenal of FoxPro for Windows data management. To master it, you need only the skills for building expressions, and the knowledge that this is one of the most heavily used and fastest of all search commands.

Selecting **Seek** brings up the Expression Builder, which usually indicates what kind of expression will be valid. You should have already selected the index (tag) you need for the Seek, since there is no means of changing index order in the Expression Builder. Unlike Locate, Seek must be used on an index key. That means you must form an expression that will correctly fit the key of the index (tag) currently ordering the table. For example, if the index tag key is LASTNAME, then you need to form a character expression that can reasonably be matched in this key, such as "JOHNSON". Seek can work with any legitimate key expression—numeric, character, date, or logical and with compound keys.

Compound keys are a special case. Just like the key itself, your search expression needs to be of character type only. For instance, if the key is LASTNAME+DTOC(ENTERDATE,1), then you need to make a search string like this: "JOHNSON"+DTOC("12/02/92", 1), where the Date to String (DTOC( )) function converts the date to a character type.

Seeks are always very fast, less than a second or two even in extremely large tables. That's the nature of an indexed search, and why so much of FoxPro relies on indexes. The Seek, if it finds a match for your expression, will put you on the record of the match. In many cases this is the first record of a series, in which case you may want to open a Browse window to examine them. If the Seek fails to find a match, the current record will be the End of File (EOF()).

Armed with a knowledge of variables, expressions, and the so called "navigation" commands, such as Goto, Seek, and Locate, you are ready to roam around in data tables.

Input: Append

Once you've organized your database, meaning at least a data table or two have been created, it's time to consider one of the less glamorous aspects of data management: input.

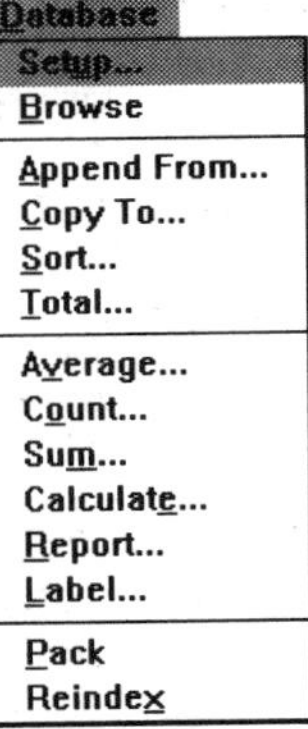

Figure 2.4
The Database menu.

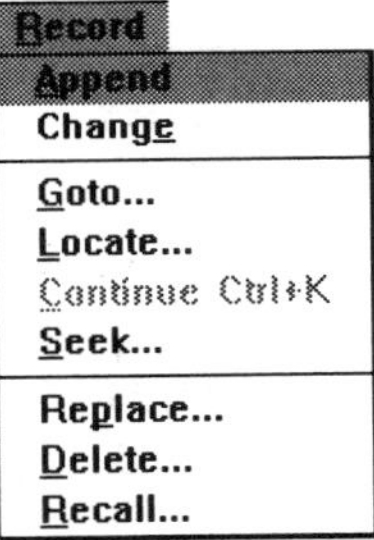

Figure 2.5
The Record menu.

Virtually all of the action is found in the Database or the Record menu. Here are your points of access for data entry and editing. It is very important to understand that from the system menu all of your options involve *direct entry*. This means you are entering data directly into a table with very little checking to see if the entry is correct or appropriate. The other approach, as you will see in much detail later, is *controlled entry*. It's done with data-entry screens (mostly created in the Screen Builder), which give you many ways to *validate* the data being entered.

But in the system menus, the only validation performed by FoxPro is on data type. For example, you can't enter anything but a legitimate date in a date field. For this reason, data entry via the system menu is normally reserved for users working in their own tables (where mistakes don't destroy other people's data), or for data management people and programmer's who *never* destroy other people's data....

Append / Change

The Append option has already been covered in the section on creating data tables. FoxPro asks if you would like to begin data entry. If you say yes, it gives you an Append dialog box, shown in Figure 2.6. For the most part, however, you'll be selecting **Append** from the Record menu **Alt-R-A**.

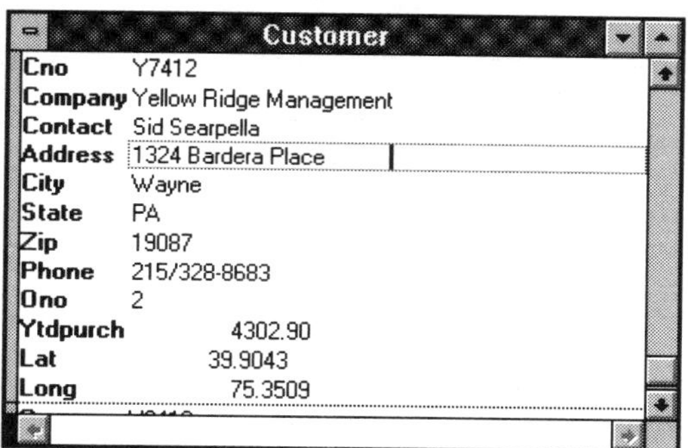

Figure 2.6 *The Append dialog box.*

Append lets you add one record at a time to a table. As you can see, each field is displayed in a vertical stack. It's homely as a mud fence, but you might be surprised how many data entry professionals prefer the format. The identical screen layout is used by the **Change** option. However, the Change dialog box lets you skip forward and backward one record at a time for editing (using **PgUp** and **PgDn**). The Append dialog box just keeps adding new records. (If you push it backward, it jumps into the Change mode.)

Append From

If given a choice, in lieu of adding a few thousand records by typing, most people prefer to add chunks of data from another source—another data file. Sometimes this may be part of a data-conversion project, or an upload from a mainframe computer, or just a simple transfer of data from one DBF to another.

As you might expect, depending on the task at hand, there are many ways to move data from one file to another. In the FoxPro system menu under the Database option, is Append From. Selecting this brings up the Append From dialog box, shown in Figure 2.7, an all-purpose screen for adding data to your tables from many kinds of files.

Figure 2.7
The Append From dialog box.

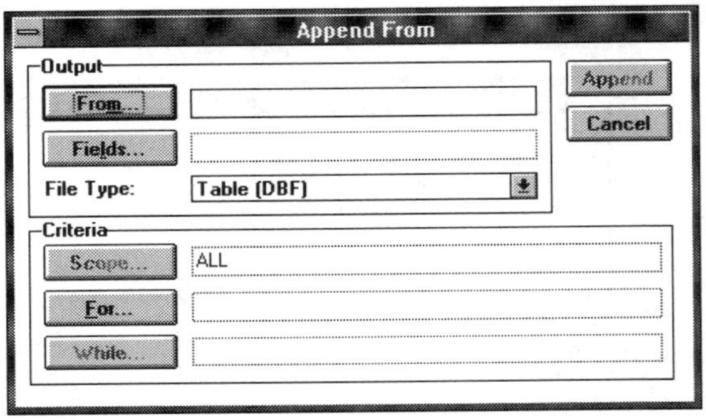

Append From assumes you have already opened an appropriate data table to receive records. It also assumes that you know something about the structure of file from which you are going to append. These are fairly significant assumptions. You may recall from the chapter on naming fields that it was recommended to give identical fields in different files the same field name, data type, and width. Append From is one place where this will pay off. In going from DBF to DBF, if the field names, data type, and width are the same, the data will transfer without a hitch. However, if the fields don't match completely, you may have a problem using Append From. Some fields may not transfer at all, especially if they're the wrong data type, or be truncated because of different field widths.

This leads to the observation that the capabilities of Append From should not be confused with a complete system for data conversion. Sooner or later you will probably have to do a data conversion—which can often be a version of data management from hell. Taking data from another system and converting that information to fit your data tables may require the services of Append From, but may well include programmed approaches of a complexity that can be astonishing.

A little of this complexity can be illustrated by the part of Append From window that handles non DBF files. In the Output section you have the option to select a **File Type**. Selecting this produces a drop-down list that shows all of the file formats supported by FoxPro for Windows for conversion to a DBF file. These are shown in Table 2.10.

Table 2.10
Supported import file formats.

Type	Source
ASCII	Comma delimited
ASCII	Tab delimited
ASCII	Space delimited
ASCII/SDF	Standard data file (row/column)
SYLK	Symbolic link format
DIF	Data interchange format
XLS	Microsoft Excel
MOD	Microsoft Multiplan v.4.01
WRK	Lotus Symphony v.1.0
WR1	Lotus Symphony v.1.2
WKS	Lotus 1-2-3 v. 1A
WK1	Lotus 1-2-3 v.2x
WK3	Lotus 1-2-3 v.3x
PDOX	Paradox
RPD	RapidFile v.1.2
FW2	Framework II

Since Fox can't directly read anything but a DBF, any incoming data that is not already in that format must be first converted. For this to work you need to know that the field from the source file matches the target field in your data table. You also need to know the order of the fields in the source file, since for the most part FoxPro maps the fields to yours in that order.

Without going into the variations between file formats (here at least), suffice it say that it is sometimes very difficult to know precisely the types, alignment, and order of data in one file to match with your own. Append From does absolutely nothing to prevent you from loading thousands of totally mismatched records. That's why, whenever possible, data conversion projects use the IMPORT command, which does the conversion by creating a new DBF based on the field information (if any) in the source file. While this may force yet more DBF to DBF transfer, it at least allows you more control over the placement and type of fields. Unfortunately this command is not available from the system menu. On the other hand IMPORT doesn't handle ASCII (text) files, which are some of the most commonly used.

Hopefully this discussion will give you a clue that data conversion, and sometimes even simple data transfer, isn't always so simple. However, Append From is used with great regularity in maintaining and manipulating DBF files.

Input: Edit

First things first. You can't edit what you can't find. Most of the time, you're going to need to use Seek, Locate, or Goto to get to the record you need to edit. However, with tables that aren't too large, say less than 5,000 records, it's not uncommon to simply open a Browse window and visually scan through the table—by brute force, so to speak.

Browse

For people new to the Xbase tradition, *browse* seems an interesting choice of word. It's remindful of cows and horses, and is in fact a form of data grazing. Actually, the Browse is one of the glories of the Xbase/FoxPro language, and in fact something being copied (word and all) by far more pedigreed data-management systems. In FoxPro the **Browse** option appears in the Database menu, and the View window. Before you click on it, first select a file, for a Browse is always based on a single file. Otherwise, a dialog box will open and ask you to select a file. Once done, you get a window that looks just like a spreadsheet screen—rows and columns. The Browse window is shown in Figure 2.8.

Figure 2.8
The Browse window.

Customer

Cno	Company	Contact	Address
14021	1st Computers	Jeff W. Culbertson	5111 Parkway
18232	1st Data Reductions	Dennis Johnson	360 Riverview Farm Street
12082	1st Software Systems Ltd.	Rance Sivren	23433 Chapel 121
12840	1st Survey	Robert Hepworth	733 Peeler 86th
A8872	A Beck Pertamina	Jim Ansarti	4001 Rowed Rd
A8818	A. Arts Computers	Darryl Roudebush	3305 Plantation Avenue
A6459	A. Bloomington Biz	Phil Putnam	6300 East Drive
A6188	AZ Inc	Tom Totah	2041 Wilshire Blvd
A5181	Abbymark Velonex	Isador Sweet	2139 Bridge Sciller
A3964	Acres Tree Solutions	Russell Kmickle	621 Ferndale Ste Park
A3882	Add Associates	Len Silverman	318 N Sante Fe Ave Office L
A1046	Add Inc	Bert Crawford	253 Mitchell St
A7249	Adder Incorporated	Brenda Cartwright	1237 Bering Belleview
A3835	Adv. Software	Barbara H. Martin	600 114th Ave Se A1a
A3061	Advantage Computer School	Duane Marshall	3784 Van Dyke Suite Street
A0169	Aerial Inc.	Lynn Williams	903 Highland Drive
A8902	Alex County Community Corp	Rance Hayden	75 Briar Ave

This window is easy to use because it reminds people of something they've already grown accustomed to using. Only here it's a window on some twenty or more records of a data table, which can be quickly scanned or just leisurely—browsed. There are many kinds of information that lend themselves to this format, and for the user it provides a convenient mode for editing and comparing data in different records.

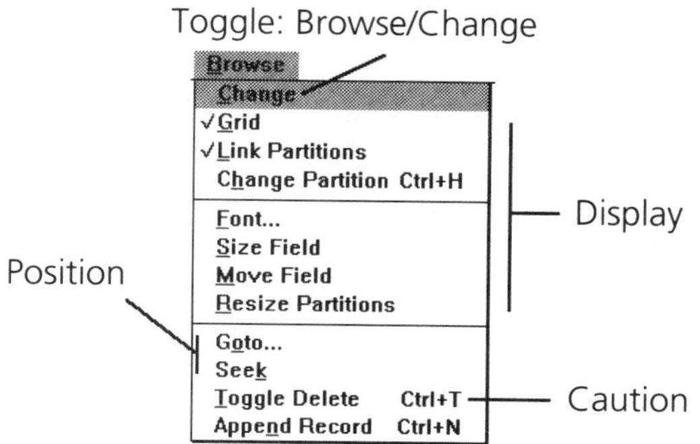

Figure 2.9
The Browse menu.

It may be helpful to point out that the Browse menu, shown in Figure 2.9, provides commands that are found elsewhere in the menu system, but are conveniently included here: Goto, Seek, Toggle Delete and Append Record. These do exactly the same thing as their nonbrowse brethren, but the appearances are different, because they relate to the Browse window. Append Record, for example, doesn't put you in an append window, but instead drops you to the bottom of the table, adds a record (a new line in the Browse), and displays the last records of the table in the Browse window along with the new blank line.

It's well worth your time to become familiar with all of the display tricks that FoxPro endows in the Browse menu. Split (partitioned) screen, moving fields, and sizing fields are all heavily used in maintaining data, and sooner or later you may want the capabilities inside a program.

It's also pertinent to mention that the Browse lends itself to damaging data. In many other situations you can change data, realize your mistake, and cancel the entry. In Browse, as soon as you go from one field into another, the data is permanently changed in the data table. Since it is very easy to move between fields, a lot of random mistakes can be introduced through the Browse screen. Later in programming, you will see how a Browse can be controlled in much the same way as a data-entry screen. But for now, keep in mind that if you enter something you don't want into a field, and you don't remember what was there in the first place, your only option is to use the **Esc** key, which drops you out of the Browse, but saves the original data in the field.

Change and Browse in Tandem

You may have noticed in the Browse menu that it contains a Change option. It's tempting to look at these options, Browse and Change, as two faces of the same coin. This is particularly true when using Browse, because you can toggle between Change and Browse with the Browse menu or **Alt B**. In fact the Browse window can be configured to show a Browse screen on one half, and a Change screen on the other half, as shown in Figure 2.10.

Figure 2.10 *Browse and Change in a split screen.*

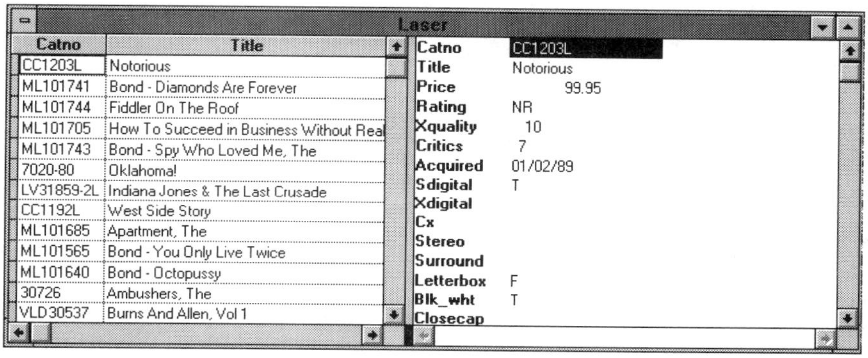

Laser

Catno	Title
CC1203L	Notorious
ML101741	Bond - Diamonds Are Forever
ML101744	Fiddler On The Roof
ML101705	How To Succeed in Business Without Real
ML101743	Bond - Spy Who Loved Me, The
7020-80	Oklahoma!
LV31859-2L	Indiana Jones & The Last Crusade
CC1192L	West Side Story
ML101685	Apartment, The
ML101565	Bond - You Only Live Twice
ML101640	Bond - Octopussy
30726	Ambushers, The
VLD30537	Burns And Allen, Vol 1

Catno	CC1203L
Title	Notorious
Price	99.95
Rating	NR
Xquality	10
Critics	7
Acquired	01/02/89
Sdigital	T
Xdigital	
Cx	
Stereo	
Surround	
Letterbox	F
Blk_wht	T
Closecap	

To do this, select **Browse** (which gets you the basic window) and either partition the window with the mouse or with the Browse menu option. Then, in one or the other partition, select the **Change** option in the Browse menu. This is an extremely useful editing configuration—one that you might want to use in applications programming.

This is a good place to point out important differences in your approach to FoxPro for Windows as you might use it yourself, and how you might approach it if it's to be used by someone else.

NOTE

When splitting a Browse window into a Change and Browse half, a lot of the Browse fields are going to be obscured, including some that might be very useful if visible. You can, of course, rearrange the field order with a mouse or more clumsily by selecting the fields to be displayed through the View window. However if its for yourself alone, you will often elect to forgo such niceties in favor of expedience. If, however, someone who doesn't know the data table as intimately has to use the Browse/Change window, then you'd better be prepared to make the field order correct before you turn it over to them.

Editing Text

You can edit text in *all* of the following:

- Memo fields
- The Command window
- Program files (PRG)
- Screen and menu snippets
- Get fields
- Browse fields

Most people clearly recognize that in a memo field you should be able to use all of FoxPro's text-editing capability—Cut and Paste, Search and Replace, and so on. The Edit menu, shown in Figure 2.11, contains all of these commands. In fact you can use these in any of the fields above. Of course, Search and Replace doesn't make a lot of sense in a twenty-character field. But cutting and pasting from one area to another can be extremely useful.

As you progress with learning FoxPro, and particularly with programming, there will be many occasions where it's a great time saver to work things out in one place and paste them over into another. Prototyping in the Command window and pasting results into a program file is a good example.

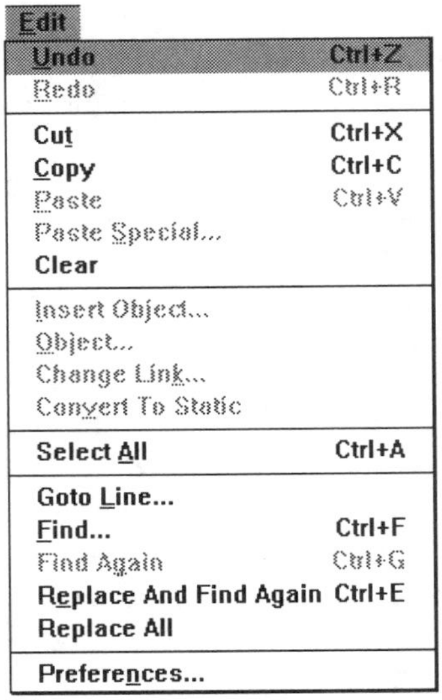

Figure 2.11
The Edit menu.

Edit

Undo	Ctrl+Z
Redo	Ctrl+R
Cut	Ctrl+X
Copy	Ctrl+C
Paste	Ctrl+V
Paste Special...	
Clear	
Insert Object...	
Object...	
Change Link...	
Convert To Static	
Select All	Ctrl+A
Goto Line...	
Find...	Ctrl+F
Find Again	Ctrl+G
Replace And Find Again	Ctrl+E
Replace All	
Preferences...	

As you work with the system menu, you might notice the options change constantly as you move through your files and screens. This relieves you from needing to know when a particular editing option is available (especially in your own programs). The Edit menu actually could be split into two quite different functions: the obvious one is for text editing, which includes the basics like Cut, Copy, Paste, Find, and Replace. The other part is for links between FoxPro for Windows and other Windows software—such as, Paste Special, Insert Object, Object, and Change Link. These are the OLE (Object Linking and Embedding) options of FoxPro for Windows to be covered later.

Text Menu

FoxPro for Windows also provides a menu to control various aspects of text display in the Text menu. The Text menu, shown in Figure 2.12, is one of those signals that FoxPro for Windows is different from its DOS predecessor. Management of screen text is a nonissue in DOS, since programs like FoxPro for the most part must assume only one type of screen output—the standard 80 character, 25 line, and IBM character set. But Windows is a GUI (Graphical User Interface) and GUIs bring a wonderful capability to the use of text—fonts. You now have the possibility of using thousands of fonts, and each with many variations and sizes. So FoxPro for Windows has added the Text menu to give you access not only to fonts, but line size, and other elements that affect the display of text. Also thrown in is Spelling (although why this isn't in the Edit menu is a mystery).

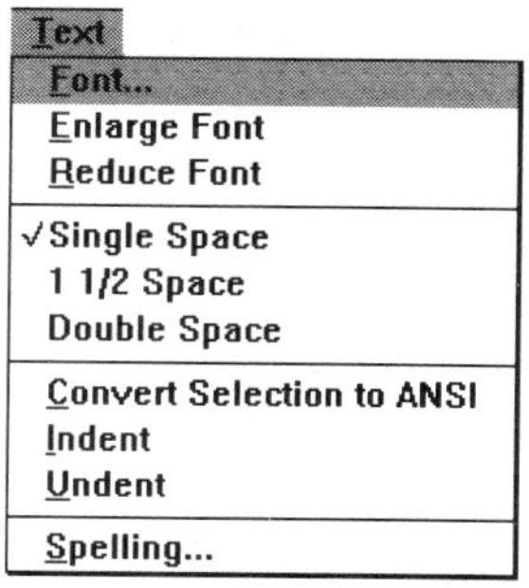

Text
Font...
Enlarge Font
Reduce Font
✓Single Space
1 1/2 Space
Double Space
Convert Selection to ANSI
Indent
Undent
Spelling...

Figure 2.12
The Text menu.

Most of the selections in this menu are aimed at text either in the Command window or general editing (such as in memo fields, programming, and screen work). If you are working with the system menus exclusively, then your needs for these options is confined to the editing of memo fields. FoxPro "remembers" your selections for the two contexts, Command window, and editing. ("Remembering" in FoxPro means it stores your selections in the resource file.) For example, if you have opened a table that contains a memo field, you can place the cursor on the field (typically in a Browse window), and either double click with the mouse or press **Ctrl - PgDn** for the keyboard. This puts you in an editing window.

This has established the "mode" as general editing, and you can go into the Text menu to select Font **Alt T F**. Any changes you make in the font window are immediately reflected in the editing window. As you'll quickly notice, the editing window does not support multiple fonts. The last font selected is the one used for *all* of the text.

Selecting Fonts

The availability of high quality fonts at very popular prices is causing an explosion not only of font libraries but in raising the font consciousness of millions of heretofore typographically illiterate PC users. It's enough to make a typesetter turn pale and retire. There are already signs that people are beginning to trade fonts like baseball cards—"I'll give you one Snowball and a Viking for the best Bookman you've got." (Not a legal trade, though). Now that FoxPro has joined the Windows parade, you too can bring the artistry of fonts to database management.

While fonts are one of the "big four" design elements (fonts, icons, pictures, and wallpaper) that help to distinguish the FoxPro for Windows programs from DOS programs, fonts aren't new to Fox. FoxBase Mac has had fonts for years.

The Font dialog box, shown in Figure 2.13, has the familiar three elements: Font, Style, and Size. All three are scrolling list boxes that let you select from the available options. The Font box is the one you use to choose a new font, of course. Some people will have literally hundreds of fonts on display here (and it will have taken eons for FoxPro for Windows to load the list and open the Font window). Others may have only the basic set provided by Windows and FoxPro for Windows. While the vast libraries of fonts are wonderful, let's start with these standard fonts.

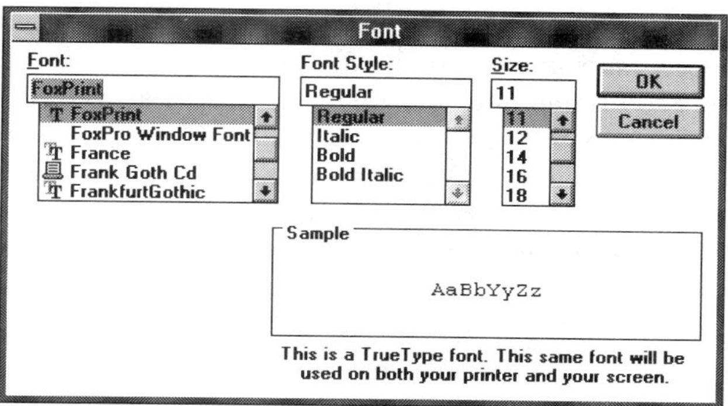

Figure 2.13 *The Font dialog box.*

It's useful to talk about the properties of the standard fonts because you need to make choices about your own text editing and Command window fonts. But when it comes to programming and providing software for other people, you also can't assume they have all those weird and wonderful fonts you may have collected. Unless you're prepared to pay for legally shipping fonts around, you may have to make do with the basic fonts—the only ones you can assume are available to everyone using FoxPro for Windows. Table 2.11 lists the standard fonts.

Table 2.11 *Standard fonts.*

Font Name	Description and Use
FoxPro Window Font	Specifically for use in FoxPro for Windows, and little else.
FoxFont	The "standard" Fox typeface, monospaced.
FoxPrint	TT Very similar to Courier, and often used in reports. Some people prefer this font for the Command Window.
COURIER NEW	TT Standard Windows font, designed to look exactly like typewriter output.
Arial	TT Standard Windows font, the TrueType Helvetica, clean and simple (sans serif).
Times New Roman	TT Standard Windows font, used for normal "book" like text (serif).

For the most part, these are serviceable yet boring fonts. As you may be aware, Windows supports several kinds of fonts—principally the old fashioned screen and printer fonts that are fixed at various sizes, and the more flexible scalable fonts that can range in size from 6 points to 72 points. The FoxPro Window Font and FoxFont, are screen/printer types. FoxPrint is a TrueType font, one of the scalable fonts that are now all the rage. Windows "officially" uses TrueType, but also supports a number of other font types, for example Adobe Type I. Courier New, Arial, and Times New Roman are the other standard TrueType fonts provided by Windows. You can go a long way, and make very fine looking output with only these fonts.

In the context of FoxPro for Windows, you can think of fonts as having three basic uses:

- Body text
- Decorative typefaces
- Programming fonts

Body text, found in the memo fields, is like the text of this book—it needs to be simple, legible, and pleasing. Decorative typefaces are used not so much to enhance text, but to provide a visual or graphic element. You can design screens using text that looks like this:

Enter your selection here: [ ]

or like this:

Enter your selection here

The only thing that counts is your artistic sensibilities. But the decorative type faces can do wonders for dull screens—provided you don't get carried away.

Fonts for programming, however, are another matter. Since FoxPro only allows one font and size in any one programming document, you should standardize on a font that looks good to you. While you can use anything, it's customary—even important—to select a *monospaced* font. In most TrueType libraries, the majority of fonts are *proportional*, which means that as you type the characters, they will automatically be justified on the page and are relative to each other with some letters (like l and m) fitting more tightly together than others. This looks good for smooth reading, but plays havoc with one of the necessities of readable program code—aligned columns. An example follows.

```
IF nTrigger = 12
    nCount=RECCOUNT()
    cNames=LASTNAME
    dToday=DATE()
ENDIF
```

(Times Roman, regular, 12 pt.)

Compare this with:

```
IF nTrigger = 12
    nCount=RECCOUNT()
    cNames=LASTNAME
    dToday=DATE()
ENDIF
```

(Courier, regular, 10 pt.)

Courier is a monospaced font, all the letters are spaced equally apart. Courier New is the only monospaced TrueType font that ships with Windows, but if you don't like its stodgy "typewriter" look, there are plenty of other monospaced TrueType fonts available.

The selection of style (regular, bold, underline, italic, and bold italic), usually a matter of emphasis, has to be considered carefully because a style is applied to all text in an editing window. Not all fonts support a wide variety of styles, which may limit their general use. Likewise, the fixed fonts are very limited in type size (usually expressed in points), while most TrueType or Adobe Type I fonts can be scaled to almost any size 4 points to 127 points. For practical reasons these generally range from about 6 points to 72 points.

(Copperplate, Regular, 4-72 point)

Fonts and other Text menu options are covered in detail in Chapter 11.

Chapter 3
Table Operations

This is the meat and potatoes of data management. Table operations loosely defined encompasses things like updating, deleting, sorting, and counting—basic-data management functions that in general operate on entire tables. Most of these operations are used in the process of maintaining and updating data, and with a few limitations are all available through the system menu.

Basic Operations

Replace

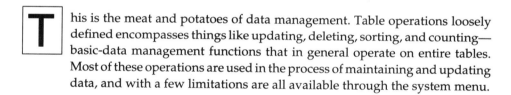

You'll find the **Replace** option under Record in the main menu. This command has a scope that ranges from one record (which is why it's in the Record menu) to the entire table (which is its more common use in the system menu). It's one of the most powerful, dangerous, and useful commands in the Xbase language. The Replace dialog box is shown in Figure 3.1 on the next page.

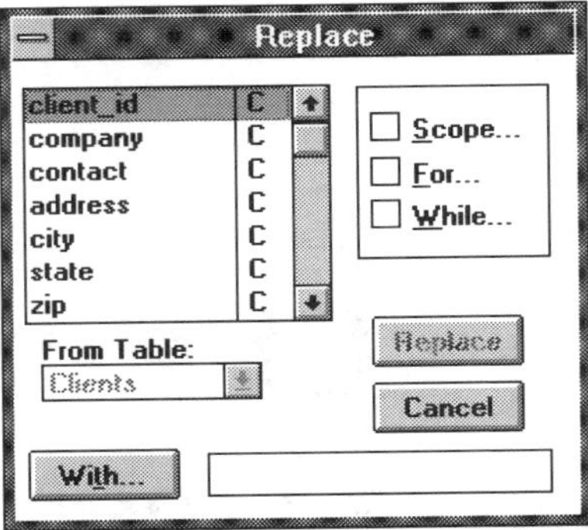

Figure 3.1
The Replace dialog box.

The basic mechanics are very simple. Using the field list in the upper left, select a field to be replaced *with* something. Selecting the **With** button brings up the Expression Builder, where you specify what should replace the field. You can also type something directly into the entry field to the right of the **With** button.

This produces a command that looks like this:

```
REPLACE CITY WITH "NOME"
```

The three check boxes in the upper right, Scope, For, and While provide your options to limit the records Replace affects. It is extremely common to use the FOR expression to have the command work on a subset of the table, for example, STATE = "CA", which limits the replacements to only those records with California listed as the state.

Replace is the most heavily used tool in the data maintenance toolkit. Here are some typical examples of its use:

- Updating fields, such as replacing a date field with the current date.
- Repairing or changing character fields, such as replacing a state field with all upper case letters.
- Replacing one field with another, for example replacing a total field with the contents of that field plus the entry in a sales field.
- Replacing one field with the contents of a field in another table. This is based on a relation being set between the tables.

The point that should be stressed about Replace is that the With component can be almost anything—another field, a field expression, a variable, a variable expression, a constant, whatever. The best approach to getting the most out of this command is to understand that it can be brought to bear on a wide range of data manipulation tasks, limited only by your understanding of how to use expressions in the With and For clauses.

There are many other aspects to Replace, including the ability to act on more than one field at a time. But these are not available in the system menu, and are introduced later.

Reindex

This menu option in the Database menu is very simple. It reindexes every open index, or every index tag in an open CDX file. If you don't already have a DBF open, you'll get a file selection dialog. After that, FoxPro does its thing and reindexes. This is a useful file-maintenance option, but you should be aware that reindexing won't help with damaged index files, nor does it re-allocate disk space when the size of the index decreases dramatically. That's why it's recommended to periodically recreate the index through the View window.

Sort

Sorting is often contrasted with indexing. A sort physically rearranges the records in a table. In fact, with FoxPro a new file is created by a sort. If you want to retain the old file name, this forces you to delete the old file, and then rename the new one to the old file name. Compared to indexing this seems rather involved. So why bother with sorting at all?

Sorting makes the most sense when a table is relatively static (doesn't change much), and is subject to frequent searches (both indexed and nonindexed). The physical sorting of a table, and particularly very large tables, can have a noticeable effect on the performance and efficiency of indexes and other forms of searching. Also, a sorted table may be faster for some kinds of output (like printing) than running through an index. In this latter case it's often practical to sort to a new file and leave the data there for use by a report.

These are all relative benefits, and the advantages of sorting a table need to be tested on a case-by-case basis. Otherwise, the strong tendency in the last decade has been to forgo sorting unless necessary.

The **Sort** option is reached through the Database menu, and brings up the Sort dialog box, shown in Figure 3.2 on the next page.

Figure 3.2
The Sort dialog box.

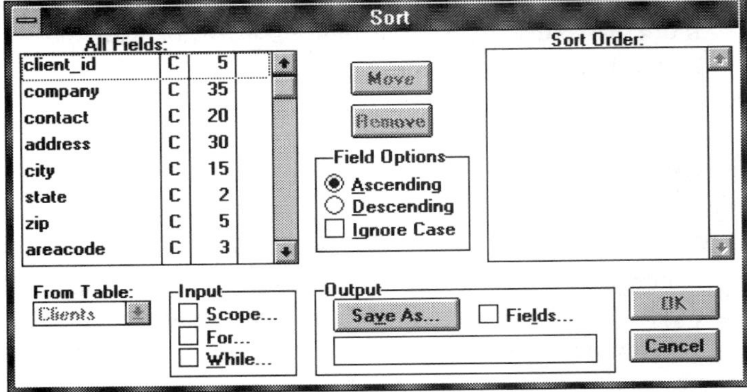

In the system menu, sorting does not allow field expressions, so you select the fields you want to sort by—up to six. The sort is performed in the order of fields you select, so you need to give some thought to what the primary sort key should be and what is the role of secondary sorts. In some cases this amounts to sorting by the same key field as the primary index (such as an ID or a unique number), then using the other sorting fields as "tie breakers." However, because of the frequent linkage between sorting and reporting, it's quite common to sort by fields that are not even indexed. (In this respect sorting can save you index space.)

Each of the sort fields can be set to sort in ascending (A-Z), or descending (Z-A) order, and whether to ignore case (upper and lower) or not. There are Field Option buttons for each of these. Like so many other commands Sort can take SCOPE, FOR, and WHILE options to limit the range of records being sorted. Finally, you can select the **Save As** button to find a file for output, or you can enter a new file name (with path) in the entry box. Sort also provides a Field Picker screen to select specific fields to be output from the sort.

WARNING

Sorting can use a tremendous amount of disk space—up to three times the size of the file being sorted. If you are working with very large files, and have some limitations on available disk space, a little math (3 x <file size>) is in order.

Delete, Recall, and Pack

Every database system has to have a method for getting rid of unwanted data. In the Xbase systems, you delete records (one or more at a time), which marks them as deleted but does not physically remove them from a file. The process of deletion is completed only when you issue the **PACK** command, which runs through an entire file and removes deleted records for evermore. Until a PACK has been run, you can still retrieve deleted records with the **RECALL** command.

Given this basic scenario for removing unwanted records, FoxPro usually requires periodic maintenance to PACK files. Pack is located in the Database menu. When selected, it gives you a chance to back out, and if you don't, proceeds to swiftly remove *all* deleted records.

Delete and **Recall** are located in the Record menu, though both can work on any command scope. They also have dialog boxes with an identical layout, as shown in Figure 3.3 and Figure 3.4.

Figure 3.3 *The Delete dialog box.*

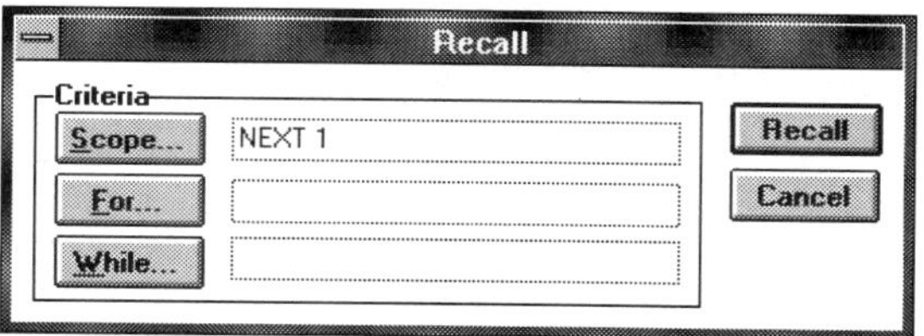

Figure 3.4 *The Recall dialog box.*

By now the criteria options in each window should be familiar—Scope, For, and While.

You can use these to select specific records, or a range of records to be deleted or recalled. This is a familiar process in many kinds of data maintenance, particularly with data conversions or data that is of very short term value.

SHORTCUT

You can also very efficiently delete or recall individual records in a Browse window by using the **Ctrl-T** key combination, or less swiftly from the Browse menu.

Chapter 4
Data Retrieval and Output

s far as most users are concerned, retrieving information is where the rubber meets the road in database management. After all of the work to create tables, enter and maintain data, now comes the time to get something back—retrieve the data in ways that are meaningful, useful, and better than the user could do without the help of a computer.

The FoxPro environment provides an embarrassment of riches to retrieve information. Perhaps a better phrase would be a confusion of riches. There are so many ways to retrieve data, people have difficulty understanding what to use when. Here's a quick list of the methods:

- RQBE, Relational Query by Example
- The Report Writer
- The Label Generator
- The Browse window
- Summarizing commands like COUNT, AVERAGE, and TOTAL
- OLE and DDE links
- Output to other programs through file transfer

- Simple listings via commands like LIST and DISPLAY
- Retrieval through programming

The good news is that each method has its own best uses, the less than good news is that the lack of consistency and overlapping capabilities, makes it difficult to choose between them. The FoxPro menu system gives you access to the first seven of these methods, obviously the lion's share. This chapter emphasizes the ways you can choose methods.

Preparing for Retrieval

In a relational database system (of almost any kind) the difficult part of retrieving data is almost invariably getting the right *setup*, such as opening data tables and indexes, and setting relations. The FoxPro retrieval tools like RQBE and the Report Writer are basically easy enough to use once the correct setup has been established.

Setting the Environment

With the partial exception of RQBE, you need to set the environment before using any of the FoxPro retrieval methods. This means opening tables and indexes, and in some cases establishing relations (one-to-many or otherwise). It may also mean choosing fields for display, setting a filter, and other global settings. In the system menu, all of this can be accomplished in one place—the View window.

Using the View Window for a Work Session

You're about to start a work session. The task is to create a couple of reports, and print them. All of the data is from a specific project, a customer database, and you expect to use at most two or three tables. What's the procedure?

Start by selecting Window, View (**Alt-W-V**) to open the View window. Since this work session involves a project, the data files (and other files as well) are located in a specific group of subdirectories (under c:\customer).

Normally, when started from the Windows Program Manager, FoxPro comes up with its default directories set to its own location (such as f:\foxprow). This should be changed, at least for this work session. If you don't change it, you'll probably wind up putting new files in the FoxPro directory instead of your work directories. From the View window select the **File** icon at the left, shown in Figure 4.1, to bring up the View: File Selection window, shown in Figure 4.2.

Figure 4.1
The View File Selection icon.

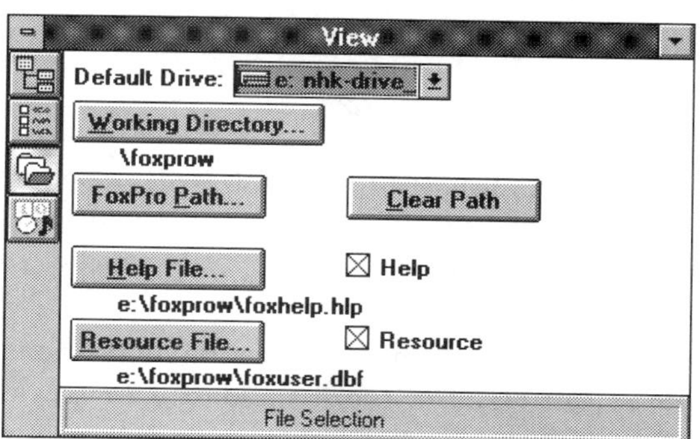

Figure 4.2
The View window.

General Directory Setup

This dialog box allows you to set most of the important default directories of FoxPro. The directory changes you make remain in effect until you change them again. (See Section II for more flexible ways of doing this.) Assuming that you are already familiar with DOS path conventions, you can review each of the options, and make any needed changes:

- **Default Drive**—A:, B:, C:, or D:, etc. In this case because the default directories are on the C: drive, you change the default to C:.
- **Working Directory**—This is the directory where the FoxPro files are

located, in this case on the network E: drive. For obvious reasons, this doesn't change often.

- **FoxPro Path**—Just like DOS, you can specify a path (a series of directories) for FoxPro to use when looking for files. This seems like a simple thing, but it can have a rather large impact on the operation and performance of your setup. In a search, FoxPro examines the working directory, then goes on to the directories of the FoxPro path. If that fails, it then goes to the DOS path. Of course, if no file is found, you'll get a message.

The path you enter should cover all of the subdirectories involved in a project (or at least all those that may have files FoxPro will use). For this example, you need to change the path to

```
c:\customer;c:\customer\dbf;c:\customer\rep
```

The first one is the project directory, below it are the directories by type of file and function—in this case c:\customer\dbf for data files and c:\customer\rep for reports.

- **Help File**—FoxPro maintains the capability to use two entirely different help systems: the traditional (DOS) FoxPro help, using FOXHELP.DBF or the Windows help system with its own FOXHELP.HLP file. Use this option to specify which help file (and thus help type) will be used.
- **Resource File**—One of the more interesting innovations of FoxPro 1.0 was to introduce a resource file, a standard DBF that contains many kinds of information about the system. It includes color schemes, window locations, browse fields, and printer drivers.

In larger projects and applications, its common to have both help and resource files customized and located in their own subdirectories.

When you've completed the general directory setup, select the **Main View** icon, shown in Figure 4.3, to get back to the View window, shown in Figure 4.4.

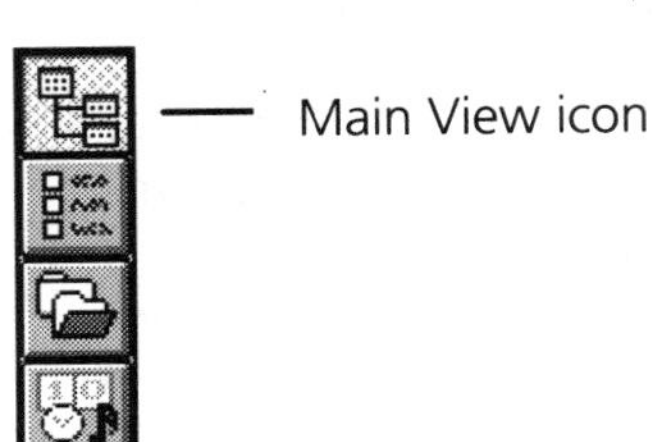

Figure 4.3 *The Main View icon.*

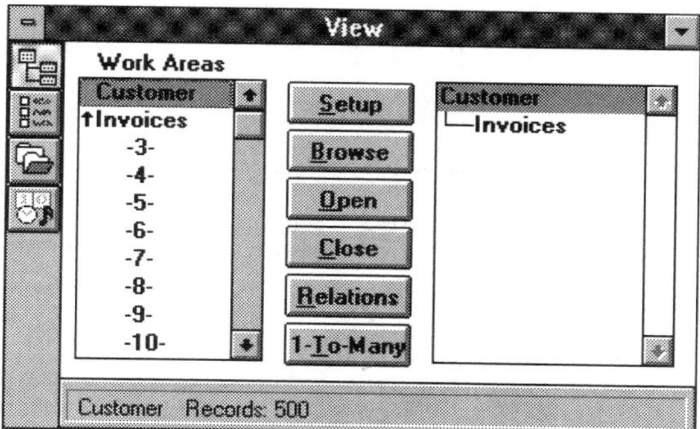

Figure 4.4 *The View window.*

At this point, you're ready to open files, indexes, and set relations. In this example only two files are opened: CUSTOMER and INVOICES, both indexed on CUSTOMERID and with a relation set from CUSTOMER into INVOICES which is defined as one-to-many (one customer may have none, one, or many invoices). This configuration of tables is the foundation for the type of retrieval you select.

System Setup: The Working Environment

There are times when you may want to get information about your system or set some of the options that control how things work. FoxPro has nearly 200 commands and functions to monitor or set options in the working environment. Of these, some 35 are available in the View window in two different screens: Set Options and Set Miscellaneous. Table 4.1 on the next page outlines the Set Options selections and Table 4.2 outlines the Set Miscellaneous selections. These topics are covered in further detail in Section II and Section III.

Table 4.1
Set Options selections.

Option		Description and Use
Carry	off	Editing: While appending, copy data from previous record into the new record.
Deleted	off	Deleted records are used/not used by command actions.
Exact	off	String search comparisons must match exactly and have same length.
Clear	on	Screen/Window cleared on leaving FoxPro for Windows.
Confirm	off	Terminating key (**Enter**) or **Tab** must be used to exit GET fields.
Exclusive	on	Files are opened for exclusive use. For networks should be off—shared use.
Lock	off	Editing: Records are automatically locked.
Multilocks	off	Editing: Enable/Disable locks in multiple records.
Near	off	On: Searches will stop at the nearest match. Off: unsuccessful search puts pointer at EOF.
Print	off	Output: Send all output to printer.
Talk	on	Output: Send processing information to the screen.
Headings	on	Output: Show field headings in screen listings.
Logerrors	on	Programming: Sends compiler errors to a file for later review.
Development	on	Programming: Checks file creation date/time for purposes of compiling.
Echo	off	Programming: Open/Close the Trace Window.
Bell	on	Enable/Disable the tinny little PC speaker beep during editing.
Clock	off	Display of the system clock in the lower right hand corner.
Escape	on	Programming: Enable/Disable use of **<Esc>** key to stop program execution.
Notify	on	Display "wait window" with informational messages for user.
Safety	on	Automatic warning for all operations that alter files.
Status Bar	on	Display of status bar at bottom of screen.

Table 4.2
Miscellaneous Options selections.

Option		Description and Use
Date	Am	Style of date format: American, European etc.
Show Century	off	Display the century in all dates- 01/02/1993 vs 01/02/93
Date Delimiter	/	Enter a special data delimiter.
Currency	$	Select the display symbol for currency.
Symbol Left	yes	Left justify (to left margin) currency symbol.
Decimals	2	Select the number of decimals to be displayed.
Clock	off	Show the system clock, set type of hours (24 or 12), and select row/column for display.
Bell	on	Turn on the PC speaker for "bell" and set the frequency and duration of tone.
Talk	on	Turn on/off command processing results, and set the interval for display.

Many of these options are quite specialized and aren't changed much. A few, such as Deleted, Exact, and Exclusive are exceedingly important in their own context. For example in using FoxPro for Windows on a local area network, if you neglect to turn *off* the Exclusive option, any files that you open will be unavailable to anyone else on the network. Deleted and Exact, if used carelessly, may cause many difficulties with search and processing operations.

Output Options

Retrieval and output are two different things. Retrieval is the query, criteria, filter, and scope that selects which data (primarily records) to retrieve from the data tables. Output determines what to do with the results of the retrieval.

There are four basic types of output:

- To the screen or a window

- To a printer or other printing device
- To a file
- To a memory variable or array

There is also an oddball output for RQBE—to a "cursor," a kind of phantom file. For any particular item only one of these output options usually is used. However, if you are creating applications for other people, then you often need to make provision to use *all* of these methods.

In the system menu, you will run across these options in connection with various commands, and particular with the Report Writer, Label Generator, and RQBE. As you will see, the basic decision of which output method to use is normally simple. The complications arise when you get to the specifics...Which window? What kind of file? Which printer?

Printing deserves special attention. It's the most common form of organized output. It's also the area that traditionally presents more problems than almost any other part of computing.

Printers and Printing

Printing from FoxPro for Windows is a far cry (or no cry at all) from what has been experienced in DOS. By comparison to the vagaries of printer drivers, LAN complications, printer selection problems, and so forth, the standardized and functional Windows approach is a relief. The most important improvement is that Windows provides all applications with the means to select printers and automatically handles matching printers with the appropriate driver. Windows supports hundreds of printers, and continues to update and upgrade the list. This, at least, is a problem in DOS that no longer exists under Windows.

In the File menu, you'll find Print Setup (**Alt-F I**), which brings up what should be a very familiar screen—the Print Setup dialog box with all of the elements common among Windows programs. The Print Setup dialog box is shown in Figure 4.5. It's here that you can select what printer (or similar output device) you want to use. You can also change the orientation (landscape or portrait), paper trays, and whatever extras your printer supports. Again, Windows handles the determination of what is supported and what's not.

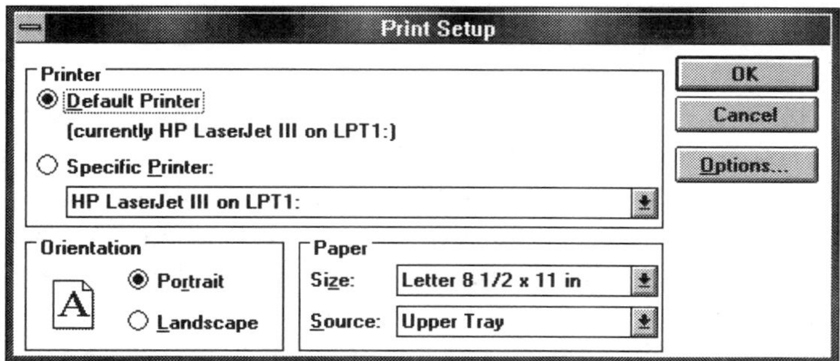

Figure 4.5
The Print Setup dialog box.

As part of setting your working environment, you may use Print Setup to select the printer.

Like all Windows programs, FoxPro for Windows has the Print menu option under File in the main menu (**Alt-F-P**). In the Print menu, shown in Figure 4.6, there are only four kinds of printing available:

1. Print from the Command dialog box.
2. Print from a File Edit dialog box.
3. Print an ASCII (text) file or other file on disk.
4. Print the Windows Clipboard.

For the most part, these are printing options most useful in the programming process, or in editing memo fields.

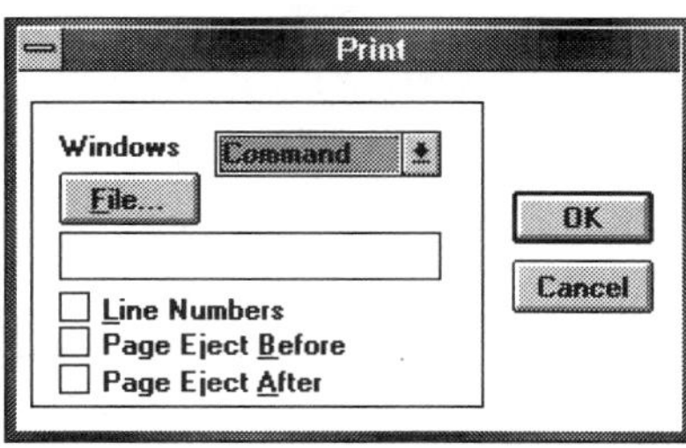

Figure 4.6
The Print window.

RQBE

FoxPro has two primary avenues of approach to query data files for information: one using commands like LOCATE coupled with conditional logic (logical expressions), the other through the Structured Query Language (SQL).

SQL, variously pronounced *sequel* or *S-Q-L*, is everywhere. The "sequel" pronunciation was originally from an IBM product. It has become standardized through official ANSI committees, shoehorned into almost every conceivable database product, and it's just about the only way to query databases across hardware and software boundaries.

SQL is deceptively simple. Depending on implementation, there are only 20 to 30 significant commands in the language. The "core" consists of the following:

Table 4.3
The SQL Core Commands.

ALTER TABLE	Change (modify) tables.
CREATE...	Create tables, indexes, views databases.
CREATE TABLE	Create a new table.
DELETE	Delete records in a table.
DROP...	Delete tables, indexes, views, databases.
GRANT/REVOKE	Grant or revoke user access privileges.
INSERT	Insert records into a table.
SELECT	Retrieve a set of records.
SHOW...	Display a list of all databases, data items, etc.
UPDATE	Update a group of records.

As you can see from the table, FoxPro for Windows supports only three of the SQL commands. That's partly because FoxPro/Xbase provides it's own way of doing the same things. FoxPro concentrates instead on the query capability of SQL, the SELECT command and its numerous clauses. Here's a *simplified* syntax:

```
SELECT [ ALL | DISTINCT ]
```

```
[ <alias> ] <select item>
       [AS <column name ]...
FROM <table>...
[[ INTO <destination> ]
       | [ TO  FILE <file>...
       | TO PRINTER...
       | TO SCREEN ]]
[ WHERE <join condition>
[ AND <join condition>... ]
[ AND|OR <filter condition>... ]]
[ GROUP BY < group column>... ]
[ HAVING <filter condition> ]
[ UNION [ALL] <SELECT command> ]
[ ORDER BY <order item> ]
```

As you can see, this looks a lot like programming. In fact there are so many different ways to do the same thing, sometimes with very subtle differences in results, that learning all the variations is demanding. While the basics of SQL SELECT can be learned in a few hours, it can take months (even years) to master. As you become proficient in Xbase programming, you'll need to add the FoxPro SQL commands to your battery of skills. But in your applications, you'll need to be careful how you expose the user to SQL.

In fact, the difficulty of "raw" SQL commands for the average user are so great, many attempts have been made to put them into a friendlier interface. The most important of these is RQBE—Relational Query by Example.

RQBE, Relational Query By Example, was introduced to the commercial Xbase world by FoxPro 2.0 for DOS. The original concept came from IBM research, and has been around for several decades. It's purpose is to simplify the process of retrieving data from tables, specifically from a relational type of database system, using SQL. There have been many versions, some more successful than others. The FoxPro implementation is utilitarian, requires a good deal of skill, and is backed by one of the finest query engines available (the Rushmore Technology).

Like so many of the more sophisticated FoxPro for Windows tools, RQBE can be quite easy to use for simple things, and gets close to being a black art for complex applications. Like the Expression Builder and conditional expressions, RQBE is designed more to *support* the use of SQL, than it is a guide or automated system. Among it's many talents, you can count on three outstanding uses:

- Interactive querying of multiple tables, often called *ad hoc queries*, to dig information out of a number of sources.

- Extracting data for reports, word processing, graphics, and other programs.
- A convenient way to create and test SQL SELECT queries for incorporation in programming.

You might add a fourth use—teaching SQL. Because RQBE generates a "standard" SQL SELECT command, you can experiment and immediately see how your configuration would be expressed in SQL. It should be pointed out, however, that RQBE is not the full SQL implementation available in FoxPro. Sub queries and clauses such as UNION are only available when using the SQL SELECT command in the Command Window or in programs.

The combination of RQBE and the Fox Report Writer provides an extremely flexible and efficient retrieval/output system. RQBE may not be the easiest tool to master, but it's worth the effort.

Using RQBE

Since an RQBE session is usually saved as a file (.QBE), a new RQBE session begins with File, New, Query (**Alt-F-N-Q**). To edit an existing file, use File, Open (setting the file type to query) and select the file you want.

The RQBE dialog box, shown in Figure 4.7, is compact, somewhat terse, and often leaves people wondering what the order of use may be. Figure 4.8 displays the "geography" of the RQBE dialog box.

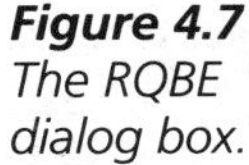

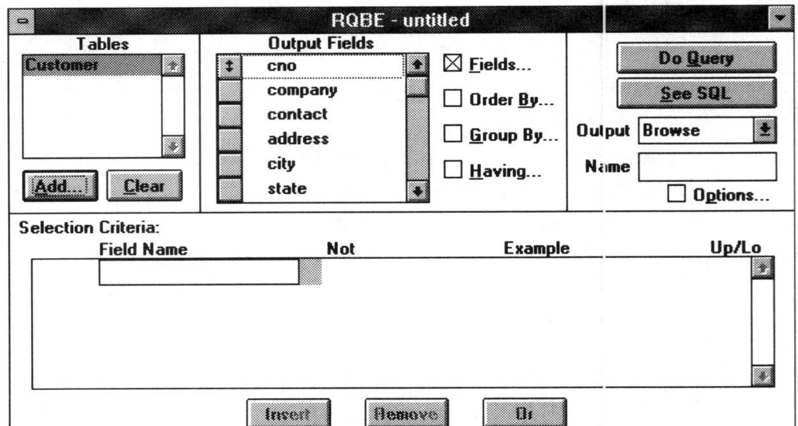

Figure 4.7 *The RQBE dialog box.*

Figure 4.8
The "geography" of the RQBE dialog box.

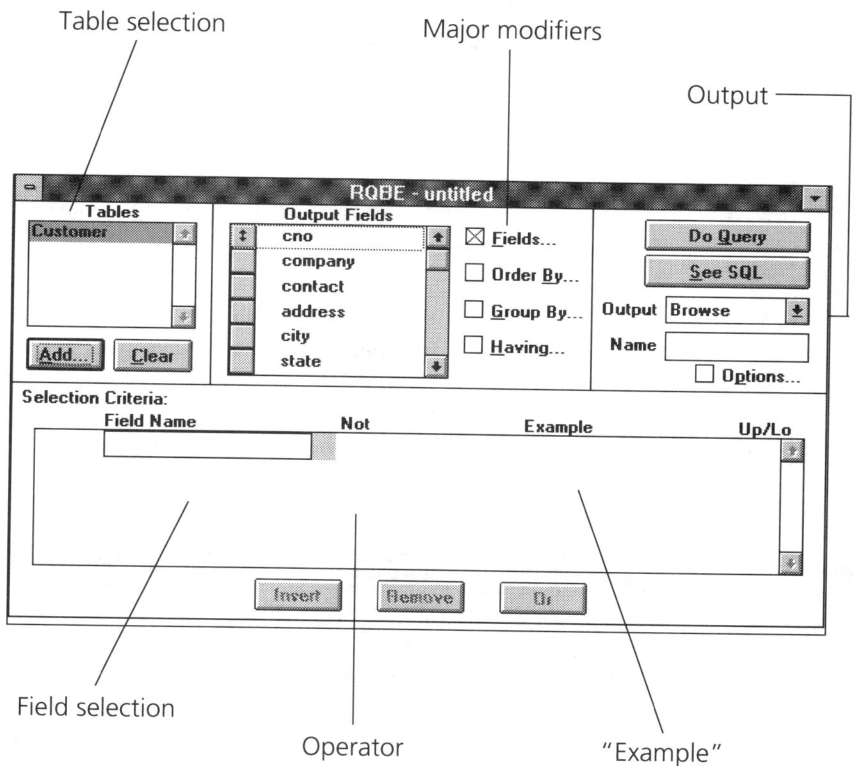

The pattern and strategy of RQBE session resembles that of any other type of retrieval: Setup, Retrieval Criteria, Output. Start by opening the relevant tables and setting relations (in SQL called *joins*). Next specify what records you want to select from the tables. Then specify the type of output and how you want the output formatted. With RQBE/SQL there are almost always multiple ways to accomplish a task, so the basic strategy is to come up with the simplest and most accurate approach.

In the upper right hand corner of the RQBE window, you'll notice the Do Query, and See SQL buttons. A standard Query window is displayed in Figure 4.9 on the next page.

Figure 4.9
A standard Query window.

Query

Cno	Company	State	Itotal
R5705	Raybank Services & Computing	AZ	1540.03
R6042	Rent-A-Tool	ID	1801.13
R2676	Rubber & Designs	IA	1435.36
S9559	Software Associates	WI	2407.79
S5632	Soltis Systems Trouble Systems	CO	1510.52
Y7497	Yergen Endeavors	AK	1347.72

Unless the query generates a lot of data or takes a great deal of time, it does little harm to continually test your query as you build it. Many people like to take it step-by-step, and at each point Do Query to see if their approach is working. If you're somewhat more experienced, you can also use the other button, See SQL, to look at the current SQL statement. A sample SQL window is displayed in Figure 4.10.

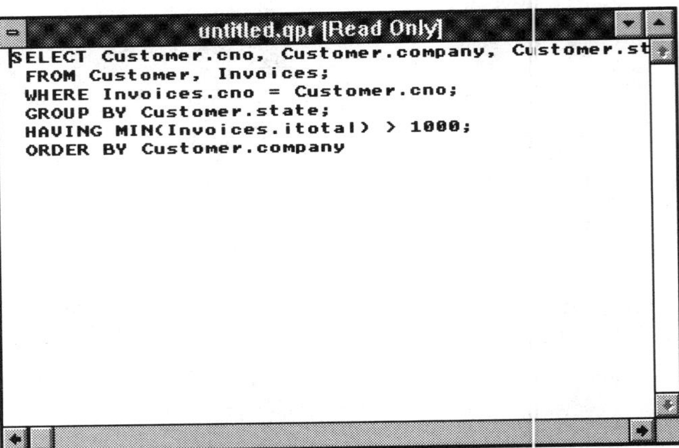

untitled.qpr [Read Only]
SELECT Customer.cno, Customer.company, Customer.st
FROM Customer, Invoices;
WHERE Invoices.cno = Customer.cno;
GROUP BY Customer.state;
HAVING MIN(Invoices.itotal) > 1000;
ORDER BY Customer.company

Figure 4.10
A sample SQL window.

This is also a great way to learn SQL, since you can immediately see what your changes in the RQBE window do to the actual syntax of the SQL statement.

Whenever you open or create an RQBE query, the RQBE menu option is displayed in the system menu. This menu basically repeats everything that's available through option buttons in the RQBE window. The exception is the

Comment option, which gives you a way to document the goals and strategy of your query. Your entries are stored in a memo field of the .QBE file. As soon as you are sure that a query is worth keeping, use File, Save or Save As (**Alt-S-S** or **Alt-S-A**) to save the query to disk.

RQBE Table Selection

In all other forms of retrieval for FoxPro, it's mandatory to do a complete setup of tables, indexes, and relations before you can start the retrieval. RQBE is somewhat different—it works with tables that are already open. In fact, the current work area will become the default open file in the Table selection box. However, any additional tables must be added explicitly—even if they're already open. Moreover, you do not set indexes for RQBE. In fact, it's probably not a good idea to have any open indexes going into an RQBE session, Rushmore Technology is particular about choosing its own indexes.

The best approach is not to do any setup outside of RQBE. Start with all work areas empty, and Add tables in RQBE as needed. As usual, the first table you add should be the main table. This is the "parent" table from which joins (relations) are created to the "child" tables.

Joins and Criteria

As you can see in Figure 4.8, the Joins and Criteria area takes up half the window, which indicates the pivotal role this has in the RQBE setup. Because both join and criteria clauses occupy the same space and have a similar format, it's easy to confuse the two. However, the function of a join is fundamentally different from a criteria.

The function of a join is fundamentally different from criteria, although they occupy the same area and have a similar format.

Joins

A *join* is SQL jargon for a relation between two tables. Every time you want to add another table to include its information, you need to create a join between it and the master table (or another joined table). In the raw SQL

SELECT command, the tables are attached to the FROM clause, and the join becomes a WHERE clause.

```
SELECT ALL FROM CUSTOMER, INVOICES ;
WHERE CUSTOMER.CNO = INVOICES.CNO
```

In most cases, the join should be between the parent table and an index key in the child table, *even though the index is not explicit*. Rushmore uses any index tag that fits your join, but not finding any may cause it to create a temporary index. This is no problem with small tables, but on large tables it could lead to an unacceptable wait.

The form of the join in the RQBE window is:

FIELD NAME	OPERATOR	FIELD NAME

When you select Add in the table selection area (after a primary table is open), you will get the Join Condition dialog box, shown in Figure 4.11.

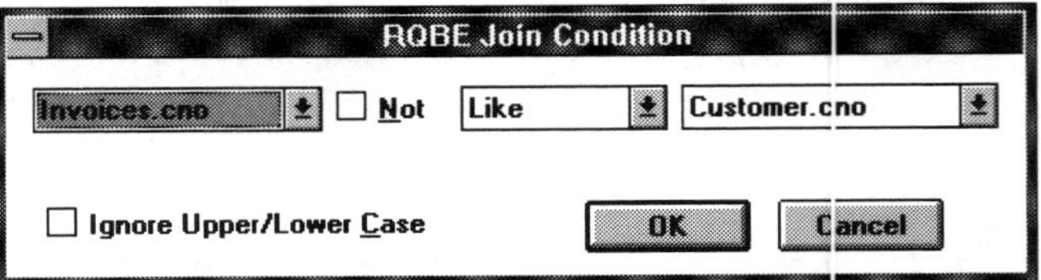

Figure 4.11 *The RQBE Join Condition dialog box.*

Specify the field in the parent table, the linking operator, and the linking field name in the child table. The *operators* of the join are what distinguish SQL from the familiar SET RELATION. A standard FoxPro relation is based on a match (equality) between keys. The SQL join can be based on the same type of equality (called an *equi-join*), but you may also use several other relational operators, which are expressed in an English equivalent. The SQL operators are displayed in Table 4.4.

Table 4.4
SQL operators.

SQL	Operator
Like	=
Exactly Like	==
More Than	>
Less Than	<

Typical joins looks like this:

```
WHERE customer.id = invoices.id

WHERE TRIM(customer.contact) == TRIM(address.contact)
```

This makes the SQL join look like a SQL criteria:

```
WHERE customer.state == "CA"
WHERE customer.state IN "MI MT MN MO"
WHERE invoices.idate > DATE() - 90
```

Criteria

As you would expect, criteria are used to specify what records you want from the tables. They perform the same function as the logical expressions in a typical FOR clause and are constructed in much the same way, except for the "Example" term on the right side of the relational operator.

FIELDNAME or Expression	OPERATOR	Example

This is the example in Relational Query By Example. Actually, you need to specify exactly what you want. If you enter:

CUSTOMER.CITY	=	San Diego

you'll get all of the records that have San Diego in the city field. If you use just "San" as the example, you'll get all the cities that begin with "San". Note that you don't need to use quotes for character strings in the example entry.

By now you may have recognized that the "example" is often simply a constant, or as FoxPro would have it; a value expression. However, you can also use functions in the example or even complex expressions. So what remains is hardly recognizable as an example, but is simply any valid FoxPro expression. And what goes for the right term, also applies to the left term. You can use either a field or any valid expression. In fact, buried way down at the end of the field list that pops up when you select the left term, you'll find the <expression> option. Selecting this will bring up the familiar Expression Builder window.

The criteria entries, like the joins, become another addition to the WHERE clause, preceded by either an AND or an OR. The AND clauses are automatic when adding another criteria. The OR must be signaled explicitly by selecting the Or button at the bottom of the window. In addition you can select the **Not** button to put a NOT in front of your right expression. All of these logical operators behave as you would expect from your experience with building expressions. They are used to combine criteria into a complex conditional expression that might look something like this in raw SQL:

```
SELECT ALL FROM customer, invoices ;
WHERE customer.cno = invoices.cno ;
AND (customer.city = "San Diego" ;
AND NOT (customer.city == "Los Angeles" ;
OR (customer.city = "San Francisco")))
```

Notice that parentheses are used to clarify the order of precedence.

In the RQBE Window, the example looks like Figure 4.12.

Figure 4.12 RQBE Window Selection criteria.

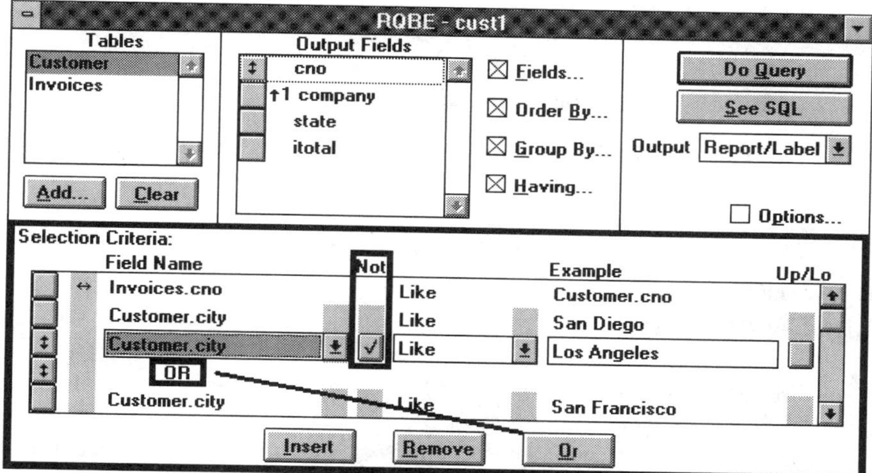

The operators for criteria are the same as for joins, with two additions: Between and In. The Between operator can take a range of two values separated by a comma. This works for numeric, date, and character values, such as: BETWEEN 1,500 or BETWEEN MN,MT. In is the "list" operator, again with any numeric, date or character values, you can enter a list separated by commas: IN 1,5,7,9 or IN CA,MI,NY,NJ. Here are some typical statements:

```
SELECT customer.id, customer.ytdpurch ;
 FROM customer ;
 WHERE customer.ytdpurch BETWEEN 1000,5000
SELECT customer.id, customer.state ;
 FROM customer ;
 WHERE customer.state IN "CA,MI,NY,NJ"
```

Both Joins and Criteria may use the Up/Lo option, located just to the right of the example area. All this does is toggle the application of the UPPER( ) function (conversion of all characters to upper case) to both left and right terms. For example, WHERE UPPER(CUSTOMER.CITY) = UPPER("MT"). This is useful if:

- You are using character expressions.
- You are not sure whether the data is in upper or lower case.
- You are reasonably sure that this is what you want.

So far, with the Table area and the Join and Criteria area, you can construct a fairly simple and quite useful query. But you have only scratched the surface of RQBE.

The Other Major Modifiers

In addition to the WHERE clause, Fields, Group By, Order By, and Having are the other major modifiers of SQL SELECT. These latter four are distinguished from the WHERE clause because they can act upon sets (groups) of records: The selection criteria in the RQBE window work on a record-by-record basis, selecting only those records that meet the criteria conditions. The other major modifiers on the other hand, work with sets of these records. In addition, Fields and Order By can manipulate the presentation of the results of the query by limiting output to specific fields, and in specific sort order.

While it is not explicit in the RQBE dialog box, there is a kind of processing order to the elements of SQL, shown in Figure 4.13.

Figure 4.13 *SQL processing order.*

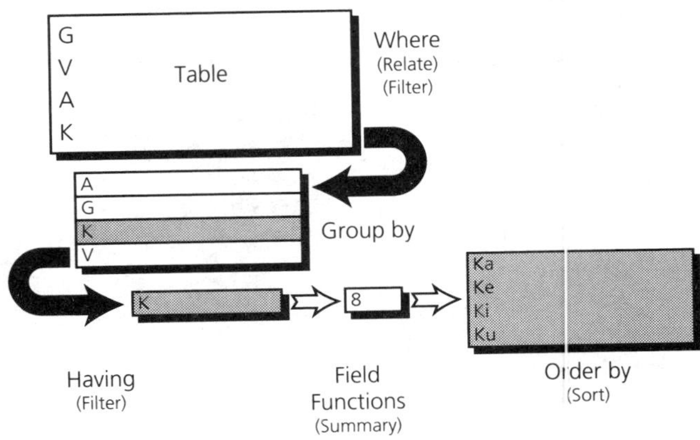

The entries you make in the RQBE window Selection Criteria area correspond to the WHERE clause. These are your initial filters that extract from the table only those records that fit the criteria. This extraction is a subset of records from the table that is passed on to the other major clauses for further refinement.

The next clause, Group By arranges anything passed through the Selection Criteria into groups, such as groups of states, or groups of products. The grouping is the setup for the Having clause to filter the grouped records by some criteria. This produces an even smaller subset of records, which are the final data. Then the Fields options and Order By clause come into play to shape, summarize, and order the data for output.

In a sense this is a classic pattern for a SQL query. None of the clauses are required. Nor is their order of use predetermined. You can have SQL queries with no Selection Criteria, but using only the Having clause. Or queries with only the Selection Criteria and nothing else. You are required to select one or more fields for output, of course. But their order, number, and complexity are all optional, and the Order By clause is completely optional.

However, in normal usage the RQBE/SQL clauses and options are not random or independent. It helps to understand that Sort By is strictly an output option and has no effect on the actual selection of records. Or that the Selection Criteria (WHERE clause) come before the other clauses and work on single records, whereas the other major modifiers work on sets of records.

Group By

For those who have worked with any kind of report generator, the concept of grouping should be quite familiar. In a table of five hundred national customers with a state field, there are bound to be some states with multiple customers. If you group the table by state, then all of the records from each state will be together. This is, in effect, another kind of sorting. (In many systems you would have to sort the table first, before the groups could be used.) In SQL and RQBE, the Group By clause can perform multiple groupings and sorts on data. These are selected in the Group By dialog box, shown in Figure 4.14 on the next page, using the familiar field picker.

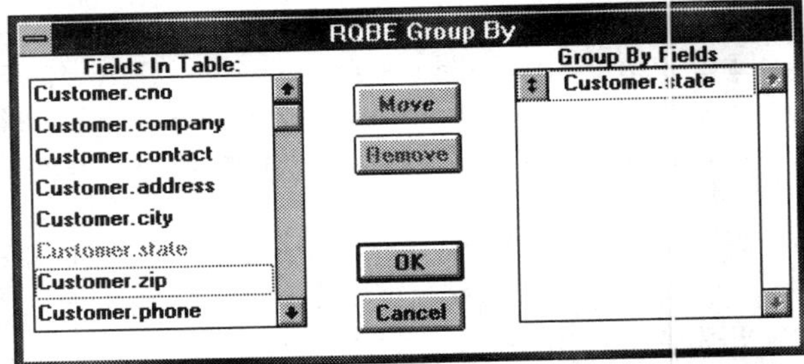

Figure 4.14 The RQBE Group By dialog box.

The result in the SQL statement looks similar to this:

```
SELECT customer.id, customer.state, customer.ytdpurch ;
 FROM customer ;
 GROUP BY customer.state
```

Having

For all practical purposes, the Having clause is exactly like the Selection Criteria for the WHERE clause, except the Selection Criteria are applied to all records of a table and the Having conditions are usually applied to the groups specified by the Group By clause. However, if you don't specify a group, then Having treats all records coming through the Selection Criteria as one big group. In other words, it still works and in fact works exactly like a Selection Criteria. Confusing? Maybe. Redundant? Definitely. But that's SQL.

Extending the example used for Group By, here's the statement so far:

```
SELECT customer.id, customer.state, customer.ytdpurch ;
 FROM customer ;
 GROUP BY customer.state ;
 HAVING customer.ytdpurch > 1000
```

The Having clause causes this statement to show *one* record from *each state* that has at least one customer with more than $1,000 in purchases.

Fields

In some queries where you have joined multiple tables, the number of fields available to be displayed can be huge. Too many, in fact, for meaningful presentation. The Fields option of RQBE (press **F** when not editing in the RQBE Select Fields dialog box) allows you to select which fields are to be included in the output from a query. The RQBE Select Fields dialog box is displayed in Figure 4.15.

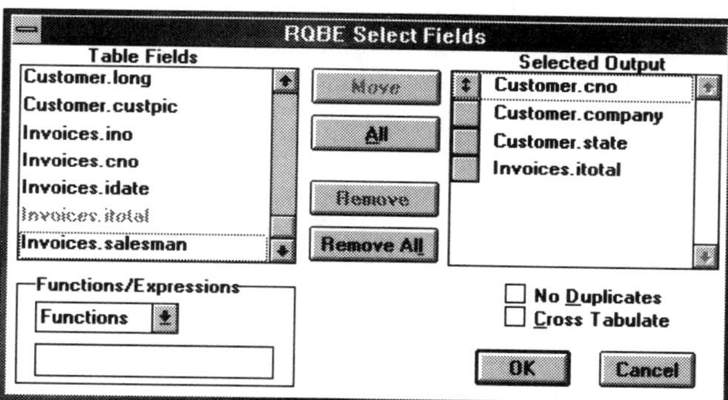

***Figure 4.15** The RQBE Select Fields dialog box.*

FoxPro defaults to display all of the fields of the master table. In most queries, this forces you to go into the RQBE Select Fields dialog box and remove unwanted fields, as well as add any others that may be needed. Fields that are used for criteria and joining do not have to be included in the RQBE Select Fields selection. However, for the other major clauses, you need to exercise some judgment about fields from other tables to be included. Be sure not to miss any fields relevant to the logic of your query.

The Fields option produces the <select item> list that follows the SELECT clause, such as in these examples:

```
SELECT customer.id, customer.contact, customer.ytdpurch ;
 FROM customer
SELECT customer.id, invoices.itotal, invoices.idate ;
 FROM customer, invoices
```

Besides the selection of fields, there are three other options available in the Fields window, two of which are quite significant: No Duplicates and Cross Tabulation.

No Duplicates Option

The No Duplicates button forces the query to output only unique records, screening out any duplicates. This produces the DISTINCT clause in the SQL SELECT command.

Cross Tabulation Option

The Cross Tabulation button, tucked away as it is in the RQBE Select Fields dialog box, is easily overlooked. It is the connection to a powerful and useful FoxPro capability. The finished product in a cross tabulation by state, salesman, and invoice may look like this:

	Crocker	Hill	Leppard	Olson	Zillertal
CA	109,123	233,040	0	355,980	255,374
NV	0	0	435,098	124,425	0
OR	189,662	278,391	0	0	243,689
WA	129,241	398,674	0	0	104,399

The only tricky part of using cross tabs is the setup. You need exactly three fields. They must be in a specific order, corresponding to the x axis, y axis, and cross-tab content. And, of course, the data in these fields should make sense for the purposes of cross tabulation. Also, because the number of fields in a table is limited to 254, you can't have a cross tab with more than 254 items on the x axis.

The example above is typical. On the left (y axis) are states, across the top (x axis) are salespeople, and the tabulation data in the middle is a total of their sales by state. The setup in the Select Fields window looks like Figure 4.16.

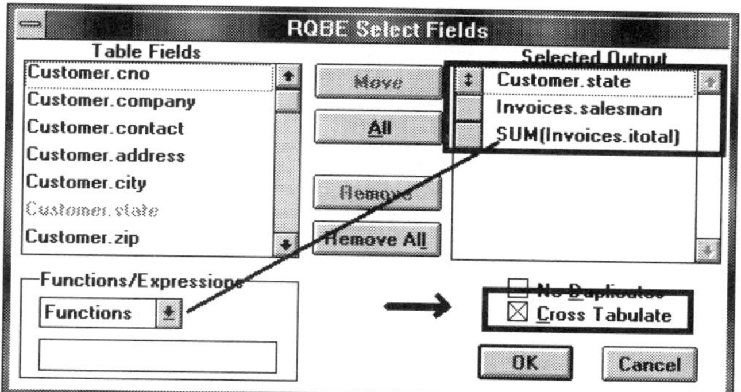

Figure 4.16 *Cross tabulation in the RQBE Select Fields dialog box.*

Once you get the hang of knowing what kind of data fits a cross tab, creating one is easy. And the payoff comes when you send the cross tabulation into the new FoxPro Graph Wizard. This nifty subsystem, originally created for Microsoft's Excel spreadsheet, is now being passed around many of the Microsoft Windows applications, including FoxPro.

The Graph Wizard guides you through a series of four steps to produce a basic graph of the data in the cross tab. There aren't many bells and whistles available, but it's extremely easy to use, and the output is useful either on screen or printed.

SQL Field Functions and Expressions

In addition to the fields of the tables, you can select from a list of SQL field functions that summarize specific information from fields, or use an expression of your own. These are constructed in the Functions/Expressions area in the lower left of the RQBE Select Fields dialog box. Type an expression or field function in the entry area, or use the Function pop-down list. Any expressions or functions used here are added to the list of <data items> following the SELECT statement. In effect, you are creating additional fields, or as they are called in the Browse, *calculated fields*. These have no existence outside of the RQBE query, but are displayed in the output just as if they were a field. Your entries can look like any of the following:

```
"This is a field title"
SUBSTR( customer.contact, 1, 20)
COUNT( DISTINCT customer.contact )
```

They shows up in the SELECT clause of the SQL statement looking like this:

```
SELECT "This is a field title", SUBSTR( customer.contact, 1,
20), ;
COUNT( DISTINCT customer.contact ) ;
FROM customer
```

Any standard FoxPro function like SUBSTR( ) above is fair game, however, these work on a record-by-record basis. By contrast, the so-called SQL field functions (elsewhere called group functions) accumulate information from all records or subsets of records from the entire table. As you will see in Section III, these are similar in operation to the FoxPro for Windows commands of the same name. Table 4.5 shows SQL field functions.

Table 4.5
SQL field functions.

COUNT(<expr>)	Count all occurrences of a (non empty) field or expression.
SUM(<expN>)	Sum all non empty occurrences of a numeric field or expression.
AVG(<expN>)	Average all occurrences of a numeric field or expression.
MIN(<expN>)	Return the minimum value of a numeric field or expression.
MAX(<expN>)	Return the maximum value of a numeric field or expression.
COUNT(DISTINCT <expN>)	Count all unique occurrences of a field or expression.
SUM(DISTINCT <expN>)	Sum all unique occurrences of a numeric field or expression.
AVG(DISTINCT <expN>)	Average all unique occurrences of a numeric field or expression.

In most cases, you would be using a field name for the required expression. However, these functions work with other expressions, including standard FoxPro functions, as appropriate.

Order By

Order By is the SORT operation, working just like all of the other sorts in FoxPro. There are no limits to the sorting levels, except those of practicality. And, as you'll notice in Figure 4.17, you can only sort on fields that have been selected in the Fields dialog box.

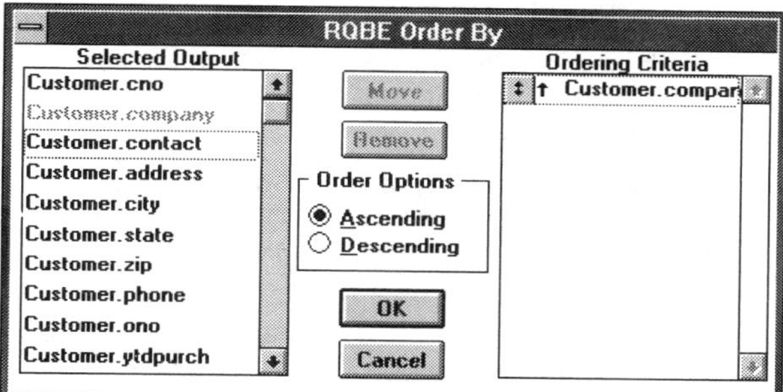

Figure 4.17 *The RQBE Order By dialog box.*

Order By is very much an output clause. It's sole function is to organize the data that is finally delivered to an output option.

Output Options

As already mentioned, the default output for RQBE is into a Browse window. This is the most useful way to develop and spot-check your query. However, when you're satisfied that the query is performing correctly, it may be time to turn to the other forms of output. RQBE has a rather rich assortment. The options are located in the output area in the upper right of the RQBE dialog box.

RQBE output options are shown in Table 4.6 on the next page.

Table 4.6
RQBE output options.

Browse	The default output for RQBE, and the most convenient way to scan the results of a query. However, the Browse window is read only and once closed the data is not saved.
Report	Outside of the Browse window, this is the most common way to use data retrieved through RQBE. Selecting this option automatically channels the data into a FoxPro report (created in the Report Writer) or creates a quick report on the spot.
Label	Similar to the Report option (actually a part of the same output screen), Label outputs the data through a label form created in the FoxPro Label Generator.
Table/DBF	This option creates a standard .DBF file on disk. After choosing this option, enter the file name into the Name Text Box, or use the file selection dialog to choose an existing file.
Cursor	The cursor (not related to a screen cursor) is SQL jargon for a somewhat shadowy temporary file. Depending on the Rushmore Technology, this may be an actual file on disk, or else a table that resides in memory. Its value is that you can "pass" a cursor to another SQL statement, or save the cursor to an actual .DBF file on disk by giving it a name in the Name Text Box, or choosing an existing file with the file selection dialog.
Graph	Connects the retrieved data with the Microsoft Graph Wizard a subsystem included with FoxPro. It guides the user through the process of creating a basic graph. There are ten graph types to choose. The graphs can be viewed on screen, printed, and saved to a file. The only requirement for using Graph output is that the data be appropriate. Generally this is used with the Cross Tabulation option in the RQBE Select Fields dialog box. Other combinations are possible. Data for the graph option can also be saved to a file by entering a filename in the Name Text Box, or selecting an existing file with the file selection dialog.

The RQBE Display Options dialog box is available only when you've selected **Report/Label** from the output options, then selected the **Options** button. The RQBE Display Options dialog box is shown in Figure 4.18.

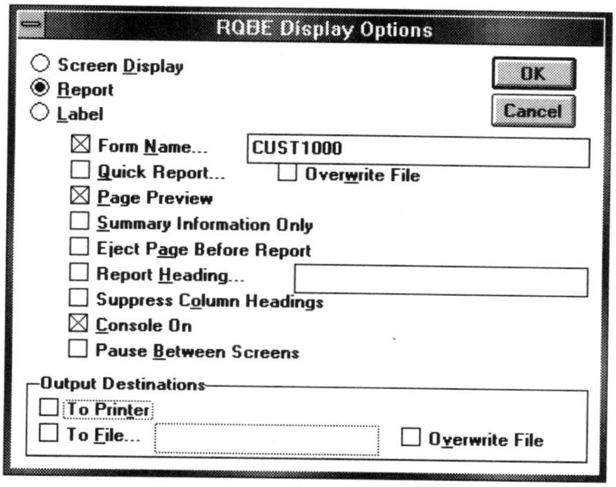

Figure 4.18 *The RQBE Display Options dialog box.*

Depending on whether you select Display, Report, or Label various option buttons are enabled or disabled. The important thing for the purposes of RQBE is that you can specify a report or label form that has already been created. You can also elect to have a Quick Report made from the RQBE data. (This option is not available for labels.)

Notes on Learning RQBE

Getting acquainted with RQBE takes practice. Lots of practice. Get together two or three tables with a limited number of records (five hundred or less), that can be easily related, and that have familiar content. When testing your RQBE/SQL concoctions, do frequent reality checks—either from your own sense of the data, or by browsing the tables.

Practice joins first. Make sure you understand what they do, and how they affect the outcome of all of the other elements of the SELECT. Remember that when you create a join, the lookup into the joined table is done on a record-by-record basis, and if it fails to find a matching record all of the logic applied thereafter are not applied against that record.

Be sure you are intuitively secure with the how SQL/FoxPro handles the processing of the major clauses. While there is a standard processing path that works, there are many other combinations of these clauses that also produce results. FoxPro checks only for the most egregious syntax errors, but does nothing for completely erroneous combinations of clauses and filter logic. This is why practice and reality checking is so important.

As you become more comfortable with RQBE, push your experimentation into complicated combinations of the WHERE criteria, the GROUP BY clause and the variations of the HAVING clause. It will help you later to achieve a greater understanding of the differences between the WHERE and the HAVING clauses, and when to use them.

The Report Writer

Transforming data into printed information is by popular impression *the* most important part of data management. Not all of this transformation takes the form of reports, but out of linguistic convenience reports and printed output have become synonymous. It's a rare project indeed that doesn't have a battery of reports.

Given the importance of reports, it's not surprising that attempts to make them easier to create are about as old as computing. Report printing lends itself to various kinds of automation—it's very repetitive and has well-understood components. The result has been a long history of report languages (like RPG) and report generators. The FoxPro report generator, the Report Writer, is already in its fifth edition. With each succeeding version, the Report Writer has matured, acquired more features, and become easier to use. The FoxPro for Windows version approaches state-of-the-art in report writers, which is saying a lot.

It wasn't too long ago, ten years or so, that microcomputer report generators were capable of only the most basic reports. Reports of any complexity usually had to be programmed—"hard coded"—one of the most nit-picking and time-consuming tasks in all of programming. Be thankful that you may never have to program a report. The FoxPro Report Writer isn't unlimited in capability, but can handle better than 90 percent of all of the reporting needed for applications.

In this chapter you'll be using the Report Writer as a menu option and a stand-alone "Power Tool." But it must be stressed that the Report Writer wouldn't be half the tool without the powerful database machinery that lies behind it, and the rich programming environment which supports it. Mastery of the Report Writer must include it's context within FoxPro for Windows as a whole. Without the services of the Rushmore Technology, RQBE, User Defined Functions, etc., the limitations of the Report Writer would be considerable.

In many ways, the Report Writer is easy to use. You probably already have a fairly clear image of what data tables and printed reports look like. But the question is how the Report Writer translates the tables into a printed format. First exposure to this kind of database reporting may seem unfamiliar. Terms like *bands*, *objects*, *groups*, and *report variables* are tossed about, along with Report Writer's way of visually representing a report. But a little practice and it will all make sense, as long as you don't start by trying to be too fancy.

To oversimplify for a moment, there is a typical path that leads from data to the printed page:

1. **Setup**—opening files, setting indexes and relations, and choosing printers.
2. **Layout**—choosing paper size, print orientation, page order, and placement of information on a page.
3. **Groups and calculations**—specifying report groups to organize a report, use of report variables for summary calculations.
4. **Objects**—placing fields, text, boxes, circles, lines, and pictures into the report layout.
5. **Design and decoration**—enhancing report objects and layout for visual effect (such as fonts and styles).
6. **Testing**—at each of the above steps, using the report Preview and actual printing to examine layout, design, and calculations.

You don't necessarily go through all of the steps above, and certainly not in detail, for every report you create. But you should learn to recognize the patterns of building a report, and plan accordingly. Although building reports can be at times tricky and at times tedious, they should never be an afterthought. They certainly aren't for the users of your applications.

Setup for a Report

You know that data tables are constructed of records and fields, and that most operations on the tables proceed from the top of the table to the bottom, in either an indexed or sequential fashion. Given the various FoxPro retrieval methods, you can select which records and fields are to be included. Putting this together, visualize a report being the result of a scan of a table (or multiple tables), as in Figure 4.19 on the next page.

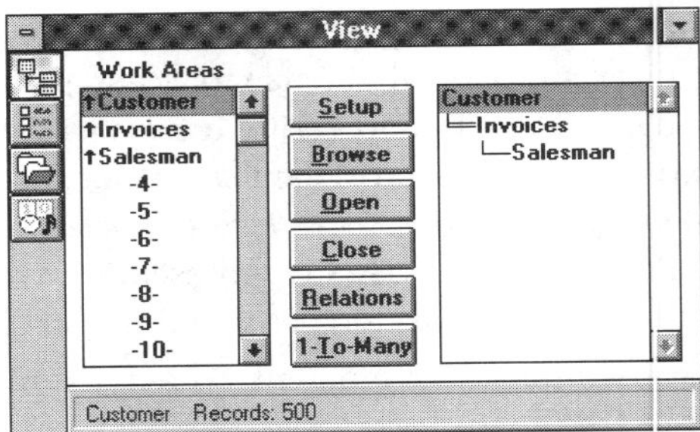

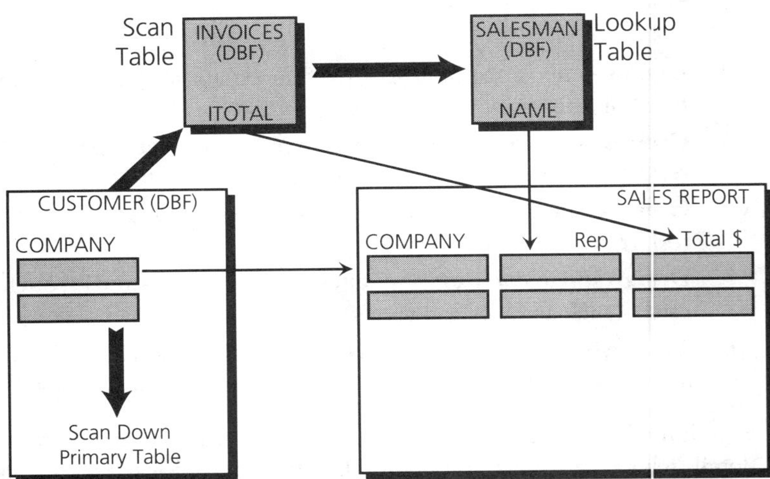

Figure 4.19 *A Report Writer setup.*

Like most of the FoxPro power tools, for the first time around, the Report Writer should have all the required files, indexes, and relations already opened and set. Thereafter, you can save the configuration—the *environment*—so it can be automatically recreated the next time you open or run the report. The Report Writer saves your report as a form in an .FRX file format. As usual, using the View dialog box is the best way to do your setup.

NOTE

All of the following Report Writer examples are based on using three files from the FoxPro tutorial material: CUSTOMER.DBF, INVOICES.DBF, and SALESMAN.DBF.

What Is This Report?

Before you lay hands on the View dialog box, it's probably a good idea to stop and ask, "What is this report?" A simple question, but often fudged until you get half way done and realize that things aren't right. In a formal preparation for a report, minimally a study would be done to see what data is needed, and a drawing made of what the report should look like. This is always a good idea. Naturally, under normal time pressures, things rarely get done this way. That doesn't make the approach less valid. The more difficult or important the report is, the more important it is to do your homework.

The starting point is to determine what the report is supposed to do and who's supposed to use it. Is it just a raw listing of data, an executive summary, a report to the board of directors using fancy graphics, or a routine business report? These are all reports for a specific audience, which to some extent dictates your approach. Not so much the basic design, but the presentation quality. More importantly, you also need to examine the purpose of the report—show profit and loss, indicate the best selling products, determine the commissions of salespeople. Frequently the purpose is obvious. But you might be surprised how many reports are created that turn out to have no real purpose. (Perhaps you're not surprised.)

The example in the Report Setup diagram is a typical business sales report. It's purpose is to show customer sales activity by state, so comparisons can be made between states and salespeople in those states.

The next piece of homework is to determine what information is supposed to be in the report. For a variety of reasons, this isn't always clear. Sometimes the subject matter of the report indicates what data to include. The users of the report can be asked what they need. However, people frequently only know in general what they want, and have difficulty expressing their requirements in words that mean something in the database context. That makes you something of a translator. Despite your best guesses as to report content, sometime it won't become clear what people really wanted until you deliver a report with information that isn't wanted or that's missing. Fortunately, the Report Writer makes it relatively easy to add or delete items from a report. It's still important, of course, to get as good a list of needed data as possible.

Files, Indexes, and Relations for Reports

The selection of files to open is, of course, determined by the information required for the report. Most reports consist of a primary table, one or two secondary scan tables, and any number of lookup tables. The primary table, as explained, controls the processing of the report. Secondary scan tables provide multiple instances of something connected to the primary table—fancy language for something like the customer with multiple orders in the example setup. Lookup tables are used for record-at-a-time lookups, typically to provide supporting information. In the example setup, the salesman table is a lookup to get the full name of salespeople listed by number in the invoices table.

The sort order, or more likely the index order, of the primary table is often extremely important for report grouping. The other tables will generally be ordered with indexes appropriate for setting relations. In the example setup CUSTOMER is opened with an index on the STATE field. INVOICES is opened with the index CNO (the customer number to link with the customer table), and SALESMAN with the index SALESMAN to link with the invoices table. Reports use relations extensively. Lookup tables have the basic relation, record at a time link. Scan tables have one-to-many relations to link with multiple records.

It should be stressed that the Report Writer isn't fussy about where it's data comes from. In this current example, standard data tables are being opened and configured in the View dialog box in preparation for making a report. You could just as easily write a program to open files, or use RQBE to generate a single "all-in-one" table that drives the report. The RQBE approach is particularly powerful, since you have the option to prepare a table that already contains all needed data, and that has already been sorted and grouped correctly. This tends to make running a report much more efficient.

Using the Report Writer

Presuming that you've already opened files, set indexes, and set relations, it's time to create a new report. From the main system menu, select **File, New, Report, New** (**Alt-F-N-R**). This brings up the default Report Writer Window and adds the Report and Object menus to the system menu.

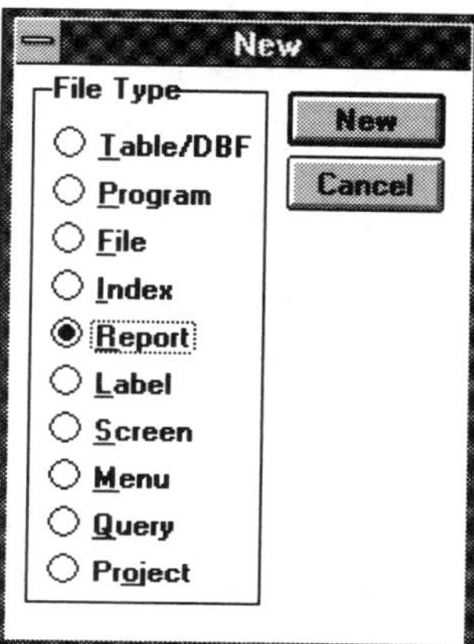

Figure 4.20
The New dialog box.

Figure 4.21
The Default Report window.

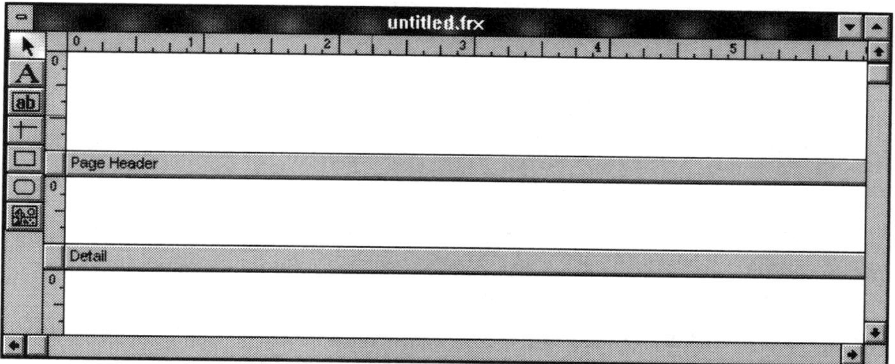

This brings up the default Report Writer window and adds the Report and Object menus to the system menu. The default window is a bare framework, and you could start immediately to add report elements to it. But you might want to take advantage of one item in the Report Menu—**Quick Report (Alt-R-Q)**.

Figure 4.22
The Report menu.

Report
Page Layout...
Page Preview... Ctrl+I
Show Position
Ruler/Grid...
✓Snap to Grid
Title/Summary...
Data Grouping...
Variables...
Quick Report...

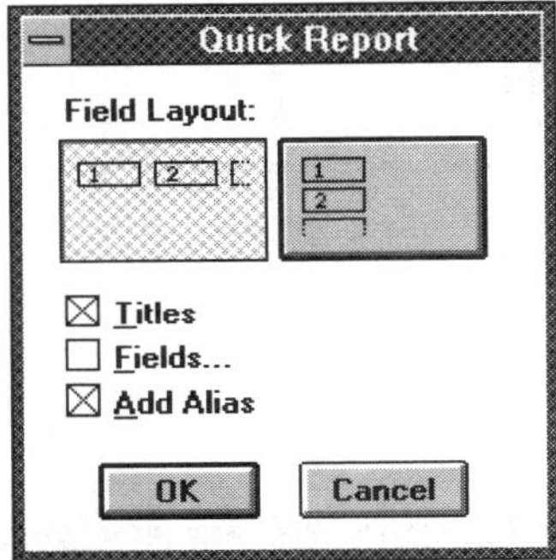

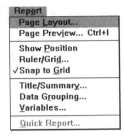

Figure 4.23
The Quick Report window.

The Quick Report option gives you the ability to select a spreadsheet layout (Browse like) or an Edit layout, and determine whether the fields should have titles, which fields are to be displayed, and whether table aliases should be applied to the fields. That's it. There are plenty of simple reports that don't need much more than this. You can always take the results of the Quick Report and modify it to be the base for much more complex reports.

As you might expect, a Quick Report isn't fancy.

If you don't choose the Quick Report, then you're ready to work with the standard Report Writer window. In contrast to the simplicity of the default window, here's an illustration (Figure 4.24) of a report that uses nearly all of the elements available in the Report Writer.

This is a completed report design, one that uses all of the bands available in the Report Writer. Bands are a screen representation for the areas in a standard report structure—title page, page header, detail, and page footer. The Report Writer is a band-oriented report generator. Bands control the structure of the report, the logic of processing, and the form of the printing. You can picture the screen like a ladder with adjustable rungs. Report space (usually printing lines) can be added or removed for any of the band areas (the white space between band bars) simply by using the band slider button on the left of each band. Alternatively, you can double click on the band buttons to pop up a Band dialog box to set the band size.

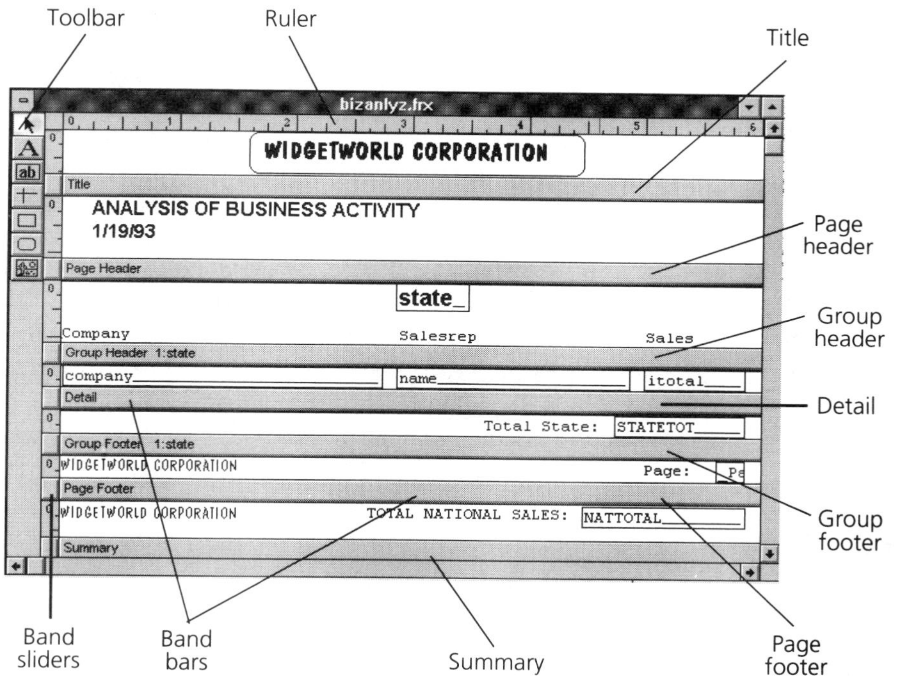

Figure 4.24 *The Report Writer window.*

Report Design and Layout

There are many ways to design and build a report. Helter skelter is probably the most common method. Some people prefer to do it systematically, starting with the main pages (title, body, summary), then adding the bands for the body (page header, detail, page footer). This might be called the "outside-in" approach. Another approach, especially appropriate for reports with complex processing requirements, is to work through the flow logic of the detail and group bands and add the trimmings later. This could be called the "inside-out" approach.

Any of the approaches can work, but you need to find methods that are most efficient. The goal of report building is to get the job done. Most projects require a lot of reports. Even a modest application might have 20-30 reports, and larger projects often have hundreds. Like it or not, much report building is necessary but repetitive work. This is aggravated by the fact that for most applications, creating reports comes in the latter part of the development cycle. That's just the time when people on the project are beginning to wind down or wear out, and when the end user is getting wound up and impatient. Coming so late in the game, complex reports can be the undoing of a good application. That's why it's important to practice with the Report Writer until you develop your own standard routine.

In time you might become an expert in all of the ways of building a report. But it doesn't hurt to master one way in the beginning. If you're going to pick an approach for practical reasons, it probably should be the inside-out method. Designing and building reports around the processing logic can head off many potential problems. It's very frustrating to put all kinds of finishing touches on a report, only to discover that it can't accurately deliver the information.

Whatever your approach, you need to form a clear picture of how the bands in the Report Design window correspond to the output on the page. The place to start is to understand report flow.

Report Flow

The concept of report flow is important. There are three kinds of "flows":

1. Flow through the data tables, (such as the processing order).
2. The flow of data in the report design.
3. The flow of printing.

For this sales analysis example, the flow in the data tables starts with the CUSTOMER table. Virtually all reports have a master or primary table. The records of this table may not even print, but the processing order of this table drives the report. As the CUSTOMER table is processed on a record-by-record basis, a relation has been set into the INVOICES table to list customer purchases, if any. If there are invoices, then flow transfers to the INVOICES table in order to print all invoices. As the INVOICES table is scanned, a lookup is made into the SALESMAN table to get the full name of the sales person (listed only as a number in the INVOICES table). After all invoices have been run, flow returns to the CUSTOMER table. This is the data flow.

The flow in the report itself starts with the order of pages. Figure 4.25 shows a typical report structure.

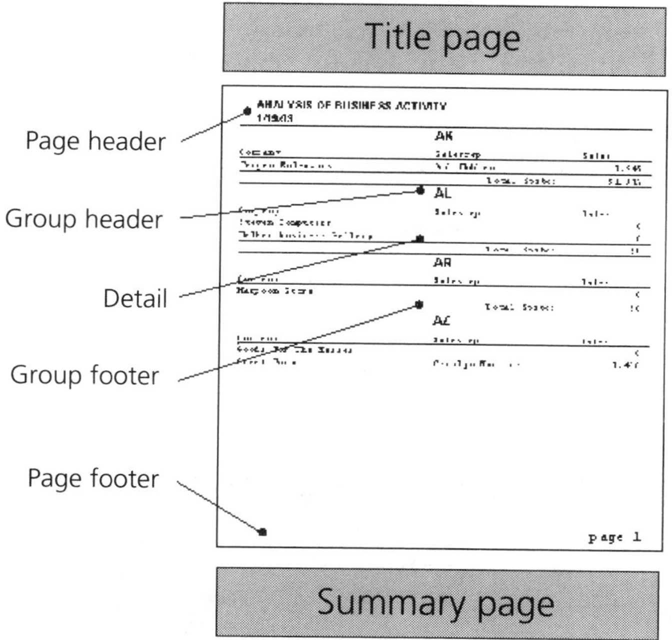

Figure 4.25 *A typical report structure.*

Many reports have a title page. Then there are the basic report pages, sometimes called the body of the report. There may also be other sections to the report that have separate pages. Finally there may be a summary page, typically for summary statistics and totals. The report flow also includes the structure of the basic report pages. As they run from top to bottom, there may be a page header identifying the report. Then there is the body of the page, called the detail in FoxPro. The body may be broken into separate sections, called groups, that may have their own group header for divider lines, column headings, and so on, and may have a group footer for totals and the like. Finally the page usually has a page footer for page numbering.

All of these flows contribute to the layout and processing of your reports. In time you need to get the feel of how data is processed in the tables, where it goes into your report pages, and how it gets printed.

The behavior of the bands at printing time is fairly straightforward, with the exception of the Detail band. Where the Title, Header, Footer, and

Summary bands are fixed—they never print more lines than you've indicated in the Layout window—the Detail band can stretch. It can add more lines as needed by whatever is being printed. This is why memo fields, which contain a variable amount of text, can only be automatically printed in the Detail band. It can stretch to accommodate variable text. The same applies to report graphics and particularly bitmap pictures. Only the Detail band can accommodate the shaping of pictures to fit with a variable amount of printed text.

The use of bands defines the areas of a report. Bands act as a guide for what data should be put in the areas, and what design elements like boxes and lines might be used. But this is not WYSIWIG. To get a picture of what the output looks like, you'll need to frequently use the Page Preview (**Ctrl-I**, or **Alt-O-I**), shown in Figure 4.26.

Figure 4.26
The Page Preview dialog box.

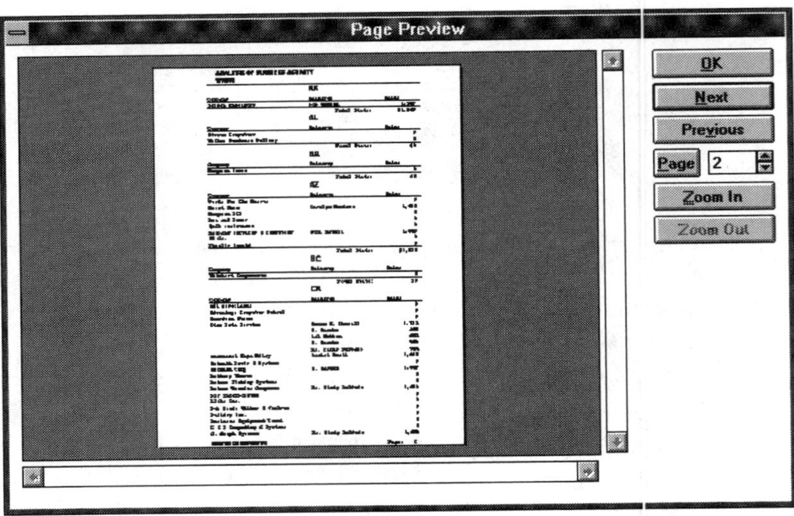

There are two modes in Page Preview, Zoom-Out (full page mode) and Zoom-in (sort of half-page mode). Unfortunately, the Zoom-Out loses many of the details, and Zoom-In shows most of the details but presents less than half a page, which loses perspective. The best choice remains an actual print of pages.

To create the basic layout, you need to set the size of paper, default font, and printing flow. It's a good idea to do this as soon as possible, and go directly into the Page Layout dialog box, Report, Layout (**Alt-O-L**), shown in Figure 4.27.

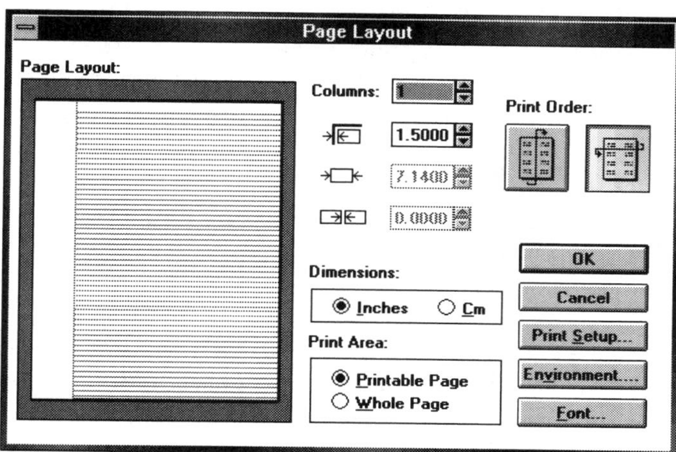

Figure 4.27
The Page Layout dialog box.

Following is a list of the options in the Page Layout dialog box:

- **Print Setup**—brings up the standard Windows Printer Setup dialog box. Here you can select portrait or landscape for page layout, and the size of paper. You can also set the printer (or similar output device) for the report.
- **Print Order**—specifies horizontal and vertical printing order. The button on the right is the standard print order—left to right across the entire page. The other option, column order (the button on the left), is new with FoxPro. It enables printing in text columns (not the same as numeric reports printed in columns), and opens the door to many kinds of formats not previously possible. Keep in mind that column order produces a "snaking" continuous print, proceeding from the column on the left—from top to bottom—to the next column in turn—from top to bottom.
- **Columns**—is to specify up to fifty columns on a page. To make the columns work properly, you'll need to carefully consider the width of data to be included, and how it will fit inside a column. What you see in the Report Writer design window is what will fit in *one* column. If you

have more data than will fit in the column size you've selected, FoxPro grays out those items that won't fit.

With a single column, only the left margin width can be adjusted. Once you have specified more than one column, then you can set the width of the columns, and the distance between columns (the *gutter*).

- **Print Area**—FoxPro lets you distinguish between the entire page or the part of the page that actually prints. This distinction only applies to laser printers, which typically have a frame of 1/4 inch that does not print around each page.
- **Font**—selects the default font for a report. Individual objects can be assigned their own fonts.
- **Dimensions**—sets the unit of measurement for the report dimensions to inches or centimeters.
- **Environment**—has nothing to do with printing or layout, which masks its importance. When you create a setup (or view) of tables, indexes, and relations for a report, you may want to save it so you don't have to go through the setup process again. The Save option in the Environment dialog box saves these three key elements of your operating environment. Later, if you select Environment when running a report, the table setup is automatically restored.

  This may sound like a very good idea. Sometimes it is, particularly when first developing a report. However, as experience will teach you, saving the environment is tantamount to hard coding the location of your files. If anything changes in these files, or they get moved to another subdirectory, your report stops running, and the user gets an error message.

You can also start your design by setting the *ruler* and *grid* (the ruler on the edge of the Design window, and the grid of lines running through the window). These are both optional, but can be very helpful for alignment, especially when combined with the Snap to Grid option in the Report menu (**Alt-R-G**). This forces alignment with a grid line, and is used to ensure that a row or column of objects are in accurate alignment.

The Title/Summary page window is reached through Report, Title/Summary (**Alt-O-Y**) in the system menu. There's not much to this—selecting Title or Summary adds those bands to the report. If you also select the page options, then each will be on a separate page.

Running a Report

During the process of creating a report, and of course to actually run it for real, FoxPro for Windows provides the Report option of the Database system menu, shown in Figure 4.28.

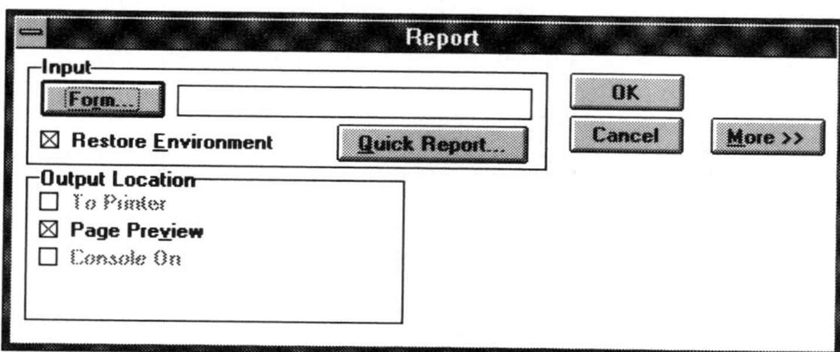

Figure 4.28 *The Report dialog box.*

The basic Report dialog box has only a few options. If you are working on a report form, then the name of that report is displayed in the Input text box. Otherwise, you need to select a report **Form** from a file on disk. Reports are stored in .FRX files, and to simplify locating them with the file open dialog, it's a good idea to put them all in one subdirectory.

The **Restore Environment** check box can be used if the report was created with the Save Environment option enabled. If it was, FoxPro opens and restores all files, indexes, and relations necessary to run the report.

The **Quick Report** option is available if you are not working with an existing report, but have an open file. As an option in this window, you will be asked to provide a name to save as a new report, before FoxPro runs the Quick Report form.

The Output Location box gives you three choices for output: To Printer, Page Preview, and Console On (to the screen).

Selecting the **More>>** button brings up an extended Report dialog box, shown in Figure 4.29 on the next page.

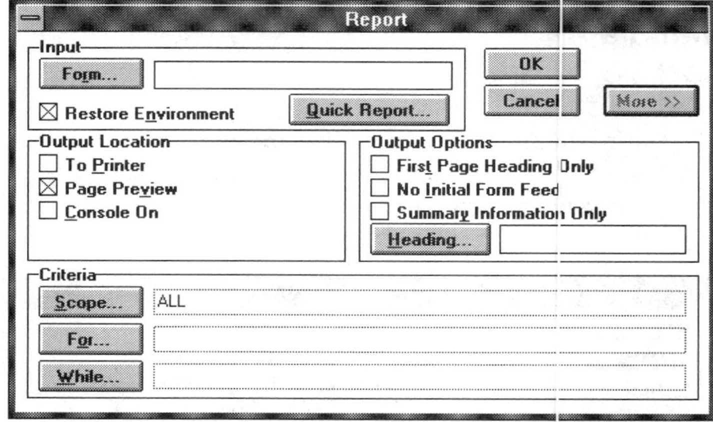

Figure 4.29 *The Report dialog box.*

Two new option boxes appear, Output Options and Criteria. The Criteria box has the familiar Scope, For and While options, for which you can use the buttons to summon the Expression Builder. These options are often used to selectively print data in the same way they are used to control other FoxPro operations.

The Output Options box has some options that are carried over from FoxPro for DOS. The First Page Heading Only does not refer to the headings bands in a report form, but rather to the Heading option in this box. If you choose to enter a report heading, or use the Heading button for the Expression Builder, this will be printed at the top of every page of the report, unless you select the First Page Heading Only checkbox.

No Initial Form Feed suppresses the printing of an initial blank page.

Summary Information Only is an oddly powerful option that can radically change the appearance and output of a report. If the report contains data that can be summarized, such as columns of numbers, then this option produces a report that shows only the totals for these columns. Other kinds of reports with varying data configurations produce very different summary reports. Some will be useless. However, as a Q&D (quick and dirty) method to get summary information, this options is very helpful.

Report Groups

There are some reports that are just simple lists—lists of customers, lists of parts, and so on. For these reports a straight listing, such as provided by a Quick Report, is all that's needed. But what if a list can be categorized, like a list of parts by car model, and you want to highlight these categories? Or what if you need to get summary sales figures by regions of the country from a list of stores? That's when a simple report crosses into the territory of report groups.

The capability to create report groups is universal among report generators, and you may recall the FoxPro RQBE can create groups as well. Groups are used any time you want to break up the data into types or categories. Groups allow you to separate different types of data, both visually on the page and for purposes of calculation. The example being used here has a classic group—it requires totals for customer purchases by state. So the customer table needs to be ordered by state, which gets all the customers from a state grouped together.

NOTE

If it isn't sorted on it, you can't group by it.

Groups fall out of the sort order of the primary table. The sort order is usually created by an index, but of course this can be done with a plain old Sort or the Order By clause of an RQBE query. In the customer database example, the sort order for this report is by state, using an index on the STATE field. This has one sort order, and can make one group. If you need additional grouping, say by state, by area code, and by city, then your sort (whether with an index or otherwise) needs to order the data first by state, then by area code, and then by city. These *cascade sorts* (or indexes) produce the ordering necessary to define three groups: state, area code, and city.

Presuming you've got your data house in order, defining groups in the Report Writer is very simple. From the main menu select Report, Data Grouping to bring up the Data Grouping dialog box, shown in Figure 4.30 on the next page.

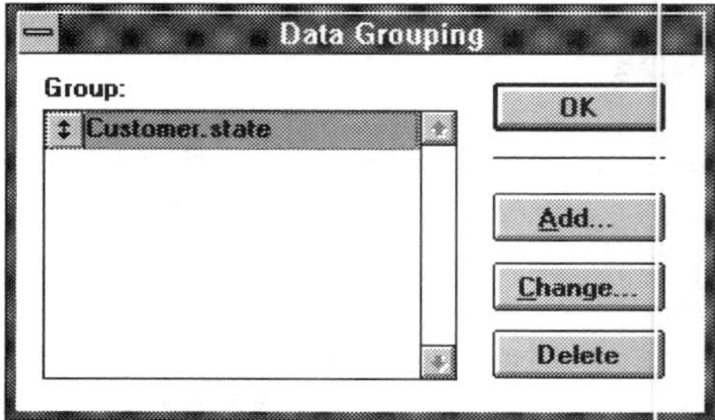

Figure 4.30 *The Data Grouping dialog box.*

The Data Grouping window is simply a list of groups, to which you can Add, Change, or Delete. If you select either Add or Change, you get the dialog box for Group Info, shown in Figure 4.31. This is where you actually define the group.

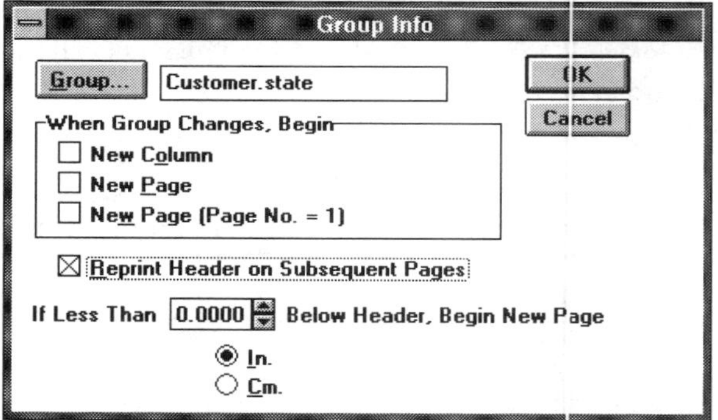

Figure 4.31 *The Group Info dialog box.*

Groups are most commonly established on fields, or more specifically, on a particular sort order. If your sort order is based on an expression, then the group should be based on the same expression. The Group button lets you define the group using the Expression Builder screen. In addition to establishing the identity of a group, you can also specify what happens when a group changes: a new column or a new page (with an option to set a new page number). The column option works in concert with columnwise printing and provides some interesting design possibilities particularly for multicolumn landscape reports.

Another check box specifies reprinting of the group header on subsequent pages of the report. This can be very useful for repeating column headings and other visual alignment elements (such as lines and boxes) of a report.

Finally the Group Information dialog box has what might be called a "widow/orphan" option for groups. By specifying the distance between a Group Header and the end of a page, FoxPro forces a page break rather than leave a Group Header without any subsequent content on the same page.

All of these options give you control over the action of a group, and in particular what happens at a group break. This is the point where one group item ends, and another begins. In the customer report, this happens when the records of one state ends, and another state begins. The break in this example also affects the scan in the invoices table, since only invoices related to the state in the customer table are part of the scan. This sets the table, so to speak, for totaling invoices by state. As you will see, group breaks have a very important role in the use of report variables.

Report Variables

Report variables are, first of all, just variables. They can store values of any kind (such as character, numeric, or date), like all other variables in FoxPro. You can make use of a report variable anywhere in a report to hold values. These values can be passed into UDFs and can persist beyond the run of the report—just like other variables. Yet the impression is that report variables are quite different than standard variables.

Perhaps what makes report variables seem different is that FoxPro provides a special screen to define them, and report variables can be linked with report summary calculations like Sum or Count. As you will see, this latter capacity is very similar to calculated fields. This causes people to get report variables and calculated fields mixed up. On the whole, report variables, and to a certain extent their connection with report groups, are probably the most perplexing part of learning the Report Writer.

In real life (or a report builder's life anyway) there are at least a million ways to use report variables. Here's three of them (using the customer report for an example):

1. **The invoice table contains the amount for each customer purchase. In this report, you'd like to have the amounts totaled by state.** This first use of a report variable is dependent on the table being ordered by state, and a state group having been defined. To define the variable, start with Report, Variable (**Alt-O-V**). Since this is a new variable, select the **Add** option, which brings up the Variable Definition dialog box.

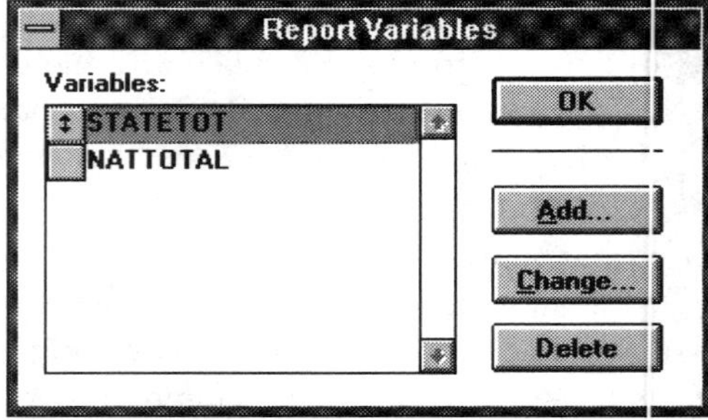

Figure 4.32 *The Report Variable window.*

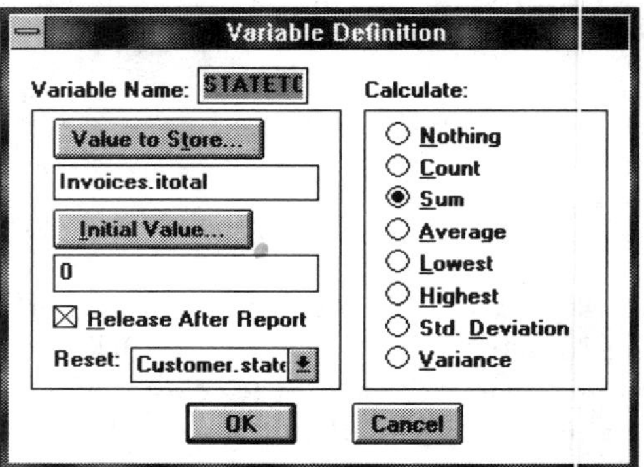

Figure 4.33 *The Report Variable Definition window.*

This report definition screen exists because you have no direct access to the workings of a FoxPro report. Unlike general programming, where you can manipulate the code surrounding a variable, in a report you can't tinker with the FoxPro code. So the definition dialog box gives you somewhat limited but useful ways of inserting and manipulating a variable in a report.

The main purpose for report variables is to store the running values of summary calculations. In the case at hand, you want a running total of invoices by state. In the Variable Definition dialog box, you enter a name for the variable, such as `statetot`, and indicate the Value to Store to be `invoices.itotal`—the invoice amount field from the invoices table. Since there is no starting value for this variable, you can leave the default of 0 in the initial value box. Likewise the default Release After Report can remain to remove the variable from memory, as soon as the report completes.

The crucial entry for this definition is the **Reset** option. Reset means "reset to zero" for summary calculations. You use this any time you want to have the calculations start over with a new grouping. Besides the standard options (End of Report, End of Page, End of Column), each group that you have defined is also displayed. In this case, `customer.state` would be selected, since you want the `state` total to be zeroed before starting a new state.

The final step for defining this variable is to select the **Sum** option to have it contain the running sum of the invoices `itotal` field. When you're done with the definition, you can display the variable in the state Group Footer band.

2. **You want to have an invoice total for the entire country.** The second variable is even simpler than the first. Again, **Add** a variable. Give it a name, `nattotal`. As with `statetotal`, the Value to Store is `invoices.itotal`. Only this time leave the **Reset** option on the default End of Report. And then set the calculate option to Sum. It's important that this variable be displayed in the Summary band, if you want it to contain the total for the entire report.
3. **You would also like to have the largest state total as a percentage of the national total.** The third report variable demonstrates the primary value of report variables—you can use them in other report variable expressions. The national total has already been calculated in `nattotal`. Now you need the highest state total. Again, **Add** a variable. Give it a name, `StateHigh`. The key to this variable is using the report variable `statetotal` for the Value to Store. This is also a variable not reset until the end of the report. Finally select **Highest** as the summary calculation. All of these variables are then used in the Summary band in this display expression:

```
(statehigh/nattotal)*100
```

This produces the ratio of the highest state sales expressed as a whole number percentage of the national sales total.

NOTE

As the FoxPro manuals point out, you need to be careful with any report variable that contains another report variable as part of its definition. The order in which variables are listed in the Report Variable window is *the order of calculation*. If you put statehigh in the list before statetot, you'll get an incorrect calculation.

Groups and Report Variables Together

Report variables do not require groups. But they are so commonly used together, that it's important to reinforce the relationship.

Groups are used to determine when report variables are reset (to 0). In the customer report example, FoxPro scans the customer file from top to bottom: one customer for AK (Alaska), another customer for AK, then one customer for AL—a new state and a group break. At the group break several things happen. FoxPro prints the Group Footer for the previous group. It then resets all designated group variables. Finally, it prints the Group Header of the new group.

Report Objects

If the report layout is the playing field, then objects are the players. All of the elements so far provide the framework to hold fields, expressions, text, lines, boxes, and pictures. These are the report objects. FoxPro like so many other contemporary products is moving towards an *object-oriented* approach to software, and particularly software development. This can be, and often is, driven beyond the edge of credibility. Microsoft is not one pushing that edge. In FoxPro the Report Writer and the other power tools borrow some object-oriented lingo, but this should not be confused with the more systematic approach of OOP (Object Oriented Programming).

Report Expression (Field) Objects

In FoxPro an *object* is simply some recognizably distinct entity that may have a number of characteristics associated with it. A field from a database table is an object. In the Report Writer it may have several characteristics. The whole package of a field can be moved around the layout screen, modified, or deleted as a unit.

The Report Expression dialog box can only be accessed by clicking with the mouse on the **Field Tool** icon in the toolbox. There is, unfortunately, no keyboard alternative. Once the field tool is selected, you use the mouse to size the field somewhere in the Report Layout window. Click on any of the six boxes surrounding the field while continuing to hold down the left mouse button, drag the field marquee to the desired size, and then let go of the mouse button. This opens the Report Expression dialog box, displayed in Figure 4.34.

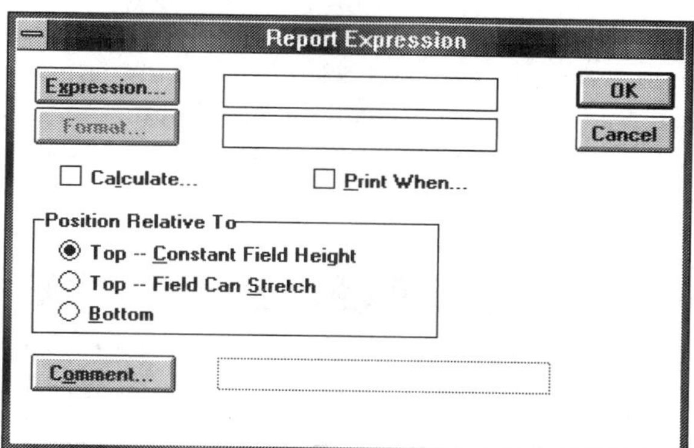

Figure 4.34 *The Report Expression dialog box.*

If you know the name (and alias) of the field or other expression, you can type it directly into the text box to the right of the Expression button. Otherwise, select the Expression button and yet another instance of this dialog box is displayed, ready for you to select a field, or construct an expression of your choosing. About 90 percent of the time, this is simply selecting a field. Another 8 percent of the time, you'll combine a field with functions or other expressions such as:

```
TRIM( customer.company ) + " ID:"+ customer.cno
```

The last 2 percent of the time will be for special expressions, for example this one based on a condition, which prints "Big Sale" if the invoice total is greater than $1,000:

```
IIF( invoices.itotal > 1000, "Big Sale", "" )
```

Once the expression object has been defined and located in the layout, there are options in the Report Expression dialog box that cover two main aspects of the objects' characteristics: Format and Printing.

Expression Formatting

Clicking on the **Format** button displays one of the three expression Format dialog boxes. Depending on the data type, the dialog box will be for a character, numeric, or date expression. FoxPro for Windows tries to "guess" the data type, but some expressions you enter may not have a clear type, and FoxPro will guess wrong. Be sure to check the radio buttons below the format text box to see if you've got the correct data type. Figures 4.35, 4.36, and 4.37 shows the Format dialog boxes for character, numeric, and date expressions, respectively.

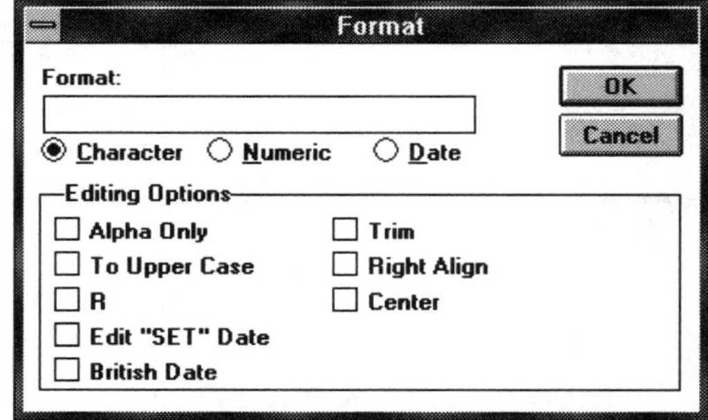

Figure 4.35 *The Format dialog box for character expressions.*

Format
Format:
OK
Cancel
Character
Numeric
Date
Editing Options
Left Justify
Blank if Zero
(Negative)
Edit "SET" Date
British Date
CR if Positive
DB if Negative
Leading Zeros
Currency
Scientific

Figure 4.36 *The Format dialog box for numeric expressions.*

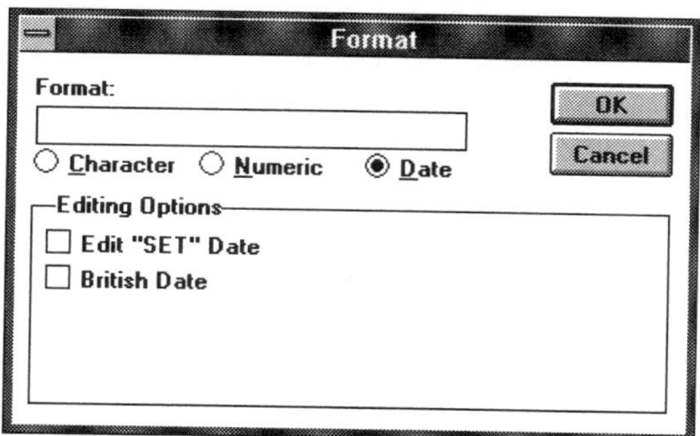

Figure 4.37
The Format dialog box for date expressions.

This may be your first contact with expression formatting, and particularly format templates. The purpose of this formatting in the Report Writer is to shape and control how an expression is output. For example, if a field expression normally produces output in lower case (johnson), but you want it in all upper case (JOHNSON), there are two ways to produce this effect. Apply the UPPER( ) function to the field in the expression definition, or use the **To Upper Case** option in the Format dialog box.

NOTE

Expression formats are displayed prominently in the programming of @SAY and @GET, the screen input/output commands. They are used again and again. This is a good time to start committing them to memory.

Tables 4.7, 4.8, and 4.9 review the available print formatting options by data type.

Table 4.7
Character data formatting functions.

Option	Code	Output and Example
Alpha Only	A	Display only alpha characters.
To Upper Case	!	All characters displayed in uppercase (all caps) `[ JOHNSON]`

(continued)

R	R	Nonformat characters displayed `[(612) 454-6547]`
Edit "SET" Date	D	Edit data as a date using current SET DATE format. `[03/21/93]`
British Date	E	Use European date format. `[21.03.93]`
Trim	T	Remove all leading and trailing blank spaces.
Right Align	J	Align text on the right of the field. `[ JUSTIFIED RIGHT]`
Center	I	Center text in the field. `[ CENTERED ]`

Table 4.8
Numeric data formatting functions.

Option	**Code**	**Output and Example**
Left Justify	B	Numeric data aligned with left side of field. `[1234 ]`
Blank if Zero	Z	If the field output is zero, then nothing will be printed.
(Negative)	(	Negative numbers placed in parentheses. `[ (3423)]`
Edit SET Date	D	Edit data as a date using current SET DATE format.
British Date	E	Use European date format.
CR if Positive	C	CR (credit) printed after number, if positive. `[ 34CR]`
DB if Negative	X	DB (debit) printed after number, if negative. `[ 34DB]`
Leading Zeros	L	Print leading zeros before number. `[0000234]`
Currency	$	Prints a currency format. `[$20,220]`
Scientific	^	Displays numbers in scientific notation. `[ 1.45E]`

Table 4.9
Date data formatting functions.

Option	Code	Output and Example
Edit Date	D	Edit field as a date in current date format. [12/12/93]
Edit British Date	E	Edit field in European date format. [21.03.93]

All of these options are available at the click of a mouse in the Format dialog boxes. You may have noticed that after clicking on the options, the code representation of your selection appears in the Format text box. You can enter the same codes directly into the box using the @ character to signify a FUNCTION followed by one or more of the codes listed above. For example, you can type **@D** to have something output as a date, or @T! to have text trimmed and output in uppercase.

Format functions affect the entire content of an expression. On the other hand format templates impose patterns on individual elements (characters, numbers, and so on) of a field. Suppose you wanted the first three letters of a field capitalized, you can use the following format template: "!!!XXXXX". These are called PICTURE template codes in the Xbase language, and *field masks* in other systems. They provide you with minute control over the output format. You'll notice in Table 4.10 that many of the options have an equivalent in the functions, only here they operate on one character at a time:

Table 4.10
PICTURE template codes.

Code	Output and Example of Use
A	Allows output of only alphabetic characters. [AAAAA]
L	Allows output of logical data only. [L]

(continued)

N	Allows letters and digits only for output. [NNN]
X	Allows any character. [XXXXXXXX]
Y	Allows Y,y,N,n only, with Y and N converted to uppercase. [Y]
9	With character data, allows only numeric entry. With numeric data, allows all number and signs. [$99.99]
#	Allows numbers (digits), blanks, and signs. [###,###]
!	Convert lower case letters to uppercase. [!!!]
$	Display current currency symbol. [$ ##.##]
*	Display asterisks in front of numeric values. [***###]
.	Specifies the decimal point. [99.99]
,	Comma separation for digits left of decimal point. [$ ###,###,###]

If you choose to enter function or template codes directly, be certain you include the @ symbol for any of the function codes. Do not use quotation marks for any of the entries. Function codes and picture templates can be combined. For example, [@B$ ###,###] is interpreted by FoxPro to format a number left justified with a leading dollar sign, and with a comma between thousands and hundreds—[$234,222].

Summary Expressions (Calculated Fields)

Summary Expressions, often called *calculated fields*, are very similar to Report Variables. By selecting **Calculate** in the Report Expression dialog box, you'll see a list of calculation options exactly like those for report variables, and a Reset list with the same alternatives.

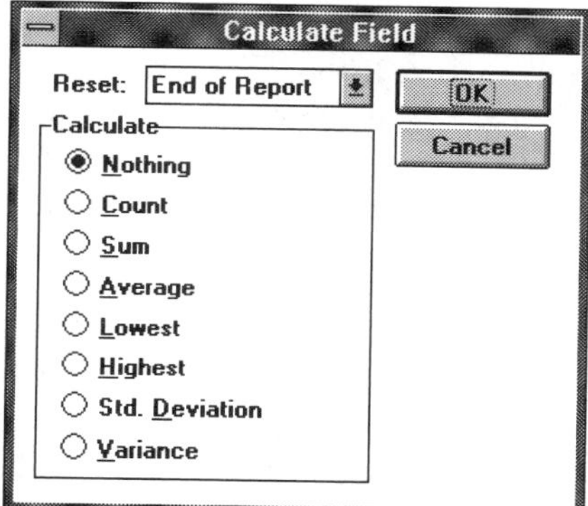

Figure 4.38
The Calculate Field dialog box.

NOTE

Calculated fields are less flexible than Report Variables. They can't be used inside other expressions, and their results can't persist beyond the running of the report. For this reason, it's recommended to stick with Report Variables for any kind of summary calculations.

The Position Relative To box provides you with three options for placement of the field/expression in a line: Top—Constant Field Height aligns the field with the top of a line and maintains its size. Top—Field Can Stretch also aligns with the top of a line, but allows the field area to expand (vertically) with the volume of text. Bottom, aligns the field with the bottom of a line. All of these options are best used to insure uniform alignment across a line.

SHORTCUT

You can get much more accurate placement of objects by moving them into position with the mouse, and then switching to the Arrow keys for one pixel at a time movement.

Text, Line, and Rectangle Objects

These objects are simple to use. They are all "decorative" objects used to highlight, segregate, and organize the visual presentation of a report. Which is also to say that they're artistic elements and you throw them into a report at the peril of making the thing a mess. All of the objects are used by selecting their corresponding tool from the toolbox, then applying them to the Report layout. Here's a brief rundown of each object:

- **Text**. Text objects are more or less obvious. They're used for titles, descriptions, and so on. The most important thing about them is that in FoxPro they become major design elements because text can take on the attributes of Font and Style. The Text dialog box is displayed in Figure 4.39.

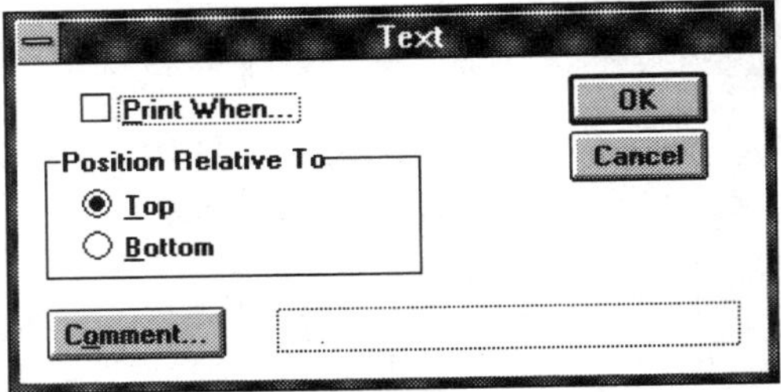

Figure 4.39 *The Text dialog box.*

- **Rectangles/Lines.** The two geometric shapes objects, which are actually four objects—squares, rectangles, lines, and circles—are very similar. Rectangles (squares) and lines share the Rectangle/Line dialog box. Like text objects they can have a Print When condition, and may be positioned at the top or bottom of a line. A rectangle can also be set to "stretch" with a band. This is particularly useful if you want to box a memo field and have it expand with the size of the text. The Rectangle/Line dialog box is displayed in Figure 4.40.

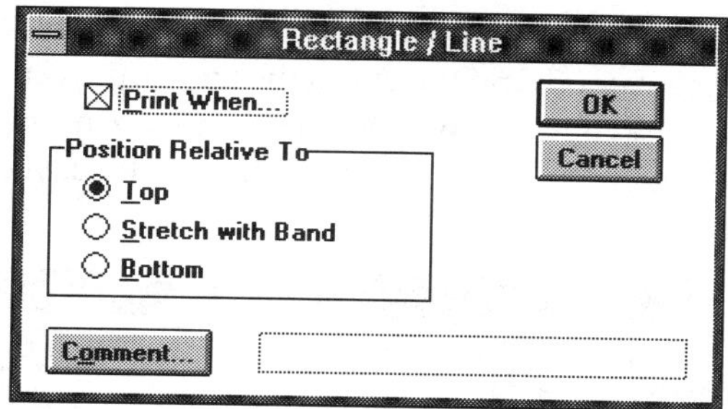

Figure 4.40
The Rectangle/Line dialog box.

- **Round Rectangles**. Round rectangles (and circles) have their own dialog box, with much the same options as the Rectangle/Line dialog box, with the exception of the choices for Style of round rectangle. There are various bevels for the corners. The one on the far right, however, turns the rectangle into a circle. This is a curious way of presenting a circle shape, but presumably you don't use many circles in printed reports. The Round Rectangle dialog box is displayed in Figure 4.41.

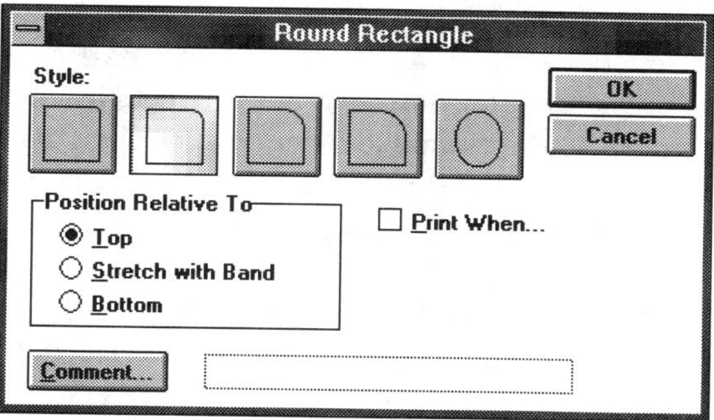

Figure 4.41
The Round Rectangle dialog box.

Picture Objects

Outside of fonts, this is the first encounter in the FoxPro system menus with the special properties of a Graphical User Interface (GUI). It takes a GUI to make the presentation of graphics (such as pictures and icons) relatively easy. The Report Writer now allows you to incorporate picture elements in a report, and the mechanics are simple. Most of your time will be spent with adjustments, sizing, and alignment to make the picture element fit properly in the report.

Like the other report objects, picture objects are only available through the toolbox. Select the **Picture** icon, and then with the mouse draw the outline of the picture frame in the Layout window. When you release the mouse button, the Report Picture dialog box, shown in Figure 4.42, is displayed.

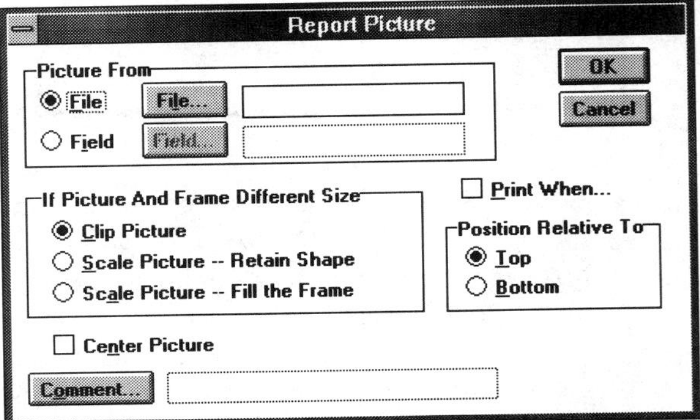

Figure 4.42 *The Report Picture dialog box.*

The first step is to identify the source of the picture (pictures are never stored in the report). You've got two options, a file on disk with a .BMP extension (or at least any true bitmap picture file), or from a General Field in a table. If you select the File option, you'll get the familiar Windows file open dialog box to select the file you want. As usual, this requires that you have an idea where to look for files. For this reason it's usually a good idea to put all .BMP files of a project in the same subdirectory.

If you select the **Field** option, you'll get the Choose Field/Variable dialog box. The only choice that makes sense is, of course, a field. The field must be of the general data type and contain something that is (or closely approximates) a bitmap image.

That's all there is to selecting the image. However, General Field images tend to come in a wide variety of shapes and sizes. They don't always fit neatly into the area you've selected in the report. So FoxPro gives you some options for shaping pictures.

In the If Picture and Frame Different Size box there are three options:

- **Clip Picture** handles pictures that are bigger than the frame you indicated. It "clips" the overlap of the picture and shows only that portion that fits in the frame. If this doesn't show what you had in mind, then you need to go back to the picture's source (usually a drawing program of some kind) and edit the picture.

- **Scale Picture—Retain Shape** resizes the picture inside the frame without losing the proportions of the original shape. In effect this allows only exactly proportional changes to the picture size.
- **Scale Picture—Fill the Frame** stretches the picture to fit the frame, regardless if that introduces any distortion of the picture.

In addition to the picture and frame options, you can also select the **Center Picture** option, if you are working with bitmaps in a general field. This automatically centers the picture in the frame instead of the default position in the upper left corner.

Different pictures react differently to these treatments. You'll frequently have to do some experimentation to find the right combination of frame, sizing, and alignment. Because of the sometimes peculiar behavior of pictures and the time it takes to print them, it's a good idea to be moderate with their use in printed reports.

When to Print

NOTE

This is a new and very powerful set of options for the Report Writer. Your time would be well spent to experiment with them.

The **Print When** options are a very welcome new addition to the capabilities of the Report Writer. They especially extend what can be placed in the Detail band of a report by making it possible to have objects, or more importantly whole lines, that do not print if there's nothing to print. This opens the door to having lookups in multiple tables, which print only when certain conditions are true.

The Print When check box is displayed with all object windows, and when selected pops the Print When dialog box. The uses of options here are not always obvious, but they are quite versatile.

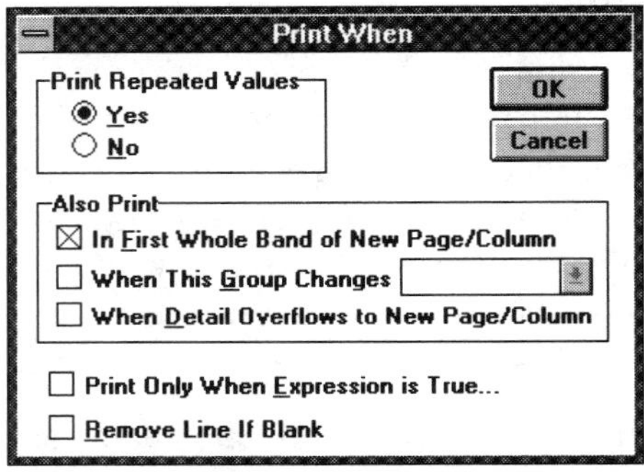

Figure 4.43 *The Print When dialog box.*

The Print Repeated Values option was available in earlier versions of the Report Writer. It's main function is to suppress repeated printing of expressions in the Detail band. The classic example is for a company name followed by a list of invoices. The company name is only needed once, so you would select **No** in the Print Once Per Band dialog box.

The Also Print dialog box contains three options that are used mostly for printing of objects in and around page, group, and column breaks.

And finally there are two inconspicuous options at the bottom of the Print When window. These two are the most important! The best way to explain the **Print Only When Expression is True** and **Remove Line if Blank** options is with a short example.

This fragment of a report illustrates only one of many possible uses of the Print When options. In this case the basic report is a list of companies from the customer table, which highlights customers belonging to three sales volume "clubs". As the report is run, the sales volumes are calculated from the invoices table. The trick is to display a customer's club membership only when appropriate, otherwise omitting the lines. In the Report Layout Window there are three lines defined to print invoice information, but in the Printed Output only one line (or none) actually print. This is the work of the **Print When** options.

The key to making this work is to follow the same basic procedure for each of the objects in the "club" lines (the text objects like Thousand Dollar Club, and the field expression objects):

1. Open the **Text Object** window or **Report Expression** window by double-clicking an object.

2. Next click on the **Print When** check box, which brings up the Print When window.
3. The business end of this technique uses the two check boxes at the bottom of the window: **Print Only When Expression is True** and **Remove Line if Blank**. Click on the **Remove Line if Blank** box. This works in concert with the **Print Only on Expression** option to omit lines that are "blank". All objects in the line should be set not to print unless they satisfy a condition. If they fail the condition, FoxPro considers them to be "blank".
4. Next, click on the **Print Only When Expression is True** option. In the Expression Builder window you define the condition when the object *should* print. In this example, for each of the "club line" objects, the condition is based on the value of the itotal field in the invoice table. For example, the "Thousand Dollar Club" uses the conditional expression,

   ```
   invoices.itotal > 1000.
   ```

   The other two lines are variations of this expression,

   ```
   BETWEEN( invoice.itotal, 500, 1000 )
   ```

   This uses the function **BETWEEN( )** to determine a range of values. These objects will print only when these expressions are satisfied. Again, important point to remember is that *every object* in a line must have the same Print When logic, if you want the line not to print.

Two final touches to this example are:

1. To mark the customer.company field for not printing repeated values (in the Print When window). This will ensure that the company name will not reprint whenever one of the "club lines" is printed.
2. Include a solid line (using the line tool) below the company field as a separator. This object should also have a **Print When, Print Only When Expression is True** setting. In this case one that will make the line print only when one of the "club lines" prints, which in this case could be:

   ```
   BETWEEN( invoices.itotal,100,1000000 )
   ```

The Object Menu

Some report objects contain information—fields and text. All report objects, however, are design elements in the report layout. They contribute to the visual presentation of the information. At some point in the creation of a full scale report, you'll turn your attention to the visual layout and decorative aspects of how the report will look when printed. In the process of refining these elements you'll need to turn to the options in the Object menu. The options of this menu can be put into two categories: positioning options, and object characteristics options, shown in Tables 4.11 and 4.12, respectively.

Table 4.11
Object menu: positioning options.

Option	Use
Align to Grid	If you select the Ruler/Grid option from the Report menu, you can force objects to align with that grid. This can be very useful in the early stages of report design, when you want to make elements line up correctly and evenly. There will be other occasions, however, when you'll need to turn the grid alignment off to allow for off center and other forms of micro positioning.
Bring to Front	Any object, or group of objects can be positioned on top of other objects. In effect, you can layer objects. How ever, you may want to change which object is on top of a stack. This option puts a selected object up front, visible above any other object underneath.
Send to Back	The opposite action from Bring to Front, this sends an object (or group) behind other objects, pushing it to the bottom layer.
Center	Automatically centers the selected object on the page between the left and right margins.
Mode	In a related characteristic to Front and Back objects, the Mode determines whether an object is transparent or opaque. If you make an object opaque, then nothing underneath it is visible. If you make it transparent, then portions of anything underneath shows through wherever white space occupies the transparent object.

Group	Either by using the mouse to draw a marquee around several objects, or using the Shift key with the Arrow keys, you can select two or more objects simultaneously. Then by using this menu option, all of the objects can become a single object as a group. This can make it much easier to move and reposition the objects. Typically, this option is used on lines of objects in the report.
Ungroup	Frequently groups are created for the sole purpose of moving a large number of objects from one part of the report to another. However, once the move has been made, it's usual to ungroup the objects for further adjustments.
Text Alignment	Text can be aligned inside the text frame you have created. The options that appear here are: Left, Center, Right, Single space, One and a Half spaces, and Double space.

Table 4.12
Object menu: object characteristics.

Menu Option	Use
Font	Depending on your collection of fonts, you can apply almost any typeface, size, and style to your report text.
Fill	Fill applies only to objects that have the space to take a fill pattern (such as hatching, lines, solid colors), most typically rectangles and circles.
Pen	Lines, text, and box edges may all have one or more pen characteristics. These include: width of pen (width of the line) that ranges from hairline to 6 points, and the style of line (dots, dashes, dots and dashes, solid).
Fill Color	In addition to a pattern, circles, and rectangles may have a specific color that fills the empty space of the object.
Pen Color	Lines, text, and edges may also have a specific color.

Testing a Report

Unless you do many reports with the Report Writer, the logic peculiar to printed reports, the use of report variables, and grouping all conspire to make problems seem more obscure. When you study your reports for accuracy, *never assume*—check your logic and the calculations. If possible, run different sets of data through the report to see if it accurately handles extremes. But of course, you won't catch everything.

Reports with scans into subsidiary tables cause more problems than those that run vertically down the primary table. This is probably obvious. But when you are testing and debugging a report, the interactions between lookup/scan tables, report groups, and summary calculations make for some very subtle errors. In many cases only a sense of how these elements work together and trial-and-error, lead to a solution.

When looking at the overall task of creating a database application, or similar projects, you should never forget that although there are simple reports that take only minutes, there are also reports of such devilish complexity that they may take days. And that's with using the Report Writer—think of how long it would take if you had to code from scratch!

The Label Designer

The Label Designer could be called "Report Writer Jr." since it has the same windows and options as the Report Writer. There are only two differences:

1. The "front end" to the label creation process directs you to select the type of label to be used.
2. In the Label Designer only the Detail band has any output.

When you start creating a label, you are making mailing labels—and that's it. Any other label application, like making name tags or product labels are done just as easily and more flexibly in the Report Writer.

To create a label, you normally open the needed file(s), typically the ones with names and addresses. If this involves any indexes (or sorts) and relations, these too should be done before you begin designing. After the label has been designed, you can save it to a file (with the extension .LBX), and also save the environment, which stores all file, index, and relation information. Later, when running the labels or modifying the label format, you can specify Restore Environment to automatically open the files.

Like creating all other files in FoxPro, you start with the File, New menu selections and then **Label**, **New** (**Alt-F-N-L**). This brings up the New Label dialog box, shown in Figure 4.44.

This dialog box is the key to the Label Designer, because you must select a label format. FoxPro has licensed the Avery Label formats, which gives you a wide selection of the most popular label sizes and shapes. Your selection of a label is then carried over into the Label Designer and Report Writer, and automatically sets the band length, width, and print characteristics. This includes automatic settings for the standard one-up, two-up, three-up, and four-up label sheets (labels printed in one to four columns).

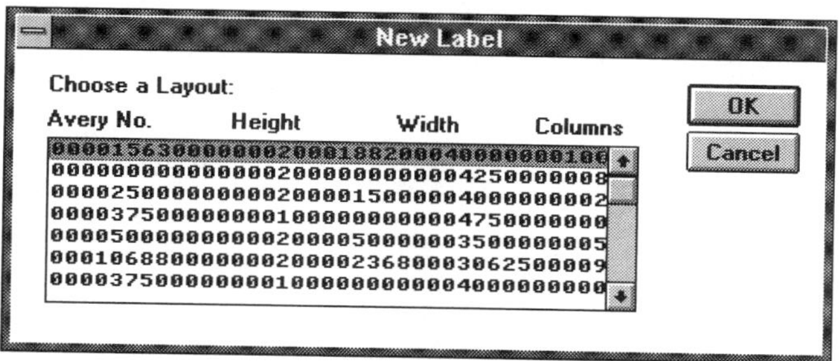

Figure 4.44
The New Label window.

The Label Layout dialog box, is a clone of the Report Writer Layout dialog box. However, though other bands are shown (depending on your label type selection), only the Detail band does anything.

The Label dialog box is also very similar to the Report Writer dialog box, except it uses the word "sample" instead of "preview," and doesn't have the heading options. Otherwise you have the standard Scope, For, and While options, and the three output locations: To Printer, Page Preview, and Console On.

Summarizing Calculations

The final data retrieval tools, called the *summarizing calculation* options—Count, Average, Sum, Calculate, and Total—give you a way to extract statistics from your tables on an *ad hoc* basis. Although these same functions are more commonly used in two other contexts, the Report Writer and RQBE, they are available from the system menu for data maintenance and quick responses to queries like, "How many widgets did we sell last month?" or "What was the average sales total per salesperson, and who had the least and the most sales?"

You can also link these operations with the Report Writer by having the results of the summarizing options stored to memory variables, which are then picked up as variable expressions in the Report Writer. You might ask, "Why would you do these calculations separately, when the Report Writer can also do them?" Normally you wouldn't, but there are certain kinds of reports that don't lend themselves to running summarizing calculations. For example, let's say you need to compare sales figures from one table with total year-to-date sales from another table. It may not be possible for the Report Writer to do a calculation pass on both tables, so you would probably use the **Sum** menu option to do the calculation on one table before running the report on the other table.

Average

Like all of the summarizing calculation options (except Count), Average requires a numeric data field. It's actually a combination of the **Sum** and the **Count** commands: average = sum/count. This implies that before an average can be computed, FoxPro has already done a sum and count, which is why in the **Calculate** command you can do all of these summarizing functions at the same time.

To set up for the Average command, open the needed file and then choose **Database, Average (Alt-D-V)** from the system menu. Next you'll see the Average dialog box, shown in Figure 4.45, which is typical for all of these commands.

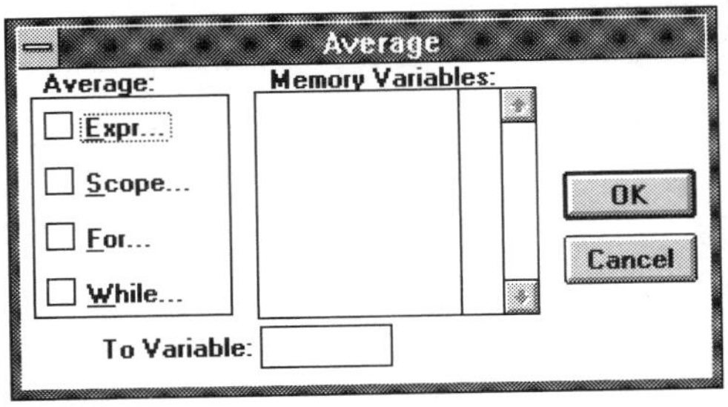

Figure 4.45 *The Average dialog box.*

The first option in the box on the left, Expr..., is required and is used to select what will be averaged. Choosing **Expr** brings forth the Expression Builder. All you really need to do is select one or more numeric fields to be averaged. If you want more than one field, create an expression with several fields separated by a comma, such as customer.ytdpurch, customer.ytdtax, customer.ytdreturn. Scope, For, and While are used as in other dialog boxes.

Like all the summary options Average can place its results in a memory variable. The Memory Variables list shows any currently active memory variables, and you can select one of those, if appropriate. Otherwise you use the To Variable edit box to enter a new variable. If you are averaging several fields at the same time, you can save the results to multiple variables. Enter a variable corresponding to each field, separated by commas.

Count

The Count option is a slight variation. You can see this right away in the Count dialog box, shown in Figure 4.46. Select Database, Count (**Alt-D O**).

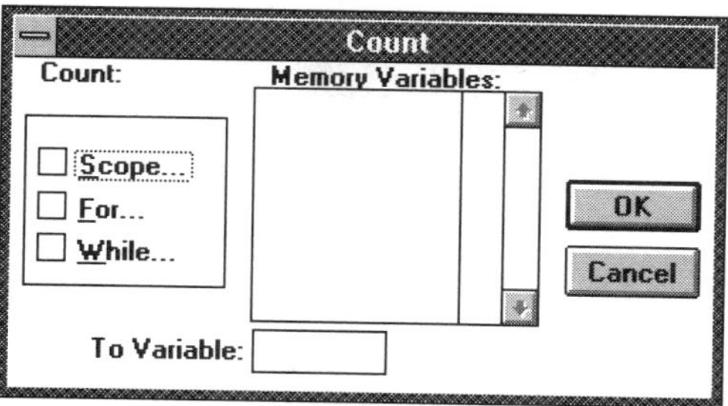

Figure 4.46 *The Count dialog box.*

The Count dialog box has no Expr...option. That's because a count is always of some logical expression, which defines what is being counted. Most typically this is a Count For. (Just counting a field would simply get you the number of records in a table—a figure easily gotten without running a count.)

Sum

Sum is a carbon copy of Average, except it sums instead of averages, of course. Reached through Database, Sum (**Alt-D-M**), the Sum dialog box requires at least one numeric field to be defined by Expr... in the Expression Builder.

Calculate

Calculate can do counts, sums, averages *and* standard deviation (STD), minimum (Min), maximum (Max), Net present value (NPV), variance (Var), *and* it can do one or more of them at the same time.

In Figure 4.47, a customer file was opened, that contains a year-to-date total purchase field (customer.ytdpurch). This field could be used for any number of the summary statistics, but in this case just minimum and maximum to find the customer with the largest purchase total, and the one with the smallest.

Figure 4.47 *Using the Calculate option.*

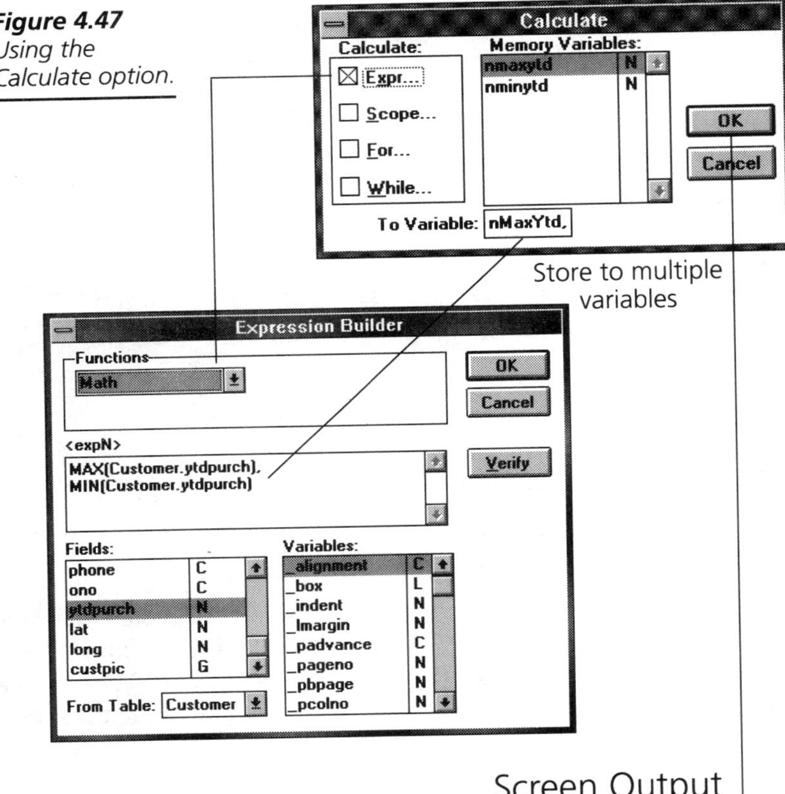

Select **Database, Calculate** from the system menu to open the Calculate dialog box. This looks and works just like the other summary calculation windows. Except where before you could only have multiple field calculations of the same type, here you can mix and match from the entire list of summary calculations.

Select the **Expr...** to reach the Expression Builder dialog box, which is specially configured for the Calculate operation. A pop-down list of Functions is available in the upper-left corner. Selecting one (in this case starting with MAX( )) puts the function into the edit box. Next select to the field to be used from the Fields list. It is automatically inserted into the highlighted text area of the MAX( ) function. The only "trick" is to add a comma to the end of each subexpression. You can add as many additional function/field expressions as you need (up to the line length limit of 1,024 characters).

Back in the Calculate dialog box, you can also assign variables the results of the calculate operations. All it takes is one variable for each of the functions used in the calculate expression. Like the subexpressions above, these too are separated by commas. When you execute the command, FoxPro places the results of each subexpression in the corresponding variable and display the results on the screen (if TALK is on). All of this occurs with a single pass through the table.

Total

Although it also does summary field calculations, the Total option is quite different from the other summarizing calculations. It sends all of its output to another .DBF. It is also dependent on the sort or index order of the source file. In many ways it is a remnant of the days before RQBE and the SQL SELECT, which can do a similar job but with more flexibility.

By default Total sums (totals) all of the numeric fields in a table, and creates a record in a new .DBF for each change in the sort order. These totals are placed in the fields of the same name of each record in the new file. This works best when the source table is largely numeric fields, as in an accounting application, and one or two fields that determine the sort order (usually by index). Otherwise, Total copies every field in the source table to the new file, in addition to totaling into the numeric fields. With very large files, this could be a problem, and at best result in a great deal of redundancy.

In most cases FoxPro places the key of the current index (tag) into the Expr... text box. This is the definition of the sort group. If it isn't correct, or you would like something different, select the Expr... button and enter the desired sort key. But remember, the table must be currently sorted or indexed on that key for Total to work.

Next, either type in the path and name of the output file in the Save As text entry box, to determine where Total sends the results, or use the Save As... button to get the Windows file dialog box and select the output file there. As usual, Scope, For, and While are available to define a subset of records to be totaled. There is also a Fields check box that brings up the Field Picker dialog box to define which numeric fields to include in the totaling. Curiously, you can't specify which of the other nonnumeric fields you want or don't want.

Copy To

Copy To is the output side of Append From. In the era before RQBE it was the primary method of extracting data from one table into another .DBF. These days, RQBE and SQL SELECT are much preferable for this task, being far more versatile and generally faster. However, Copy To still has an active role to play as the way to export data to other file formats. The list of supported formats in Table 4.13 is very similar to Append From, minus Paradox, RapidFile, and Framework.

Table 4.13
Supported export file formats.

Type	Source
ASCII	Comma delimited
ASCII	Tab delimited
ASCII	Space delimited
ASCII/SDF	Standard data file (row/column)
SYLK	Symbolic link format
DIF	Data interchange format
XLS	Microsoft Excel
MOD	Microsoft Multiplan v. 4.01

WRK	Lotus Symphony v. 1.0
WR1	Lotus Symphony v. 1.2
WKS	Lotus 1-2-3 v. 1A
WK1	Lotus 1-2-3 v. 2x
WK3	Lotus 1-2-3 v. 3x

Unlike Append From, where data type compatibility is a concern, Copy To is quite simple. Call up the Copy To dialog box, shown in Figure 4.48, by selecting Database, Copy To (**Alt-D C**) from the system menu.

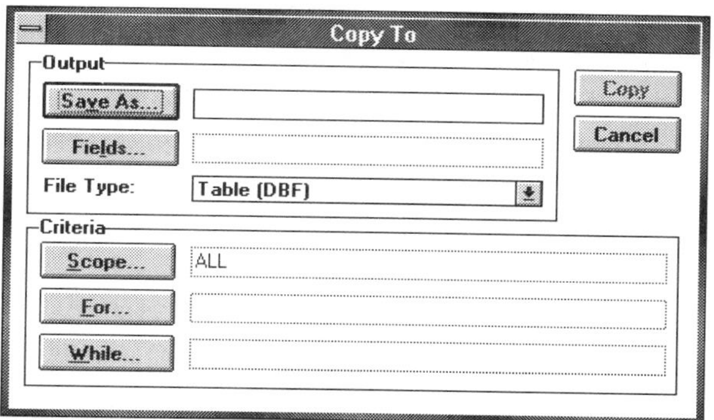

Figure 4.48 *The Copy To dialog box.*

Start with selecting the output file format, if other than a .DBF, from the File Type drop list. Then go to the Save As area and either enter the path and file name (without extension) in the entry box, or select the Save As button to use the Windows file dialog box. Incidentally, the file dialog box resets your default subdirectory to the location of the new file. This is no problem if you're aware that's what happens.

Finally, you can use the old standbys Scope, For, While to select a subset of records to be exported. And you're done.

Chapter 5
Miscellaneous Menu Options

his chapter covers the final bits and pieces of the nonprogramming part of the FoxPro for Windows menu system.

Keyboard Macros

In some software *macros* represent a transition from simple use of an application to the act of programming. A lot of innocent people were led into a most Byzantine endeavor called "macro programming" by prominent spreadsheet software. However, in the GUI, mouse-driven world of FoxPro, keyboard macros are a far cry from anything like real Xbase programming. Yet Macros is on the Program menu, as if it were meant solely for programmers.

Not so. In fact, it's for those people who want to maximize their use of the system menus and not necessarily get into programming, that macros find their best use.

Above all, a macro is a shortcut. In the case of FoxPro, it's a keyboard shortcut, consisting of one or two keystrokes that invoke a stored routine of Xbase commands. Instead of clicking here and there and everywhere to execute a commonly used data management routine, you automate it with a macro. Here are some examples:

- Automate the opening of frequently used files.
- FoxPro assigns some common command macros (DISPLAY, CLEAR, BROWSE, etc.) to the function keys, you can use these or create your own set.
- There are many operations in the text editor which can be enhanced with a macro. This is especially true for programming, for instance you can use macros to add comment markers and many other often repeated text elements.

Before you start to make a macro, you should practice what you intend to "macroize" (this is not really a word). At least mentally run through the steps. When you're ready, open the Macro dialog box, shown in Figure 5.1, by selecting Program, Macro (**Alt-P-A**) from the system menu.

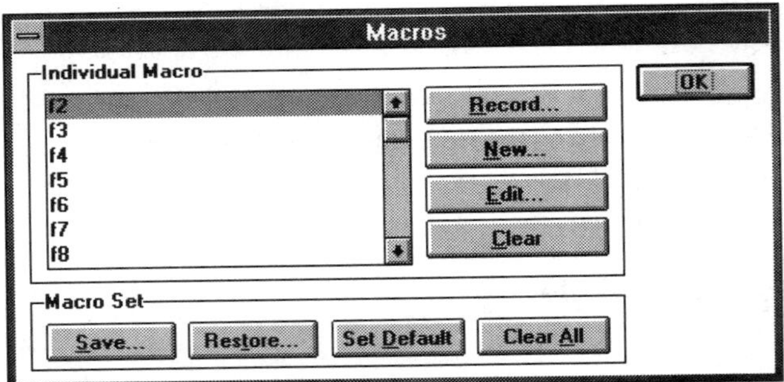

Figure 5.1
The Macro dialog box.

From the main Macro dialog box you can start a new macro, re-record an existing macro, edit a macro, clear a macro, and work with a macro set. The starting set of macros, provided by FoxPro, are for the standard IBM style keyboard function keys F2 through F9 (**F1** is reserved for system Help, and **F10** for ending a macro). These are fairly useless, so you can start by overwriting most of them.

To start the recording process, select **New** or **Record**, then you'll get the Macro Key Definition dialog box, shown in Figure 5.2. Press the key, or key combination (function keys, ctrl + key, alt + key, shift + key). If the key combination isn't already assigned to a macro, recording begins immediately. Otherwise, you'll get the Overwrite Macro dialog. Normally, you'd choose to overwrite. Then recording commences with a Wait Window in the upper right corner to remind you that **<ctrl> F10** will end the macro.

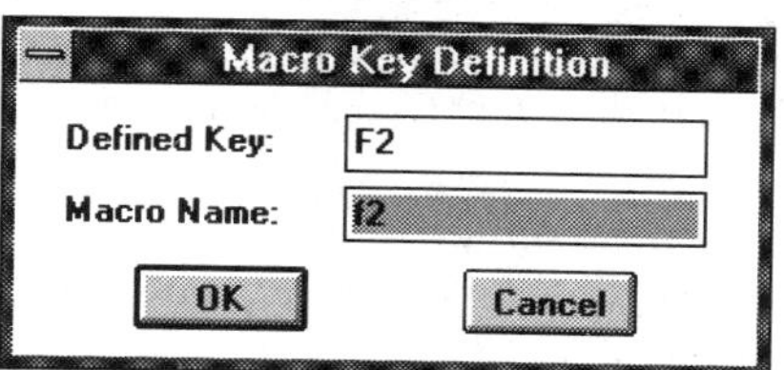

Figure 5.2 *The Macro Key Definition dialog box.*

The macro recorder is very literally a keystroke recorder. It records only keystrokes. Mouse clicks are not recorded, and in fact they can invalidate your entire macro. You should exercise care in hitting keys so that they record cleanly and in the correct order, although you can edit the macro later.

At any point during the recording, you can stop by pressing **Ctrl-F10.** This brings up the Stop Recording Macro dialog box, shown in Figure 5.3. This allows you to add Pauses or Literal keyboard input, or otherwise terminate the macro. Then you're done. You should test the macro to make sure you didn't leave out a step. If there are problems, you can re-record or edit the macro.

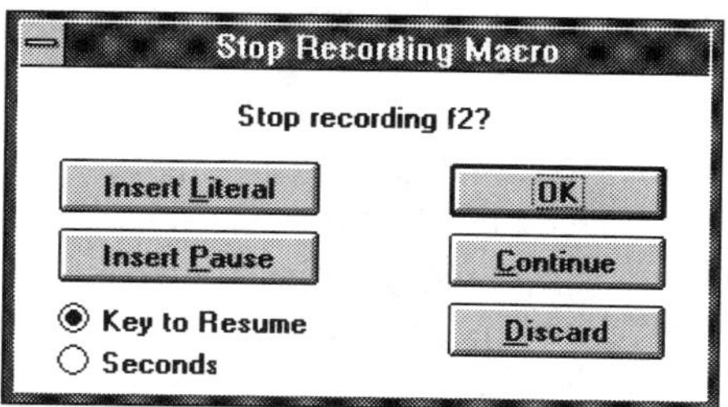

Figure 5.3 *The Stop Recording Macro dialog box.*

The mechanics are simple. But people find that creating the "perfect" macro is not so easy. You forget parts of the sequence. You forget to turn off the recorder. You forget it can't read mouse clicks. And it should also be mentioned that macros *inside* programs don't mix. Leave the macro work for the system menu. Given it's limitations, some people hate macros. They find them a nuisance to create, remember, and use. Yet other people find them indispensable, and create a library of macro sets. Fortunately, there's no mandate involved. You can find your own best methods.

Help Menu

The Help Menu in FoxPro is a grab bag. Besides the access to the help system, it contains a number of bits and pieces that were in the System menu of FoxPro for DOS 2.0—Calculator, Calendar/Diary, Filer, and Puzzle. It also provides access to the About information—general FoxPro configuration info. The description and usage of these options is covered in some detail in the *Getting Started and Interface Guide*, which won't be repeated here. However here are some annotations, which might be useful.

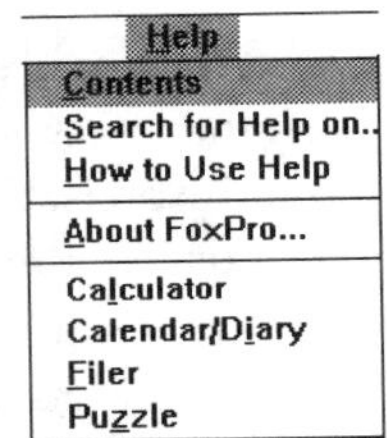

Figure 5.4 *The Help menu.*

Dual Help Systems

FoxPro has two help systems, one is the normal Windows Help and the other a legacy system from FoxPro for DOS. This duality belies a problem for the application developer. The standard Windows Help system is not editable through FoxPro, which means you need third-party tools to make modifications. The FoxPro for DOS help is editable, and in fact is an integral part of most FoxPro for DOS applications—another reason for including it here. However, this DOS-based system doesn't look like a Windows program and doesn't operate like the standard Windows Help.

The content of either Help system is uneven. When it comes to language elements, Help is *the* most current and complete source of information. It gets updated with each minor revision of the code, the manuals do not. However, the information on the user interface and other general operations of FoxPro are at best sketchy. There are some topics that are thoroughly covered, and many others not covered at all. You generally learn to use the Help system command reference frequently, and the manuals for the rest of it.

About FoxPro

The About FoxPro option contains information that is occasionally useful. In particular, information about the version of FoxPro and the hardware configuration are important when doing installations, testing, and sometimes debugging. You should know what information is here, and how to read it.

The Calculator, Calendar/Diary, Filer, and Puzzle options are in some ways merely trimming. However, since the early days of FoxPro, they can be included—lock, stock and barrel—in applications. As a result, they've been widely distributed with developer's programs, which is why Microsoft was loath to remove them from FoxPro for Windows. Besides, a good case can be made for their usefulness. (Well, the Puzzle option is a little low on the utility score.)

All of these options are part of the standard system menu, of course, and as long as you leave the Help menu intact in your applications, they will be available. You can also remove any of the options simply by deleting their entries from the menu list—more of this in Chapter 14.

When it makes sense for an application, you can include the Calculator option. While this is a limited "basic" calculator, it can be handy for users to do spot calculations. There are two system variables (_CALCMEM and _CALCVALUE) that can be used to incorporate totals into your programs. The Calculator is a simple screen to use, which simplifies its documentation and it has few side effects on the application environment.

The Calendar/Diary option, on the other hand, presents some problems. It's so easy to include this "applet" (a small application within an application), that you may forget there are files being created for each person who uses the calendar or diary. These files have a tendency to grow in size, until one fine day somebody discovers megabytes of disk space have disappeared. If you use the Calendar/Diary option, be sure you include a way to maintain the files—monitor their size and number, and be able to delete them as necessary.

Because it's direct and simple, many people find the FoxPro for Windows Filer to be on of the best file and directory managers around. It's also been spruced up for the Windows environment and deserves serious use, in and out of applications. You can use this to prune your subdirectories, move files around, and perform general file maintenance. Of course, this functionality is also part of the Windows environment—the Windows File Manager, specifically—but many people prefer the simplicity and speed of the FoxPro

Filer. You can also inlcude it with your applications as a way for users to do certain kinds of file maintenance on their systems.

Run Menu

The Run menu provides a conveniently central point of access to many of the Power Tools of FoxPro for Winodws. Other than that, all of these options are found elsewhere in the System menu with the exception of Application. This option can be the gateway into your own programs. But it raises an interesting point for the design of a user interface.

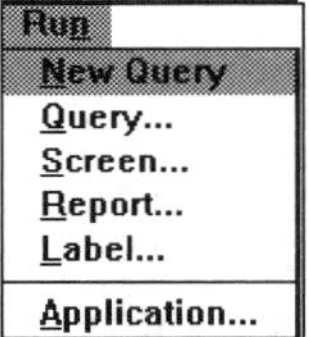

Figure 5.5 *The Run menu.*

Microsoft added the Run menu rather late in the history of FoxPro, mostly to highlight the PowerTools and to provide an "official" access to applications. For each of the options, Query, Screen, Report, Label, and Application, a file open dialog box appears, which asks the user to select which query, screen, application, etc. to run. That's fine, as long as the user is familiar with navigating DOS subdirectories and file names, and knows what files should be opened. There are many environments where these are some very big assumptions.

Most of the time, application developers would never rely on such a direct and potentially confusing method for launching programs, reports, etc. It leaves the user with too many ways to do the wrong thing. But you must decide for yourself, in each application, whether this direct approach is better than one which provides more support (and control) of the user's choices.

Chapter 6
The FoxPro Database Engine

The FoxPro Database Engine is a general topic, one of several in the book, that covers a subject that doesn't fit neatly into the progression of learning FoxPro for Windows. The topic is important, however, for a general understanding of FoxPro.

The point of using a database management program is to manipulate information—gather it, store it, order it, and retrieve it. Issues concerning the user interface and fancy graphic display, while important, are not the heart of the program. There has been a strong trend in the computer industry to separate the *back end* of database management—the "engine" that does the storing, ordering, and retrieving of data—from the *front end*, where the data is gathered and displayed through the user interface. The buzz phrase client/server is commonly used to express the two approaches.

FoxPro version 2.5 (in all its variations including FoxPro for Windows) derives from the days when a database management program did both ends of the job. In fact, FoxPro still combines one of the finest database engines available with the capability of creating a state-of-the-art user interface (especially with FoxPro for Windows). But in some ways it sits uncomfortably between the industrial-strength database servers like those from Oracle and Sybase/Microsoft, and the user-oriented capabilities of programs intended to manage smaller volumes of data.

FoxPro for Windows is not intended to run the entirety of a Fortune 500 company, or to provide real-time transaction processing for the airline industry. Its database engine is good, but not that deep. On the other hand, a lot of MIS people would be surprised to see how easily FoxPro for Windows can handle databases with millions of records. Nor does FoxPro pretend to be the ultimate answer in a user friendly database (aside from occasional lapses in marketing hype). Yet with thoughtful programming, it can create many different kinds of user-friendly environments.

All things being relative, FoxPro for Windows stands out as being the fastest microcomputer-based data manager and one of the most flexible. It's a superb developer's tool. It has lots of muscle to handle bigger jobs, and lots of control to handle the finesse. Two more points need to be reinforced:

1. The FoxPro database engine does not require a degree in database administration to operate.
2. Complete access to the FoxPro engine is through one of the world's most popular business programming language—Xbase. This makes FoxPro accessible and maintainable in ways less mainstream micro products could never hope to be.

The Rushmore Technology

The newest and most important part of the Microsoft database engine is a patented system called *Rushmore Technology*. (The name actually comes from Hitchcock's movie, *North by Northwest*, filmed at Mount Rushmore.) This technology has been variously praised as "utterly revolutionary" and dismissed as "a parlor trick." Fortunately it is a little less than revolutionary, and a lot more than a parlor trick. If it were a parlor trick—flashy but without substance—then it would quickly be dismissed. And if it were completely revolutionary, it would probably be incomprehensible and difficult to implement, which would lessen its impact on the database industry.

Rushmore Technology is more than a "query" capability, although that's one of its most impressive features. It is a number of file management techniques—indexing, data compression, bitmap storage, query optimization, I/O management, memory management—under one roof. Behind much of the Rushmore Technology are some rather simple ideas, the kind that make people slap their forehead and say "Why didn't I think of that!" But the results, like the best of magic, are astonishing.

How this is accomplished is a mix of innovative microcomputer thinking and mainframe technical savvy. The "secret" Microsoft/Fox has consistently exploited is to avoid data management on the disk drives. Do it in memory, do it with clever algorithms, but don't do it on the disk. Of course, the Rushmore Technology *is* secret (patented), so nobody publicly has the definitive description of how it works. However, a reasonably accurate outline is helpful in understanding how you can approach the use of Rushmore Technology.

"Look Ma, We Shrunk the Indexes!"

As is well known, computing done in memory (RAM) is much faster than using disks drives. However, though memory is becoming cheaper and thereby more plentiful, a software company can't compete on the assumption that everyone has 8 MB or more of RAM. So, while it works best to use memory for fast database processing, the lack of it is a major roadblock. You can't put massive databases (or even relatively small ones) entirely in RAM. Ah, but the indexes...that's much more possible. It becomes even more possible when you apply compression techniques to the index, shrinking it to one sixth (or more) of its original size, which Rushmore does.

Indexing a database has long been one of the most potent techniques for rapid access to information. Most data-management systems use indexing to one degree or another. The Rushmore Technology positively *feeds* on indexes. That's one point of FoxPro's attack. It's compressed (compact) indexes are quicker to access on disk, and often can be loaded completely into RAM—part of an elaborate *cache* scheme. Plus, since the indexes take less disk space, you are encouraged to make more of them.

However, compressed or not, manipulating indexes and data in memory is tricky. With hindsight, it can be said Microsoft/Fox was fortunate to have struggled with the memory limitations of microcomputers. That hard won experience has paid off in a new memory management system introduced in FoxPro 2.0 and refined in the more liberal RAM atmosphere of FoxPro for Windows, which on the low end maximizes memory use on PC's with limited memory, and on the high end can use extended memory, the native RAM of 386 processors, by the bucketful. The memory-management system works hand-in-glove with the database engine to provide the fastest possible computing environment.

Putting Data Management on the Bitmap

The next point of attack: FoxPro does much of its data management using the indexed data and bitmapped images of the search results and only goes to the actual database files on disk when absolutely necessary. This is one of the core techniques. For example, when you specify a search value `LOCATE ALL FOR product.type = "WIDGET"` the "Widget" search value is transformed into a bitmap image. If "Widget" occurs in an indexed field, Rushmore also attempts to store a bitmap image of the index in RAM. (This is gross oversimplification, of course.) If you follow the first query with a second similar query, something like `LOCATE ALL FOR product.type = "WIDGET" AND product.color = "BLUE"`, Rushmore uses the results of the first query and the bitmap of the index in conjunction with a read on the index of the new piece of the query. This can have dramatic effect on the speed of successive retrievals.

The moral for usage is to build your queries a piece at a time and let Rushmore continue to build its bitmaps and figure out the best way to manipulate the search. And don't try to force-feed Rushmore. Setting indexes is one way to make it work overtime. You can't second guess (or first guess either) what Rushmore will need. Moreover, when you set an index order, Rushmore is required to go back to the index from the *non-ordered* bitmap image and construct a sorted list. This takes time. So if at all possible, don't invoke Rushmore with a table order set. This is automatically true for an RQBE query or an SQL SELECT, but standard commands with FOR and WHILE clauses are also Rushmore optimizable and might be hampered by tables with an index order.

Searching for the Optimal Optimizer

So Rushmore Technology loves to do its own thing with indexes. But for any given file operation, and especially for SQL queries, how does it choose which indexes to use (or create)? What kind of search algorithms are used? This involves selecting the best way to retrieve data, called *query optimization.*

Optimizers, the generic term for software that manages the query operation, are notoriously complex and difficult. It's significant that Microsoft is attempting with Rushmore to build a most ambitious and innovative optimizer, and plans to make it the centerpiece of future development. Many other data-management companies don't even have optimizers, much less showcase them. Microsoft has already publicly committed to years of "tuning" its optimizer, as the heart of Rushmore Technology.

Without getting into the details of how an optimizer works (and in this case nobody outside of Microsoft knows for sure how the Rushmore optimizer works), it's basic job is to determine the query you pose: what indexes and other resources are available, which should be used, what logic should be applied, and how the found data should be prepared. This is a heady mixture, concocted of classic search algorithms, RAM caching, bitmap techniques, common sense, ingenuity, and practical experience.

The Rushmore optimizer is one smart query cutter, but it's not omnipotent. For one thing you can make it impossible for the optimizer to do its job. This is what Microsoft means when it says you must build "optimizable" queries.

The proscribed format for an optimizable query should look quite familiar:

```
<index expression> <relational operator> <constant expression>
FIRSTNAME = "Mark"
```

The simple example contains the classic format. FIRSTNAME is a key field (all or the first part of an index key). Rushmore must find an index expression in the table that matches your query index expression. If it doesn't, it may decide to build an index. Then again, it might not. If you have an index on the table such as LASTNAME+FIRSTNAME, it does nothing for Rushmore. With character expressions it must compare index keys against the <constant expression> values on a character by character basis, moving from left to right. If it had to search long concatenated keys, it's speed would be drastically cut. So it doesn't bother to look for buried key values. This is also why you can't use the substring search operator—$—in an optimizable query.

Your best queries are those that don't vary much from the classic format. Try to make the index expression match single expression index keys. And keep your constant expressions simple. Although you can use functions that result in a constant expression, they take extra processing time.

As a database user or developer, you've got a tremendous ally in Rushmore. But in the real world of database management, even the best of allies can let you down. There are plenty of queries that Rushmore can turn into an absolute mess. And as outlined above, it does have restrictions that often don't meet real world requirements. As you get into the programming aspects of FoxPro, you'll also discover that nothing beats a direct SEEK into a table coupled with a SCAN/ENDSCAN loop, as long as the return data set isn't too large, and you're not working with multiple tables.

For data retrieval, you're better off exploiting Rushmore to the hilt, especially in RQBE and the SQL SELECT capacity. Other parts of data management, notably data maintenance, use a mixture of Rushmore oriented technique and plain old Xbase approaches. That's part of the fun of FoxPro, you can learn to be your own optimizer.

Section II

Basic Programming

At some point, either by temperament or by necessity, many people decide the commands available through the FoxPro system menus just aren't enough. This is the point where you start to deal with the essential FoxPro—the programming language. This also used to be known as "hitting the wall." In the days of dBase II and dBase III+ you could do some database management without programming, but sooner rather than later you had to face the steep part of the learning curve—the "wall" called programming. With FoxPro the wall has been kicked over a bit and shaped into something more closely resembling a curve, but it's still a formidable barrier for people. It doesn't need to be.

If you've already learned some data management through the FoxPro system menu, then you already know about the basic database management operations. For the most part, the menu options are the same as the programming language commands. You probably noticed that your menu choices were echoed to the Command window. This is a major clue that FoxPro is pointed in the direction of software programmers and developers. Now you need to learn about the different ways in which you can use the programming language, beginning with the Command window and simple program files.

Before launching into the first elements of the Xbase/FoxPro language, there are a few of observations about learning a language that might be helpful.

1. There is no substitute for doing.
2. There is a difference between knowing by heart and knowing about.

There are 612 commands and functions in the FoxPro for Windows version of the Xbase language. Not to mention the hundreds of modifier clauses attached to these commands and functions. This is the world of programming *syntax*, the form and expression of a language. If you've been around computers more than a few minutes, you've already noticed how picky they are. Press the wrong key and an hour's work might be consigned to digital history. And programming, which places you much closer to the basic operations of your computer, is even more sensitive. Programming syntax is unforgiving, it is often complex, and it is unavoidable. There are about one hundred or so commands and functions that are truly important. The rest you keep on mental file for potential use. Hopefully this section will help you make the distinction between the two.

Chapter 7
Command Window Programming

Previous chapters have dealt with using the FoxPro menus to do your database work. That is the most visual method of working with Fox, but sooner or later the migration begins at the Command window—the window that shows up whenever you begin a FoxPro session. The Command window, shown in Figure 7.1, is for just what it says—entering commands. In this age of sophisticated user interfaces, it's a hallmark of FoxPro and other Xbase products that the ability to type direct commands remains so prominent.

Using the Command window has two main advantages: it's very direct, and it can do things not available in the menus. It's direct because you type the exact commands you want and FoxPro executes them immediately. While there are some limitations, the Command window gives people a sense of control over their data that is very satisfying. It's also a great place to experiment, prototype, and learn.

However, there's no hand holding. This is one big step down the road to programming. You are responsible for knowing what commands to use, and how to put them together. This may be initially more difficult than using menus, but it is one of the best ways to learn how commands and functions work. In fact, the standard advice is to start learning the Xbase/FoxPro language in the Command window. It's interactive, which means you can see the results of your command immediately. The instant feedback, even if its an error message, helps the learning process.

Figure 7.1
The Command window.

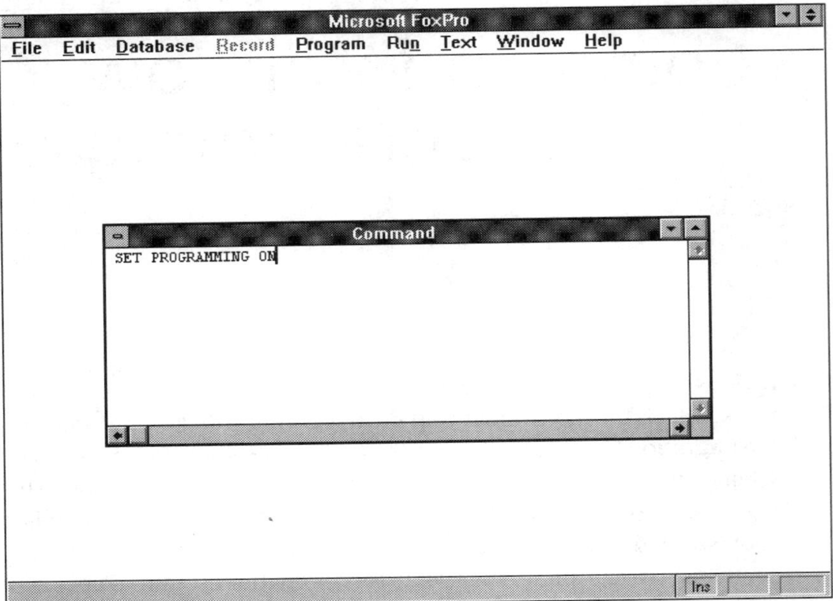

It also helps to have some real database work, or at the very least a good set of practice files. Some of the files in the tutorial are readily available, though on the small side. The ideal set of practice files would have one primary table of at least one thousand records, two or three secondary scan tables (containing multiple records related to the primary tables), and two to five lookup tables. This is enough to cut your relational teeth, and a get a feel for the performance of FoxPro.

For the most part, the approach in this chapter is to stick with the Command window as the maintenance center of FoxPro. The examples are common data maintenance exercises—each and every one of them drawn from real-life experiences—as bizarre as some of them may seem.

Using the Command Window

Editing in the Command Window

Get comfy. Depending on your eyesight, sense of aesthetics, and other subjective factors, size the Command window so you have plenty of room for long commands, and use the font picker in the system menu to select a font and size that serves the same purpose. In most cases a monospaced font (all letters are the same size) like Courier New (TT), or FoxFont work best. You can type command lines longer than the window and either have the window scroll (which is a nuisance, since you can't see the beginning of the line) or use a semi-colon (;) to continue the command on the line below, for example:

```
REPLACE ALL contact WITH customer.fullname ;
FOR NOT EMPTY(customer.fullname) ;
AND customer.enterdate > DTOC("11/01/92")
```

It's a good idea to put the continuation marker after an operator or keyword, and leave a space between it and the end of the line. Not only is this usually easier to read, but it avoids the possibility of the FoxPro interpreter/compiler gluing the lines together in a way that causes an error.

Keep in mind the Command window is not quite the same as entering a program—for one thing you can't do loops or conditional structures. However, as an editing surface, the Command window is like working with a slightly eccentric version of the standard FoxPro program editor. You have Cut, Paste, and Find, as you would expect. However you can't really clear the Command window, because it stores a history of the commands you enter. Every time you press **Enter** to execute a command, the window is redrawn and replaces any command you may have edited or cut. Actually, this running history is very useful. Not only can you see where you've been, but you can cut and paste any of the previous commands and modify them to make a new command statement.

Although this is a little early to go into details, from the point of view of learning, it's a good idea to use the same approach to programming in the Command Window as you would in a program file. Develop the same habits for formatting, naming conventions, and so on. Sometimes this seems like overkill, but in the long run the consistency pays off.

An example of this is the use of abbreviated commands. FoxPro interprets a command with only the first four letters of the command phrase, so APPE BLAN works just as well as APPEND BLANK. Being work minimizers, programmers naturally want to reduce the number of keystrokes. So it would seem appropriate to use the four-letter shortcuts. Problem is, most of the Xbase commands were intended to look like English for ease of readability. You might become accustomed to APPE BLAN, but it doesn't look much like English, especially to someone not familiar with the abbreviations. The rule for programming, where somebody else has to read the code is four-letter shortcuts are dirty words.

Typical Uses of the Command Window

Not much database work gets done without setting the working environment and opening one or more files. Some people prefer the View window to do this. For others, it's faster to use a series of commands typed directly into the Command window.

Setting the Environment

There are dozens of SET commands in FoxPro (101 to be exact). Not all of them pertain to setting the environment of a working Command window session. Many of them are used only in the context of a program. In addition, most of them have direct equivalents in the FoxPro configuration file (CONFIG.FPW), which is commonly used to set the environment in programming. A few, however, are useful in the Command window on a regular basis.

SET TALK

The Syntax for SET TALK is:

```
SET TALK ON | OFF | WINDOW [<window name>] | NOWINDOW
```

Typical usage of this command is:

```
SET TALK OFF
```

Talk is the quaint Xbase term for displaying the intermediate results or status of these commands:

- APPEND FROM
- COUNT
- PACK
- SORT
- AVERAGE
- DELETE
- REINDEX
- SUM
- CALCULATE
- INDEX
- REPLACE
- TOTAL
- COPY TO
- SELECT SQL

The default for this Set command is on, which is just fine for the Command window. In FoxPro, the talk is always sent to the status bar at the bottom of the screen and the WINDOW | NOWINDOW options are meaningless for the Command window. There is a performance hit for having talk on, since the CPU has to spend some time doing the status bar display. Not much of a hit, though, even on very large tables. Most users would rather have some idea if a lengthy table operation is still running or if it's getting any results, and sacrifice a few seconds.

SET SAFETY

By default, FoxPro warns you about attempting an operation that deletes all of the data in a table (or the file itself)—such as ZAP and ERASE. Usually in the Command window the warning is a good idea. However, if you have a particularly destructive work session in mind, you can turn the safety off, and be, as they say, "on your own recognizance."

The syntax for SET SAFETY is:

```
SET SAFETY ON | OFF
```

SET DELETED

This is one of those "innocent" commands that can cause a lot of trouble. When you DELETE a record, a marker (*) is placed in the record. From then on, depending on the status of SET DELETED, you will or won't be able to see that record in common operations like BROWSE or CHANGE. This is a global setting, meaning that it applies to all open tables.

The syntax for SET DELETED is:

```
SET DELETED ON | OFF
```

If SET DELETED is on, deleted records are ignored by table processing commands and not visible in the access commands like BROWSE.

If SET DELETED is off, all records are included in table operations, and visible to the user in access commands.

The default setting is OFF, meaning all records are visible. This may not be appropriate for some commands or for screening. However, if you change the status, you need to keep track of it because of the impact it can have on the scope of processing.

SET EXCLUSIVE

When you work on tables in the Command window, you will frequently perform operations that "lock" files or records. In a multiuser system unless you SET EXCLUSIVE OFF, you may suddenly shut out people from their applications. This might mean a lot of very angry network users.

Its syntax is:

```
SET EXCLUSIVE ON | OFF
```

With exclusive off, you are telling FoxPro to treat the tables as "shared," and to exercise the automatic locking mechanisms in the context of a multiuser environment. There are times when you need to perform a database task that requires a complete file lock (such as PACK and REINDEX). If you are working on a LAN, you need to use SET EXCLUSIVE ON, or open the file in exclusive mode to execute these commands.

What Files Are on Disk?

DIR

The DIR command lists the files in a directory. The syntax for DIR is:

```
DIR | DIRECTORY [ON <drive>] [[LIKE] [<path>] [<skel>]]

[TO PRINTER [PROMPT] | TO FILE <file>]
```

- DIR shows all database (.DBF) files in the current subdirectory.
- DIR *.* shows *all* files on the current subdirectory. This command works just like the DOS DIR command, including the use of the wildcards * and ?.
- DIR \<path>\ shows database files on some other directory, for example DIR F:\WORK\.

Alternate commands are LIST FILES, LIST FILES LIKE *.*, and DISPLAY FILES.

Open Database Files in Work Areas

USE

The syntax for USE is:

```
USE [<file> | ?] [IN <expN1>]      [AGAIN] [INDEX <index file;
list> | ?
[ORDER [<expN2> | <idx index file> | [TAG] <tag name> [OF <cdx;
file>]
[ASCENDING | DESCENDING]]]] [ALIAS <alias>] [EXCLUSIVE][SHARE];
[NOUPDATE]
```

Typical usage of this command is:

```
USE <file> IN 0
USE customer IN 0
```

The generic command to open a database file (.DBF) is USE, but the Xbase language requires that a specific work area be designated for each open file. (A work area is really an allocation of memory to hold file information and variables.) FoxPro allows up to 225 work areas. The IN 0 clause automatically finds the first available work area and opens the file in it. There is usually no reason for you to keep track of what work areas are assigned.

It's not required to specify an index to be opened with a file, but most of the time you will. FoxPro automatically opens the .CDX file, but it won't select an index (tag) for you. To specify an index, use the syntax:

```
USE <file> IN 0 ORDER <index tag>
USE customer IN 0 ORDER company
```

As an alternative, SELECT 0 selects the lowest open work area and has to be on a line of its own. IN 0 also selects the lowest open work area, while IN SELECT(1) uses the highest open work area.

Do yourself a favor, use it. An alias is an alternate name for a file that FoxPro defaults to the full file name. When you need to refer to the file, such as identifying a field, the long filename gets tedious to type and makes for very long command lines. One sensible convention is to use a somewhat mnemonic three letter alias for each file, such as INV for INVENTORY. Then a reference to a field in that file is simply INV.ITEMCOST. The syntax to use an alias is:

```
USE <file> IN 0 ORDER <index tag> ALIAS <alias name>
USE customer IN 0 ORDER company ALIAS cus
```

The inclusion of the little word "again" is a potent addition to the Xbase language. It means you can have multiple copies of a database file open at the same time. Just like you might open separate windows on the same word processing document, AGAIN does the same thing for a database file. This is a more advanced use, but it's occasionally needed in the Command Window. Note that you normally use an alias with the AGAIN clause so that the file has a different name than the originally opened file. The syntax to use AGAIN is:

```
USE <file> ALIAS <alias name> AGAIN
USE customer ALIAS cus2 AGAIN
```

Multiuser: If you are working in a network environment, most of the time SET EXCLUSIVE OFF will be in effect. This means that all files are opened to be shared with other people by default. For some operations, notably those that can affect an entire file (such as PACK, REPLACE ALL and REINDEX) it's necessary to open the file for exclusive use (one person only). This isn't always possible, since FoxPro does not open a file exclusively if somebody is already working in it. Use the syntax:

```
USE <file> EXCLUSIVE
USE customer EXCLUSIVE
```

Set Relations Between Tables

SET RELATION TO

Not everybody uses FoxPro to create a relational database system, and, as you'll see later, a "preset relation" isn't always the best for performance, but it's very common in the Command window to use relations so you can browse data.

The sytax to set a relation is:

```
SET RELATION TO [<expr1> INTO <expN1> | <expC1> [, <expr2> INTO
<expN2> |
<expC2> ...] [ADDITIVE]]
```

Typical usage of this command is:

```
SET RELATION TO <field name> INTO <file alias/name>
SET RELATION TO cno INTO ord
```

Remember the rules concerning what you can link with a relation. This expression is used for the first relation of a file.

The following expression is used for any additional relations of a file.

```
SET RELATION TO <field name> INTO <file alias/name> ADDITIVE
SET RELATION TO cno INTO ord ADDITIVE
```

SET SKIPTO

To establish a one-to-many relationship between the file in this work area and the file named in the expression, use:

```
SET SKIP TO <file/alias>
```

Opening a Command Window Session

Putting the previous commands together, the following is typical code for opening a Command window session:

```
SET EXCLUSIVE OFF
DIR
USE customer ALIAS cus ORDER cno IN 0
USE orders ALIAS ord ORDER cno IN 0
USE details ALIAS det ORDER ino IN 0
SELECT ord
SET RELATION TO ino INTO det
SET SKIP TO ino
SELECT cus
SET RELATION TO cno INTO ord
SET SKIP TO cno
```

This opens three files and two relations, the typical business transaction sequence.

Creating New Files and Indexes

If it doesn't exist, you have to CREATE it. Files, indexes, reports, labels, and queries fall into this category. For the most part creating files is done using the menu system or the View window, but if you insist typing is faster. There are two ways to create a database file from the keyboard.

CREATE

Typical usage of this command is:

```
CREATE <filename>
CREATE customer
```

This drops you into the Modify Structure dialog box (see Chapter 1 for details).

CREATE TABLE

The most direct method of creating a table is:

```
CREATE TABLE | DBF <dbf name> ( <fieldname1> <type>
[(<precision>[,<scale>])[ , <fieldname2>]])
```

This is a SQL command that was incorporated into FoxPro 2.0 and instantly replaced the older "workaround" methods of creating a table in programs, which used COPY TO STRUCTURE EXTENDED. Although it's syntax looks murky, it's actually quite simple. In the following example, the only "trick" is to define each field the same way you would in the Modify Structure window—<fieldname>, <data type>, <width>, <decimal>.

```
CREATE DBF customer ( cno c (8), company c (30), ytdpurch n;
(8.2))
```

Of course, if you're creating a file with many fields, this command is somewhat cumbersome in the Command window. But for smallish files, particularly temporaries, it's a convenient method.

Incidentally, you don't need to select an unused work area for this command, it uses the next open area automatically.

Creating and Deleting Indexes

Much more commonly used in the Command window are the commands that create and delete indexes (tags). As mentioned before, the "old style" indexes (.IDX) are still legitimate and may be found in many legacy programs. For the vast majority of new cases, however, using the structural .CDX file and TAGs is the only way to fly.

Multiuser: A file must be opened EXCLUSIVE before using any of the following commands.

INDEX ON

The syntax for creating an index is:

```
INDEX ON <expr> TO <idx file> | TAG <tag name> [OF <cdx file>]
[FOR <expL>] [COMPACT] [ASCENDING | DESCENDING] [UNIQUE]:
[ADDITIVE]
```

This is the standard and simplest form for building an index:

```
INDEX ON <field name expression> TAG <tag name>
INDEX ON company TAG company
INDEX ON lastname+firstname TAG lastfirst
```

One of the glories of the Xbase language is its extreme flexibility for what can be used in the `<field name expression>`. First and foremost, it can use concatenated (compound) indexes composed of more than one field. It can also accept modification of the index fields by a wide array of functions. Finally, you can also have a UDF (User Defined Function) for the index expression, such as:

```
INDEX ON CapFirst(lastname) TAG mixlast
```

where the CapFirst( ) function changes all last names to a capitalized first letter, and lower case for the rest. Such flexibility is not free. UDFs and complex indexes are much slower to build, and usually make much larger indexes. They are also often unusable by the Rushmore technology. Use fancy indexes only when needed.

NOTE

It helps to have tag names follow a convention. For example, simple tags are the same name as the field. Compound or other tags (attempt) to remind the user of how the tag is built or what it does. Why? Among other things, when you're busy coding, it's a pain to have to look up a tag name and is much simpler if it's the same name as the field.

Another common use is:

```
INDEX ON <field name expression> TAG <tag name> FOR <logical;
expression>
```

```
INDEX ON lastname + firstname TAG lastfirst FOR lastname =;
"JOHNSON"
```

Besides building an index tag, this command attaches a condition to the indexing, which says in effect "include only those records specified by the FOR expression."

This makes for highly specialized indexes and usually a lot of tag management, but it can really enhance the performance of some applications where the data in the FOR expression is fairly static and there is a limited number of such indexes needed. Otherwise the SQL SELECT command combined with general indexing is a much more flexible method (and just about as quick).

One of the criticisms of the Xbase language is that it allows duplicate entries to a "key" (file index). However, you can put the UNIQUE clause into building the index and only unique occurrences of the information in the field will be included in the index.

```
INDEX ON <field name expression> TAG <tag name> UNIQUE
INDEX ON TRIM(contact) TAG contact UNIQUE
```

Using this syntax, you could have sixteen "Johnsons" in the file, but only one (the first one) is in the index.

Using the SET UNIQUE ON command accomplishes the same thing, however, this is a *global* setting, affecting every index you create. It's not a good idea to use this approach, unless you're sure it's appropriate.

Occasionally it's desirable to reverse the order of an index, for example with dates or dollars. By default indexes are created in ascending order, which you can override with the DESCENDING clause:

```
INDEX ON <field name expression> TAG <tag name> DESCENDING
INDEX ON TRM (contact) TAG contact DESCENDING
```

REINDEX

This command reindexes all of the tags in a .CDX file. Unfortunately, it does not clear unused space from the .CDX, which means that periodically you should delete the tag, and then use the basic INDEX ON command to make sure the indexing is cleared properly.

DELETE TAG

To immediately remove—without warning—the named index tag from a .CDX file, use:

```
DELETE TAG <tag name1> [OF <cdx file1>] [, <tag name2> [OF <cdx
file2>]] ...
```

or

```
DELETE TAG ALL [OF <cdx file>]
```

A common use is:

```
DELETE TAG <tag name>
DELETE TAG lastfirst
```

Getting Information About a Work Session

FoxPro has several places to get information about the work session. The status bar at the bottom of the screen carries some information. The View window is the best way to get a visual representation of table status. There are also several useful commands.

DISPLAY STATUS

DISPLAY STATUS is a quick, though visually messy way of seeing what files are open, what index tags exist (and which one is currently the master index), along with a lot of other information about the SET options, open windows, and so on. Someday we may get a more discriminating way of checking on the status of our programs and work sessions. Some of the same information is available using the View window. The output of this command can be sent to a printer or a file, although the default goes to the screen.

The syntax for DISPLAY STATUS is:

```
DISPLAY STATUS [TO PRINTER [PROMPT] | TO FILE <file>];
[NOCONSOLE]
```

DISPLAY MEMORY

This is a "dump" of the contents of any active memory variables.

```
DISPLAY MEMORY [LIKE <skel>] [TO PRINTER [PROMPT] | TO FILE;
<file>]
[NOCONSOLE]
DISPLAY MEMORY TO PRINTER
```

If you use the LIKE option, you can have the list restricted to variables that begin with the same characters. As you will see, the naming of variables by data type (such as a=array: aStates, aCounties) makes this variation of DISPLAY MEMORY quite useful. This command will see limited use in the Command window, until you get into programming.

```
DISPLAY MEMORY LIKE  <skeleton>
DISPLAY MEMORY LIKE A*
```

Creating Files the Easy Way

Creating and loading files with data is a time-consuming process. If you can get the data from another file, already loaded, then you can jump-start your work. Of the four commands in FoxPro that do this, two are available from the system menu (APPEND FROM, COPY TO) and two are not (IMPORT, EXPORT). All of them can work with file formats other than the native .DBF. The first two commands are also used extensively to swap data from one .DBF table to another.

There are subtle differences between all four of these commands, both in their clauses and supported file formats. You may find yourself having to pick and choose carefully. It must be said this is one area of FoxPro that badly needs consolidation and updating.

APPEND FROM

APPEND FROM can be classified as one of the workhorse commands in FoxPro for Windows data maintenance. Its syntax is on the next page.

```
APPEND FROM <file> [FIELDS <field list>]
[FOR <expL>]
[[TYPE] [DELIMITED [WITH TAB | WITH <delimiter> | WITH BLANK] |
DIF | FW2 | MOD | PDOX | RPD | SDF | SYLK | WK1 | WK3 | WKS |
WR1 | WRK | XLS]]
```

Some common examples are:

```
APPEND FROM <filename> FIELDS <field list> FOR <expL>
APPEND FROM customer FIELDS cno, company, state;
FOR state = "CA" TYPE SDF
APPEND FROM <filename> DELIMITED WITH <delimiter>
APPEND FROM sales DELIMITED WITH CHR(254)
APPEND FROM <filename> FOR <expL> TYPE <type>
APPEND FROM regions FOR region="EAST" TYPE WK3
```

It's capabilities fall into two broad areas: .DBF to .DBF data transfer, and transfer from external file formats into a .DBF. The key element of an APPEND FROM is that it is always bringing data into an *existing* .DBF table structure. If the data being appended does not exactly fit the structure—different size, different data type, different number of fields—things happen to the data, mostly unpleasant things.

When transferring data from one .DBF to another, first check the structures of both files so that you're sure what fields are going to transfer and what changes, if any, might occur. Transfers from "foreign" file formats may be more difficult because the exact field names, sizes, and types may not be known or may have no equivalent in the .DBF format. This is particularly true of ASCII files, which are all text files and come in a variety of flavors. ASCII file options are listed in Table 7.1.

Table 7.1
ASCII file options.

Type/syntax clause	Sample/description
ASCII, comma delimited DELIMITED WITH ","	`"ATLANTA", 345, "GRAY", 45.95` This is a very common format from mini-computer and mainframe systems. It's advantage is a more compact format compared to SDF.

ASCII, tab delimited DELIMITED WITH TAB	`ATLANTA 345 GRAY 45.95` This format used to be quite common, but has fallen into disuse, probably because of the problems a tab delimiter causes in word processing.
ASCII, space delimited DELIMITED WITH BLANK	`ATLANTA 345 GRAY 45.95` This is a simple variation of the DELIMITED WITH option.

ASCII, SDF (Standard Data File)
SDF
	`ATLANTA 345 GRAY 45.95`
	`BOSTON 111 BLUE 109.95`
	This is probably *the* most common format for data transfer. It's a typical format for spreadsheet output as an ASCII file, and for many minicomputer and mainframe export files. For appending it requires precise alignment within the fields of the receiving .DBF.

ASCII,variable delimiter DELIMITED WITH CHR(254)	`ATLANTA 345 GRAY 45.95` The actual character for a delimiter can be almost anything. This is a seldom-used option.

ASCII files have no header to define the contents, so you need to examine them carefully to decide what will actually append into a .DBF. The appending process looks something like this:

Appending from ASCII Files

This example begins with a text file, PARCOST.TXT, from a spreadsheet that contains cost figures for the components of parts sold. The first task is to load this file into a .DBF. Study the layout of the PARCOST.TXT file to determine, as best you can, the widths of each field and their data types.

Next, create a temporary table, PARTCOST.

```
CREATE DBF partcost(pno c(6),component c(30),
cost n(6.2),vendno c(8))
```

Append data from the text file in Standard Data File (.SDF) format.

```
APPEND FROM parcost.txt TYPE SDF
```

Now index the relevant fields.

```
INDEX ON pno TAG pno
```

```
INDEX ON cost TAG cost
```

At this point, the file is ready to be linked (in a relation) with PARTS.DBF.

Table 7.2 shows the complete list of foreign file types supported by APPEND FROM. You might notice that some major formats, including Microsoft's own Access files, are not included.

Table 7.2
Supported APPEND FROM file formats.

Type	Source
ASCII	Comma delimited
ASCII	Tab delimited
ASCII	Space delimited
ASCII/SDF	Standard data file (row/column)
SYLK	Symbolic link format
DIF	Data interchange format
XLS	Microsoft Excel
MOD	Microsoft Multiplan v. 4.01
WRK	Lotus Symphony 1.0
WR1	Lotus Symphony 1.2
WKS	Lotus 1-2-3 v. 1A
WK1	Lotus 1-2-3 v. 2x
WK3	Lotus 1-2-3 v. 3x
PDOX	Paradox v. 3.0, 3.5, 4.0
RPD	RapidFile v. 1.2
FW2	Framework II

COPY TO

Like its workmate APPEND FROM, COPY TO handles both .DBF files and foreign file formats. The syntax for COPY TO is:

```
COPY TO <file> [FIELDS <field list>] [<scope>]
```

```
[FOR <expL1>]
[WHILE <expL2>]
[[WITH] CDX] | [[WITH] PRODUCTION]
[NOOPTIMIZE]
[[TYPE] [FOXPLUS | DIF | MOD | SDF | SYLK| WK1 | WKS | WR1 |
WRK | XLS |
DELIMITED [WITH <delimiter> WITH BLANK | WITH TAB]]]
```

Common uses are:

```
COPY TO <filename> FIELDS <field list> FOR <expL> WITH CDX
COPY TO test1 FIELDS id, testno, count1, avg1 ;
FOR testno > 100 WITH CDX
COPY TO <filename> FIELDS <field list> TYPE <type>
COPY TO customer2 FIELDS cno, ytdpurch TYPE XLS
COPY TO <filename> FIELDS <field list> DELIMITED WITH
<delimiter>
COPY TO work1.txt FIELDS cno, ytdpurch DELIMITED WITH ","
```

Table 7.3 lists the supported COPY TO file formats.

Table 7.3
Supported COPY TO file formats.

Type	Source
ASCII	Any delimiter
ASCII/SDF	Standard data file (row/column)
FOXPLUS	.DBF with a converted memo file
SYLK	Symbolic link format
DIF	Data interchange format
XLS	Microsoft Excel
MOD	Microsoft Multiplan v. 4.01
WRK	Lotus Symphony v. 1.0
WR1	Lotus Symphony v. 1.2
WKS	Lotus 1-2-3 v. 1A
WK1	Lotus 1-2-3 v. 2 x
WK3	Lotus 1-2-3 v. 3x

COPY TO always creates a new file composed of the fields you've specified, or all the fields in the source file. It supports SCOPE, FOR, and WHILE to give you complete control over what records are copied. The WITH CDX clause creates a matching structural index file with the same tags as the source file.

You may also use COPY STRUCTURE TO <filename> to copy the structure of a .DBF file to a new .DBF file *without* transferring any data. This is used a great deal to take the structure of one file, modify it, and then load data.

A COPY TO Session

For this example, start with:

```
USE customer ALIAS cus IN 0
```

Then send data to a Lotus 1-2-3 file for consolidations.

```
COPY TO lotus22 FIELDS cus.company, cus.ytdpurch ;
FOR cus.ytdpurch > 1000 TYPE WK1
```

Finally create a temporary .DBF complete with an index file for a report lookup. Note that in very large files the SEEK coupled with the WHILE saves time over any other approach.

```
SET ORDER TO state
SEEK "CA"
COPY TO calytd WHILE state="CA" WITH CDX
```

IMPORT FROM

Whereas APPEND FROM must deposit data into an already existing .DBF table (and must conform to its structure), IMPORT creates a new .DBF based on the structure of the file being imported. This gives you more latitude in processing data from other tables. However, IMPORT is limited to foreign file formats and doesn't support the common ASCII text file formats. It also has no FIELDS or FOR options to control what data is being imported. This makes it a bulk importer of a table that probably needs further pruning and massaging with either the APPEND FROM or COPY TO commands.

The syntax is:

```
IMPORT FROM <file>  [TYPE]
FW2 | MOD | PDOX | RPD | WK1 | WK3 | WKS | WR1 | WRK | XLST
```

An example is:

```
IMPORT FROM d:\acct\billable TYPE PDOX
```

The file formats supported are listed in Table 7.4.

Table 7.4
Supported import file formats.

Type	Source
XLS	Microsoft Excel v. 3.0, 4.0
WRK	Lotus Symphony v. 1.0
WR1	Lotus Symphony v. 1.2
WKS	Lotus 1-2-3 v. 1A
WK1	Lotus 1-2-3 v. 2x
WK3	Lotus 1-2-3 v. 3x
MOD	Microsoft Multiplan v. 4.01
PDOX	Paradox v. 3.0, 3.5, 4.0
RPD	RapidFile v. 1.2
FW2	Framework II

EXPORT TO

EXPORT TO used to be the companion command to IMPORT, but since COPY TO now not only matches the capabilities but exceeds them, most people use COPY TO instead. The syntax for EXPORT TO is:

```
EXPORT TO <file> [FIELDS <field list>] [<scope>] [FOR <expL1>]
[WHILE <expL2>]
[NOOPTIMIZE]
[[TYPE] DIF | MOD | SYLK | WK1 | WKS | WR1 | WRK | XLS]
```

An example is:

```
EXPORT TO E:\TEST\CUSTCALC FIELDS cno, company, state, ytdpurch
FOR state="CA" TYPE XLS
```

NOTE

It's very typical in a Command window session to jump around the work areas, closing some, opening others, changing index order, and setting relations. If you open the View window as you work, you can see it display the changes, and it will help you build your own mental image for manipulating work areas.

COPY TO versus SQL SELECT

Hopefully you have become familiar with the RQBE PowerTool, and are aware of its command alternative, the SQL SELECT statement. SELECT can also be used in the Command window. Short statements like:

```
SELECT customer.cno, invoices.ino ;
      FROM customer, invoices ;
      WHERE invoices.cno = customer.cno ;
             AND customer.state = "CA" ;
INTO TABLE test
```

are easy enough to enter, and produce the same results as:

```
USE invoices IN 0 INDEX cno
USE customer IN 0
SET RELATION TO cno INTO invoices
COPY TO test FIELDS customer.cno, invoices.ino ;
FOR customer.state = "CA"
```

Both approaches can create an extract of data from multiple tables, and both give you plenty of ways to control what records are selected. However, SELECT is far more flexible and extendible than COPY TO. So why not always use SELECT in the Command window?

Unfortunately, extracting tables with SQL SELECT in the Command window is inconvenient and inefficient. For simple SQL statements, you're probably better off using RQBE. And for complex statements, especially those that involve subqueries, it would be better to work with a program file. Editing almost any SQL statement in the Command window, especially a lengthy one, is messy. You get a lot of repeated lines jammed together that are very hard to read. And above all, the Command window makes no attempt to save your work. RQBE and the program file allow you to retain a complex statement for future use.

Some people say this is hair-splitting. Doubtless personal preferences may play a larger role than any inherent quality of one approach being better than another. Certainly, you can use SQL SELECT in the Command window. But for ongoing editing sessions, COPY TO is a simpler command that suits the rather simple maneuvers common to data maintenance. Moreover, mixing the Command window with a program file that contains a SQL statement is a very convenient approach in its own right.

Getting Located in a Table

FoxPro maintains a *table pointer* for every open file. It has five basic positions, which you need to recognize:

1. Beginning of file (BOF)
2. First record of the table
3. Other records of the table
4. Last record of the table
5. End of file (EOF)

Figure 7.2 displays tables and pointers.

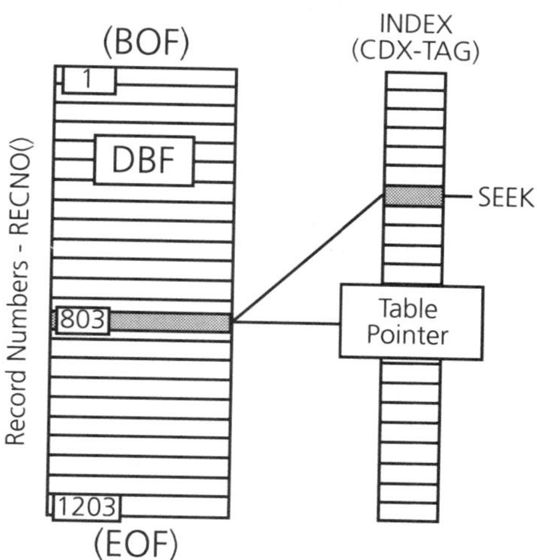

Figure 7.2
Tables and pointers.

The pointer tracks the currently selected record. Each record is automatically assigned a number (RECNO), which is part of the pointer. There are, however, two positions that do not correspond to a record—beginning of file and end of file. These are actually *beyond* the scope of the table.

You might wonder what purpose do these phantom positions serve? When you search for something in a table and it's found, the pointer is on the located record. What happens if nothing is found? You wouldn't want the pointer on a record. The solution was EOF, an end-of-file position for the pointer, which has the characteristics of an empty record. The BOF position exists for much the same purpose, although it is hardly ever used. If you try to go beyond these positions using the GOTO or SKIP command, you'll get an error message.

Most of the FoxPro table operation and search commands have specific behaviors with the table pointer. Table 7.5 lists pointer positions, after execution, for some of them.

Table 7.5
Command pointer positions.

Command	Pointer position
SEEK	Found: RECNO
	Not found: EOF
LOCATE	Found: RECNO
	Not found: EOF
INDEX, REINDEX	First record
REPLACE ALL	EOF
DELETE / RECALL ALL	EOF
SUM, AVERAGE	EOF
TOTAL	EOF
COPY TO	EOF

Once the table(s) for a session are open, the real work begins. One of the most important aspects is getting to the right place in a table. This could mean finding some specific piece of data, or selecting a group (set) of related information, or putting the table pointer at some specific place in the table. There are a number of ways to do this, each useful in its own way. These commands can collectively be viewed as pointer-setting commands, because they put the table pointer in specific locations.

SELECT

More often than not, you need to make sure you're in the right work area. It's always better to be safe. SELECT allows you to choose your work area. Its syntax is:

```
SELECT <work area/alias>
SELECT CUS
```

This is where using short aliases begins to pay off. This is also another place where the View window is often more expedient than typing, since all you have to do is click on the work area you want to select.

SKIP

In this age of spinner buttons and slide controls, SKIP is a mighty crude way of navigating a table, but it works. Its syntax is:

```
SKIP [<expN1>] [IN <expN2> | <expC>]
```

Some common expressions of SKIP are:

```
SKIP <numeric expression>
SKIP 20
SKIP -1
nRecs = 20
SKIP nRecs IN CUS
```

To go forward (toward the bottom of the file), use any positive number, or expression that evaluates positive. To go backward (toward the top of the file), use negatives. In practice, this command is used mostly in programming routines.

GO and GO RECORD

All records in a file are automatically "numbered" by FoxPro; that is, they are in an ordinal sequence. If you know the number of a record, you can go to it directly. The syntax for GO is:

```
GO [RECORD] <expN1> [IN <expN2> | IN <expC>] [TOP | BOTTOM]
```

Or, more simply:

```
GO <numeric expression>
```

Some examples are:

```
GO 1203
GOTO 1203
nPointer = RECNO( )
GO nPointer
```

Some people regard this as a stone-age technique. It's unreliable in a sense, because in a changing file the record numbers do not stay the same. It should be noted that of all ways to get to a specific record, this is the fastest, provided you know the record number.

SET ORDER TO

If you didn't open a file with a specific index tag, or want to change an index, use the SETORDER TO command. Its syntax is:

```
SET ORDER TO [<expN1> | <idx index file> | [TAG] <tag name> [OF
<cdx file>]
[IN <expN2> | <expC>] [ASCENDING | DESCENDING]
```

Or, most commonly:

```
SET ORDER TO <tag name>
SET ORDER TO contact
```

This makes the named tag the master index. Don't confuse SET ORDER with SET INDEX. The latter is used with old style .IDX files, where each file was one index. In FoxPro using the CDX file, where there may be several tags, you set the order (read as "sort order") by designating one of the tags as master index. With this command you can also refer to the tag by its number in the tag list—1,2,3, and so on. In the Command window this may be okay, but it's not suited for programming, since it masks the content of the index, and may cause problems if anyone changes the tag list order.

One of the benefits of how FoxPro for Windows uses indexes is that a "reverse" order is available at any time on any indexed field—without re-indexing. Use this syntax for that purpose:

```
SET ORDER TO <tag name> DESCENDING
```

A to Z, 1 to n is the default ASCENDING order, Z to A, n to 1 is DESCENDING.

SEEK

SEEK is one of the bedrock commands of the Xbase language. It's also relatively uncomplicated. It does a search based on an index. Its syntax is:

```
SEEK <data expression>
SEEK "JOHNSON"
cLook = "JOHNSON"
SEEK cLook
```

To use it, the file being searched has to have a controlling index (master tag), and the data expression needs to be something that could be found in that index. If there is a match, the file pointer is put on that record. If there is no match, the pointer is located on the last record of the file and EOF( ) is set to true (.t.). The data expression itself can be just about anything, including a UDF or other complex expressions. The only requirement is that the expression evaluate to the same data type as the index being used.

This command is used incessantly in both the interactive part of FoxPro and in programming. In the Command window the most common use is to find some piece of information in a file, and then go to a BROWSE or similar command to look at the data.

Note that a companion function, SEEK(<data expression>, <work area/alias>) does the same thing, but is mostly used in programming routines. There is also some linguistic deadwood, the FIND command, which does an indexed search like the SEEK but only with character data. It's obsolete, but still found in old (dBase III type) programs.

SET FILTER TO

Before the days of SQL and the Query by Example, people used this command to isolate a specific "set" of records. It had a bad reputation, however, for being intolerably slow in very large files. It's slightly ironic that the Rushmore Technology, which gave us the powerful SELECT command, also gave new life to the old SET FILTER TO. It's good news, because unlike SELECT which produces a new table (or cursor), SET FILTER TO works within an active file. Different applications use either of these techniques for set oriented work, and it's good to have both of them functional. Its syntax is:

```
SET FILTER TO <logical expression>
SET FILTER TO lastname = "JOHNSON"
```

The "logical expression" refers to the sky's-the limit-capability (see Chapter 1) for creating conditionals in database files.

LOCATE FOR

Like SET FILTER TO, this is a command that was resurrected by the Rushmore Technology. There's only one reason for using it, as opposed to using the SEEK command: It can be followed by a CONTINUE command, to continue finding matches for the same logical expression. This can be useful in the Command Window, where you can't set up a search loop. Its syntax is:

```
LOCATE FOR <expL1> [<scope>] [WHILE <expL2>] [NOOPTIMIZE]
LOCATE FOR <logical expression>
LOCATE FOR lastname = "JORDAN"
```

For example, to find all "Johnsons"s, do this:

```
LOCATE FOR lastname = "JOHNSON"
EDIT
CONTINUE
EDIT
```

DOT OPERATOR

```
<filename/alias>.<field name>
cus.contact
```

The dot operator can be loosely translated as "the thing on the right belongs to the thing on the left." In the most common case, the thing on the left is a file name or alias, and the thing on the right is a field in that file.

Tables often have fields of the same name. In fact, for most relational systems identical field names for index keys is recommended. However, if files with identical key fields are open at the same time, you have to use the file identifier to avoid confusion (yours and the computer's). Some people recommend that all fields be identified in this way to avoid any problem with overlap and to make the code crystal clear as to what file and field combination is meant.

There is an alternate to the dot operator, which looks something like an arrow, for example: cus->contact. This is the old dBase III format and is still common in dBase and Clipper code. However, because the dot operator is quicker to type and is very much akin to the dot operator in the "C" language, it's become the standard for FoxPro.

Ready for Entry

Having opened all the needed files, and if necessary located information, you're ready to input new data or editing existing data. In this case the entry is by hand—typing. In most cases data entry into FoxPro applications is done by controlled screens, but when it comes to data maintenance it's often most expedient just to get into the files and modify them manually.

APPEND

Simple and direct, APPEND adds one record to the file and puts you into a screen for direct entry of the fields.

Alternate commands—APPEND BLANK, INSERT, and INSERT-SQL—also create new records and are covered extensively in the programming section.

BROWSE

Basically this is a table or spreadsheet view of data with rows of records and a column for each field. It allows users to compare a number of records at a glance, which puts information in context. For most kinds of data review, and many kinds of editing, this is the most convenient format. Users like the control it gives them over the data.

The FoxPro BROWSE is extremely flexible, both in selection of data and how it is presented. It supports forty clauses that modify and augment the basic command, most of which are relevant only to programming. Some clauses are obscure, and others confer on BROWSE a power and flexibility found in no other programming language. It's well worth your time to practice with the BROWSE and all its facets. The following are some of the forms that are most useful in the Command window.

BROWSE LAST

When doing data maintenance and moving back-and-forth between files, you can use this form to tell FoxPro to use the same configuration (such as window size and column arrangement) as the last time you used this browse. It's a good habit.

BROWSE LAST FOR

With the addition of the FOR clause in FoxPro version 2.0, and its' link to the Rushmore Technology, the BROWSE command became one of the most sophisticated in the arsenal. Similar effects could be achieved with doing a SET FILTER TO before a BROWSE, but this new form was at once more elegant and better integrated. For one thing you don't have to remember to close the filter when leaving the browse. It does it for you. Its syntax is:

```
BROWSE LAST FOR <logical expression>
BROWSE LAST FOR lastname="JOHNSON"
```

BROWSE FIELDS

One of the drawbacks of the browse format is that fields are often hidden beyond the right edge of the browse window. Of course you can scroll your way over to them, but this defeats some of the purpose of instant data comparison. One solution is to restrict the number of fields available to only those most useful. Hopefully to one screenful. The FIELDS clause lets you set the order and number of fields as they appear in the browse window. Its syntax is:

```
BROWSE FIELDS <field list> LAST
BROWSE FIELDS lastname, firstname, city, state LAST
```

EDIT/CHANGE

EDIT and CHANGE have the same syntax as BROWSE.

These two commands do exactly the same thing. So why both? History. In older versions of Xbase they were different. Today they're an example of language bloat. Most people use the CHANGE form. As you've may have already seen in the system menu, the CHANGE option is a toggle with the Browse option. The fields are stacked vertically, which usually means that you can see more fields on the screen than you can in the browse format, but only one or two records at a time. In programming applications, the Edit window is seldom used, because people create much more elaborate and controlled screens. But in the interactive Command window mode, this is still a very useful format.

A Typical Editing Session

Its time to do some routine updating of information in the CUSTOMER table. Some addresses have changed, as well as phone numbers, and other information. As is so often the case, the primary source of information is a list on a piece of paper—so much for the paperless office.

```
SET EXCLUSIVE OFF
SET SAFETY ON
USE customer IN 0 ORDER company ALIAS cus1
USE customer IN 0 ORDER city ALIAS cus2 AGAIN
SELECT cus1
SEEK "Merganthau Real Estate"
```

Notice the use of AGAIN. This allows you to have more than one copy of the customer file open at a time, each with its own index order. This speeds up searches.

Since nothing was found on the company search, try a city search. It's less precise, but perhaps the spelling of the company was incorrect. So the best thing to do is use a search that gets you more "in the neighborhood".

```
SELECT cus2
SEEK "Atlanta"
```

The BROWSE gives you a chance to scan a number of entries at once, in this case looking for a company that looks like Merganthau. The FIELDS restriction to one field makes a more focused BROWSE screen for easy searching. However, use a CHANGE so that all fields are visible to do any editing you would need to drop out of the BROWSE.

```
BROWSE KEY "Atlanta" FIELDS company
CHANGE
```

For the next search, you don't have any company name or city, just a last name. Unfortunately, there is no last name field in the customer table, just a CONTACTs field that has last names buried in a long character string. This becomes a job for LOCATE, which can do the substring search, and continue until you come upon the right person with the last name.

```
SELECT cus1
LOCATE FOR "Barker" $ contact
CHANGE
CONTINUE
CHANGE
```

Table Operations

This is the heart of database management and these are some of the most powerful commands in the Xbase language. They are also potentially the most dangerous. They are capable of making changes throughout an entire table, and doing them very quickly.

Multiuser: A table must be opened as EXCLUSIVE before using any of the following commands on the whole table.

REPLACE

This is another fundamental command with more uses than a Swiss Army knife. In this form, particularly where the "scope" is ALL, REPLACE is used constantly to perform many kinds of database maintenance and data conversion tasks. Its syntax is:

```
REPLACE <field1> WITH <expr1> [ADDITIVE] [, <field2> WITH
<expr2> [ADDITIVE]] ...
[<scope>] [FOR <expL1>] [WHILE <expL2>] [NOOPTIMIZE]
```

Three examples are:

```
REPLACE <scope> <field> WITH <value>
REPLACE ALL cus.contact WITH UPPER(cus.contact)
REPLACE NEXT 20 firstname WITH ALLTRIM(firstname)
```

In data maintenance another form of the command is used all the time to "fix" data that has been erroneously entered, improperly formatted, and so on.

```
REPLACE <field> WITH <value> FOR <logical expression>
REPLACE state WITH "CA" FOR state="CAL"
```

The FOR clause creates the set of records to be acted upon, and then the replacement occurs only on those records. It is very easy, however, to create incorrect expressions—and ruin a lot of records if you're not careful. Always test this kind of REPLACE on either a sample file, or on one record, before unleashing it on the rest of the live data.

The next form isn't too common in the Command window. For it to work you need to do a SEEK or LOCATE so that the file pointer is on the first occurrence of the while condition. Its syntax is:

```
REPLACE <field> WITH <value> WHILE <logical expression>
REPLACE state WITH "CA", zip WITH "10023" WHILE state="CAL"
```

Code for a Replace Session

This example is fairly typical of data conversion jobs. A new table is being created from data contained in three other tables. Few of the field names, or in some cases even data types, are common between the tables, so you can't use APPEND FROM or COPY TO. This is a job for REPLACE.

```
CLEAR ALL
SET TALK ON
SET SAFETY ON
SET EXCLUSIVE OFF
```

Open all four files and set relations. The order of the vendor file is based on the expression vendno+ventotal, which in descending order sorts the vendor with the highest sales at the point where the relation from the distven table does it's first lookup.

```
USE e:\acctg\vendors IN 0 ORDER vendtot DESCENDING ALIAS ven
USE f:\sales\offices IN 0 ORDER officeid ALIAS ofc

USE e:\acctg\distven IN 0 ORDER distId ALIAS dst
USE c:\temp\vendhist IN 0 ORDER distid ALIAS vhs EXCLUSIVE
```

This forms a one-one-two relation with the distven (district vendors) table feeding data by relation from the vendors and offices files into the new vendhist (vendor history) file.

```
SELECT dst
SET RELATION TO vendor INTO ven
SET RELATION TO office INTO ofc ADDITIVE
SELECT vhs
SET RELATION TO distid INTO dst
```

Having set all of the needed relations, the REPLACE command can pull data from all three "feeder" files to load the vendhist records. Notice the use of continuation markers. This could be done with a series of REPLACE commands, but would take much longer to type, and this method executes in one pass.

```
REPLACE state WITH dst.state,;
        office WITH ofc.officeid,;
        vendor WITH ven.vendno,;
        distyr WITH dst.yearstart,;
        vendyr WITH ven.ventotal ;
FOR dst.state = "CA" AND ven.ventotal > 1000
```

Check to see if what was supposed to happen did in fact happen.

```
BROWSE LAST
```

UPDATE ON

In a sense, this is a two table version of the REPLACE command. It's a little complicated to set up, but it can accomplish a lot of work in a single pass. It's important to keep in mind that being an index-oriented command, updates only occur if matches from the key are found in the FROM table. With UPDATE, the file being updated (the current work area) must also be indexed on the <key field>. Its syntax is:

```
UPDATE ON <field> FROM <expN> | <expC> REPLACE <field1> WITH
<expr1>
[, <field2> WITH <expr2> ...] [RANDOM]
```

An example is:

```
UPDATE ON <key field> FROM <work area/alias> REPLACE <field>
WITH <value>
UPDATE ON contact FROM cus ;
REPLACE name WITH cus.contact+","+ord.firstname
```

DELETE and RECALL

As mentioned before, deletions in the Xbase language are a two-step process. This first step marks records in the table as deleted—a* appears on screen (it is actually the marker in the file as well). Until you do a PACK, you can always go back and use the RECALL command to remove the deletion. This is a handy safety net. The syntax for DELETE is:

```
DELETE [<scope>] [FOR <expL1>] [WHILE <expL2>] [NOOPTIMIZE]
```

Examples are:

```
DELETE <scope>
DELETE ALL
DELETE <scope> FOR <logical expressions>
DELETE ALL FOR lastname = "JOHNSON"
```

The syntax for RECALL is:

```
RECALL <scope> [FOR <expL1>] [WHILE <expL2>] [NOOPTIMIZE]
```

Examples are:

```
RECALL <scope>
RECALL ALL
RECALL <scope> FOR <logical expression>
RECALL ALL FOR lastname="JOHNSON"
```

Like many other commands, DELETE and RECALL have the services of the Rushmore active FOR clause.

PACK

This is the point of no return for deletions. The PACK command physically removes all records marked for deletion, and there is no way to get them back.

ZAP

This is a vicious little command. At one stroke you can wipe out every record in a table. However, it's useful and if "Safety" is turned on, harmless. Otherwise, use this command only when necessary.

MODIFY STRUCTURE

Modifying the structure of a data table is done in the same way as creating it. Issuing this command puts you into the Table Structure dialog box. Here you can add or remove fields, change widths and data types, and set single-field indexes.

A Table Year-end Cleanup Session

It's the first of the year and its time to clean out customers who haven't done any business in the previous year, and flag those who did less than $100 (for future sales calls).

```
SET TALK ON
SET EXCLUSIVE ON
```

Since this session will be deleting records, delete should be turned off so that you can see the deleted records.

```
SET DELETE OFF
USE invoices IN 0 ORDER cno ALIAS inv
USE customer IN 0 ORDER cno ALIAS cus
SET RELATION TO cno INTO inv
SET SKIP TO cno
```

This is the typical pattern for deleting—delete using a FOR clause, BROWSE to make sure the right records were deleted (if not, just use RECALL to bring them back). Finally, a PACK to get rid of the records physically.

```
DELETE ALL FOR cus.ytdpurch = 0
BROWSE LAST FOR DELETED( )
PACK
```

When the deletions are done, use REPLACE to flag customers with less than $100 of business.

```
REPLACE ALL cus.status WITH "C" FOR inv.itotal < 100
BROWSE FIELDS cus.company, cus.status
```

Standard Command Window Output

For the purposes of reviewing and maintaining data, most people lean on the services of the BROWSE. But there are many other situations where simply seeing information on the screen or getting summary totals is more appropriate.

Output usually comes in one of three forms—screen, print, or file. In the Command window, output is generally to the screen, with occasional use of a printer or file. The idea here is speed and convenience. Programmer's most often speak of Command window output as *dumps*, unformatted listings of things like table contents and directories.

All of the following commands send their output to the screen by default. They can also take these output clauses (one at a time): TO PRINT, TO FILE <file name>.

DISPLAY

This is one of the most basic commands in the Xbase language. It's not terribly sophisticated in format, but it serves the job of delivering screen loads of data—one screen at a time.

```
DISPLAY [[FIELDS] <field list>] [<scope>] [FOR <expL1>] [WHILE
<expL2>] [OFF]
[TO PRINTER [PROMPT] | TO FILE <file>] [NOCONSOLE] [NOOPTIMIZE]
```

A most common example is:

```
DISPLAY <scope> FOR <logical expression>
DISPLAY ALL FOR lastname="SMYTHE"
DISPLAY ALL FOR lastname="SMYTHE" TO PRINT
```

If you want to get a little more control into the screen output, you can add some of the following:

```
DISPLAY <scope> FIELDS <field list> OFF
DISPLAY ALL FIELDS TRIM(lastname), firstname, midname, status
OFF
```

This last example restricts the fields displayed to those in the field list. You can also use functions to format the fields, as in TRIM(lastname)above. The OFF clause removes the record number from the display.

LIST has exactly the same form and capabilities as DISPLAY but it produces a continuous listing with no pauses at each screen. For that reason it's used to dump data to a printer or a file. DISPLAY STRUCTURE, DISPLAY MEMORY, and DISPLAY STATUS show screens of information about your data tables, memory variables, and other system items. They are very useful from time to time to notice how many files are open, and what their indexes are.

COUNT

This is a very interesting command because of its astonishing speed. Any count done on an indexed field, even with huge files, happens in a matter of split seconds. This speed really encourages querying tables to get counts of various things—a very useful yardstick in all kinds of data maintenance.

```
COUNT [<scope>] [FOR <expL1>] [WHILE <expL2>] [TO <memvar>]
```

```
[NOOPTIMIZE]
COUNT <scope> FOR <logical expression>
COUNT ALL FOR lastname = "SMITH"
```

For example, before you delete a particular type of data entry error you might run a COUNT FOR to see how many errors there are. Its syntax is:

```
COUNT ALL FOR lastname="SMOUTHE"
```

TOTAL TO

```
TOTAL TO
```

As mentioned in menu system section, this command used to be the only way to create a summary file containing totals from numeric fields. Now, the job is usually better performed with RQBE or the SQL SELECT statement. The syntax for TOTAL TO is:

```
TOTAL TO <file> ON <expr> [FIELDS <field list>] [<scope>] [FOR
<expL1>]
[WHILE <expL2>] [NOOPTIMIZE]
```

An example is:

```
TOTAL TO <file> ON <expr> <scope> FOR <logical expression>
TOTAL TO test1 ON ytdpurch ALL FOR state = "CA"
```

CALCULATE

Even if you don't have multiple calculations to perform, this is still the command to learn and use. Its syntax is:

```
CALCULATE <expr list> [<scope>] [FOR <expL1>] [WHILE <expL2>]
[TO <memvar list> | TO ARRAY <array>] [NOOPTIMIZE]
```

An example is:

```
CALCULATE <expr list> FOR <expL>
CALCULATE CNT( ), SUM(ytdpurch), AVG(ytdpurch), MIN(ytdpurch);
MAX(ytdpurch) FOR state = "CA"
```

In one pass of a table it can make any combination of the calculations in Table 7.6.

Table 7.6
Calculating functions in an expression list.

Calculation Expression	Description
AVG(<expN>)	Average = sum / count of a numeric field.
CNT( )	Count of records matching SCOPE/FOR/WHILE.
MAX(<expr>)	Maximum value of a field.
MIN(<expr>)	Minimum value of a field.
NPV(<expN1>, <expN2>[, <expN3>])	Net present value of a numeric field.
STD(<expN>)	Standard deviation of a numeric field.
SUM(<expN>)	Sum of a numeric field.
VAR(<expN>)	Variance of a numeric field.

Alternates commands for CALCULATE are AVERAGE, SUM, and COUNT.

Screen Output

The Command window is one of the few places in FoxPro where output to the screen, or *desktop*, is the default. The desktop is the area between the system menu at the top and the status bar at the bottom. The Command window itself cannot display anything, so if you use any commands or functions that return results to be displayed, you can use one of the following methods.

CLEAR | CLEAR SCREEN

This clears the current output window, which may also be the desktop.

QUESTION MARK (?)

How the question mark became the command for "output the following," we may never know. A lot of people have seen it for the first time, and had their own "?"

Its syntax is:

```
? | ?? <expr1> [PICTURE <expC1>] | [FUNCTION <expC2>] [AT
<expN1>]
[FONT <expC3>[, <expN2>]] [STYLE <expC4> | <expr2>] [, <expr3>]
...
```

Some examples are:

```
? "Now is the time for all good men to come to."
? RECCOUNT( )
? 345 + 456
```

As crude, unformatted and simple as it is, the ? gets used all of the time in the Command window to display field content, variables, function results, and many other things. However, when output has been directed to the printer, the ? forces a carriage return and a line feed. If that's not what you want, use ??, as in the following example:

```
?? "Now is the time..."
```

The double question mark creates neither carriage return nor line feed, so in essence it merely butts its text up to the previous text (provided you don't get a word wrap).

```
?? "NOW " ?? "Is the time" ?? " for all."
```

produces

```
NOW Is the time for all.
```

You can add PICTURE clauses, AT to define a location, and FONT and STYLE to jazz up the text.

```
?? "This is customer number: " AT 10
? nCustCount PICTURE "###,###" FONT "Arial", 14 STYLE B
```

Why you would want to do this, instead of using the more precise and versatile @ ..SAY, is not clear. But there are always circumstances, especially if you are reduced to programming printed reports, where this may be useful.

Again, by default, ? and ?? send their output to the screen. However you can redirect the output by using any of the following commands:

- SET PRINT ON
- SET PRINT OFF
- SET DEVICE TO PRINT
- SET DEVICE TO SCREEN
- SET ALTERNATE TO <filename>
- SET ALTERNATE ON

The last two commands direct to a file all output and anything you type into the Command window. This can be useful for retaining table and directory listings, and so forth.

Screening Information

The following code example may be used for screening information:

```
SET EXCLUSIVE OFF
SET TALK ON
CLEAR
USE customer IN 0 ORDER cno ALIAS cus
```

First, find out how many customers are from the western states.

```
COUNT FOR state $ "MT WA OR CA NV AZ CO WY UT NM" TO nWest
CLEAR
```

Having cleared the screen, the value of nWest can still be brought back.

```
? nWest
DISPLAY ALL FIELDS company, contact FOR state = "NV"
```

As a matter of routine, you should make sure the file pointer is at the top of the table before you run any table wide commands.

```
GO TOP
```

```
CALCULATE AVG(ytdpurch) TO nPurch
```

The value of the average purchase to date has been stored to a memory variable. Now it needs to be used in a new field as the customer file. But first modify customer to add the field PCTAVG as the field where the percentage of sales above/below the average is stored.

```
MODIFY STRUCTURE
REPLACE ALL pctavg WITH ((ytdpurch-npurch)/nPurch)*100
DISPLAY ALL FIELDS company, pctavg, ytdpurch FOR pctavg > 50
CLEAR
DISPLAY ALL FIELDS company, pctavg, ytdpurch FOR pctavg > 150
```

Cleaning Up and Shutting Down

Every database program under the sun admonishes users never to reboot or turn off their computer before exiting the program correctly. Why? Because there is always the chance that the software is doing something in those files, and when you cut it off without warning, the program loses track of things like the end of the file, or the synchronization of indexes. Fortunately, FoxPro is quite robust in this respect, and for the most part the damage of abrupt shutdown is the loss of maybe the last record of data entered. Still closing things down properly is every user's responsibility.

CLOSE DATABASES

A simple and direct command that does one thing, close every open table and index.

CLEAR ALL

This command clears most of the decks. Tables, variables, windows, all disappear. This one command is used to "start from scratch" in the Command window. (With a program a few more commands may be necessary to accomplish the same thing.)

ERASE

This command erases any unopened file from disk. You need to provide the complete path and file name, including extension. DOS wildcard symbols (?, *) are not supported. If you use the ? option, the Windows File Open dialog box is displayed. Remember when erasing .DBF files, also get the memo file, .FPT, if there is one.

The syntax for ERASE is:

```
ERASE <file> | ?
```

or alternatively

```
DELETE FILE <file> | ?
```

QUIT

This is the "correct" way to exit from FoxPro. Quitting allows proper closing of all files and other forms of final cleanup.

A Maintenance Session

Following is a sample database maintenance session:

```
SET TALK ON
SET EXCLUSIVE OFF
SET DELETE ON
CLEAR ALL
```

For convenience, open all of the files that might be needed.

```
USE customer IN 0 ALIAS cus
USE invoices IN 0 ALIAS inv
USE parts IN 0 ALIAS par
USE detail IN 0 ALIAS det
USE salesmen IN 0 ALIAS sls
USE office IN 0 ALIAS ofc
```

The task here is to produce a file of salespeople, by office, with year-to-date sales, percent of total, and percent of maximum sales, to be sent to regional offices. First create the file to hold the information.

```
CREATE DBF salestat(ono c (1), office c (20),salesman c (4), ;
name c (30),ytdsales n (8.2),pcttotal n (3.1),pctofmax n (3.1))
```

Go to the SALESMAN file and get the total statistics.

```
SELECT sls
CALCULATE SUM(sls.ytdsales), MAX(sls.ytdsales) TO ARRAY aSales
```

Load the SALESTAT file with data from SALESMAN (ono, salesman, name, ytdsales fields).

```
SELECT salestat
APPEND FROM salesman
```

Update the statistics fields from the calculated array.

```
REPLACE ALL pcttotal WITH (ytdsales/aSales[1])*100,;
pctofmax WITH (ytdsales/aSales[2])*100
```

Finally, fill in the name of the office from the office file.

```
SELECT ofc
SET ORDER TO ono
SELECT salestat
SET RELATION TO ono INTO ofc
REPLACE ALL office WITH ofc.city
```

The SALESTAT file is ready for distribution.

It was discovered that all parts records in PARTS.DBF are duplicated. Getting rid of them is not so hard because *every* record is duplicated...

```
SELECT par
```

Indexing with UNIQUE creates a table without duplicates in the key, which when copied to a temporary file makes a table without duplicates.

```
INDEX ON pno TAG uniqpno UNIQUE
COPY TO partemp
```

Clear out the PARTS.DBF and re-load it from the temporary file.

```
ZAP
DELETE TAG uniqpno
```

```
APPEND FROM partemp
ERASE partemp.dbf
```

Next, print a list and delete parts that show no sales in the previous year.

```
SELECT det
```

Check to make sure DETAIL file has an index on pno.

```
DISPLAY STATUS
```

It doesn't, so make one.

```
INDEX ON pno TAG pno
```

Shift to the parts file and set a relation to look for parts that don't show up in any invoice detail.

```
SELECT par
SET RELATION TO pno INTO det
COUNT ALL FOR NOT FOUND("det")
```

Two parts did not sell during the calendar year. Do a print dump of them, and then delete.

```
LIST ALL FOR NOT FOUND("det") TO PRINT
DELETE ALL FOR NOT FOUND("det")
```

You're done for the session, so clean up.

```
CLEAR ALL
QUIT
```

Using Functions in the Command Window

What's the difference between a command and a function? They look different: DISPLAY vs RECCOUNT (), but this is only superficial. Commands are like their name, they generally go do something. Classic functions are subroutines that simply return information. Also, there can only be one command in a line of code. In certain circumstances a line of code might have several functions. In fact, those functions that are most useful in the Command window are those which can be combined in the same line with commands like REPLACE and TOTAL.

FoxPro for Windows has 292 functions. Too many to learn all at once. Fortunately, a few functions are used more than others. Even fewer are used with regularity in the Command window, and these are some of the most important functions in any context. In the next chapter, functions will be taken apart anatomically, and you'll learn how to stitch them together in your own User Defined Functions. But here in the Command window, there are only three points about functions which are important to understand:

1. **Functions are "in line"**—you can place them inside of commands, other functions, or just about anywhere it makes sense to use a function. In the Command window a function can be used "standalone" as long as it's preceded by the ? (if you want to see the results). Otherwise you can use the equal sign "=" instead. The function will work, but you won't see the results on the screen.

   ```
   ? RECOUNT ()
   = RECOUNT ()
   ```

   An extremely common use of functions is to provide input for a field as part of the REPLACE command. There are literally millions of variations for this, many of which you will discover for yourself. One example is:

   ```
   REPLACE ALL LASTDATE WITH DATE( )
   ```

   Following is an example of one function "nested" inside of another function.

   ```
   REPLACE ALL MIDINIT WITH ;
   SUBSTR(FIRSTNAME,AT(".",FIRSTNAME)-1,2)
   ```

   This too is very common. In this example the AT( ) function returns the location of a period in the FIRSTNAME field, which is then used by the SUBSTR( ) function as an argument for where the substring should begin. This finally returns a single character and a period—"B."—to be placed into the middle initial field, MIDINIT.

2. **Functions always return a value.** Some care needs to be taken that functions returning values into other functions or command clauses have the correct data type.

   In this example, the DATE( ) function always returns a date data type—which the SUBSTR( ) function doesn't recognize—and generates a syntax error.

```
REPLACE START WITH SUBSTR(DATE( ),1,6)
```

You have to use one of the date conversion functions like DTOC( ) (date to character) to produce the character string that the SUBSTR( ) function is expecting.

```
REPLACE START WITH SUBSTR(DTOC(DATE( ),1,6)
```

3. **Functions are fussy about their "arguments."** (Arguments are parameters you pass to the function). Unlike command verbs, where the order of the clauses is generally not important, function arguments must be in the correct order and the correct data type.

   WRONG:

   ```
   REPLACE COMPANY WITH SUBSTR( TITLE, 1, AT( TITLE, "."))
   ```

   RIGHT:

   ```
   REPLACE COMPANY WITH SUBSTR( TITLE, 1, AT( ".", TITLE))
   ```

   The little shift in the arguments of the AT( ) function sometimes produces a syntax error. However, since this syntax returns a 0 (equivalent to TITLE not found in "."), it sometimes won't generate an error message. Instead it may produce an incorrect value, which is much harder to detect and track down.

   Errors like the above are easy to make because there are a lot of functions, and many of them take rather complicated arguments. Of course, most of the time you'll get a syntax error message, but at least with the more important functions (like the ones that follow), you should try to learn the argument requirements, just as you would learn the clauses for a command verb.

General Use Functions

Following are some utilitarian functions that get used here, there, and about everywhere. They are not associated with any particular data type, or any specific situation.

EMPTY

This function is used extensively to test if a field or variable is "empty," that is, has no content. Its syntax is:

```
EMPTY( <expr> )
```

<expr> is an expression of any data type.

```
=EMPTY ( ctext )
```

In common usage, this function is very straightforward. However, from a computer science point of view you should be aware of some issues. EMPTY() reports a 0 (zero) numeric value as empty. As a mathematician will tell you, a zero is not nothing. Likewise, EMPTY() reports both characterr expressions " " (a space) and "" (a null) as empty. For one thing, these two expressions are not the same. For another, a space is not truly empty. It's an ASCII 32 - a space, which is just as valid as any letter of the alphabet. While these distinctions may seem fine, there are circumstances where you need to be careful what you're asking EMPTY() to test.

This is especially true for .dbf files because numeric fields can be truly "empty," have nothing at all in them whatsoever, or they may have zeroes. In an accounting application, for example, this difference between a truly empty (null) value, and a zero value can be very signifcant. The null field indicates that no entry has been made at all. A zero could be a legitimate entry. Other functions, notably LEN(), which test the length of a value, can be more accurate than EMPTY() in this kind of situation.

Cautionary words aside, EMPTY() is used frequently in table maintenance to update field information. A typical use might be:

```
REPLACE ALL STATUS WITH "?" FOR EMPTY( STATUS )
```

BETWEEN

The syntax is:

```
BETWEEN <expr1>, <expr2>, <expr3>
```

<expr1> is the value to be tested for "betweeness."

<expr2> is the minimum value of the test range.

<expr3> is the maximum value of the test range.

```
= BETWEEN( 8, 2, 10 )
= BETWEEN( "DOG", "AARDVARK", "ZEBRA" )
```

Returns: .t. (true) if the value of <expr1> is between <expr2> and <expr3>, otherwise it returns .f. (false).

Mathematically this is very easy to express: x >= min, x <= max.

A Programming Function

There are literally hundreds of functions that are really only practicable in the programming environment. One, however, stands out as a useful tool anywhere: IIF.

IIF

Of all the "testing" functions, and there are many, this is by far the most important. It's often referred to by its mnemonic moniker—the Immediate IF—because of its relationship to the programming construct IF...ELSE...ENDIF. It does the same job, but as a function and in one line of code. Its syntax is:

```
IIF( <expL>, <expr1>, <expr2> )
```

<expL> is the "test," a logical expression, that evaluates to true or false (.t./.f.).

<expr1> is the value to be returned if the test expression is true (.t.)

<expr2> is the value to be returned if the test expression is false (.f.).

For example:

```
= IIF( SALES > 10000, SALES, 0 )
```

Returns SALES, if sales are greater than $10,000, otherwise it returns 0.

It's relatively easy to get a handle on IIF( ) by looking at it this way:

```
IIF( a true or false test , return this if true, return this if
false )
```

One thing this IF function has in common with all functions is that it can be nested: one function can be placed inside of another function. In fact, it is commonly nested with itself:

```
REPLACE ALL STATUS WITH IIF( SALES>10000, "A", IIF( SALES >
5000, "B", "C"))
```

As the REPLACE command scans the table, the IIF( ) is testing each record, first to see if the value in the SALES field is greater than $10,000. If it is, then the STATUS field is set to "A." If it is not, the another test is made, this time to see if SALES are greater than $5000. If they are, the status will be set to "B," and if not will be set to "C." This construction is sometimes called a *cascading if,* and is fairly common in both the Command window and programming. There are theoretical limits to how deeply you can nest the IIF( )s, but in practice it becomes very hard to follow the logic beyond three or four levels.

It's tempting to become very reliant on the IIF( ), especially in the Command window. Even in the programming environment, IIF( ) is often preferred because of its compact format, and because it usually executes somewhat faster than an identical IF...ELSE...ENDIF.

Character Functions

Since a large percentage of the fields in a table are of the character or memo type, it makes sense that there are a large number of functions to manipulate and test character data. (Keep in mind that functions work on variables and constants, as well as fields.) In the Command window, you will often be doing various kinds of editing and housekeeping tasks with the character fields. The following functions should be the most useful.

To illustrate the uses of these functions, here's a ungainly character string that might be found in a field:

```
" My dog, Horst, has fleas "
```

Let's also store it to a memory variable, so it won't need to be written out every time:

```
cText = " My dog, Horst, has fleas "
```

Position in Character Strings

The most common task in manipulating character strings is counting "positions" in the string. For example here are the positions for the sample text:

```
" My dog, Horst, has fleas "
12345678901234567890123456789
         10        20
```

The text begins at 1, a blank. The dog's name, Horst, begins at position 11 and ends at position 15. The string has a total length of 29 characters. Of course, you will seldom have the opportunity (or time) to lay out every text string for this kind of visual analysis. And in programs, no chance at all. So, FoxPro provides a number of functions to help locate and position things within a character expression. These functions are used a lot inside other functions that change the character expression.

AT, RAT

```
AT(<expC1>,<expC2>,<expN1>)
RAT(<expC1>,<expC2>,<expN1>)
```

<expC1> is the character expression to search for

<expC2> is the character expression to be searched

<expN1> specifies the occurrence of the search expression to return a position.

```
? AT( ",", " My dog, Horst, has fleas ",2)
```

Returns: 16

```
? RAT(",", " My dog, Horst, has fleas ",2)
```

Returns: 9

In both cases above, the function is asked to return the position of the second comma in the search string. AT( ) searches from left to right, counts from the left, and returns 16. RAT( ) searches from right to left, also counts from the left, returning 9. Most of the time people use AT( ) because we are accustomed to counting from left to right. But when there are cases where counting from the right is the shortest distance, or makes the most sense, use RAT( ).

LEN

In the context of character expressions, this function is used to get the end position of a character string.

```
LEN( <expC> )
```

Returns: 29

<expC> is any character expression.

Modify Character String

This second group of functions is used to change the shape and content of a character string.

The Trimming Family

You may have noticed in the text sample there are spaces at the beginning and the end. These are called *leading* and *trailing* blanks. While in some cases this is harmless, there are many more examples where unwanted blanks can mess up a composite character string. For example if you wanted to add to this text " - and ticks." You'd get " My dog, Horst, has fleas - and ticks." Depending on which spaces you wish to expunge, you can use one or more of these functions:

ALLTRIM

Like the name implies, this function trims both leading and trailing blanks from a character string.

```
ALLTRIM(<expC>)
```

<expC> is any character expression.

```
? ALLTRIM(" My dog, Horst, has fleas ")
```

Returns: "My dog, Horst, has fleas"

There is one school of thought that says to use ALLTRIM( ) all of the time since it covers all of the bases. The other school says, that wastes processing time, and it's not clear what you want trimmed. Clarity of intention *is* one of the cardinal virtues of good programming.

TRIM and RTRIM

Both of these functions do exactly the same thing, trim off trailing blanks. The syntax for TRIM is:

```
TRIM <expc> / RTRIM (<expc>)
```

Returns: " My dog, Horst, has fleas"

<expC> is any character expression.

LTRIM

The syntax is:

```
LTRIM( <expC> )
```

<expC> is any character expression.
Returns: "My dog, Horst, has fleas."

The Padding Family

Let's say you want to make the sample text a title for a paper. You need to put it into the title page, neatly centered. You could count the width of the page, usually eighty characters, then count the characters in the string, and then subtract that from eighty, and divide that by two, and add that many spaces to the front and back of the text. Or, you could use one of the padding functions, as you will see below, in this case PADC( ).

The padding family of functions works on any character string by adding a character (any character) left, right, or both left and right. They are used most often to pad serial ID numbers (such as 00000123), amounts in checks (such as SUM OF ********1.00), and so forth.

The syntax is:

```
PADL(<expr>,<expN>[,<expC>)
PADC(<expr>,<expN>[,<expC>)
PADR(<expr>,<expN>[,<expC>)
```

<expr> is anything you want padded

<expN> is the length of the expression after padding.

<expC> is the character you want to use for padding.

```
? PADC (" My dog, Horst, has fleas ", 10, " * ")
```

Returns: `"********** My dog, Horst, has fleas **********"`

REPLICATE

This function takes any character or text and repeats it a specified number of times.

```
REPLICATE( <expC>, <expN>)
```

<expC> is any character expression.

<expN> is the number of times to replicate the character expression.

```
= REPLICATE( cText, 2 )
```

Returns: `" My dog, Horst, has fleas  My dog, Horst, has fleas "`

The function is best used where a variable number of characters need to be replicated, or where the programmer doesn't want to type a hundred asterisks, as in this example:

```
REPLACE ALL title WITH "Not Available "+REPLICATE("*", 100);
FOR status = "Inactive"
```

The Case Family

Case, if you haven't encountered it already, is a big deal in computer circles. Whether text is upper case (capitalized), or lower case, or mixed case, can make a difference to a number of computer operations, particularly searches.

This whole issue of case sensitivity is too broad to cover in detail here, but suffice it to say that from time to time you will need to adjust data in tables to particular case requirements. There are five functions provided by FoxPro to do the job, three of which are included here (ISUPPER( ) and ISLOWER( ) are not).

UPPER

This function converts all text to upper case (capitals). Its syntax is:

```
UPPER(<expC>)
```

<expC> is any character expression.

```
? UPPER(ctext)
```

Returns: `"MY DOG, HORST, HAS FLEAS"`

LOWER

This converts all text to lower case. Its syntax is:

```
LOWER(<expC>)
```

<expC> is any character expression.

```
? LOWER(ctext)
```

Returns: `"My dog, Horst, has fleas"`

PROPER

```
PROPER(<expC>
```

<expC> is any character expression.

```
? PROPER( cText )
```

Returns: `" My Dog, Horst, Has Fleas "`

Because PROPER( ) converts the first letter of every word in a character string to a capital, it is frequently used to change an all lower case name field to a mixed case field.

Unfortunately, its operational rule doesn't know what to do with names like "mcdonald" (McDonald), so people have created their own functions for capitalizing names.

The Space Function

Despite its seemingly innocuous appearance, the SPACE( ) function has many uses. Its syntax is:

```
SPACE(<expN>)
```

<expN> is the number of spaces to return.

```
? ctext + SPACE(10)
```

Returns: `"My dog, Horst, has fleas          "`

In most cases, as above, it's used as a specialized REPLICATE( ) to add blanks to character strings. It's used even more in programming as a shorthand for initializing character variables, since cFirstName = SPACE(24) is a lot clearer than cFirstName = "   ".

The Substring Functions

The substring function is probably the most heavily used function for character strings, possibly the most used of any function for general table maintenance. Its' ability to pluck a string out of another string is used all of the time in data conversion and field to field transfer.

SUBSTR

This is called the "substring" function, and is probably the most heavily used function for character string manipulation, and one of the most used functions for all kinds of general table maintenance. Its syntax is:

```
SUBSTR( <expC>, <expN1>[, <expN2>])
```

<expC> is the character string from which to extract a substring.

<expN1> is the starting position for the substring to extract.

<expN2> is the number of characters to extract.

```
? SUBSTR(" My dog, Horst, has fleas    ",11,5)
```

Returns: `"Horst"`

The substring function has the ability to pluck one character string out of another string. This has an enormous number of uses in data conversion, field maintenance, and other character manipulations. the trick to using it is to understand the arguments <expN1> and <expN2>. These are the boundary positions of the string to be extracted, which in English read like: "Starting at character position <expN1>, stop <expN2> characters to the right."

In the example above, it's known what the character position and length of "Horst" happens to be. It starts on the 11th character from the left, and ends 5 characters to the right of that position. But what if you don't know the precise position and length of a substring? That's when you call on the services of other functions to determine various character positions. The three most common, AT(), RAT(), and LEN() are described in this chapter. An example of how they work is on the next page.

```
REPLACE dogname WITH SUBSTR( cText, AT("Horst",cText),5)
```

In this case, the substring "Horst" has a known length (5), but not its position in the main string. This position is provided by the AT() function. Manipulating character strings can be very detailed work. That's why even experienced programmers use the Command window to prototype and test expressions like these.

The next two functions are relatively complex and high powered string manipulators.

STRTRAN

Usually pronounced *stringtran*, this function replaces one substring in text with another substring. Its' uses are manifold to change or fix substrings in fields. Its syntax is:

```
STRTRAN(<expC1>,<expC2>[,<expC3>][,<expN1>][,<expN2>] )
```

<expC1> is the string to search

<expC2> is the substring to search for

<expC3> is the string to replace the search substring

<expN1> is the first occurrence to search for (optional, by default the first one)

<expN2> is the number of occurrences to replace (also optional).

```
? STRINGTRAN( ctext, "Horst," :Fluffy," . , .)
```

Returns: `"My dog, Fluffy, has fleas"`

Another example, say you have a field called COMPANY, which in several hundred records has the company name MyDogs Inc. Then you find out the company has changed its name to MyPuppy, Inc. Use the following command in the Command window:

```
REPLACE ALL COMPANY WITH STRTRAN (COMPANY,"MyDogs", "MyPuppy");
     FOR "MyDogs" $ COMPANY
```

STUFF

In many ways STUFF( ) is more difficult to use than STRTRAN( ), but it is more precise. With STUFF( ) you often need to know, or test for, the exact position of the substring you plan to replace and also the exact length of that substring. This is not always easy, and some complex expressions may be needed. Its syntax is:

```
STUFF(<expC1>,<expN1>,<expN2>,<expC2>)
```

<expC1> is the character expression to be stuffed (the stuffee).

<expN1> is the starting position for the substring to be stuffed.

<expN2> is the ending position for the substring to be stuffed.

<expC2> is the character expression to stuff.

The name "stuff" is a good clue as to what this function really does. By adjusting the <expN2> argument, you can change the number of characters to be replaced. A zero (0) does not remove any characters, and quite literally "stuff " the new string into place. The <expC2> argument can also be set to a null string (""), and then the number of characters indicated by <expN2> are removed from the current string. Both of these options are useful, as in the following examples:

```
cText = STUFF( cText, 1, 2, "")
```

Returns: `"My dog, Horst, has fleas "`

```
cText = STUFF( cText, LEN(TRIM(cText)), 0, ".")
```

Returns: `" My dog, Horst, has fleas. "`

Character position manipulation is hardly an art, but it does take practice.

Logical Searching in Strings

This group of functions are similar to the AT( )/RAT( ) family since they search for a character expression in other character expressions. But instead of returning a position number, they return either true or false (.t./.f.).

The Substring Operator ($)

As inauspicious as it may seem, the substring operator (sometimes called a function in the manuals) is one of the most frequently used for character work.

```
<expC1> $ <expC2>
```

<expC1> is the string to search for.

<expC2> is the string to be searched.

```
? "Horst" $ " My dog, Horst, has fleas "
```

Returns: .t.

This simply tests whether the first string can be found in the second string, or put another way: the first expression is *contained in* the second expression. The test is case sensitive, so you have to be careful that you're not comparing upper case apples with lower case oranges, so to speak. Here's a simple ex-ample of it's day-to-day use that takes into account a possible difference in case:

```
COUNT ALL FOR "DOG" $ UPPER( TITLE )
```

This gets a count of all of the records where "DOG" (note the capitals) is contained in a field called TITLE. Note the use of the UPPER( ) function to be sure that the search string and the search field have the same case.

The substring operator $ lends itself to logical expression conditions like those of the FOR and WHILE clauses, but be warned—*A $ expression is not optimizable by the Rushmore Technology*. Which means that any time you use this operator, you're going to get a pure sequential search—from one end of the table to the other.

INLIST

This is really a "general" function, since it can work with any kind of expression. In this case it's used for character strings. Its syntax is:

```
INLIST(<expr1>, <expr2> [, <expr3>... ])
```

<expr1> is the expression (any data type) to search for.

<expr2>[, <expr3>...] is a list of expressions to search in, separated by commas. It must be of same data type as <expr1>.

```
? INLIST("dog," "horst," "fleas," "my," "dog")
```

Returns: .t.

When working in data tables that have fields with a single character or character string (a character, word, or phrase), you can use INLIST( ) to test if the string is in a specific list. For example, in a field that's supposed to contain nothing but certain codes, you could use this run:

```
COUNT ALL FOR NOT INLIST( CODEFIELD, "A", "C", "E", "F", "Z" )
LIST ALL FIELDS RECNO( ), LASTNAME, CODEFIELD ;
FOR NOT INLIST( CODEFIELD, "A", "C", "E", "F", "Z" ) TO PRINT
```

The first command line gets a count of how many codes in the codefield are not legit. If there aren't too many of them to reasonably print, the second command line then prints the offending records with the record numbers and the last name. In large tables, it's usually a good idea to know the size of your "problem" before you print a list—unless you don't mind using a ream of paper.

LIKE

This function returns a true (.t.) only if all of the characters in the first expression exactly match all of the characters in the second expression. Its syntax is:

```
LIKE(<expC1>, <expC2>)
```

<expC1> is the character expression to be matched, including wildcard symbols.

<expC2> is the character expression to test.

```
? LIKE("dog," ctext)
```

Returns: .t.

If this were all it could do, LIKE( ) would be very limited in use, since exact matches can be tested in other ways. You can use wildcard symbols, just like those from DOS, in the first expression:

- * matches anything.
- ? matches any single character.

If you're familiar with doing DOS file searches, then you'll understand how LIKE( ) can be used to determine if a certain word or phrase fragment exists in another character string. This will almost always be used with an operational command, something like this:

```
COUNT ALL FOR LIKE( "Dog*", NAME )
BROWSE FOR LIKE( "flea?" , INSECTTYPE )
```

The first command gets a count of all names (records) where "Horst" is the first five letters, and might include such names as "Horstlein," "Horstlchen," "Horst," or "Horstundgraben." The second command displays in a browse window only those records where the insect type begins with "flea" and any single letter after that. This could include "fleas," but not "flease."

Putting Character Manipulation to Work

At this point, there are enough character related functions to do some work. First, let's fix the sample text, " `My dog, Horst, has fleas` ".

```
cText = ALLTRIM(" My dog, Horst, has fleas ")
```

Returns: "`My dog, Horst, has fleas`"

```
cText = cText + "."
```

Returns: "`My dog, Horst, has fleas.`"

```
cText = STRTRAN( cText, "Horst", "Spot" )
```

Returns: "`My dog, Spot, has fleas.`"

In fact, let's fix it all in one line:

```
? STRTRAN(ALLTRIM(" My dog, Horst, has fleas
")+".","Horst","Spot")
```

Returns: `"My dog, Spot, has fleas."`

So much for silly examples. Real work in the Command window character functions means working with the fields of a table and the operational commands. Here's a tale of the "real world":

In the process of building a customer database, a number of temporary data entry people were hired to input information about customers from old sales slips. Unfortunately, they were not schooled on some of the finer points of data entry, and there was no standardization on the way to enter "Mr. and Mrs.". Consequently, the NAME field of the CUSTOMER table contained numerous variations:

```
Mr. and Mrs. Johnson
Mr and Mrs Works
Mr. John J. and Dora Whitely
MR., MRS. HARRY CLAUSS
Mr. & Mrs. Brotelli
Mr. Bruce T. and Mrs. Martha Timmer
MR./MRS. FINLAYSON
```

Worse, some of these had extra spaces inserted at various locations. All of this might have been relatively harmless had not the owner of the company decided that a uniform salutation was mandatory because she wanted to specifically target husband and wife customers. She also wanted the first names kept separately for husband and wife, so that a separate mailing could be made.

The resident data-management guru, who happened to be one of the data entry people, decided to use the powers of the Command window like this:

```
USE CUSTOMER ALIAS CUS ORDER FIRSTNAME
```

Opens the customer table.

```
MODIFY STRUCTURE
```

Add the fields SALUTATION C 10, HUSBAND C 12, and WIFE C 12 to the table.

```
COUNT ALL FOR "MR" $ UPPER(NAME) AND ;
 ("AND" $ UPPER(NAME) OR "&" $ NAME OR "/" $ NAME OR "," $
NAME)
```

When faced with a problem like this, find out how big a problem there is by getting a count. If you check the examples above, it catches all of the husband and wife listings without including miscellaneous company names and such. Doing the COUNT also tests a FOR condition that will be similar to one used for making the changes. Remember you can cut and paste freely in the Command window, which makes all commands reusable.

To take care of loading the salutation field, use:

```
REPLACE ALL SALUTATION WITH "Mr. and Mrs." ;
 FOR "MR" $ UPPER(NAME) AND ;
 ("AND" $ UPPER(NAME) OR "&" $ NAME OR "/" $ NAME OR "," $
NAME)
```

Now it's necessary to get rid of the various Mr./Mrs. combinations and parse out the first names, if any. This is where things get tricky. First the scans for Mr. and Mrs. with first names:

```
REPLACE ALL HUSBAND WITH SUBSTR( NAME, AT("MR",UPPER(NAME))+4 ,
;
(AT( "AND", UPPER(NAME)) -(AT ("MR", UPPER (NAME)) + 4)));
FOR "MR" $ UPPER(NAME) AND ("AND" $ UPPER(NAME));
AND LEN( SUBSTR( NAME, AT("MR",UPPER(NAME))+2 , ;
AT( "AND", UPPER(NAME)) -2)) > 2
```

This is where prototyping in the Command window becomes invaluable. The character string logic is picky. The first SUBSTR( ) function extracts any name lying between the period of MR. and the space before an AND. The LEN( ) function is used to screen out instances where there is a MR but not followed by a name. (Two spaces between the MR and the AND might contain an initial, but not likely.) This example is only for the "AND" case. A very similar construction is used for the "&", "/", "," cases in turn.

Now to do the Mrs. part. Guess what? You can't do the Mrs. part. There is nothing on which to "anchor" a function between the MRS and a last name. FoxPro can't tell the difference between a last name and a first name. You might try to use the spaces—there's two of them where a Mrs and a first name exists. But there can be plenty of exceptions. Sometimes its better to "eyeball" the table and make corrections based on the wisdom of the human brain. This being the case, you should leave the original field untouched until the visual proofing has been completed.

In any case but eyeballing Mr. John J. and Dora Whitely will fall through the cracks.

This entry, and names where the "Mr." is separated by more than two spaces from the "and" complicate the search beyond usefulness. This was labeled as a real world example, and in fact there are some lessons here:

1. Design the table right in the first place. If there had been a SALUTATION, HUSBAND, WIFE, and LASTNAME field, most of the problem would have been eliminated.
2. Some things are not possible with FoxPro. A perfect solution to this problem would require Artificial Intelligence programming, not a FoxPro strong suit.
3. Some things may be do able with FoxPro, but compared to using human intelligence and old-fashioned "eyeballing," may be impractical.

The final cleanup of the name field is fairly accurate and simple:

```
REPLACE ALL NAME WITH STUFF( NAME, 1, AT("MRS", UPPER(NAME))
+2),"") ;
 FOR "MR" $ UPPER(NAME) AND ;
 ("AND" $ UPPER(NAME) OR "&" $ NAME OR "/" $ NAME OR "," $
NAME)
```

Date and Time Functions

Basic to the Command window toolkit are some date and time functions.

DATE

Keep in mind that DATE( ) is no more accurate than the clock in your computer.

```
DATE()
? DATE( )
```

Returns: 12/12/92, the current system date as a date expression.

MONTH, DAY, and YEAR

The FoxPro set of MONTH( ), DAY( ), YEAR( ) functions all return numeric results. Only for months, there is a function, CMONTH( ), that returns a character string. This is a bit inconvenient, since frequently the breakdown of a date into month, day, or year is to display or print it, which is done more easily if these are in character strings. The variable <expD> is any date expression. The syntax for MONTH is:

```
MONTH( <expD> )
```

or

```
CMONTH( <expD> )
? MONTH( DATE( ) )
```

Returns: the month as a number.

```
? CMONTH( DATE( ) )
```

Returns: the month as a character expression.

```
DAY( <expD> )
? DAY( DATE( ) )
```

Returns: the day of the month as a number.

```
YEAR( <expD> )
? YEAR( DATE( ) )
```

Returns: the year as a number.

To get the year expressed as a number is generally inconvenient, so much of the time the function is used like this to return a character string:

```
= STR( YEAR( DATE( ) ), 4)
```

Once in this form, you can cut the year down to "93," and so on, for use in display or with indexing.

The Date Conversion Family

It is fairly common to convert dates back and forth between a character expression and a date expression, as there are a number of situations where conversion is necessary. The most common are for compound indexes (multiple fields), which must be of a single data type, and for conversion of dates entered as text.

CTOD

Keeping in mind that FoxPro stores dates internally in a numeric format, this function accepts any legitimate date expressed in character format. Its syntax is:

```
CTOD( <expC> )
```

<expC> is a date expressed as a character string, such as "12/12/92."

```
cStart = "12/12/92"
dStart = CTOD( cStart )
dStart = CTOD( "12/12/92" )
```

Returns: - an Xbase date (12/12/92).

If a bad date is encountered, such as " /23/92", CTOD() simply turns it into a blank date, (/ /).

DTOC

The main use for this function is to make an expression appropriate for indexing. Its syntax is:

```
DTOC( <expD> [,1] )
```

<expD> is a date expression and [,1] is an optional argument (to return a date as a pure string).

```
? DTOC( DATE( ) )
```

Returns: "12/22/93," a date as a character expression.

```
? DTOC( DATE( ), 1 )
```

Returns: "19931222," a character expression date without slashes.

In its standard form (without the 1 argument), it returns a date with slashes. This causes problems with index order, lookup, and space. With the second argument turned "on" with a 1, the function returns a compact string for the date. This should always be used when combining a date field with a character field in a compound index:

```
INDEX ON LASTNAME+DTOC( BIRTHDATE, 1) TAG NAMEBIRTH
```

There is an alternate function, DTOS( ), that also produces the date character expression without the slashes. However it's probably better to stick with DTOC( ) because of its greater familiarity.

In the "old days" before a number of other date functions showed up, it was necessary to convert a date to a character so you could parse out the month, day, year components. Now this is seldom done.

DATE BRACES { }

```
{ }
{  /  /  }
{ <date in characters> }
```

<date in characters> is a date without quotes, simply the numbers and separators.

```
dStart = {12/12/93}
dStart = {  /  /  }
dStart = {  }
```

Returns: an Xbase standard date value. In the latter two examples, a blank date.

This isn't exactly a function. Nor are the brackets formally an operator. So, what is this? It's a weird curly brace date thing that does what CTOD() does, but is simpler to use. It's also distinctive and can be quickly learned for shorthand date entry. For example, the following sets a date field in all records of a table with a blank (empty) date:

```
REPLACE ALL firstdate WITH { }
```

TIME

The syntax for TIME is:

```
TIME( )
cNow = TIME( )
```

Returns: "12:30:24"

The time is returned as an eight-character string, and it includes hours, minutes and seconds. Since displaying seconds is often unnecessary, you can use some of the character string functions, namely SUBSTR( ) to extract a shortened time:

```
cNow = SUBSTR( TIME( ), 1, 5)
```

Returns: - "12:30"

Remember that this time is always expressed in 24-hour form (so-called military time). The time returned depends on you computer's system clock, and like the DATE( ) function, won't be any more accurate.

Numeric Functions

The vast majority of numeric functions pertain to various aspects of mathematics (SIN( ), ACOS( )), or with financial calculations (PAYMENT( ), PV( )), and so on. These are useful but specialized. Numeric functions are one area in which FoxPro is often enhanced by third-party function libraries. A few functions for use in the Command window are covered below.

INT

This function returns the integer portion of any numeric expression. It's main use is similar to that of the "parsing" functions for character strings—breaking down component parts of a numeric expression in this case the integer portion. Its syntax is:

```
INT( <expN> )
```

<expN> is any numeric expression.

```
? INT( 2.1416 )
```

Returns: 2.

ROUND

The syntax for ROUND is:

```
ROUND( <expN1>, <expN2> )
```

<expN1> is the numeric expression to be rounded.

<expN2> is the number of decimals places to round to.

```
? ROUND( 2.1416, 2)
```

Returns: 2.14

The usual rules for rounding apply here: decimal values five and greater round up, four and less round down.

VAL

The syntax for VAL is:

```
VAL( <expC> )
```

<expC> Any number expressed as a character.

```
? VAL( "567" )
```

Returns: 567.

As a conversion function, VAL( ) is usually paired with the character string counterpart, STR( ), which changes numbers into character strings. It's not at all unusual to convert field values one way or another, using these functions, to manipulate them. You should take some care with numbers that contain values to the right of the decimal, or that contain the "E" marker of scientific notation. The decimals may be rounded depending on the current value of SET DECIMAL TO, and "E" causes VAL( ) to convert to decimal values like

```
= VAL( "345.3e2" )
```

which returns 34530.

Table-Oriented Functions

There are over forty functions that work in conjunction with operational commands like REPLACE. However, most of these are valuable largely in the programming environment. Eight have been selected here, because of their common use in the Command window.

RECNO

The syntax for RECNO is:

```
RECNO( [<expC> | <expN>] )
```

<expC> is the optional name of an alias or file name.

<expN> is the optional work area number.

```
? RECNO( )
```

Returns: 125.

As with RECCOUNT( ), the current record number is display in the bottom information bar. However, it is used on occasion in the operational command to create a scope, for instance:

```
REPLACE ALL CITY WITH "NEW YORK" FOR RECNO( )>= 100
```

In this case, it changes the city for all records with a record number greater than or equal to 100.

DELETED

This function tests whether a record has been deleted or not. Its syntax is:

```
DELETED( [<expC> | <expN>] )
```

<expC> is the optional name of an alias or file name.

<expN> is the optional work area number.

```
? DELETED( )
```

Returns: .t. (true), or .f. (false).

It's used quite frequently for table maintenance, for example to archive a group of records that have been deleted before they are purged (PACKed) from the file, for example:

```
COPY TO NAMEBAK FOR DELETED( )
```

RECCOUNT

RECCOUNT provides a count of records in a table, taken from the file header. This is one of those innocuous functions that you tend to use daily (hourly?). However, in FoxPro for Windows, with its constant record count displayed in the information bar at the bottom, this function is less necessary. As with most table functions, an <alias> can be used to select a table not in the current work area. This is used mostly in the programming environment. The syntax for RECCOUNT is:

```
RECCOUNT( [<expC> | <expN>] )
```

<expC> is the optional name of an alias or file name.

<expN> is the optional work area number.

```
? RECCOUNT( )
```

Returns; 103000.

FOUND

As the name implies, this function is used to verify if a SEEK, LOCATE or other search has found a match. Its syntax is:

```
FOUND( [<expC> | <expN>] )
```

<expC> is the optional name of an alias or file name.

<expN> is the optional work area number.

```
? FOUND("CUS")
```

Returns: .t. (true) or .f. (false).

Once upon a time, FOUND( ) was used after every SEEK, but with the advent of the SEEK( ) function in FoxPro 1.0, it's largely been replaced. It's currently used the most in the Command window (or programming) to test whether an indexed search (usually a relation) from a parent table, has found a match in a child table. For example:

```
USE CUSTOMER ALIAS CUS ORDER CITY IN 2
USE ORDER ALIAS ORD IN 1
SET RELATION TO CITY INTO CUS
REPLACE ALL ORD.CITY WITH CUS.CITY FOR FOUND("CUS")
```

Here there are two files opened, CUSTOMER and ORDER, with the customer table indexed on city. A relation is set on the city field between order and customer tables, and then the REPLACE command is used with a FOR clause to change each city name in the order file with the city name in the customer file, if one is found. There are innumerable variations of this format, as it is used frequently in table maintenance.

Putting It All Together in the Command Window

An End-of-Year Data Maintenance Example

In many kinds of database applications, and especially those involving financial or accounting activity, there is a great deal of data maintenance associated with the end of the year. In a complete application this maintenance work would be programmed and available through menu choices. However, in some cases it's more convenient or even more efficient to do EOY maintenance in the Command window.

In this abbreviated example, the customer database needs some work at the turn of each fiscal year (Jan. 1). A date field needs to be reset, a status flag changed, customers checked for activity, data checked for integrity, and some reports and listings run. This uses some very common Command window functions and commands, and it's a good way to show the process of "thinking data manipulation."

As usual, make any configuration settings you need, open the relevant files and index tags:

```
SET SAFETY ON
SET TALK ON

USE invoices ALIAS inv ORDER custid IN 0
USE customer ALIAS cus ORDER custid IN 0
```

The customer file is a good place to start EOY maintenance, since it's usually the master file for reports and queries. It's appropriate to do data integrity checking first, because the accuracy of reporting may change, as you repair or remove bad data. In the customer file, the most vital field is CUSTID, the key field for the table.

```
SELECT cus
LIST ALL FOR EMPTY(custid) OR LEN(custid) < 8 TO PRINT
```

This produces a listing of customer records which are missing a customer ID or where the ID is not a standard length. Both cases are not legitimate identification numbers and need to be removed or fixed. The printout is used to check each case. If there are any customer IDs which should be repaired, you could find individuals by using a lookup on the name:

```
SET ORDER TO lastname
SEEK "Johnson"
EDIT
```

Or if there are a lot of changes, use:

```
BROWSE FOR EMPTY(custid) OR LEN(custid) < 8
```

However, let's say that several dozen IDs are all less than the required 8 characters, because somebody forgot to enter leading zeros. You can fix these with a single command, rather than doing it manually:

```
REPLACE ALL custid WITH PADL(custid,"0") ;
 FOR LEN(custid) < 8
```

It's very characteristic of maintenance work that you often make choices about what should be done manually (one at a time), and what can be done with a command. Sometimes it takes longer to formulate and test a command, than it does to manually fix the problem records.

When you're satisfied that the customer ID field is ready, go ahead and mark all the remaining records for deletion:

```
DELETE ALL FOR EMPTY(custid) OR LEN(custid) < 8
```

And when you've done all the data integrity checking and record deleting in the file, you might go on to removing the records permanently:

```
PACK
```

Now that the customer table has been cleaned (or at least the primary key), there's still some checking of relations between the customer and the invoices file. Assuming a *business rule* that only customers with invoice records are listed in the customer file, a printout can be run to check for any "widowed" customers.

```
SELECT cus
SET ORDER TO custid
SET RELATION TO custid INTO inv

LIST ALL FOR NOT FOUND("inv") TO PRINT
```

Likewise you should reverse the relation and check for any "orphan" invoices, where an ID in the invoice file doesn't match an ID in the customer file:

```
SELECT cus
SET RELATION OFF INTO inv
SELECT inv
SET RELATION TO custid INTO cus

LIST ALL FOR NOT FOUND("cus") TO PRINT
```

If this turns up any errors, you'd repeat a process similar to the one used for weeding out invalid ID fields, and either correct or remove records that are not part of a relation. When this has been accomplished, you're ready to do some updating:

```
SELECT inv
SET RELATION OFF INTO cus
SELECT cus
SET RELATION TO custid INTO inv
SET SKIP TO inv

REPLACE ALL cus.lastdate WITH {12/31/92} ;
 FOR inv.invdate <= {12/31/92}
```

This creates a 1-to-Many relationship between the customer table and the invoices table in order to check the invoice dates. If they fall before the end-of-year, then the LASTDATE field in customer is updated. In this example, LASTDATE is used for reference and updating of monthly totals. In some circumstances it might be worthwhile to run a listing of customers who were **not** updated:

```
LIST FIELDS cus.custid, cus.lastname, inv.invdate, inv.custotal
;
 FOR cus.lastdate <> {12/31/92} TO PRINT
```

Presumably, most of these customers were entered after 12/31/92, and you might want to flag them for checking the accuracy of the entry, the amounts ordered after that date, and so forth. This could also be done by using the customer—invoice table relation again, but sometimes flags are logically clearer and are better for performance, especially for complex reports:

```
REPLACE ALL cus.flag WITH "N" FOR cus.lastdate >= {1/1/93}
```

Finally, the tables are ready to run a major End-of-Year report:

```
CLEAR ALL
REPORT FORM EOYCUST1 ENVIRONMENT TO PRINT
```

Chapter 8
Good Old-Fashioned Coding

Until two years ago, all programming in the Xbase world was accomplished with an ASCII text file and a favorite editing program. FoxPro 2.0 changed that, irrevocably, but incompletely. As you will see, the FoxPro for Windows "Power Tools" are a continuation down the path towards an integrated application development environment and moving away from the program file (.PRG). But FoxPro for Windows isn't there yet. Much of what you do for developing applications with the Power Tools is built upon a prerequisite knowledge of the "old" way of doing things—program files, functions, procedures, control structures, and so forth. That's the topic of this chapter.

From here on, you are in programming land. Programming is often an acquired taste, driven by a love of problem solving and the pleasure of seeing something you create come alive on the screen—being used, presumably, to the benefit of somebody or something.

The Setup for Programming

So far in this book, little attention has been paid to the kind of hardware and software you are using, and how it relates to

FoxPro. When you venture into programming, however, these things become more critical. The "setup" includes:

- Hardware: CPU, memory, disks, and so forth
- Operating system, memory manager, and so on
- FoxPro for Windows configuration
- Choice of program editors

Basic Configuration

Because FoxPro is a Windows program, the basic hardware and software configuration requirements are simplified (especially compared to the DOS version). This is mostly considered on the basis of a stand alone setup—one programmer, one CPU. You may be connected to a network, but this won't affect your hardware requirements much, except in the area of disk space.

Your CPU choice is simple: buy the fastest you can afford. FoxPro runs well on all 386 and 486 models at 20 MHz or better. However, as you are or about to become a FoxPro programmer, and no doubt will use the Power Tools, you should be aware of a few points:

- Whenever you create an application with the Power Tools (Screen Generator, Menu Generator, and Project Manager), there is a two-step process: the program is generated, which creates an output file, then the output file is compiled. This generate-and-compile sequence is repeated every time you change portions of your program.
- Depending on the size and complexity of the code you create, the generate-and-compile time can vary from a few seconds to several minutes. One thing is certain, however, the CPU, memory, and disks of your system receive a healthy exercise during these operations.
- Studies have shown that between six and eight generate-and-compile cycles are done an hour. That's fifty to seventy cycles in an eight hour day. Simple math says if you can shave a half minute off the cycle, you save about half an hour a day.

The most effective way to save time is to invest in the fastest CPU you can afford.

Because so much of the FoxPro activity is disk oriented, it also pays to get a fast and big hard disk. This isn't much of a burden these days, since 120 MB to 200 MB hard disks with less than 19 ms seek times are common and relatively inexpensive. Of course, you may need much bigger disks, depending on the volume of data to be handled. If you plan to do any distribution of your software, you should have both 5.25" and 3.5" floppy drives.

Memory is *the* one place not to play cheap. Microsoft has already put the recommended level of RAM for FoxPro at 4 MB (6 MB if you haven't designated a swap disk). With this you will get adequate memory, if you don't run more than one other program of any size. However, if you plan to use OLE or DDE to connect with another Windows program such as Excel or Ami Pro, then you need to factor in 1 MB to 2 MB for each additional program. In the Windows environment, it is also easy enough to keep two copies of FoxPro running, perhaps one for editing and debugging and one for testing and running. Although there are some potential file use conflicts in doing this, a little practice can make it a useful approach. In any case, this eats RAM like a bear eats bacon. For programming, a more realistic memory size is 8 MB up to about 16 MB, at which point the law of diminishing returns sets in.

In the area of memory management, the delivered software with MS DOS 5.0 or 6.0 and MS Windows (such as HIMEM.SYS) works. Other products, especially Quarterdeck's QEMM or Qualitas 386Max, are other programs people swear by (and occasionally at). So far, all of these products seem to operate with FoxPro with stability, and in general provide greater control over memory than the DOS programs.

FoxPro for Windows Configuration Options

The FoxPro for Windows configuration file, CONFIG.FPW, is an important element in the operation of FoxPro and FoxPro applications. It's one of the places where you can optimize and customize the FoxPro environment without going into programming or typing a lot of commands each time you get to the Command window. However, of the ninety-five or so options in the configuration file, only about twenty are used with regularity. Almost all of these options are also available through the standard SET commands (such as SET PATH TO and SET COLOR TO), that you can use in the Command window. This is another reason why minor variations are rarely set in the CONFIG.FPW file. Table 8.1 on the next page lists all options with the most commonly used highlighted.

Table 8.1
SET values in CONFIG.FPW.

Command	Values	Default	Description
_BEAUTIFY	<file path>		Program path—BEAUTIFY.APP
_FOXDOC	<file path>		Program path—FOXDOC.DLL
_GENGRAPH	<file path>		Program path—GENGRAPH.APP
_GENMENU	<file path>		Program path—GENMENU.PRG
_GENPD	<file path>		Program path—GENPD.APP
_GENSCRN	<file path>		Program path—GENSCRN.PRG
_GENXTAB	<file path>		Program path—GENXTAB.PRG
_SPELLCHK	<file path>		Program path—SPELLCHK.APP
_STARTUP	<file path>		Program path—FOXSTART.APP
_TRANSPORTER	<file path>		Program path—TRANSPRT.PRG
ALTERNATE	<file>		Output to file <name>
ALTERNATE	OFF|ON	OFF	Output to file
ANSI	OFF|ON	OFF	ANSI compatibility
AUTOSAVE	OFF|ON	OFF	Automatically save text
BELL	ON|OFF	ON	PC tone/bell
BELL	frequency	512	Tone of bell
BLOCKSIZE	<expN>	64	Size of memo field blocks
BORDER	<attribute>	SINGLE	Type of window border
BRSTATUS	OFF|ON	OFF	Browse status bar
CARRY	OFF|ON	OFF	Copy edit data to next record
CENTURY	OFF|ON	OFF*	Specify year format in dates
CLEAR	ON|OFF	ON	Clear screen on startup
CLOCK	OFF|ON	OFF	Clock display
CLOCK	row, column	| STATUS	Location of clock
COLOR	<color attrib>		Set color pairs
COLOR OF SCHEME	<ColorPairList> | <ColorScheme>	Current settings	Set color scheme
COLOR SET	<ColorSetName>	DEFAULT	Name a color set
COMMAND	DO <proc name>		DO a program on startup

<table>
<tr><td>COMPATIBLE</td><td>OFF|ON</td><td>OFF (FOXPLUS|DB4)</td><td>FoxPlus compatibility</td></tr>
<tr><td>**CONFIRM**</td><td>OFF|ON</td><td>OFF</td><td>**Enter** on edit required</td></tr>
<tr><td>CONSOLE</td><td>ON|OFF</td><td>ON</td><td>Direct output to screen</td></tr>
<tr><td>CURRENCY</td><td><expC></td><td>"$"</td><td>Symbol for currency</td></tr>
<tr><td>CURRENCY</td><td>LEFT|RIGHT</td><td>LEFT*</td><td>Location of currency symbol</td></tr>
<tr><td>CURSOR</td><td>ON|OFF</td><td>ON</td><td>Screen cursor</td></tr>
<tr><td>DATE</td><td><expC></td><td>AMERICAN*</td><td>Set date format</td></tr>
<tr><td>DEBUG</td><td>ON|OFF</td><td>ON</td><td>Debug/Trace windows</td></tr>
<tr><td>**DECIMALS**</td><td><0 to 18></td><td>2*</td><td>Number of decimal places</td></tr>
<tr><td>**DEFAULT**</td><td><drive>|<dir></td><td></td><td>Default drive or directory</td></tr>
<tr><td>**DELETED**</td><td>OFF|ON</td><td>OFF</td><td>Deleted records are active</td></tr>
<tr><td>DELIMITERS</td><td>OFF|ON</td><td>OFF</td><td>Delimiters</td></tr>
<tr><td>DELIMITERS</td><td><expC>|DEFAULT</td><td></td><td>Delimiter symbol</td></tr>
<tr><td>**DEVELOPMENT**</td><td>ON|OFF</td><td>ON</td><td>Check file date and times</td></tr>
<tr><td>DEVICE</td><td>SCREEN|PRINT|FILE</td><td>SCREEN <file></td><td>Current output device</td></tr>
<tr><td>ECHO</td><td>OFF|ON</td><td>OFF</td><td>Open trace window</td></tr>
<tr><td>**EDITWORK**</td><td><file path></td><td></td><td>Path to text edit directory</td></tr>
<tr><td>ESCAPE</td><td>ON|OFF</td><td>ON</td><td>**Esc** key</td></tr>
<tr><td>EXACT</td><td>OFF|ON</td><td>OFF</td><td>Exact string match</td></tr>
<tr><td>**EXCLUSIVE**</td><td>ON|OFF</td><td>ON</td><td>Exclusive use of files</td></tr>
<tr><td>FULLPATH</td><td>ON|OFF</td><td>ON</td><td>Display full path names</td></tr>
<tr><td>F<num></td><td><char str></td><td></td><td>Set function keys</td></tr>
<tr><td>HEADING</td><td>ON|OFF</td><td>ON</td><td>Display field headings</td></tr>
<tr><td>HELP</td><td>ON|OFF</td><td>ON</td><td>Help system enable</td></tr>
<tr><td>**HELP**</td><td><file></td><td>FOXHELP</td><td>Name of help file</td></tr>
<tr><td>HOURS</td><td>12|24</td><td>12*</td><td>12 or 24 hour time format</td></tr>
<tr><td>INDEX</td><td><file extension></td><td>IDX</td><td>Default index file extension</td></tr>
<tr><td>INTENSITY</td><td>ON|OFF</td><td>ON</td><td>Highlight input fields</td></tr>
<tr><td>LABEL</td><td><file extension></td><td>.LBL</td><td>Default label file extension</td></tr>
<tr><td>LOGERROR</td><td>ON|OFF</td><td>ON</td><td>Compiler error log</td></tr>
<tr><td>MACKEY</td><td><expC></td><td>SHIFT + F10</td><td>Macro recorder key</td></tr>
<tr><td>MARGIN</td><td><0 to 254></td><td>0</td><td>Left margin setting</td></tr>
<tr><td>MARK</td><td><expC></td><td>"/"*</td><td>Specify date delimiter</td></tr>
</table>

(continued)

<table>
<tr><td>MEMLIMIT</td><td><%available memory></td><td>[min K][max K]</td><td>Limit of memory use by FoxPro</td></tr>
<tr><td>MEMOWIDTH</td><td><8 to 256></td><td>50</td><td>Width of memo display</td></tr>
<tr><td>MVCOUNT</td><td>128-3,600</td><td>256</td><td>Number of variables allowed</td></tr>
<tr><td>NEAR</td><td>OFF|ON</td><td>OFF</td><td>Near pointer set on search</td></tr>
<tr><td>NOTIFY</td><td>OFF|ON</td><td>ON</td><td>Display system messages</td></tr>
<tr><td>ODOMETER</td><td><1 to 32,767></td><td>100</td><td>Record report interval</td></tr>
<tr><td>OPTIMIZE</td><td>OFF|ON</td><td>ON</td><td>Rushmore optimization</td></tr>
<tr><td>OUTSHOW</td><td>OFF|ON</td><td>ON</td><td>Shift-Ctrl-Alt window hide</td></tr>
<tr><td>PATH</td><td><path></td><td></td><td>Set default path</td></tr>
<tr><td>POINT</td><td><expC></td><td>"."*</td><td>Set decimal character</td></tr>
<tr><td>PRINT</td><td>ON|OFF</td><td>OFF</td><td>Set output to printer</td></tr>
<tr><td>PROGWORK</td><td><file path></td><td></td><td>Program cache directory</td></tr>
<tr><td>REPORT</td><td><file extension></td><td>.FRX</td><td>Default report file extension</td></tr>
<tr><td>REPROCESS</td><td><-2 to 32,000 > 0</td><td>|AUTOMATIC</td><td>Retry for locking interval</td></tr>
<tr><td>RESOURCE</td><td>ON|OFF</td><td>ON</td><td>Resource file</td></tr>
<tr><td>RESOURCE</td><td><file></td><td>FOXUSER</td><td>Name of resource file</td></tr>
<tr><td>SAFETY</td><td>ON|OFF</td><td>ON</td><td>Warning for file actions</td></tr>
<tr><td>SCOREBOARD</td><td>OFF|ON</td><td>OFF</td><td>Display scoreboard</td></tr>
<tr><td>SEPARATOR</td><td><expC></td><td>","*</td><td>Set default separator</td></tr>
<tr><td>SORTWORK</td><td><file path></td><td></td><td>Default sorting directory</td></tr>
<tr><td>SPACE</td><td>ON|OFF</td><td>ON</td><td>Space between fields</td></tr>
<tr><td>STATUS</td><td>OFF|ON</td><td>OFF</td><td>Status bar display</td></tr>
<tr><td>STATUS BAR</td><td>OFF|ON</td><td>ON</td><td>Status bar display</td></tr>
<tr><td>STEP</td><td>OFF|ON</td><td>OFF</td><td>Open Trace window</td></tr>
<tr><td>SYSMENU</td><td>ON|OFF|AUTOMATIC</td><td>ON</td><td>System menu</td></tr>
<tr><td>TALK</td><td>ON|OFF</td><td>ON</td><td>Display processing info.</td></tr>
<tr><td>TEDIT</td><td><expN>
<editor></td><td></td><td>Call external text editor</td></tr>
<tr><td>TEXTMERGE</td><td>OFF|ON</td><td>OFF</td><td>Text merge with fields</td></tr>
<tr><td>TMPFILES</td><td><file path></td><td></td><td>Working files directory</td></tr>
<tr><td>TRBETWEEN</td><td>ON|OFF</td><td>ON</td><td>Trace between functions</td></tr>
<tr><td>TYPEAHEAD</td><td><0 to 128></td><td>20</td><td>Typeahead buffer size (bytes)</td></tr>
<tr><td>UDFPARMS</td><td>VALUE|REFERENCE</td><td>VALUE</td><td>Type of UDF parameters</td></tr>
<tr><td>UNIQUE</td><td>OFF|ON</td><td>OFF</td><td>Unique indexing</td></tr>
</table>

Following is an example of a representative `CONFIG.FPW` file called specifically at the DOS command line with `FOXPROW /cF:\PROJ\CONFIG.FPW`.

```
MEMLIMIT     = 1024
MVCOUNT      = 512
DEFAULT      = F
PATH         = \PROJ;\PROJ\SCR;\PROJ\MNU;\PROJ\REP
SORTFILES    = C:\TEMP
PROGFILES    = C:\TEMP
WORKFILES    = C:\TEMP
EDITFILES    = C:\TEMP
_BEAUTIFY    = F:\FPW\BEAUTIFY.APP
_FOXDOC      = F:\FPW\FOXDOC.DLL
_GENGRAPH    = ""
_GENMENU     = F:\FPW\GEMENU.FXP
_GENPD       = F:\FPW\GENPD.FXP
_GENSCRN     = F:\FPW\GENSCRN.FXP
_GENXTAB     = ""
_SPELLCHK    = ""
_STARTUP     = ""
_TRANSPORTER = ""
```

Directory Configuration

The most important of the CONFIG.FPW file settings have something to do with location of files, directory work areas, and the like. This is the heart of configuration for FoxPro. As you might expect, there are two different approaches to this configuration: one for the standalone computer, and one for networks. There are some similarities in the approach that can be emphasized:

You are laying the directory groundwork for all your projects, be it one or many. The goal is to organize and simplify, so that locating, copying, deleting, and all of the other file housekeeping activities are easier to accomplish. You also want to optimize your resources—fast hard disks, RAM disks, and so on.

The convention used in this book for project files keeps directory structure and directory names as short and simple as possible, and, above all, consistent from project to project:

Project Root Directory

Project files
Resource files
config.fpw

(Project Sub-directories)

PRG	**DBF**	**SCR**
Program files	Data files	Screen files
MNU	**REP**	**BMP**
Menu files	Report files	Bitmap files

It doesn't matter much whether this is on a network drive or a local drive. As a rule, the FoxPro program and support files are in their own subdirectory system elsewhere on the network or your own hard disk. If you have enough memory for a RAM disk, then you might want to consider loading some of the FoxPro program files there. Specifically, GENMENU.FXP, GENSCRN.FXP can benefit from being on a RAM disk. In general, however, FoxPro for Windows doesn't get much of a boost from a RAM disk.

At this point in the book, you aren't officially using the screen, menu, and bitmap directories, but your projects will eventually grow into them. There are other types of files, (.FMT, .QBE, etc.) which you may also eventually want in a separate subdirectory. Whatever directory structure you adopt, be sure to set up the PATH statement in the config.fpw so FoxPro can find the files.

The FoxPro Editor and Others

Choosing program editors used to be like choosing underwear—a relatively personal matter. However, all of the major programming language vendors, including Microsoft, are moving in the direction of a fully integrated development environment. The program editor is a big part of this environment, and all vendors provide their own, while making it relatively inconvenient to use a different editor. Not that this ever stopped programmers.

However, with FoxPro, a cautionary word is in order: Don't get too attached to a non-Fox way of doing things. Because the Power Tools use .DBF files instead of ASCII text files, the code stored in memo fields is not accessible (at least yet) to third-party editors. This can limit these editors to use only in standalone .PRG files of procedures and functions. Besides, not only does the combination of Windows and the current development system form a fairly integrated package, but it's no secret the next version of FoxPro will make major changes in the development environment. You can count on those changes to build from the existing way of doing things, making anything less "mainstream" difficult to fit into the scheme.

Finally, the FoxPro text editor isn't half bad...in fact it may be more than half good. Consider some of these enhancements from the FoxPro 2.0 DOS version:

- Drag-and-drop editing—the ability to select, copy, and move text with only the mouse.
- Indenting and undenting of selected text for proper clegic display.
- Ability to change fonts, size, and line spacing.

And as always, the built-in editor is linked to the debugging facilities, so that opening the appropriate file puts the cursor on the line with a problem (more or less).

Still, the FoxPro editor is not a sophisticated program like Brief, or as nimble as Qedit (two old favorites of programmers). If you're already familiar with these programs, you can still continue to use them, at least some of the time, by using the RUN command from the Command window something like this:

```
RUN QEDIT GSTEST.PRG /n50
```

You can also use the CONFIG.FPW to set a default text editor. The TEDIT option can be set to invoke your favorite editor whenever FoxPro goes into edit mode with memo fields:

```
TEDIT = F:\ED\QEDIT
```

But not, unfortunately, in the Power Tools.

Moving to a Simple Program

Using the Command window to enter FoxPro commands is part of programming. But there comes a time when the limitations of the Command window get in the way of what you need to do. Or perhaps you're sick of re-entering often repeated commands. Whatever.

It's time to create a program file to contain the sequence of commands you need. This is a very reasonable way to start programming. It's an extension of the work you've already done in the Command window, only now you can begin to take advantage of control structures (loops, conditionals), and the fact that your work can be repeated at any time (and by anybody). Your first efforts may look nothing more fancy than the example on the next page.

```
* MAINT.PRG
USE CUSTOMER ORDER CUSTID IN 1
USE ORDERS ORDER CUSTID IN 2
SELECT CUSTOMER
SET RELATION TO CUSTID INTO ORDERS
SCAN
IF STATUS="I" AND LASTORD<DATE()-365
DELETE
IF FOUND("ORDERS")
SELECT ORDERS
SCAN WHILE CUSTID=CUSTOMER.CUSTID
DELETE
ENDSCAN
ENDIF
ENDIF
SELECT CUSTOMER
ENDSCAN
```

This *is* a program. The coding cannot be duplicated in the Command window, because of the IF..THEN and SCAN..ENDSCAN control structures. Using the FoxPro editor, you create programs by typing commands into a text file (which have the .PRG extension added automatically). The file can be started with the system menu—File, New, (select program), New (**Alt-F N New**) or with the following command in the Command Window—MODIFY COMMAND MAINT.

Once the file is finished and you've saved it—File, Save, or Save As (**Alt-F S**)—you can run it as many times as you like with a DO MAINT command in the Command window, or by using the Run OR Program option of the system menu.

Assuming that you're not yet familiar with IF..ENDIF and SCAN..ENDSCAN constructions (though you might well be), the format of this little program may not bother you. Even so, it's probably difficult to follow exactly what's going on. There's no annotation, documentation, or any other visual cues. And that's where the issue of programming conventions begins.

Some Basic Programming Conventions

Contrast the following version of MAINT.PRG with the one above.

```
* MAINT.PRG
* 1/25/93
* Locates and Deletes Order and Customer records, where the
account is no longer active.
USE customer ALIAS cus ORDER custid IN 1
USE orders ALIAS ord ORDER custid IN 2
SELECT cus
SET RELATION TO custid INTO ord
*Customer File Processing Loop
SCAN
 * Delete only customers who are inactive, "I", and who have
 • not ordered in over a year.
 IF cus.status = "I" AND cus.lastord < DATE() - 365
   DELETE
   *Check order file
   IF FOUND( "ord" )
     SELECT ord
     *Order File Processing Loop
     SCAN WHILE ord.custid = cus.custid
       DELETE
     ENDSCAN
   ENDIF
 ENDIF
 SELECT cus
ENDSCAN // cus loop
```

It has the same code, but with two additions: indented lines and a liberal use of the * (comment) marker to enter documentation. This is hardly a polished example, but the shape of the program is beginning to be visible.

"Shape?" you ask. Consider looking at the code for an average application—about ten thousand lines. If all of these lines were entered as in the first MAINT.PRG example, it would be one big uninterrupted vertical column about 105 feet long. A little difficult to comprehend. So, you break it up into separate programs, say ten (.PRG) files. Now you have ten files of about ten feet in length. Still somewhat cumbersome. Go the next step, and break each of the files into sections and probably some related procedures and functions. Each time you break up the programming into smaller pieces, hopefully for some reason, the program becomes a little easier to understand (unless you go off the deep end and make a thousand little program pieces).

To make this easier, coding conventions are established. The idea is to create a consistent pattern that can be instantly recognized. If all of your code is structured consistently, it will be easier to read. And if you manage to follow some generally accepted conventions, other people will be able to read it easily too. So things like conditional structures and control loops are indented, to show that they are nested, one inside the other:

```
   SCAN
    IF <test>
      DO WHILE
        <do something>
     ENDDO
   ELSE

     <do something>
   ENDIF
ENDSCAN
```

This has the fancy name, *clegic display*. It is one of the more obvious programming conventions—nested structures are indented a certain number of spaces with the beginning and end of the structure at the same position. There are many other conventions. Some have to do with distinguishing commands from variables, others with variable data types, and so forth.

Here's an annotated version of the MAINT.PRG program, describing some of the conventions being used...

1. There should be a header, a top section of the program, that describes what the program is called and what it is supposed to do.

```
* MAINT.PRG
* 1/25/93
* Locates and Deletes Order and Customer records,
• where the account is no longer active.
```

2. Segments of code with different purposes are separated by blank lines.

```
* Open files.
```

3. FoxPro commands are all upper case. Fields, variables, and aliases are lower case.

```
USE customer ALIAS cus ORDER custid IN 1
USE orders ALIAS ord ORDER custid IN 2
SELECT cus
SET RELATION TO custid INTO ord
```

4. Significant elements in the program are annotated.

```
*Customer File Processing Loop
SCAN
```

5. Logic or processing that is not self-evident should be explained.

```
 * Include only customers who are inactive,"I", and  who
have not ordered in over a year.
 IF Cus.Status = "I" AND Cus.Lastord > DATE() - 365
```

6. Don't jam code together, leave room for easier reading.

```
DELETE
```

7. Program structures like IFs and loops should be indented.

```
*Check order file
IF FOUND( "ord" )
  SELECT ord
  *Order File Processing Loop
```

8. Identify the table (using the alias) for all field references.

```
SCAN WHILE ord.custid = cus.custid
               DELETE
    ENDSCAN
ENDIF
```

9. Annotate the ends of structures that are not easily connected to their beginnings.

```
ENDIF // status = i
 SELECT CUS
ENDSCAN // cus loop
```

You may be wondering, "Why bother?" If your honest answer is, "Nobody cares," then perhaps you don't need to bother. Presumably nobody but you is going to see the code, and a year later you will remember clearly what you were doing. On the other hand, if your programs need to be shared with other people, or you'd like a little help in reconstructing what you were doing, then conventions that make your code more legible and better documented are more than worth the effort.

Of course, we're talking habit here. None of the coding conventions are difficult or even time consuming, especially if you make them automatic and habitual. The problem, as in so many other endeavors, is how to acquire good habits. The process of learning these conventions is about one-third knowing some generally accepted conventions, and two-thirds common sense. This book uses numerous conventions that are generally accepted, and tries to explain them as it goes along. However, as always, there is no one way for everybody.

Files, Procedures, and UDFs

Programming in the FoxPro context should flow from the natural use of data tables, database operations, and information retrieval. That's what distinguishes Xbase programming (of any kind) from other languages like C or Basic. If you've cut your learning teeth in the system menu and the Command window, you already know 80 percent to 90 percent of the relevant database commands and functions. Now it's time to put that knowledge into a bigger framework, one that can take you all the way into building applications.

Program Files

All along you've been writing code to manage your data. Now you want to save your work and expand your capabilities. This means putting your code into a program file. As already mentioned, you can simply open a .PRG file with the File, New, or type MODIFY COMMAND <filename> in the COMMAND window and start programming.

However, over time and hopefully lots of programs, there's more to a program file than just batting out some code. In fact there's a natural structure of a program file that appears again and again, although, of course, not all programs look like this:

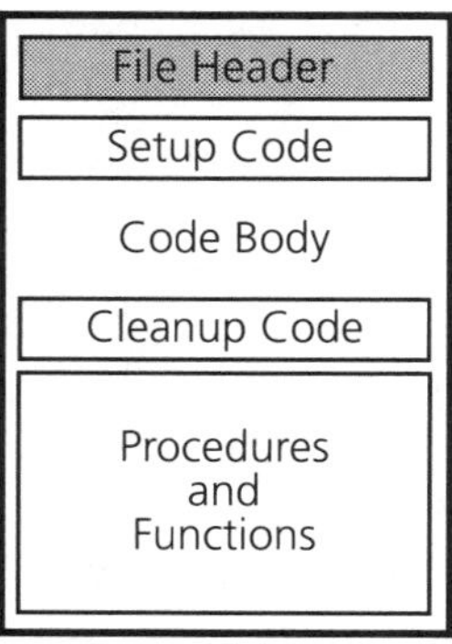

Figure 8.1 *Program file structure.*

The program file (.PRG) is the largest "object" in the typical application. Of course, some applications may consist of several program files. The program file is the container for all of the other elements—file header, setup code, code body, cleanup code, and especially procedures and functions.

File Header

Just like a header in a report, the program file header usually conveys basic information about the program—what it's called, what it does, who made it and when, and perhaps most importantly, a log of changes. The format below is merely a suggestion, but keeps things simple and reasonably clear.

```
******************************************************************
*      PROGRAM:       DUPECHEK.PRG
* DESCRIPTION:       CHECKS FOR DUPLICATES IN THE TABLE
*      CREATED:       12/12/92
*   PROGRAMMER:       NK
*
*        Notes:
* Needed a generalized program to search any data table for
* duplicate
* key fields (where duplicates are not allowed). Routine
* maintenance
* program to be included with applications.
*
*
* Revision History:
* 3/31/93    Corrected SCAN loop problem. NK
*
*
*
******************************************************************
```

The asterisks in the left column are required to indicate these are comments and not code lines. The FoxPro compiler ignores all of these lines. Once upon a time, programmers were told not to include too many comment lines in a program, because the compilers would spend too much time processing them. Even if compilers did (and they sure don't now), that was lousy advice. *Never* be stingy with in-code documentation. This is the place where information means the most. Don't waste the opportunity to clarify what you're trying to do with liberal notation.

However, as the old hands say, "SET VERBOSE OFF." Too much or too wordy documentation probably won't be read. Keep the commentary reasonably terse, accurate, and relevant. In the header, it's very helpful to document the purpose of the file and any tricks, quirks, or problems in the code. In some cases where the program is extremely complicated, programmers will put "pseudo code" here to illustrate the general approach.

Setup Code

Most programs, although by no means all, need to set up the working environment—declare variables, open files, set relations—before launching into the heart of the programming. Quite naturally setup is the first working part of a program file. There's no "standard" way to do a setup, but a reasonable approach looks something like this:

```
*——————————————[ SETUP
*> Set Environment
cTalk = SET("TALK") && save current status
cExact = SET("EXACT")      && save current status
SET TALK OFF
SET SAFETY OFF
SET EXACT OFF

*> Open file to be checked
* (This file and/or key field will be changed as needed.)
USE customer ALIAS cus ORDER cno IN 0

*> Open file to hold list of duplicates
USE dupes   ALIAS dup IN 0

*>Initialize local variables
PRIVATE cNewKey, cOldKey
cNewKey = ""          && holds new key value
cOldKey = ""          && holds old key value
```

The setup for this program is minimal. In larger application files, the setup may run to a hundred lines of code or more. But the purpose is always the same—get ready for the main body of programming. It helps to be consistent with the order of setup elements, so you can get used to looking in the same place.

Code Body

There is no such thing as a typical code body, of course. It could be an entry screen, a processing loop (like this example), a math algorithm...almost anything.

```
SELECT cus
cOldKey = cus.cno    && store first key value

*——————————[ DUPLICATE SCAN LOOP
SCAN

  *Compare current key vs old key
  IF cOldKey = cus.cno
    * If keys values match, process a duplicate
    DO DupFile WITH cOldKey, cus.cno, RECNO()
  ENDIF

  cOldKey = cus.cno && store current key

  SELECT cus
ENDSCAN // end of scan loop
```

In this example, the program is looking through the customer table one record at a time to find duplicate values in the customer number (CNO) field. Since the table is indexed on CNO, all duplicates should be sorted together. To find them, you just compare the value in the previous record with the value in the current record. If they match, there is a duplicate. When duplicates are found, a DO command calls a procedure that logs the duplicate into another table for later review.

Cleanup Code

Just as the name implies, the cleanup section does all of the housekeeping necessary before leaving the program—closing files, releasing variables, windows, and resetting environmental values.

```
*——————————[ Cleanup
*> Close files
```

```
SELECT cus
USE
SELECT dup
USE

*> Reset environment
SET EXACT(cExact)
SET TALK (cTalk)
```

This DUPECHK.PRG is a "standalone" program. It's not designed to be run in conjunction with any other programs. For this reason it doesn't need to make many adjustments to what comes before it, or what comes after it. It's setup and cleanup are almost entirely for its own purposes. Such independence is not often the case. Many, if not most, programs you write need to coexist with other programs or the general environment of an application. In this case the cleanup and the setup sections of a program are responsible for being "good citizens." They need to preserve the environment before the code body of the program is run, and restore that environment when done.

Program Nesting

Actually, the statement "They need to preserve the environment before the code body of the program is run, and restore that environment when done." is not necessarily true. This is where you get into the programming jargon of the "calling" and "called" program. In FoxPro one program calls (starts, invokes, runs) another program by using the DO command. This same command applies to procedures. Functions are also "called," but as you've seen, they can be embedded in a line of code or called independently with the equal sign.

An important concept related to calling/called programs is that they can be "nested," as in Figure 8.2.

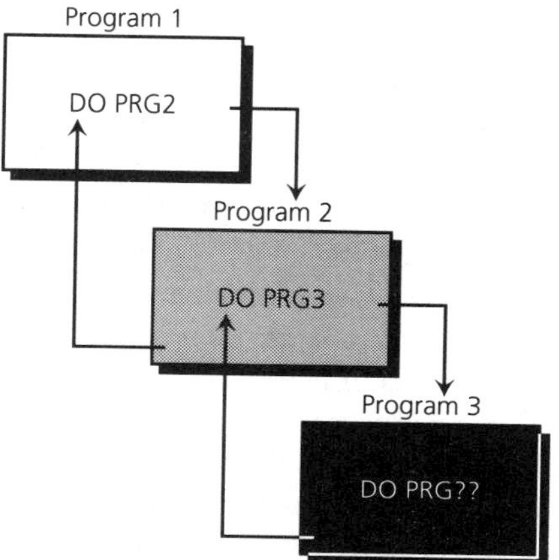

Figure 8.2
Nested programs.

Typically, in a series of nested programs, this is an "out and back" cycle. Program 1 calls program 2. Program 2 calls program 3. When program 3 is done, it returns program control back to program 2, which continues executing from the command line after the DO. When program 2 is finished, it returns control to program 1.

The cycle doesn't have to complete. A program can be terminated at any time, and FoxPro has a RETURN TO MASTER command that jumps control back to the original calling program. However, most of the time nested programs complete their operation and return to the program level above them. (It's common to describe nested programs in a two-dimensional way, just like the diagram, with nesting levels and words like top, bottom, above, below.)

Technically, when one program calls another program, there are three possibilities for setup and cleanup.

1. The calling program does it.
2. The called program does it.
3. They both do it.

This is an important responsibility. To use a very crude example, if you run a program that has several tables open, and then you call another program that closes some of these tables without restoring them, when you go back to your first program, it will crash. Which program should have the responsibility for seeing to it open tables either stay open, or are restored?

The common rationale is for the *called* program to do it. Program 1 shouldn't be required to know how program 2 needs to be set up. The called program is supposed to do a job independently of any particular calling program, which means it has to take care of its own setup. In the process it can save information about the environment it received when starting, and restore it when done. The only "official" connection it may have with the calling program is through information passed explicitly (called *parameters*).

This is but the merest taste of the approach involved in object-oriented programming, and a much simpler idea—reusable code. The idea is to build programs, procedures, and functions that are independent, "modular," and capable of being used in a variety of situations.

However, the real world of programming isn't always so clean and independent. In FoxPro there are at least three hundred to four hundred possible environmental settings, open tables, relations, filters, that might apply to a program. There is no way a called program can deal with even a fraction of these settings. So as a rule, the called program only takes care of those things that it will modify during its run. Knowing this is the approach, a calling program that has some very complex configurations might want to protect itself and save some of that configuration before issuing a call. In this case both the calling and called programs are participating in the setup and cleanup.

Procedures and UDFs

If a program file is the superstructure of a program, then procedures and user defined functions (UDFs) are the building blocks.

In form UDFs and procedures are very similar:

- Both procedures and UDFs must be inside a program or procedure file.
- Procedures begin with the key word PROCEDURE followed by up to a ten-character name.
- UDFs begin with the key word FUNCTION and then a ten-character name.

- Both can take a PARAMETER statement to receive values from the calling program.
- A UDF and a procedure may have a RETURN, but it's not required.

This is what a procedure looks like:

```
*Sample Procedure
PROCEDURE countit
PARAMETER nCount

PRIVATE nStateCnt, nTopCust

SELECT cus
COUNT FOR cus.state = "CA" TO nStateCnt
COUNT FOR cus.ytdpurch > 1000 TO nTopCust
nNatCount = nCount + nStateCnt
nNatRatio = nStateCnt / nNatCount
@ 10,20 SAY nStateCnt PICTURE "###,###"
@ 11,20 SAY nNatRatio PICTURE "##.##%"
```

This is what a function looks like:

```
*Sample User Defined Function
FUNCTION CountIt
PARAMETER nCount

PRIVATE nStateCnt, nTopCust

SELECT cus
COUNT FOR cus.state = "CA" TO nStateCnt
COUNT FOR cus.ytdpurch > 1000 TO nTopCust
nNatCount = nCount + nStateCnt
nNatRatio = nStateCnt / nNatCount
@ 10,20 SAY nStateCnt PICTURE "###,###"
@ 11,20 SAY nNatRatio PICTURE "##.##%"

RETURN nNatCount
```

There is not a whole lot of difference between them. The real difference shows up in the calling program. Procedures are only available this way:

```
DO <procedure name> [WITH <parameter 1, parameter 2,...>]
```

For example:

```
DO countit WITH nCurCount
```

UDFs can be used just like any other function...

```
IF CountIt( nCurCount ) > 200
```

or

```
= CountIt( nCurCount )
```

Other than the usual RETURN <value> of a UDF, the compiler in FoxPro treats procedures and UDFs as if they are the same thing. Given the greater flexibility of UDFs, is there any reason to use procedures? No functional reason. No performance reason. No compiler reason. No efficiency reason. It's a habit. And now Microsoft has added to the confusion by introducing new terminology, a User Named Procedure, which they freely mix with the standard terms in the sample code. A case can be made for maintaining the logical distinction between functions with their in-line capability, and procedures for their direct call. That is, use DO <procedure> instead of = <Function>. This is a fine distinction. In the end, however, some people favor functions, some people favor procedures, and most people mix the two.

There are three major reasons for making extensive use of procedures and UDFs:

1. UDFs in particular are more flexible in their use than program files.
2. You can make libraries that are available throughout a program.
3. They help clarify the structure and operation within a program.

In many cases, various ways of programming are adopted not because they are easier, or faster, but because they help make sense out of a very complex process. Using simple building blocks, functions, and procedures, is one way to construct even the largest of applications. This is what the modularity of User Defined Functions (and procedures) has done for the Xbase language.

Before Xbase developed the ability to include function definitions in any program file, the only way you could use generic procedures of your own making was to create a procedure file. This was limited to 32 procedures. Even if you used a procedure file, applications tended to have dozens, if not hundreds, of small program files. This tended to make the structure of an application very fragmented, if not downright chaotic.

In the FoxPro of today, you can create an unlimited number of UDFs or procedures and put them into a procedure file. You can also include UDFs and procedures within any program file. This makes it possible to develop a library of generic functions that can be used in many projects, and at the same time create any number of functions that are specific to a single project—or even a part of a single project. It also means that you can create relatively large program files around specific functionality—true "modules" of an application—and greatly reduce the fragmentation of an application.

Building UDFs

Few skills will be as important for your programming as the mastery of building functions. Even in simple program files, you will use functions. In the Screen Builder you will use functions. In the Menu Builder you will use functions. In a typical application you will create hundreds, yes hundreds, of functions. And to top it off, you should begin (now) to create your own library of functions (and procedures) that can be used from project to project.

Beside the actual function structure, all functions need a *function call* (that is if you want to *use* the function). The syntax for this is:

```
[=] <function name>( [[<argument1>][, <argument2>],...] )
```

At places in the FoxPro documentation, the arguments of calling functions are also referred to as *parameters*. In the C programming language, the function call has *arguments* and the function itself has *parameters*. This keeps the two distinct. Most Xbase programming follows this convention. FoxPro allows up to twenty-four parameters in a function, although you'd be foolhardy to create one that complex.

NOTE

When your programs make a function call, The FoxPro runtime engine searches for the function first in the file of origin, then in an open procedure file. Next it backtracks through all open program files, and finally it searches the path on the disk for a file the same name as the function. This search sequence gives you a clue of how to place your functions for maximum performance. Obviously if you leave them out on the disk, that's the last place searched and therefore slowest place to put them. Functions that need frequent and immediate response, for instance in rapidly executing loops, should be in the same program file as the function call.

The basic structure of a function is not complicated, as in Figure 8.3.

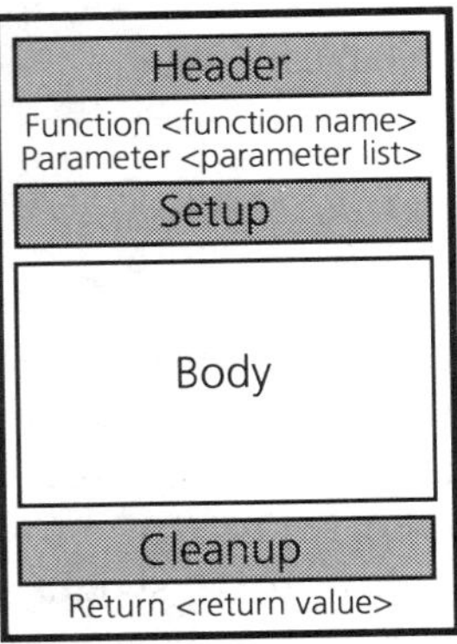

Figure 8.3 *Function structure.*

Function Header

Like a program file, functions (and procedures) should have some kind of header. How much information you put into the header depends on its purpose. It would seem like overkill to have a thirty line header for a three line function. (Don't believe there are three line functions? How about this:

```
FUNCTION MarkUp
PARAMETERS nCost, nPrice
RETURN ((nPrice - nCost) / nCost) * 100
```

Even two line functions are not uncommon.) For comparison, here's a very basic header used inside of an application file, followed by a full-blown header for a library of functions.

Short Format Header

```
*____________________________________________
* FUNCTION NAME: CheckIt()
* DESCRIPTION: VALID, lookup for fee
* PARAMETERS: nFeeTotal = Total fee from FEE table.
* CALLED BY: FEELIST.PRG
*____________________________________________
```

Long Format Header

```
*****************************************************************
* FUNCTION NAME.. MakePass()
* DESCRIPTION.... MAKE A PASSWORD ENTRY IN USERS FILE
* DATE CREATED... Fri 11-15-1991
* PROGRAMMERS.... NK
* REVISIONS...... Wed 02-05-1992 added parameter,nk.
* PARAMETERS..... cStfId = cMStaffId = Staff ID (initials)
* SYNTAX......... MakePass( cMstaffid )
* USAGE.......... IIF( PassWord(3,2), MakePass( cMstaffid ),
"")
* RETURN......... .t./.f.
* NOTES.......... Uses CIPHER Library
* CALLED BY...... GUF (General Use Function)
* CALLS.......... Encrypt()
*****************************************************************
```

Function Name and Parameters

The function header is immediately followed by two of the three official function clauses:

```
FUNCTION <function name> and PARAMETER <parameter list>.
```

You are allowed up to ten characters for a function name. By convention these should be as mnemonic (memory jogging) as possible, and are written in mixed case—Microsoft C programming style: PriceCheck( ), CalcCost( ), FeeLook( ). This helps to distinguish UDFs from the native functions of FoxPro, which are all capitals by convention. Some programmers also like to data type their functions in the name, since FoxPro for Windows doesn't really care what they are (unlike C and most other languages). The typing reflects the data type returned by the functions and is often indicated like this: nCalcCost(), cNameFind() where the n is for numeric, c for character etc. As you will see, this is the same convention used for variables.

You may have already gathered the PARAMETER <parameter list> corresponds directly to the <function name>([[<argument1>][, <argument2>],...]) of the function call. For the most part, this is a one-to-one linkage with argument 1 said to be *passed* to parameter 1, and so on.

```
YourFunc( arg1, arg2, arg3, arg4 )
FUNCTION YourFunc
PARAMETER parm1, parm2, parm3, parm4
```

Stop a moment, however, and ask yourself: "*What* is being passed?" Which might lead to an even better question, "*Why* do we bother with parameters?"

This may be your first encounter with *scoping*, one of the more esoteric topics in programming. Scoping can be phrased as a question: "What is the scope of the program? What is the scope of the variable?" In both cases, the question asks: "When is this program/variable available to other programs?" And if available, can it be modified?

Perhaps the real motivator behind scoping is bug avoidance. Programs that pay no attention to the availability of their variables, functions and procedures, may find themselves crashing on corrupted variables or missing functions.

However one of the more positive reasons for functions and procedures is to, in a sense, isolate their workings and their information (variables) from the rest of a program. This relative independence is what makes it possible for the same function to be used in a variety of different places. The theory is that a function shouldn't care about the environment of the function call. It should only accept the information it needs, and then go about its business without affecting anything around it. This needed information is passed by parameters.

Parameters are normally part of the insulation process. Instead of a function needing to know about variables that exist, somewhere out in the calling programs, it gets a very specific list of variables. All other variables that it needs are created for local use and disappear when the function returns. However, the insulation is relative. A function that requires data very specific to a particular calling program is said to be *tightly bound*, and conversely a more general function is *loosely bound*—or in truth not bound at all. Some functions require no parameters. Most, however, do need parameters as inputs.

Another aspect of this binding—which answers the question "*What* is being passed?"—is that parameters of functions may be passed *by value* and *by reference*. What's the difference? The default is by value. If <argument 1> of the function call is a variable with assigned value of 2, then the receiving <parameter 1> of the function is also assigned the value of 2.

```
nCount = 2
= CalcCount( nCount )
...
```

```
FUNCTION CalcCount
PARAMETER nCnt
? nCnt
2
```

No matter what happens to the parameter variable in the function, the value of the originating variable remains the same.

When a parameter is passed by reference, something quite different happens. The receiving parameter gets the memory location of the variable in the calling argument, instead of the value. The receiving parameter is a *reference* to the argument variable. This means when any new value is assigned to the parameter variable, the value of the original variable is changed.

```
nCount = 1
SET UDFPARMS TO REFERENCE
= CalcCount( nCount )
SET UDFPARMS TO VALUE
? nCount
3
...
FUNCTION CalcCount
PARAMETER nCnt
nCnt = 3
RETURN
```

You may have noticed SET UDFPARMS TO REFERENCE | VALUE in the above example. This is the command that switches the method of passing for function parameters. (It does not apply to procedure parameters.) Functions that use parameters by reference are more tightly bound to their calling programs. This tends to make them less independent and less reusable. Functions and procedures that cannot be reused or used in different programs, are *structural*, they exist primarily to simplify the structure and maintenance of a program. This is not a dishonorable purpose, but in the coming world of object orientation it is often considered second rate.

From a more practical point of view, you create functions to clarify your code, modularize structure, and when possible generalize module use. Whether you use parameters by value or by reference should depend on what you need the function to do. You *are* trying to avoid having the function step on any variables or processes that occur outside of itself. You are *not* trying to turn FoxPro into an object oriented-programming language…not yet.

Also in the practical and useful category, one of the innovations of the Xbase/FoxPro language is you don't need to have all of the arguments for all the parameters. For example:

```
= YesNo("Continue Entering?", 8, "Y")
...
FUNCTION YesNo
PARAMETER cMessage, nAtRow, cDefault, cWithColor
```

There are three arguments and four parameters. And FoxPro won't complain. (However, if you skip a parameter or have more arguments than parameters, it *will* complain.) This feature is a "growth enabler." If a function could use another parameter, for example you could add a timeout parameter to the example above, just put it at the end of the parameter list.

```
PARAMETER cMessage, nAtRow, cDefault, cWithColor, nTimeOut
```

All of the old function calls will still work flawlessly, but new calls and retrofits can take advantage of the enhanced function.

Function Setup

There are no formal rules about what goes into a function setup, or even that such a thing exists. Still, there is some practical reasoning behind having a segment of a function so named. It's the place to define variables, set tables, and other housekeeping before launching into the main purpose of the function. If you're consistent about the order of things in a setup, over time maintenance will be easier, because you will know where to find things.

```
*————————————————————[ SETUP

*[1] Trapping for bad parameters
IF EMPTY( cName )           && must have a name
 RETURN (.f.)               && if not, bug out
ENDIF

*[2] Initialize local variables
PRIVATE is_ok, nCount, cBuildName
is_ok = .f.
nCount = 1
cBuildName = SPACE(30)
```

```
*[3] Save needed calling environment
cOldAlias = ALIAS()
cOldOrder = ORDER()
cOldWin = WONTOP()
cSetExact = SET("EXACT")

*[4] Set local environment and tables
SET EXACT ON
SELECT cus
SET ORDER TO lastname

*[5] Set user interface elements
DEFINE WINDOW bLname FROM 1,0 TO 23,79 ;
  TITLE "Customer Names" ;
  FLOAT GROW ZOOM CLOSE ;
  COLOR SCHEME 10
ACTIVATE WINDOW bLname
```

In this rather typical example, the first order of business is to decide whether the function should be executed at all. There's no point in going through the rest of the code, if some needed precondition is missing. In this case a RETURN is used to abort the function. In some programming circles this is forbidden. On the other hand, this use of RETURN is very clear, requires no additional code, and has no side effects.

More will be said later about the meaning of the PRIVATE <variable list>, another item of scoping. It simply ensures that variables used only in this function will in fact be visible (in scope) only in this function.

Any function that must use a table, and especially if any of the conditions of the table need to be changed, is responsible for saving the original conditions (and restoring them before returning). This is also true of important environmental settings, in this case SET EXACT.

Finally, the setup usually handles any initial user interface elements such as windows, screen colors, and menus.

Function Body

The body of the function is where the real action takes place. It can, of course, be almost anything. Processing, user interface, logic, loops, and in any combination whatsoever.

Function Cleanup

Cleanup is the bookend to the setup. What gets saved, should be restored.

```
*——————————————————[ Cleanup
* Close Tables, Windows etc.
SELECT fee
USE
RELEASE WINDOW bLname

* Reset Windows
IF NOT EMPTY( cOldWin )
  IF WEXIST( cOldWin )
    ACTIVATE WINDOW ( cOldWin )
  ENDIF
ENDIF

* Reset the tables
IF NOT EMPTY( cOldAlias )
  SELECT (cOldAlias)
  IF NOT EMPTY( cOldOrd )
    SET ORDER TO (cOldOrd)
  ENDIF
ENDIF
* Reset environment
SET EXACT ( cSetExact )
```

Just like entering an ENDIF for every IF, most functions need to have things restored that were saved in the beginning. If you forget, you'll probably be rudely reminded. Matching elements of the setup with the cleanup should be automatic. Some programmers go so far as to do setup and cleanup at the same time, before going on to programming the body of the function.

Return of the Function

Contrary to the practice in C, FoxPro does not require a RETURN, either in a function or a procedure. However, if you want the function to return a value, which it usually does, then you must include the RETURN command followed by an expression that produces the value to be returned. Some programmers also feel that always including a RETURN makes it clearer where one function or procedure ends, and another begins. It's a visual cue, even if a few more keystrokes. In fact, you can be downright graphic about the end of a function.

```
RETURN IIF( nCount > 10, .t., .f.)
*** End of function FeeCounter() ***
```

Example Function

Having taken functions apart and examined them for meaning and secrets, it's now time to offer a complete function. This is a short example, but reasonably useful. It does error checking on a user's entry of a time. There are precious few time-oriented functions in FoxPro, which leaves the doorway open to produce an number of variations for yourself. (This same function is reworked in Section III to take advantage of the new Spinner control.)

```
***********************************************************************
* FUNCTION NAME.. ValTime()
* DESCRIPTION.... VALIDATE A STANDARD TIME ENTRY.
* DATE........... 2/27/91
* PROGRAMMERS.... NHK
* LAST CHANGE.... na
* PARAMETERS..... cTime = <time value> : string - "##:##"
* SYNTAX......... ValTime( <time str> )
* USAGE.......... = ValTime( M.enter_time )
* RETURN......... .t./.f.
* NOTES.......... Simple validation of a time entry. Presumes -
            * 1. a five character time field, "##:##" and
            * 2. the use of a 24 hour clock (military time).
* CALLED BY...... Many and various, a GUF (General Use
* Function).
* CALLS.......... none
***********************************************************************
FUNCTION ValTime
PARAMETER cTime

PRIVATE ret_val, cT1, cT2, i, nK
ret_val = .t.

*> Parse the entered time & pad with zeros.
cT1 = ALLTRIM( SUBSTR(cTime,1,2) )
cT2 = ALLTRIM( SUBSTR(cTime,4,2) )
cT1 = PADL( cT1, 2, "0" )
cT2 = PADL( cT2, 2, "0" )

*> Test 1: Look for non numbers
```

```
FOR i = 1 TO 4              && loop to check characters.
  nK = ASC( SUBSTR(cT1+cT2,i,1) )
  ret_val = IIF( BETWEEN( nK, 48, 58), .t., .f. )
  IF ret_val = .f.          && set return as false.
   = ErrLine("Please use only numbers.", 2)
  EXIT
 ENDIF
ENDFOR

IF ret_val = .t.
  *>Test 2: Check the Range of Values
  nT1 = VAL( cT1 )  && convert string to number
  nT2 = VAL( cT2 )
  ret_val = IIF( nT1 < 23 .and. nT2 < 60, .t., .f.)
  = IIF( ret_val = .f., ErrLine("Not a valid time. Please use a
24 hour clock.",2),.f.)
ENDIF
RETURN ( ret_val )
*
```

Program Control Structures

Control structures have the ability to turn, direct, change, cycle, and corral the flow of a program. There are four types: conditionals, loops, calls, and menus. The conditionals are the traffic cops, forever separating yes from no and channeling program flow. The loops capture the flow of a program and make it repeat, until meeting a conditional end. The calls—to programs, procedures and functions—move the flow off and usually bring it back. Menus, much like calls, move the program flow out and back, but only at the user's choice. Control structures are shown in Figure 8.4.

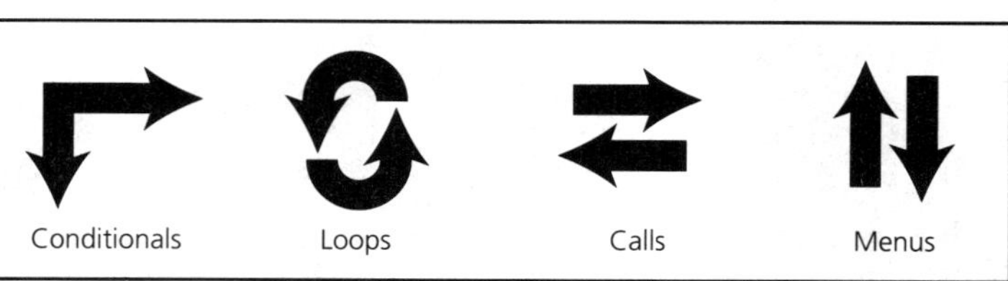

Figure 8.4 *Control structures.*

Conditionals

There are only three conditional structures, but how important! They provide the logical framework for programming and exist in almost the same syntax for nearly every modern programming language.

The Standard IF

IF you want a million bucks, THEN you'll write a great piece of software, ELSE you'll sell computer printer paper. So begins the logic of the IF. The English syntax works, always, when formulating a computer IF statement. In some languages IF...THEN...ELSE is the actual syntax. In Xbase generally, the formal syntax is a little different:

```
IF <expL>
   <statements>
[ELSE
   <statements>]
ENDIF
```

It is loosely translated like this:

```
IF < some logical test that is either true or false >
   The test was true, do some stuff here.
ELSE (control structure separator)
   The test was false, so do something else here.
ENDIF (end of the control structure marker)
```

Since you've already encountered the logical expression throughout the menu system and the Command window, you already know that the logical test for the IF can be almost anything:

Very simple	`IF 1+1 = 2`
Relatively simple	`IF cWorldPeace = "InterNet"`
Somewhat complex	`IF SUBSTR( cus.company, 1, 3 ) = "IBM"`
Moderately complex	`IF MIN(ACOS(nRoof)/30,4.35) >;` `SQRT(ATAN(nRoof)/60)`

Complex	`IF wYesNo("Are you sure.?",8,.t.,"GR+/R,W+/B")AND ; cus.ytdpurch > 1000`
Very complex	`IF SEEK("Home", "CUS") AND NOT(; MONTH(DATE())=12 OR ; nOverDue < IIF(inv.due > 100, inv.due, 0))`

The only requirement is, of course, that the statement evaluate true or false. If the logical expression is true, then program control goes first to the code between the IF and the ELSE (or if no else, then the ENDIF).

```
IF SEEK(cus.cno, "inv")
  SELECT inv
  cSalesPerson = inv.salesman
  SKIP
  SELECT cus
ENDIF
```

Once the code inside is completed, program control resumes at the first line beyond the ENDIF. If the logical expression evaluates to false, in the example above control drops immediately to the line beyond the ENDIF. If there is an ELSE, however, control is passed to the code between the ELSE and the ENDIF:

```
IF SEEK(cus.cno, "inv")
  SELECT inv
  cSalesPerson = inv.salesman
  SKIP
  SELECT cus
ELSE
  WAIT "No invoices for this customer!" WINDOW NOWAIT
ENDIF
```

The IF, <logical expression>, and ENDIF are required. Everything else is up to you and the needs of your program for a conditional test or branching, as it is sometimes called. You can also *nest* the IF statements:

```
IF nYrTotal > 1000
  SELECT cus
  SEEK cno
  IF cus.ytdpurch > 50?
     SELECT inv
     SEEK cno
     IF inv.itotal > 250
       cAward = "We have a winner!"
     ENDIF
```

```
   ENDIF //cus.ytdpurch
ENDIF //nYrTotal
```

There are three observations to note about this example:

1. This could not be done with a single logical expression in the first IF, because it was necessary to execute a command before going to the next IF.
2. The two slashes (//) following the ENDIFs are an element of documentation style. Actually the FoxPro compiler ignores any commentary following keywords like ENDIF. No special markers like && or * are required. However, the slashes visually help to reinforce the structure of the IF/ENDIF and the notation of the key logic element helps to relate the end of the control structure back to the original IF. In this example, which spans only a few lines, it is no big deal. But some IF/ENDIF structures run to hundreds of lines and many nested levels. Without some attention to detail formatting, you can waste a lot of time trying to figure out what belongs to what.
3. The indentation convention used is three spaces. There is no standard for this. However, it helps to keep program lines inside the boundary of a standard eighty characters (screen and paper width). Since constant scrolling to the right is a pain in the pupils, this makes viewing much easier. If you use a deep indentation, you can quickly get nested structures that push lines outside the area of the screen. Three spaces is a workable compromise.

The In-Line IF

IF you were sharp eyed OR bothered to look, THEN you may have noticed in one of the logic samples above a little ringer—the in-line IF or IIF( ):

```
IF SEEK("Home", "CUS") AND NOT( MONTH(DATE())=12 OR :
  nOverDue < IIF(inv.due > 100, inv.due, 0))
```

The IIF( ) is a function, and for that reason can be nested inside lines of code. It can perform the same kind of duty as the standard IF, setting a conditional expression that returns a true or false. However, the IIF is much more versatile. It can return *any* kind of value. Here's the general syntax:

```
IIF(<expL>, <expr1>, <expr2>)
```

This actually reads like: IIF(<logical expression>, THEN <some expression>, ELSE <another expression>). The difference between the THEN and ELSE areas and that of a standard IF is that you can't use any commands. Any other kind of expression—functions, other logical conditions, constants—are fair game. In this sense the IIF reads like this:

```
IIF(For an expression that is either true or false , if true
RETURN the value of this expression ,
else if false RETURN the value of this expression )
```

For example:

```
IIF( cus.ytdpurch > 1000, cus.ytdpurch, 0 )
```

This tests to see if a customer's purchase exceeds $1,000. If so, then return the actual value of their purchases, otherwise return zero. Normally the values in either part of the return expressions are of the same data type (in this case numeric). In the Xbase language this data type agreement is not a requirement. Here's an example of a nested IIF:

```
= IIF(nTotPaid >= 500,DATE(),IIF(nTotPaid >=
250,inv.paydate,"HOLD")
```

As long as the receiving function, command, or expression doesn't have a problem with getting different data type, IIF can provide it. In this case the = simply evaluates the expression, but this could have worked with a ? in the Command window, or the other screen display command @ SAY.

The in-line IF is one of the most versatile logic structures in the Xbase language, and is used constantly. It has the added benefit of executing more rapidly than the standard IF, so in any case where lots of IF logic is required, the IIF( ) is the form of choice.

The CASE

All conditional logic is bifurcating. (Ahem.) That means it's either true or false. But that doesn't mean the logic has to have only two elements to the condition. There are plenty of cases where the logic isn't either/or but rather a series of cases. This is a "list" of conditions, only one of which is true, that is expressed in the DO CASE/ENDCASE structure.

```
DO CASE
```

```
CASE <expL1>
  <statements>
[CASE <expL2>
  <statements>
 ...
CASE <expLN>
  <statements>]
[OTHERWISE
  <statements>]
ENDCASE
```

The simplest example is the CASE structure following a menu selection (or in FoxPro screens after a push button option):

```
DO CASE
CASE cMenuChoice = "Add"
  APPEND
CASE cMenuChoice = "Edit"
  EDIT
CASE cMenuChoice = "Delete"
  DELETE
CASE cMenuChoice = "Quit"
  CANCEL
OTHERWISE
  WAIT "Please make a selection." WINDOW NOWAIT
ENDCASE
```

Program flow starts at the top CASE and works its way down each condition. If one is true, then the code following is executed, after which program flow drops to the next line after the ENDCASE. If none of the cases are true, the optional OTHERWISE can be included to provide a response. Because of the top-down, one-hit only approach of the CASE structure, you have to be careful with the logic so that all of the choices are actually possible. Here's an example of one that doesn't work:

```
DO CASE
CASE nCount <= 500
CASE nCount <= 300
CASE nCount <= 100
ENDCASE
```

The last two cases will never fire. This is an obvious example, but it's easier than you might think to create a similar, if more sophisticated, mistake.

Loops

There are four *iterative control structures*, or *loops* in FoxPro—DO WHILE, FOR, SCAN, READ. Each has its own characteristics, typical use, and peculiarities, however, there are some things that are common to all the loops, as illustrated in Figure 8.5 on the next page.

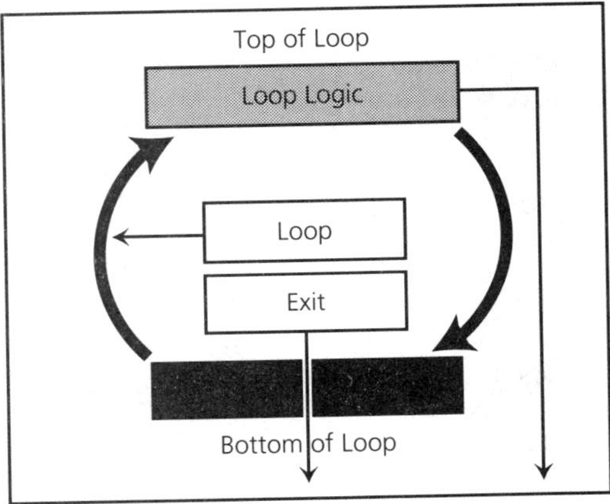

Figure 8.5 *Structure of loops.*

The primary logic that sustains the loop is located at the top. These are the conditions or counters that determine whether the loop should continue, or "drop out" to the first line beyond the end of the control structure. Curiously, the Xbase language has no formal loops that test for an exit at the bottom of the loop (the READ loop actually does). However there is the EXIT clause, which can be used with an IF/ENDIF at the bottom to simulate such loops. The EXIT causes program flow to immediately drop out of the loop at the bottom. The LOOP clause causes an immediate return to the top of the loop.

The General Loop

The DO WHILE is the graybeard of Xbase loops, being the one and only loop present at the creation. It was the "generalist" loop, often formed and twisted to perform more specialized looping functions. Then Clipper added the FOR/NEXT loop in 1986, and FoxPro added the SCAN/ENDSCAN in 1990.

These are specialist loops that removed the necessity of doing the same tasks with DO WHILE. These days the DO WHILE loop is often used for very large program loops, those intended to enclose a great deal of program code. The syntax is very simple:

```
DO WHILE <expL>
  <statements>
  [LOOP]
  [EXIT]
ENDDO
```

This loop requires a logical expression at the top, one that returns either true or false (.t. or .f.). If true, then the loop continues. If false, the loop exits at the bottom without executing any further code inside the loop. It's hard to illustrate the structural use of the DO WHILE but perhaps this compressed example might serve:

```
DO WHILE .t.
  DO CASE
  CASE USED("cus")
    BROWSE FIELDS <customer fields>
    DO CustFix
  CASE USED("inv")
    BROWSE FIELDS <invoice fields>
    DO InvFix
  CASE USED("det")
    BROWSE FIELDS <detail fields>
    DO DetFix
  OTHERWISE
    EXIT
  ENDCASE
ENDDO
```

This is a "permanent" loop because the logic at the top is always true. The escape hatch has to be somewhere else in the code, using the EXIT clause. A more typical DO WHILE with a conditional expression that actually tests for something looks like this:

```
*Gas Chromatograph Input Loop
*Run until outside of test parameter.

nSpike = 0


nNorm = 0
```

```
nTest = 0
DO WHILE MAX( nSpike, nNorm, nTest ) < 100
  nSpike = GCHigh()
  nNorm = GCTable( nSpike, 2.1)
  nTest = GCTest(nSpike, nNorm, "EC")
ENDDO
```

The Counting Loop

The FOR loop gets hauled out whenever a loop needs to run a specific number of times. This can be emulated with the DO WHILE, but the FOR is specifically designed for the task and executes more rapidly. The key part of the syntax is the unique FOR condition:

```
FOR <memvar> = <expN1> TO <expN2> [STEP <expN3>]
  <statements>
  [EXIT]
  [LOOP]
ENDFOR | NEXT
```

Translated, this reads: Continue looping FOR the value of <a memory variable> to increment from <starting value> TO <ending value> , in STEPs of <size of increment>. The code looks something like this:

```
FOR i = 1 TO 10
  nValue = IIF( nTotal/i > 100, nTotal, 0)
ENDFOR
```

Most of the time the counting is by addition: the progression is from a lower value to a higher value, however the loop can also go in the other direction:

```
FOR i = 10 TO 1 STEP -1
  nValue = IIF( nTotal/i > 100, nTotal, 0)
ENDFOR
```

In this case the optional STEP clause is used to indicate the subtraction. Otherwise STEP has a default value of 1. Although it's most common to use constants for the <expN1> and <expN2> values, they can also be any kind of expression, for example:

```
nCount = 1
FOR k = dStartDate TO dEndDate+365 STEP 7
```

```
    aWeekIncome[nCount] = WeekLook()
    nCount = nCount+1
  ENDFOR
```

The original Clipper FOR loop used the FOR / NEXT construction, and FoxPro accepts that variation. The native form, however, is FOR / ENDFOR.

The Table Loop

The only task of the SCAN loop is to scan a data table, traversing from top to bottom. This replaces the old DO WHILE construction:

```
DO WHILE NOT EOF()
  SKIP
ENDDO
```

In effect SCAN has the SKIP command built-in at the bottom of the loop, and executes 10 percent to 15 percent faster than the DO WHILE. It's by far the preferred way to move through a data table.

```
SCAN
 [<scope>]
 [FOR <expL1>]
 [WHILE <expL2>]
 [NOOPTIMIZE]
 [<statements>]
 [LOOP]
 [EXIT]
ENDSCAN
```

You should notice right away that SCAN has the hallmarks of a table operation command—SCOPE, FOR, WHILE—the data table filters that determine what records are included in the SCAN. Otherwise this looks and works like a normal loop.

An *extremely* common construction for the SCAN loop looks like this:

```
SELECT cus
IF SEEK( cus.cno, "inv")

  SELECT inv
  SCAN WHILE cus.cno = inv.cno
  IF inv.itotal > 500
```

```
      cAward = "We Have a Winner!"
    ENDIF
    ENDSCAN
  ENDIF
```

A SEEK, SEEK( ), or LOCATE is used to find something in a table, then SCAN is used to check the following records that still match the initial search. In this connection notice the use of the WHILE clause, as is customary in a table where the pointer is already located on the desired starting record.

Just to indicate the flexibility of a SCAN loop, here's an *untypical* construction:

```
SELECT cus
SET ORDER TO lastdate
SEEK dYearEnd
SCAN FOR cus.state = "CA" ;
     WHILE dYearEnd <= cus.lastdate ;
     REST
   IF cus.ono <> "1"
     nCustTotal = nCustTotal - cus.ytdpurch
   ELSE
     nCustTotal = nCustTotal + cus.ytdpurch
   ENDIF
ENDSCAN //cus.state = "CA"
```

This loop starts with the record pointer on the first record that matches the dYearEnd value, say 1/31/92. It then scans forward while that value is less than or equal to the last date of customer activity. However, it only includes those records of customers whose state is California.

SCAN loops are one of the most useful of all control structures. General table commands like SUM, TOTAL, and REPLACE are one-trick ponies compared to SCAN. It gives you the opportunity to work with a table on a record by record basis, inserting within the confines of the SCAN...ENDSCAN construction almost any kind of logic, table updating, and conversions.

Program Calls

The wording control structure isn't all that accurate for a program call, but it still fits. When you DO a program, or call a function (= <function>), you are most definitely changing program flow. Whether this amounts to invoking a simple subroutine, or an entire subsystem, program calls should be treated with some care.

In most cases a program call goes off to the called procedure or function, does some work there, then returns to the calling program. In the meantime, a lot can change. Not only is program control changed and channeled by program calls, but the entire environment of a program is often involved. Hence the concern for thinking about a program call as a special event.

With your common UDF, you probably don't need to be very concerned. But any call to a procedure or function that potentially changes table status or environmental settings should be at least highlighted—even in the code. For example:

```
IF cus.state = "CA"
  SELECT inv
  SEEK cus.ono
  IF inv.itotal > 1000
    *======UPDATE OFFICE=======>>
    DO OFFICEUP
  ENDIF
ENDIF
```

Or if there is a lot of setup and cleanup to be done:

```
*Setup for Test Codes Lookup
SELECT test
nTestPtr = RECNO()
cOldAlias = ALIAS()
cOldOrder = ORDER()
*========TEST CODE LOOKUP=====>>
DO TESTCODE
*<<============================
*Cleanup on return
SELECT (cOldAlias)
SET ORDER TO (cOldOrder)
GO nTestPtr
```

This makes it clear the program call is not to be taken lightly. If there are problems that occur later, it will be much easier to spot where they might be.

Menus

Menus are also control structures. They are the only structures that to some degree are under user control. The programmer decides what options should be offered in the menus, and the user chooses the options to do their work. This makes menus a critical element of the user interface *and* a critical element of the program flow.

As a control structure, menus most resemble program calls. In fact, that's largely what most menus do—offer a choice of program calls. You've probably heard the expression *menu tree*, the hierarchy of menu options with one menu choice leading to another menu, and so on. This is often the structure of a program from the user's point of view. However, FoxPro 2.0 added another dimension to menus with the Menu Builder. Menus are now a structure for programming in their own right. The file generated by the Menu Builder, an .MPR file, is much like a program file (.PRG), but more formally structured with well-defined segments for setup, cleanup and other program material, in addition to the code for the menu itself.

FoxPro now contains four generations of menuing commands—mostly an unfortunate legacy. Unless you are converting programs older than FoxPro 2.0, you probably should remain deliberately ignorant of details concerning any menu commands other than those used for the standard Windows menus of FoxPro. For the record, however, Table 8.2 lists the other menu approaches:

Table 8.2
Obsolete menu commands.

Command	Description
@ <row>,<col> PROMPT MENU TO <memvar> SET MESSAGE TO <row>	This is often called the "Lotus 1-2-3" menu approach—the single line of menu options at the top of the screen. There are no popup options. This style has one thing going for it—no READ is necessary. It can also provide a menu message explaining each option, a feature missing from the standard Windows menus.
MENU BAR <array1>, <expN1>MENU <expN2>,<array2>, <expN3>... READ MENU BAR TO <memvar1>, <memvar2> [SAVE]	This menu approach seemed to come out of nowhere, and is just as quickly returning. It has been totally obviated by the menu system in FoxPro 2.0 and 2.5.
@ <row>,<col> MENU <array>, <expN1>..[TITLE <expC>] [SHADOW] READ MENU TO <memvar> SAVE	This is a menu popup, similar to other @..GET popups.

The "real" FoxPro menu system, which is very complicated at the programming level, is covered in section III.

Screens and READs

Do you recall the old argument about giving kids calculators in elementary school? If they use them they will never learn how to do math in their head. It will stunt their intellectual growth. By analogy, there's a similar philosophical question about learning the "old fashioned" way of creating a data-entry screen. These days everybody uses the Screen Builder Power Tool. You move objects around the screen and the Screen Builder cranks out the code. Does this mean you should skip learning about the hand coded screen using the old @ SAY / GET construction? Or will this stunt your comprehension of programming? The same argument applies to the use of the Menu Builder Power Tool versus learning how to code menus.

This book comes down hard on the side of learning screen-related commands from the ground up, and conversely touches down only briefly on the menuing commands. The FoxPro menu system, its way of creating the standard Windows menus, is complex—to the point of being ugly. But it is also extremely repetitive. So much so, that even if you were to master all of its options, you'd still wind up copying code all over the place—so much of it is the same. That's why learning the Menu Builder thoroughly, with only a minimum of knowledge about the basic menu coding, is not only defensible but practical.

Screen work is something else. Whereas menus in FoxPro essentially all look and work the same, screens can be, often are, highly individualistic. They represent an almost infinite variety of processes, functions, and approaches. It's true, parts of screens can be "canned" through the Screen Builder, but large parts of them cannot. Furthermore, the most intricate and difficult elements of the user interface occur in screens. It's hard to make good design and coding decisions about these elements unless you are more or less intimately aware of the underlying commands. For these and other reasons, this book takes the view that learning screen command basics is worth the time, perhaps even vital, to achieving mastery of the user interface techniques available through the Screen Builder.

The Basic Surfaces

You will find some confusing terminology in FoxPro manuals: *Screen, windows, main window,* and *desktop* are used profusely and often seem interchangeable. They're not. Part of the confusion is historical. Until only five years ago or so, the Xbase language didn't do "windows." There was only one "screen," the normal display area of your monitor, and all commands used the word "screen" (such as SAVE SCREEN). These days, all Xbase products have elaborate windowing capabilities with dozens of commands like SAVE WINDOWS. FoxPro for Windows lives up to its name by making windows central to the whole user interface. Yet it's central Power Tool is called the *Screen* Builder, and the basic unit of construction is a *Screen* Set.

Perhaps recognizing that screen and windows were sometimes being confused, Fox threw in another term, which is emphasized in FoxPro for Windows: the desktop. Actually, it means almost the same as the old term screen—the entire area of your display without menus, windows, status bars, icons, tool bars or any other user interface paraphernalia. However, because this is a Windows program, there is always the basic FoxPro window frame. This is what is sometimes called in the manuals the main window.

One way to visualize the user interface is as the screen as a base or background, on top of which the other elements are placed.Some of the elements are movable (windows and Tool Bars) while others are fixed in position (menus and the status bar), although they all may be completely removed from the screen. Some programmers like to call these elements surfaces, as in *design surfaces*. Other programmers, and Microsoft, tend to call them *screen objects*. Whatever you choose to call them, it's important to keep their spatial and figurative relationships in mind. There is a definite hierarchy, running from bottom to top in spatial terms:

1. **Windows desktop**—The "bare" Microsoft Windows screen with no programs or desktop shell.
2. **Program Manager/other desktop**—Most people run Program Manager, Norton Desktop for Windows, or another screen "shell" on top of the basic Windows screen.
3. **FoxPro for Windows main window**—When FoxPro is started, it creates its own program window, that can cover the entire screen or be minimized inside of the desktop.

4. **FoxPro desktop or screen**—The area inside the main FoxPro window is what's available to the programmer for modification. All elements, including menus and status bar are optional.
5. **Windows, dialog boxes, tool bars**—Although confined to the main FoxPro window, the number, placement and depth of other windows and dialog boxes is unlimited, up to and through the point of visual chaos.

Most of these elements float on the screen surface, and can be layered one on top of the other. This is particularly true of FoxPro windows, which have a whole repertoire of commands and functions to manage their position in a stack of windows.

Relative Screen Position

One of the most compelling reasons for using the Screen Builder in FoxPro is its ability to automatically generate the coordinates of screen positioning in a GUI environment. Those of you who have worked with screens in the DOS environment are in for a jolt. In DOS the screen is considered to be twenty-four lines high and eighty characters wide. Position on the screen is simply stated as a row and column coordinate—2,30 for instance being row two, column thirty. With a little practice it's quite possible to place objects in this coordinate system simply by guestimate.

The FoxPro for Windows environment is different. Instead of the uniform characters of DOS, in Windows each font generates its own height, width and justification—for TrueType fonts this means anything within the entire scalable range of point sizes. So one line could be 70 points high (but also include some 20-point characters), and others 8 points high. Some fonts are monospaced, but most of them have unique spacing characteristics, which means in one font the word *antidisestablishmentarianism* is 4 inches long and in another font 2.5 inches long. This flexibility presents some problems for accurate screen positioning.

Most GUI systems use screen *pixels* as the coordinate measurement. However, as a concession to compatibility with the DOS coordinate system, FoxPro still uses a <row,column> format, but the rows and columns can be expressed as fractions significant to the nearest thousandth—2.826,20.394. The DOS row, column coordinates loosely map to the FoxPro screen. A window defined from 0,0 to 35,80 almost covers the screen area, depending on the current window font. However, it might require 0,0 to 35.15,79.955 to make a completely full-screen window. Try figuring these in your head.

The Screen Builder is very good at laying out a "permanent" screen that doesn't have any physical changes during its use. But it's not uncommon for screen design to call for modification of screen layout while the program is running. Sometimes these screen changes are subtle, sometimes dramatic. Usually it requires a combination of putting on screen elements, and also taking them off. This random putting and taking is almost impossible to orchestrate on the Screen Builder's design surface. It's usually done "behind the scenes" with sequences of manually coded commands. Unfortunately, positioning these individual commands will drive you crazy. Their behavior is so dependent on the fonts, that it's extremely difficult to predict where they will take effect. The only "method" is trial and error, which works, but is very time consuming.

Having said all of this about the difficulties of manually positioning screen elements in FoxPro, let's plunge into the most basic commands that require screen positions.

The Basic SAY

One might say this is mother of all screen elements. @..SAY puts text on the screen. In its simplest form, it reads: AT (@) this specific row and column SAY (display) the following text. Of course, the complete syntax is a bit more involved:

```
@ <row, column> SAY <expr>
     [FUNCTION <expC1>]
     [PICTURE <expC2>]
     [SIZE <expN1>, <expN2>]
     [FONT <expC3>[, <expN3]]
     [STYLE <expC4>]
     [COLOR SCHEME <expN4> | COLOR <color pair list>]
```

But the task remains the same: @..SAY positions text, such as prompts, titles, and descriptions on the screen. The rest of the clauses merely modify the appearance of that text. Here are some basic samples:

```
@ 10,10 SAY "Now is the time for all good persons to come to."
@ 10,10 SAY 2 + 2
```

```
@ 10,10 SAY cLastName
@ 10,10+LEN(cLastName) SAY "Needs to pay "+STR(nDueAmount)
@ 10,10 SAY TRIM(customer.lastname)+", "+customer.firstname
```

You'll notice that @..SAY can display any data type, even the results of calculations. It just can't display mixed data types. The display expression must be all of one type, which may require conversion, as in the fourth example line. @..SAY can be used with a wide variety of expressions, in fact, all of them: fields, calculations, functions, and constants.

The FUNCTION and PICTURE clauses you may recognize from the chapter on the Report Writer. Since @..SAY shares most of these options with @..GET, the tables of FUNCTIONs and PICTUREs are in that topic.

By default, @..SAY displays in the current screen font, colors, and style. All of these can be modified.

The @..SAY is a comparatively simple screen element. Compared to what? Compared to the next topic, one of the most important user interface *and* data management elements in FoxPro, the @..GET.

The Anatomy of a GET

Data entry is not simple. Paste that thought into your brain's clipboard for a moment, and take a look at the diagram below of FoxPro's main tool for data entry—the @ GET.

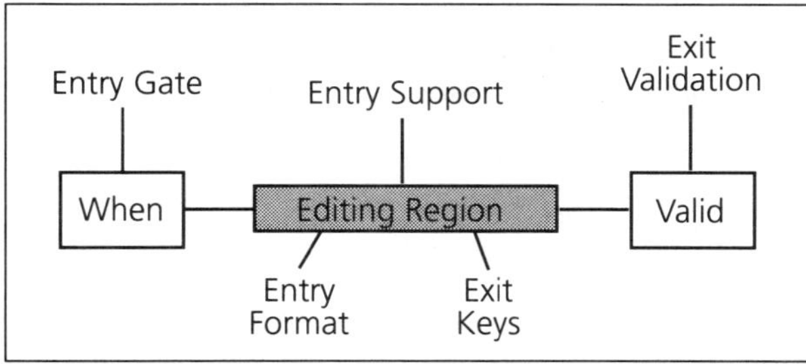

Figure 8.6
Anatomy of a GET.

The act of typing each item of data into a computer is like a little drama. It has a beginning, a middle, and an end. It is subject to almost infinite variation, but the goal remains the felicitous entry of valid information. The job of checking and supporting data entry may begin before a single key is struck, and may end only when all of the entry meets an appropriate validation. At least this is how FoxPro is structured to handle the process.

The syntax for a GET is elaborate:

```
@ <row, column> GET <memvar> | <field>
     [FUNCTION <expC1>]
     [PICTURE <expC2>]
     [FONT <expC3>[, <expN1>]]
     [STYLE <expC4>]
     [DEFAULT <expr1>]
     [ENABLE | DISABLE]
     [MESSAGE <expC5>]
     [[OPEN] WINDOW <window name>]
     [RANGE [<expr2>] [, <expr3>]]
     [SIZE <expN2>, <expN3>]
     [VALID <expL1> | <expN4> [ERROR <expC6>]]
     [WHEN <expL2>]
     [COLOR SCHEME <expN5> | COLOR <color pair list>
```

This syntax has been evolving for over a decade, like most of the Xbase language, and Fox's role has been large. The original syntax of a GET in dBase II was:

```
@ <coordinates> GET <exp> PICTURE <format>
```

Even though most programmers are starting to use the Screen Builder to create their GETs without ever dirtying their fingers with much of the syntax, a thorough knowledge of the data entry process—and how it relates to all forms of the GET—is vital.

The @..GET at it's simplest is a screen element designed to take user entry, and place it into either a variable or a table field:

```
@ 10,10 GET cLastName                && variable
@ 10,10 GET customer.lastname        && field READ
```

The READ normally accompanies GETs, and is required to activate them for entry. Technically, this is all that's required to build a data-entry screen. But this is hardly the end of the story. For just a moment, put yourself in the shoes of a data entry person, about to start typing in a single GET field. You're supposed to enter a specific piece of information, keystroke by keystroke. No typos. No incorrect data. And do it as fast as possible, because you have 4,357 more entries to make, before noon.

Now, get back into your own shoes, and observe the nervous data-entry person who knows absolutely nothing about the data being entered, but has to go like heck to finish 4,357 entries before noon. And you wonder just how much of the data entered is accurate.

This is the basic scenario for data entry, on each and every item. It's also why good screen design begins with a series of decisions about how to handle entry (and edit) at the level of the individual GET.

Entry Gate

The first decision on a GET field is: "When is this open for entry?" This is sometimes called the precondition, because it tests for specific conditions before allowing entry. The GET clause for the precondition is [WHEN <expL2>]. For example, say you wanted to not allow any entry into a salary editing region, unless the data-entry person had a high enough security clearance. To do this, somewhere along the way the data-entry person has logged in (probably with a password), and a variable with a security level has been initialized: nSecurity1 = 4. Then you test for this condition in the GET:

```
@ 10,10 GET nTotSalary WHEN nSecurity1 >= 4
```

Another example involves any situation where entry into a previous GET is a precondition for entry into another GET. It might look like this:

```
@ 10,10 GET cSocialSec && Social Security Number
@ 11,10 GET cLastName WHEN NOT EMPTY( cSocialSec )
```

If the precondition in the WHEN is not met, the user is not able to move into the GET editing region, either with the keyboard or the mouse. In all other respects, however, the region looks the same and the user is given no clue as to its condition, or why they may have failed the precondition. If you're building a user-friendly, or at least user-considerate screen, you might want to try a UDF in the WHEN clause to put up a message, something like this:

```
@ 10,10 GET cSocialSec && Social Security Number
@ 11,10 GET cLastName WHEN SSNCheck()
...
FUNCTION SSNCheck
IF EMPTY( cSocialSec )
  WAIT "Your name can't be entered without a ";
  Social Security Number." WINDOW NOWAIT
```

```
  RETURN .f.
ELSE
  RETURN .t.
ENDIF
```

There is another "gate keeper" approach, which is a combination of the [ENABLE | DISABLE] clause of the @..GET and the SHOW GET command. Using the social security number example from above, this approach looks like this:

```
@ 10,10 GET cSocialSec
@ 11,10 GET cLastName DISABLE
```

The advantage to the DISABLE is that FoxPro supports a different color display for disabled editing regions. By default, the color is usually something that makes the area barely visible. This makes it easy for the user to see what is available for entry, besides not being able to move into the editing region. The "catch," however, is how to ENABLE the editing region. Although this is jumping ahead just a bit, the usual approach is through a UDF in the VALID clause of a *related* GET:

```
@ 10,10 GET cSocialSec VALID ShowName()
@ 11,10 GET cLastName DISABLE
...
FUNCTION ShowName
  IF NOT EMPTY( cSocialSec ) AND nSecurity1 >= 4
    SHOW GET cLastName ENABLE
  ENDIF
RETURN .t.
```

The SHOW GET used in the example above has a relatively simple syntax:

```
SHOW GET <var>
     [, <expN1> [PROMPT <expC>]]
     [ENABLE | DISABLE]
     [LEVEL <expN2>]
     [COLOR SCHEME <expN3> | COLOR <color pair list>]
```

The <var> is the name of the variable to be shown. FoxPro knows when you type in cLastName for the variable that it indeed has an active variable CLASTNAME in its list. (If it doesn't, you'll get an error message.) Although SHOW GET is mostly associated with the Screen Builder (the <expN1>, PROMPT, LEVEL clauses make most sense in that context), don't get into the rut of thinking that's the only place to use it.

Entry Format

The user is now past the entry gate, the WHEN or DISABLE clause, and the cursor is in the editing region of the GET, ready to type. Is this free-form entry? If the data type is character, it might be. But often, you may want to have data entered using the same format—standardization of dates, or phone numbers that look like (123) 456-7890, and so forth. This is the territory of the entry format, or sometimes called the entry *mask*. In effect you specify the template for the edit region to which the data entry must conform.

You may recall from the section on the Report Writer that you had a number of ways of specifying how data would look, its format, when printing. The formatting options for @..GET and @..SAY are similar, there's just more of them. They fall into two groups, FUNCTION formats, and PICTURE formats. The FUNCTION options affect the entire editing region, and in fact they are used by Microsoft to create the suite of controls that are so crucial to the FoxPro interface. The PICTURE options work on a character-by-character basis, and are highly specific.

The FoxPro manuals and help system do a reasonable job of explaining and outlining the FUNCTION and PICTURE options. Rather than repeat all of that here, the following Tables 8.3 and 8.4 emphasize the context of use for each of the options. Notice that all of the FUNCTION options can be used in the PICTURE clause if preceded by the @. Both forms are used in the examples, however PICTURE is often more compact and just as clear, especially when both function and picture options are being used.

Table 8.3
Format functions.

Option	Code	Output and Example

Alpha only	A	Allows only alpha characters. There are a few data entries that must be letters only, state abbreviations for example.
		`@ 1,20 GET cState FUNCTION "A"`
		`@ 1,20 GET cState PICTURE "@A"`

(continued)

Upper case only — !

Converts all alpha characters to uppercase (all caps). In some database schemes all character data is stored in uppercase for searching purposes (noncase-sensitive searching). In FoxPro this is not necessary since fields can be indexed with the UPPER( ) function to accomplish the same thing. However some fields, again like state abbreviations might require uppercase only.

```
@ 2,20 GET cState FUNCTION "!A"
@ 2,20 GET cState PICTURE "@!A"
```

Display mask only — R

This format function allows you to create an entry mask (same as a PICTURE template) such as:

```
@ 3,20 GET cWphone FUNCTION "R(###)###-
#### |####"
@ 3,20 GET cWphone PICTURE "@R (###)###-
####|####"
```

Also, the mask characters are *not* stored to the variable or field, only the characters or numbers actually entered. This is sometimes used to save disk storage space. However, it also makes casual browsing of data more difficult. For instance, reading phone numbers like 61234356542345, which displayed under program control with the R option would be (612) 343-5654 x 2345.

Trim all — T

Removes all leading and trailing blank spaces, like the ALLTRIM() function. This option makes little sense for input, except where the variable is going to be immediately concatenated with other variables. More typically this is used with the @ SAY.

```
@ 4,20 SAY cus.lastname FUNCTION "T"
@ 4,20 SAY cus.lastname PICTURE "@T"
```

Multiple list — M

Once upon a time, this little option was very handy. You create a comma delimited list of acceptable values (character only), something like this:

```
@ 5,20 GET cCusType FUNCTION "M
Active,Inactive,; Deadbeat,Prospective?
```

If the variable or field is not initialized to one of the values, the first value becomes the default. Users then can press **Spacebar** or enter the first letter of values to move between values, and press **Enter** to select one. However, in this day and age of popup everything the M function is stylistically something of a throwback, or at least inconsistent.

Select edit region	K	This function makes sense only with GETs. It automatically selects the editing region, just as if you'd marked a selection with the mouse or keyboard. Then, like other selected areas, if you begin entering something different, the original selection is immediately cleared. However if you use the Arrow keys, normal (nondestructive) editing can also be done.
		`@ 6,20 GET dStartDate FUNCTION "KD"`
		`@ 6,20 GET dStartDate PICTURE "@KD"`
		One interesting side effect of using this option is that a selected editing region is automatically set to a different color (usually red or something bright). This acts like a very big cursor, and can visually help the user identify where they are in the screen.

Scroll edit region	S	It often happens in crowded screens that a long text field (or variable) may not fit. By using this scroll format, you can set the length of the editing region to be displayed and FoxPro allows the user to scroll (right) to see the remainder. This can be very helpful, as long as the user is aware this capability is available.
		`@ 7,20 GET cComment FUNCTION "S40"`
		`@ 7,20 GET cComment PICTURE "@S40"`

Right align text	J	Right justifies data in the editing region.
		`@ 8,20 GET cVar FUNCTION "J"`
		`@ 8,20 GET cVar PICTURE "@J"`

Center text	I	Centers data in the editing region. For example if a variable (cVar) contains `"        Dog"` then `@ 9,20 SAY cVar FUNCTION "I"` displays `" Dog "`

Left justify text	B	Left justifies data in the editing region.
		`@ 10,20 GET cVar FUNCTION "B"`
		`@ 10,20 GET cVar PICTURE "@B"`

(Negative)	(	Negative numbers are placed in parentheses. This is often used in accounting procedures. The Report Writer also supports printing DB and CR (debit and credit) following numbers, but not in the GET/SAY.
		`@ 11,20 GET nProfit FUNCTION "("`
		`@ 11,20 GET nProfit PICTURE "@("`

(continued)

Edit date	D	Edits a field or variable as a date in current date format. This is the automatic mask for dates—mm/dd/yy. It assures that only legitimate dates are entered.
		`@ 12,20 GET dDay FUNCTION "D"`
		`@ 12,20 GET dDay PICTURE "@D"`

British date	E	Edit field or variable in European date format—dd/mm/yy.
		`@ 13,20 GET dEuroDay FUNCTION "E"`
		`@ 13,20 GET dEuroDay PICTURE "@E"`

Leading zeros	L	Displays leading zeros before numbers. The zeros will not be stored with the variable or field. For example, if nCount = 9 is put into `@ 14,20 SAY nCount FUNCTION "L"` the output is "0000000009," following the default value of ten significant digits to the left of the decimal. About the only use for this option is in check printing.

Currency format	$	Displays a number in currency format. This also does not store with the variable or field. The $ is always flush right with the last number, which means that if the last number is at the left hand edge of the edit region, the $ does not display, hence this option won't work with the "L" option or with SET CURRENCY LEFT.
		`@ 15,20 GET nTotalPay FUNCTION "$"`
		`@ 15,20 GET nTotalPay PICTURE "@$"`

Scientific notation	^	Displays numbers in scientific notation, such as 12.5E7.
		`@ 16,20 SAY nEmc2 FUNCTION "^"`
		`@ 16,20 SAY nEmc2 PICTURE "@^"`

Table 8.4
PICTURE template codes.

Code	Description and Example
A	Allows only alphabetic characters. Same effect as the "A" function, but applied to individual entry positions. If all characters should be alpha, then the function should be used instead. Here's an example of a mixed template with "A:" `@ 1,20 GET cPartId PICTURE "AAA9999A"`

	This allows only input like "COM1234B."
L	Allows logical data entry only, meaning that only T / t, F / f, Y / y, or N / n are accepted. All valid entries are converted to .t. or .f. for storing in the variable or field. This is only for entries of width 1. This format has largely been replaced by control buttons. `@ 2,20 GET nTorF PICTURE "L"`
N	Allows letters and digits only, meaning it excludes diacritical marks, and things like #$%. It can be used only with character data. `@ 3,20 GET nControl PICTURE "NNN"`
X	Allows any character whatsoever. So why bother? It simply describes how wide the editing region should be, up to the length of the variable or field being edited. In other words it can create an editing region shorter than the data, but not longer. `@ 4,20 GET nRandom PICTURE "XXXXXXXX"`
Y	Allows Y,y, N,n only, with y and n converted to uppercase. This is often used as the equivalent of a logical entry. `@ 5,20 GET nYorN PICTURE "Y"`
9	With character data, allows only numeric entry. With numeric data, allows all numbers and signs. `@ 6,20 GET nWholeAmt PICTURE "999999"` For example: 345432
#	Allows numbers (digits), blanks, and signs. This is often mixed with the "9" option to control entry of numeric values. `@ 7,20 GET nTimeOut PICTURE "####.9"` For example: - 324.8
!	Converts lowercase letters to uppercase. Again, this works on a character by character basis, and is most useful in a "mixed" template. Otherwise the function @! should be used to convert all characters. `@ 8,20 GET cCpuId PICTURE "!!!999"` For example: AMD286
$	Displays current currency symbol. The template option designates the exact placement for the currency symbol. The currency function @$ always places the symbol flush to the left number. `@ 9,20 GET nBigBucks PICTURE "$ ###,999,999"`
*	Displays asterisks in front of numeric values. This is another check writing option. `@ 10,20 GET nAmount PICTURE "$*9,999.99"`

(continued)

For example: $*****2,300.34

. Specifies the decimal point (numeric data only).

```
@ 11,20 GET nTiming PICTURE "###.99"
```

For example: -99.99

, Comma separation for digits left of decimal point (numeric data only).

```
@ 12,20 GET nTotalPay PICTURE "@$ 999,999"
```

For example: $300,000

Entry Support

Not all of the GET editing region activity is purely preventative. Give the users a break. Create data entry and edit conditions that support them, as well as check on them. Entry support is a big issue. Much of the innovation behind GUIs has been to help the user with entering things into the computer, or simply telling it what to do. If you run down the list of elements that are aimed at user input, you'll probably find many of them familiar: popup lists, text editing regions, check boxes, radio buttons, icon buttons, tool bars, and context sensitive help.

In FoxPro, all of these things are part of the @..GET (or slight variations of it). For the purposes of description, the support elements can be put into three categories.

1. Control and selection support: such as popups and lists.
2. Information on demand, support by key or icon access.
3. Default conditions support.

Control and Selection Support

One of the key tenets of a good user interface is that user options should be clear and easy to choose. This applies to both the entry of data, and the programmatic choices like those of menus. FoxPro follows through on this tenet with the so called *controls*, variations of the @..GET that provide data entry and selection support (such as lists), or on-screen menu-like options (such as push buttons), or frequently both. Most of these radically change the appearance of the @..GET. The standard editing region is replaced by a variety of boxes, icons, popups, and so forth. Table 8.5 lists the options:

Table 8.5
@..GET control and selection elements.

Type of input Element	Basic Command
Standard editing regions	@..GET
Text editing regions	@..EDIT
Push buttons	@..GET FUNCTION *
Picture push buttons	@..GET FUNCTION *B
Radio buttons	@..GET FUNCTION *R
Check boxes	@..GET FUNCTION *C
Invisible buttons	@..GET FUNCTION *I
Popup lists	@..GET FUNCTION ^
Lists	@..GET FUNCTION &
Spinners	@..GET SPINNER

Most of these are covered in detail Section III.

Information on Demand

Not all of the support needs to have a direct effect on the entry or editing. Users also need to have contextual information that helps them decide what to enter and how to enter it. However, for any data-entry screen with more than a handful of editing regions, it's impossible to display all of the relevant information on the screen at the same time. Thus arises the need for *information and support on demand*. In FoxPro, there are three main avenues of approach, context sensitive help, On Key Labels (OKLs), and popup information.

The built-in FoxPro help system is always available through the system menu, or by pressing **F1**. You can also take it several steps further by modifying its contents, and linking the help to individual GETs—a very specific context sensitive help.

OKLs, or On Key Labels, are another major topic and user-interface issue. Even in a visual and mouse-oriented environment like Windows, the use of function keys and other key combinations is still an important way to allow users to call up information and program functions on demand.

The final techniques for information on demand are based on using screen elements that can be used simultaneously with data entry.

Default Conditions

In many instances the simplest support you can give a user is to insert a default value into the editing region. A most obvious example is to put the current date into a date region that's likely to use the current date. All this requires is to "initialize" the GET variable before the user goes into the editing region. You can do this before the screen is displayed, with the DEFAULT clause, or change the values during entry or edit in a VALID function, and use SHOW GET to update the display.

```
dToday  =  DATE()
@ 10,30  GET  dToday  PICTURE   @D
```

The [DEFAULT <expr1>] clause of the @..GET creates a variable of the name specified as the GET variable, and assigns it the value of <expr1>. This is a compact and easily understood approach. However, if the variable already exists, DEFAULT does *not* reset the value.

```
@ 10,30  GET  dToday  PICTURE   @D   DEFAULT  DATE()
```

One of the optional GET clauses, [MESSAGE <expC5>], allows you to display a descriptive message for each GET. In FoxPro, the message appears in the status bar at the bottom of the screen. This is an unobtrusive and efficient way to help users understand where they are in the screen, what the expected entry values may be, and other keystroke options available at that point. For example:

```
@ 10,20  GET  nTotal  PICTURE   ##,###   ;
  MESSAGE  Enter  the  total  salary  in  thousands.
```

```
@ 11,20 GET nTax PICTURE "##.##%" ;
 MESSAGE "Enter tax percent or <F2> for tax table."
```

Exit Keys

During the time that a user is in the editing region, FoxPro provides no direct way of monitoring the exact keystrokes being used. There are ways to get around this, but most of them are very slow and usually unnecessary. For the most part you rely on the editing format, default values, and entry support to guide the user correctly. However, at the point where a user exits the editing region, the keystroke(s) used may be much more important. Did the user update anything? Do they want to leave the region without change? Are they done editing? Table 8. 6 lists the valid exit keys.

Table 8.6
Valid exit keys.

Tab, Shift-Tab	Move between editing regions *without* activating VALIDs.
Enter, Tab	Depending on the status of SET CONFIRM, exits a region and triggers a VALID check. (SET CONFIRM ON requires an **Enter** or **Tab** to exit an editing region.)
Right Arrow, Left Arrow	If at the beginning or end of an editing region, exits and triggers a VALID.
Up Arrow, Down Arrow	Moves forward or backward one editing region and triggers a VALID.
PgUp, PgDn	Signals an end to the editing session for a standard READ. With a READ CYCLE these keys have no effect.
Ctrl-S	Signals a "quit editing without saving."
Ctrl-W	Signals a "quit editing and save."
Esc	Signals a "quit editing without saving."

The exit keys are a transition between editing (or just being in the editing region) and the exit validation routines. Depending on what the user was doing in the region, you may need to inspect the exit key and decide what if any response is necessary. Typically this is done in a UDF.

Exit Validation

Traditionally, this has been one of the most important elements of data entry. Exit validation means checking the user's entry as they leave the editing region (via the exit keys mentioned above). The VALID clause, introduced by the Clipper compiler in 1987, has been the inspiration for more UDFs than any other aspect of the Xbase language. It still plays a very big role in the FoxPro Screen Builder.

The syntax for a VALID is fairly simple:

```
[VALID <expL1> | <expN4> [ERROR <expC6>]]
```

You have two options for the type of valid expression, one logical, the other numeric. If either of these options produces a false (.f.) result, then you have the option of displaying an error message to the user through the ERROR <expC6> clause. That appears to be all of it. But in fact the VALID has at least three potent functions: error trapping (obviously), user support, and further processing.

VALID: Error Trapping

Users make mistakes. This is known. User's make many mistakes in data entry. This is a given. It's your responsibility (to your data, and to the user) to catch—*trap*—as many mistakes as you can. Some of this trapping may be very simple, like trying to catch typos or forcing an entry. Other trapping can be extremely complex, involving table lookups, and calculations. The VALID clause allows for all cases.

There are many kinds of error trapping that can be done without leaving the GET line. Any logical condition (the <exprL1>, a logical expression to use Fox's terminology) is fair game, as long as it feeds a .t. or .f. to the VALID. The first example traps for an empty social security number—it's a required entry. The second example checks to make sure a starting date is not pre-dated.

```
@ 10,20 GET nSocSec PICTURE "999-99-9999" ;
      VALID IIF(EMPTY(nSocSec),.f.,.t.) ;
      ERROR "Your social security number must be entered."
@ 10,20 GET dStartDate PICTURE "@D" VALID dStartDate <= DATE()
```

FoxPro also allows a numerical expression <exprN2> to be returned to the VALID. If the expression returns 0, it is interpreted as a false (.f.). Any other number is interpreted as the number of entry regions to move forward or backward. This feature was added a few years ago to allow programmers to move the entry point around a screen in response to an entry. It is now completely obsolete. The numbering system falls apart as soon as you introduce any new GETs, plus it's hard to follow. Use the approach you see in the Screen Builder chapters instead.

When the trapping gets tough, it's time to haul out the UDFs. Inside the confines of a function you can do almost anything, literally. In an error trapping situation, a validation function typically goes through one or more conditions, possibly does lookups in tables, and then generally informs the user if there's a problem. Of course, there are a million and one variations, but here's a simple example:

```
*Create a counter for number of failed pass code attempts
nPassCount = 0
*Enter pass code
@ 10,20 GET cPassCode ;
  PICTURE "!!99AA" ;
  VALID PassLook( cPassCode ) ;
  ERROR "Incorrect code entry. You have one more try."

...

FUNCTION PassLook
PARAMETER cPass

PRIVATE is_OK, cPart1, cPart2, cPart3, nPassCount
is_OK = .t.
nPassCount=1

* Break out each component of the code
cPart1 = SUBSTR( cPass, 1, 2)
cPart2 = SUBSTR( cPass, 3, 2)
cPart3 = SUBSTR( cPass, 5, 2)

*Test each of the components. This is a cascade if, so if
*one proves false, the subsequent tests are skipped.
```

```
is_OK = IIF( cPart1 $ "AA BB CC DD", .t., .f.)
IF is_OK
  is_OK = IIF( BETWEEN( VAL(cPart2), 10, 50), .t., .f.)
  IF is_OK
    is_OK = IIF( cPart3 = "XX", .t., .f.)
  ENDIF
ENDIF
nPassCount = nPassCount + 1 && increment pass counter
IF nPassCount = 3 && blow the user off.
  QUIT
ENDIF

RETURN ( is_ok )
*
```

VALID: User Support

The line between error trapping and user support can be very thin. There are many cases where you may want to allow the user to make an entry, and only if it is wrong, bring in some machinery to support them. Code entry is a typical example.

Most applications require users to enter a number of codes (such as codes for type of parts, category of people, and job codes). Typically, codes are ugly, unmemorable strings, like AKP03892L3. Users generally can't be assumed to know all of the codes. On the other hand, maybe you can't assume they don't know any. In some cases, they may actually learn the codes and find it much quicker to type them in. In these cases, you should allow the user the ability to enter a code on their own. Only if the code is wrong, or the user signals they don't know the code, do you intervene with some kind of support. Here's how you might set that up:

```
@ 10,20 GET cPartCode PICTURE "@R !!!99" ;
 VALID PartCode()
...

FUNCTION PartCode

PRIVATE cOldAlias
cOldAlias = ALIAS()

IF LASTKEY()=13 AND EMPTY( cPartCode ) && User wants help
```

```
    * Do a BROWSE "pick list?
    SELECT par
    BROWSE FIELDS partcode, description, price, location ;
      TITLE "Highlight a code and use <Ctrl>W to select" ;
      NOAPPEND NODELETE NOMODIFY LAST
    * Put selection into the GET variable
    cPartCode = par.partcod?
  ELSE         && Entry was made
    * Look it up
    IF NOT SEEK( cPartCode, "PAR" ) && Couldn't find it
      * Do a BROWSE "pick list?
      SELECT par
      BROWSE FIELDS partcode, description, price, location ;
        TITLE "Highlight a code and use <Ctrl>W to select" ;
        NOAPPEND, NODELETE, NOMODIFY LAST
      * Put selection into the GET variable
      cPartCode = par.partcod?
    ENDIF
  ENDIF
  SELECT ( cOldAlias ) && Back to original table
  RETURN .t.
  *
```

This is *far* from the last word on handling codes entry. But this example should give you some of the flavor of using a UDF to help support data entry. By providing pick lists, further description, perhaps intermediate entries leading to a selection, you can help the user make a correct entry, or no entry at all.

VALID: Further Processing

It often happens during the course of entry or edit that processing is waiting on the users entry. Let's say that after the user has entered their birth date, a sequence of calculations take place and a data table should be updated. Yet there is more editing to be done, and you don't want the user to leave the current screen. This is when you'd use the VALID and a UDF to do further processing. Here's the example:

```
@ 10,20 GET dBirthDate PICTURE "@D" VALID BirthCalc( dBirthDate
)
...
FUNCTION BirthCalc
```

```
PARAMETER dBd

PRIVATE nAge, cLevel, nLevel, nFee

*Calculate person's age.
nAge = (DATE() - dBd)/365

*Look up their age group.
DO CASE
CASE nAge <= 22
  cLevel = "Junior"
  nLevel = 5
CASE nAge <= 35
  cLevel = "Young Adult"
  nLevel = 4
CASE nAge <= 60
  cLevel = "Mature Adult"
  nLevel = 3
CASE nAge <= 75
  cLevel = "Senior"
  nLevel = 2
OTHERWISE
  cLevel = "Ancient"
  nLevel = 1
ENDCASE

*Calculate the fee level.
* (Age level x fee x twice a year)
nFee = nLevel * 10.95 * 2

*Update the Fee Table.
cOldAlias = ALIAS() && save current alias
SELECT fee
REPLACE Fee.age WITH nAge,;
  Fee.group WITH cLevel,;
  Fee.feetype WITH nLevel,;
  Fee.feeamt WITH nFee

* Return to original table
SELECT ( cOldAlias )

RETURN .t.
*
```

As a point of fact, whenever you call a UDF from a VALID, it can do almost anything—provided, of course, that you don't mess up the original calling program. Whole subsystems can be opened, if necessary. The amount of processing and updating you do is probably limited only by the patience of the user, who is waiting to get on with data entry.

Using RANGE Validation

The RANGE clause historically preceded the VALID and for a time was the only "in-line" method for doing post-edit validation. However, RANGE is limited to single-character alpha entries A through Z, numerics, and dates—a rather small range of validation. The syntax is simple, and so are some examples:

```
[RANGE [<expr2>] [, <expr3>]]
```

<expr2> is the low value in the range, <expr3> the high value. The range is automatically considered continuous as unit integers (1,2,3..., days, ASCII character values).

```
@ 10,20 GET nAge RANGE 22,110
@ 11,20 GET cCode RANGE “A”,"F”
@ 12,20 GET dBirth RANGE {1/1/1873},{1/1/1972}
```

Like a lot of FoxPro commands and options, this sort of range validation can be done other ways. But the RANGE option has the advantage of being explicit in its task, which makes it easy to understand (self documenting), and requires no calls to external functions—which executes faster. For this kind of validation, try to use RANGE first, and go to more elaborate UDFs only if necessary.

Cosmetics

Appearances, certainly aren't the most important part of data entry. Yet, for experienced programmers this aspect frequently becomes one of the most time-consuming parts of their work.

The plain and simple @..GET takes on its default visual attributes from the current window or screen settings. For lots of reasons, however, you may want to enhance the display by changing fonts, font style, or the color of the editing region. That's what these three clauses of the GET do:

```
[FONT <expC3>[, <expN1>]]
```

```
[STYLE <expC4>]
[COLOR SCHEME <expN5> | COLOR <color pair list>]
```

The FONT clause presumes you know what fonts are available and what type size you need. It reads FONT <official font name>, <valid font size>. If you know that you want the TrueType font Arial at 16 points, then your entry would look like this:

```
@ 10,20 GET cPartName PICTURE "@!" FONT "Arial",16
```

If you wish, you can also add one of the following style codes:

- **B**—Bold
- **I**—Italic
- **N**—Normal
- **O**—Outline
- **Q**—Opaque
- **S**—Shadow
- **-**—Strikeout
- **T**—Transparent
- **U**—Underline

Such as in:

```
@ 10,20 GET cPartName ;
 PICTURE "@!" ;
 FONT "Arial",16 ;
 STYLE "BI"
```

Finally, you can specify the color of the editing region, both as it appears for display and as it appears when someone is editing in it:

```
@ 10,20 GET cPartName ;
 PICTURE "@!" ;
 FONT "Arial",16 ;
 STYLE "BI" ;
 COLOR W+/BG,GR+/B
```

Hard coding the cosmetic aspects of a GET is hard work. These days most people do it through the automatic facilities of the Screen Builder. You point to a font from the font list, and the Screen Builder inserts the code.

Many pages ago, this segment led off with "Data entry is not simple." At least it's not simple if you're aiming at professional standards. Because data entry is so important to a database application, and because the users of an application spend so much time with data entry, it's worth the effort to consider the details of validation and user support. Very often, this is the difference between a successful and unsuccessful application.

End with a Clean Screen

The previous topics filled the screen with titles, descriptions, and editing regions. It's time to clean up. All of the following commands work the same in user-defined windows as they do in the FoxPro desktop.

If you expect to return to a screen and would like to restore it to a previous state, you can use the following command:

```
SAVE SCREEN [ TO <memvar> ]
RESTORE SCREEN [ FROM <memvar> ]
```

For example:

```
SAVE SCREEN TO sMainScreen
...
RESTORE SCREEN FROM sMainScreen
```

This command saves the entire screen, which takes anywhere from 4 to 24K of memory—don't get carried away with using SAVE SCREEN.

There is a command for saving user-defined windows, SAVE WINDOW, but this does not save the image in the window, only the window definition.

```
CLEAR
```

It's simple, direct, and effective. This clears the entire screen. However, if you want to be a little more selective on what gets cleared, you can use one of these:

```
@ <row,col> CLEAR
@ 10,00 CLEAR
```

This wipes out the screen display of a single row, beginning with the column specified to the end of the screen.

```
@ <row,col> CLEAR TO <row,col>
@ 10,30 CLEAR TO 20,50
```

This clears out a rectangular area of the coordinates you specify—the first <row,col> are the upper left corner, the second <row,col> are the lower right corner.

Creating screens the old fashioned way frequently requires some trial and error to get correct placements, but there's nothing mysterious about it. Here's a brief example of a "hand coded" screen:

```
CLEAR
@ 05,20 SAY "This is an example of setting the screen" COLOR
GR+/B
@ 06,20 SAY "using only the most primitive methods."   COLOR
GR+/B

*> Set the table
SELECT customer
SET ORDER TO fullname          && Last+first+mid

*> Get the user's full name
cFirst = SPACE(15)
cMid   = SPACE(20)
cLast  = SPACE(30)

@ 10,20 SAY "PLEASE ENTER YOUR FULL NAME BELOW:"
@ 12,20 SAY " First Name: "
@ 12,32 GET cFirst PICTURE "@K!T" ;
       VALID NOT EMPTY(cFirst);
       MESSAGE "A first name is required."
@ 13,20 SAY "Middle Name: " GET cMid   PICTURE "@K!T"
@ 14,20 SAY "  Last Name: "
@ 14,32 GET cLast PICTURE "@K!T" ;
       VALID NameLook( cLast, cFirst )
READ

IF LASTKEY() <> 27               && User hit escape key
  *> Load the table with the customer's name.
  SELECT customer
  REPLACE lastname  WITH cLast,;
          firstname WITH cFirst,;
          midname   WITH cMid
ENDIF

CLEAR
CANCEL

*> Validation Function
```

```
FUNCTION NameLook
PARAMETER clname, cfname

PRIVATE is_ok
is_ok = .f.

*> Do a lookup on the last+first name.
IF NOT SEEK( clname + cfname )
   @ 22,20 SAY "Customer not located. Please enter again." ;
          COLOR GR+/R
   =INKEY(3)                        && Pause for 3 seconds
   @ 22,20 CLEAR                    && Clear the message line
   is_ok = .f.
ELSE
   @ 22,20 SAY "User located. Program completed." COLOR GR+/B
   is_ok = .t.
ENDIF
RETURN (is_ok)
*
```

Variables & Arrays

Basic variables were introduced in Part 1. Here are variables that are vital to some important techniques in FoxPro. This is where things get fancy: macro substitution, name expressions, variable scoping, and last but not least, arrays.

Naming Variables

FoxPro doesn't care what gets put in a variable. However, if you're sloppy you will get errors, and you'll also probably get confused. Variables float around from place to place carrying important raw materials for the ongoing processes. But they are not all alike. If you want to know what's going on, and make best use of them, you should data type your variables. Fortunately, the method for type determination is very easy: put the first letter of the data type, in lower case, at the beginning of every variable:

- **c**Character
- **n**Numeric
- **d**Date

- **f**Float
- **g**General
- **m**Memo
- **a**Array
- **is**_logical

Then you see the ringer at the bottom, is_logical. Every programmer can be eccentric, to a point. Besides, compare... is_true, is_ok, is_done with lTrue, lOk, lDone, and see which is more quickly recognized. The l looks almost exactly like a 1. A matter of personal preference, of course, where consistency is the only virtue.

Once you've decided to type a variable, it's highly recommended to *initialize* it. That means assign a value to it of the data type you desire. This is usually a neutral or null value of the length or characteristics most likely to be needed:

```
cName = SPACE(30)
dToday = {}
nTotal = 00.00
```

For one thing, if you don't initialize variables, they don't exist. That is, unless you declare them, using PUBLIC. But then they have only false (.f.) for a value, which may cause errors in your code. Initializing variables also serves the purpose of documenting the length or format of data that's supposed to be stored in them.

There is one other kind of variable naming that is generated by FoxPro, and you probably will use yourself. That's the official representation of a field variable: m.<field name> or in the old Xbase style m-><field name>. Whenever FoxPro creates field variables, usually through the SCATTER command, they will be in the first form m.lastname, m.firstname. This format helps FoxPro distinguish between the original fields and the field variables, so it's a very good idea to honor this convention consistently.

Variables and Scoping

The concept of *scoping* was introduced for programs, procedures, and functions. Even there, scoping is about variables. As procedures are called and exited, when are variables created? How long do they last? These questions arise because FoxPro has definite rules about the scope of a variable, and supports four different types of variables relative to their scope: default, public, private, and regional, as shown in Figure 8.7.

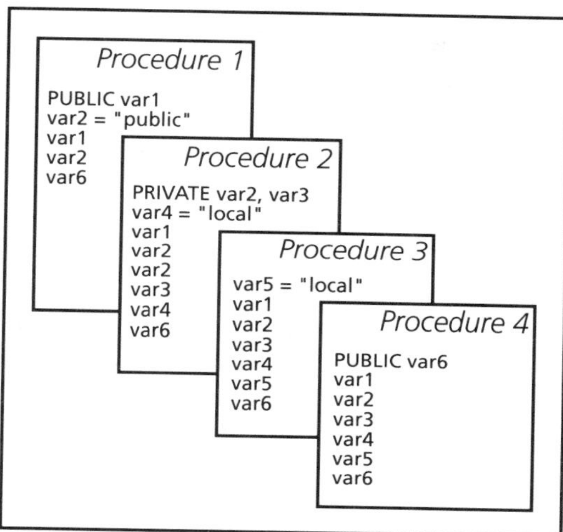

Figure 8.7 *Scoping variables.*

Default Scoping

When you create a variable of any kind in a program, procedure, or function, it has two scoping characteristics by default:

1. It remains in memory (persists) as long as that program, procedure, or function persists.
2. The variable is available (visible) to all procedures below the originating procedure, unless explicitly hidden.

As in the diagram above, if you create a variable in procedure 1 by assignment—var2="public"—it persists as long as procedure 1 is active. FoxPro automatically releases the variable, as it exits the procedure. In this way FoxPro takes care of a lot of the housekeeping (typical of Xbase systems). The second characteristic means that all variables created in procedure 1 are visible (can be read) and available (can be changed) by any procedure called in sequence from procedure 1. In this way variables initialized in the very first program file are in effect global, for all that follows.

This default scoping is quite forgiving and versatile. But it's not perfect. Far from it. What happens if you don't want a variable created in another part of the application to be available in other parts? Or what if you want to create a variable somewhere other than the first file that will persist both "above" and "below" the procedure in which it was created? For needs like these, FoxPro supports three explicit forms of variables, PUBLIC, PRIVATE, and REGIONAL.

Public Variables

From the moment of its creation, a public variable is visible and available to *all* programs. It persists until you explicitly RELEASE it, or until program execution is stopped through a QUIT. Var1 and var6 in the diagram are public variables. The first (var1) is global throughout the run of the program, while var6 becomes available only after Procedure 4 is executed. Public variables are created using this syntax:

```
PUBLIC <memvar list>
PUBLIC nCount, cTable
PUBLIC [ARRAY] <array1>(<expN1>[, <expN2>])
[, <array2>(<expN3>[, <expN4>])] .
PUBLIC aStates, aCounty
```

Be careful not to declare the same variable PUBUC more than once. It will generate a generic SYNTAX ERROR, which may be difficult to interpret as a scoping problem.

Private Variables

As you might expect, private variables are restricted in some way. Actually, they behave just like any normal variable created by assignment, with one important exception. You can name a variable PRIVATE that has the *same name* as another already existing variable. In effect making a private variable *hides* the original variable, and its contents can neither be read nor changed. In the diagram, var2 is first created in procedure 1, and then declared PRIVATE in procedure 2. Only this local var2 is then available. This technique has many uses, but it's greatest value is in keeping the variables of one procedure or function from inadvertently overlapping (*cross referencing*) with variables of the same name in other procedures or functions. For example, suppose you like to use the variable nCount as a generic holder for table COUNTs. You want it to be used in many different functions, but in each case you don't want it to contain the value from another function. So you make it PRIVATE:

```
PRIVATE <memvar list>
PRIVATE nCount, cTable, cFirstName
PRIVATE ALL [LIKE <skel> | EXCEPT <skel>]
PRIVATE ALL LIKE nCount*
PRIVATE ALL EXCEPT nCount*
```

Private variables are still visible to procedures below, and they disappear when you leave the originating procedure. It's good programming technique to write your function (or procedure), then go back and make all of the variables used in it private. It's good insurance against a bad cross reference, like a variable's data type being changed, mysteriously.

Regional Variables

Private variables are protected from cross referencing in other programs, procedures, and functions. But in FoxPro there is another program construction that you will meet in Section III—the screen set. A screen set may be composed of several screens, each a separate "program" (.SCX). However, when a screen set is generated, FoxPro lumps a large portion of code from all screens together. This makes PRIVATE variables meaningless. To handle this situation, FoxPro 2.0 introduced the REGIONAL variable definition. As you will see, #REGION, a generator directive, and REGIONAL are commonly used in all screen sets. But more on that later.

Removing Variables

Getting rid of variables, releasing them, can often be left to FoxPro. In small programs, this almost always is sufficient. But in larger programs, you have two limitations that need to be kept in mind: available memory and the total number of variables.

RAM, even in robust Windows systems, is finite. Variables chew up memory. A FoxPro out-of-memory error may be your first clue that you've got too many variables. By then, however, you've already got a big problem. It would be better to limit variables within the minimum required by your program. In short, get rid of variables when they're not needed. For one thing, keep the number of public variables to the absolute minimum.

There are also some limitations to the total number of variables you can have at one time—sixty-four thousand to be exact. Since this is hardly a limitation, the only other fact you *do* need to know is that by default FoxPro allows 256 variables. This isn't many for large applications, and you may need to put a line in your CONFIG.FPW file (MVCOUNT=512)to bump the number up, say to 512.

On the other hand, with a little attention you can probably keep an application's crop of variables pruned to a trim count. Your tools for the job are:

```
RELEASE <memvar list>
RELEASE nCount, cTable, cFirstName
```

And

```
RELEASE ALL
[LIKE <skel> | EXCEPT <skel>]
RELEASE ALL
RELEASE ALL LIKE nCount*
RELEASE ALL EXCEPT aStat*
```

Typically, you would put variable RELEASEs in the cleanup section of your programs and functions, along with releases for other objects like windows and menus.

On the other hand, perhaps you'd rather not deep six all your working variables. Just send them on vacation. FoxPro can do that too:

```
SAVE TO <file> | TO MEMO <memo field>
      [ALL LIKE <skel> | ALL EXCEPT <skel>]
SAVE TO taxvars ALL LIKE nTx*
SAVE TO MEMO comment ALL LIKE cNote*
```

Then later, at your discretion, you can bring the variables back into play:

```
RESTORE FROM <file> | FROM MEMO <memo field>
     [ADDITIVE]
```

```
RESTORE FROM taxvars ADDITIVE
RESTORE FROM comment ADDITIVE
```

Be sure not to forget that little clause ADDITIVE. If you do, you can say bye-bye to *all* of the existing variables.

Variable Substitution Techniques

This is a tough but important topic. It's important because of the role these variable substitution capabilities play in making your code more generic, especially in the building of functions and procedures. For example, if you code a file opening statement like:

```
USE f:\sales\customer ALIAS cus ORDER lastname
```

then this is the only file, alias, and index tag it can open. On the other hand, if you use a substitution technique—in this case a name expression—you can make a generic file opening statement that can open any number of different files.

```
*> These variables can be loaded with any file.
cFilename = "f:\sales\customer"
cAlias = "cus"
cTag = "lastname"
USE (cFileName) ALIAS (cAlias) ORDER (cTag)
```

This example is the core of the data dictionary system presented in this book. There are thousands of other uses for the variable substitution techniques, including some that can be astonishing. The three techniques available are name expressions, the EVALUATE function, and macro substitution. They are all *run-time* substitutions, because they occur at the time you run your programs, not during generation or compilation. This means they let you alter the content of commands (and even the commands themselves) on the fly.

Name Expressions

Whenever you encounter a command that can be read like COMMAND <Name of Something>, then you can probably use a name expression. The

<Name of Something> is always the name of some FoxPro object: a file name, a table name or alias, a variable name, window name, or project name. To use a name expression requires a variable (as do all three techniques). First you assign a variable with the name of something. Then, using parentheses, you include the variable with the command. Here are some common examples:

- **Tables** `cTableName = "customer"`
  `USE ( cTableName )`
- **Programs** `cFileName = "taxcount.dbf"`
  `DO ( cFileName )`
- **Fields** `cFieldName = "customer.lastname"`
  `REPLACE ( cFieldName ) WITH cLastName`
- **Views** `cViewFile = "taxtable.vue"`
  `SET VIEW TO ( cViewFile )`
- **Aliases** `cOldAlias = ALIAS()`
  `SELECT ( cOldAlias )`
- **Indexes** `cOldOrder = ORDER()`
  `SET ORDER TO ( cOldOrder )`
- **Windows** `cOldWind = WONTOP()`
  `ACTIVATE WINDOW ( cOldWin )`
- **Color sets** `cColorSet = "GR+/B,W/B,W/B,W+/B,GR+/BG,B/W,W+/W,;`
  `B/W,W/B,N/N"`
  `SET COLOR SET 10 TO ( cColorSet )`

Named expressions are ubiquitous in well-written programs. They can be used in a myriad of places where you might have variable content for a command. Suppose you want to change a color. If you've hard coded colors, then you need to manually replace them every time you change your mind about a color scheme. On the other hand, if you've been using name expressions for a variable—like cColorSet—then all you need to do is change the colors assigned to that variable once, usually in the setup for your program, and all of the occurrences of that variable are automatically changed.

Another example that should be used in almost every program, function, or procedure stores the work area (alias) and the current index tag, if any, to a variable:

```
cOldAlias = ALIAS()
cOldOrder = ORDER()
...
* Restore original file and index, trap for no file or index.
```

```
IF NOT EMPTY( cOldAlias )
  SELECT ( cOldAlias )
  IF NOT EMPTY( cOldOrder ) AND ORDER() <> cOldOrder
    SET ORDER TO ( cOldOrder )
  ENDIF
ENDIF
```

Since your program has no idea what file and index, if any, may be open when it's called, there's no way to hard code this. The variables and name expressions (cOldAlias)and (cOldOrder) take care of that by storing and restoring any file and index tag that comes along. What works for files can also work for many other conditions that you may want to preserve and restore in a procedure or function.

EVALUATE

Where the named expression merely passes the content of a variable, as a character string, to a command, EVALUATE( ) processes (evaluates) the expression stored in the variable. The expression *must* be a character string or a character variable:

```
nTotal = 50
? EVALUATE( "nTotal" )
```

Returns: 50

```
? EVALUATE( nTotal )
```

Returns: *! Invalid function argument value, type, or count.*

```
cValue = "2+2"
? EVALUATE( cValue )
```

Returns: 4

```
cDateLine = "{12/01/93}-{12/01/92}"
? EVALUATE( cDateLine )
```

Returns: 365

```
cLogic = "nTotal > 100"
? EVALUATE( cLogic )
```

Returns: .f. or .t.

There are no rules for when to use EVALUATE, except that it's faster than a macro substitution for any expression that needs to be evaluated before being passed to a command. It's also overkill (both computationally and as a matter of typing) for situations that can use a name expression. It's best use is in places where an evaluated substitution must be repeated often, as in certain kinds of loops like this one:

```
nTotal = 0
FOR i = 1 TO 10,000
  IF EVALUATE("nTotal > 500")
    EXIT
  ELSE

    nTotal = GetTotal()
  ENDIF
ENDFOR
```

Macro Substitution

Macro substitutions are the granddaddy of all the variable substitution techniques. They have been around since dBase II. They've also been used and abused more than any single little operator.

It looks harmless enough: the simple ampersand (&). Put this in front of a variable, and FoxPro substitutes the contents of the variable into the command or expression being executed.

```
cFileName = "f:\sales\customer"
USE &cFileName
```

This works exactly like a name expression. But there's more:

```
cValue = "2+2"
? &cValue
```

This returns 4, just like EVALUATE( ). The macro substitution also evaluates an expression stored in the variable as a character string. But there's still more:

```
cCommand = "USE customer ALIAS cus ORDER cno"
? &cCommand
```

The macro substitution will execute this command! This is possible because FoxPro is an "interpreter" processing engine. It's already been mentioned that when you're working in the Command window, FoxPro immediately executes your commands. In reality this is also true all the time, even when your programs are compiled.

Xbase systems are never totally compiled. There is always a run-time engine that acts as the interpreter. Some parts of your code will bypass this run-time interpreter, and thereby execute faster. A macro substitution, however, always invokes the interpreter. It works something like this in a program:

```
cOpenClause = "customer ALIAS cus ORDER lastname"
USE &cOpenClause
```

It runs like this in the run-time interpreter:

Pass 1: `USE "customer ALIAS cus ORDER lastname"`
`<= &cOpenClause`

Pass 2: `USE customer ALIAS cus ORDER lastname`

On the first pass, FoxPro "unloads" the macro, pulling out its contents. On the second pass, it interprets (parses) the contents and includes them with the current instructions, if any. This two-pass approach is what makes macro substitutions so powerful. It also makes them slow. In fact because of all of the machinery necessary to load the interpreter and run two passes, macro substitutions are the slowest operation in FoxPro.

Yet some really incredible things can be done with macro substitution, and only with macro substitutions. Like all the other substitution techniques, & is used to make things generic. Perhaps the most common example is in the processing of table operation commands, like COUNT, and AVERAGE, that use a FOR clause. There are many situations where you want to run one of these command, but have the user alter the conditions, without getting into your code. With a macro substitution it would be done something like this:

```
*Get the user's input on the dates to run.
dStartDate = {}
dStopDate = {}
@ 10,20 SAY "Enter the starting date: " GET dStartDate PICTURE;
"@D"
@ 11,20 SAY " Enter the ending date: " GET dStopDate PICTURE;
"@D"
READ

*> Compose the FOR expression, note date brackets.
```

```
cFor = "cus.startdate >= {"+DTOC(dStartDate)+ ;
       "} AND cus.stopdate <= {"+DTOC(dStopDate)+"}"

*> Run the operations with macro substitution
SELECT cus
COUNT ALL FOR &cFor TO nCount
AVERAGE ALL FIELD cus.totalpurch FOR &cFor TO nAvg
```

Comparison of All Three Techniques

Each of the three techniques has it's place. When possible, name expressions and EVALUATE( ) are always used in lieu of a macro substitution, because they execute much faster. Name expressions are simple to use, but limited in application. EVALUATE is more flexible, but also limited. Macro substitutions almost always work, but slowly.

Still, at a practical level, the three techniques are easy to confuse. In truth there will be times when only experimentation will show you what works and what doesn't. However, some comparative examples might help frame the options. Here's the setup:

The standard FoxPro for Windows expression would be:

```
USE f:\foxprow\tutorial\customer IN 4
```

First, break down the components of the command (except the USE) and put them into variables for later substitution:

```
c1 = "f:\foxprow\tutorial\customer"
c2 = "2+2"
c3 = "IN"
```

Each of the following comparisons show the results for a "naked" variable, a name expression, the EVALUATE() function, and for a macro substitution.

- **Comparison 1—Substitution for the file name.**
  - `USE c1`
    Returns: the message *! File cf.dbf does not exist.* FoxPro has no way of knowing that c1 is a variable and not a file name.
  - `USE (c1)`
    works.

- `USE EVALUATE(c1)`
  works.
- `USE &c1`
  works.

- **Comparison 2—Substitution for the work area/alias.**
  - `USE (c1) IN c2`
    Returns: the message *! Alias c2 not found.* It fails for the same reason as in comparison 1 above: c2 looks like an alias, not a variable.
  - `USE (c1) IN (c2)`
    returns the message *! Alias 2+2 not found.* The name expression merely presents the expression as a "name" string, which of course isn't a valid alias name.
  - `USE EVALUATE(c1)IN EVALUATE(c2)`
    works.
  - `USE &c1 IN &c2`
    works.
- **Comparison 3—Substitution for the IN clause.**
  - `USE (c1) c3 &c2`
    Returns: the message *! Unrecognized phrase/keyword in command.*
  - `USE (c1) (c3) &c2`
    Returns: the message *! Unrecognized phrase/keyword in command.*
  - `USE EVALUATE(c1) EVALUATE(c3) EVALUATE(c2)`
    Returns: the message *! Unrecognized phrase/keyword in command.*
  - `USE &c1 &c3 &c2`
    works.

None of the other techniques can substitute for a command or command clause.

System Variables

As a program itself, FoxPro uses thousands of variables. Almost all of these are unknown and unavailable to you as an Xbase programmer. However, FoxPro does provide a class of *system variables* that provide some information about values being stored for internal use. For the most part, these behave just like ordinary variables—you can read and change them at will. If you try to release them, FoxPro politely ignores it.

These variables fall into five categories: printing, programming, applications, versions, and setup. All have their uses, from time to time, in programming. Only _CUROBJ, however, is used with regularity. The rest of them you should know about, and be ready to use, without necessarily knowing each and every variable.

Table 8.7
FoxPro system variables.

System Variable	T	Default	Description/Use
PRINTING			Many of these variables are used extensively in the DOS version of FoxPro. In FoxPro for Windows, only the variables of use in the Report Writer are of much interest. These have been marked below.
_ALIGNMENT	C	LEFT	Settings are the usual LEFT, RIGHT, CENTER.
_BOX	L	.T.	Boxes will be displayed around text.
_INDENT	N	0	Indent of the first line, in characters.
_LMARGIN	N	0	Position of the left margin, in characters 0 to 254. Active when wrap equals true.
_MLINE	N	0	Returns specific lines from a memo field.
_PADVANCE	C	FORMFEED	Page advance method: FORMFEED, LINEFEED.
_PAGENO	N	1	Useful for putting page numbers into reports.
_PBPAGE	N	1	First page to print.
_PCOLNO	N	Current	Current column number.
_PCOPIES	N	1	Number of copies.
_PDRIVER	C	Null	Name of the printer driver (DOS).
_PDSETUP	C	Null	Invokes the Printer Driver setup screen (DOS).
_PECODE	C	Null	Ending printer codes (printer reset).
_PEJECT	C	BEFORE	Eject paper BEFORE, AFTER, NONE Both printing.

Variable	Type	Default	Description
_PEPAGE	N	32,767	Ending page.
_PLENGTH	N	66	Length of page in lines.
PLINENO	N	0	Current line number.
PLOFFSET	N	0	Page offset.
PPITCH	C	DEFAULT	Printer pitch: PICA, ELITE, CONDENSED, DEFAULT.
PQUALITY	L	.F.	Printer Quality: draft = .f., letter quality=.t.
PRETEXT	C	Null	Character to preface text merge lines.
_PSCODE	C	Null	Startup printer codes.
_PSPACING	N	1	Printer line spacing—1, 2, or 3.
_PWAIT	L	.F.	Pause between pages, .t. or .f.
_RMARGIN	N	80	Setting (in columns) for the right margin.
_TABS	C	Null	Tab settings: such as 8, 16, 24, 32, 40.
_TEXT	N	-1	Text merge output.
_WRAP	L	.F.	Status of word wrap on or off = .t. or .f.
APPS			
_CALCMEM	N	0.0	The current value of the Calculator memory.
_CALCVALUE	N	0.0	The current value in the Calculator screen.
_DIARYDATE	D		Current date for the FoxPro diary.
VERSIONS			These variables are used to identify on which platform (machine type) the program is currently running.
_DOS	L		.t. if FoxPro for MS-DOS
_MAC	L		.t. if FoxPro for Macintosh
_UNIX	L		.t. if FoxPro for UNIX
_WINDOWS	L		.t. if FoxPro for Windows
SETUP			These are all variables that contain the path to FoxPro support files. Many are (or should be) set in the CONFIG.FPW file.
_BEAUTIFY	C		Path to BEAUTIFY.APP
_FOXDOC	C		Path to FOXDOC.EXE
_FOXGRAPH	C		Path to FOXGRAPH.EXE
_GENGRAPH	C		Path to GENGRAPH.PRG
_GENMENU	C		Path to GENMENU.PRG

(continued)

_GENPD	C		Path to GENPD.APP
_GENSCRN	C		Path to GENSCRN.PRG
_GENXTAB	C		Path to GENXTAB.PRG
_SPELLCHECK	C		Path to SPELLCHK.APP
_STARTUP	C		Path to STARTUP.APP
_TRANSPORT	C		Path to TRANSPRT.PRG
PROGRAMMING			
_CLIPTEXT	C	Null	Contents of the FoxPro/Windows clipboard.
_CUROBJ	N	0	Number of the current GET object.
_DBLCLICK	N	0.5	The amount of time to measure between mouse clicks.
_TALLY	N	0	The count of records returned from an RQBE/SQL search, a COUNT or other command that returns a record count.
_THROTTLE	N	0	The speed with which program text is displayed in the TRACE window.

Using Arrays

An array is an indexed variable. In the old days, only five or six years ago, Xbase didn't have arrays (believe it or not). People would fake them in a variety of ways. A simple minded example: state1, state2, state3.... That's three variables to hold the names of states, indexed 1 to 3. And why would they bother to fake an array? For one thing, keeping related data in a "set" of variables is logically convenient. For another, with an index scheme, you can loop through the variables, counting off and checking each one as you go. Remember what was said about using macro substitution in loops? Faking an array for counting was very clumsy:

```
FOR i = 1 TO 10
  cI = LTRIM(STR(i))
  state&cI = state.statename
ENDFOR
```

Fortunately Clipper and then FoxPro finally provided real arrays. They look like this: aState[1], aState[2], aState[3].... Each variable, called an *element* of an array, has an "index" value, the *subscript*, enclosed by brackets. This makes loops much easier, and faster:

```
FOR i = 1 TO 10
  aState[i] = state.statename
ENDFOR
```

Arrays don't look like regular variables, and they're not created like one either. For one thing, they must be explicitly created by one of two commands:

```
DECLARE <array1>(<expN1>[, <expN2>])

[, <array2>(<expN3>[, <expN4>])]
DECLARE aState[51]
DECLARE aCounty[36], aCity[1000]
DECLARE aState[51,4]
```

or

```
DIMENSION <array1>(<expN1>[, <expN2>])
[, <array2>(<expN3>[, <expN4>])]
DIMENSION aState[51]
DIMENSION aCounty[36], aCity[1000]
DIMENSION aState[51,4]
```

The syntax of the two commands looks exactly alike. And they are. Why, you ask, are there two of them? The answer, yet again, is history. Clipper used DECLARE and Basic used DIMENSION. Fox decided to carry both. You can also use parentheses instead of brackets to enclose the subscript, again a bow in the direction of other programming languages. Xbase has never been too proud to steal language and syntax from anything. Making the best of a redundancy, some people like to use DECLARE to create an array, and DIMENSION to redefine it, but it matters not a whit to FoxPro.

There are three things about arrays in FoxPro that are well worth remembering:

1. **An array can have one or two dimensions.** Speaking like a mathematician, two dimensional arrays are the same as a matrice and a one-

dimension array is a vector. They are created like this: DECLARE aState[51,4]. This means there are fifty-one element *rows*, and four element *columns*. You can picture a two dimensional array like this:

	1]	2]	3]	4]
aState [1,	IA	IOWA	Des Moines	Midwest
aState [2,	ID	IDAHO	Boise	West
aState [3,	IL	ILLINOIS	Springfield	Midwest
aState [4,	IN	INDIANA	Indianapolis	Midwest

Does this remind you of a data table? That's another important feature of arrays—they can mimic a data table. Moreover, since they are RAM based, you can perform some database-like actions on an array much more rapidly than from a table on disk. The disadvantage is that you may not have enough memory to dump a table into an array. FoxPro gives you three commands that support the "array as table" concept:

```
COPY TO ARRAY <array> [FIELDS <field list>] [<scope>]
[FOR <expL1>] [WHILE <expL2>] [NOOPTIMIZE]
COPY TO ARRAY aState FIELDS state.abbrev, state.name,
state.capitol, state.region
APPEND FROM ARRAY <array> [FOR <expL>] [FIELDS <field
list>]
APPEND FROM aState FIELDS state.abbrev, state.name
SELECT...INTO ARRAY <array>
SELECT DISTINCT state.abbrev ;
FROM state ;
ORDER BY state
INTO ARRAY aState
```

If you specify more than one field, these commands automatically produce a two-dimensional array with as many columns as there are fields, and as many records as are in the original table (or in the subset you create with the FOR, WHILE, and other options in the SELECT).

Arrays can be used in several of the FoxPro for Windows controls to contain a list of items, for example in a popup list. In this connection, the SQL SELECT approach is used frequently to load the array.

2. **Arrays can be re-dimensioned at any time without losing content.** There are some common sense rules for this. Suppose you start by

creating a ten-by-four array (ten rows, four column) and load it with blanks using the STORE command, which initializes all of the elements at once:

```
DECLARE aName[10,4]
STORE " " TO aName
```

Over time the elements become filled with data (names of people), and you decide that ten entries (rows) isn't enough and you need a couple more columns. Adding more is simple: DIMENSION aName[100,6]. FoxPro adds the new elements (all ninty by two of them) without disturbing the data in the original forty elements. Now, however, you can't load the array with the STORE command, because you don't want to overwrite those first ten rows. You need a loop that starts at the eleventh row:

```
FOR i = 11 TO 100          && outer loop for rows
  FOR j = 1 TO 6           && inner loop for columns
    aName[i, j] = SPACE(3)
  ENDFOR
ENDFOR
```

Suppose this array fills with sixty names, then you decide to trim the size down a bit to conserve memory: DIMENSION aName[50,6]. This is a mistake. You've just lost ten array rows containing data. You need to exercise some caution in reducing the number of elements in an array.

3. **Arrays can contain data of any kind, in any element**. An array like the following one, is perfectly okay, even useful, because it "packages" a set of related information:

```
DECLARE aPerson[10,6]
STORE " " TO aPerson
aPerson[1,1] = "Johnson"              && last name
aPerson[1,2] = "Herbert"              && first name
aPerson[1,3] = "M."                          && midinit
aPerson[1,4] = {09/22/36}                    && birthdate
aPerson[1,5] = DATE()- aPerson[1,4]          && age
aPerson[1,6] = "999-00-9999"                 && social sec.
```

As a side benefit, you can take this package (which is analogous to a *structure* in C), and pass it to a function *by reference*, like this: = PeopleCalc(@aPerson). The use of the @ has the same effect as SET UDFPARMS TO REFERENCE. The function can then modify the elements of the array, without needing to make the array PUBLIC.

The Array Toolkit

Plain and simple arrays are useful. But FoxPro includes a number of functions that increase the usefulness of arrays many fold. Some of these functions perform tasks very similar to those for a data table—such as sorting and searching.

ALEN( )

```
ALEN(<array>[, <expN>])
DECLARE aState[52,4]
? ALEN( aState )
```

Returns: 208.

```
? ALEN( aState,1 )
```

Returns: 52.

```
? ALEN( aState,2 )
```

Returns: 4.

The ALEN function, the *Length of an Array*, clearly illustrates how FoxPro views an array as a continuous "stack" of elements. Without the <expN> qualifier, you get the total number of elements. Using 1 IN <expN> gets the number of rows, and 2 returns the number of columns. This function is frequently used to control a FOR/ENDFOR loop:

```
FOR i = 1 TO ALEN(aState,1)
  FOR j = 1 TO ALEN(aState,2)
      aState[i,j] = SPACE(12)
  ENDFOR
ENDFOR
```

The standard LEN( ) function is *not* an alternative, and if used on an array will cause an error.

AINS( )

```
AINS(<array>, <expN>[, 2])
DECLARE aState[48,4]
=AINS( aState, 3) && Inserts a row before row 3
```

Returns: 1, if successful.

```
=AINS( aState,2,2) && Inserts a column before column 2
```

This is the "insert array elements" function. It's very important to remember this does not make the array bigger. If you insert ten elements into a twenty element array, the last ten elements get "pushed" out of the array—lost, and all the data in them. In cases where you truly want the array to expand, you need to first make room for the insertion:

```
DECLARE aState[48,4]          && an array of states
DIMENSION aState[51,4]        && re-dimension by 3 rows
=AINS( aState, 3)             && insert rows for 3 missing
=AINS( aState, 13)            && states
=AINS( aState, 42)
aState[3,1] = "AK"            && load new rows
aState[3,2] = "Alaska"
aState[3,3] = "Juneau"
aState[3,4] = "Western"
...
```

If you do a lot of work with arrays, it's more than worth your while to develop some generic functions that extend the FoxPro array functions and make them more convenient to use. For example, this function both inserts a row and makes the physical increase in the size of the array:

```
*___________________________________________
*      FUNCTION: ArowIns()
*   DESCRIPTION: INSERTS A ROW INTO A 2-D ARRAY
*       CREATED: 10/12/90
*    PARAMETERS: cAname = Name of the array to insert into.
*                  nRowPos = The insertion point(row).
*         NOTES: Redimensions the array to physically add
*                the row at the bottom of the array.
*___________________________________________
FUNCTION ArowIns
PARAMETER cAname, nRowPos
  DIMENSION &cAname[ ALEN(&cAname,1)+ 1, ALEN(&cAname,2) ]
RETURN IIF( ADEL( &cAname, nRowPos ) = 1 ,.t.,.f.)
*
```

ADEL( )

The syntax is:

```
ADEL(<array>, <expN>[, 2])
```

```
DECLARE aState[51,4]
=ADEL[ aState, 3] && Deletes row 3
=ADEL[ aState, 3, 2] && Deletes column 3
```

Returns: 1, if successful.

As the reverse of AINS( ), this is the "delete array elements" function. The principles are similar. Deleting elements, rows, or columns does not change the size of the array. It simply "fills in the gap" by causing the array elements to be moved up from the bottom of the array into the space (element, row, or column) being deleted. In a one-dimensional array, the <expN> indicates the element to be deleted. In a two-dimensional array it indicates the row. And if you want to delete a column, add the 2 option.

As with AINS( ), if you really want to make the array smaller and at the same time delete a row, you need to re-dimension the array—*after* the deletion. Perhaps if you do this often, the best thing to do is create a function:

```
*______________________________
*     FUNCTION: ArowDel()
* DESCRIPTION: DELETES A ROW FROM A 2-D ARRAY
*      CREATED: 10/12/90
*   PARAMETERS: cAname = Name of the array to delete from.
*                 nRowPos = The deletion point(row).
*        NOTES: Redimensions the array to physically remove
*               the row at the bottom of the array.
*______________________________
FUNCTION ArowDel
PARAMETER cAname, nRowPos
  IF ADEL( &cAname, nRowPos ) = 1
    DIMENSION &cAname[ ALEN(&cAname,1)-1, ALEN(&cAname,2) ]
   RETURN .t.
 ELSE
   RETURN .t.
 ENDIF
*
```

AELEMENT( )/ ASUBSCRIPT( )

Before you can go on to some very useful array functions, particularly ASCAN( ), you need to get into some fairly confusing details with AELEMENT() and ASUBSCRIPT( ). However, let's keep this as simple as possible.

```
AELEMENT(<array>, <expN1>[, <expN2>])
```

<array> is the name of the array to use.

<expN1> is the row subscript.

<expN2> is the column subscript.

```
DECLARE aState[51,2]
= AELEMENT( aState, 10, 1)
```

Returns: 19.

```
ASUBSCRIPT(<array>, <expN1>, <expN2>)
```

<array> is the name of the array to use.

<expN1> is the element number.

<expN2> use 1 to return a row subscript, 2 to return a column subscript.

```
DECLARE aState[51,2]
= ASUBSCRIPT( aState, 19, 1) && row subscript
```

Returns: 10.

```
= ASUBSCRIPT( aState, 19, 2) && column subscript
```

Returns: 1.

One of the realities behind arrays is that while you can visualize them as two dimensional, internally FoxPro treats them as one dimensional. An array declared as [5,4] doesn't really have five rows and four columns. It has twenty elements, numbered one through twenty. That's why several functions require that you provide the element of the array to work on, and won't accept subscripts. This is no problem with one-dimensional arrays, since there is only one reference number. But with two-dimensional arrays, it isn't so easy. So FoxPro provides you with a couple of functions to make conversions.

These are another "bookend" pair of functions that can tell you the element number from a given subscript (AELEMENT( )), or the subscripts from a given array element (ASUBSCRIPT).

Only their two dimension syntax is useful.

ASCAN()

Similar to the LOCATE command, this "search an array" function does a sequential search of an array looking for a match to the <expr> you've specified. If the search is successful, it returns the number of the element found, otherwise it returns 0. The returned element can be used to directly reference an array, since FoxPro accepts both an element or subscripts: aState[20,1] = aState[19] = aState[ASCAN(aState,"IL")]. Its syntax is:

```
ASCAN(<array>, <expr>[, <expN1>[, <expN2>]])
```

<array> is the name of the array to scan. (This can be a literal ("astate") or a variable expression).

<expr> is the expression of any data type to be located in the array.

<expN1> is the starting array element to begin searching (the default is element 1).

<expN2> is the number of elements to search (the default is all elements).

```
DECLARE aState[51,2]
=ASCAN( aState, "AK")
```

Returns: 3.

```
=ASCAN( aState, "IL", AELEMENT(aState,10,1))
```

Returns: 19.

It's important to keep in mind that ASCAN() by default searches *all* of the elements. It knows nothing about rows and columns. Even if what you're looking for has to be in the second column (the "state name column" for example), there's no way to make ASCAN search just that column. Two-dimensional arrays can mimic data tables, but you don't have the same depth of tools for working arrays, unless you build them yourself.

ASORT()

Sorting an array is usually in preparation for use in display, either in one of the list type controls, or popups. The syntax is similar to the other array functions:

```
ASORT(<array>[, <expN1>[, <expN2>[, <expN3>]]])
```

where <array> is the name of the array to sort.

<expN1> is the element or row to begin sorting.

<expN2> is the number of elements or rows to sort.

<expN3> is the sort order (0=ascending, 1=descending).

```
DECLARE aState[51,2]
= ASORT( aState )
```

Returns: 1 if successful, otherwise it returns -1.

```
=ASORT( aState, AELEMENT(aState,10,1),30) &sort from element
10,1
=ASORT( aState, 1, 51, 1) && Sort array in descending order.
```

Limitations of Arrays

Given all of the things that can be done with arrays and their relative efficiency, you might be tempted to ask, "Why bother with regular variables?" The answer is, "The problem is human." Arrays present two difficulties to mortals, they are relatively anonymous, and the business of subscript versus element number in two-dimensional arrays is cumbersome to manage.

However, only the first issue causes real problems. While you might be clear what goes into an array, like aThermoDyn[900,50], at the time you create it (and hopefully document it), six months later when you look at code (pages away from the documentation) will you know what aThermoDyn[603,37] contains? And code filled with hundreds of array elements only makes the readability problem worse.

All in all, limitations of memory and ease of use included, arrays are one of the most under-utilized features of FoxPro. You are strongly encouraged to "say array" when thinking about fast data manipulation.

More Basic Commands and Functions

You've already been introduced to a fair sampling of commands and functions through the system menu and the Command window. Now comes the time to add those commands and functions that are most at home in the program file (and later in screen and menu files as well). A few other items are included to round out your introduction to the most basic commands and functions.

Program Control

COMPILE

Although FoxPro automatically compiles any executable program file that you call, you can also invoke the compiler from the Command window. These days, however, most compiling is done under the control of the Project Manager.

```
COMPILE <file> | <skel> [ENCRYPT]  [NODEBUG]
```

<file> is the name of the file to compile (if it is other than .PRG, specify the extension).

<skel> is a valid DOS file skeleton using the wild cards "*" and "?"

[ENCRYPT] provides protection against software theft.

[NODEBUG] does not include debugging information, especially line numbers, in the compiled files (this cuts the size of the files by about 10 percent).

```
COMPILE customer.prg
COMPILE *.PRG NODEBUG
```

Part of the programming cycle in FoxPro is to *compile* all executable files (such as .PRG, .SPR, or .MPR). During the compilation process, code is analyzed for syntax errors, variable references, program modules and calls, then converted to an *object file* containing what is called pseudo code (no longer FoxPro code, but not quite machine language—pure binary code). These compiled files are then executed through the FoxPro run-time engine, which does a complex mixture of interpreter work (like in the Command window) and binary execution—like regular compiled programs.

CANCEL

To terminate program execution, and release all *private* memory variables, use CANCEL.

CLEAR ALL

Use CLEAR ALL as kind of an all purpose, wipe-the-slate-clean command. It closes all files, releases all memory variables, and releases all window and menu definitions.

Numeric Functions

Here are some more relatively generic numeric functions that can be used in a variety of situations. There are many more, specifically math oriented functions that are available with a quick look in the *Language Reference* manual.

ABS

```
ABS( <expN> )
= ABS( -45 )
```

Returns: 45, the absolute value of <expN>.

MOD

```
MOD( <expN1>, <expN2> )
```

<expN1> is the dividend.

<expN2> is the divisor.

```
=MOD( 31 , 2 )
```

Returns: 1.

This one of two forms of the *modulus*, which returns the remainder of a division. This may seem like a somewhat esoteric function, but it is frequently used in calculations to determine whether a number is odd or even.

You can use <expN1> % <expN2> as an alternative.

RAND

```
RAND( <expN> )
```

<expN> is a seed value. If none, a default of 100001 is used. A negative number will be substituted with the time of the system clock in seconds.

```
=RAND( )
=RAND(-1)
=RAND(48930)
```

Returns .42—a two-decimal place number between 0 and 1.

(See the *Language Reference* for excellent coverage of RAND.)

SIGN

```
SIGN( <expN> )
```

<expN> is any valid numeric expression.

```
=SIGN( nMytaxReturn )
```

Returns: -1—the sign of any number as 1 = positive, 0 = zero, -1 = negative.

MIN

```
MIN ( <expr1>,<expr2>[,<expr3>...] )
```

<expr1>,<expr2> is a list of at least two numbers, dates, or characters.

```
=MIN( 22,5,67,8,34,54)
```

Returns: 5—the lowest value in a list of numbers.

```
=MIN( DATE(), dNextPay, dLastPay, dWorkDay )
```

Returns: 11/12/91—the date value with the oldest date.

```
=MIN( "ACE", "CEA", "AAB", "CBE" )
```

Returns: "AAB"—the character expression with the minimum ASCII value.

MIN/MAX play the same role for testing expressions as do their data-table bretheren.

MAX

```
MAX ( <expr1>,<expr2>[,<expr3...] )
```

<expr1>,<expr2> are a list of at least two numbers, dates, or characters.

```
=MAX( 22,5,67,8,34,54)
```

Returns: 67—the highest value in a list of numbers.

```
=MAX( DATE(), dNextPay, dLastPay, dWorkDay )
```

Returns: 12/12/92—the date value with the most recent or future date.

```
=MAX( "ACE", "CEA", "AAB", "CBE" )
```

Returns: "CBE"—the character expression with the highest ASCII value.

Numeric functions lend themselves to extension through creation of UDFs. Here's a simple example:

```
*___________________________________________
*    FUNCTION: OddEven( <expN> )
* DESCRIPTION: DETERMINES IF A NUMBER IS ODD OR EVEN.
*     CREATED: 12/22/92
```

```
*  PARAMETERS: nNum = Any valid numeric expression.
*     RETURNS: "ODD" or "EVEN"
*       NOTES: Use anywhere to sort or organize numeric
* information,
*              such as columns in printing, or page numbering
* etc.
*       USAGE: cChoice = OddEven( RAND() )
*       CALLS: None
*   CALLED BY: This is a GUF (General Use Function)
*___________________________________________
FUNCTION OddEven
PARAMETER nNum
RETURN IIF( MOD( nNum, 2 )> 0, "ODD", "EVEN")
*
```

Conversion Functions

In addition to the two data conversion functions already introduced, VAL( ) and STR( ), here are more useful tools in moving data from one format and type to another.

TYPE

TYPE( ) currently recognizes six data types: C—character, N—numeric, L—logical, D—date, M—memo, and U—undefined. The argument of this function is really a *name expression*, which does a lookup in FoxPro's internal memory variable table. Its syntax is:

```
TYPE(<expC>)
```

<expC> is the name of a variable, array, or field to be analyzed for type, as a character expression.

```
=TYPE("nStart")
```

Returns: N—the data type as a letter.

A very common use of TYPE( ) is to check a parameter list of functions and procedures, as in this example fragment:

```
FUNCTION CheckPart
PARAMETER cPartId, nOnHand, dPurch
```

```
  IF TYPE("CPARTID") <> "C"
  WAIT "Invalid Part ID" WINDOW NOWAIT
  RETURN .f.
ENDIF
IF TYPE("NONHAND") <> "N"
  WAIT "Invalid On Hand Count" WINDOW NOWAIT
  RETURN .f.
ENDIF
IF TYPE("DPURCH") <> "D"
  WAIT "Invalid Purchase Date" WINDOW NOWAIT
  RETURN .f.
ENDIF
```

This same approach would apply to any type of conversion routines where you must be sure that the data types are accurate.

CHR

There are two principal uses for this function: to send printer codes to printers, and to put on screen or into tables characters that cannot be entered directly from the keyboard. No doubt you've seen (or even used) some of the smiley faces, check marks, boxes, and such that are part of the IBM/compatible character set. None of these are available directly from the keyboard, but can be created in a program using the CHR( ) function. (You do need to know what the ASCII number is for the character you want to use.) Its syntax is:

```
CHR(<expN>)
```

<expN> is a valid ASCII number.

```
=CHR(251)
```

Returns: the character represented by the ASCII number.

The following is an example of using CHR( ), which puts a check mark (ASCII 251) in a field, as part of loading a data table:

```
REPLACE ALL customer.ok WITH CHR(251)
```

ASC

The main use for this function is in checking keyboard entry for a particular range of letters, numbers, or symbols. Its syntax is:

```
ASC(<expC>)
```

<expc> is any valid ASCII character.

```
= ASC("G")
```

Returns: 71—the ASCII code value of the character entered.

This example checks for a valid alpha entry:

```
IF BETWEEN( ASC(cLetter), 65, 90)
  DO ENTRYLOOK
ENDIF
```

TRANSFORM

The effectiveness of this function is that you can impose the *mask* or editing templates used for @..SAY on either numeric or character data. The important part of its work is that it automatically takes the significant digits, characters, or date elements from the item to be transformed, and maps them one-to-one from left to right into the placeholder symbols in the template. For example a variable containing 234, will map into a template like "(###)" as (234). In forming the picture template, you have at your disposal most of the PICTURE functions. The syntax for TRANSFORM is:

```
TRANSFORM(<expr>, <expC>)
```

<expr> is any numeric or character expression.

<expC> is the picture template to be used (the same as for @..SAY PICTURE).

```
=TRANSFORM( 2343235, "$###,###,###")
```

Returns: $2,343,235.

```
=TRANSFORM( "Modem256 ","@R !!!!!###")
```

Returns: MODEM256.

In converting data, TRANSFORM has many possible uses, such as this one for loading a table with memory variables of different data types and formats:

```
REPLACE ALL PHONEH WITH TRANSFORM( nAreaCode,"(###)")+;
 TRANSFORM( cPnumber,"###-####")+;
TRANSFORM( nExten,"| ####")
```

IS_ALPHA and IS_DIGIT

The syntax for IS_ALPHA is:

```
ISALPHA( <expC> )
```

<expC> is any valid character expression.

```
=ISALPHA("2342")
```

Returns: .F.—it's true if the first character is an alphabet character, otherwise it's false.

The syntax for IS_DIGIT is:

```
ISDIGIT( <expC> )
```

<expC> is any valid character expression.

```
=ISALPHA("2342")
```

Returns: .T.—it's true if the first character is a numeric character, otherwise it's false.

These two functions can be helpful in converting character fields or variables by testing the content for numeric or character values. Sometimes this needs to become fairly elaborate, if for example, you wanted to make sure that data in a field is all numeric (or alpha). Here's a routine that would do that checking:

```
*____________________________________
*     FUNCTION: AlphOrNum(<expC>)
* DESCRIPTION: DETERMINES IF A CHARACTER STRING IS ALPHA OR
* NUMERIC.
*     CREATED: 1/23/92
*   PARAMETERS: cWord = Any valid character expression.
*        NOTES: This checks every character. If all of them are
* numeric
*               then false is returned. Otherwise this will be
* called
*               an alpha, even if it contains some numbers, and
* return
*               true (.t.).
*        USAGE: = AlphOrNum("98098")
*        CALLS: None
*    CALLED BY: This is a GUF (General Use Function)
*____________________________________
FUNCTION AlphOrNum
PARAMETER cWord
PRIVATE i
FOR i = 1 TO LEN(ALLTRIM(cWord)) && loop to test each character
  IF ISALPHA( SUBSTR(cWord, i,1)) && one alpha and the whole
thing
```

```
        RETURN .t. && is alpha, so drop out.
    ENDIF
ENDFOR
RETURN .f.
*
```

Date and Time

There really aren't many date and time functions in the FoxPro basic stock. Traditionally this is an area that has been enhanced by people creating their own UDFs, or by third-party libraries of functions.

CDOW

```
CDOW( <expD> )
```

<expD> is any date or date expression.

```
= CDOW( DATE() )
```

Returns: Thursday—the day of the week as a complete word.

DOW

```
DOW( <expD> )
```

<expD> is any date expression.

```
        = DOW( DATE() )
```

Returns: 2—the day of the week as a number (1=Sunday).

DAY

```
DAY( <expD> )
```

<expD> is any date expression.

```
< = DAY( )
```

Returns: 24—the day of the month as a number.

CMONTH

```
CMONTH( <expD> )
```

<expD> is any date expression.

```
< = CMONTH( )
```

Returns: June—the complete name of the month as a character string.

MONTH

```
MONTH( <expD> )
```

<expD> is any date expression.

```
< = MONTH( )
```

Returns: 10—the number of the month in the date expression.

YEAR

```
YEAR( <expD> )
```

<expD> is any date expression.

```
< = YEAR( )
```

Returns: 1993—the year of the date expression as a number.

SECONDS

```
SECONDS( )
< = SECONDS( )
```

Returns: 199.260—the number of seconds elapsed since midnight. SYS(2) is an alternate function.

These following two functions are typical of how easily you can enhance or vary existing date and time functions.

```
*_____________________________________________
*     FUNCTION: CYear(<date expr>)
*  DESCRIPTION: RETURNS THE YEAR AS A CHARACTER FROM A DATE
*      CREATED: 11/22/92
*   PARAMETERS: dYr = Any valid date expression.
*        NOTES: FoxPro for Windows has only the YEAR()function
*               which produces the date as a number. Not very
```

```
*               convenient for use in printing or screen work.
*        USAGE: = CYear(DATE())
*        CALLS: None
*    CALLED BY: This is a GUF (General Use Function)
*___________________________________________________
FUNCTION CYear
PARAMETER dYr
RETURN LTRIM(STR(YEAR(dYr)))
*
*___________________________________________________
*     FUNCTION: ElapseTime()
*  DESCRIPTION: RETURNS THE MINUTES BETWEEN TWO TIMES
*      CREATED: 11/23/92
*   PARAMETERS: cStart = Starting time as TIME() expression -
* character.
*               cFinish = Ending time as TIME() expression -
* character.
*        NOTES: The function converts the character time to its
* numeric
*               equivalent and then does the subtraction of
* starting
*               time from ending time.
*        USAGE: cTime1 = TIME()
*               = ElapseTime( cTime1, TIME() )
*        CALLS: None
*    CALLED BY: This is a GUF (General Use Function)
*___________________________________________________
FUNCTION ElapseTime
PARAMETERS cStart, cFinish
nStart = (VAL(SUBSTR(cStart,1,2))/60)+VAL(SUBSTR(cStart,4,2))
nFinish = (VAL(SUBSTR(cFinish,1,2))/
60)+VAL(SUBSTR(cFinish,4,2))
RETURN nFinish - nStart
*
```

Some Nice Big Chunks

True, this is an odd heading. But these are some very handy routines that FoxPro provides, complete, for your use. Programming from scratch to imitate the Windows file management dialogs, or the FoxPro Expression Builder is no simple matter. Be thankful you can get the benefit of these routines with a single command.

Select Directory Dialog Box

This function brings up the Select Directory standard dialog box. The user can navigate the disk directory tree and select an appropriate directory. If the user selects **Cancel** or uses the **Esc** key, a null string ("") is returned.

```
GETDIR([<expC1>[, <expC2>]]
```

<expC1> is the directory to be initially selected.

<expC2> is the prompt to be displayed at the top of the dialog box.

```
cDir = GETDIR()
cDir = GETDIR("F:\SALES\","SELECT A SALESPERSON'S DIRECTORY")
```

Returns: f:\sales\ron—the name of a directory as a character string.

Open File Dialog Box

This opens the Open File dialog box.

```
GETFILE([<expC1>] [, <expC2>] [, <expC3>] [, <expN>])
```

<expC1> is the filename extensions to limit files displayed in dialog box.

<expC2> is the prompt displayed at the top of the dialog box.

<expC3> is the text in the Open push button.

<expN> specifies the number and type of push buttons in the dialog box.

```
cFile = GETFILE("DBF")
cFile = GETFILE("PRG;SPR;MPR","Edit Program","Edit",1)
```

Returns: f:\sales\ron\totals.spr—the path and file name selected. Otherwise, a null string is returned.

The standard Windows Open File dialog box has been opened, to allow you some leeway in controlling user's file selection. You have three options to work with:

1. Control what files to display, using one of the following approaches:

   - **Single extension**—Only files of this extension will be displayed.

- **Multiple extensions with unique file names**—Only files of these extensions will be displayed. If more than one file of the same name exists, then only the first one will display.
- **Multiple extensions, all files**—All files with these extensions will be displayed.
- **Files without extensions**—All files that have no extension.
- **All files**—All files in the directory will be displayed.
- **Wild card files**—Files will be displayed according to the DOS wildcards used.

2. Select the buttons to be displayed based on the following number in <expN>:

   - **0 or empty**—<Open>, <Cancel>
   - **1**—<New>, <Open>, <Cancel>
   - **2**—<None>, <Open>, <Cancel>

3. Change the name of the "action" button. The default above is Open. You could substitute Browse, Edit, or Delete.

Although you may wonder how you know what the user selected from the list of buttons, FoxPro relies on basic logic: If a file is selected, then whatever you had for the Open option was selected. If the returned value is a null (""), then either None, New, or Cancel was selected, depending on your choice of options. How you distinguish New or None from Cancel, however, is not clear. The "secret" is buried in the *Language Reference* manual's code example: CASE "Untitled" $ dbf_file. If New is selected, then of course it won't have a name, and FoxPro automatically assigns it "Untitled." If None is selected, well that's the same as Cancel. This is mighty convoluted, but it works.

Locate a File

This is sort of a two-stage GETFILE. Its syntax is:

```
LOCFILE(<expC1>[, <expC2>] [, <expC3>])
```

<expC1> is the file (path and name) to be located.

<expC2> is a list of alternate file extensions to be displayed if no file is found.

<expC3> is the prompt for the Open File dialog box.

```
cFile = LOCFILE("CUSTOMER.PRG","PRG;SPR;MPR","Find Customer
File")
```

Returns: e:\sales\customer.prg—the path and filename if selected, otherwise it returns a null ("").

First there will be a search for the file in <expC1>. If it is not found, then the Open File dialog box will be invoked. The order of search goes first to the default directory (the one currently selected), and then to the FoxPro path. If the specified file isn't located, then FoxPro uses the file extensions listed in <expC2>, if any, and retries the path search for each of them. If that search fails, then the Open File dialog box is called, and <expC2> becomes the list of files to be displayed.

Save As Dialog Box

The standard Save As Dialog is called by this function. This allows the user to select a file to be saved, or create a new file and file name. Its syntax is:

```
PUTFILE([<expC1>] [, <expC2>] [, <expC3>])
```

<expC1> is the prompt to be displayed above the list of file name.

<expC2> is the default file name to be displayed in the selection box.

<expC3> is the extensions of the file names to be displayed.

```
= PUTFILE("Program Files","Customer.prg","PRG;SPR;MPR")
```

Returns: e:\sales\customer.prg—the file name selected or entered, otherwise it returns a null ("").

File Maintenance Desk Accessory

The FoxPro File Manager, a.k.a. File Maintenance Desk Accessory, is a surprisingly useful tool. It's not the sort of thing you'd let every user have access to for every application. But there are situations where this rather complex subsystem will be most handy. Its syntax is:

```
FILER        [LIKE <skel>]  [NOWAIT] [IN [WINDOW] <window name>
| SCREEN]
```

<skel> is a file skeleton, using DOS wildcards.

<window name> is the name of the window to be used.

```
FILER LIKE *.PRG IN WINDOW wGeneral
```

Expression Builder

The Expression Builder is a fairly complex tool to unleash on the user, but when circumstances warrant, it's a very useful support mechanism. The validation of the expression alone, makes it worthwhile to use this command in your programs. Its syntax is:

```
GETEXPR [<expC1>] TO <memvar> [TYPE <expC2>[; <expC3>]]
[DEFAULT <expC4>]
```

<expC1> is the prompt in the title of Expression Builder window.

<memvar> is the memory variable or array element to store constructed expression.

<expC2> is one of the four types of expressions that can be created in the Expression Builder (C=character, N=numeric, D=date, L=logical).

<expC3> is the error message to use, if the constructed expression isn't valid.

<expC4> is a default expression to be initially displayed.

```
GETEXPR "" TO aCarType TYPE "C"
GETEXPR "Create Fruits Expression" TO cFruit TYPE "L;You must;
have your fruit.";
DEFAULT '"APPLE" $ fruit.name'
```

Windows Font List Dialog Box

GETFONT( ) opens the FoxPro Font dialog box and allows the user to select a font from the Windows font list. The name of the font is returned.

These commands and functions are especially useful in creating generic table maintenance routines (what this exercise in simple programming is all about). Getting the names of files to open, is often a part of such routines, as well as constructing FOR or WHILE clauses.

Debugging

No chapter on Good Old-Fashioned Coding would be complete without covering Good Old-Fashioned Debugging. These are the Siamese twins of software, joined at the head of the programmer.

The meaning of the word "bug" in this context is now part of the common language. You know what is meant when somebody says, "It's buggy." So you may understand the intent, if not the source of the statement: "*All* software is buggy." That shining shrink-wrapped software is buggy. The software cranked out by corporate programming is buggy. Your code is buggy. This can be said not only with confidence, but conviction. It is the nature of the software beast.

But there is an important qualifier. How buggy? And this can be further classified by two criteria, How bad and how often? Table 8.8 lists a handy bug classification matrix. Pick one from each column (mix and match), according to the circumstances.

Table 8.8
Bug classification matrix.

Severity of Bugs	Frequency of Bugs	Consequence of Bugs
Causes system crash.	Every time it's used.	Programmer/staff is fired, disgraced, or hung.
Program crashes.	Several times a day.	Program is discredited, abandoned, or ignored.
Program causes data errors.	Once or twice a day.	Program is used but disliked or distrusted.
Program fails to perform some function.	A couple of times a week.	Program is marginally acceptable.
Program has nonfatal errors.	Once in a while.	Program is okay, but could use some polishing.
Program has harmless but irritating glitches.	Happened only once.	Program is okay. Take care of things as they crop up.

This matrix may appear light-hearted in spirit, but there is pain within it. Real people have had really bad experiences with buggy software—both the users and the makers. The subject is not trivial.

You can start with classifying software problems in two very broad categories: design problems and programming errors. The first category is usually not considered part of debugging, although it's every bit as important (and potentially lethal). It represents a whole class of problems, including missing functionality, difficulty of use, bad documentation, and awkward design. However, programming errors are the focus here.

Under the category of programming errors, there are three generally recognized types: *syntax errors, run-time errors*, and *functional errors*. Syntax errors are mistakes in the mechanics of programming—typos, missing clauses, and command structure errors. Most, but not all, of these are caught by the FoxPro compiler. Then there are the errors that don't show up until you run the program—the run-time errors. These can be of many kinds, but are exemplified by problems with variables—bad data types, missing data—or with program environment errors, like running out of memory, or not being able to open a file. The third type, functional errors, are things that run well (they don't crash), but don't do what they're supposed to do. Calculation errors, data mix-ups, and missing information fall into this type.

When you debug a program, you have to deal with all three types of errors. Sometimes simultaneously. There is no magic formula. Debugging is one part setup (the tools you have at your disposal for analyzing and fixing bugs), one part knowledge and experience (errors are frequently not what the error messages say they are), and one part black art and luck.

Sometimes you fix a bug, not by finding it, but by doing something a different way. Sometimes you change one thing, which fixes a bug, and then two more bugs are caused by what you changed. If you've done very much debugging at all, you'll understand why it can be said all software is buggy.

It's a great challenge to be a good debugger. And a necessary skill. The better you become at it, the better your software is likely to be, not to mention reducing the time spent dealing with it.

The Edit/Compile/Debug Cycle

There are a lot of "cycles" in programming. Few have more impact on the life of a professional programmer than the edit/compile/debug cycle. The reason is simple to state:

```
Edit/Compile/Debug Cycle = TIME = $
```

It takes time to create and edit a program. It takes time to compile it. It takes a lot of time to debug it. And this is a cycle—you do it over and over again. Write some code. Compile it. Run it. Encounter bugs. Fix bugs. Write some more code. As mentioned before, in an eight-hour day, a programmer working at an "average" pace (if there is such a thing) probably goes through this cycle fifty to seventy times a day.

Given this repetitive cycle and its relationship to time and money, it's no wonder that professional programmers (and management) pay considerable attention to the speed and efficiency of performing the various elements of the cycle. In fact it's usually close to an obsession.

If you're not a professional programmer, does this cycle affect you? That all depends on your attitude about time spent programming. If this is basically leisure time, and you have few goals for programming other than enjoyment (lucky you), then the timing of the cycle is probably a non-issue. However, if your time is more limited, your goals more ambitious, or any combination thereof, then you too will probably become interested in the efficiency of your edit/compile/debug cycle. Note that with FoxPro the full cycle becomes edit/generate/compile/build/debug.

Of course, this is a complicated issue. Hardware plays a role. The software development environment, in this case FoxPro, plays a huge role. Your own habits and approaches are extremely important. As they say, it all adds up.

The two worst thieves of time in programming are "simple modifications," and debugging. Programmers sometimes go improvement happy and are forever tweaking their code. They can also become mired in a seemingly endless process of debugging. On projects that require working with users, it's estimated that program modification and debugging take up to 60 percent of the project time. Of that, easily half is debugging. Anything that takes up to 30 percent of your programming time, is worth a good hard look.

Dealing with a Bug By Stages

Your first problem is finding the source of the bug. You actually have several levels or stages of possible response:

1. Rely on the error message, experience, and a look at the code.
2. Bring in one or more of the FoxPro debugging tools.
3. Set up a complete debugging session.
4. Quit looking for the bug, and program around it.

This last one is partly tongue-in-cheek. Programmers' don't generally go around categorizing bug hunting like the a civil emergency plan. On the other hand, maybe they should. Call it what you like, but debugging is not all the same. For one thing, you don't necessarily haul out all of the debugging machinery. It takes time to set up a debug session of any thoroughness. Sometimes a lot of time. So the course of first choice is to use your noodle, and perhaps to go poking in the code at the point of suspected trouble. That point, is sometimes indicated by the error message, shown in Figures 8.8 and 8.9.

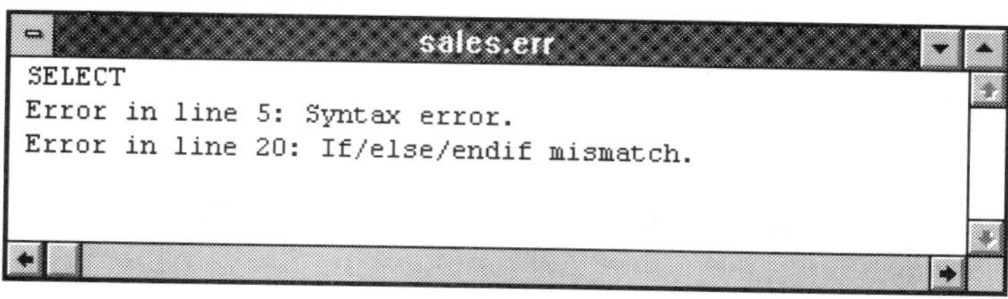

Figure 8.8 *Compiler error messages.*

Figure 8.9 *Run-time error messages.*

The official FoxPro error messages are helpful, but they don't go very far. In fact sometimes they are downright wrong, or worse, misleading. You'll quickly learn that bugs may produce "symptoms" via the error message that only hint at the underlying cause(s). To find the actual cause of a bug, you may need to carefully scrutinize the program's condition and vital signs at the time the bug occurred. What files and indexes were open? What windows and variables were active? Depending on the type of error message, there may be dozens of pieces of information that could help to lead you to a diagnosis. What you need is more information, which FoxPro doesn't automatically give you.

Commands and Functions for Debugging

There are about twenty commands and functions that are primarily used for debugging and error trapping. Their range of capabilities is quite large, but unfortunately in FoxPro their use is not integrated—with anything. Here's a brief run-down of what's available:

Compiler Error

SETLOGERRORS

SET LOGERRORS sends or does not send errors found by the FoxPro compiler to an error file (<name of current program file>.ERR). The default is on. Its syntax is:

```
SET LOGERRORS ON | OFF
```

MODIFY FILE

You can use MODIFY FILE in the Command window to open the log of errors file after compiling a program. If you're working in the Project Manager, this is available from a menu option. The extensions of the error file is .ERR and the file name is the same as that of the compiled program file. The syntax of MODIFY FILE is:

```
MODIFY FILE [ <file> | ? ]
MODIFY FILE customer.err
MODIFY FILE ?
```

Run-Time Error

The following commands are for handling run-time errors.

ERROR

```
= ERROR( )
```

Returns: the number of the most recent error, as catalogued in the *Developer's Guide*.

LINENO

```
LINENO( [1] )
```

[1] is the line number returned is relative to current function or procedure, rather than file.

```
= LINEND(1)
```

Returns: the line number of the currently executing program.

This could be more useful than it is. Unfortunately, program editors, including FoxPro's, are unable to number lines from the beginning of procedures/functions that are inside a file. This makes the relative line number something less than automatically applicable.

MESSAGE

```
MESSAGE( [1] )
```

[1] returns the program source code that (presumably) caused the error.

```
= Message(1) >
```

Returns: the current error message.

SYS

```
SYS(2018)
= SYS(2018)
```

Returns: additional information about an error (the error message parameter), usually the name of a file or variable that was missing.

ON ERROR

ON ERROR invokes a user-defined error handler, that is, if you've written one. This is an important part of building a complete application, though for most programmers it seems to constitute a pain in the patootie. In the context of debugging, this command can also be used to route error handling to a debugging routine. Its syntax is:

```
ON ERROR [<command>]
```

<command> is the procedure or function to execute.

```
ON ERROR DO ERRLOG WITH ERROR(), LINENO(), MESSAGE(),;
MESSAGE(1)
```

PROGRAM

The syntax for PROGRAM is:

```
PROGRAM(<expN>)
```

<expN> lists, from 0= master program, backwards through program levels: 1,2,3,...

```
=PROGRAM(3)
```

Returns: the name of the program back 3 levels.

SYS(16 [,<expN>]) is an alternate function.

SUSPEND

SUSPEND stops the execution of a program, but does not clear memory variables or any other element of the working environment. The program is in suspension until either CANCEL or RESUME is issued. This is mostly used to halt a program so you can get a leisurely look at the current environment, using DISPLAY MEMORY and DISPLAY STATUS.

RESUME

This command resumes execution of a program from the point where it was suspended.

RETRY

After an error has occurred, you have the option (usually) to RETRY. This reruns the code that caused the error.

VARREAD

The syntax for this command is:

```
VARREAD( )
```

Returns: the name of the field, variable, or array element for the currently active GET or Browse field, if any.

This function has a variety of uses, including context sensitive help and field processing, but for debugging it is often useful to know the current field or variable. This is particularly true in the FoxPro environment, where line numbers in the Screen Builder output files (.SPR) are not helpful to locating errors in the screen file (.SCX).

SYS(18) is an alternate function.

General Debugging

The following commands can be entered in the Command window, or embedded in program code as part of the setup for debugging.

SET DEBUG ON | OFF

This command enables or disables access to the Trace and Debug windows through the system menu. Either window is still available through program control. The default is off.

ACTIVATE WINDOW DEBUG and DEACTIVATE WINDOW DEBUG

These commands open or close the Debug window.

SET ECHO ON | OFF

SET ECHO opens or closes the Trace window for program debugging. The default is off.

An alternate command is ACTIVATE/DEACTIVATE WINDOW TRACE

SET STEP ON | OFF

This function opens or closes the Trace window and automatically sets the trace option to Step. This halts execution until you use either the Resume or Step option in the Trace menu to continue the program. The default is off.

SET TRBETWEEN ON | OFF

This command is a companion command to SET STEP and SET ECHO, this sets the Trace window to display all lines of code, if on, and only the line of code at a breakpoint, if off. This is the same as the Trace Between Breaks option in the Trace window menu. The default is on.

THROTTLE

Another companion command to SET STEP and SET ECHO, this system variable specifies how fast lines of code will be displayed in the Trace window. Its syntax is:

```
_THROTTLE = <expN>
```

<expN> is the delay in seconds between execution of program lines.

The default speed, <expN>, is set to 0, with no delay between display of each line. The allowed range is from 0 (fastest) to 5.5 (slowest). For the most part, code zips by so fast at anything under .3 seconds, that trying to read it is futile. This value can also be set through the Trace window menu option, Throttle.

SET DOHISTORY ON | OFF

When set on, this places the commands of a program into the Command window as the program executes. For most purposes, it's better to use the Trace window. However, if you need to test something in the code by altering it, this is a way to be able to edit and then execute any line of code. The default is off.

SET TALK

The syntax for SET TALK is:

```
SET TALK ON | OFF | WINDOW [<window name>] | NOWINDOW
```

With talk on, you can see the results of calculations, variable assignments, and the status of most table operation commands (such as COUNT and INDEX). The output can be directed to the screen/desktop [NOWINDOW] or to a specific window (which must already be defined). The default is on.

SET ODOMETER

The syntax for this function is:

```
SET ODOMETER TO <expN>
```

It is a companion command to SET TALK, this sets the reporting interval (how many records processed between update of display), when talk is set on. The default is one hundred records. Unless the table being processed is very large or very small, this should be sufficient to keep the user informed on the progress of a table operation.

Rolling Your Own Debug Screen

You could use some of the commands and functions described above to cobble together your own debugging information. However, the following is an example, something you can use and modify for your own purposes and approaches. It's called StatLook( ), and it's designed to provide easy access to a lot of FoxPro information that could help you analyze an error. It's working surface looks like Figure 8.10.

Figure 8.10
Statlook debug screen.

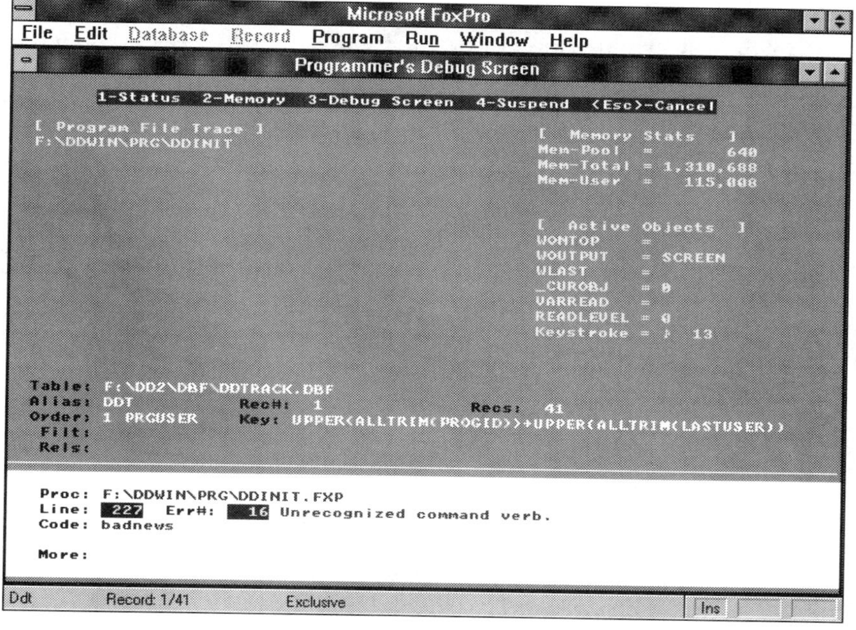

Hooking this error trapping system into your program is simple, and shows how the various error related functions can be used. First move the STATLOOK() function from the distribution disk into your own procedure file. Then somewhere in the initialization of your programs, you insert this code:

```
ON ERROR DO STATLOOK WITH ERROR(), MESSAGE(), MESSAGE(1),
SYS(16),;
   LINENO(1), SYS(102), SYS(100), SYS(101), WOUTPUT(),
LASTKEY()
```

This "arms" the FoxPro error trapping to intercept error calls and send them to STATLOOK(). The various arguments used in calling STATLOOK() provide the information needed to analyze an error. You can also assign the same code to a function key, so that STATLOOK() can be invoked at almost any time during the run of a program. For example:

```
ON KEY F12 DO STATLOOK WITH ERROR(), MESSAGE(), MESSAGE(1),
SYS(16),;
    LINENO(1), SYS(102), SYS(100), SYS(101), WOUTPUT(),
LASTKEY()
```

This screen has no READ, and a very simple menu, in order to reduce conflicts with the program environment at the time and error occurs. When the screen first appears, pressing any key will bring up the options menu. Any keystroke other than a menu option will resume execution of the program. The options menu will let you inspect the current status (files, indexes etc.) and memory variables. Otherwise you can suspend the program, cancel but retain the operating status, or cancel and clear everything. STATLOOK() is designed for programmers, and is usually removed in favor of a less technical error reporting system for users.

If the source of the bug is not apparent from the information, or from examining code, you then make a decision about how much debugging machinery to use. Is this a level 2 debug? There are two main pieces—the Debug window, and the Trace window. Both of them take time to set up, time to run, and complicate the searching process. But sometimes there is no other way. Of the two, the quickest to use is the Debug window.

The Debug Window

The Debug window, shown in Figure 8.11, can be started by selecting Program, Debug from the system menu, or with ACTIVATE WINDOW

DEBUG in the Command window or a program. Most of the time, you activate the window from the menu and Command window and proceed to enter expressions.

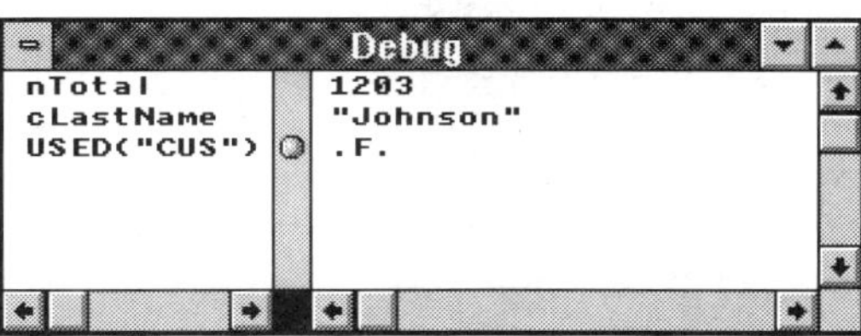

Figure 8.11 *The Debug window.*

The main purpose of the Debug window is to allow you to watch the changing values of *expressions* as the program executes. Again, this is expressions in the broad FoxPro sense of the term—variables, functions, and logical expressions. About the only thing you can't put in the expression area of the Debug window is a macro. You can type one in, but FoxPro sends out a weak beep of complaint, and then proceeds to ignore your entry. Otherwise, you can enter any expression that you think would be helpful to isolate a problem.

Naturally there are a gazillion circumstances for an error, and just as many approaches to using the Debug window. But here's a rather typical example, which should illustrate the flavor of the process, where the error message is:

```
! Invalid function argument value, type, or count.
```

This message indicates that a FoxPro function (*not* a UDF) has been passed an invalid argument. It's most likely a parameter receiving the wrong data type, but at this point you don't know that for sure. There might be something wrong with several parameters.

From the StatLook() window you see the currently executing procedure is a program file—cuscalc.prg—and you have a line number, 34, and the offending line:

```
REPLACE ALL cus.district WITH;
STUFF(cDistrict,cOld,cNew,nStart,nTimes)
```

The offending function is STUFF(), and you have five parameters that could be wrong. It's time to turn on the Debug window and have a look at these variables as they change just preceding the function call. Write down the names of the five variables. If this were the Trace window, you could use **Copy** and **Paste** to save the variable names, but when FoxPro first detects an error, it gives you nothing in the way of an integrated path to debugging.

Open the Debug window, and enter the five variables in the expression area. The value side should evaluate to null or empty values, since the program has stopped execution. (Unless some of the variables were Public.) Before you go back to run the program again, there's one more step you can take in the Debug window, set a breakpoint.

The second purpose of the Debug window is to get the program to stop, when it gets to some critical point in the code. This could be at the beginning of a function, or when a file opens, or when a variable takes on a certain value. To do this, the Debug window lets you set a *breakpoint* on a specific expression. If that expression evaluates to true, then program execution is halted, and you can decide whether to open the Trace window, look at memory and file status, and so on. You can also either RESUME execution, which is usually entered in the Command window, or CANCEL the program.

In the case of the example at hand, you might want to enter a breakpoint expression (an expression intended to make the program halt at a specific location). You would enter something like this:

```
PROGRAM()="CUSCALC" AND LINENO()=34.
```

When this evaluates to true, you'll be at the line in the program where the original error message was generated.

Now it's time to re-run the program and watch the memory variables in the Debug window: DO CUSCALC

When the program execution hits your breakpoint, the program stops (but does not cancel), and you can examine the values in the five argument variables:

```
cDistrict     "West South"
cOld          "South"
cNew          324
nStart        6
nTimes        1
```

If you have followed the convention of indicating the data type of variables with the first letter of the name being the type, then you will immediately spot that cNew should be a character, but instead has a numeric value. Otherwise, you'd have to know that the third argument of STUFF is an <expC>.

Now you know the offending variable, but you still need to find out *where* it's being set to the wrong value. In real life, you'd probably open the program file at this point, and go right to the spot where this variable takes on a value (by using the program editor's search capability). But for the sake of edification, let's say that cNew takes on several values along the way to the function call, and you don't have any idea which one is the source of the error. It's time to bring in the Trace window.

The Trace Window

The Trace window, shown in Figure 8.12, is as close as programming gets to motion pictures. The window displays your code as it executes, highlighting one line at a time. It's impressive to watch hours of your coding zip by like a train at high speed. Useless too, because at anywhere near that speed you can't read it. The real purpose of the Trace window is to allow you to inspect the code as it goes by, looking for the flaws that might be causing a bug. In the debug example from above, the Trace window would be used to examine lines of code as the value in the problem variable changes. From that you might be able to detect if you've got some kind of false interaction with a table, or a calculation has gone astray.

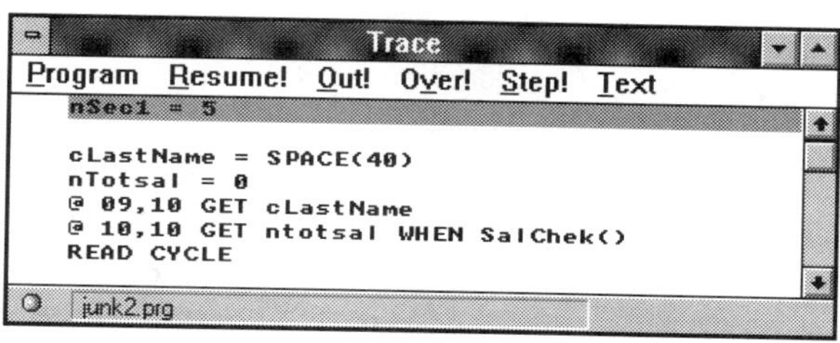

Figure 8.12 *The Trace window.*

There are many ways to invoke the Trace window. Which one you use depends on your judgment of two things: *When* you need to have the window open, and *how fast* it should run. There are a surprising number of choices, including two speed options—Throttle mode and STEP mode. Throttle is the speed at which the lines of a program are executed through the Trace window. This can be anywhere from 0 (full speed) to a delay of 5.5 seconds. The usual reading speeds are between .35 and .6. STEP mode, like it sounds, moves through the code one line at a time and under manual control. You have to click on the Step! option of the Trace menu to make the program continue. Here are the various options (but not all the combinations) for opening the Trace window and starting programs:

- **System menu**—Program, Trace (open window)

- **Trace menu**—Program, Throttle (set throttle speed)
  Program, Open, Do! (start the program at throttle speed) or
  Program, Do! (start the program in STEP mode)
- **Command window**—SET STEP ON, DO <program>
- **Program code**—ACTIVATE WINDOW TRACE, DO <program>
  SET ECHO ON, DO <program>

Once the Trace window is open, many of the options in the Trace menu apply only to execution in the STEP mode. Step! moves the program execution one line at a time. Over! causes program execution to perform subroutines (procedures, functions etc.) without tracing through them. This can be an enormous time saver, since you are often not interested in seeing the code of many subroutines. Out! is seldom used, but signals for execution to continue until it returns to a calling program, where the program halts (suspend) on the first line after the program call. While in STEP mode, or at any other time program execution has been suspended, you can use the Resume! option to start execution again (at throttle speed).

As you'll quickly see, it takes a lot of time to flow code through the Trace window. Since good debugging is also the art of not wasting time, there are a couple of things you can do to reduce the amount of time spent in the Trace window. One of these is to use breakpoints, very similar in concept to the Debug window. You can set breakpoints on most lines in the Trace window (when execution is suspended) simply by clicking with the mouse on the highlighted line, and with the **Spacebar** or **Enter** keys. A bullet is displayed in the breakpoint column at the left of the Trace window. Having set the breakpoints, program execution stops at each, allowing you to inspect variables. Then you can continue with the Resume! menu option.

If you don't want to see all of the code between the breakpoints, use Program, Trace Between Breaks to set display between breaks off. This speeds program execution greatly. However, the approach is cumbersome. The alternate is to put debugging control code into the program itself. Some people prefer this method for its clarity of purpose, although it's hardly less cumbersome than setting breakpoints.

Program Setup

Because of the huge speed penalty for running the Trace and Debug windows, if you're in a situation where repeated testing or bug searching is necessary, it may be more expedient to control debugging within the program. The advantage here is that you can set up more than one "start/stop" areas, have a look at one place, and then move at full speed to the next place. Here's a sample setup:

```
*>>>> START: TESTING/DEBUG <<<<<
ACTIVATE WINDOW DEBUG
ACTIVATE WINDOW TRACE
_THROTTLE = .4

* Execute some code
...
* Temporarily go to step
SET STEP ON

* Execute more code
...

SET STEP OFF
DEACTIVATE WINDOW TRACE
DEACTIVATE WINDOW DEBUG
*>>>> END: TESTING/DEBUG <<<<<
```

The obvious disadvantage to this approach is that you have to go back and clean-up when you're done. None of the methods for tightly controlling Trace window execution is quick and easy. But then you wouldn't be getting this deep into the mechanics of debugging unless you're dealing with a real doozy of a bug (would you?).

Test and Debug Setup

Figure 8.13 is a representation of a level 3 debug, including the Trace window, Debug window, in-program debugging code, the works. You hope you don't have to do this very often, but once in a while, an intractable bug shows up and you have to haul out all of the heavy machinery.

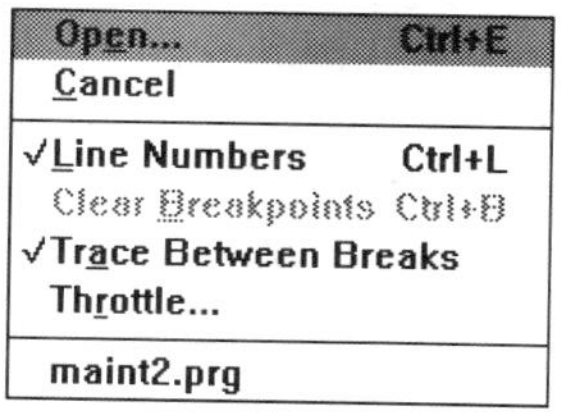

Open... Ctrl+E
Cancel
✓Line Numbers Ctrl+L
Clear Breakpoints Ctrl+B
✓Trace Between Breaks
Throttle...
maint2.prg

Figure 8.13
The Debug setup.

One problem, which you can see immediately, is that there's no place for the program to execute on the screen. You've got so much debugging junk in the way, that something is always going to be covering something else. Which suggests that you can't very effectively use complex debugging setups with user interface and display problems.

Fortunately, the really bad debugging problems are usually environmental or deeply procedural, and only peripherally involve the user interface. And what are these "really bad" bugs? The environmental sort arise from conflicts and interactions of elements outside your program control, for example: Subtle effects of running short on memory. Trouble with TSRs or third-party function libraries. Bugs and anomalies in FoxPro. Bugs and anomalies in Windows or other Windows programs. These are really bad because they have "normal" symptoms and generate normal error messages, but you can never quite seem to find the cause of the problem (because it's not in your program).

The deeply procedural bugs are those that arise from the structure of your program, the interaction of variables, or the way your program handles the data tables (among the most common occurrences). Switching between program modules in particular, the hallmark of event-driven programming, is notorious for "side-effect" bugs. Some of these problems can literally take hours to narrow options, test theories, and try fixes. And sometimes, you simply have to throw up your hands and say, "I don't know what's causing the problem. I'll just work around it." That's when you've reached level 4 debugging.

Most debugging is of the variety in which you spend most of the time rooting and snorting through code and the debug machinery, only to find something you can fix in one or two minutes (or less). It's the analyzing and information gathering part of the process that's key, and why there's no real substitute for experience. Still, if it's any motivation to beginners, it's true that experienced programmers almost never make syntax errors!

Building Short Programs

Leaving the horrors of debugging encountered in the last section, it's time to get back to the purpose of good old fashioned coding—writing programs. Basic programs are just that—basic. The cleaner, clearer, and more direct they are, the better. Even if you become an absolute whiz at the event-driven, user-interface dominated, object-oriented programming of the Power Tools, there are times when you'll come back to these simple program files for solace and grounding. They fit in your head, from beginning to end. They accomplish something specific. And they don't take weeks to write, test, and debug.

Almost by definition, these programs should fit in a single file (.PRG). They may or may not include a number of subsidiary procedures and functions, also in the same file. For the most part, these short programs should be extensions or outgrowths of the kind of data maintenance you've done in the Command window. Only here your work can be repeated, enhanced, and even multiplied.

The form of the programs is also basic:

1. Say what the program is about (header).
2. Save and reset the environment.
3. Open tables, indexes, and relations.
4. Get any user input needed for setup.
5. Do the job—process something.
6. Cleanup and quit.

The samples program below fits this mold.

Sample Program

In the chapter on functions, an example of a very primitive duplicate field checker was introduced. Here's its bigger brother. The program, DUPECHK.PRG (on the accompanying disk), has some elements and techniques that more or less summarize the basic coding presented in previous chapters:

1. DUPECHK.PRG is a maintenance routine, not far removed from the sort of thing you might do in the Command window.
2. The program has some rudimentary elements of a user interface, but not much. You could enhance it, if the spirit moves.
3. It makes use of all three kinds of variable substitution (name expressions, the EVALUATE() function and macro substitution) in order to make the program generic. You can select any DBF table, any field in that table, and the program will still work.
4. The use of the IIF() is a good example of function nesting. It's used here to determine the data type of the selected field. You might note how the function has been formatted to emphasize the nesting and keep the logic clear.

5. The program uses an array as a substitute data table, plus the ASCAN() function to read the array.
6. It has some slightly tricky logic to check for index tags and locate duplicates. You might read through the code to follow the processing logic.
7. The output options are primitive, but typical for this kind of maintenance program.

```
*************************************************************************
* PROGRAM NAME... DUPECHK.PRG
* DESCRIPTION.... CHECKS FOR DUPLICATE FIELD VALUES
* DATE........... 11/22/92
* PROGRAMMERS.... NK
* NOTES.......... This program can be used for locating
*duplicate values
* in any DBF field. It's primary use would be for index
*key fields where
* duplicates are not allowed. The user must select the
*file to search, and
* then select the field to use for the duplicate search.
*If the field does
* not have a simple index tag (same name as the field),
*then the program
* will alert the user and create one. When the search is
*complete, the user
* has the option to review the duplicate with a Browse, a
*printed list, or
* a screen list.
*
* CALLED BY...... General Use
* CALLS.......... None
* REVISIONS...... 6/22/93 Additional user interface bells
and whistles, nk
*************************************************************************

*——————————————————————[ SETUP
PRIVATE cChkFile, i, n, is_tag, cField, cYn
PRIVATE newfield, oldfield, aLog, cLook

cTalk = SET("TALK")                       && save talk and
safety
cSafe = SET("SAFETY")                     && for restoration
SET TALK OFF
SET SAFETY OFF
```

```
CLEAR
@ 2,20 SAY "* KEY FIELD DUPLICATE CHECKING PROGRAM *"
COLOR GR+/B

*————————[ Get the file to work on
cChkFile = GETFILE("DBF","Select the file to test for
duplicates.")

IF NOT EMPTY( cChkFile )                  && user must select
a file

  *Note macro substitution use.
  USE &cChkFile ALIAS chk

  *————————[ Get the field to check
  = AFIELD( aChkField )                   && field list to an
array
  cField = SPACE(10)
  @ 8,20 SAY "Select the field to check"
  @ 9,20 GET cField FROM aChkField PICTURE "@^T"
  READ

  IF NOT EMPTY( cField )                  && user must select
a field
    *————————[ Find out if this is an indexed field.
    i=1                                   && tag counter
    is_tag = .f.                          && tag flag
    *> Loop through tags for this file
    DO WHILE .t.
      *> Look for a match between the selected field and
tag keys
      IF NOT EMPTY( SYS(14,i))            && sys(14) returns
tag keys
        IF TRIM(cField) == SYS(14,i)
      is_tag = .t.                   && if a tag exists, set
flag
      EXIT                           && and drop out of loop
    ENDIF
  ELSE                               && no more tags
    EXIT                             && exit loop
  ENDIF
  i=i+1
ENDDO

IF NOT is_tag                        && if field not indexed
```

```
      cYn = "Y"
      @ 13,20 SAY "The field is not indexed. Create a temporary
index? ";
              GET cYn PICTURE "@Y"
      READ

      *> If user agrees, index field - or else end program.
      IF cYn = "Y"
        * Note name expression use.
        INDEX ON (cField) TAG (cField)
      ELSE
        WAIT "Program completed." WINDOW NOWAIT
        CLEAR ALL
        CLEAR
        CANCEL
      ENDIF
    ENDIF
  ENDIF // field selection
ELSE                                      && no file selected
  WAIT "Program completed." WINDOW NOWAIT
  CLEAR ALL
  CLEAR
  CANCEL
ENDIF // file selection

*————————[ SETUP FOR DUPLICATE SEARCH
* Create a holding array for the record numbers of all
* duplicates that are located. This will later be tied to
* output for user inspection.

DECLARE aLog[1,2]
i = 1                                     && array counter
n = 1                                     && loop counter

* Duplicates are located by comparing the field value from the
* previous record with the field value of the current record.
* These values are stored in two variables: oldfield and
*newfield.
* The complex looking initialization for the oldfield variable
*is
* needed so that it will have the same data type as the
*newfield
* variable, but not contain the same value.

newfield = &cField                        && comparison variables
```

```
oldfield = IIF(TYPE("&cField")="C","",;
           IIF(TYPE("&cField")="D",{},;
           IIF(TYPE("&cField")="N",0,;
           IIF(TYPE("&cField")="L",.f.,;
           IIF(TYPE("&cField")="F",0,"")))))
*> User messaging
@ 15,20 SAY "Searching - Record #: "
@ 15,48 SAY " of "
@ 15,52 SAY RECCOUNT() PICTURE "@B"

GO TOP
*————————[ SCAN LOOP FOR DUPES
SCAN

  @ 15,43 SAY n PICTURE "@B #####"

  * Load the comparison variable. Note substitution method
  * to use the field selected.
  newfield = EVALUATE( cField )

  *————————[ Find a duplicate
  IF newfield == oldfield                && note "exact" match:
==

    *————————[ Log both records to the array
    DIMENSION aLog[i,2]
    aLog[i,1] = RECNO("chk")             && log record number
    aLog[i,2] = EVALUATE( cField )       && and content of field
    i=i+1

    *> Get the previous record and log it.
    SKIP -1
    DIMENSION aLog[i,2]
    aLog[i,1] = RECNO("chk")
    aLog[i,2] = EVALUATE( cField )
    i=i+1

    SKIP

  ENDIF

  *> Load previous field variable for comparison.
  oldfield = EVALUATE( cField )
  n=n+1

ENDSCAN // end of checking loop
```

```
*——————————————[ USER OUTPUT OPTIONS

cLook = "Browse"                            && default
@ 17,20 SAY "Select output to:"
@ 18,20 GET cLook PICTURE "@*HT \<Browse;\<Print;\<Screen"
READ

*> Process output options. Note the use of ASCAN to drive
*  the lookup into the logging array, and the use of IIF to
*  feed a .t. or .f. to the FOR clause.
DO CASE
CASE cLook = "Browse"
  BROWSE FOR IIF(ASCAN( aLog, RECNO())>0,.t.,.f.)
CASE cLook = "Print"
  GO TOP
  LIST ALL FOR IIF(ASCAN( aLog, RECNO())>0,.t.,.f.) TO PRINT
CASE cLook = "Screen"
  GO TOP
  DISPLAY ALL FOR IIF( ASCAN( aLog, RECNO()) >0, .t., .f.)
ENDCASE

*——————————————————[ CLEANUP

*> If there is a temporary tag, get rid of it.
IF NOT is_tag
  DELETE TAG (cField)
ENDIF

*> Restore orginal settings
= SET("TALK", ctalk )
= SET("SAFETY", cSafe )

CLEAR ALL
CLEAR
CANCEL
*
```

Building Your Library

With books, CDs, and functions and procedures it's never too early to start a library. But just what is this *library*, and how do you get one?

In the beginning, a library of functions and procedures is a file—a program file. It contains your efforts at building useful, generic, functions and procedures. It contains similar items cadged from bulletin boards, magazines, and friends. And it will grow, evolve, improve, and refine—at your hands. Without question you will see your early efforts in the library and feel like all programmers do when confronted with their own ignorance—appalled. But you'll fix it. You're learning, after all. The library is the repository of the best of your learning.

But what goes into a library? Or what *should* go into it?

The only real criteria are:

1. Any routine that goes into the library should work.
2. The routine can be used in multiple applications. That is, it is in some degree generic.

After that, there are all kinds of things that might qualify for selection. You might, for example, be interested in mathematics. FoxPro has an impoverished selection of math functions and commands. So make some more. Get some from the bulletin boards, and fix those the way you like them. The same goes for many areas of the FoxPro function catalog.

Later, when you have understood how screen sets, snippets, and event-driven programming are supposed to work, you can begin adding elements from that world into your library. This library is going to span many files, and probably will take some housekeeping to keep it all straight.

There's no formula for library construction. But here are some guidelines:

1. The guiding force in building your library will be your developing intuition of what constitutes a generic procedure. The day will come when you are programming something, and the proverbial light bulb (15 watt) will come on. "I could have used this before!" When you begin to realize that a function might have uses beyond the current project, it's time to start thinking about being more rigorously generic.
2. Rigorously generic simply means to be more careful and systematic about preparing the code. Think about how it might be used in other places, and what it would take to make sure that's both possible and safe. For one thing, start right away with giving it good documentation, a complete header with plenty of explanation about what's going on, and beef up the in-code explanations.

3. Then examine the variables used in the procedure. Where do they come from? Which ones are local, which public? Are the parameters (if any) generic, or are they tightly bound to an application? Make every attempt to have only private variables in the procedure, or those that are passed through the parameters.
4. Pay special attention to the use of tables. Are specific tables required in the routine? As a matter of fact many generic routines don't use tables at all. It they do use tables, they've got to be generic tables, or at least ones that share a common set of fields.
5. Check the routine for all cases where the program environment is changed, such as SET commands and redefined system variables. It's the responsibility of the library routine to preserve things the way they were when it started, and restore them before it returns.
6. As you look at variables, tables and the program environment, start thinking about side effects. Does your routine close anything, rename anything, redefine anything? Does it do anything that might adversely affect other procedures? Work these out so that you're reasonably sure there are no side effects.
7. Test your creation. Really test it. If possible have other people test it.

That's it. A library is meant to be used. You take things out, and put things in. It's a dynamic place. It's also the basis of what will become your object-oriented class library—but thankfully you won't have to start worrying about that until FoxPro for Windows version 3.0.

Section III

Application Development

The basic programming in FoxPro (as covered in Section II) can take you a long way. For many situations, especially when you're doing *ad hoc* data management, it may be all you need. But as the programming becomes more complex, and especially if the software will be used by other people, then the task quickly becomes much bigger. The requirements and responsibilities multiply, as do the components of your projects. This is application country.

An *application* in FoxPro jargon is typically software designed and programmed to do a definable job—inventory, purchasing, contact management, whatever—and is complete with database files, program modules, and reports. In most cases it is assumed an application will have some kind of distribution, that it will be used by people other than the programmer or data manager.

In the old days (before FoxPro 2.0) this was standard programming territory. It still can be, but Microsoft/Fox now provides a set of Power Tools to help automate and organize the process of building applications:

- Project Manager
- Screen Builder
- Menu Builder
- Report Writer/Label Generator
- RQBE

The importance of these tools in the overall scheme of FoxPro cannot be stressed enough. This is where the action is, now, and even more in the future. Master these tools, and you are in a world of database software development. However, they take time to master. And, as you will see, for the most part they are not geared toward programming on the Q&D (quick and dirty). These are tools for building full-scale applications.

Any attempt to describe the process of building an application is going to run afoul of scale. A large-scale application, say a customized accounting system intended for commercial sale, is very different from an application you can create in an afternoon. Yet they are both applications. The approach taken in this book is to list and explain most of the myriad elements and options for building large-scale applications, but at the same time help you decide which of them you need for *your* application. The trick, if you can call it that, is to know when you don't need it without compromising the success of the project. Loading an application with things it doesn't need, wastes time, confuses users, and makes maintenance more difficult. Leaving something out, especially something that might be needed in the long run, can also be disastrous.

There's nothing this book can provide that will replace the experience of actually building several applications. Mistakes will teach you more than any chapter. In fact a lot of the things covered here will make more sense once you've been there and sweated through your first couple of applications with FoxPro. But then again, sometimes looking at a road map helps, most especially when you've never been to a place before.

Chapter 9
Organizing Applications

It's important to remember, FoxPro for Windows is a huge system of data management and programming tools, and as such, it is a means to an end. Using FoxPro isn't (or shouldn't be) the whole story of developing an application.

Even the smallest and least complex of applications arises from somebody's need to computerize something. This "somebody" is usually other people, who have their own needs, personalities, schedules, relationships, money, equipment, and so forth. This is the context of your application. While it would be comfortable to sit down by yourself with FoxPro and bang out the perfect application with its powerful tools, you'll find that the context of your application will often not be so tidy.

Unless you are developing applications strictly for yourself, there is always the fact that other people have an interest, perhaps a stake, in what you create. The computer industry likes to lump these other people into the broadest possible category—users. However, you know them as customers, clients, employers, colleagues, or friends. Much of the time you even know them by name. And their wishes are often what started the application in the first place.

Two facts are the driving force behind most application development: Applications are *for somebody* and are supposed to *do something*. Throughout the process of building an application you'll be bumping into one or both of these touchstones. Do yourself a favor and embrace them, often and honestly. It's all too easy to become engulfed by (or enamored of) the complex working environment of FoxPro for Windows. Turning the learning of FoxPro into the object of the project may be fun, but that's not what building a particular application is really about.

The Application Development Cycle

There are many ways of describing the application development cycle. Some of them are academic (in at least two senses of the word), some are proprietary (the concept belongs to a company), some are based on experience and common sense. And some are...crazy. Most of them, programmers find unappealing or unnecessary. Programmers seem to prefer the footwear slogan, "Just Do It."

Just doing it can work, as long as the project is simple enough to keep in your head, and doesn't need to be communicated to anyone. Such projects do exist, and programmers relish them. But most application projects are more complex. They may take a long time, involve many people, require detailed communication, and need to be carefully designed. Which means that most applications have an application development cycle, whether the developer chooses to deal with it explicitly or not.

The underlying steps and concepts of an Application Development Cycle are very straight-forward:

1. **Analysis.** Find out what the application is supposed to do, what data is involved, and who's supposed to use it.
2. **Design**. Know something about the application and figure out what the data tables should look like and what pieces of programming (such as modules and screens) are needed.
3. **Programming**.

As Ross Perot would say, "It's that simple."

At least it can be that simple. A slightly more detailed view of the steps and concepts are represented in Figure 9.1. This is just one view of the cycle, one that is adapted for database applications.

Real development is not this sequential, of course. Steps overlap, get lost, cycle among themselves, and generally move forward in a much more messy fashion.

Figure 9.1 *Application development cycle.*

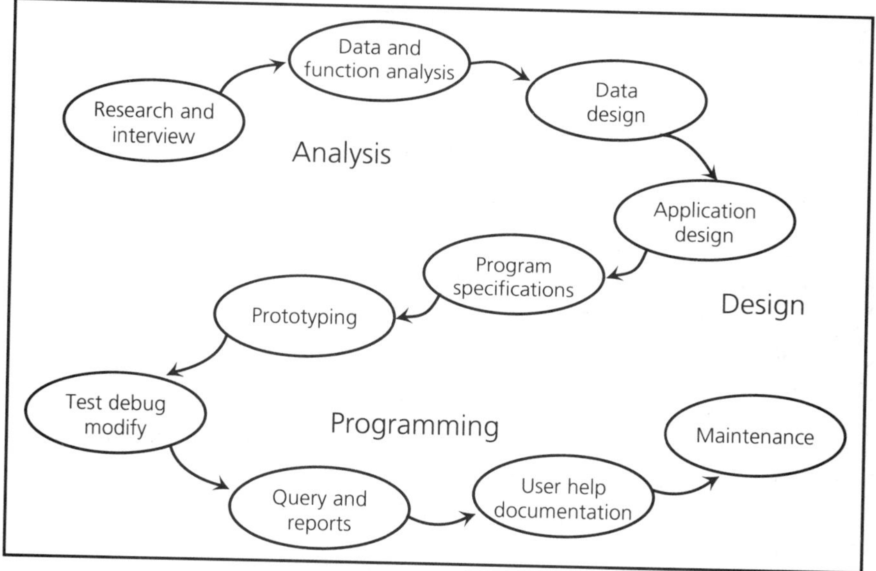

Research and Interview

On one project, the guy down the hall comes in and says, "Hey, we need a program to collect the stock trades for the day. Can you whip something up?" Another project, a half million dollar application, is expected to require over a year to develop and will involve half the people in the company. The scale of research, interview and analysis phases for these two projects is quite different. But not objective. In both cases you need to sit down with the principal(s) and find out what they want. You need to see documents and other information that will help you decide what data is involved. And you need to understand who will use the application—their environment, habits, and needs. It's just that one project can be researched in a day, and the other might take months.

More projects are made or broken at this stage of the development cycle than at any other point. That's because most applications fail by not understanding what the user wants. Sometimes the user's requirements are misunderstood. As a result, some projects are scaled way too large and have a tendency to founder. Likewise, missing important features can lead to rejection. At other times, the developer's eagerness to push a certain approach will inhibit the user from expressing what they really want.

Above and beyond what the users tell you about their requirements, many applications can only be understood if you take the time to learn about the user's business. How do they work? What is their working environment, including computers? What business rules do they apply to the area of the application? Much of this can only be learned by observation, interview, and even participation. On some projects, particularly those which have extensive or intricate user interface requirements, this can be make or break research.

The few paragraphs above don't begin to do justice to the importance or subtleties of the subject. Analysis is one area where it's highly recommended to read specialized literature, perhaps take a course in school, and if possible talk to people who do this kind of work. Keep in mind that application analysis is a profession in its own right. That says volumes about just how complex and special it can be.

Fortunately, outside of mega-projects (however that is defined), common sense is a reasonable guide to researching an application. As you learn to develop applications, there's no need to be paranoid about lack of special knowledge. Just be aware of your limits, and try to be systematic.

Data and Functional Analysis

It's a reasonable assumption that FoxPro is used mostly to develop applications that have a large data-management component. Or at least where having access to an underlying database is important. At this step of analysis, you spread out the collected documents and notes about project data, and start to identify individual items of information (often called data items, or data elements). While making this identification, you can also begin to categorize the data by type, and make some estimations of volume, turnover rates, and so on.

The object of the data analysis is to understand what information the user believes is needed, where it is located, and who uses it. This is a user-centered approach to data analysis, reflecting the most common type of application for FoxPro. There are many other approaches. Some applications have little or no user participation. In these cases, approaches like transaction analysis and data flow diagrams may be more useful. You also need to cover external data requirements; some projects will require connection to other computers, or to convert existing data. Either case requires a careful analysis of the type of data, formatting of files, and means of communications.

Data analysis is the technical side of researching an application. Again, this is an area of considerable specialization. This is also the step where CASE (Computer Assisted Software Engineering) tools are often employed. Although CASE techniques are outside the scope of this book, you should be aware that a growing number of companies and government agencies require analysis that uses one or more diagrammatic analysis techniques, such as Entity-Relation (E-R), Gane/Sarson, and Chen/Martin.

The other part of the analysis step, functional analysis, takes many forms. However, essentially it's a blending of data flow and an analysis of processes and procedures (human or computer). Generally this means looking at the jobs performed by people who will use the computer application, and relate that to computer processes like data entry, data update, and reporting.

As an example, here's a line from an analyst's notebook: "Sally in PR generates the piece, but Bill in management needs to read and approve it before it's moved to the layout editor." In such notes, you read that a document is written by Sally, which in a FoxPro application means editing in a memo field, or else either an OLE or DDE connection to a word processor. On Sally's command, the document is stored in a memo or general field of a FoxPro table, and made available to Bill. There you will need a screen to present the document for revision and a way to capture an approval signature. Finally, the approved document is transferred to the appropriate person in the art room, who will acknowledge the receipt (needing an entry screen) and then export the document to layout software.

That one note called for at least three review and entry screens, a notification process, data transfer of two different kinds, and a running documentation of the procedure (such as dates and time). You would also make explicit note that the system obviously needs to be running on a network, probably requires specialized work with OLE or DDE and a Windows based word processor, and needs some minimal security for sign-off and archiving. All of these become elements in the design of the application.

Data Design

This step is characteristic of applications built around data management. Of course not all of the applications you build will need dozens of tables and complex relations. But enough of them will be big enough to spend time with data design.

The difference between data design and data analysis is that you are moving from generic data to data that will be captured by specific FoxPro tables. You may have made a list of items on a current (typewritten) report. Now you will decide what data type they are (or should be), what their length is, and finally how they should be named as a field in a FoxPro table. At the same time you are identifying fields, the table design should be taking shape. It's part of this process to develop the *relational schema*, usually a diagram, that outlines the tables and the relations between them. At the same time, you are also identifying indexes (tags), and other aspects of the data system like filters and one-to-many relations.

Application Design

Once the data tables have been defined (provisionally, of course), the next step is to design the structure of the application. Usually this means defining modules, screens, menus, and other major structural elements. You will also be making numerous decisions about what elements of a complete application apply: application security, system codes, output management, and help systems, etc.

Program Specification

Program specifications, "the specs," are more typical of applications being built on contract (or bid). But generally, most applications benefit from having the details spelled out. How many screens, reports, and other program elements? Time estimates. Cost estimates. Materials needed. Hardware required. Communications and LAN requirements. This can be as simple as a list of time and materials, or a complete work order that specifies who should be doing what-where-when.

Prototyping

It's becoming part of the chapter and verse of modern programming that applications begin as prototypes. The prototypes are subjected to review (with the user/client), and then go into the refine and modify phase. However, with FoxPro Power Tools, much of what used to be called prototyping is now closer to a "finished" product from the moment a screen or menu has been created. This is largely an illusion. With most projects, there is almost constant tweaking of screen layout and other elements to suit the needs (and frequently the whims) of the users. That's what prototyping is all about—getting the user's understanding and consent before you complete the programming.

Test, Debug, and Modify

As the prototypes of modules are completed, they go into the test, debug, and modification phase. This may or may not involve the users in review and testing as well. Generally, software needs considerable debugging at this stage, and is subject to major and minor modifications both at the discretion of the programmer and the user. For most projects, this is the most time consuming phase of the work.

Queries and Reports

Often, queries and reports begin development somewhat after initial module prototyping. (Not always, of course.) The reason for this is to wait for data definitions and data entry to be accepted and stabilized. This avoids needing to change reports every time a small change occurs in the data. In FoxPro there are principally three forms of output: RQBE, Report Writer, and Label maker. The three are often used in concert, or in connection with external programs, like Microsoft's Word for Windows, to produce many kinds of reports and label runs.

User Help and Documentation

There are three kinds of help and documentation. For the user there is on-line help, the help that is part of the application. In FoxPro you have the choice of using the native Windows help system, or using the system developed for FoxPro for DOS. In many cases, user documentation includes printed material as well, in the form of manuals and procedure books. The third kind of documentation is for the programmer. Maintenance and modifications to the program are based on a foundation of having appropriate information about how the system was designed, specified, and then coded.

Maintenance

You don't just throw your application over the wall and run. (although sometimes you might like to). Delivered software has an afterlife called *maintenance*. Whether this means commercial revision of your product, or visits to a client site to fix bugs, all software needs maintenance. Data-based applications in particular need maintenance, because no matter how well they are designed or how robust their machinery, data tables become corrupted and accumulate bad data. Some of this maintenance can be built into your application, and at other times it will take your direct attention.

This "completes" the cycle. Of course, being a cycle, it could very well start over—a new version. Buried in the sweep of this cycle, or whatever form it may take for your applications, are major decisions about your approach, scheduling, and requirements. If you take up application building professionally, these decisions frequently become the basis of profit or loss.

Components of an Application

Having taken a quick look at the development cycle, drop down a level and consider your application from the point of view of what needs to be in it (in addition to the functions required by the main task of the application). For example, you know that the application keeps track of video tapes, so you have a database of tapes, suppliers, and customers. You have screens to look up tapes, enter rentals, and buy more tapes. You will also need reports of various kinds. What else?

People are often surprised by all of the things that go into a complete software application. These are things that require programming, or at least specific work by a programmer/data manager. Luckily, not all of the elements are needed for every project. But many of them are. Table 9.1 lists the components of a complete application.

Table 9.1
Components of a complete application.

Data tables	The usual complement of data tables, indexes, and memo files that form the underlying database of the application.
Data dictionary	A system for recording what tables, indexes, and so forth are used in the application.
Configuration and initialization	External and internal setup for starting the application. Includes the CONFIG.FPW and WIN.INI files, as well as specific startup routines for the application.
Login and security	User login, with or without password, and the application security. This usually includes access checking for menu options and data entry and edit privileges.
Processing routines	Table updating and other purely processing elements of an application that don't need user interfacing.

(continued)

Screens	Data entry and edit, informational, and all other user interface screens of the application.
Menus	System and screen level menus for the entire application.
Reports	Printed reports.
Labels	Mailing lists and label printing.
Queries	Queries (RQBE and SQL-SELECT) independent of printed reports. This might also include the Graphics Wizard.
Report management	Routines for selection of reports and various output methods.
OLE/DDE support	Connection to other Windows software via OLE or DDE.
Multiuser operation	Routines for multiple users (typically on a LAN).
Communications/fax	Ability of the application to use telephone services.
Data transfer	Transfer of data, usually via files, to and from other systems, either over LAN, direct cable, telephone connection, or sneaker net (floppies).
Peripheral input	Input from bar-code devices, scanners, and analog equipment, though specialized, occurs in many applications.
Printer management	Control and access to multiple printers and print forms. (This is fortunately not usually an issue in FoxPro for Windows.)
System parameters	Operational parameters, such as system date, and name of owner, that are used to set up and operate the application.
System codes	Most applications have data that is stored in the form of codes. This is a data table and management system for handling all codes used in the application.
Help system	On-line help system for the user. Either Windows/FoxPro or FoxPro DOS style.
Maintenance routines	User-accessible routines for data-integrity checking, re-indexing, and packing.
Maintenance	Version control and a system for defining and performing application maintenance over a period of time.

Programmer documentation	Documentation specifically for the programmer, including runs of FoxDoc, system diagrams, analytical notes, business rules, and other forms of system documentation.
Error trapping and recovery	A system for replacing the FoxPro error messages with something more meaningful to users.
Data archiving	The ability to archive and retrieve data (off-line access).
Data backup and restore	Routine (daily) data backup and restoration capability.
Distribution	Distribution of an application via compiling as an .EXE or through FoxPro .APP files. Many issues concerning packaging, costs, and pricing.
Installation/setup procedures	Routines for first-time installation, and other application setup.
Data loading/ conversion	Many applications require loading of databases, or conversion of existing data before they become useful. A system for identifying and managing conversion issues is important.
User documentation	Creation of manuals and procedure books to support the user.
User training	User training in the operation and use of the application.
User support	Support of the user in case of emergencies, debug situations, and other assorted crises common to application implementation.

Taken as a whole, the list is daunting. As with the steps of the application development cycle, decisions about what components of an application to include are often critical. Or put more accurately, after the decision to include a component has been made, the real decision is how much of an effort will be made to produce it. User documentation might consist of ten 8 1/2-by-11 sheets stapled together, or a professionally produced and bound book of about four hundred pages. What does a particular application need? User requirements, competitive pressures, and your resources and skills all play a role in such decisions.

Chapter 10
Analysis and Design

Chapter 9 presented an overview of an application. This chapter goes back to the "front end" of an application—analysis and design—to get a better feel for this part of development. It's the area where everybody says "The more time spent here, the more time saved later." There's truth in that. But it isn't always true. You can just as easily over-analyze and over-design.

In some institutional settings—large corporations, government—the tradition of mainframe software development places a high value on analysis and design. As well they should when most applications require months, if not years, and cost hundreds of thousands of dollars, if not millions. In that context, what's a month or two for study and design?

On the personal computer side, things have tended to be much more relaxed about organizing and planning software development. Programming by the seat-of-the-pants is considered normal, even noble. After all, didn't the early successes come from people writing software in their garage? The beauty of personal computers was the freedom to just do a program—without asking for computer time, or needing a degree in computer science.

This is still true of programming with personal computers. But our vision of what can be done with a PC has changed.

Back in 1981 it was great fun to write a database program to catalog a stamp collection. Today, there are probably many of you who are contemplating applications that will run a company—perhaps a big company.

Such large scale and ambitious programming, sometimes called an *industrial strength* application, is not kid stuff. Creating this kind of application wasn't simple for the mainframe programmers, and it isn't simple for PC programmers. While PC development may be faster and less expensive, it still pays to know what you want to do before you do it.

The question for application developers becomes, "What's the right balance of knowing where you're going, and just doing it on the fly?" When using personal computers and FoxPro, how much time and effort do you really need to spend with front end research, analysis, and design?

Part of the answer, if there really is an answer, has to do with personal preferences, talents, and work habits. But surely another part of the answer depends on the nature of the application, it's size, complexity, and context. What follows in this section of the book attempts to explain some of the analysis and design machinery that can be brought to bear on larger projects without going overboard on the technicalities.

Analyzing a Project

It might be a phone call. Or a visit from someone. Or your boss sends you a memo. Perhaps you won a bid. The start of an application development process is exciting. (It better be, or you're in the wrong business.) It represents a new challenge—a challenge to your powers of analysis, your skill with people, your judgment of time, your programming acumen.

You need to confront the more or less blank slate of project definition, the tools and techniques you bring to the story (as well as some you may need to learn along the way), and get busy. Following are some points about the sample project we will be following in this chapter.

- The job at hand is to analyze the needs of a school district for a human resources management system, and design computer software to satisfy those needs.
- The first impression of this project is that school employment practices are complicated. Unions, administrations, teachers, kids, parents, school boards, and local politicians are all involved.

- Some assumptions about this project are that you'll be doing the project with FoxPro (...thank goodness), and it will be done with one type of computer (IBM/compatibles) on a Local Area Network.
- Your first step is to go talk to somebody. Preferably the person who is paying for the project.

Analysis seems like an exercise in parallelism, a lot of things going on simultaneously. For one thing the source of your information is always multifarious. Much of it will come from meetings or interviews with people. Some of it will come from documents or existing computer data. And some of it will come from observation. To get started with the HR application, there are two major efforts: meet and talk with all the principal players—the Director of Personnel, the Director of Finance, and the Superintendent, then with the people who actually do the work: the payroll clerks, personnel, secretaries and so on. At the same time, start collecting stuff. Ask for all the relevant reports, documents, papers, computer printouts, and whatnot that have any bearing on what people do for human resources management in the district. And you tell them not to try to second guess what you need. You want it *all*.

As this information comes flowing in, it's time to start crunching it into those little categorical boxes so beloved by analysts. In this case we'll use the terms *data analysis*, *functional analysis*, and *business rules analysis*. (There are lots of other terminology and approaches, but let's keep this relatively uncomplicated.)

Data Analysis

FoxPro is a data-management system, so one of the first approaches to a new project is normally to find out what data is involved. As a rule, this isn't very difficult. If you're dealing with a business or other organization, there are always reports. Tons of reports. These are invaluable as a starting point, because they indicate what people want by way of information, at least as of the moment. You can expect a percentage of data in the reports is useless, and there will be new data not in the reports—but still, a good 80 percent or better of the data in the current reports will show up in the new system.

The school district involved in the human resources (HR) system, like school districts everywhere, generates reams of report data—daily. However, much of it is coming from a distant mainframe system, maintained by a consortium of schools. It is the remoteness of this system and the inability to get reports containing what they wanted and how they wanted it, that is one of the motivations for this district's move to a PC system.

Downsizing has been going on for a while. In frustration, some of the people of the district have "taken it upon themselves" to put some of their information on PCs and crunch their own reports. Unfortunately, none of their efforts are coordinated. Another perceived reason for developing a new HR application.

Both the mainframe and the PC systems have documentation about the data involved. The mainframe produces a voluminous report from its data dictionary. The best the PC can do is the equivalent of the FoxPro command LIST STRUCTURE TO FILE. Nevertheless, both sources make it easy to identify specific items of information, the data items.

Not all of the reporting is computer generated. A good 20 percent is being done the old-fashioned way—with a typewriter and a copier. In addition, the district has produced a number of handbooks, pamphlets, and worksheets aimed at new employees. A large amount of "on the spot" HR activity—change notices—are also on sheets of paper, or canned forms of one kind or another. These too are fair game for identifying data items.

Some of the best information comes from scribbled worksheets, often tucked among the more official papers. These sometimes reveal what the official reports and documents fail to contain, information that the staff had to collect "on the side."

All told, this particular district officially collected over eight hundred unique data items, and unofficially perhaps another one to two hundred. However, the amount of redundancy is stunning, the original item count tops fifteen hundred. For example, names, addresses, phone numbers in all their variations appear in over sixty documents and databases. Because of the scale of this project, all of the potentially useful data items were catalogued in what was called a "General Data Dictionary" (itself a FoxPro program).

Even a superficial scan of the district's data items shows the information falling in two large groupings: information about employees, and information about their jobs. Although the two types of information are often combined in documents, they are handled as different types of information by the people working with it. As a matter of administrative routine, an expected stock of employee data is maintained by clerical staff. Position information is treated as a matter for management.

At the planning level, many school districts work with a budgeting system based on a somewhat unique concept—a "Full Time Equivalent"(FTE)—usually defined as working for 2,080 hours a year. (Actually this district has three distinct definitions of an FTE, which is a source of some problems.) Jobs are defined both by salary and by FTE. The school financial people track the salary, and everybody else uses the FTE. This is one of those "quirks" that you're looking for when doing data analysis. There is no lack of Human Resource software for general business, but not a great deal for school administration. And the reason is precisely because of things like the FTE. Given peculiarities like this, standard HR software doesn't translate well or easily. It takes another approach, often tailored to the business practices of the school district involved. Which is another reason why this district had decided to roll their own system.

The two primary groups of data, employee and positions is clearly the most important parts of the HR database, but how they should be linked—via data as well as in form—will have to wait for functional analysis.

Functional Analysis

Functional analysis encompasses any kind of analysis that attempts to outline what people will actually do with an application. It could include data flow analysis, job function description, transaction analysis, or any other form of analysis that will be useful in defining the purpose and structure of a computer program.

With the HR system, this part of the analysis starts with a diagram of the personnel/HR job functions such as hiring, payroll, and contract management, as in Figure 10.1. Each of these functions is staffed by at least one person. Any computerization of the HR system, involves these people, and it is very important to include their work patterns and requirements in the functional analysis. Eventually specific screens and menu options are needed to cover their work.

Figure 10.1
Function analysis.

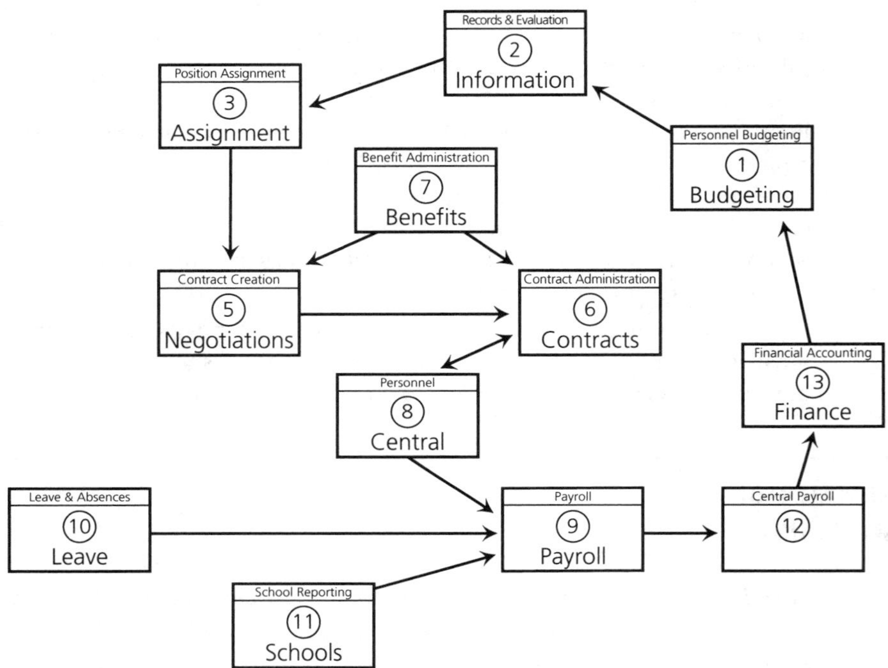

There are many other perspectives to functional analysis. In the HR application, diagrams of the data flow, decision making process, and computerization levels help to clarify who did what, to whom, when, and why. Other applications require different approaches—whatever it takes to gain a clear picture of the functionality you're being asked to computerize. This is the part of analysis that can benefit the most from observation. Spending time observing what people do, and perhaps even doing some of it yourself, can be invaluable. Your knowledge of what people are currently doing, what they would like from a new system, and how things work in general, form the basis of your application design.

Business Rules Analysis

There are rules, written or unwritten, for every job and task in business. When you set about building an application to computerize one or more of these tasks, you'll need to embed these rules in your coding. They could be something as simple as rules for calculation (formulas) of certain percentages, or as complicated as a series of IF, ELSE conditions concerning the steps for hiring a new employee. For example to always calculate the district-wide salary average on the basis of gross salary capacity for each school, minus the average rate of position change for the district. By formula this is district salary average = sum of (school salaries /(school salary capacity - average position change)).

Business rules may be a little too restrictive in connotation. Sometimes what is meant are *business procedures*. For example that accounting must receive all open purchase orders from district departments by the first Friday of each month.

Whatever you choose to call them, there is a growing school of practice that says business rules analysis is an important part of building most applications, equal to relational design and functional analysis. There's good reason for taking this stance. All too often, calculations, logic, and procedural steps are all too "embedded" in the code. Nobody can find them or identify them, although they may be crucial to the operation of a company, and the application.

In FoxPro applications, many of these rules are going to show up in the VALID clauses of the data entry screens, but they could be buried anywhere, or even be part of the design and structure of how the program works. The goal is to make these rules explicit. Track them from the day you discover them (and discover is often the right word), through the day they become part of the program coding, and on into the maintenance documentation.

This part of business rules analysis proved to be very influential in deciding several crucial things about the school district HR system:

- The role of the computer program will be weighted toward supporting and recording personnel decisions and actions, rather than have a decision making role.
- There are areas of HR activity so complex as to be best left out of the initial project.

- Privacy and security should be at or near the top of the list in design of a new system.

CASE Tools for FoxPro

All of the forms of analysis covered above can be approached through specific analysis *methodologies*. This tends to be a fancy word for *diagramming*. Diagrams can be wonderful. At their best, they communicate complex ideas quickly and clearly, even to nonspecialists. Diagrams can also be a nightmare. They can be extremely time consuming, frustrating, and at worst a completely unintelligible hodge-podge of boxes, arrows, and arcane symbols. The difference between the worst and the best, is practice, commitment to the diagramming technique, and usually a CASE tool (or tools).

There are two major approaches to CASE (computer assisted software engineering), usually referred to as *upper CASE* and *lower CASE*. Upper CASE is about software analysis and design, the topics of this chapter. Lower CASE is about code generation from design tools—in short, *the FoxPro Power Tools are CASE tools*. But FoxPro has nothing to offer for upper CASE, the analysis part.

Table Design

In most FoxPro applications, the underlying database is one of the most important components. Your design of this database, sometimes called the *database schema*, is usually the first design step and one that has repercussions throughout the rest of your application. Most of your screens, reports, and other application components are dependent on the database and table design.

Table Design Factors

Table design is about making decisions of balance. There are many factors, as in Figure 10.2, that enter into your decisions about what tables to create, what data items should go into them, how they should be indexed, and how they are related to other tables.

Figure 10.2
Table design factors.

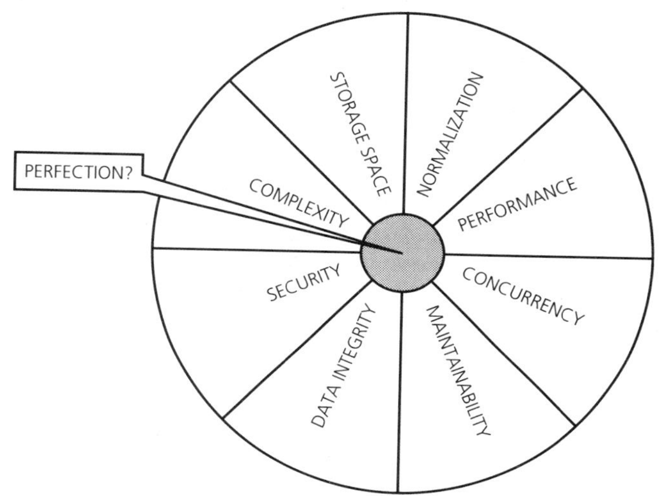

For any specific application, some factors are going to be more important than others. Some, like data integrity, are always important. But most of the time you need to be asking yourself what your tradeoffs are. This is like the famous truism of programming: GOOD, FAST, CHEAP. Pick any two.

Keeping in mind there's a great deal of overlap, following is a run-down of the factors, some of the implicit tradeoffs, and illustration of these considerations in the school district HR application.

Data Integrity

The tolerance for "dirty data" is very low. If a database system introduces data errors, or allows users to create them, it won't be trusted for very long. All data systems develop errors. And some errors are more important than others. In fact, with certain kinds of data, a great deal of error can be tolerated—specifically, any data that isn't being used but is still in the tables. Your understanding of how much data integrity is required by a system will guide decisions concerning such items as maintenance routines and data validation.

For the most part, data integrity is enforced by validating data entry, and running integrity checking routines on a regular basis. In a sense, data integrity isn't something you can design into a system. However, some of the other factors contribute to having more or less data integrity. For example, if a system is extremely complex, it may be more difficult to measure or define data integrity.

In the HR system, most of the personnel data is factual information used in a large number of official calculations and governmental reporting. Accuracy in the description of people, their jobs, and their payment is a primary consideration. For these reasons, this system has a very low threshold of tolerance for bad data. Hardware reliability, network stability, and data entry control are major considerations in the design of the database.

Security

Data security means access control. Who can get at the data, and what can they do when the get there? There are many levels of security, ranging from single password control at the beginning of an application (or no control at all), to completely encrypted data files. If you're working with a network multiuser application, then network security plays an important part in the physical location and distribution of a database schema.

The more extreme security measures, such as complete file encryption, have very definite performance consequences. Distribution, and rights control over subdirectories and files, adds to the complexity of a system. And as a rule, the tighter the security, the less user-friendly the system tends to become.

As might be expected, personnel records are both very private and very sensitive. However, a school district is a public institution, and most of the personnel data is legally a matter of public record. These conflicting mandates require some special security considerations. The system is designed to prevent random accesses to information—break in by hackers, or the snoopy public—while providing sufficiently easy official means for providing the information to required reports and on demand to the general public. This meant incorporating data encryption in a number of fields within tables, and the encryption of one entire table.

Complexity

It's not unusual for an "average" system to have fifty to one hundred data-related files. If most of these tables have multiple relations with other tables, the design of a schema very quickly begins to look like the web of a mad spider. It might work, but who can check it? As the complexity level rises, so too do the problems with maintenance, concurrency, performance, and data integrity.

The usual rule of thumb is to keep it simple. Don't create more files than you absolutely need. Don't throw in relations, indexes, and other linking devices like OLE or DDE unless they are necessary. Of course, some applications *are* complex, and your design will have to reflect that fact. Sometimes throwing in extra files may help to simplify the *content* of a design, even while it adds to the complexity of the *structure*. For example, in the HR system it was noted that most of the personnel had at least two and sometimes three addresses and phone numbers associated with them: home, office, and after school location (such as coaching). To keep all of this information in the main personnel file would mean a lot of "dead fields" for some records. So it was decided to create an address table to contain nothing but address related information. This simplified the content of the personnel file considerably, but it did add another permanent relation and two more files to the system.

Storage Space

In some theoretical circles, it is desirable not to consider "physical factors"—storage space, and performance for example—when designing tables and the database schema. However, hardware considerations are very important. A database system that is underpowered, and particularly one that is plagued with a slow and small hard disk, is going to have performance problems, at least, and quite likely data integrity and concurrency problems as well.

The storage capacity of a database system is no longer the bear it was only five or ten years ago. Hard drives with a gigabyte (1,000 Mb) or more of space are approaching the $1,000 mark. Only a few years ago, 1 G drives for mainframe computers cost $15,000 to $25,000. While space is never unlimited, it's a lot more inexpensive than it was, and hence there's usually a lot more of it to use. This is not to imply that a database design can simply ignore data storage completely. But if you really need fifty characters in a field, you don't usually need to cut back to thirty characters, and let the users "make do" with that.

Plans called for the HR system to be implemented on a LAN that has two 1.2 G drives, and a running usage level of about 30 percent. This made storage space for the database, estimated at a maximum of 25 Mb, a total nonissue.

Normalization

As mentioned in Section I, normalization is the process of organizing data tables so that they carry no redundant data. There are both practical and theoretical reasons for the concern over redundancy. The main reason for most designers is that redundant data poses large data integrity problems. What if you have an address for one person in three different places. When something changes in that address, in one file, then it's the responsibility of the system to update all of the other occurrences of that address. This isn't always easy.

Normalization also helps to break data into logically consistent units (tables)—all addresses in one file, all personal information in another, and so on. This can help the maintenance of a system by making it easier to change data structures (a noted characteristic of relational database systems). Each table, if properly normalized, can have a dynamic life of its own without compromising any other table, as long as the relational links are maintained.

Performance

Performance is near and dear to the heart of the Microsoft/FoxPro people. FoxPro for Winodws represents a monumental effort to coax speed out of a system not noted for that attribute. It's success in that regard will be a major selling point. But when it comes to *your* application, you need to get the accurate measure of the performance requirement just as you would any other factor.

Not all applications need blazing speed. In fact many applications can easily trade performance for such items as security and data integrity. On the other hand, most FoxPro applications will have a lot of user interaction. Users don't generally sit in front of their applications with a stop-watch (if they do, you're probably in deep trouble), but neither are they impervious. Most of them have experience with other software, and will instantly detect if your application is slow.

Designing a database for performance usually means balancing many of the other factors. Almost all of them may contribute to diminishing performance. Too many relations and a very complex file structure have a heavy performance penalty. Heavy multiuser activity obviously diminishes performance. This is one area where de-normalization is sometimes "required." It's no secret that relational systems can founder when burdened with a large number of indexes and relations pointing every-which-way. Occasionally it's necessary to put data back into a single file (flat-file style), or to put redundant data into files so that relational lookups are not necessary.

The HR application has very low requirements for performance. Most of the data tables are small (less than fifteen thousand records), and relatively little of the system is used for "real time" retrieval of data. Thus, the HR program is leaning more in the direction of security, data integrity, and maintainability than in the direction of maximum performance.

Concurrency

This is a fancy name for sharing files. It's safe to say these days that most applications are going to be run on LANs or some other form of multiuser system—even if they weren't intended to in the first place. As soon as more than one person at a time needs to have access to tables, you have a concurrency issue. This is a big subject, and warrants a chapter to itself. However, in the realm of table design, consideration for multiuser operation may influence the distribution of tables, including the use of "local" files (files located on the hard disks of workstations rather than on network servers), and the careful management of the FoxPro SET EXCLUSIVE and SET REPROCESS commands.

Concurrency also has an impact on data security, data integrity, and performance. The more people that use a system, the more opportunities for the data to be compromised. Protecting files against unwanted access, and sudden hardware failure needs to be part of the design and utilization plan for the system.

In the HR system, it is expected that between ten and fifteen people will almost constantly be working with the data tables. This is not a high degree of concurrency, but enough to make it necessary to review every table from the point of view of how it will be shared on the network and in some cases how the sequencing of record edits should be handled.

Maintainability

Overall, the design of the database schema and the structure of the individual tables need to be extremely well documented. Most of the maintenance of an application is applied to the data tables, indexes, and other files in the system. Badly designed or badly documented systems make maintenance much more difficult by obscuring important fields or indexes. Over normalized systems require a lot of data maintenance routines, while the use of too many consolidated files tends to make very big files that take a long time to process and maintain.

Relational Design

When all is designed and done, the table structures and table content are supposed to be an accurate and useful representation of the subject matter of the application. A working model, in other words. The tables should capture all of the information needed by the application, and at the same time do it efficiently and accurately.

A system of tables can achieve these goals by luck. But don't bet on it. Some approaches work better than others, and in general a deliberate approach works best. In thinking through a design, it also helps to have some framework on which to base your decisions. That's what the relational design principles provide.

This may be the place, but not the time, to go into the formal terminology and concepts of relational design. But a "rule-of-thumb" or intuitive description of the relational approach might be helpful at this point, and won't require a six month course of study.

Figure 10.3 shows a sample diagram of what a relational database system is going to look like when you're done.

Ultimately, each item in this diagram is a .DBF, and each file contains data related to the titles in each item. This overview, somewhat simplified to keep things neat, depicts what is sometimes called the *database schema*. The arrows indicate the relationships, or more precisely the *functional dependencies*, between tables. A one-way arrow, for example between Employees and Addresses, indicates that the information in the Employee table in some way depends on the Address table, but the Address table is not dependent on information in the Employees table. Two way arrows indicate mutual dependency.

In a Personnel System, employee information is obviously important, but it is also diverse. For example, besides having a name employees also live somewhere and work somewhere—they have one or more addresses. The Address table provides additional information that's a necessary part of the profile of an employee. In this sense information in the Employee table isn't complete without the Address information. However, the Employee table doesn't provide any information needed by the Address table.

OK, but why do these different tables exist?

Whether you've been gathering information about your application for two hours or two months, the time comes when you take all you have—the data, the intuitions, the observations—and turn them into one or more data tables with specific content (fields). First you need to work your way into defining the tables. There are many ways to do this. Most of the time, your clues come from examining together the results from the "big three" elements of analysis outlined above: data, function, and rules.

Figure 10.3
Database schema.

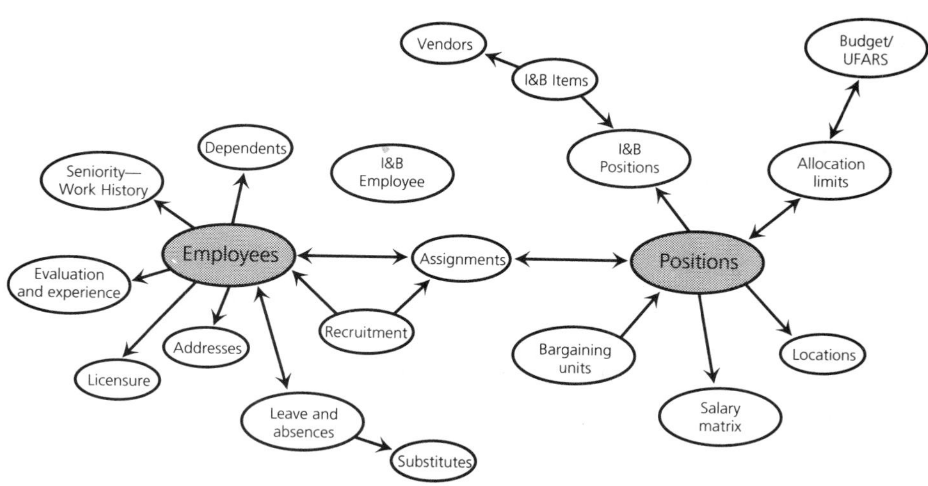

Data Groups

Even a superficial study of the information you've gathered from existing reports, documents,and such usually suggests various groupings of data. The amount of data in a particular area might suggest groupings. Interviews and meetings with users show they too tend to lump certain kinds of information together into categories, such as "employee profile", or "contract data." These categorizations may not wind up as tables, but they point in a useful direction.

Functional Groups

The functional approach isn't the same as following groups. Bringing functionality into the design is more a matter of orientation: what the data is used for, who gets access to it, and what are the information needs for various functional areas. While certainly payroll has a need for data that is grouped by being "payroll data," several other functional areas have a strong need for the same data—in this case financial administration and personnel management. This suggests that perhaps a payroll file isn't the only way to organize the data.

Business Rules

The key role played by business rules, in the broadest sense of that phrase, is to provide a definition for the relationships between data and functional groups. The arrows in the diagram are, more often than not, business rules. In the HR system, it becomes clear that a crucial pair of business rules can have two definitions:

1. An employee may have several positions.
   A position may be held by one and only one employee.
2. An employee may have several positions.
   A position may be shared by more than one employee.

One of the primary goals of the HR system is to establish *Position Control*: an accountability and an accounting for the assignment of positions. The personnel management needs to know, at any time, how many people are employed, what jobs they hold, how many jobs are unfilled, and what the budget and actual figures are for those positions. Given this goal, the two sets of business rules above have strong implications. A position shared by more than one employee is harder to track and account for than one employee. Within the goals of the HR system, the stricter rule provide greater accountability. And with that, the primary table structure in Figure 10.4 is suggested.

Figure 10.4
Primary table structure.

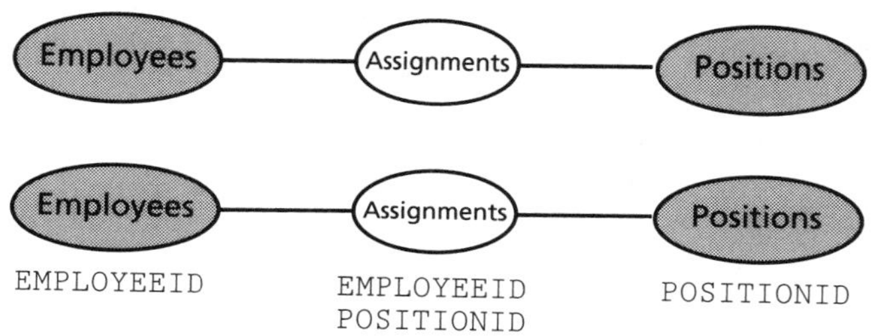

It is hardly an insight to know that the HR system needs some kind of table with employee information and a table for information about positions. The important part, however, is the decision on how to link these two tables. The adopted business rules suggest that a way is needed to allow an employee to have more than one position, but regulating the positions to no more than one employee per position. One answer to the requirements, is to create an Assignments table.

This table contains mostly *references* to information in the Employee and Positions tables, and a few data items specific to an assignment. For each employee in the Employee table there is one or more records in the Assignment table, as defined by one and only one position in the Position table. The key is the combining of an Employee ID, which links to the Employee table, and a Position ID, which links to the Position table.

This is a relatively uncomplicated and obvious relationship. From this nucleus of most important tables, there is now the task of defining other tables that have direct relations with these three. You could start by first dumping all employee data into the Employee table, all position information into the Position table, and so on. Very quickly you'd see that both tables would be a bloated mish-mash. This is the time to call on the two most important rules of *normalization*.

1. Remove redundancy.
2. Remove derived facts.

The easiest rule is number 2. If the data item is something that can be calculated, inferred, or otherwise derived from other data items, you don't need it. This can also be called the "let the report writer do it" rule. If net sales is gross sales minus costs, you don't need to put net sales in a table, just costs and gross sales. You do the calculation in a report or on the screen. Throwing out derived data items helps reduce the number of fields, but it doesn't get you very far down the relational road.

Rule number 1 hinges on what is considered a redundancy. This might not be what you think.

Removing redundant data can be done systematically. You might start with a broad list of data items, such as one for Employees, and attempt to move them into other tables in a series of steps. As an example (abbreviated for space), Table 10.1 is *not* normalized:

Table 10.1
An employee table without normalization.

Employee-ID	Start-date	Seniority	Class-contents
A110	12/01/54	B	Class-num size 101 3 142 3
A111	12/10/33	A	Class-num size 101 10 124 4 122 1
A112	12/11/46	B	Classnum size 101 44

The field CLASS-CONTENTS does not have a simple value because there are really two sub-fields, CLASS-NUM and QTY. Displayed this way, the table looks pretty ridiculous, but in so-called *flat file* data managers, it's easy enough to create something like CLASS-CONTENTS:CLASS-NUM and CLASS-CONTENTS:QTY. Anyway, the fix is easy, as in Table 10.2.

Table 10.2
A normalized employee table.

Employee-ID	Start-date	Seniority	Class-num	Size
A110	12/01/54	B	101	3
A110	12/01/54	B	142	3
A111	12/10/33	A	101	10
A111	12/10/33	A	124	4
A111	12/10/33	A	122	1
A112	12/11/46	B	101	44

Hopefully, this still doesn't look right to you, but for the record it's now in *first normal form*. The normal forms are a sequence of five steps that can be used to normalize a table. The rule for first normal form (1NF) simply states that all field values must be simple (one item of data per field).

One glance at the table above and it's obvious that first normal form does not get rid of redundancies, so on to *second normal form*. Its rules are:

1. The table must be in first normal form.
2. All nonprimary fields must be functionally dependent on the table key.

Nonprimary fields are those that are not part of the table key. The table key for Employee is Employee-ID. The start-date is dependent on an individual employee (although not necessarily unique), however class number and class size do not depend on any particular employee. Normalizing to second normal form (2NF) means creating more tables out of one. Table 10.3 on the next page shows the Employee table, and Table 10.4 shows the Class table.

Table 10.3
The Employee table.

Employee-ID	Start-date	Seniority
A110	12/01/54	B
A111	12/10/33	A
A112	12/11/46	B

Table 10.4
The Class table.

Employee-ID	Class-num	Size
A110	101	3
A110	142	3
A111	101	10
A111	124	4
A111	122	1
A112	101	44

This is looking pretty good. But, by the book, not good enough. The redundant culprit is seniority. This is true in two senses—it's dependent on the start-date for its determination, and its a derived data item. Seniority is based on the number of years an employee has worked, which starts with a calculation of current date minus the start date, and then matches the range of years with a seniority level (A,B,C) This should be in another table. The Employee table is shown in Table 10.5, the newly created Seniority table is shown in Table 10.6.

Table 10.5
The Employee table.

Employee-ID	Start-date
A110	12/01/54
A111	12/10/33
A112	12/11/46

Table 10.6
The Seniority table.

Age1	Age2	Seniority
1	5	C
6	25	B
26	50	A

With this move, the original table has arrived at *third normal form* (3NF). The rules used are:

1. The table must be in second normal form.
2. The table does not contain any functional dependencies between nonprimary fields.

The relationship between start-date and seniority is a functional dependency, hence the creation of a new table.

There are two more normal forms, fourth and fifth. Both deal with repeated values for primary key fields. Even though a table may be in third normal form, all fields being part of a primary key (Employee-ID+Licensure+Classlevel), each key value is unique, and there are no field dependencies, there may still be redundancy of repeated values, as in Table 10.7.

Table 10.7
The Employee table.

Employee-ID	Licensure	Class level
A110	English	5-12
A110	French	3-6
A111	French	3-6
A111	Russian	10-12
A111	English	5-12
A112	French	7-12

As before, the case above is resolved by creating an additional table to hold licensure and class level certification (K-12).

Through this exercise, the design goal is to have tables with no redundancies. The approach is to move toward a relatively simple rule: *Tables should only store facts about their primary keys.* Primary keys should have unique values.

Hopefully the pattern of normalization may be emerging. You start with a conglomeration of data items, and progressively sort them into functionally coherent groups. The groups are then assigned to tables, while providing relational links for other tables to use as lookups. The process does make sense, although both in practice and in theory there are many refinements and complications. Still, with experience, you will be able to normalize tables fairly easily.

Binder Diagram

There are many ways to represent a relational system of tables (a schema). The approach illustrated below was chosen because of its emphasis on relations, indexes (keys), table fields, and its suitability for Xbase development. It's called a *Binder diagram*, after Robert V. Binder. In the slightly modified form used in Figure 10.5a and 10.5b, it contains additional information about the names of tables and aliases. About the only thing that's missing is a complete file struc-ture, which could be included, but the diagram would become unwieldy.

Figure 10.5a
Binder diagram.

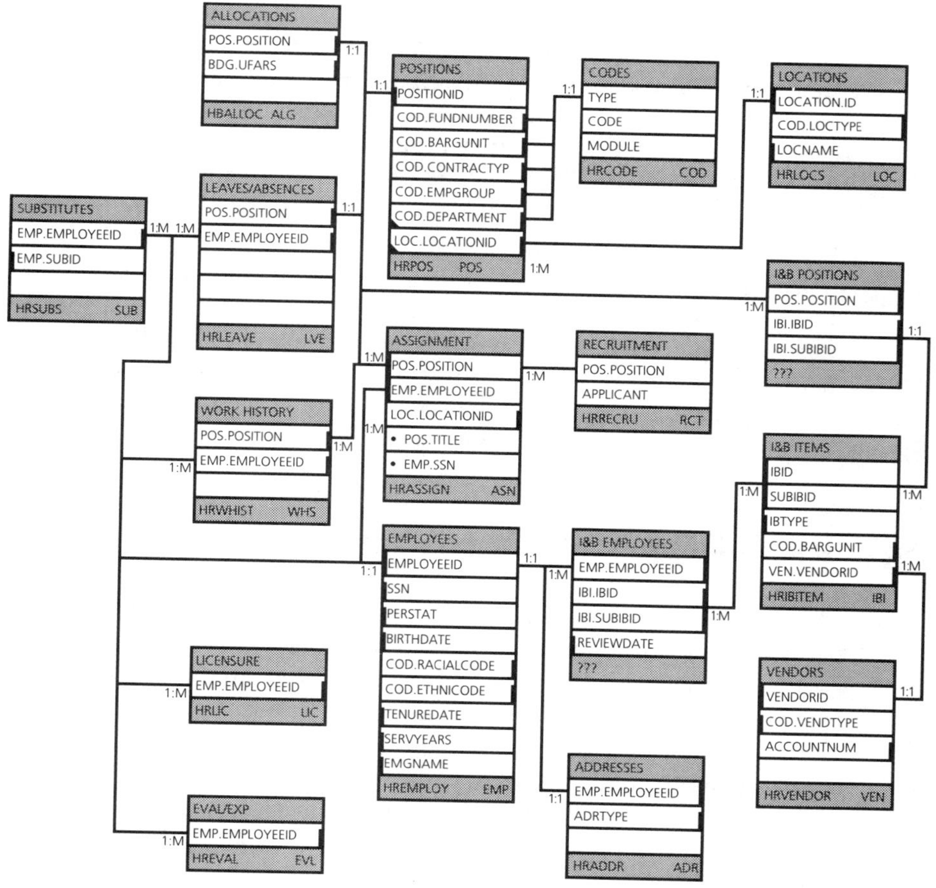

Figure 10.5b
Binder legend.

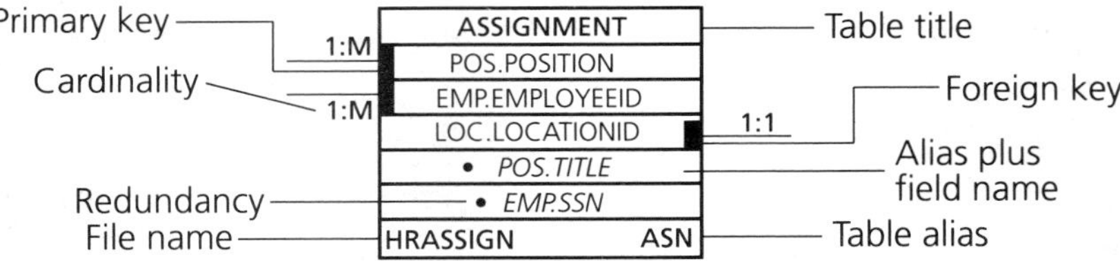

The Binder diagram is also noted for its ability to document redundancy. It accepts that real word relational systems often include redundant fields that should be explicitly noted in the diagram. Overall, this approach provides a good road map to a database schema. Of course it sometimes leaves out details, and not all of the relational routes are included. But the point of a diagram like this is to clarify the underlying data structure, not catalog the details. It summarizes a lot of thinking, a lot of rules, and of course most of the table design in a very compact format.

The endgame of table design is to arrive at something you can turn into FoxPro tables and fields, and understand how these can be linked to form the relational system. This version of a Binder diagram includes the actual file names and aliases to be used in an application. However the diagram only indicates that relations are possible, not which ones should actually be used in an application. That's part of application design.

Application Design

Application design should be holistic. It's the part of the application development process where you can afford to take the long view—try to see the whole as being greater than the parts. Consider the process from the very beginning to the day when you go into permanent maintenance mode.

Application design has two tasks: deciding what should go into the application (the components) and how the application should be structured (such as program modules). These two tasks are considered in two contexts: the user's and the developer's (programmers). As always, the amount of work and detail you put into application design depends on the scale and complexity of the application. You're always trying to balance the need for understanding what you want to do with an application, and the potential for blowing the job out of proportion.

Required Elements

By the time you sit down to figure out what goes into your application, you should have a good notion of what it's supposed to do, and what information is involved. Now's the time to decide what components of a "standard" application are needed, and what are the elements special to this particular application. Standard components include:

- Data tables
- Data dictionary
- Configuration and initialization
- Login and security
- Processing routines
- Screens
- Menus
- Reports
- Labels
- Queries
- Report management
- OLE/DDE support
- Multiuser operation
- Communications and fax
- Data transfer
- Peripheral input
- Printer management
- System parameter
- System codes
- Help system
- Maintenance routines
- Maintenance
- Programmer documentation

- Error trapping and recovery
- Data archiving
- Data backup and restoration
- Distribution
- Installation and setup procedures
- Data loading and conversion
- User documentation
- User training
- User support

Most applications have:

- Data tables
- Processing routines
- Screens
- Menus
- Reports

That leaves twenty-four other options (and no doubt more). A quick-and-dirty application won't have much more than the minimum. An application that has to be used by other people and hold up over time will probably add these components:

- Configuration and initialization
- Report management
- Multiuser operation
- System parameters
- System codes
- Help system
- Maintenance routines
- Programmer documentation
- Error trapping and recovery
- User documentation

More heavy-duty applications, such as the HR system being used as an example, may add these components:

- Data dictionary
- Login and security

- Printer management
- System maintenance
- Installation and setup procedures
- Data loading and conversion
- User training
- User support

Over time you will develop your own standard routines for some of these components. Their use becomes so easy, perhaps even automatic, that you'll include them in almost every application. However, in almost every application there will be modifications to standard routines, and perhaps other components that must be built from scratch. You're not only listing what will be needed, but trying to get a feel for how much work there is to do.

Most of the other options on the standard list depend on the nature of the application, and in fact may blend into some of the application specific components. For example, OLE and DDE are gateways into other Windows programs. They might be part of a complex data transfer scheme, or simply a way to put graphics into a database. They might be part of the context in which the use of graphics is application specific, such as capturing architectural diagrams, or very general as part of the user interface.

The point of considering application-specific components is to isolate areas that require special attention (and presumably extra work). The list of such possible components is of course as varied and endless as the types of applications. In the HR System, the Assignments component requires specialized calculations for salary and other benefits, and so a processing and table updating component needs to be added to the list. The HR System also needed several subsystems to handle personnel functions such as leaves and absences, substitute teachers, hiring, and insurances and benefits.

Module Design

The next part of design does the structural layout, including the screens, menus, and reports. This goes through phases, ranging from "the best shot" to "the real thing." Seriously, this type of design is the one that is most subject to major revision, probably because it is also most subject to the complex interaction between you, the content of the application, and the user.

What you are attempting to do is pin down (diagram or describe) the components of an application in terms of the modules (program units), and then the programming elements used in those modules.

The program modules are a kind of high level description of functionality from the programmer's point of view. It's not the same as the data structure, although that's a big part of it. It's also not the same as the components, since several of them might be included in a single module. With FoxPro this is most typically a *screen set*, one or more screens used together with a menu, reports, processes, and tables. But this is a very loosely defined concept. Modules are really an administrative approach, so you can say, "this week we're working on the <x> module." For that reason modules tend to be focused on functionality: the "maintenance module," the "planning module." Figure 10.6 diagrams module design.

Figure 10.6
Module design.

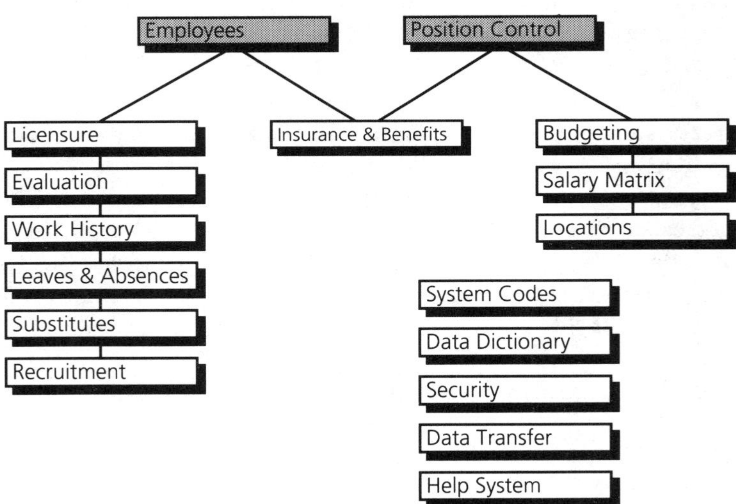

Some applications won't be big enough to warrant modularization, but most benefit from it. It's all part of making complexity a little easier to deal with. The bigger the project, the more you need to break it down into modules just to make it manageable.

Once you've decided on the modules for the application, then you can design the programming elements that go into them, shown in Figure 10.7.

Figure 10.7
Programming elements.

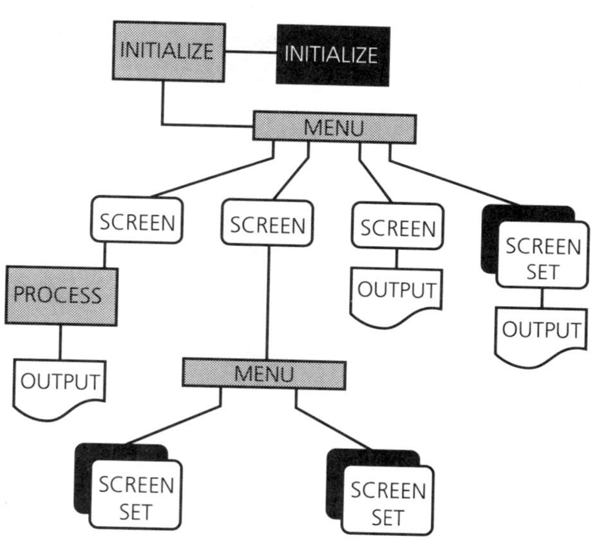

These are mostly quite basic: screens (data entry, edit), processes (calculations, table updating), retrieval and output (reports, labels, queries), and menus. How specific you choose to be (written description or diagram) probably depends on how much there is to do, who has to do it, and how long it is expected to take. The point of this part of the design is to make things clear for the developer/programmer, without restricting creativity and judgment. If you're doing the work by yourself, obviously you may only need enough notation to maintain an outline of what's to be done. If other people are involved, and especially if the client/user needs to be informed, then the required level of documentation goes up.

The layout of the application modules and their component elements helps to spell out the relationship between various parts of the application, and particularly how the user will be able to use the system. This is, after all, the big pieces of the user interface. The layout should also specify how the program modules relate to the application database.

From the HR System, diagram 10.x is a small portion of the module elements design. A couple of elements should be highlighted: initialization and procedures library.

It's become standard practice in FoxPro applications to begin with an initialization program. This is usually a .PRG, although it doesn't have to be. The purpose of the program, as you might guess, is to set the stage for the application—initialize the system. This can include anything from soup to nuts, help to security. It's very convenient to have all of the public variables, major file openings, security setup, and so forth all in one place. The sample init file below, has more areas than usual, but for that reason provides a good example of the diversity of things that can be initialized before launching into a major application.

```
*+————————————————————————————————————————————*
*| Program: HRINIT.PRG
*| Description: Initialization of Main Program Environment
*| Date: Thu 12-05-1991
*| Time: 18:28:01
*| Programmer: NK, LJ
*| Revisions: Mon 10-26-1992 New ChkLogin(), nk
*| Thu 01-02-1992 Revisions to Security Variables nk
*| Generic Version Rev. 3.0 - Fri 12-06-1991
*+————————————————————————————————————————————*

*——————————[ Network Settings
IF NETWORK()
 SET EXCLUSIVE OFF
 SET REFRESH TO 0,999
 SET REPROCESS TO AUTOMATIC
ENDIF

*——————————[ DEFINE ENVIRONMENT
CLEAR
CLEAR ALL
SET PROCEDURE TO HRPROC
RESTORE FROM SYS
SET TALK OFF
SET SAFETY OFF
SET BELL OFF
SET DELETED ON
SET CONFIRM ON

*——————————[ PUBLIC Variables
*> General
```

```
PUBLIC cMform, cMprocname, cOwner, cMtmpfile,; cLongowner,
cRephead
PUBLIC dMdate1, dMdate2, nColorCnt, nLastClk, cName,; cMuname

cMprocname = "" && Calling Procedure/Function
cMform = "" && Report Form Variable
cOwner = "Schools" && Reports/Titles
cLongOwner = "School District" && Official Name
cRepHead = "Personnel" && Report Header
cMtmpfile = "" && holder for PickTag() file
dMdate1 = {" / / "} && Generic date holders
dMdate2 = {" / / "}
nColorCnt = 0 && Counter for PushColor()
nLastClk = 0 && Mouse double click counter
cName = "" && Generic Name Holder
cMuname = "" && Alternate user name

*——————————[ Error Trapping
*> Developer's Error Trapping
is_debug = .t.
ON KEY LABEL F12 DO STATLOOK WITH ERROR(), MESSAGE(),;
MESSAGE(1), ;
 SYS(16), LINENO(1), SYS(102), SYS(100), SYS(101),; WOUTPUT(),
LASTKEY()
ON ERROR DO STATLOOK WITH ERROR(), MESSAGE(),; MESSAGE(1), ;
 SYS(16), LINENO(1), SYS(102), SYS(100), SYS(101),; WOUTPUT(),
LASTKEY()

*——————————[ Video Variables
IF ISCOLOR()


 *> Define Interface Environment
 SET MESSAGE TO 1 LEFT
 *————————————————[ STANDARD COLOR SCHEMES
 * PRIMARY COLOR SET IS BLUE_TIE (Modified)

 *> 1 User Windows - LEVEL 1
 SET COLOR OF SCHEME 1 TO ;
 N/BG,N/W,W+/BG,W+/BG,BG+/BG,B/W*,GR+/BG,N+/N,W+/BG,;
W+/BG,+
 *> 2 User Menus
 SET COLOR OF SCHEME 2 TO ;
 BG/B,W+/B,W+/B,W+/BG,BG+/BG,B/W*,GR+/B,N+/N,W+/B,W/B,+
 *> 3 Menu Bar
 SET COLOR OF SCHEME 3 TO W/B,N/BG,W+/BG,W+/BG,W/BG,;
W+/B,W+/BG,N+/N,W+/B,W/B,+
```

```
*> 4 Menu Pops
SET COLOR OF SCHEME 4 TO W/BG,N/BG,BG+/BG,W+/BG;
W/BG,W+/B,W+/BG,N+/N,W+/B,W/B,+
*> 5 Dialogs
SET COLOR OF SCHEME 5 TO ;
B+/RB,W+/BG,W+/RB,W+/N,W/N,GR+/B,GR+/RB,N+/N,;
W+/RB,RB+/RB
*> 6 Dialog Pops
SET COLOR OF SCHEME 6 TO N+/B,W+/B,W+/B,W+/N,W/N,;
N/BG,GR+/B,N+/N,W+/N,W/N
*> 7 Alerts
SET COLOR OF SCHEME 7 TO GR+/R,W+/R,W+/R,N+/W,N/W,;
GR+/R,R+/R,N+/N,W+/R,RB/R
*> 8 Windows
SET COLOR OF SCHEME 8 TO ;
W+/W,W+/B,W+/B,GR+/B,RB/B,GR+/B,GR+/BG,N+/N,B/BG,;
BG+/BG
*> 9 Window Pops
SET COLOR OF SCHEME 9 TO N+/B,W+/B,W+/B,N+/W,N/W,;
GR+/RB,N/W,N+/N,W+/N,W/N
*> 10 Browses
SET COLOR OF SCHEME 10 TO N/W,GR+/B,W+/B,GR+/B,;
RB/B,GR+/RB,W+/B,N+/N,W+/N,W/N
*> 11 Reports
SET COLOR OF SCHEME 11 TO W+/N,W+/N,N/W,N+/W,N/W,;
N/W,N/W,N+/N,N+/B,W/N
*> 12 Alert Popups
*SET COLOR OF SCHEME 12 TO GR+/R,N/W,GR+/R,W+/R,;
N+/R,W+/N,GR+/R,N+/N,W+/R,N+/R

ELSE
*————————[ Monochrome Defaults
BRIGHT = 'W+'
ULBRIGHT = 'U+'
BLINKBRITE = 'W*'
REVERSE = 'N/W'
REVBRITE = 'N/W+'
INVISIBLE = 'N/N'
NORMAL = 'W/N'
ENDIF

*————————[ Load Data Dictionary
*
* Once development is completed, this routine in the
* INIT file should
* only load the "M", MAIN file variables. Application
```

```
* specific file
* variables should be loaded in the top scr/prg of the * app.
*
IF FileUse( DDFILE ,"FIL",.t.,"","",.f.)
 SCAN
 STORE TRIM(FILENAME) TO Mfile
 STORE TRIM(PATH) TO &Mfile
 ENDSCAN
ELSE
 RETURN
ENDIF

*_______________________________________
*> Open Tracking Information file (DDTRACK) and its
* .CDX file
*_______________________________________
IF ! FileUSE( DDTRACK ,"DDT",.T.,"PRGUSER","A",.T.)
 =ErrLine("Can't open DDTRACK.DBF",4)
 RETURN .F.
ENDIF


*_______________________________________
*> Open Codes Information file (DDCODE) and its .CDX
* file
*_______________________________________
IF ! FileUSE( DDCODE ,"COD",.T.,"TYPECODE","A",.T.)
 =ErrLine("Can't open DDCODE.DBF",4)
 RETURN .F.
ENDIF
*________________________[ Login/Security
PUBLIC nSec1, nSec2, aDept, wWin, cDept
PUBLIC cMusername, cMstaffid
nSec1 = 0     && ACCESS Level
nSec2 = 0     && RIGHTS Level
cDept = ""    && DEPARTMENTAL access
wWin = ""     && Current Active Window
is_sec = .t.  && Turn Security ON/OFF

*=======================>> Get USERNAME from Network
= ChkLogin()

*______________[ Security Matrix Load
IF is_sec
 IF NOT USED("SEC")
 IF NOT FileUse( DDSEC ,"SEC",.t.,1,"A",.t.)
 RETURN
```

```
  ENDIF
  ELSE
  SELECT SEC
  ENDIF
  PUBLIC aSecLoc
  DECLARE aSecLoc[RECCOUNT(),4]
  COPY TO ARRAY aSecLoc FIELDS SECLOCID,SEC1,SEC2,DEPT
  USE
ENDIF

*——————————[ Help System
*> TURN ON FOR PRODUCTION and HELP LOADING!
PUBLIC cHelpKey
cHelpKey = " The Human Resources System"
SET HELP TO ( HRHELP )
SET HELP ON

*——————————[ Permanent OKLs
ON KEY LABEL F2 DO SetPbm

*=======================[ FOUNDATION READ SECTION
*]========================*
*> Setup for menu & read
PUBLIC is_Quit, cToBeDone
is_Quit = .f.
cToBeDone = ""

PUSH MENU _MSYSMENU
SET SYSMENU AUTOMATIC

*========================>> CALL MAIN MENU
DO HRMENU.MPR

KEYBOARD "{ALT+P}"
*========================>> FOUNDATION READ
READ VALID FRHandler()

*=====================[ END FOUNDATION READ
*]=============================*

*> Clean up
POP MENU _MSYSMENU
SET SYSMENU TO DEFAULT
CLEAR ALL
ACTIVATE SCREEN
CLEAR
ON KEY
```

```
ON ERROR
CLOSE PROCEDURE
CLEAR PROGRAM
SET TALK ON
SET HELP TO
SET DELETED OFF
ON KEY LABEL F2
*> For Development only, back to COMMAND window
KEYBOARD "{CTRL F2}"
*
*===================[ EOF HRINIT.PRG
*]=======================================*
```

The application design also includes a procedure library. As was suggested in Section II, it pays to develop your own library of procedures and functions, in generic format, so they can be used in a wide variety of applications. Although it is not a requirement of FoxPro, it is convenient and programmatically clear to use SET PROCEDURE TO <procedure file name> early in the program. This provides the entire application with a library of functions. It also raises the issue of how to position functions and variables so that they are available but under control in your application.

Scoping an Application

Scale and scoping go together. The bigger the application, the more modules it contains, the more you need to pay attention to the scoping of procedures, functions, and variables. The goal of scoping is to not crowd the memory of your application, and keep procedures, functions, and especially variables from stepping on each other. If you're consistent with scoping, it also helps the organization and maintainability of an application, since you (or other people) will know where to look for certain kinds of routines or variables.

For example, functions that are part of your library (used in many projects) are stored in the procedure file. Functions that are used throughout an application are stored in the initialization file. Functions used throughout an application module are stored in the top file of that module. And finally there are the "local" functions attached to specific screens, processes, and so on. Variables follow a similar pattern with PUBLICs being declared in the initialization file, Xbase public variables (those created by assignment: cName = LASTNAME) created in the top file of a module, REGIONAL variables for screen sets, and then PRIVATE variables used in all other local functions and procedures.

User-Interface Design

As you contemplate the prospect of building an application, kick back in your chair with your eyes closed and visualize: How do you "see" it? What's the user going to see? Screens go floating by your mind's eye, full of colors, shapes, and textures, since this is Windows. Maybe you see pictures, and icons, colorful backgrounds, push buttons, and popup lists, and spinners. Welcome to user-interface design.

You are about to launch into a topic that really distinguishes FoxPro for *Windows*. Almost all of the "new" stuff, (as opposed to the "old" stuff in FoxPro for DOS), is user interface capability—fonts, bitmaps, and icons.

This is a new "look and feel" that will have profound impact on your applications. In fact, the whole realm of design for a GUI (Graphical User Interface) is so complex and time consuming, there's a strong tendency for user interface issues to dominate your applications.

This is not, necessarily, a bad thing. It seems to be true that as we head into the twenty-first century, the issues of the user interface are becoming paramount in computer applications. Commercial application developers now say that for a typical application, about 60 percent to 70 percent of their time is spent on user-interface related work. But that doesn't mean you should develop amnesia concerning the rest of your application. The processing, data manipulation, and maintenance are still there. In most cases, these remain the backbone of your application.

Still, the user-interface design is challenging. Although there are some emerging standards, you have a lot of latitude—enough to make or break an application. The ways in which a computer program interacts with the user—mouse clicks, keystrokes, colors, flow of modules, windowing, menu options, information support, to name just a few—are some of the most interesting and creative aspects of programming. Not to mention that an application with a well-designed user-interface has a much better chance of success.

There are many, many issues in user interface design. This book can cover only a small fraction of them. For building applications, however, you need to make a few but important user interface decisions up front. These can be broken down into three topics:

- Transportability

- Modes versus modeless
- Event Driven Programming

Transportability

Because you are working with FoxPro for Windows, you've already made one major commitment to user interface design—Windows. As you're probably already well aware, there is a Windows way of doing things. It's one of the prime selling points (especially in competition with the Apple Macintosh)—"Learn one program, and you've learned them all." Although Microsoft doesn't enforce the user interface conventions with as much zeal as Apple, you'd better think twice or thrice before wandering very far away from "Windows normal" in your designs.

FoxPro for Windows does carry the tools that allow you to change the look of menus and windows. At the least, you should have a very good reason for bypassing the general look and feel of Windows. That reason might just be *transportability*.

FoxPro, version 2.5, is positioned in the database market as the "cross-platform" solution. Write one set of code, and use it on DOS, Windows, Macintosh, and Unix. If you're a commercial developer, or building applications for a company that has more than one of these computer platforms, then you'll lick your chops at increasing your market or distribution four-fold. FoxPro even offers a rather sophisticated pair of tools to do the job, the Transporter and the Screen Builder.

The reason for these tools is almost exclusively user-interface design. The underlying code of FoxPro, especially the database commands and functions, work flawlessly in any environment (not all of the same performance characteristics, but close enough). Where the code differs most is in the user interface. Windows in DOS are not the same in MS Windows, which are not the same as the Macintosh, and definitely not the same as Unix (Motif, Open Look, Xwindow). Yes, you can use the same FoxPro commands to create a window, but they are going to look substantially different, have different sizing characteristics, titling, and so on. This kind of difference appears in a myriad of other user interface elements. All of this affects your user-interface design.

FoxPro 2.5 provides a translation tool, the Cross Platform Transporter. Run your program through the Transporter and it turns out code suitable for a different computer environment. Of necessity, however, the Transporter takes a rather minimalist approach. It can make your application use some of the same design conventions as the new host computer system, but it can't explore all of the possibilities.

Fortunately, FoxPro 2.5 meets you at least half way. The Screen Builder has been enhanced to generate sections of code, each one specific for a particular computer system. With small applications, this combination of the Transporter to help you get started with cross-platform development, and the multiple-platform support of the Screen Builder, makes this sort of development incredibly easy. On larger projects, however, you're going to face some serious bloat (thousands of "extra" lines of code). This is a problem for maintenance and development (such as long generate and compile times).

You do need to be aware that choice of user-interface approach, computer operating environment, and cross-platform development is a fairly complex mixture that may require some very careful planning, execution, and housekeeping.

Modes versus Modeless

This topic and the next (event-driven programming) are at the heart of the most important issue in user interface design: Who's in control? If you answer, "the user," then you've understood the power of the Macintosh and all that has come after it. If you answer, "the company," meaning the requirements of an employer, then you've understood what MIS has been grappling with ever since the invention of the PC.

Control, in an application, usually means "what can the user do now?" A *mode* is a strict functional limitation on what the user can do. If you are in Edit mode, then only text may be edited. You can't calculate numbers, run another part of the module, or play Solitaire. The modal approach says, "The program is in control (as a surrogate), and you (the user) can only do what is allowed at a given point." The nonmodal or *modeless* approach says, "The user is king. Users may go anywhere and do anything at any time." Both approaches may sound extreme. They are.

In practice, most applications employ a mixture of modal control and modeless freedom. The questions really are how much and when. These are your design decisions.

Part of your answer has to come from the computer environment. FoxPro is of and by the Windows environment. MS Windows is largely modeless.

Within the limitations of hardware, the user can have as many programs running and be doing as many different activities as they wish. Windows applications for the most part follow suit, and tend to allow the user great control over the flow of the program, as well as permitting free access to any of the other Windows capabilities.

Another part of your answer, which may run counter to the openness of the Windows environment, is the requirements of your application. An accounting system does not need, and probably shouldn't have, the wide open accessibility of a word processing program. The needs for security, efficiency, and similar factors may increase the use of a modal approach. Likewise, a decision support type of application, which provides information in a number of ways, leans far more in the direction of a modeless approach.

The modeless approach is much more difficult to program. The next four chapters will probably convince you why. But let's start with the main concept, event-driven programming.

Event-Driven Programming

If, after examining the needs of your application, you have decided that an open, modeless approach is the best, you are then going to be entering the world of event-driven programming.

There are many ways to characterize event-driven programming, but a useful starting point is to label it "control passive." You design your user interface programming to basically set the table for the user, and sit there waiting for the user to do something. Your program is waiting for an *event*. Events have very special meaning. They are the life force of this kind of programming, which is why it's called event *driven*. The user signals to your application, through the use of certain events—a mouse click, a keystroke, or a menu selection—what should be done. Then your program reacts to the user event.

Other than the initial setup, the user is in control. Your program needs to passively monitor the user signals, providing response and support as appropriate. Since the user can, and will, go in any conceivable direction, it becomes the software designers' and programmers' responsibility to keep the options open, while at the same time not create conflicts and disasters within the program. This is usually not easy.

Chapter 11
Elements of the User Interface

Stepping into the user interface possibilities of FoxPro for Windows is like what it must have been for medieval artists discovering perspective—liberating. It's not that you couldn't make a decent screen in FoxPro for DOS, but compared to FoxPro for Windows, the DOS screen is visually flat, inflexible, and, well, crude. As you design and build screens, menus, and reports, at your disposal are literally dozens of user-interface elements. Some of them are for visual enhancement, others provide information to the user, and still others control the user's options. Together they make up the "look and feel" of your application.

With so many possibilities, there's always a temptation to make your apps look good, sometimes at the expense of making them work well. This doesn't need to be the tradeoff. The best user-interface design has the quality of being easy to use and is visually stimulating. In fact, some would say that is the real "art" of software design.

Some User-Interface Goals

In addition to the issues of transportability, modal versus modeless design, and event-driven programming, there are many goals and purposes for developing a good user interface.

Information Support

Users are not mushrooms. You don't keep them in the dark and feed them compost. Put yourself in the user's shoes (which shouldn't be hard). You like to know what's going on with software. Support the user with information when they need it. Tell them what's happening when the program goes off for processing. Leave signposts and messages. Give them full descriptions and titles in comprehensible English. Provide popup information when appropriate. Almost every screen, and then every application as a whole, deserves a "pass" to check for adequate user messaging, titles, and other clues that help users understand where they are in a program, and what they're expected to do.

Quick and Easy Choosing

Take a look at your favorite commercial software. How often do you make choices when using it? Scores, maybe hundreds, of times an hour, using menus, tool bars, icons, dialog boxes—you name it. Most of the active user interface has something to do with the user making choices. It stands to reason that anything this common and this important should receive a lot of your attention when building a user interface for your application.

Perhaps you have heard the phrase *Point and Shoot*. This is a selection technique. FoxPro supports it full measure with push buttons, popup lists, radio buttons, check boxes, and all of the system menu. The goal is to make user's selections quick and easy.

Save Keystrokes

Here's another user interface objective of which you are probably aware: saving keystrokes and mouse clicks. It's an old story in user-interface design—making something easy to use doesn't always make it faster to use. Mousing is a good example. Using a mouse is easy for people to understand and master. But when it comes to editing and data entry, the mouse is a pest. It's more inconvenient, hence slower, to be continually reaching for a mouse, than to use keystroke shortcuts.

All actions should be available to both keyboard and mouse and try to save keystrokes and clicks. This is not always possible, but a worthy goal. There are many ways to do this—appropriate defaults (the user doesn't have to type today's date, for example), common keyboard and mouse sequences combined into a single icon choice or function key, and keeping mouseable targets large enough for easy hits.

Self-Documenting Screens

You've probably heard it said before, "The best software doesn't need a manual." This is very difficult to accomplish with all but the most simple of applications. But it's certainly a goal. You would like your screens to be "self documenting." It spares the users from constantly pushing **F1**, thumbing through manuals, or worse, calling you.

But how do you achieve a self-documenting application? Mostly through a combination of many user-interface elements. Good messaging, titles, and such are important. Appropriate user support with timely information helps. So does good screen layout and use of color. The visual aspects of the user interface help to organize, clarify, and guide the eye of the user.

Visual Pleasure

Although this is highly subjective, almost everyone can think of a piece of software they consider "fun" in the visual sense. It might be the use of color, or icons, or interesting user-interface items like pick lists. It might also be the attention to detail, or the elegance of the tools provided. Whatever. The point is that making your application aesthetically pleasing is not an esoteric goal. It can pay off with happy users. It provides some of those intangibles that make a marginal piece of software into a winner. On the other hand good looks, as in people, are no substitute for real capability.

Go with the Flow

Let the user-interface elements *flow* properly for the work at hand. This is both a matter of major design choices, like event-driven programming, and also the placement and timing of most of the smaller user-interface elements. The result, or rather the goal, is software that seems to fit the user's purposes and enhances their work flow. Of all of the goals, this is one most dependent on good research and planning. A smoothly flowing data-entry screen, for example, is no accident. It's usually the result of a lot of study of the users doing entry, a good basic design, then hours of revision and tweaking to get it right.

Color

Color has become the dominant monitor type on today's PC. There are many good reasons, but the only two that count are: people prefer color, and the expense of a color monitor is no longer a barrier. For a while, during the mid-eighties, programmers had to contend with the decision to support or not support first color, then monochrome. And support didn't just mean display on the screen. Supporting color means choosing colors that are pleasing and appropriate, and a lot of other design considerations. It wasn't easy to "support" both color and monochrome. Anyway, that's a moot point in FoxPro for Windows. You can assume color, unless you're intending your applications to work on other platforms where color is not a given.

What you cannot assume, however, is that everybody has the capability to display all 16,777,216 colors possible with the FoxPro system. Hopefully you don't have to plan for CGA graphics (the first and oldest IBM graphic standard), which allows only eight atrocious colors. But you might have to contend with having only sixteen colors, which is the level for older VGA systems. In some applications this is no problem. After all, in FoxPro for DOS the sixteen-color limit has been the norm many years. But the graphical capabilities of FoxPro for Windows beckon the designer to let the palette go. Which is fine, as long as the target hardware supports it.

Controlling color is a problem in FoxPro for Windows. For one thing, it's a complicated system with several layers of use. For another thing, the native FoxPro system has to compete with the Windows Control Panel system. And finally, the documentation is skimpy (most of it being in the on-line help). There is a sense that FoxPro color management got stuck halfway between Windows and DOS. Given the problems and level of complexity, the temptation to leave color settings to automatic generation by the Screen Builder becomes strong. Unfortunately for the application builder, there are plenty of reasons why you might want to set your own colors. For example, if you are planning to use more than the sixteen-color palette.

Good color design is nit-picking work, but that belies its importance. Color is everywhere in an application. While it rarely is a make or break feature, there's no doubt of it's importance in the overall look. Which makes it worth the time to tackle the intricacies of the FoxPro color system.

The Color System Explained

Although the FoxPro color system is very powerful, it can be confusing. This section gives an overview of the components that is designed to clarify the color system.

RGB Values

FoxPro gives you two choices for representing color at the lowest level. Of the two, the new RGB( ) function is by far the most fundamental. It takes the three most basic colors of light, the primaries—red, green, and blue—and allows you to mix them. You have 256 levels of intensity for each primary color (0 through 255), with 0 being an absence of the color (black), and 255 being the brightest. The graduation of each primary color is in terms of "shading," the amount of black, so you can expect each color to "lighten" as you go up the scale toward 255. At the lower end, about 100 and less, the colors will be dark, muddy, even gray. Around 200, each of the colors will be closest to what people would call their "true color." At the top end, they will be bright but less intense (less saturated).

NOTE

Don't expect these gradations between colors to be very precise. This is extremely hardware dependent, and if your color adapter doesn't handle sixteen million colors, it substitutes the nearest shade, which might not be all that near. If you're trying to be creative with coloring, without unpleasant hardware surprises, avoid the lower end of the settings.

When you start to mix the three colors, your palette extends to the fullest. At the bottom end with each color set to zero (0,0,0) through (32,32,32) and you get black. Values (33,33,33) through (64,64,64) are gray. Values (65,65,65)through (191,191,191) are white. Finally, with all three colors at (192,192,192) or above, you get high-intensity colors. Mixing with all three colors changes the "hue" (mixture of white) in the color.

Foreground and Background

For reasons that have much to do with the text orientation of DOS, all of FoxPro for Windows colors are arranged as *color pairs*—foreground and background. Typically, the text itself is foreground, in a background setting, something appropriately readable like white on blue. Of course foreground and background applies to more than text on the screen, but it's sometimes harder to visualize. In any case, the RGB( ) function reflects this color pair arrangement. The first three arguments, RGB(<expN1>,<expN2>,expN3.. are the foreground color, and ..<expN4>,<expN5>,<expN6>) are the background. A complete RGB expression for a color pair looks like this:

```
RGB(255;0,0,255,255,255).
```

Color Pairs

The alternate expression for this same color pair is R/W—red on white. This is the "old" Xbase approach to color. The foreground/background combination is represented by letters for colors and a "+" for a brighter version of the color. Here's the table of contents for this color system:

■ **N**	Black	**N+**	Gray
■ **B**	Blue	**B+**	Bright blue
■ **GR**	Brown	**GR+**	Yellow
■ **BG**	Cyan (blue green)	**BG+**	Light blue
■ **G**	Green	**G+**	Light green
■ **RB**	Magenta (red blue)	**RB+**	Pink
■ **R**	Red	**R+**	Light red
■ **W**	White (gray white)	**W+**	Bright white
■ **GR+**	Yellow		

The interaction of foreground on background produces some results in FoxPro for Windows that are different from FoxPro for DOS. Notably, the symbol *, which in DOS produces the brightest version of a color, in FoxPro for Windows always turns the background to bright. This produces blue on bright white, whereas B/W+ is the same as B/W (blue on gray white). It's probably possible to memorize the various combinations, but few have tried. Mostly colors are decided by trial and error.

Coloring Objects

So far, you've seen how color pairs in either RGB or character code are used to vary foreground and background colors. The next step is to apply them to something—screen objects. There are over 160 screen objects recognized by FoxPro, including various parts of windows, browses, and menus. The simplest to understand is the @..GET object. You may remember the syntax as it relates to color:

```
@ <row>,<col> GET <expr> COLOR <expC>
```

The <expC> is a color pair of either RGB or character variety, for example:

```
@ 10,20 GET cLastname COLOR R/W
@ 10,20 GET cLastname COLOR RGB(255,0,0,255,255,255)
```

In FoxPro, the syntax for the color pair does not require quotes to designate a character expression. The use of color pairs in the @..GET, and likewise in the @..SAY is the "classic" foreground/background coloration and can be used in a variety of situations, for example to set the foreground and background of a window.

```
DEFINE WINDOW wrNewColor FROM 1,0 TO 20,50 COLOR R/W
```

But windows, like many other screen elements in FoxPro, are a lot more complex than simply foreground and background. And that's where a series of color pairs, a *color list*, are used to define colors for objects within those elements.

Color Schemes

FoxPro defines a *color scheme* as a list of ten color pairs, separated by commas:

```
W+/B,GR+/B,GR+/B,W+/BG,GR+/BG,N+/N,R/W,GR+/BG,BG/W,BG+/W
```

The alpha version is relatively compact, compared to an RGB version:

```
RGB(255,255,255,0,0,255),RGB(150,150,0,0,0,255),RGB(255,255,255,0,150,150),
RGB(150,150,0,0,0,255)...
```

These color schemes have no meaning in themselves. They become active when assigned to particular *interface elements*, which themselves are composed of up to ten screen objects.

Interface Elements

This is where the coloring system gets sticky. There are currently twenty-eight interface elements recognized by FoxPro that can use a color scheme for definition of color.

- User-defined windows

- User-defined menus
- System menu bars
- System menu popups
- System dialog boxes
- System dialog popups
- System alerts
- System windows
- System window popups
- Browse windows
- Report layout windows
- Alert dialog boxes
- @..SAY/GET
- @..GET—Check boxes
- @..GET—Invisible buttons
- @..GET—Lists
- @..GET—Popups
- @..GET—Push buttons
- @..GET—Radio buttons
- @..GET—Text edit regions
- @..GET—Spinners
- @..FILL
- @..TO
- CHANGE
- EDIT
- SHOW GET/GETS
- SHOW OBJECT
- READ

Within each of these screen elements there are one or more "objects" to which the color pairs of the color scheme correspond. This may seem clearer after an example of the screen element user-defined windows, using Table 11.1 on the next page.

Table 11.1
User-defined window objects and color pairs.

Pair #	Object	Pair #	Object
1	@..SAY	6	Selected item (lists, etc.)
2	@..GET	7	Hot-key items (control buttons)
3	N/A (DOS window border)	8	N/A (DOS shadow)
4	N/A (DOS title [active])	9	Enabled object (GETs)
5	N/A (DOS title [inactive])	10	Disabled object

If you noticed the number of N/As (pairs not available), FoxPro cedes control of the "outer" window elements—border and title—to the default colors of MS Windows. This also applies to push button controls (another major screen element). To change these colors you need to use the Windows Control Panel, Color options. Something you can't do within a program. This can be a design problem. The Windows colors are *global* to all Windows programs in a particular configuration of Windows.

Following the color pair "mapping" in the above table, a color statement for defining a window might look something like this:

```
DEFINE WINDOW wrTEST AT 2,1 SIZE 10,50 TITLE "TEST WINDOW" ;
 COLOR GR+/B,B/W,,,,GR+/RB,GR+/B,,W+/B,W/B
```

The consecutive commas are necessary so that FoxPro knows these color pairs have been skipped. In this case they are nonfunctional anyway. You could, of course, also use the RGB notation in all of its lengthy glory. Which brings up a point. It could become quite inconvenient to type these long color expressions (especially RGB format!) every time you wanted to define colors for a window or any of the other screen elements. Fortunately, FoxPro provides an easy solution, standard color schemes.

Standard Color Schemes

FoxPro defines twenty four "standard" color schemes for the use of a programmer. The first twelve of these are assigned to specific screen elements, four are reserved, and eight more are user definable. These are referred to by their numbers, as in Table 11.2.

Table 11.2
Standard color schemes.

Scheme #	Assigned Use
1	User-defined windows
2	User-defined menus
3	System menu bars
4	System menu popups
5	System dialog boxes
6	System dialog popups
7	System alerts
8	System windows
9	System window popups
10	Browse windows
11	Report layout window
12	Alert dialog boxes
13-16	Reserved
17-24	User definable

For any of the twenty eight commands that support the COLOR SCHEME clause, you can use the scheme number instead of a lengthy COLOR expression. For example,

```
BROWSE TITLE "EMPLOYEES" COLOR SCHEME 5
```

This actually substitutes for the default color scheme of the Browse window (scheme 10) to whatever the scheme is for system dialog boxes. You could also define and use any of the eight user-defined color schemes (17 through 24).

There are four ways that color schemes can be defined in FoxPro:

1. Using SET COLOR OF SCHEME TO.
2. In the CONFIG.FPW file.
3. By default from the Windows Control Center Color settings.
4. By loading a color set from the resource file.

The first approach to defining a color scheme is most commonly used in programming. The syntax is:

```
SET COLOR OF SCHEME <expN1> TO [ SCHEME <expN2> | <expC> ]
```

<expN1> is the number of a color scheme to be changed.

<expN2> is the number of a color scheme to change to.

<expC> is the color pair list used to define the color scheme.

```
SET COLOR OF SCHEME 1 TO SCHEME 23
SET COLOR OF SCHEME 1 TO GR+/B,B/W,,,,GR+/RB,GR+/B,,W+/B,W/B
```

This approach can be used to program schemes "on the fly," and substitute them freely with the screen elements. The second approach is similar, but is put into the configuration file, CONFIG.FPW, to act as default settings. These look like this:

```
COLOR OF SCHEME 1 = GR+/B,B/W,,,,GR+/RB,GR+/B,,W+/B,W/B
```

Default Windows Colors

The first twelve color schemes are automatically loaded from the Windows default color settings (defined through the Windows Control Panel, Color access). Unless you change them in the CONFIG.FPW or in your program, these are the color settings for your application. This is an uncomfortable position on a two-edged sword. It's considered user-friendly to allow people to design their own colors, which to a certain extent this system does. On the other hand, color design—especially good color design—not only helps make an application distinctive but can also make it easier to follow and use. These two positions are not diametrically opposed, but close. The best way to solve this is to use color sets.

Color Sets

Having gone to all of the work of defining up to twenty color schemes (that's about 150 color pairs or three hundred RGB statements), a job that may take hours if you're designing schemes for a major project, you'd hardly want to lock them up in a single program. Again, FoxPro provides a simple solution—make a *color set* out of your schemes, and save them to the FoxPro Resource File.

A color set is a named collection of up to twenty color schemes (twenty four minus the reserved schemes). To save the schemes for future use, simply issue this command (probably from the Command window):

```
CREATE COLOR SET <color set name>
```

Later you can restore any color set from the current resource file with:

```
SET COLOR SET TO [<color set name>]
```

Using Color Schemes

Having gone through the rather lengthy description of *what* the FoxPro color system is, you may now be wondering *how* in the world do you use it, practically speaking. You've got several options. For simple coloring, such as tacking on a color statement to a @..GET, you can rely on the Screen Builder or insert your own code. However, if you're more ambitious and want to create a (more or less) unique color design for an application, then you've got to painstakingly put together one or more color sets.

For FoxPro DOS there are at least three excellent color-picker programs (two shipped with the FoxPro, and one commercial product). These help immensely by showing you the results of your color choices in the objects of the major screen elements. As of this writing, no such product exists for FoxPro for Windows, although it desperately needs one to handle the RGB capability. Keep a lookout.

NOTE

The disk that accompanies this book has a "stub" utility (one that begs to be extended), to help with creating RGB color schemes. The name of the screen set is COLORMKR (scx,sct) and you can run it with DO colormkr.spr. It has spinner dials for each of the six RGB values of a color pair. You can see what colors they produce in a user defined window, and when satisfied, the values are transferred to the Windows Clipboard for incorporation into programs, and so forth.

Whether you build color schemes (and color sets) using the RGB or Character Code styles, the usual approach for FoxPro is to redefine (a better word is override) the default Windows colors for the first twelve standard color schemes. That is, if you choose to not have your application colors be user definable. Then define the remaining eight schemes (17 through 24) as substitutes for the first twelve, or as special settings for a particular type of screen element.

Although you have no direct control over the Windows colors for window borders, titles and push buttons, you could use one of two functions, RGBSCHEME( ) or SCHEME( ), to test for the default values and adjust your own color schemes accordingly. These functions return as a character string in the color list for a scheme in either RGB format or character codes. For example:

```
* Get the default Windows scheme for user defined windows.
* cScheme1 = SCHEME(1)
* Test for the default window border color (color pair 3). This
* could
* be any length from 0 to 7.
cBorder = SUBSTR(cScheme1,AT(",",cScheme,2)+1,AT
(",",cScheme,3)-;
AT(",",cScheme,2)-1)
* Look at the background color and decide if its "warm" (reds)
* or
* "cold" (blues). Set your color schemes to match.
```

```
cBkGd = SUBSTR(cBorder,AT("/",cBorder)+1,LEN(cBorder)-AT("/
",cBorder))
DO CASE
CASE INLIST(cBkGd,"B", "BG", "RB", "B+", "BG+", "G", "G+")
   SET COLOR SET TO Cools
CASE INLIST(cBkGd,"R", "R+", "RB+", "GR+", "GR")
   SET COLOR SET TO Warms
OTHERWISE
  *probably gray, black, or white.
 SET COLOR SET TO Neutrals
ENDCASE
```

There's no guarantee this will work the way you want it to, but it may be better than leaving the color design to pure chance.

Designing with Color

The possibility of using "millions" of colors, doesn't mean that you should have them all in one screen, and that they should all be the brightest, flashiest available. In fact, what you really have in Windows is the possibility to finally use some subtle coloration, something not very easy to do with the usual sixteen colors of DOS.

Naturally, beauty is in the eye of the beholder. Which absolutely does not mean that good color selection and coordination is totally relative. It simply means that not everybody would do it your way.

Outside of being a trained graphics artist or designer, there's no "short course" in how to pick colors for software. But there is a good starting point:

- **Guide the eye to the most important things on the screen.** Nine times out of ten, that's going to be functional objects or important pieces of information. Normally, it shouldn't be to draw attention to design elements. That's why very bright colors for things like borders are usually poor design. They draw attention to themselves without doing anything to highlight the important material in the screen. A second point, useful in most situations is,
- **Consider the colors on the basis of regular use.** All too often, screens are designed with colors that make them look flashy and attractive, but in the long haul (daily use) become distracting and even irritating to the user. It's hard on the eyes to do hours of data entry on a screen with screaming yellow and eye-popping pink.

Even with these simple guidelines, the selection of colors for the many different screen objects can become complex. The screens in FoxPro tend to become layered, sometimes three or four deep. Color can play a large role in how these layers are clear (or confusing) to the user. Sometimes colors are chosen to identify a type of screen, or the module to which a screen belongs. There are many legitimate "reasons" for applying color schemes. The only real test, however, is how the user actually perceives them. This is difficult to measure, but worth your time to consider.

Text and Fonts

In a broad sense, a large percentage of the visual material on the screen is text. Data entry is text, push-button prompts are text, messages are text, titles are text, and instructions are text. With the advent of icons and picture buttons in FoxPro, there are now other options for decorating a screen. But text is still a major, if not always dominant, element.

By adding the selection of *font*, *size*, and *style*, the presentation of text becomes even more of a design element. Windows 3.1 and the availability of inexpensive TrueType fonts, has turned font-mongering into trend. But the warnings mentioned earlier still apply—you can make few assumptions about what fonts other computer systems will have.

When Windows (3.1) encounters a font that it does not have in the local repertoire, it makes a "substitution"—a best guess as to which of the available fonts is closest to the one that's requested. The guesses, based on point size, serif, and pitch are not usually very accurate, for example an actual case:

Original:

TESTING (COPPERPLATE, 14PT)

Substitute:

TESTING(Prestige Elite, 14pt)

Not only does this obviously look different, it also changes the spacing and layout of text. Although the two fonts are the same "size" (14pt), they don't have the same spacing or dimensions. A screen spaced properly for one, looks awful in the other.

It is possible to test for active fonts using either WFONT( ) or FONTMETRIC( ). Both of these return information about the currently active window font. (They won't help you with other types of screen objects.)

Presumably you could check to see if the font you specified is the one actually used, but your corrective opportunities are limited. The point is simply, not to use fancy fonts unless you plan to ship (legal) copies along with your application.

Windows

What's the most obvious user interface element in a Windows program? Windows. FoxPro can do windows, lots of windows—user windows, alert windows, dialog windows, browse windows. These are all "standard" Microsoft Windows formats. Most of them allow for considerable user manipulation, including sizing, moving, and zooming . All of these capabilities are available under program control.

It's important to remember that a window isn't just a decoration (a frame), it's a *container*. It's a very special screen entity, or object, with its own properties, that also becomes a unit of program organization. Most FoxPro applications can be seen as a collection of windows. True, the jargon of the Screen Builder refers to *screens* and *screen sets*, however with very few exceptions these screens are windows.

As you go deeper into application building, you'll find that control and manipulation of windows is one of the most important, and most difficult, of your programming tasks.

Basic Windowing

Creating a window is one of the "mega" commands in FoxPro. There are forty options.

```
DEFINE WINDOW <window name1> FROM <row1, column1> TO <row2,
column2> |
AT <row3, column3> SIZE <row4, column4>
     [IN [WINDOW] <window name2> | IN SCREEN | IN DESKTOP]
     [FONT <expC1>[, <expN1>]]
     [STYLE <expC2>]
     [TITLE <expC4>]
     [HALFHEIGHT]
     [PANEL | NONE | SYSTEM]
```

```
[CLOSE | NOCLOSE]
[FLOAT | NOFLOAT]
[GROW | NOGROW]
[MDI | NOMDI]
[MINIMIZE]
[ZOOM | NOZOOM]
[ICON FILE <expC5>]
[FILL FILE <bmp file>]
[COLOR SCHEME <expN2> | COLOR <color pair list>]
```

Rather than trying to explicate this mass at once, the following sections break the window clauses into three topics—naming, shaping, and decorating.

Naming Windows

```
DEFINE <window name1>
DEFINE WINDOW wrEmployee FROM 10,1 TO 15,30
```

Technically, you can define windows until you run out of user memory. (Don't be alarmed by the DISPLAY MEMORY reading for windows which shows 256 K or so for a full screen window.) For most purposes, five to seven windows is about all most programmers can comfortable control, although special circumstances may call for more.

Because a window is an object that can be specifically referenced by commands, every window must have a name. Although you can call them anything up to ten characters long, there is good reason to adopt a naming convention for windows. Later, you may be creating routines to track and control window behavior based on the type of window. These types are not official FoxPro designations, but have become widely used (thanks to Y. Allan Griver's work). The naming convention is simple: window names begin with a lower case *w* followed by a lower case letter for the type of window:

- **wr**—Read window, used in conjunction with a READ.
- **wb**—Browse window, used to contain a BROWSE.
- **wp**—Plain window, no read, no browse, just a plain window.
- **wm**—Modal window, designated as modal.
- **wc**—Control window, used for push button controls.

So a Browse window for an employee list might be *wbEmpList*. Making the last part of the name meaningful to the content of the window can be very helpful.

Which reinforces one of the points for these conventions—they make identifying and understanding a window much easier.

Keep in mind that a window *name* and a window *title* are usually not the same thing. The exception is one form of a Browse window. If you give a window a title, and then open a browse in that window, the browse then has the window title as its window name. This can lead to some strange window names. For example:

```
DEFINE WINDOW wTest AT 10,0 SIZE 10,50 TITLE "DETAIL AND;
PAYMENT"
BROWSE WINDOW wTest
```

The "name" of the Browse window is DETAIL AND PAYMENT, however you can refer to the name of this window as DETAIL. FoxPro only recognizes the word or character before the first blank space in a character string as a window name.

Shaping and Locating Windows

From the time you create a window (define it) to the time you make it go away (release it), the "shape" of a window and its location on the screen are important determinations. All sizing is affected by the current window font and font size:

```
FROM <row1, column1> TO <row2, column2> |
DEFINE WINDOW wbLookup FROM 20,0 TO 23,79
```

This is the conventional method for Xbase to specify the location of a window. It is a fixed-size window, meaning that although the window may be moved around the screen, it will always have the same size. The location coordinates are relative to what the window is in—in the screen or in another window.

Introduced with FoxPro for Windows, the AT method for specifying location is identical in its use of coordinates with FROM, however SIZE means the depth and length of the window in rows and columns.

Its syntax is:

```
AT <row3, column3> SIZE <row4, column4>
DEFINE WINDOW wrPositions AT 10,1 SIZE 5,30
```

The key words AT/SIZE tell FoxPro to automatically adjust the window size to accommodate changes in the window font. Most of the time, this is desirable, although by enlarging the window font you can easily make the borders of the window move out past the edges of the screen.

Using one of these clauses, you can specify the containment of a window IN some other object, specifically the Windows desktop, the FoxPro screen, or another window.

```
[IN [WINDOW] <window name2> | IN SCREEN | IN DESKTOP]
DEFINE WINDOW wrDaily AT 0,0 SIZE 4,20 IN WINDOW wpTruth
DEFINE WINDOW wrDaily AT 2,2 SIZE 10,30 IN DESKTOP
```

The normal placement is in the screen, which is the default value. However, IN WINDOW and IN DESKTOP have their uses. IN WINDOW is used to create a "parent-child" relationship between windows. If you define a window this way, it cannot be moved outside of the parent window, and shapes and moves with that window. IN DESKTOP lets you create a rogue window in the Windows desktop itself.

```
[HALFHEIGHT]
DEFINE WINDOW wrEmploy AT 2,3 SIZE 10,60 HALFHEIGHT
```

This clause is used to maintain compatibility with DOS FoxPro Windows, specifically in the size of the Title area.

The next five clauses all determine the users ability to move, size, and close a window. The defaults are always the no option. The ones you choose for a window depend on content. For instance, many windows have fixed positions for SAY and GET; changing size—GROW—makes no sense.

With this clause,the user is able to close a window.

```
[CLOSE | NOCLOSE]
DEFINE WINDOW wbPick AT 3,10 SIZE 20,40 CLOSE
```

This can be an important trigger for the DEACTIVATE clause of a READ.

A "floatable" window can be moved around the screen by a user.

```
[FLOAT | NOFLOAT]
DEFINE WINDOW wbPick AT 3,10 SIZE 20,40 CLOSE FLOAT
```

This is a very common and useful attribute, since it makes it possible to uncover information underneath a window.

Resizing a window using GROW makes sense only when the window has something like a picture or memo field.

Its syntax is:

```
[GROW | NOGROW]
```

```
DEFINE WINDOW wbPick AT 3,10 SIZE 20,40 CLOSE FLOAT GROW
```

In FoxPro, MINIMIZE reduces the screen to an icon in the Windows Desktop. For example:

```
DEFINE WINDOW wbPick AT 3,10 SIZE 20,40 CLOSE FLOAT GROW
MINIMIZE
```

If you wish, you can use the ICON FILE option to specify a particular icon for the minimized window.

Unlike GROW, which allows the user to determine any size for a window (up to full screen), ZOOM allows only two stages, full screen and the original size (whatever you set that to be).

```
[ZOOM | NOZOOM]
DEFINE WINDOW wbPick AT 3,10 SIZE 20,40 CLOSE FLOAT GROW
MINIMIZE ZOOM
```

While it might be tempting to simply list all of the shaping clauses for each window, you need to consider the effect. Closing a window may mean that it disappears forever—not necessarily what you might want. Resizing windows might cover important information. And so on. Each collection of windows (or screen set if you're using the Screen Builder) has its own purpose and characteristics, and you need to decide which of these shaping attributes are appropriate.

Decorating Windows

This group of clauses for DEFINE WINDOW or MODIFY WINDOW change the appearance but not the shape or basic attributes. They "decorate" a window with color, pictures, and frames. In a large application, one that may have dozens of screens, it can sometimes be important to consciously design windows as a means of helping the user identify where they are in a program. To a certain extent this is an extension of the conventions used by Microsoft in Windows or FoxPro, where dialog boxes have more or less standard shapes and colors.

FoxPro for Windows inherits the Microsoft Windows system for windowing. On one hand, this gives you the ability to MODIFY WINDOW on the fly, something that cannot be done with DOS FoxPro windows. On the other hand, no more creative borders (frames) for your windows.

```
[ PANEL | NONE | SYSTEM ]
DEFINE WINDOW wbList AT 2,20 SIZE 10,60 SYSTEM
```

You now have three border choices: none, single line, and standard Windows, shown in Figure 11.1. And as mentioned before, you no longer have control over border colors within FoxPro for Windows. They must be set from the Windows Control Panel.

Figure 11.1
Window borders.

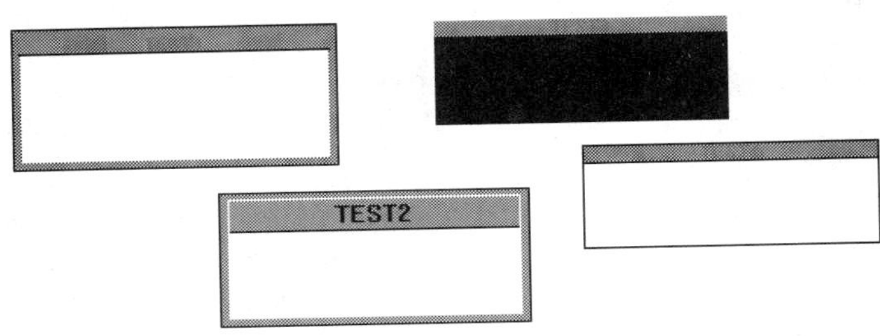

Here is your familiar trio for fonts: font, size, and style:

```
[FONT <expC1>[, <expN1>]] [STYLE <expC2>]
DEFINE WINDOW wrDaFonz AT 10,20 SIZE 6,10 FONT "Arial",14;
STYLE "BI"
```

With these clauses each window can have its own defaults for these three settings. If you don't set it, you'll get the homely and utilitarian FoxFont. All text displayed in the window (including SAYs and GETs) will have these attributes, unless otherwise specified.

It's tempting to put user instructions in the title, such as *Enter your name here and press* **F2**. There isn't much room for this, and it may lead to some problems later when window titles are used in identifying windows with the WTITLE( ) function.

```
[TITLE <expC4>]
DEFINE WINDOW wrVonPrinz AT 2,20 SIZE 10,40 TITLE "DATABASE;
CHAMP"
```

In general it's better practice to leave window titles generic and if possible short, such as *Employees* and *Invoice Detail*.

Color schemes for windows, though limited because of the Microsoft Windows defaults, can still be useful, especially for text and other objects inside the window.

```
[COLOR SCHEME <expN2> | COLOR <color pair list>]
DEFINE WINDOW wbRoygBiv AT 0,0 SIZE 36.5,79.6 COLOR SCHEME 22
DEFINE WINDOW wrHalfBlu AT 0,0 SIZE 22.5,33.5 COLOR GR+/B,W+/B
```

Most of the standard FoxPro color schemes apply to windows or windowed objects:

- **1**—User-defined windows
- **5**—System dialog boxes
- **6**—System dialog popups
- **7**—System alerts
- **8**—System windows
- **9**—System window popups
- **10**—Browse windows
- **11**—Report layout window
- **12**—Alert dialog boxes

FoxPro opens the floodgates for using bitmaps and icons as part of the user interface. This clause allows you to fill your windows with pictures and images from a universe of choices:

```
[FILL FILE <bmp file>]
DEFINE WINDOW wrFillUp AT 0,0 SIZE 36.6,79.6;
FILL FILE F:\BMP...\CLOUDS.BMP
```

As a design element, this is a dramatic and even dominant new opportunity. The technique requires nothing more than an appropriate bitmap file (.BMP) containing the image you want to use, then using FILL FILE with a valid path to the file. FoxPro takes care of sizing the bitmap (tiling) to the window. There are a few caveats, however.

- Bitmap fills require additional memory, just like Windows wallpaper, they take a bigger byte of your system resources.
- Unless they are extremely neutral, background pictures have a tendency to totally dominate text and other screen elements, and can lead to very messy, even unreadable, screens.
- Keeping track of the .BMP files may present problems.

For windows that you have designated MINIMIZE, the following clause specifies an icon file to create the minimized icon on the Windows desktop. This is a minor point, but a nice touch for applications where you intend to keep several windows active at the same time:

```
[ICON FILE <expC5>]
DEFINE WINDOW wrMinIt AT 10,2 SIZE 10,30;
ICON FILE F:\ICO\REDFOX.ICO
```

Basic Windowing Commands

Having been introduced to the properties of windows (size, location, color), its time for the commands that manipulate windows.

SHOW WINDOW

The syntax for SHOW WINDOW is:

```
SHOW WINDOW <window name1> [, <window name2> ... ] | ALL [IN;
[WINDOW]
<window name3> | IN SCREEN] [REFRESH] [TOP | BOTTOM | SAME];
SAVE]
```

One named window is required for this command, but you can string together a comma separated list.

```
ALL [IN [WINDOW] <window name3> | IN SCREEN]
```

This displays all windows, or only those windows contained in a specified window or in the FoxPro main window.

```
[TOP | BOTTOM | SAME]
```

This clause specifies the placement of a window in a stack of two or more windows in the screen.

```
REFRESH
```

This is an important option for Browse windows. If your application is operating on a network, it causes the data to be updated (refreshed) to show any changes made by other users. It has a side benefit on any system in that if forces the cursor into this window. For example:

```
DEFINE WINDOW wrToys AT 1,0 SIZE 22,70 TITLE "Toy Inventory"
```

```
SHOW WINDOW wrToys TOP
DEFINE WINDOW wbEmploy AT 0,0 SIZE 33.6,79.6 TITLE "Employees"
BROWSE WINDOW wbEmploy NOWAIT
...
SHOW WINDOW wbEmploy REFRESH
```

Both SHOW WINDOW and ACTIVATE WINDOW are used to display a window, once it has been defined. It helps to consider windows in two states, defined but not visible, or visible. You can keep a number of windows defined, and then shuttle them on and off the screen with SHOW WINDOW and HIDE WINDOW, placing them at any level on the screen (top, bottom, same).

ACTIVATE WINDOW

```
ACTIVATE WINDOW [<window name1> [, <window name2> ... ]] | ALL
[IN [WINDOW] <window name3> | SCREEN]      [BOTTOM | TOP |
SAME] [NOSHOW]
```

NO SHOW

```
DEFINE WINDOW wrDetails AT 2,20 SIZE 10,40 TITLE "Part Details"
ACTIVATE WINDOW wrDetails
ACTIVATE WINDOW wrDetails TOP
```

NOSHOW prepares the window to accept placement of SAYs and GETs without actually showing them on the screen. This technique is used by the Screen Builder to create a "flashless" screen.

Other than the single exception of the NOSHOW clause, this command is identical to SHOW WINDOW.

HIDE WINDOW

Use this command to specify one or more named windows to be hidden:

```
HIDE WINDOW [<window name1> [, <window name2>] ... ] | ALL [IN
[WINDOW] <window nameN> | SCREEN]
```

Before you can hide a window, it first needs to be defined. (Hiding a window that is already hidden causes no problem.) While the window is hidden the definition is retained, as well as a complete record of the content. When you redisplay the window with SHOW WINDOW, the contents, location, and other attributes remain the same.

DEACTIVATE WINDOW is an alternate command for HIDE WINDOW:

```
DEACTIVATE WINDOW <window name1> [, <window name2> ... ] | ALL
```

This command matches the ACTIVATE WINDOW command, and is a leftover from the days when FoxPro tried to stay compatible with Ashton-Tate's dBase.

MOVE WINDOW

The only advantage to using this command over MODIFY WINDOW is that it is explicitly about moving, and it supports the relative movement "by." Neither of these is enough to fully justify having both commands. Its syntax is:

```
MOVE WINDOW <window name> TO <row>, <column> | BY <expN1>,
<expN2> |CENTER
```

<window name> is the name of any previously defined window.

TO <row>,<column> are the absolute coordinates of the upper-left corner of the window.

BY <expN1>,<expN2> is the relative distance for the window to move (for example, 5,10 is down five rows and over 10 columns; -5,-10 is up 5 rows and left 10 columns).

CENTER automatically centers the window inside of the screen or window where it was defined.

```
DEFINE WINDOW wrMover AT 2,20 SIZE 10,30
SHOW WINDOW wrMover
MOVE WINDOW wrMover TO 3,20
MOVE WINDOW wrMover BY 5,10
```

ZOOM WINDOW

The only reason to use this command is to "zoom" the window to and from icon, full screen, and normal sizes. Otherwise MODIFY SCREEN is a better choice for resizing, since it has more options and is clearer in purpose. The syntax for ZOOM WINDOW is:

```
ZOOM WINDOW <window name> MIN | MAX | NORM [AT <row1, col1> |
FROM <row1, col1> [SIZE <row2, col2> | TO <row2, col2>]]
```

MIN | MAX | NORM size the window to an icon (MIN), a full screen (MAX), and back to the size of the current definition (NORM).

[AT <row1, col1> [SIZE <row2, col2>]] and [FROM <row1, col1> TO <row2,col2>]] also resize the window completely, using either the FoxPro for DOS or FoxPro for Windows coordinate systems. This capability is exactly the same as in MODIFY WINDOW.

For example:

```
DEFINE WINDOW wrPayroll AT 2,0 SIZE 30,80 MINIMIZE FLOAT
SHOW WINDOW wrPayroll
ZOOM WINDOW wrPayroll MIN
```

MODIFY WINDOW

The syntax for MODIFY WINDOW is:

```
MODIFY WINDOW <window name> | SCREEN
[FROM <row1, column1> TO <row2, column2> |
 AT <row3, column3> SIZE <row4, column4>]
[FONT <expC1>[, <expN1>]]
[STYLE <expC2>]
[TITLE <expC3>]
[HALFHEIGHT]
[DOUBLE | PANEL | NONE | SYSTEM]
[CLOSE | NOCLOSE]
[FLOAT | NOFLOAT]
[GROW | NOGROW]
[MINIMIZE]
[ZOOM | NOZOOM]
[ICON FILE <expC4>]
[FILL FILE <bmp file>]
[COLOR SCHEME <expN2> | COLOR <color pair list>]
```

(See DEFINE WINDOW for an explanation of clauses.)

For example:

```
DEFINE WINDOW wrTest AT 2,0 SIZE 20,70 TITLE "TESTING"
MODIFY WINDOW wrTest GROW CLOSE FLOAT COLOR SCHEME 23
MODIFY WINDOW wrTest NOGROW NOCLOSE NOFLOAT COLOR SCHEME1
```

This command is a relatively important enhancement to the manipulation of the user interface. It makes it possible to redefine the characteristics and properties of a window "on the fly" and without "blipping" (removing and redisplaying). This makes windows much more responsive to user selections and current conditions. For example, if the user chooses a particular action, you could immediately change the color of the window and its title to reflect the selection. Prior to MODIFY WINDOW you would probably have used a RELEASE WINDOW and DEFINE WINDOW to accomplish the effect, only it would have taken much longer and been a lot less smooth.

SAVE WINDOWS

The syntax is:

```
SAVE WINDOWS <window list> | ALL TO <file> | TO MEMO <memo
field>
```

<window list> | ALL is a list of currently defined windows, or all defined windows.

TO <file> specifies that the window definitions may be saved to a file and later restored.

TO MEMO <memo field> specifies that window definitions may also be saved to a memo field in a standard .DBF, like the resource file.

```
DEFINE WINDOW wrPosition AT 3,4 SIZE 20,66 TITLE "Positions"
SAVE WINDOW TO wrPosition F:\win\FoxWinds.win
```

In some very complex applications where windows are being changed frequently between modules, it may be expedient to save the window definitions to a file or memo field and restore them later. In most other situations, however, it's probably safer to code window definitions rather than rely on the availability and integrity of external files.

RESTORE WINDOW

RESTORE WINDOW is the complement to SAVE WINDOW. Its syntax is:

```
RESTORE WINDOW <window list> | ALL
FROM <file> | FROM MEMO <memo field>
RESTORE WINDOW ALL FROM F:\win\FoxWinds.win
```

CLEAR WINDOWS

This command removes *all* windows from the screen and their definitions from memory.

RELEASE WINDOW

This allows you to specify which windows should be removed from the screen and from memory. Its syntax is:

```
RELEASE WINDOW <window list>
```

Window Functions

DEFINE WINDOW and MODIFY WINDOW let you specify how a window should look, it's location and size. The other commands let you move the window around, show or hide them, and ultimately save or release them. The final pieces necessary for controlling windows are the functions that monitor information about windows and the screen. There are twenty of these functions. Some are used constantly and others only for special occasions.

Figure 11.2
Window functions.

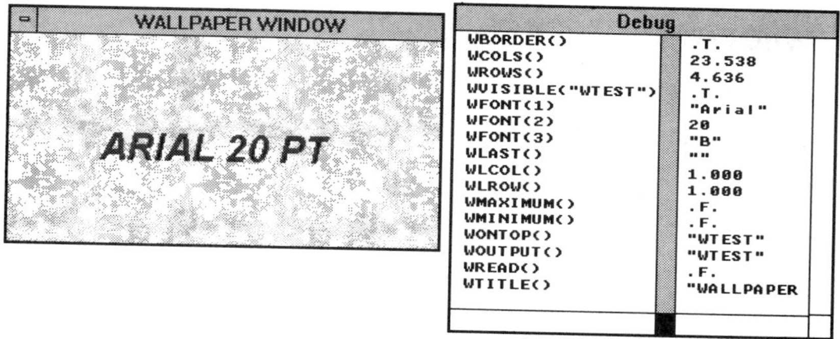

This diagram illustrates some of the more common window functions. You should note that the status of most of these functions will not change until you SHOW or HIDE a window. As with the options of DEFINE WINDOW, the following list of functions is broken down into shaping and location, and decoration.

Shape and Location Functions

Shape and location functions are listed on the next page.

WCOLS

```
WCOLS([<window name>])
```

The number of columns is sensitive to the font and font size of the window.

```
=WCOLS("WTEST")
```

Returns: 77.444, the number of columns in the specified window.

```
=WCOLS( )
```

Returns: 45.777, the number of columns in the current window.

```
=WCOLS("")
```

Returns: 80, use of the null string ("") returns the size of the FoxPro main screen.

WROWS

```
WROWS([<window name>])
```

In all cases the number of rows is sensitive to the font and font size of the window.

```
=WROWS("WTEST")
```

Returns: 23.124, the number of rows in the specified window.

```
=WROWS( )
```

Returns: 30, the number of rows in the current window.

```
=WROWS("")
```

Returns: 25, use of the null string ("") returns the rows of the main screen.

WLCOL

```
WLCOL([<window name>])
=WLCOL("WTEST")
```

Returns: 2, the upper-left column coordinate of the current or named window.

WLROW

```
WLROW([<window name>])
=WLROW("WTEST")
```

Returns: 10, the upper-left row coordinate of the current or named window.

NOTE

This pair of functions, WLCOLS and WLROWS, provide the upper-left coordinates of a window. This can be used in a number of calculations for moving or resizing a window.

WEXIST

```
WEXIST(<window name>)
=WEXIST("WTEST")
```

Returns: .t. or .f. If the named window exists (is defined), returns .t., otherwise it returns .f..

WVISIBLE

```
WVISIBLE(<window name>)
=WVISIBLE("WTEST")
```

Returns: .t. if the named window is visible, otherwise it returns.f..

WLAST

```
WLAST([<window name>])
=WLAST()
```

Returns: wtest, the name of the last window active on the screen.

```
=WLAST("WTEST")
```

Returns: .t. if the named window was the last active window, otherwise it returns .f.

WONTOP

```
WONTOP([<window name>])
=WONTOP()
```

Returns: wtest the name of the window currently on the top of the screen. It returns "" (null string) if the window is the main screen or Command window.

```
=WONTOP("WTEST")
```

Returns: .t. if the named window is on top, otherwise it returns.f.

WOUTPUT

```
WOUTPUT([<window name>])
=WOUTPUT()
```

Returns: wtest, the name of the window currently the active output window. It returns "" (null string) if the output window is the main screen or Command window.

```
=WOUTPUT("WTEST")
```

Returns: .t. if the named window the current output window, otherwise it returns.f.

Output in this context means where screen output is sent.

WREAD

```
WREAD([<window name>])
=WREAD()
=WREAD("WTEST")
```

Returns: .t. if then current or named window is a Read window, otherwise it returns.f.

Windows are involved as a READ window if they are included in the READ WITH clause, or are part of a control window used in many screens but with a single READ.

WMAXIMUM

```
WMAXIMUM([<window name>])
=WMAXIMUM()
```

```
=WMAXIMUM("WTEST")
```

Returns: .t. if the current or named window is at full screen size, otherwise it returns.f.

WMINIMUM

```
WMINIMUM([<window name>])
=WMINIMUM()
=WINIMUM("WTEST")
```

Returns: .t. if the current or named window is minimized, otherwise it returns .f.

WCHILD

```
WCHILD([<window name>] [<expN>])
```

<expN> is 0 for the bottom child window, any positive number for consecutive window names.

```
=WCHILD(0)
```

Returns: wTest1, the name of the window on the bottom of a window stack.

```
=WCHILD("WTEST")
```

Returns: 3, the number of child windows in the named window.

WPARENT

```
WPARENT([<window name>])
=WPARENT()
```

Returns: wtest1, the name of the current parent window.

```
=WPARENT("WTEST1")
```

Returns: .t. if the named window is a parent, otherwise it returns .f.

Decoration Functions

Following are the decoration functions.

WBORDER

```
WBORDER([<window name>])
=WBORDER("WTEST1")
```

Returns: .t. if the named or current window has a border.

WFONT

```
WFONT(<expN>[, <window name>])
=WFONT(1)
```

Returns: Arial, the font name for the current or named window.

```
=WFONT(2)
```

Returns: 16, the point size for the current font.

```
=WFONT(3)
```

Returns: B, the current font style.

WTITLE

```
WTITLE([<window name>])
=WTITLE()
```

Returns: Payroll, the title of the current or named window.

Browses

The BROWSE was introduced in Parts 1 and 2 as a powerful, interactive, and relatively simple tool for viewing and editing data. Now it's time to haul out the heavy programming machinery and deal with BROWSE as one of the most important user interface elements in FoxPro. While it's a bit of a stretch, whole applications could be built using nothing but the BROWSE. It's that flexible and multifaceted.

The BROWSE syntax has more clauses than a congressional appropriations bill:

```
BROWSE
     [FIELDS <field list>]
     [FONT <expC1>[, <expN1>]]
     [STYLE <expC2>]
```

```
[FOR <expL1>]
[FORMAT]
[FREEZE <field>]
[KEY <expr1>[, <expr2>]]
[LAST]
[LEDIT] [REDIT]
[LOCK <expN2>]
[LPARTITION]
[NOAPPEND]
[NOCLEAR]
[NODELETE]
[NOEDIT | NOMODIFY]
[NOLGRID] [NORGRID]
[NOLINK]
[NOMENU]
[NOOPTIMIZE]
[NOREFRESH]
[NORMAL]
[NOWAIT]
[PARTITION <expN3>]
[PREFERENCE <expC3>]
[REST]
[SAVE]
[TIMEOUT <expN4>]
[TITLE <expC4>]
[VALID [:F] <expL2> [ERROR <expC5>]]
[WHEN <expL3>]
[WIDTH <expN5>]
[[WINDOW <window name1>]
      [IN [WINDOW] <window name2> | IN SCREEN]]
[COLOR SCHEME <expN6> | COLOR <color pair list>]
```

To make the syntax a little more tractable, these clauses can be categorized for either editing or windowing.

Browse Editing

One of the features of the FoxPro BROWSE that has contributed greatly to its use in applications, is the ability to have nearly the same sophisticated control and validation of data entry and edit, as you have with the @..GET. This control exists on two levels, for records and for the individual fields. Since the

BROWSE may display and allow editing in more than one table, you need to distinguish between those actions like deleting which affect a record—and only the "primary" table in the current work area—and those which affect the fields in any table.

Record Level

As a screen object, you don't have to always think of the Browse as an "editing surface," a place to do data entry and edit. It obviously can have many read-only (nonediting) functions, and can serve as a very efficient way to display a lot of data. Browses are also used extensively in pick-list routines (as you will see later in this chapter), which are also mostly read-only. To set this mode, you can use any or all of the following three clauses:

- **[NOAPPEND].** No new records may be added to the primary table being browsed.
- **[NODELETE].** Records may not be deleted from the table in the current work area.
- **[NOEDIT | NOMODIFY].** `(BROWSE NOAPPEND NODELETE NOMODIFY)` No editing of fields is permitted. When all three clauses are combined, the Browse effectively becomes a read-only screen. These clauses are *not* the default values for a Browse, and must be explicitly included.

As the next step toward editing "rights," the BROWSE features the familiar WHEN and VALID clauses as applied to records in the current table.

WHEN

The syntax for WHEN is:

```
[WHEN <expL3>]
```

<expL3> is a logical expression that evaluates to .t./.f. or 1/0.

```
BROWSE WHEN nSecurity > 3       && BROWSE table level control
BROWSE WHEN cus.totsale > 500   && Record level control
```

Both WHEN and VALID are a little tricky to understand in the Browse. They don't prevent you from entering the Browse. *They operate only when you move the cursor from one record to another*. The WHEN is used as the gateway into the next record. If the expression in <expL3> evaluates to true or > 0, then editing in the next record (row of the browse) is allowed, otherwise the record becomes read-only. This is applied to the first record of the browse, so that a user can be effectively put in NOMODIFY mode for the entire table. In other cases you can set a WHEN that acts like selective editing filter, allowing edits only on data where the record meets a specific criteria.

As a user interface control, the WHEN allows the situation where the user can see the full spread of items—say a parts list—while being able to edit only selected items, for instance based on their security clearance or department affiliation.

VALID

The syntax for VALID is:

```
[VALID [:F] <expL2> [ERROR <expC5>]]
```

:F forces the validation for a field (all movement out of the field will be validated).

<expL2> is any expression (function, expression etc.) that evaluates .t./.f. or 1/0.

ERROR is an optional clause to provide an error message to the user.

<expC5> is any valid character expression.

```
BROWSE WHEN nSecurity > 3 VALID :F NOT EMPTY(cus.lastname);
   ERROR "You must enter a last name."
BROWSE VALID CheckVal( cus.total )
BROWSE VALID IdLook( ) ERROR IdMessage( )
```

When included with the BROWSE this "post-entry" validation occurs any time the user makes a change in a record. The :F forces a validation, even if nothing has changed. Since you have ample tools to validate individual fields, this record level validation is most commonly used to check values between fields, for example adding three fields to make sure they don't go over a limit.

Although FoxPro doesn't let you access the internal operations of the BROWSE, like all WHENs and VALIDs, you can consider this a break in the action, a way you can insert your own UDF to do things inside the Browse. The only restrictions are that you don't destroy the original table setup of the BROWSE (like changing relations to external fields), and any changes to the defined characteristics like the field list won't have any effect.

Selecting What to Edit

Like many of the major commands in FoxPro, BROWSE supports a way to limit the visible records (screen only a subset of records). Previously this could only be done by means of SET FILTER TO, which was very slow and had to be carefully managed. In FoxPro the Browse now is attached to the Rushmore engine, which gets you performance, and it also means that BROWSE conditions do not persist beyond the use of the Browse.

FOR

The syntax for FOR is

```
[FOR <expL1>]
```

<expL1> is any expression that returns .t. or .f., in mold of the classic logical expression.

```
BROWSE FOR "J" $ lastname       && Not Rushmore Optimizable
BROWSE FOR lastname = "JOHNSON" && Rushmore Optimizable
```

In many ways the inclusion of the FOR clause in the BROWSE of FoxPro 2.0 was one of the most important enhancements in the history of the Browse. It made it practical (it had already been possible) to use the Browse for subsets of data of almost any type.

Although you can't change the value of the FOR clause on the fly, you can put the BROWSE into a loop, provide a way for the user to redefine the FOR values while still in the Browse, and then leave the BROWSE to recreate it with the new values. The code below is a skeleton of a way to do this.

```
DO WHILE .t.
  cFor = "lastname='JOHNSON'"       && Store logical expression;
to variable
  * Use macro substitution in BROWSE to set the FOR expression.
```

```
  * The valid function is triggered whenever leaving a record.
  BROWSE FOR &cFor VALID MakeFor()
  IF EMPTY(cFor)    && any mechanism to exit the loop
    EXIT
  ENDIF
ENDDO

FUNCTION MakeFor
 *Code to allow user input of value to change in the cFor;
variable.
 * or else make cFor blank to exit the BROWSE and loop.
 ...
 cTempFor = "lastname = "+cUserInput
 IF cFor <> cTempFor && Only do anything if FOR is changed.
   * Force termination of the BROWSE with a <ctrl> W;
equivalent.
   * KEYBOARD stuffs the keyboard buffer with any valid;
keystroke.
   KEYBOARD CHR(23)
   cFor = cTempFor
 ENDIF
 RETURN .t.
 *
```

KEY

The syntax for KEY is:

```
[KEY <expr1>[, <expr2>]]
```

<expr1> is the lower limit of the index value.

<expr2> is the upper limit of the index value (optional).

```
SELECT customer
SET ORDER TO lastname
BROWSE KEY "JOHNSON"
BROWSE KEY "JACKSON", "JOHNSON"
BROWSE KEY "JOHSON" FOR FIRSTNAME = "JOHN"
```

The KEY clause preceded the FOR clause by one version (FoxPro 1.0), and in many respects has been superceded by the more flexible newcomer. However, the KEY clause is index dependent, meaning that you have to set the table to a specific index for the KEY to work. Like all single-table indexed lookups this is faster because it does not need to invoke the Rushmore machinery. In cases where the values of the lookup are known (either as constants or as predictable values for variables), the KEY clause may be quicker than using the FOR.

The two expressions, <expr1> and <expr2>, are the *scope*, the lower and upper limits of the lookup values to be found in the index. These values must match the data type of the index being used for the KEY clause.

The KEY clause can be mixed with the FOR clause, although this will probably lose any performance advantage of the simple index lookup of the KEY.

Field Level Editing

The syntax for FIELD is:

```
[FIELDS <field list>]
BROWSE FIELDS cus.lastname, cus.midinits, cus.firstname,
cus.custid
```

The field list is the structure on which you hang the many and various field editing options of the Browse. The order of the list corresponds to the order in which columns of the Browse screen appear. One of the difficulties of the Browse is the horizontal orientation, which tends to stretch tables with many fields way out on the right, and require a lot of tabbing by the user. To avoid some of this problem, most Browse screens prune the number of fields and place them from left to right in the most logical and practical order for the needs of the user.

Browse Field Options

In addition to the FOR clause, the other feature that truly distinguishes the FoxPro Browse is the degree of control you have over the fields. In almost all respects, you have the same capabilities as the @..GET, a truly amazing capacity given the huge number of fields present on the screen in even a simple Browse. These can be summarized by naming them with their @..GET equivalents, as in Table 11.3.

Table 11.3
Browse field options.

Code	Meaning
:R	Read-only
:<expN>	Column width
:V	Valid
:F	Force valid
:E	Error message
:P	Picture
:B	Range
:H	Title of column
:W	When

The syntax for the Browse Field Options is compact and, as a result, a bit cryptic:

- `<field1>...`
- `[:R]` set the field to READ ONLY. `(FIELDS cus.custid:R)`
- `[:column width]` fixes the column width at <n> spaces. `(FIELDS cus.custsales:9)`
- `[:V=<expr1> [:F] [:E=<expC1>]`
  - :V=<expr1> is any validation expression or function that returns .t./ .f. or 1/0.
  - :F forces validation regardless of keystroke or status of field.
  - :E=<expC1> is any character expression for a user message.

For example:

```
FIELDS cus.total:V=CheckTotal():F:E="Must be greater than;
100"
```

This has the same characteristics and capabilities as the VALID and ERROR clauses of the standard @..GET. Using the :F option forces the expression in :V to be evaluated, whether the field has changed or not.

You would use this option primarily to trap for empty values. Using UDFs for the valid is the most compact form, but you can still use full expressions in the option:

```
:V=cus.totsales > 500 AND NOT EMPTY(cus.lastname)
```

- [:P=<expC2>], The "Picture" option, supports exactly the same codes and functions as the PICTURE clause of the @..GET, @..SAY (with the exception of the @M function).

```
FIELDS cus.custsales:9:P="$##,###.##"
```

- [:B=<expr2>,<expr3>[:F]], the "Range" options, are yet another mirror of the @..GET RANGE clause. Adding the :F forces the verification of the entry to be between the range values, whether the field has been changed or not.

```
FIELDS cus.custype:B=0,9:F
```

- [:H=<expC3>] From the user interface point of view, this is one of the most useful of options. Many, if not most field names are awkward, if not downright incomprehensible—cus.prtotgrsal, det.newprdprc. By using this "Column Heading" option, you can create headings for the fields that might even tell the user what's in the field. Another use is to save space by shortening fields or using abbreviations.

```
FIELDS cus.custype:H="Type"
```

- [:W=<expL1>], "When" option, corresponds exactly to the @..GET WHEN clause. It allows you to control access into a field (column).

```
FIELDS cus.custid:W=SecureChk(3,4)
```

Putting these options together for the fields of a Browse looks like this:

```
BROWSE FIELDS ;
   cus.lastname:30:P="@!":H="Last Name":V=NameChk():F,;
   cus.midinit:P="@!":H="Mid.Initials",;
   cus.firstname:15:P="@!":H="First Name":V=NameChk():F,;
   cus.custid:W=SecChk():H="ID":V=IdChk():F
```

As you can see, a full-blown field list with all of the options can become lengthy. There is a limit of 2,048 characters per command line. It's theoretically possible to exceed that with a BROWSE on a very large table (or group of tables), loaded with options, but not likely. However, if you run into a situation that does have many fields and many options, you might consider using a format file (.FMT).

FORMAT signals FoxPro that you are using a format file to set definitions. Format files go way back in the history of Xbase. They've come in and out of favor at least three times. Just when it looked like FoxPro would kill them for good, this option to link format files with a BROWSE came along.

A format file is essentially a screen file, composed almost solely of @..SAY and @..GET statements. It has a .FMT extension instead of a .PRG, but it's still really a program file (to differentiate it from anything the Screen Builder does). Historically, the format file was the only way to create multi-screen data entry, but has been almost completely displaced by the techniques of the Screen Builder. However, it's value in the Browse is that FoxPro picks up all of the field definitions and transfers them to the fields of the Browse. In this approach, there is no 2,048 characters per line limit to contend with, and it does provide a way to organize the many field validation options.

The steps for including a format file are straightforward:

1. Create the format file as you would a program file. Include only @..SAY and @..GET statements complete with all necessary clauses. Save the file with a .FMT extension.
2. Before defining the Browse in your program, use SET FORMAT TO <format file> to load the format file.
3. Include the FORMAT clause in your BROWSE command line.

   ```
   BROWSE KEY M.lastname FORMAT
   ```

4. When you're done with the Browse and format file use SET FORMAT TO.

Calculated Fields

In a Browse screen the equivalent of an @..SAY is a *calculated field*. The term is slightly misleading, an "evaluated field" might be more accurate. The format for the field looks like this:

```
< (field name) column header > = <any valid FoxPro expression>
```

For example:

```
BROWSE FIELDS ;
  Total = cus.totalsale + cus.totaltax,;
  NewId = MakeId(),;
  OK = IIF(nCount>10, "OK", "NA")
```

The Calculated field name becomes the text for the column header, although it must follow all of the conventions of a legitimate field name. The valid expression is any kind of expression (in the FoxPro sense) which evaluates to something that will be displayed in the fields. For obvious reasons, all calculated fields are read-only.

While it takes only a few sentences to describe a calculated field, and the concept is easy enough to grasp, it should be emphasized: The sky's the limit. The kind of information you put into a calculated field is really limited only by your imagination.

Two final clauses to round out the Editing options: WIDTH and FREEZE.

The syntax for WIDTH is:

```
[WIDTH <expN5>]
BROWSE WIDTH 10
```

This clause sets the width of all fields. It is not used very often.

The syntax for FREEZE is:

```
[FREEZE <field>]
BROWSE FIELDS ;
  cus.lastname,;
  cus.firstname,;
  cus.address,;
  cus.city ;
  FREEZE cus.lastname
```

In one of its many uses, a Browse may be made into a pick-list display, allowing the user to scroll through records to select one. In some of these cases, the FREEZE clause, which fixes the Browse highlight cursor in one field, can be an indicator to the user.

Browse Windowing

In many ways, the Browse is the most sophisticated window in FoxPro. It is also a chameleon, being able to live inside of other windows and take on their attributes, while maintaining its own unique capabilities. Partitions, grids, locks, and freezes, shown in Figure 11.3, are just some of the windowing capabilities unique to the Browse.

Figure 11.3
The Browse window.

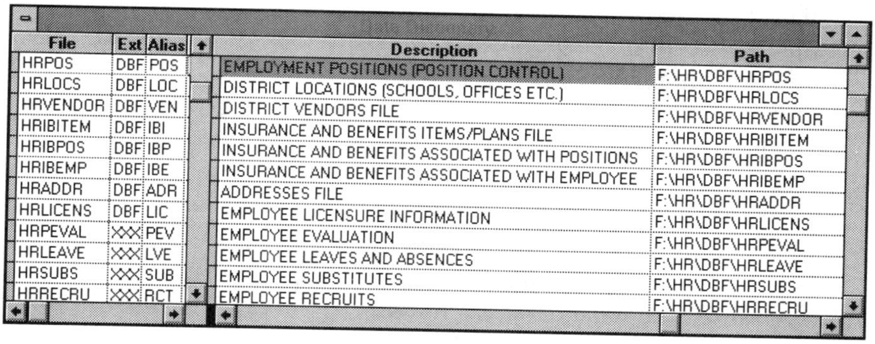

File	Ext	Alias	Description	Path
HRPOS	DBF	POS	EMPLOYMENT POSITIONS (POSITION CONTROL)	F:\HR\DBF\HRPOS
HRLOCS	DBF	LOC	DISTRICT LOCATIONS (SCHOOLS, OFFICES ETC.)	F:\HR\DBF\HRLOCS
HRVENDOR	DBF	VEN	DISTRICT VENDORS FILE	F:\HR\DBF\HRVENDOR
HRIBITEM	DBF	IBI	INSURANCE AND BENEFITS ITEMS/PLANS FILE	F:\HR\DBF\HRIBITEM
HRIBPOS	DBF	IBP	INSURANCE AND BENEFITS ASSOCIATED WITH POSITIONS	F:\HR\DBF\HRIBPOS
HRIBEMP	DBF	IBE	INSURANCE AND BENEFITS ASSOCIATED WITH EMPLOYEE	F:\HR\DBF\HRIBEMP
HRADDR	DBF	ADR	ADDRESSES FILE	F:\HR\DBF\HRADDR
HRLICENS	DBF	LIC	EMPLOYEE LICENSURE INFORMATION	F:\HR\DBF\HRLICENS
HRPEVAL	XXX	PEV	EMPLOYEE EVALUATION	F:\HR\DBF\HRPEVAL
HRLEAVE	XXX	LVE	EMPLOYEE LEAVES AND ABSENCES	F:\HR\DBF\HRLEAVE
HRSUBS	XXX	SUB	EMPLOYEE SUBSTITUTES	F:\HR\DBF\HRSUBS
HRRECRU	XXX	RCT	EMPLOYEE RECRUITS	F:\HR\DBF\HRRECRU

The Browse is also the most user-configurable of all windows. Besides the usual window attributes of size, location, and zoom, you can add all of the partitioning, change/browse display, column sizing and movement, and so forth. FoxPro also provides you with ways to preserve Browse configurations using the LAST or PREFERENCE clauses. Incidentally, you need to alert users to the fact that leaving the Browse with **CTRL-Q** does not save their Browse configuration.

LAST is by far the simplest form. By including this with your BROWSE command, the "last" configuration is retrieved from the FoxPro resource file.

```
[PREFERENCE <expC3>]
Browse PREFERENCE "EMPLIST"
```

Preferences work much like the LAST clause, except they are named and specific to a Browse configuration. This allows the developer to create predefined configurations (the preferences) and store them to the FoxPro resource file. If you wish, these preferences can be made read-only, so the user cannot make permanent modification to the Browse window (although they can make all the changes they want during one session).

The Resource File

As mentioned above, one of the functions of the FoxPro resource file is to store configurations of windows and a number of other items of system information, like color sets. The resource file is an integral part of the FoxPro operation. A resource file will always exist, and it will always be open while you run the program. Consequently one school of thought says, "Go with it. Use the resource file as much as FoxPro for Windows does itself."

The other school of thought says, "Are you crazy? Resource files get erased, damaged, moved out of the path. Put anything vital to your application in the resource file and you're playing roulette with disaster."

The resource file, which in most respects is just another .DBF, is as robust as any other FoxPro file, which is to say, very robust. However, because it is open all of the time, and frequently used by FoxPro, it *is* vulnerable, however slightly. That vulnerability, even if it's one in a thousand, makes relying on the resource file to keep your application running somewhat more risky than it is with most of the other files. If it's important, make sure you have a backup scheme. You'll need a way to detect if the resource file is missing. FoxPro won't warn you, it simply creates a new one if it can't find a resource file. (It does warn you if the resource file has been damaged.) If you detect the resource file has been changed or simply not the one you need for your application, then you'll need a way to restore it with the information required.

There are many ways to do this. As an example, the default FoxPro resource files are called FOXUSER.DBF and FOXUSER.FPT. Let's say you've stored a number of application specific color sets, Browse and window settings in these files. Keep a copy of the additional settings in another file—something like APPUSER.DBF/.FPT. Also, select one or more of the settings, such as a named preference for a Browse, or flag something to test for to see if the resource file has changed. Then put this routine (with your own variations) into the initialization file of your application:

```
*—————[ Resource File Test
SET RESOURCE OFF
USE FOXUSER
LOCATE FOR NAME="EMPFILE"
IF NOT FOUND()
  APPEND FROM APPUSER
ENDIF
USE
SET RESOURCE ON
```

There's a big difference between using the resource file to store user choices and configurations, and relying on the resource file to define critical operating conditions. How important this factor is may depend on the type of application you are building. If your application leans toward the more controlled data-entry or modal type, then you probably should code all window and Browse definitions. On the other hand, if your application leans in the direction of a more user-controlled, interactive style, then relying on the resource file is probably the way to go.

Windows, Colors, and Fonts

By default, the Browse is its own window. This is convenient in some respects, especially in the interactive environment, where the user is shaping the window as they wish, and probably using the LAST clause to save their configurations. But in the programming environment, the Browse window leaves some things to be desired—it can't be positioned, or sized under program control, unless you go the convoluted route of defining read-only PREFERENCEs in the FoxPro resource file.

To get around this limitation, you can use one or the other of the WINDOW clauses:

- `[WINDOW <window name1>]` In this clause, the Browse takes on all of the characteristics of the named window. It's the responsibility of the programmer to define the window before calling the BROWSE, then to release the window definition afterwards. The window does not need to be activated prior to the call. This approach is common practice for applications where the Browse is more tightly controlled. For example:

  ```
  DEFINE WINDOW wbEmployee AT 2,0 SIZE 10,40 FLOAT GROW ZOOM
  TITLE "Employees"
  ```

```
BROWSE WINDOW wbEmployee
RELEASE WINDOW wbEmployee
```

- `[IN [WINDOW] <window name2> | IN SCREEN]` The Browse with this clause *does not* take on the characteristics of the window. It merely places the normal Browse window inside the named window (or screen). The Browse Window can't be moved outside the parent window, but is free to be configured as needed within it. For example:

```
BROWSE IN WINDOW nrPosition
BROWSE IN SCREEN
```

- `[TITLE <expC4>]` The titling of a Browse window is a simple thing to do. It's behavior is not simple. Because the Browse window has no "name" of its own, it can take on a name from a variety of sources, in this order:
  1. By default from the name of the current table or table alias.
  2. From the current user defined output window, if any.
  3. From the Browse TITLE, if any.

  If you specify a Browse TITLE, FoxPro uses the letters up to the first space as the name of the Browse window. For example *Employee Listing* produces a window named *Employee*.
- `[NORMAL]` Regardless of the window in which the Browse appears, you can use this clause to make the Browse window characteristics default to the "normal" Browse settings for color, size, position, title, and control options.
- `[COLOR SCHEME <expN6> | COLOR <color pair list>]`

  ```
  SET COLOR OF SCHEME 10 TO SCHEME 22
  BROWSE LAST COLOR SCHEME 10
  ```

  With a Browse, you have three choices for setting its colors: By default, by the current output window (with the WINDOW clause), or explicitly by the COLOR SCHEME or COLOR clause. As with the other windowing clauses, anything done explicitly to the BROWSE overrides all other settings. If you are controlling the Browse through a user-defined window, then put the color statements with that window. If you are using the Browse Window in a standalone, interactive mode, then set the colors in the BROWSE definition.
- `[FONT <expC1>[, <expN1>]]` Like other windows, the Browse Window may be assigned a default font and font size.
- `BROWSE FONT"Arial", 12`

`[STYLE <expC2>]` This sets the default style for the default font in the Browse Window.

```
BROWSE FONT"Courier New", 10 TYPE "BI"
```

Partitioning

The Browse window is unique among windows for its ability to be partitioned, changed from one format to another, and to display a grid. The following clauses give you program control over the use and definition of these options.

- `[PARTITION <expN3>]` is the clause that defines a partition in the Browse window. The <expN3> is the column location for the placement of the window splitter. Since the spacing of the Browse window is dependent on the font and font size, you may need to do some experimentation to get the partition to fall where you want it between field columns.

  ```
  BROWSE KEY m.lastname PARTITION 20
  ```
- `[LPARTITION]` By default the Browse highlight cursor is placed into the first field of the right partition. This clause puts it in the first field of the left partition.
- `[NOLGRID]` and `[NORGRID]` turn off the grid markings in either the left or the right partition.
- `[NOLINK]` By default, the records in each partition are synchronized (as you move between records in one partition, the other partition follows). If you specify NOLINK, the partitions are no longer synchronized. This might be useful to do a lookup in the table with one partition, and then use a UDF to bring the two partitions back in line.
- `[LOCK <expN2>]`

  ```
  BROWSE FIELDS sales , tax, item, cost LOCK 3 PARTITION
  40
  ```

  When the Browse window is partitioned, you can use the LOCK clause to specify how many field columns will be visible in the left partition. This is useful for Browses used for pick lists, lookups, and similar work where the information in the left partition is a "must see", while the right partition remains open to move freely among the fields.
- `[LEDIT]` and `[REDIT]` One of the more interesting of the Browse's capabilities is the ability to shift from Browse (tabular) mode to Change

(vertical) mode on the fly. This is one of the options in the Browse menu. You can accomplish the same thing in a program using LEDIT or REDIT to change either left or right partition into the Change format. Here's an example of a complete Browse/Change partition setup:

```
BROWSE FIELDS item,cost,sale,tax,qty,vendor PARTITION 30;
LOCK 2 ;
   NOLGRID LPARTITION REDIT
```

Programming Options

Finally, there are several Browse clauses that have meaning largely within programs.

- `[NOMENU]` Normally invoking the Browse window adds the Browse menu option to the system menu. While this is very useful for an interactive session, there are several options in the menu which could cause trouble, such as delete and append. You can suppress the Browse menu with the NOMENU clause. Incidentally, the Browse menu is one of the few you can't modify.
- `[NOREFRESH]` By default, on a local area network, the Browse window will be updated periodically to reflect changes by other users (see Chapter 16 on Networking for details). You can suppress this updating with NOREFRESH. This speeds processing and Browse scrolling, especially for tables opened with the NOUPDATE option.
- `[NOWAIT]` By default a Browse window is open and active only as long as the user remains in that window. With the NOWAIT clause, program execution continues on the first line after the BROWSE definition, while retaining the Browse window. This is an important clause for integrating Browse windows with multiple screen applications.
- `[REST]` Normally, the table pointer is placed at the first-record-of-table position coming into a Browse. However, if you've already positioned the table on a record, then you might want to use REST to force the Browse to keep the pointer in its current position.
- `[SAVE]` With this clause FoxPro keeps the Browse window open as you cycle from one window to another.
- `[TIMEOUT <expN4>]` In situations where users might leave the Browse window open indefinitely, posing security or performance

problems, you can include the TIMEOUT clause with the number of seconds to wait for user input before closing the Browse.

A sigh of relief might be in order. This was the last BROWSE clause. Definitely a mega-command, and also one of the most important. As mentioned before, the Browse is such a rich and versatile environment, that it's worth becoming fully acquainted with its capabilities. It should be a big part of any application builder's user interface options.

As a final example, here's a complete setup for a browse in a controlled environment:

```
DEFINE WINDOW wbEmployee AT 1,0 SIZE 30,80 FONT "Arial",10 ;
  FLOAT GROW ZOOM TITLE "Employees" COLOR SCHEME 10
SELECT emp
BROWSE FIELDS ;
   emp.lastname:30:H="Last Name":P="@!":V=NameChk(),;
   emp.firstname:15:H="First Name":P="@!":V=NameChk():F,;
   id = MakeEmpID(),;
   emp.startdate:H="Start":P="@D",;
   emp.department:40:P="@!":V=DeptLook(),;
   emp.age:P="99":B=18,60,;
   emp.position:30:V=PosPick(:F:E="Please select a position.",;
   emp.operator,;
   emp.sysdate ;
   WINDOW wbEmployee ;
   FOR emp.startdate > {10/01/92} ;
   NODELETE ;
   NOMENU ;
   WHEN SecChk() ;
   VALID DataChk() ;
   TIMEOUT 600
RELEASE WINDOW wbEmployee
```

Menus

Menus are obviously part of the user interface. All applications have menus, if for no other reason than in FoxPro for Winodws you haven't got much choice. As mentioned earlier, you'd have to be truly stubborn not to fall in line with the standard Windows menu scheme, as managed in FoxPro for Windows via the Menu Builder. Anything else would be a lot more work, and wouldn't look like a Windows program.

This may not be very pleasing to some application builders coming from DOS versions of FoxPro or other environments. They may be used to choosing from four or five different menuing schemes. You can still do that in FoxPro for Windows. But as far as the design of the user interface is concerned, the strength of Windows is consistency.

Screen Elements

If windows, Browses, and menus are the "macro" user-interface elements, then fields, control buttons, and the like, shown in Figure 11.4, are the "micro" elements. FoxPro gives you a wide selection of basic elements and from these you can construct many more elements.

This is your "get acquainted" section on the user-interface screen elements. Later, in the Screen Builder, they become the stuff of which much of your application is made. However, the mechanics of the Screen Builder and the READ are complex enough without overloading you with the details of all these screen elements. It's also true that from time to time, you may need to use these elements in a context outside of the Screen Builder. While you don't need to remember every jot and tittle of the syntax, it helps to have a clear picture in your head of what these elements look like, what they're used for, and how (basically) they're constructed.

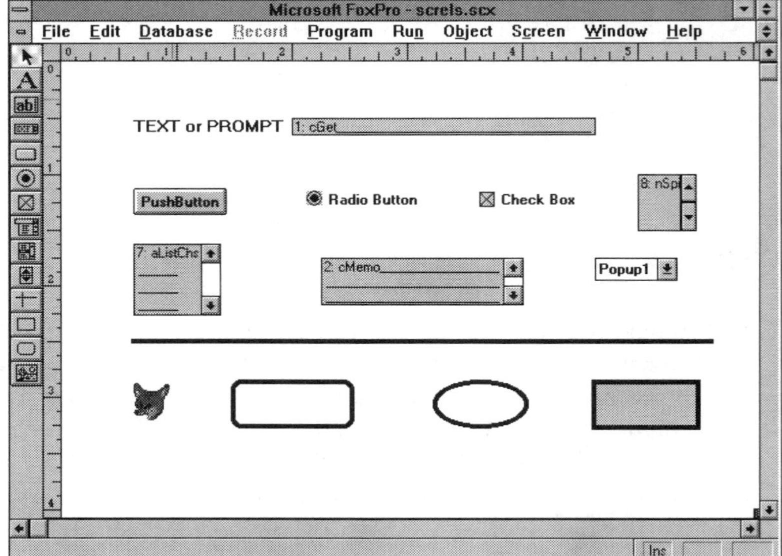

Figure 11.4 Screen elements.

Like most of the user interface elements already covered, these screen elements generally fall into one of three categories: data entry/edit, control structures, and screen decoration. As you build your user interface, you can ask yourself three questions that apply to these elements:

1. What does the data require?
2. What does the user need?
3. What does the program need?

These questions are simplistic, of course. But they belie a complex mix that comprises a user interface. In most cases your screens will have something to do with data—entering, editing, viewing, selecting. The user needs to know where they are and what they can do.Your application also needs guidance from the user as to what to do next.

GETs and SAYs

Hopefully you are already excruciatingly familiar with the use of GETs and SAYs, at least in their more mundane application. Despite all the "fancy" new buttons and other screen elements, these remain the mainstay of the user interface in data entry and editing screens.

As presented in Part 2, the standard GET has many facets to its user interface: ability to access, support during entry, and post entry validation. Managing these facets can lead to substantial user-interface elements in their own right, particularly through the use of the VALID clause. In fact it's not uncommon to use some of the controls, popup lists in particular, in conjunction with the VALID of a standard GET.

One small item of user interface design new with FoxPro is the SET READBORDER ON | OFF command. When set on, this places a "box" (black line) around the entry area of a GET. In some cases this works aesthetically, some cases not. The real reason for it is to indicate to the user that the area usually contains information, although it may be empty at the moment. A similar effect can be achieved by using colors, typically by using a light foreground (text) on a dark background:

```
@ 2,10 GET cLastName PICTURE "@!" COLOR GR+/B,W+/B
```

The role of the @..SAY has been greatly expanded in FoxPro. Besides the method used for displaying text and field prompts on the screen, variations of the SAY now make it possible to display pictures, bitmaps, and other OLE information on the screen. This is covered as a special topic later in this chapter.

Controls

Microsoft calls a number of screen elements *Controls*. What they have in common is a basis in the @..GET command, and that's about it. Some of them are indeed primarily program control elements (push buttons, radio buttons). Others however are definitely for data entry/edit (edit fields), or user selection of data (popup lists, lists, spinners). Most of them can do multiple duty. As a group these are some of the newest and most interesting of the use-interface elements available in FoxPro. You'd do well to experiment with all of them, get to know their characteristics, and then find ways to incorporate them in your application's screens.

Standard Control Clauses

Because all of the controls are derivatives of the @..GET they share many clauses in common. In fact there are only a handful of syntax differences. Rather than repeat the detail of these clauses, for each control, here's a list of the "standard" clauses and their definitions. Unless otherwise noted, you can assume they are handled identically for all controls.

- `@ <row, column> GET <memvar> | <field>` As in all @..GET/SAYs, the row and column coordinates are relative to the screen or window they are in, and to the font and font size. Since many of the controls are in fact small windows in their own right, you need to pay attention to the amount of screen estate (a neologism, similar in meaning to real estate) they require as the font size grows. All of the controls require a variable or field to receive the results of the GET.
- `[FONT <expC3>[, <expN1>]]` For all of the controls, the font and font size apply to the text contained in the control such as for lists and spinner numbers. While the size of the control area will adjust to the size of the font, you may find it necessary to resize (or use the SIZE clause) to get the are to properly fit the font.

- [STYLE <expC4>] The usual cast of character attributes applies (B) bold, (I) italic, (N) normal, (O) outline, (S) shadow, (-) strikeout, and (U) underline.
- [DEFAULT <expr>] Using DEFAULT should become automatic with all GET related commands. Since you already must specify the receiving variable for the GET, the default allows FoxPro to create the variable and load it with a starting value. Using this clause is self documenting, not prone to mistakes, and reliably creates the variable if needed, or do nothing if it already exists. (It does not change the value in an existing variable.)
- [ENABLE | DISABLE] Using these clauses to control which GETs are available to users is one of the more important techniques. Used in the context of the original GET these are the starting position, which may be changed at any time with the SHOW GET or SHOW GETS commands.
- [VALID <expL1> | <expN5>] The VALID plays an extremely important role with most of the controls. Not only is it used to test the validity of data entered or selected, but in many cases it contains the logic that processes the selection. A typical example is the Push Button (@..GET..PICTURE "@*"):

```
@ 10,20 GET cChoice ;
  PICTURE "@*H \<Add;\<Edit;\<Delete;\<Cancel;\<Quit" ;
  DEFAULT "Edit" ;
  VALID ValChoice( )
READ
...
FUNCTION ValChoice
DO CASE
CASE cChoice = "Add"
   DO ADDAREC
CASE cChoice = "Edit"
   DO EDITAREC
CASE cChoice = "Delete"
   IF NOT DELETED()
     DELETE
   ELSE
     RECALL
   ENDIF
CASE cChoice = "Cancel"
  CANCEL
CASE cChoice = "Quit"
  QUIT
```

```
ENDCASE
RETURN
```

This is, for all practical purposes, a menu—a "push-button menu". The CASE structure serves to sort out the user's selection and take the appropriate action.

NOTE

Note that the controls (except Spinners and Edit) do not support the ERROR option of the VALID, which is found in the normal @..GET.

- [MESSAGE <expC5>] This is another of those seemingly small, but often very important elements (from the user's point of view). It displays a message in the Status Bar at the bottom of the screen (provided SET STATUS BAR ON), and is used to give the user information about the GET they are currently in. For most applications, use this standard.
- [WHEN <expL2>] The "gateway" clause is common to all controls, and is used to determine if the options are active for a user.

*Check Boxes "@*C"*

Check Boxes, shown in Figure 11.5, are a screen device for yes or no selections. Each check box is a single data item (unlike most of the other controls, which often present more than one option at a time). A checked box is selected, unchecked is not selected, and the receiving variable is returned with either .t. or .f. (1 or 0, if initialized with a number).

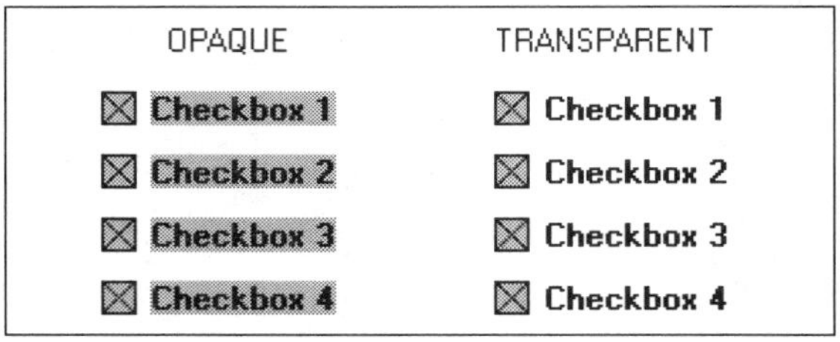

Figure 11.5 *Check boxes.*

OPAQUE	TRANSPARENT
☒ Checkbox 1	☒ Checkbox 1
☒ Checkbox 2	☒ Checkbox 2
☒ Checkbox 3	☒ Checkbox 3
☒ Checkbox 4	☒ Checkbox 4

The syntax is:

```
@ <row, column> GET <memvar> | <field>
FUNCTION <expC1> | PICTURE <expC2>
```

The distinguishing code for a check box is the use of *C either in the FUNCTION or the PICTURE clause. This is also where the text for the Check Box prompt is located:

```
@ 2,10 GET is_ok PICTURE "@*CN Is the user under 15 years old?"
@ 2,10 GET is_ok FUNCTION "*C" PICTURE "Is the user under 15?"
@ 3,10 GET is_adult PICTURE "@*CN \<Adult"
@ 4,10 GET is_child PICTURE "@*CT \<Child"
```

Its clauses are:

- **[DEFAULT <expr>]**
- **[ENABLE | DISABLE]**
- **[VALID <expL1> | <expN5>]**
- **[MESSAGE <expC5>]**
- **[WHEN <expL2>]**
- **[FONT <expC3>[, <expN1>]]**
- **[STYLE <expC4>]** The check box supports two additional font styles: Q for Opaque, and T for Transparent. As you can see in the example above, these can make a significant difference in the appearance of the check box, depending on color selection. The Opaque option makes the Check Boxes and their prompts ride "on top" of the underlying material, whereas the Transparent option lets the underlying material be visible through the check box—often not a desirable effect.
- **[COLOR SCHEME <expN6> | COLOR <color pair list>]** Like most of the controls, the check box coloration is affected only by changing a few of the ten color pairs.

*Invisible Buttons "@*I"*

Invisible buttons "activate" other screen objects. The typical use of an invisible button is to make something, like a box or region of the screen, "active." Invisible buttons are generally created as a sequence of areas, for example covering quadrants of the screen, and are numbered consecutively by FoxPro.

When you select an invisible button area, the text on top of it is highlighted. Selecting a button places the number of that button in the receiving variable, field, or array element.

In FoxPro there are other buttons that perform much like an invisible button, but none cover as much screen territory so easily. The ideal combination is the @..SAY..BITMAP, which puts a picture on the screen, followed by an invisible button sufficiently large to cover the same area, making the picture "selectable." Its syntax is:

```
@ <row, column> GET <memvar> | <field>
FUNCTION <expC1>
| PICTURE <expC2>
```

The distinguishing code for an Invisible Button is the use of *I either in the FUNCTION or the PICTURE clause. There is no "prompt" for this button. Options are listed in Table 11.4.

Table 11.4
FUNCTION and PICTURE options.

Options	Description
N	Do not terminate the READ when box is chosen (Default).
T	Terminate the READ when box is chosen.
H	Invisible buttons are displayed horizontally.
V	Buttons are displayed vertically.
\\	Disabled Invisible Button

For example:

```
* Create a bitmap picture on the screen.
@ 2,10 SAY "F:\bmp\stars.bmp" BITMAP CENTER SIZE 10,30
* Put an Invisible Button underneath
@ 2,10 GET nInv PICTURE "@*IT" SIZE 10,30
READ
[SIZE <expN2>, <expN3>[, <expN4>]]
```

<expN2> Height in rows.

<expN3> Width in columns.

<expN4> Space between buttons, in rows if vertical display and in columns if horizontal.

These are important parameters for Invisible Buttons, which usually must be sized to fit under an existing object like a screen picture, box, etc.

```
[DEFAULT <expr>]
[ENABLE | DISABLE]
[VALID <expL1> | <expN5>]
[MESSAGE <expC5>]
[WHEN <expL2>]
[COLOR SCHEME <expN6> | COLOR <color pair list>]
```

The only active "color" for an Invisible Button (which sounds like a conundrum) is color pair 6. Actually, some care needs to be taken to make sure the Invisible button doesn't clash with the object(s) on top of it.

Push Buttons
"@"*

Push buttons, shown in Figure 11.6, are most often used for "action options" selection. Because of their true button shape, push buttons are usually associated with the user selecting some kind of "action"—something happens after the button has been "pushed". As a result, push buttons are used often as an alternate form of menu, gateways to subsystems, or to move from one screen to another. Of course, like any other button they can also be used to select items of information, although their button shape doesn't have that kind of connotation as much as some of the "list" controls.

Figure 11.6
Push buttons.

The starting syntax is:

```
@ <row, column> GET <memvar> | <field>
```

Depending on the DEFAULT setting or other initialization of the variable (usual), field, or array element, the push button returns with a character string of the prompt selected, or the number of the button order. It's customary to use the character string approach, because it's much easier for the programmer to see what's been chosen. For example:

```
@ 2,10 GET cChoice PICTURE "@*T More;Less"
READ
? cChoice
```

Returns: "More", or "Less", depending on the selection.

The distinguishing code for a push button is the use of * either in the FUNCTION or the PICTURE clause. You may define a series of buttons with one command using a semicolon delimited character string:

```
@ 2,10 GET cOptions PICTURE "@* Yes;No;Maybe;Quit"
@ 2,10 GET cOptions FUNCTION "*" PICTURE "Yes;No;Maybe;Quit"
```

Options are listed in Table 11.5.

Table 11.5
FUNCTION and PICTURE options.

Options	Description	Hot Keys	Description
N	Do not terminate the READ when box is chosen (default).	\\	Disabled button.
T	Terminate the READ when box is chosen.	\<	Highlighted selection - hot key
H	Buttons arranged horizontally.	\?	Escape button.
V	Buttons arranged vertically.	\!	Default button.

NOTE

There are two options here that are easy to overlook, but shouldn't be. Because of the frequent use of push buttons as an alternate form of menu, the \? and \! options are very good additions to the micro-management of the user interface. The

\! option selects one push button as the default—the one selected and highlighted from the beginning. This will usually be the most important option in a push button series. The \? option is even more subtle. It defines one button (and only one per READ) that will be automatically selected if the user presses the Escape key. Normally this terminates the READ and drop out of a screen, but with the \? a button instead is highlighted—typically the Cancel button. This gives the user a second chance to decide if they want to leave the screen or not, and for the programmer to test and do cleanup prior to letting the user leave.

For example:

```
@2,10 GET cMenu PICTURE "@*H KAdd;\!\<Edit;\?\<Cancel;\<Quit"
```

The next piece of syntax is:

```
[SIZE <expN2>, <expN3>[, <expN4>]]
```

<expN2> is the height in rows.

<expN3> is the width in columns.

<expN4> is the space between buttons, in rows if there is vertical display and in columns if there is horizontal display.

By default, the size of a push button is adjusted to the text and font content.

`[DEFAULT <expr>]` specifies that the default value determines the type of return—if its a character, then the return value is a button prompt as character string, if its numeric, then the position number of the button is returned.

*Radio Buttons "@*R"*

Radio buttons, shown in Figure 11.7 on the next page, are used to select "one of" a set of options. This screen device is handy for representing a set of choices, all of which need to be constantly visible. When you select one, any other selected button is deselected—just like punching up radio stations on the old fashioned car radios. In reality, this functions almost identically to push buttons, but of course looks very different.

```
[ENABLE | DISABLE]
[VALID <expL1> | <expN5>]
[MESSAGE <expC5>]
[WHEN <expL2>]
[FONT <expC3>[, <expN1>]]
[STYLE <expC4>]
[COLOR SCHEME <expN6> | COLOR <color pair list>]
```

As mentioned before, Push Button colors can only be set from the Windows Control Center, Color. (A minor exception - color pair 5 will set the **MESSAGE** color. Big deal.)

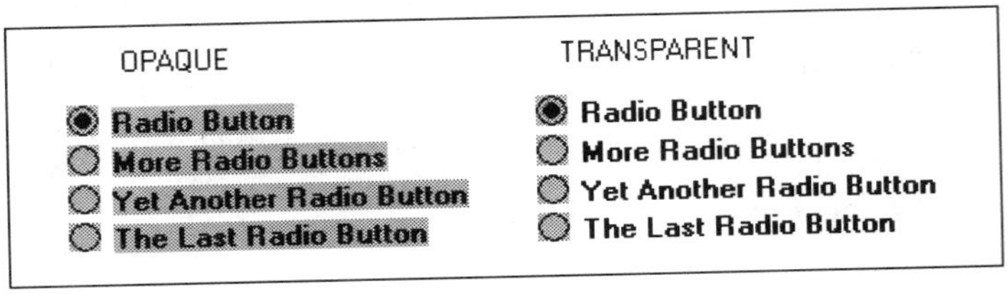

Figure 11.7
Radio buttons.

OPAQUE	TRANSPARENT
Radio Button	Radio Button
More Radio Buttons	More Radio Buttons
Yet Another Radio Button	Yet Another Radio Button
The Last Radio Button	The Last Radio Button

Its syntax follows:

```
@ <row, column> GET <memvar> | <field>
```

Depending on the DEFAULT setting or other initialization of the variable, field, or array element, the radio button will return with a character string of the prompt selected, or the number of the button position.

The distinguishing code for a radio button is the use of *R either in the FUNCTION or the PICTURE clause. You may define a series of buttons with one command using a semicolon delimited character string:

```
@ 2,10 GET cOptions PICTURE "@*R Dog;Cat;Parrot;None"
@ 2,10 GET cOptions FUNCTION "*R" PICTURE "Dog;Cat;Orynx;None"
```

Table 11.6
FUNCTION and PICTURE options.

Options	Description	Hot Keys	Description
N	Do not terminate the READ when box is chosen (Default).	\\	Disabled button.
T	Terminate the READ when box is chosen.	\<	Highlighted selection - hot key.
H	Buttons arranged horizontally.		
V	Buttons arranged vertically.		

`[DEFAULT <expr>]` Specifying the default value determines the type of return - if character, then the return value will be a button prompt as character string. If numeric, then the position number of the button will be returned.

```
[ENABLE | DISABLE]
[VALID <expL1> | <expN5>]
[MESSAGE <expC5>]
[WHEN <expL2>]
[FONT <expC3>[, <expN1>]]
```

`[STYLE <expC4>]` Like the Check Box, Radio Buttons support two additional font styles: **Q** for Opaque, and **T** for Transparent. The Opaque option makes the buttons and their prompts ride "on top" of the underlying material, whereas the Transparent option lets the underlying material be visible through the button prompts.

```
[COLOR SCHEME <expN6> | COLOR <color pair list>]
```

Of all the buttons, this is about the only one in FoxPro for Windows that allows complete color definition under program control.

Table 11.7
Radio button colors.

Color Pair Number	Attribute Affected
5	Message
6	Selected radio prompt
7	Hot keys
9	Enabled radio prompt
10	Disabled radio prompt

Spinners

The spinner, shown in Figure 11.8, offers an alternative method for entering numeric values. It can be used for any situation where the user is supposed to enter a numeric value, which could be numbers, dollars, or a date. It's principal claim to fame is that it allows mouse-only selection of numbers, by "dialing" with the up and down buttons. The spinner also allows direct manual entry, as any normal GET. In general, a spinner works best with relatively small numbers. Larger numbers take too long to dial, and it would be better not to entice people to use the mouse.

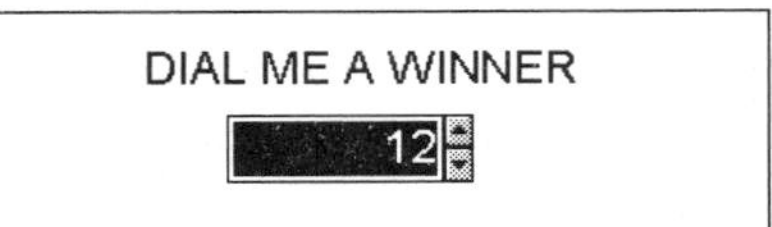

Figure 11.8
A spinner.

The Spinner is a bit unusual for a control in that it has no built-in prompt. You'll need to provide text or a prompt of your own to describe the values to be entered.

```
@ <row, column> GET <memvar> | <field>
SPINNER <expN1>[, <expN2>[, <expN3>]]
```

<expN1> increments (or step) the value for the spinner.

<expN2> is the minimum value allowed by mouse spinning.

<expN3> is the maximum value allowed by mouse spinning.

The Spinner always returns a numeric value. The increment value, by default 1, can be set appropriately for the values being requested. For example, if you're asking for centuries, then <expN1> should be 100. In sort of a weird arrangement, the minimum and maximum mouse values do not apply to keyboard input. You'll need to use the RANGE clause to check on that sort of entry.

```
@ 2,10 SAY "Enter day of the month: " ;
       GET nDay SPINNER 1,1,31 RANGE 1,31
```

The Spinner uses the full complement of @..GET..FUNCTION..PICTURE numeric options as in Table 11.8.

Table 11.8
FUNCTION and PICTURE options.

<expC1>	Purpose
B	Left justifies values in the Spinner Box.
I	Centers value in the Spinner Box.
J	Right justifies value in the Spinner Box.
K	Selects the value for editing (highlight).
L	Displays leading zeros before the value.
Z	Displays the value as blank if 0.
^	Displays the value using scientific notation.
$	Displays the value with $ sign in current currency format.

<expC2>	Purpose
9	Allows entry of only digits and signs.
#	Allows entry of digits, blanks, and signs.
*	Asterisks are displayed to the left of value.
.	Specifies decimal point position.
,	Specifies comma position(s).
$	Displays the $ sign in the current currency format.

```
@ 2,4  SAY "Date: "
@ 2,10 GET nMonth SPINNER 1,1,12 RANGE 1,12 PICTURE "99"
@ 2,12 SAY "/"
@ 2,13 GET nDay   SPINNER 1,1,MonthNum() RANGE 1,MonthNum()
PICTURE "99"
@ 2,15 SAY "/"
@ 2,17 GET nYear  SPINNER 1,1990,9999 RANGE 1990,9999 PICTURE
"9999"

FUNCTION MonthNum
RETURN IIF(INLIST(nMonth,1,3,5,7,8,10,12),31,IIF(2,29,30))
```

```
[SIZE <expN6>, <expN7>]
```

`[RANGE [<expN8>] [, <expN9>]]` The SPINNER clause only knows mice. To validate keyboard entry of numbers, use this clause with <expN8> being the Minimum value, and <expN9> being the Maximum value. HOWEVER, this only works when the user has made a change in the value. Otherwise, no validation will occur. To cover *that*, you'll need to use the VALID clause.

```
[DEFAULT <expr>]
[ENABLE | DISABLE]
[VALID <expL1> | <expN5>]
[MESSAGE <expC5>]
[WHEN <expL2>]
[FONT <expC3>[, <expN1>]]
[STYLE <expC4>]
[COLOR SCHEME <expN6> | COLOR <color pair list>]
```

A Spinner responds only to the color of pair 2 (the normal GET color), and that applies only to the value entry box.

Picklists

A lot of database work is picky business. Data entry, information support, work lists, file openings and so on. Every application needs users to pick something:

1. [Apples, Oranges, Pears, Kumquats, Ugli Fruit], pick one.
2. A database of 4,000 employees, pick one.

3. [An array of 24 elements containing colors], pick ten, put some back.
4. A database of 10,000 car parts, pick any number of them, put some back.

And how do your users pick something? It depends. FoxPro gives you a fairly wide choice of picking devices for the user interface. A picking device is a user-interface element to let users select one or more items from a list. It's such a common element in applications, developers have taken to using a generic name: *picklists*. Along the lines of the four examples above, these come in a variety of forms. FoxPro has some built-in options: @..GET—Popup, @..GET—List, DEFINE POPUP. Many other picklists tend to be constructed by programmers, especially those based on a BROWSE. The first two of these are directly available through the Screen Builder, all the others must be added to screens by the programmer.

The data items to be selected for some of these are based on programmer-coded lists, some are drawn from arrays, and still others get their items from a table. In their various forms, they cover most of the four basics, which can be more generically categorized:

1. Small number of items (two to about one hundred), one selection.
2. Large number of items (over one hundred), one selection.
3. Small number of items, pick or put back one or more.
4. Large number of items, pick or put back one or more.

The quantity of items is significant because of the difference between picklists based on arrays or data tables. Although the theoretical limits on an array in FoxPro are very large (sixty four thousand elements), memory limits are much more real. Arrays require RAM, and although they are relatively efficient use of memory space, a large array takes a chunk. And, as you will discover, large arrays in picklists have performance problems. So, when the number of items starts to get large, your picklist device usually switches to using tables.

NOTE

None of the FoxPro built-in picklists works (directly) with data tables. They all use arrays. Also none of them let the user both select and deselect items. That means out of the four major categories of picklists, FoxPro takes care of one of them. This leaves the door wide open for third-party and programmer developed picklists.

Here's a run-down of the available picklist elements, and a start on some that you can build yourself. The first two are FoxPro controls based on the @..GET. As before, you can refer to the generic description in the previous section for most of the command clauses. To spare you the redundancy, only those that are different are described in detail here.

PopUps "@^"

The popup control, shown in Figure 11.9, is one of the smallest picklist elements. As in the example below, it's dormant state is simply a box, usually with a default item visible. When selected by the mouse, it pops open to reveal the other items for selection, and the goes back to the compact form, after selection has been made.

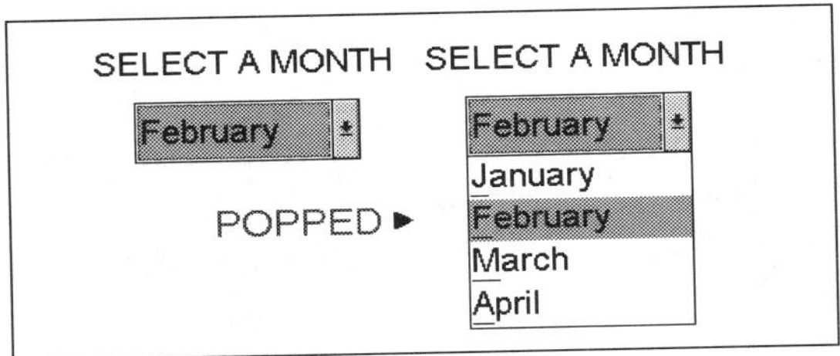

Figure 11.9 *Popup lists.*

This Picklist is relatively "light duty" and has no frills. It can only display items in a single column, is dependent on hand coding or an array for its data, and selects only one item at a time. Because of these limitations, the popup tends to be used for relatively short lists, and as user support in data-entry screens, where the user is given the option of entering data manually or of using the popup.

As with most of the other controls, using a character variable/field means that FoxPro returns the text of the item selected. Defining the variable as numeric causes the return of the item's position number.

The sequence of syntax clauses is:

```
@<row, column> GET <memvar> | <field>
FUNCTION <expC1>
PICTURE <expC2>
```

The distinguishing code for a popup is the use of ^ either in the FUNCTION or the PICTURE clause. Here too, you may define items in the list with one command using a semicolon delimited character string:

```
@ 2,10 GET cRegions PICTURE "@^ East;South;Midwest;West"
@ 2,10 GET cRegions FUNCTION "^" PICTURE
"East;South;Midwest;West"
```

```
[FROM <array>]
```

Where the number of items to select becomes unwieldy for coding within the Popup control itself, or the list of items changes over time, it's common to use an array to load the popup. There are number of ways to do this. Here's an example of three of them:

- **Hardcoded**:

```
DECLARE aRegion[5]
aRegion[1] = "East"
aRegion[2] = "South"
aRegion[3] = "Midwest"
aRegion[4] = "West"
aRegion[5] = "Pacific"
@ 2,10 GET cRegion FROM aRegion FUNCTION "^" DEFAULT "East"
```

- **Lookup**:

```
DECLARE aRegion[1]          && Don't know how many yet.
SELECT codes                && Draws data from a table
SEEK "REGIONS"              && Locate a code type
i=1                         && a loop counter
SCAN WHILE codes.type
= "REGIONS"                 && Load the array loop
 DIMENSION aRegion[i]       && resize as it goes along
 aRegion[i] = codes.descript
 i=i+1
ENDSCAN
@ 2,10 GET cRegion FROM aRegion FUNCTION "^" DEFAULT "East"
```

- **SQL-Select**:

```
SELECT codes.descript ;
FROM codes ;
WHERE codes.type = "REGIONS" ;
INTO ARRAY aRegion
@ 2,10 GET cRegion FROM aRegion FUNCTION "^" DEFAULT "East"
```

From the standpoint of performance, the hardcoded version is the most efficient, but also the most inflexible. Every time a data item would change, a programmer would have to re-code the array and rebuild the application. Use it only with very static data. It would also appear that the SQL-Select version would be the most economical of the methods for getting the item list from a table. It is, and sometimes the fastest too. However, the Lookup method may often be faster for situations like the above, where the lookup values are known exactly.

```
[RANGE <expN2> [,
       <expN3>]]
```

The range clause is somewhat unique in Popups and Lists. <expN2> represents the starting element of the array (if one is used), and <expN3> the number of elements of the array to be displayed. The first parameter is quite important for working with arrays of more than one column (two dimensional arrays). For example in an array with four columns, using 3 for <expN2> will signal that the third column of elements should be used for the popup display of items.

```
[SIZE <expN4>, <expN5>]
[DEFAULT <expr>]
[ENABLE | DISABLE]
[VALID <expL1>|<expN6>]
[MESSAGE <expC6>]
[WHEN <expL2>]
[FONT <expC3> [, <expN1>]]
[STYLE <expC4>]
[COLOR SCHEME <expN7> [, <expN8>]|COLOR <color pair list>]
```

Popups have a unique color attribute table, using two parameters for the COLOR SCHEME clause, as in Table 11.9.

Table 11.9
Popup list colors.

Color pair number	Popup box	Options and border
1	NA	Disabled options
2	NA	Enabled options
3	NA	Border
5	Message	NA
6	Selected popup	Select option
7	NA	Hot keys
9	Enabled popups	NA
10	Disabled popups	NA

Because this color table is so unique, it raises a couple of issues concerning manipulation of colors in the FoxPro environment. First of all, the ten color pairs look unusual because of the "blanks" wherever a pair is skipped (as in the NA above): ",,,,W+/B,W+/B,,,GR+/B,N+/B". Building these color lists for each screen element can be time consuming (especially if you're using the RGB approach). So for convenience, you could build a standard list for all popups and assign it to a color scheme. But for popups you need *two* color schemes, and then there are all of the other screen elements—controls, windows, browses—that can have their own color schemes. Since you only have eight user-definable color schemes, it's obvious not every screen element is going to have its own color scheme waiting in the wings.

This essentially leaves the application developer with two approaches: Keep the color schemes to an absolute minimum, or invent some system to shuttle color sets in and out (which can change all twenty-four color schemes). The choice boils down to the size of an application (and presumably it's need for varied color schemes), the tastes of the developer, and the priority given to color in the design.

Lists "@&"

About the only difference between a list control and a popup control, is that a list doesn't pop up. It remains on the screen as a fixed size display of the items. This generally makes it less economical of space than a popup. It also marks a subtle change in emphasis for the user interface. The popup displays only the currently selected value, and thus highlights it. The list, shown in Figure 11.10, always shows the items, which makes the list itself seem at least as important as the current selection. In this respect a list is like another form of push button, choices are visible, pick one.

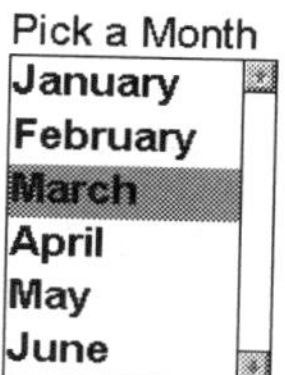

Figure 11.10
A list.

In most other respects, the list has a syntax very similar to the popup.

```
<row, column> GET <mpmnar>|<field>
```

As in all of the GET family, the positioning is relative to the window or screen currently active. The receiving variable can be either a field, an array element, or a memory variable.

```
[FUNCTION <expC1>]
[PICTURE <expC2>]
```

The defining characteristic of the list is an ampersand, &, used in either the FUNCTION or PICTURE clause. The only additional options to these clauses are N for Non-Terminating, and T for terminating the READ on exit.

```
@ 2,10 GET cState FUNCTION "&T"
@ 2,10 GET cState PICTURE "@&N"
```

```
[FROM <array>]
```

Like the popup, a list may be defined by the elements of an array (one or two dimensional). If it is more than one dimension (multiple columns), you'll need to use the RANGE clause to specify which column to use.

```
[RANGE <expN1>,[,<expN2>]
```

The range clause is somewhat unusual in popups and lists.

<expN1> represents the starting element of the array (if one is used).

<expN2> the number of elements of the array to be displayed.

The first parameter is quite important for working with arrays of more than one column (two dimensional arrays). For example in an array with four columns, using 3 for <expN2> signals that the third column of elements should be used for the list's display of items.

```
DIMENSION aState[2,3]
aState[1,1] = "Maine"
aState[1,2] = "Minnesota"
aState[1,3] = "California"
aState[2,1] = "New York"
aState[2,2] = "Iowa"
aState[2,3] = "Oregon"
@ 3,10 GET cState FROM aState RANGE 2,1 DEFAULT "New York"
PICTURE "@&"
```

| **POPUP <popup name>** The popup named here is no relation to the Popup control. This is a throwback to an earlier age of FoxPro (1.0), when

controls were still exclusive to the Macintosh FoxBase + product. Fox created a **POPUP** device (described below) as its most flexible Picklist. It shared with the menu system a capability to use a "defined popup", essentially an array of selection items. You can use any named popup in a List, however, it's a clumsy substitute for using a simple array.

[SIZE <expN4>, <expN5>] Although you can use this clause to size the List's window, in FoxPro for Windows with its variety of fonts, it's much saner to let Fox do the sizing by default.

```
[DEFAULT <expr>]
[ENABLE | DISABLE]
[VALID <expL1> | <expN5>]
[MESSAGE <expC5>]
[WHEN <expL2>]
[FONT <expC3>[, <expN1>]]
[STYLE <expC4>]
[COLOR SCHEME <expN6> | COLOR <color pair list>]
```

Table 11.10
List colors.

Color Pair Number	Attribute Affected
1	Disabled option
2	Enabled Option
3	Border and scroll bar
5	Message
6	Selected list item
9	Enabled list
10	Disabled list

Like other color scheme tables above, this one has "holes" where the color pair is not used. Actually, the List table uses an unusual number of pairs, which makes it one of the more color flexible screen elements.

The Popup Picklist

DEFINE POPUP is one of the most unique and yet unsung commands in FoxPro. It is an integral part of the FoxPro menu system, which, thanks to the Menu Builder, may be one reason people ignore it. But it can be used quite nicely for a sophisticated picklist device, and it can be plugged into the list control (as covered above). A popup picklist is shown in Figure 11.11.

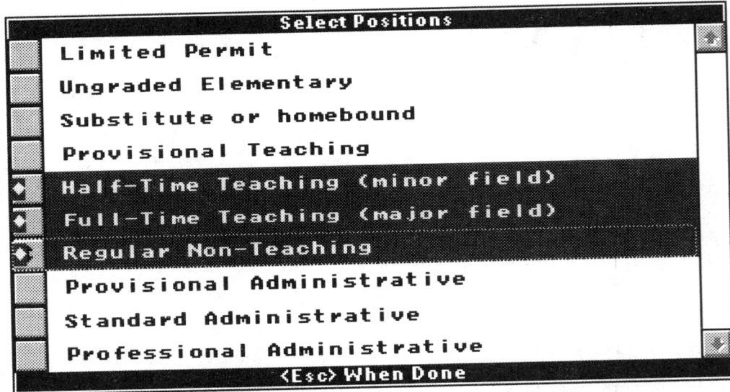

Figure 11.11
A Popup picklist.

It's other claims to fame, which so few seem to know about, are:

1. It allows multiple selections from the list.
2. The user can rearrange items in the list.
3. It can automatically load file names, field names and field content into the list.

Unfortunately, it can't do all three at once. There is an awkwardness to the POPUP command, which more than anything has discouraged its use. It has an elaborate syntax, and seems to have been jammed with options that later became more common in other commands. Moreover, the DEFINE POPUP command really has two lives, one as the way to load menu popup definitions, and the other as a standalone screen object—a picklist. In the following definition of its syntax the menu use of DEFINE POPUP is ignored, and it's use as a picklist emphasized. It's well worth consideration in this role. DEFINE POPUP has a lengthy syntax. To make it clearer, it's broken down into three sections.

Defining the POPUP Window

- `DEFINE POPUP <popup name>` Naming popups is done the same way as naming windows or other FoxPro objects.
- `[FROM <row1, column1>]` specifies the upper-left corner of the popup window. Although there are two sizing clauses (FROM and TO), this is the only one that should normally be used. FoxPro sizes the popup window for you, which in most cases is the preferred route.
- `[TO <row2, column2>]` You can also specify the lower-right corner, if you know exactly how big the popup window should be (not normally the case). However, in some cases you may need to specify the size of the popup this way, because it's internal calculator doesn't always get it right, especially when using the PROMPT FILES clause.
- `[IN [WINDOW] <window name> | IN SCREEN]` Although popups create their own window, you can put them into specific windows. There is not much reason to do this, however.
- `[TITLE <expC4>] [FOOTER <expC1>]` In a departure from Windows convention, you can give a popup window both a title and a footer. This can be useful to name the window for the user at the top, and give instructions on the bottom.
- `[KEY <key label>]` This may be the only command in the FoxPro canon that has a clause to specify a hotkey. Treat it exactly as you would an ON KEY LABEL statement.
- `[MESSAGE <expC3>]` specifies a message to be displayed in the Windows status bar.
- `[SCROLL]` Using this options allows the popup to have scroll bars on the right side, if the list is longer than the available display space. It's almost always included.
- `[RELATIVE]` is used in conjunction with menu options. It allows insertion of bar items.
- `[COLOR SCHEME <expN> | COLOR <color pair list>]` By default, popups use color scheme two for their colors.

Example for defining a POPUP window:

```
DEFINE POPUP pnPOSITION FROM 1,10;
TITLE "SELLECT POSITIONS";
FOOTER "<Esc>When Donw";
KEY F3;
```

```
SCROLL;
MESSAGE "Please select a position for this employee."
```

Defining the Popup Features

The following two clauses provide some unique properties to the popup. Both of them require that one or more item DEFINE BARs are created to be used as an item list:

```
DEFINE BAR 1 OF positions PROMPT "Janitor"
DEFINE BAR 2 OF positions PROMPT "Clerk"
DEFINE BAR 3 OF positions PROMPT "Cook"
...
```

- `[MOVER]` This clause enables the user to move, and rearrange the items in the list. The capability is unique among FoxPro commands, and can be exploited in a number of situations where you would want the user to order a list. For example, the user is given a list of five personality traits, and then asked to order them in importance (from top to bottom).
- `[MULTISELECT]` Using this clause enables the ability to select one or more items from the POPUP list. Selections are made by using the Enter key, after highlighting the item with either the mouse or the Arrow keys. In FoxPro, the user holds down the Shift key while selecting more than one item. The selection process does not conform to standard Windows selection practice. MULTISELECT is normally accompanied by the MARGIN clause so that a "mark" (a bullet) can be displayed for each selection.
- `[MARGIN]` is required only if the list is a MULTISELECT list. It provides an extra column at the left of the list for the marker.

For example:

```
DEFINE POPUP positions FROM 1.0 MULTISELECT MARGIN SCROLL TITLE
"Select Positions"
DEFINE BAR 1 OF positions PROMPT "Janitor"
DEFINE BAR 2 OF positions PROMPT "Clerk"
DEFINE BAR 3 OF positions PROMPT "Cook"
ACTIVATE POPUP positions
```

Defining Popup Content

The popup can have the values of its list automatically loaded in three ways:

1. The contents of a field from every record in a table.

2. The name of all files in a directory that fit a file skeleton.
3. The names of all fields in the current work area table.

A popup list loaded in one of these ways is *not* related to the DEFINE BARs of the menu popup. You can't use MOVER or MULTISELECT clauses, because these require bars.

- `[PROMPT FIELD <expr>` This is the most flexible, and probably most useful of the three options. It loads the value(s) from *every record* in the table for the field(s) specified by <expr>. You may recognize this as the very open ended FoxPro type expression, which can contain anything from the name of a single field, to a concatenated extravaganza with UDFs. Here are some examples:

```
DEFINE POPUP bigpop PROMPT FIELD emp.employee
DEFINE POPUP bigpop PROMPT FIELD "*"+emp.employee+"
"+adr.city
DEFINE POPUP bigpop PROMPT FIELD SelectEmp()
```

WARNING

While there is no limit on the number of items in the popup list, unleashing this option on a table of unknown size can chew up a lot of memory. It might be wise to restrict its use to tables of known (modest) size, or ones that are accompanied by a SET FILTER TO that limits the scope.

- `| PROMPT FILES [LIKE <skel>]` To load a popup with the names of files from a selected directory, use this clause accompanied by a "file skeleton"—a path plus filename with or without DOS wildcard symbols. For example:

```
DEFINE POPUP pfcurfile FROM 2,20 PROMPT FILES;
LIKE F:\EMP\*.DBF
DEFINE POPUP pfcurfile FROM 2,20 PROMPT FILES
```

  As a bonus, the popup window actually turns into a "file browser," which let's you move from directory to directory (and even between drives) until you find the file you're looking for.

- `| PROMPT STRUCTURE]` This option loads the field names of the current work area table.

Note that all popups require ACTIVATE POPUP <popup name>, or a designated hot key (the KEY clause) to make them appear on the screen, which is how they come to be popups.

Using a POPUP

Given the flexibility of the popup, and its relative obscurity, here's a few ways to make a good thing more useful. This is an example of loading, defining, and processing selections from a popup. It includes three small functions that help take some of the complexity out of using the command.

```
*———————————————[ LOAD AN ARRAY
*> In this example, load the popup array with SQL-Select.
USE F:\hr\dbf\ddcode
SELECT descript ;
FROM ddcode ;
WHERE ddcode.type = "LICLEVEL" ;
INTO ARRAY apos

*———————————————[ DEFINE POPUP
DEFINE POPUP pos ;
 FROM 2,20 ;
 TITLE "Select Positions" ;
 FOOTER "<Esc> When Done" ;
 MARGIN RELATIVE SCROLL ;
 MOVER MULTISELECT ;
 COLOR B/W*,B/W*,B/W+*,W+/B,GR+/BG,GR+/RB

*———————————————[ BUILD POPUP BARS
* Feed the popup array you've created to a function that
* turns the array list into a series of DEFINE BARs for
* the DEFINE POPUP. The parameters are the name of the
* POPUP to be defined, and the array being used. Note the
* @ "by reference" argument.

=BuildPop( "POS", @aPos )

*———————————————[ SHOW THE POPUP
ACTIVATE POPUP pos
*———————————————[ PROCESS SELECTION(S)
* This example provides three options for processing the
* results of using a POPUP. Each has a function that handles
```

```
* the somewhat tricky array manipulations required.
*
*> OPTION 1: Return a single item selection.
* The function arguments are: Name of the POPUP, Name of the
array,
* and a 1 to signal the return of a single choice.
*cCh = GetMark( "POS", "APOS", 1 )

*> OPTION 2: Return multiple selections as an augmented array.
* The function arguments are: Name of the POPUP, Name of the
array,
* and a 2 to signal the return of multiple selections. Note:
The
* array being used MUST be single dimension. It will be
returned
* with two dimensions by the function, with the second column
used
* to store .t./.f. for selection.
= GetMark( "POS", "APOS", 2 )
*> OPTION 3: Return a re-arranged list.
* The function arguments are: Name of the POPUP, Name of the
Array.
* The function will return the named array in its re-arranged
form.
*= GetList( "POS", "APOS" )

*--------------[ USE THE SELECTION(S)
* In this example, OPTION 2 was used to produce a changed
* array containing multiple selections.
k=1
FOR i = 1 TO ALEN( aPos,1 )
  IF aPos[i,2]
    @ k,10 SAY aPos[i,1] FONT "ARIAL",9 STYLE "B"
    k=k+1
  ENDIF
ENDFOR

*==========================[ Support Functions
]======================
* Three "little" functions with a ton of macro substitutions,
name
* expressions, and other legerdemain with arrays.

*-----------------------------------
*    FUNCTION: BuildPop()
* DESCRIPTION: CONVERT AN ARRAY LIST INTO THE BARS (ITEMS) OF A
```

```
POPUP
*        SYNTAX: BuildPop( <POPUP name>, @<array name>)
*    PARAMETERS: cPopName = Name of DEFINEd POPUP.
*                aPopItems = The array of items, passed by
reference.
*____________________________________
FUNCTION BuildPop
PARAMETER cPopName, aPopItems
FOR i = 1 TO ALEN(aPopItems)
   DEFINE BAR i OF (cPopName) PROMPT aPopItems[i]
ENDFOR
RETURN .t.
*
*____________________________________
*     FUNCTION: GetMark()
*  DESCRIPTION: RETURN SELECTION(s) MADE WITH A DEFINED POPUP
*       SYNTAX: GetMark( <POPUP name>, @<array name>, <expN>)
*   PARAMETERS: cPopName = Name of DEFINEd POPUP.
*               cPopItems = The name of the array of items.
*               nMarked = 1, single choice; 2, multiple
selection.
*        Notes:
* This function has two types of returns, one for single item
choice,
* and one for multiple item selections. The first is
straightforward
* and the function itself RETURNs the value of the item chosen.
The
* second type is unconventional. It takes the one dimensional
array
* of items (presumably the same one used by BuildPop()), and
converts
* it to a two dimensional array. Then it loads the 2nd column
with
* .t. or .f. depending on whether the item was selected or not.
*____________________________________
FUNCTION GetMark
PARAMETER cPopName, cPopItems, nMarked
PRIVATE nA,aTemp,i,cChoice
cChoice = ""

* More than one selection
IF nMarked > 1
  nA = ALEN(&cPopItems)      && Get length of array
  DIMENSION aTemp[nA]        && Make a temporary holding array
```

```
   FOR i = 1 TO nA && Load it with other array
      aTemp[i] = &cPopItems[i]
   ENDFOR
   DIMENSION &cPopItems[nA,2]        && Re-dimension other array
 to 2
   STORE .F. TO &cPopItems   && Clean it out
   FOR i = 1 TO nA && Re-load from temporary array
      &cPopItems[i,1] = aTemp[i]&& but in first element.
  ENDFOR
 ENDIF

 *> Loop the array for selection marks.
 * NOTE: the IIF is used to keep from running off the array,
 since it
 * could be either one or two dimensional.
 FOR i = 1 TO ALEN( &cPopItems ) / IIF(nMarked=1,1,2)
    IF MRKBAR( cPopName , i) && MRKBAR does the job of noting
      IF nMarked = 1 && if the array element has been
        cChoice = &cPopItems[i,1]&& selected, then depending if
        EXIT && this a one or multi-select
      ELSE && load a selection or fill the
        &cPopItems[i,2] = .t.       && new 2D array.
     ENDIF
   ENDIF
 ENDFOR
 RETURN (cChoice)
 *
 *___________________________________________
 *     FUNCTION: GetList()
 * DESCRIPTION: RETURN AN ARRAY WITH THE RE-ARRANGED LIST OF
 ITEMS.
 *       SYNTAX: GetList( <POPUP name>, <array name>)
 *   PARAMETERS: cPopName = Name of DEFINEd POPUP.
 *               cPopItems = The name of the array to hold the
 items.
 *        Notes:
 * The function presumes that the array to hold the items is the
 same
 * one used to define the bars of the POPUP in BuildPop(). Or at
 least
 * an array of the same length.
 *___________________________________________
 FUNCTION GetList
 PARAMETER cPopName, cPopItems
 FOR i = 1 TO ALEN( &cPopItems )
```

```
  &cPopItems[i] = PRMBAR( cPopName, GETBAR(cPopName,i ))
ENDFOR
RETURN .T.
*
```

Browse Picklists

One of the most venerable of picklists are those created with the BROWSE. There's one obvious reason why Browse picklists are so useful—they're connected to tables, which means access to lists with an almost unlimited number of items and all the manipulation tools of the database engine. Browse picklists are a natural for selecting from a very large number of items, or of course, from a database table of any kind.

Browse picklists have been around for many years, but when Clipper and FoxPro gave the developer control over keyboard values, it became much simpler to put up a Browse window with a list, let the user scroll around, then select an item by using a keystroke that terminated the Browse. This basic Browse picklist is illustrated below.

```
DEFINE WINDOW wbEmp AT 2,0 SIZE 20,79 FLOAT GROW ZOOM ;
  TITLE "Select an Employee" COLOR SCHEME 22
SELECT employee

* Define a key to terminate the Browse, in this case <Enter>
* which triggers a <Ctrl>W (chr(23)).
ON KEY LABEL ENTER KEYBOARD CHR(23)

BROWSE FIELDS ;
  lastname:H="Last Name",;
  firstname:H="First Name",;
  city,;
  state ;
  FOR state = "CA" ;
 WINDOW wbEmp

RELEASE WINDOW wbEmp

* Pick up the selection if one was made
IF LASTKEY( ) <> 27
   cEmpchoice = employee.empid
ENDIF
ON KEY LABEL ENTER  && Reset the enter key
```

Some of the keyboard manipulation used here will be covered a few sections down in this chapter. It's also possible to include "mouse picking," as is illustrated in the following large scale Browse picklist.

A Multi-Feature Browse Picklist

Over the years, Browse picklists have become increasingly sophisticated. Partly because the Browse itself has grown more powerful, and partly because the need for table based selection is so prevalent, the original simple picklist has added features like indexed lookup based on keystroke entry (you type in a name and the picklist searches as you type), mouse control, multiple column searching, and more.

There are even third-party products that provide additional speed and flexibility to the Browse picklist.

Given that a Browse picklist should be part of every developer's user-interface library, this book includes one of the "whopper" variety of the species. It has incremental searching, meaning that it searches for a match with each keystroke. It supports this kind of searching in any column (field) with a simple index. It displays the search value to the user. It supports mouse selection. It's a lot of code. So for reasons of paper conservation, it won't be listed in it's entirety here—the fruits of the library are in the accompanying disk.

It should be pointed out that this is also a "hand-me-down" utility, born in the minds of at least three (known) programmer's, and begs for embellishment in your own fashion. This is a great and necessary tradition of the Xbase language. You learn by looking at other people's code, and if you like the ideas, you expand on them. Hopefully, to pass them onward to the next sharp pair of eyes. There is never, ever, one way to do these utility routines. Thus, good ideas, and not so good ideas, abound. The point is not perfection, but determined reworking. Trying to make the routine simpler, faster, cleaner, more understandable. There's never enough time for this. But many programmers love to do it anyway.

Here's the function's header, which will serve to introduce it. It could have also been created as a procedure.

```
**************************************************************************
* FUNCTION NAME.. BrsMultKey()
* DESCRIPTION.... KEYSTROKE SEARCH IN A BROWSE, MULTIPLE FIELDS
```

```
VERSION
* DATE........... Sun 05-10-1992 03:09:55
* PROGRAMMERS.... Unknown/G.Goley/NK/LJ
* LAST CHANGE.... Wed 06-03-1992 Minor fixes, nk
* Mon 12-30-1991 FoxPro2 Version Single Field
* PARAMETERS..... cMode = ON or OFF, ie. Turn function on/off
*                  cTitle = Title for new BROWSE window, if
any.
*                  cWindow = Name of Current BROWSE window, if
any.
* SYNTAX......... BrsMultKey( <"ON/OFF">, <window title>,
<window name> )
* USAGE.......... = BrsMultKey( "ON", "Select Inspectors",
"WINSP" )
* RETURN......... .t.
* NOTES.......... As the user enters keystrokes, a seek string
is built and a
* seek done for a match. Good for looking up names, products,
etc. in large
* indexed files. This version supports this kind of search on
any indexed
* field where the field name and the index tag name are the
same. The only
* exception is date fields which cannot use a 'partial date'
search. The user
* can make a selection with either an <Enter> or with a double
mouse click.
*
* This version uses line 24 to display the search buffer.
*
* IMPORTANT: The file being searched must be indexed with
*            UPPER(), or else be all upper case naturally.
*
*      NOTE: This version resets the file order (index) with
*            BrsMultKey("OFF") to the original index, but keeps
*           the selected record.
*
* WARNING!....This function disables all ON KEY LABELS! If
program crashes
*              while this function is on, there will be no
keyboard input.
*              All keys are restored after use of function, of
course.
*
* INSTALLATION....
```

```
*
* 1. Be sure the function MouseHit() is available, so that
selection can be
*    made with a double-click.
* 2. Open appropriate file with index on a search key.
* 3. Set the Browse with the following suggested pattern:
*
*    *> Define a browse window
*    DEFINE WINDOW wBrowPop FROM 2,0 TO 23,79 ;
*     DOUBLE COLOR SCHEME 10 ;
*     TITLE "Show Window" ;
*
*    = BrsMultKey( "ON", "", "WBROWPOP" )
*
*    *> Set browse fields with a marker for those that are
indexed for search
*    BROWSE FIELDS ;
*      GSCSVID:H="*ID", ;
*      FIRSTNAME:H="*First Name", ;
*      LASTNAME:H="*Last Name" , ;
*      TEST:H="*Num" ,;
*      SERVUNIT:H="*Unit" ,;
*      DISTRICT ;
*      NOMODIFY NODELETE NOAPPEND IN WINDOW wBrowPop
*
*    = BrsMultKey( "OFF", "" )
*
* CALLED BY...... GUF (only when in a BROWSE)
* CALLS.......... GetaKey(), BldSeek(), MouseHit()
******************************************************************************
FUNCTION BrsMultKey
PARAMETER cMode, cTitle, cWindow
```

Memo Editing

In a very welcome tradition started by dBase III, the Xbase language has supported memo fields for a long time (ten years in the computer business *is* a long time). These variable length fields, which live in their own file (the .FPT), have become the basis of much of the FoxPro extensions into OLE and other graphic management. But they remain the stalwart keeper of unlimited text entry.

There are a couple of decisions that need to be made before implementing memo editing in your applications. The first of these is really a data issue: How much text needs to be entered? There's no strong reason *not* to use memo fields, but as a rule of thumb developers shy away from creating unneeded files. And it is true, memo files are not quite as robust as the main .DBF files, and from time to time become corrupt. A corrupt or missing memo file means your application is unable to use the associated .DBF. This is not a major issue, but you should think about it. If all your users need to do is enter a line or two of text, for example a brief description, then perhaps a memo field is not necessary and an ordinary character field might do.

However, if the users will be entering text of unknown length, then you really have no choice but to use a memo field. From a disk storage point of view, the memo field is relatively economical (at least at first). It requires only 10 bytes in the .DBF and reserves essentially only the space needed in the .FPT. Any questions about the efficacy of memo fields and files, should be answered by recalling that the business end of *all* FoxPro Power Tools is stored in memo files.

The second memo editing issue does concern the user interface. How much of the text should be visible? Naturally, there are many factors: How important is the text? If it's vital information, then you'd make an effort to show it. How much of it is there? If there's a lot of it, you probably can't show it all at once. How often is text entered or edited. Again, if it's used a lot, then you'd probably want it visible. All of these questions are bounded by the limitation of screen space. Memo editing screen objects do tend to be large. They require a reasonable amount of space to display intelligible sentences. Do your screens have the room?

If not, then you need to create memo editing on demand, via menu choice or push buttons. This decision, visible or pop-up memo editing, then determines your choice of the two memo editing commands available to the programmer: @..EDIT or MODIFY MEMO. The former is best suited to a permanent screen display, and the latter for a popup.

Fortunately, unlike many of the other user-interface elements, memo editing is one of the easiest to implement. That's mostly because once you get the editing area activated, FoxPro handles all of the complexity of the text editing. While it's not full-featured word processor capability, it's certainly very good for database editing. And it all happens automatically.

@..EDIT

Very similar in syntax and approach to the @..GET, the @..EDIT, shown in Figure 11.12, can be added directly to a screen by the Screen Builder (MODIFY MEMO is not a default Screen Builder option).

The syntax will look very familiar, and again redundant clause definitions will be elided.

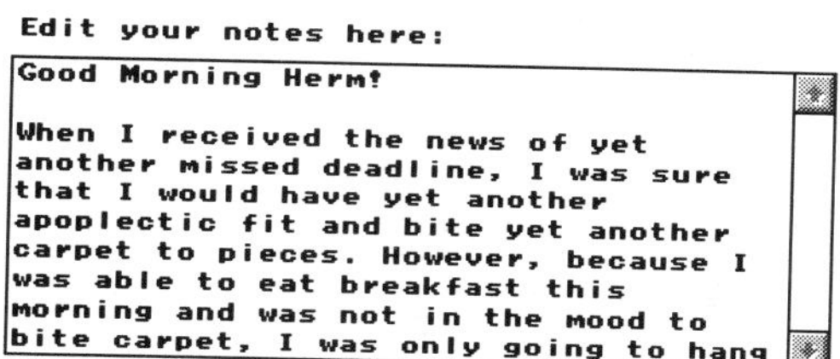

Figure 11.12
The Edit region.

There is a tendency to think of all editing commands as being memo field related. This is not true of @..EDIT. It's just at home with character memory variables, array elements, and plain old text fields, as it is with memo fields. Its syntax is:

```
@ <row, column> EDIT <memvar> | <field>
```

- SIZE <expN1>, <expN2>[, <expN3>] Unlike the sizing in many of the @..GET commands, FoxPro for Windows can't do it for you here. For one thing, it's a required clause. The editing area is a fixed feature of the screen with this command, and you need to determine just how big it should be. In the Screen Builder this is a simple sizing of the edit area marquee with the mouse. Manually, <expN1> determines the length (number of lines), and <expN2> determines the width of the area (number of columns). <expN3> determines the number of characters from a field or variable that will be placed in the editing area. For example:

```
@ 2,10 EDIT m.notes SIZE 5,40
@ 2,10 EDIT cus.notes SIZE 2,70,256
```

- `[FUNCTION <expC1>]` This clause has only two options: J to right justify text, and I to center text. This is also the only @.. without a PICTURE clause.
- `[NOMODIFY]` When included, the text area becomes read-only.
- `[SCROLL]` This places a scroll bar on the right side of the edit area, if the text is too long to be displayed in the editing area.
- `[TAB]` Normally the Tab key is used to move between fields, even from the editing area. If, for some good reason, you need to have tabs for editing, then include this clause and make it clear to users that **Ctrl-Tab** will move them out of the editing area.

```
[FONT <expC2>[, <expN4>]]
[STYLE <expC3>]
[DEFAULT <expr>]
[ENABLE | DISABLE]
[MESSAGE <expC4>]
[VALID <expL1> | <expN5> [ERROR <expC5>]]
[WHEN <expL2>]
[COLOR SCHEME <expN6> | COLOR <color pair list>]
```

Table 11.11
Edit colors.

Color Pair Number	Attribute Affected
2	Enabled text editing region
3	Scroll bar
4	Message
5	Selectedtext editing region
10	Disabled text editing region

You may notice that the “frame” around an edit region is quite anemic. It’s customary to put some other box, or even window, around **@..EDIT** regions to give them a more Windows-like appearance. This is easily done in the Screen Builder.

MODIFY MEMO

This command is for memo fields only, unlike @..EDIT, and lends itself to being summoned by a push button control, used for editing, and then closed. Operationally, you might think of MODIFY MEMO as "son of BROWSE." The two have very similar windowing characteristics, which is to say eccentric. Although MODIFY MEMO creates a window, you have no control over its size, color, or other characteristics—just like the Browse—unless you put it into another defined window. Also like the Browse, a memo window is not directly available from the Screen Builder, and must be grafted into it by the programmer. As you will see later, this presents some problems. Like Browse, managing the memo editing window along with other windows is problematic, which is why @..EDIT is preferred for a persistent editing region.

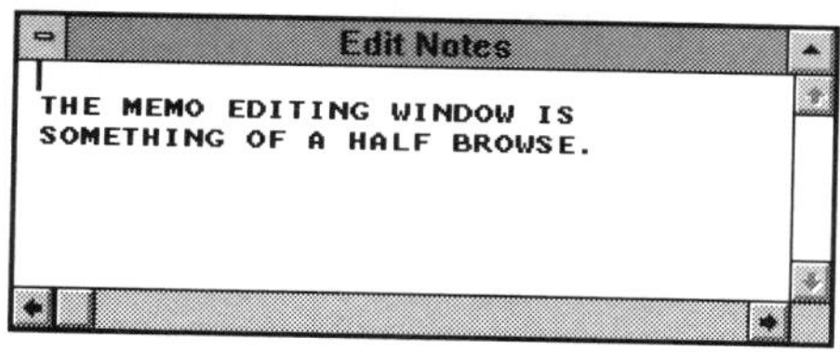

Figure 11.13
A Memo Edit window.

- MODIFY MEMO <memo field1> [, <memo field2> ...] This command permits opening an editing window for as many memo fields as there are in the current work area table. This is sometimes used to set up an interactive session for the user, and let them size, move and otherwise manipulate the memo editing windows.
- [NOEDIT] The memo editing region is opened as read-only.
- [NOWAIT] Available only in programs, this clause allows the memo editing window to be opened, and then execution of the program continues. This behaves exactly like it does for the BROWSE command, and would be used in the same way—to open one or more editing windows before calling a main screen.
- [RANGE <expN1>, <expN2>] This is a strange detail of a feature, which allows you to specify a range of characters (<expN1> = starting character, <expN2>=ending character) to be highlighted (selected) when the editing window is displayed.

- `[[WINDOW <window name1>] [IN [WINDOW] <window name2> | IN SCREEN]]` You can specify a window for each open memo editing region, or place the region in the main FoxPro screen area. As usual, IN WINDOW means that the editing region does not inherit the characteristics of the host window.
- `[SAME]` This clause prevents the editing window from becoming activated.
- `[SAVE]` Using this clause preserves an image of the edit region after the region has been exited and closed.
- `CLOSE MEMO <memo field>[,<memo field2>...] | ALL` This command can be used to close one or more memo editing windows from within a program.

Here's a sample:

```
*Select the table with the memo field(s)
SELECT cus
*Somewhere on the screen, a button to invoke the editing:
@ 10,20 GET cMemoEdit PICTURE "@* \<Notes" VALID EditNote()
...
FUNCTION EditNote
DEFINE WINDOW weNotes AT 2,1 SIZE 10,78;
  FLOAT GROW ZOOM TITLE "Enter your notes here" COLOR SCHEME 10
MODIFY MEMO cus.notes WINDOW weNotes
RETURN .t.
*
```

Pictures

Probably more than any other feature of the user interface, pictures are associated with what separates FoxPro for Windows from its DOS parent. Certainly the ability to add picture material to the screens of your application opens a new dimension in color and design. This feature is a derivative of the basic @..SAY command, logically, because pictures can only be displayed and are not modifiable within FoxPro.

One of the nice surprises of FoxPro is how easy it is to display pictures (images) and bitmaps. The main route is through the Screen Builder, which has its own dialog box for setting up a picture. The appropriate code is then generated by the Screen Builder. The code looks like this:

```
@ 2,10 SAY "c:\bmp\waves.bmp" BITMAP ISOMETRIC SIZE 10,30
```

It's not very complicated, even when done manually. With BITMAP, the effect is very much like that of the window fill capacity (covered in the section on windows), except that this has no frame or other window characteristics. You're simply laying down an image on a specific part of the screen or in a window. With the <general field> option, you're displaying an image created by some other program and placed into a general field, an OLE operation. This is somewhat different than handling bitmaps, and more flexible. The bitmap is handled as a pattern to be evenly spread across the designated area. The image from a general field can be anything, including photos, and graphics, and is independently sized within the area specified.

Bitmaps and images for the general field must be created externally. Most any kind of Windows program that can create graphics might act as a source. All that's required is the ability to produce a .BMP file or another type of file that is registered as an OLE image. Bitmaps are displayed directly from the files. General field images must first be placed into the general field, either by using APPEND GENERAL from a file, or by using Edit, Paste, Edit, Paste Special, Edit, Insert Object from the Edit Menu. (More on this in Chapter 15.)

The syntax of the @..SAY-Picture is quite simple:

```
@ <row, column> SAY
```

- `<file> BITMAP` If you're using a bitmap for an area pattern, you need to specify the actual path and filename, including the .bmp.
- `| <general field>` The name of the general field does not have to be in the current work area.
- `[SIZE <expN1>, <expN2>]` Although usually done by the Screen Builder, you can manually set the size of the picture, with <expN1> being the rows and <expN2> being the column width.
- `[STYLE <expC1>]` The only style options which are relevant are O (opaque) and T (transparent), and these apply only to bitmaps. In opaque mode, the bitmap covers and hides anything below it. In the transparent mode, any white space in the bitmap is transparent and material below the bitmap is visible.
- `[CENTER]` As you would expect, this clause centers images in the area specified.
- `[ISOMETRIC]` This clause causes FoxPro to fill the specified area with the bitmap or general field image by proportionately changing their size.
- `| STRETCH]` This clause causes the image to be scaled to fit an area, but is not scaled proportionately.

All images on the screen are subject to the current font and font size of the area. This can sometimes have strange effects on the shaping of screen pictures. You also need to pay close attention to the resolution quality of the images being displayed. Some may not take too kindly to enlargement.

Picture Buttons and Tool Bars

The urge to build Picture Buttons and Tool Bars for your applications will be irresistible, once you discover how easy it is. There are three controls that support picture images:

- Push buttons
- Radio buttons
- Check boxes

In each case, you specify a file with either an .ICO (icon) or .BMP (bitmap) extension, and FoxPro creates a button on the screen with the image from the file. The button will not look like a radio button, check box, or push button per se. They'll all look like Figure 11.14 (more or less):

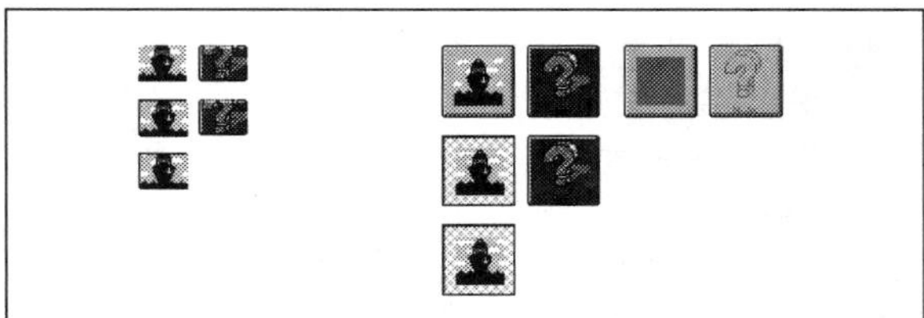

Figure 11.14
Picture buttons.

While all picture buttons don't look alike, they operate in the same way as their basic type: push buttons and radio buttons return a number for the button selected. Radio buttons always have one (and only one) button selected, and the rest unselected. The check boxes return either .t. or .f., depending on whether they've been selected or not.

You'll notice that the size of the button plays a role. Images in an .ICO file are limited to 32-by-32 pixels. If you enlarge a button beyond that size, FoxPro automatically increases the size of the button frame but the image remains the same size. All picture buttons have three visual "states," up (selected), down (unselected), and disabled. Depending on the image used, the size of the button, and the background colors, these states are not always easy to distinguish (leading to a fourth state called confusion). You'll need to exercise considerable care in the choice of .BMP or .ICO image, if you want maximum "button behavior."

Traditionally the images in an .ICO file are *icons*, highly symbolic or suggestive images and are extremely suitable for picture buttons. Bitmap images, on the other hand, were largely created as "fill" or "wallpaper" designs, meant to be spread evenly over a surface of any size. However, the traditions are not always the way it is done. You'll find bitmap images that have the same design characteristics as icons. The result will almost inevitably be a large and growing collection of both .BMP and .ICO files (plus other files that house more of both).

If you really get into this aspect of user-interface design (a dignified description for graphical playtime), it's highly recommended you invest in some commercial graphics software. There are a number of shareware and inexpensive icon and .BMP editors available. Images are also available by the thousands on almost every bulletin board. Make yourself a special subdirectory to hold your image library, and get organized.

The syntax for adding pictures to the button controls is nearly identical: You add a B to the PICTURE or FUNCTION clause, followed by the path and name(s) of the .BMP or .ICO files to be used.

```
*> PUSH BUTTON PICTURE
@ 2,35 GET nPB ;
  PICTURE "@*BH \bmp\ship.ico;\bmp\help.bmp" ;
  SIZE 4,6,1 DEFAULT 1

 *> RADIO BUTTON PICTURE
@ 7,35 GET nRB ;
  PICTURE "@*RBH \bmp\ship.ico;\bmp\help.bmp";
  SIZE 4,6,1 DEFAULT 1

*> CHECK BOX PICTURE
@ 12,35 GET nCB ;
  PICTURE "@*CBH \bmp\ship.ico" ;
  SIZE 4,6,1 DEFAULT 1
```

Caveats

Since picture buttons are relatively new to the Xbase world, and likely will be greeted with largely unrestrained enthusiasm, a few cautionary words are also in order:

When you specify an .ICO or .BMP file, FoxPro has to make a trip to disk to fetch the image, format it, and then put it on the screen. It's a quick operation, if you have high speed hardware, but it still takes time. Be aware that adding many picture buttons to a screen is going to have an appreciable effect on the speed the screen is painted. On some slower computers, the redraw times may become excruciatingly slow.

Most of the time you'll be creating picture buttons and tool bars with the Screen Builder, which makes the sizing very simple. However, there is one aspect of the Screen Builder's handling of picture buttons, which you need to consider a potential problem.

The Screen Builder requires a complete and real path to bitmap and icon files. You can't create a picture button unless the file actually exists, and at the same time you are hard coding the location into your application. About 90 percent of the time, you can get away with this, if your files are somewhere on the FoxPro path. But when applications are distributed, the paths to files may not always be where (or what) you expect. If your .BMP and .ICO files stray, suddenly your windows and buttons are going to stop working—along with your application.

In part, this is a proliferation of files problem. It's not hard to imagine an application using a hundred or more icon and bitmap files. The more files you have, the greater the chances for one or more of them to become damaged, lost, or misplaced. This is a numbers game. You either play it, or you don't.

The other part of the problem is directory management. Your application needs to have a reliable source directory for bitmap and icon files. If you've used the Screen Builder, and hard coded dozens of file locations (worst case, mostly not in the same place), every time you change the configuration of your directories, the application may choke. Solid directory discipline might avoid this problem. But when the application gets out of your own hands, you can't control this.

An unhappy and partial solution to this problem is to use *indirect file reference*. That is, put the path to all bitmap and icon files into a variable, and use that variable with a name expression or macro substitution in the picture button controls and other screen elements. For example:

```
cBmpPath = "f:\bmp\"                     && Path to bitmaps
DEFINE WINDOW wdTest AT 1,1 SIZE 15,39 TITLE "WALLPAPER
WINDOW";
  FILL FILE (cBmpPath)+"waves.bmp" PANEL ;
  FONT "Arial",20 STYLE "B" FLOAT GROW
ACTIVATE WINDOW wdTest
```

This is a very unhappy approach, because the Screen Builder won't allow indirect reference. You would need to edit the output of the Screen Builder, and this is definitely not recommended. Which means, there is no perfect solution to a potential problem. For the most part you will hard code your file locations, and cross your fingers.

Masks

It is fortunate that you'll rarely, if ever, need to mess with a mask. This is a painstaking procedure. It requires special graphics software, patience, and a lot of mouse work. It's sometimes needed because the *white space* of your graphics images (.BMP or .ICO) are treated as being *transparent*, that is, color and text underneath a white space will show through—usually ruining the image. As long as you are displaying your picture buttons on a white background, or they don't contain any white space, no problem.

If you do run into a problem, and you can't solve it by removing white space or a colored background, then you must resort to creating a *mask*. In FoxPro this means using a graphics manipulation program (an icon editor or similar) to take the original picture button image, and produce a monochrome (black and white) copy of it. Then modify the copy by making completely black any area where white space bleed is a problem, and save the file with a .MSK extension to the same subdirectory of the original .BMP file.

Decorative Elements

There are things you can do in the FoxPro for Windows environment that can add a great deal of polish to your screens. They can also take a great deal of time. And there is never enough time. This is a dynamic pressure you will face often, if you build many applications.

The most important dimension for the look of FoxPro applications is a third dimension. The illusion of depth and three dimensionality is available in a GUI, because you have control over individual screen pixels and a much broader color palette. You can use subtle color shades, and place them with maximum accuracy on the screen to create the bevels, shadows, and edges which give objects that 3-D look, as in Figure 11.15.

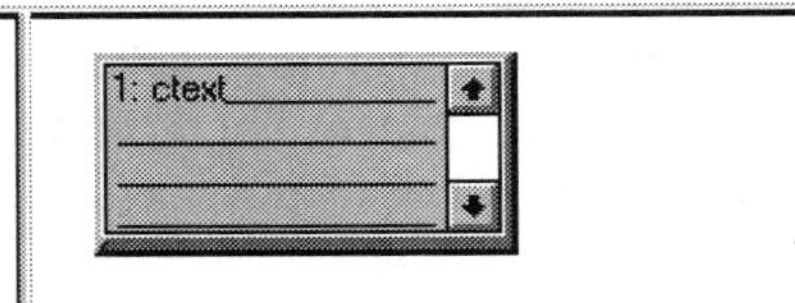

Figure 11.15
3-D modeling.

If you want to know how to create these illusions, simply study the lines and edges on the screen in FoxPro. Most of the effects are the combination of three lines, with a variation in color from dark to light. You can vary the pen width from 1 to 4 points, and the pen fill color through a variety of colors (although the FoxPro Screen Builder color palette is unfortunately limited). Corner bevels are the most difficult, because again the Screen Builder doesn't give you pixel-by-pixel control. But you can "fake it" by butting contrasting lines together at the corners.

All of this hair-line pixel splitting wouldn't be worth the effort, if it weren't for the growing use of the 3-D look in commercial products. It's rapidly approaching the point that if you want your application to look like a Windows application, then you need to incorporate a truly 3-D look. Fortunately, FoxPro helps by providing a degree of "built-in" 3D, such as the push buttons. But there are plenty of areas - divider lines, edit regions (as in the illustration above), where you'll be on your own.

It seems almost inevitable that one day, maybe even fairly soon, the tools you have to create the look of your applications will be as sophisticated as those currently available to graphics artists. It's almost frightening to think of how far that will have come from the eight color, fixed font, 24-by-80 screens of DOS. You can bet it will put a greater premium on artistic talent. Whether that has anything to do with good data management, or even user friendly programming, is another issue.

User Messaging

This is one of the minor user-interface subjects that isn't minor. Many people, including some developers, are oblivious to the number of user messages in commercial software. It can be said, almost unequivocally, that a good program keeps up a constant chatter with the user. Chatter doesn't mean verbally (quite yet, maybe in a year or two). It does mean a host of signs, signals, dialog boxes, and other devices for informing the user of what the program is up to, and what options the user has.

This is an area where treatises on the user interface abound. But to keep things compact, you can think of user messages falling into four basic categories:

- **Status.** Most status information is along the lines of "You are here," and "This is what's happening now." Keeping the user posted about the status of operations is standard practice. The status bar is, of course, the perfect example. Among other things, it tells the user the status of any open table.
- **Procedural.** These are more likely to be popup signs and dialog boxes that inform the user about what to do next, and the options available. In some cases, like the FoxPro graph wizard, it can be a whole series of dialog windows that guide the user through a complex process.
- **Cautionary.** Warnings, alerts, and other cautionary messages are almost always popups, often accompanied with user selectable options.
- **Error.** There are several kinds of errors: software problems (including bugs), procedural errors (user made a wrong choice), invalid entry errors, hardware errors (disk full etc.). In most cases your program must provide responses to errors as well as the messages themselves.

One of the reasons for categorizing user messages is to decide how you want your application to present them. You have at your disposal a number of specific message elements:

- Dialog boxes
- Wait windows
- Other popup windows

- Status bar
- Message line
- Screen text

You match one of these elements with the type of message to be presented, something along the lines suggested below.

Message element: Dialog box **Description:** The all purpose message and response interface. These come in an almost unlimited number of forms, because they are often tied to specific content. There are a few built-in dialog boxes, and most are programmer constructed. **Use:** As the name implies, a dialog with the user. There is both message information, and response input. This may be as simple as a Yes or No answer, to a number of GETs in a sequence of entries. **Types:** Procedural (often), sometimes cautionary and error.

Message element: Wait window **Description:** This is a standard FoxPro element, a popup message in a window in the upper right of the screen. Although limited to one line, it can handle several kinds of messages. **Use:** Generally used for quick, no response, messages, or process status reporting. The big advantage is the convenience of a native command. **Types:** Status (often), sometimes cautionary or error.

Message element: Popup window **Description:** A user-defined window (often in a UDF), of almost unlimited form and content. Does not take user response. **Use:** Like the Wait window, this is used for quick popup messaging, but without the one line and other restrictions. **Types:** Status, cautionary, error.

Message element: Status bar **Description:** A "static," built-in information source at the bottom of the screen. It is either on or off. (SET STATUS BAR) **Use:** Not needed sometimes, but in most cases where tables are open, or the user is manipulating data, should be left on. **Types:** Status only.

Message element: Message line **Description:** Almost all screen input elements (GETs of all kinds) support a user message to define what should be entered. The line is displayed in the bottom row of the status bar. **Use:** If you use the MESSAGE clause in a GET, you'll be doing lots of them. But users find them helpful, at least in the beginning. **Types:** Procedural

Message element: Screen text **Description:** Messages can be simply displayed on the screen. Sometimes popup boxing of areas, color changes, and other highlighting can be very important messaging. **Use:** Modifying or augmenting screen text and highlights to guide the user or reflect changes. **Types:** Procedural, Status.

It's generally agreed that different kinds of messages should look different, but that each class of message should be consistent within itself. This is chapter and verse of the *Microsoft Windows Style Book*. The conservative and probably correct approach is to stay within the interface guidelines promulgated by Microsoft. However, FoxPro does not give you much access to the internal Windows mechanisms (the Open File dialog box is an exception). This leaves you to create your own messaging system.

Actually, FoxPro itself is a mixture of standard Windows message elements—the dialog boxes, file browsers, status bar, and error messages—and "old" standard FoxPro messages. If you build your own set of message elements, it seems reasonable to use the tools provided by Fox/Windows first, and then invent those that are missing or needed specifically by your application(s).

Waits and Other Messages

In both procedural and status messages, there is a heavy use of "spot" messaging—quick popups that give the user a piece of information and then continue the program. At one time, the Xbase language gave the programmer no opportunity for such messages. The extent of it was WAIT, which paused the program with a prompt: *Press any key to continue.* In FoxPro for Windows, the WAIT is more useful:

```
WAIT [<expC>] [TO <memvar>] [WINDOW [NOWAIT]] [CLEAR] [TIMEOUT
<expN>]
```

WAIT used without any other clauses is still the ancient Xbase command. It pauses the program and says *Press any key to continue.* on the screen or currently active window. Using WAIT WINDOW puts the message into the standard FoxPro message window. Here are the rest of the syntax clauses:

- `[<expC>]` Any message that will fit in one line on the screen. As an expression, this can be something in quotes "Your Message Here," a variable, or a function that evaluates to a message, such as:

  ```
  WAIT "Press any key to continue."
  ```

- `[TO <memvar>]` If the user presses a key to exit the WAIT, including this clause with a variable, will save the keystroke to the variable. This can be used to monitor a response to questions in the wait message, such as:

  ```
  WAIT "Press Y if you are happy." TO nHappyDay
  ```

- [WINDOW] Including this clause places the message inside the standard FoxPro message window. It is automatically sized for the message (one line only), and clears itself as soon as the user presses a key.
- [NOWAIT] If you don't want the program to pause while the message is being displayed, use this clause.

```
WAIT "And that's the way it is." WINDOW NOWAIT
```

- [CLEAR] While a program is executing, you can clear a wait message with WAIT CLEAR.
- [TIMEOUT <expN>] Wait windows are often put on the screen to notify the user that some process (printing, updating) has been completed. There are times when you'd like the program to continue after a reasonable time, whether the user presses a key or not. TIMEOUT serves this purpose. It can be set to any number <expN> of seconds.

```
WAIT "The Printing Has Completed" WINDOW TIMEOUT 200
```

Although the WAIT can capture a keystroke, for example "Y" or "N", it's not a mouseable option. If you're following the rule that all user interaction must be available from both the keyboard and the mouse, you need another device for the typical yes or no dialog box. Here's an example of a UDF to do this:

```
**********************************************************************
* FUNCTION NAME.. YesNo()
* DESCRIPTION.... BASIC YES/NO USER DIALOG
* DATE........... FoxPro 2.0 version Wed 08-14-1991
* PROGRAMMERS.... NK
* LAST CHANGE.... Wed 08-14-1991
* PARAMETERS..... cYNq = Yes/No Question.
*                 nYNline = Line for Window.
*                 cYNdef = Default Y/N position.
*                 cYNcolor = Say/Get color pairs for Yes/No.
* SYNTAX......... YesNo( <question>,<line>,<default Y/N>,<Y/N
color> )
* USAGE.......... IF YesNo( "Continue?", 4, "Y", "GR+/B,GR+/R"
)
* RETURN......... .t./.f.
* NOTES.......... A simple yes/no dialog box and mouseable
reply.
* CALLED BY...... GUF
* CALLS.......... None
```

```
***********************************************************************
FUNCTION YesNo
PARAMETER cYNq, nYNline, cYNdef, cYNcolor
*>Trap options not specified in the parameters.
IF TYPE("nYNline") = "U"
  nYNline = 2        && set display line to 2
ENDIF
IF TYPE("cYNdef") = "U"
  cYNdef = "Y"       && set default answer to Yes.
ENDIF
IF TYPE("cYNcolor") = "U"
  cYNcolor = "W+/RB,GR+/R"  && set default color.
ENDIF

*> Centering the window
nYNcol= 39-(.5*(LEN(cYNq)))
nP2col= nYNcol+LEN(cYNq)+10

DEFINE WINDOW YNwin FROM nYNline-1,nYNcol-4 TO nYNline+1,nP2col
;
 DOUBLE FLOAT NOZOOM NOGROW COLOR SCHEME 10
ACTIVATE WINDOW YNwin

@ 0,2 SAY cYNq
nMessRow = SET("MESSAGE")
cMessLoc = SET("MESSAGE",1)
SET MESSAGE TO

cColor = SET("COLOR")              && save current color
SET COLOR TO "N+/W,GR+*/R"
* Use a non READ method (to save on READS).
* This is the old "Light Bar" menu system.
@ 0,2+LEN(cYNq)+2 PROMPT "YES"
@ 0,2+LEN(cYNq)+6 PROMPT "NO"
nYN = IIF( NOT EMPTY( cYNdef ), IIF( cYNdef="N", 2, 1), 1)
MENU TO nYN

*> Clean Out
SET COLOR TO &cColor
SET MESSAGE TO &nMessRow , &cMessLoc
RELEASE WINDOW YNwin

RETURN ( IIF( nYN = 1, .t., .f. ) )
*
```

This yes or no function is really a dialog box, of a very simple kind.

Dialog Boxes

If ever the were a "catch all" user-interface element, it would be dialog boxes. Essentially, these are windows that pop up on the screen, contain some informational text, and provide space for the user to make entries or selections. Some dialog boxes are largely informational, and may ask the user only for a continue or cancel. Others may be part of a series of steps in a procedure, and might require data entry or other specific information from the user. There are no set rules. Even in Windows itself, there is only a shred of uniformity—the dialog box is about the only thing that's standard. This means dialog boxes are fair game to be customized for your application.

A certain amount of standardization is usually welcomed by the user. Being able to identify what a dialog box is about, and what the user is expected to do, is part of giving uniform visual cues. For example, if it's customary to provide dialog box options like "more, cancel", then they should always be "more, cancel" and not "continue, quit" in one place and "done, more" in another. To accomplish this takes either a little foresight and planning in design, or a considerable amount of time later in the development cycle to proof all dialog boxes for consistency.

Another issue often raised about dialog boxes is whether they should be modal or not. The majority of dialog boxes are intended to be displayed only temporarily, and are frequently only steps in a procedure or a momentary request for information from the user. As a rule, there is little or no reason for the user to do anything else but view the dialog box and respond. Hence dialog boxes tend to be modal. They don't allow the user to move to another window or make menu choices.

However in some circumstances, you may find that a number of dialog boxes open on the screen may be a useful user interface technique. Doing this becomes the responsibility of the programmer to manage the open windows, the user input, and the sequence of events so that the program doesn't trip over itself.

Keyboard Elements

Even mice have "keys." They're called buttons, of course, but the purpose is the same. Even in this day and age of the computer mouse, never forget the keyboard. Especially with database work, which like word processing has data entry that is and will remain a keyboard enterprise. It is an article of principle in the Microsoft approach to Windows, that (unlike the Macintosh) *all* capabilities of a program are available through both keyboard and mouse.

In the world of event-driven programming, keystrokes and mouse clicks take on special significance. They are one of the prime events. But even in the workaday world of simple data-entry screens, the ability to monitor and respond to specific keystrokes can be very important. Managing keyboard input (including mouse clicks) takes on two forms:

1. Whatkey(s) did the user just press?
2. Should anything be done?

FoxPro gives you a varied and extremely complete set of tools to deal with these two questions.

Keystroke Functions

These functions give you a way to monitor the user's keyboard action. Actually, what they do is have a look at the keyboard buffer to see what's in it. Operating systems and commercial software packages maintain this buffer, a storage space in memory to hold the key codes sent from the keyboard for processing by the CPU. This allows the accumulation of keystrokes as words or command, before being executed. It also makes it possible to type faster than the computer can process the input. That's why in FoxPro this buffer is referred to as the *typeahead buffer*.

The size of the typeahead buffer can be set with the SET TYPEAHEAD TO <expN> command. If you set <expN> to 0, then all keyboard monitoring functions are disabled. Normally, the buffer is set to twenty characters, but for an application being used by very fast typists you might want to increase the size to forty or sixty characters (128 is maximum).

All keyboard functions are useful at one time or another, however INKEY( ) and LASTKEY( ) are used in the largest number of situations. To some extent many of these functions overlap in capabilities, which can be confusing. There is also the matter of the "key codes" returned by these functions (the values given to various keys and key combinations). They are not all the same codes for the same key.

INKEY

The syntax is:

```
INKEY( [<expN>] [, <expC>] )
```

- `[<expN>]` The number of seconds to pause the program execution. A value of 0 pauses the program indefinitely, until a key is pressed.
- `[, <expC>]` There are four codes which can be used here (mix and match):
  - **H** hides the cursor.
  - **S** shows the cursor.
  - **M** checks for both mouse click or key press.
  - **E** executes a keyboard macro expansion.

```
= INKEY( 1000, "HM")
= INKEY(0)
```

Returns: 121, the value of the first key (or mouse click) in the typeahead buffer.

There about 560 possible keystrokes and keystroke combinations that return a unique value. (A complete listing is in the *Language Reference*, under INKEY().)

This is the most common program pauser. Place this function anywhere in a program, and you can stop program execution for a controlled number of seconds, or until somebody presses a key. As a second benefit, the key value is returned by INKEY( ), which you can use to determine the user's action.

LASTKEY( )

```
=LASTKEY()
```

Returns: 124, the value of the last key pressed, that is the last key in the buffer.

LASTKEY( ) and INKEY( ) return exactly the same key codes. The difference between the two functions is that INKEY( ) pauses the program, then terminates on any keypress and returns the first key in the buffer. LASTKEY( ) looks at the buffer (any time) and returns the last key in it. That makes LASTKEY( ) a better keyboard monitor, and it's used in a great many situations where knowing the last keystroke is important.

For example, during data entry, it's often important to know if the user pressed one of the "exit" keys—Esc, Ctrl-W, Ctrl-Q. You can put LASTKEY() in the VALID of a field or the READ to do this.

```
cName = SPACE(15)
@ 2,10 GET cName PICTURE "@!" VALID CheckName( )
READ
...
FUNCTION Checkname
IF LASTKEY() = 27           && Esc key pressed.
  *user wants out, clear the variable.
  cName = SPACE(15)
ENDIF
RETURN .t.
*
```

READKEY

The syntax is:

```
READKEY( <expN> )
```

<expN> is any value, 1 will do, to have the function return a number indicating how the previous READ was terminated.

As the name sort of implies, it was designed to see what key the user pressed to exit an editing area. In this capacity, it returns two different key codes, one for exiting without having changed the data, and one for having changed data. The unchanged values (no update) are between 0 and 36, the changed values (updated) are from 256 to 292. Using these codes, a routine could use the READKEY( ) value to determine if the user had changed the value in the field or variable being edited. For example:

```
cLastName = cus.lastname
@ 2,10 GET cLastname PICTURE "@!"
READ
IF READKEY() > 255
  IF NOT YesNo("Do you want to keep your changes?",6,"Y")
     cLastName = cus.lastname
  ENDIF
ENDIF
```

CHRSAW

The syntax is:

```
CHRSAW( <expN> )
```

<expN> is the number of seconds to pause while waiting to see if there has been any keyboard input.

```
=CHRSAW(5)
```

Returns: .t. or .f., depending on if a keystroke is waiting in the keyboard buffer.

Because CHRSAW( ) makes no distinction about which key was pressed, it's most often used to trigger events simply when somebody uses (or doesn't use) the keyboard.

```
DEFINE WINDOW wmOkDokey AT 2,10 SIZE 4,50
ACTIVATE WINDOW wmOkDokey NOSHOW && Notice the NOSHOW
@ 1,0 SAY "KEEP ON TRUCKIN'.."
IF CHRSAW(5)
  ACTIVATE WINDOW wmOkDokey
  =INKEY(3)
  RELEASE WINDOW wmOkDokey
ENDIF
```

You can also use CHRSAW( ) in loops to act like a TIMEOUT clause, for example:

```
DO WHILE .t.
  *> Do something
  DO CheckWork
  * Check keyboard buffer to see if any action.
  IF CHRSAW(60)
    EXIT
  ENDIF
ENDDO
```

Handling Mouse Clicks

It's been a longstanding rap against Xbase that it took years to add mouse support, and when it came, it couldn't automatically handle a double click. It still can't on the PC. If you're developing programs for cross platform use on FoxPro Mac(intosh), this may be a problem, since the Mac has had a double mouse click since day one. There are various workarounds available. They all use the _DBLCLICK internal variable to measure the amount of time between mouse clicks. Here's one of the simplest, although it does require a PUBLIC variable.

```
************************************************************************
* FUNCTION NAME.. MouseHit()
* DESCRIPTION.... DOUBLE CLICK MOUSE BUTTON FOR ENTER
* DATE........... Fri 11-29-1991 20:58:42
* PROGRAMMERS.... NHK
* LAST CHANGE.... Fri 11-29-1991
* PARAMETERS..... cType = Type of Call: Browse or Enter
* SYNTAX......... MouseHit( <type> )
* USAGE.......... PUBLIC nLastClk && required, put in init file
*                 nLastClk = 0
*                 ON KEY LABEL LEFTMOUSE DO MouseHit WITH
"BROWSE"
*
* RETURN......... .t.
* NOTES:
* Idea from Walt Kennamer (MS/Fox), slightly modified. The
function
* traps for a double mouse click to signify either a selection
in a
* browse, or an entry (enter key)in other applications. The
parameter
* specifies the difference.
*
* REQUIRED SETUP: Create the PUBLIC variable nLastClk and set
it to 0, * this keeps a record of the last time a mouse key was
clicked.
*
* Kennamer's original function also kept track of where
* the mouse cursor was on the screen so that clicks outside
* the window or with a moving cursor would not activate
* a response. Reasonable trapping, except that it required
* hard coding the function for the specific browse
* window/title. Decided not to use it, but the code is
* provided below.
*
*         mr = MROW('browse')
*         mc = MCOL('browse')
*         IF (lastmr = mr) and (lastmc = mc) ;
```

```
*           and ((ti - lastclk) <= _DBLCLICK) ;
*           and (mr >= 0) and (mc >= 0)
*           KEYBOARD CHR(23)
*         ENDIF
*         lastmr = mr
*         lastmc = mc
*
* CALLED BY...... GUF: ON KEY LABEL LEFTMOUSE
* CALLS.......... None
***************************************************************************
FUNCTION MouseHit
PARAMETER cType

PRIVATE ti

ti = SECONDS()
IF ti-nLastClk <= _DBLCLICK
  DO CASE
  CASE cType = "BROWSE"
    KEYBOARD CHR(23)
  CASE cType = "ENTER"
    KEYBOARD CHR(13)
  ENDCASE
ENDIF

nLastClk = ti

RETURN (.t.)
*
```

Keys and Commands

The previous section covered ways to monitor the user's keystrokes. This section explains the ways FoxPro let's you change what the keystrokes do. This is a surprisingly rich field of commands. Keyboard commands, typified by using function keys should join menus and push buttons as the big three for making "programs on demand." All three act as a way of executing other routines.

This is a big part of event-driven programming—to allow the user to execute routines on demand, which means the routines are available and merely waiting the menu selection, push button, or keystroke to invoke them. The commands that do this are often referred to as *event handlers*. You're already aware of **F1** being the help key. It has a permanently attached FoxPro routine to summon the help system. Other than **F1**, every other function key and key combination (using **Ctrl**, **Alt**, or **Shift**) is available to be assigned routines.

In FoxPro for Windows it's doubtful you'd want to take function key mania as far as it goes with some DOS programs (word processors in particular). But there are many applications where a quick slap of a key is a lot quicker and more efficient than hunting down a menu selection with a mouse.

SET FUNCTION TO

```
SET FUNCTION <expN> | <key label> TO [<expr>]
```

<expN> is the number of the function key, F2=2 etc., to be assigned a command macro.

| <key label> uses any valid key label to be assigned a macro.

[<expr>] is a command macro, or a string of commands, using a semi-colon to execute individual commands within the macro.

```
SET FUNCTION 1 TO "DO CLEARSCR"
SET FUNCTION F2 TO "USE customer;BROWSE"
SET FUNCTION CTRL-F3 TO "MODIFY COMMAND MYPROG"
```

This is the oldest Xbase function key command. It's a one-trick pony, which allows you to assign a macro, or a string of commands, to a "key label" (function key or key combination). It's greatest value is usually to the programmer, who can shortcut routine commands. But from time to time, it can help users by putting common data entry values into function keys etc.

ON KEY LABEL

```
ON KEY [LABEL <key label>] [<command>]
```

[LABEL <key label>] is any of the 28 supported "key labels".

[<command>] is any legitimate FoxPro command, most commonly DO.

```
ON KEY LABEL F3 DO WorkList
ON KEY LABEL F4 DO LISTING.PRG
ON KEY LABEL RIGHTMOUSE CLEAR
ON KEY LABEL CTRL+HOME GO TOP
ON KEY LABEL INS BROWSE LAST PREFERENCE worklist
```

The use of ON KEY LABELs has become so popular, that a new piece of jargon is making the rounds: OKLs. The reason for this popularity is simplicity. Once you become familiar with the available key combinations, the mechanics of key assignment are easy. You can assign functions, procedures, and program files. The combinations are nearly endless, bounded only by bwhat makes sense at any given point in your application. For more about working with OKLs, see Key Management below.

NOTE

Certain mouse clicks, like those involved with selecting menus and using scroll bars, are taken by Windows routines and can't be trapped by FoxPro for your ON KEY LABEL MOUSE, RIGHTMOUSE, or LEFTMOUSE. This doesn't mean you can't use mouse input to trigger a routine, but it won't always be reliable, and might confuse the user.

ON KEY=

```
ON KEY [ = <expN>] [<command>]
```

[= <expN>] is one of a series of key codes.

[<command>] is any legitimate FoxPro command, usually a DO.

```
ON KEY 329 DO CleanUp
```

Only one ON KEY = may be active at a time. This command predates ON KEY LABEL by many years and has almost totally been superseded by the more flexible and versatile newcomer.

ON KEY COMMAND

```
ON KEY <command>
```

In a way this is a dangerous command. It says, simply, on every keystroke execute the <command> specified. Obviously, you wouldn't want to leave this active for very long. It is occasionally used in situations where a user message has been activated, and you want to have it cleared as soon as someone begins using the keyboard again. Here's a brief example:

```
DEFINE WINDOW wmWaitWin AT 2,0 SIZE 4,79
ACTIVATE WINDOW wmWaitWin
@ 1,0 SAY "Please enter your selection or use Cancel."
ON KEY DO ClrWait
```

```
...

PROCEDURE ClrWait
RELEASE WINDOW wmWaitWin
ON KEY
```

KEYBOARD

```
KEYBOARD <expC> [PLAIN]
```

<expC> is any valid character expression.

[PLAIN] causes the command to ignore key assignments in <expC>.

```
KEYBOARD "NOT APPLICABLE"
KEYBOARD "{CTRL+HOME}"
KEYBOARD UserName( )
```

All previous keyboard commands assign commands to keystrokes. This command assigns keystrokes to the keyboard. What it does, is stuff the typeahead buffer (keyboard buffer) with a string or string of key equivalents, to be executed by your program. KEYBOARD has been around a while, but FoxPro gave it an enormous shot in the arm by making it possible to include specific key equivalents. KEYBOARD is used often, and in some surprising circumstances, for example positioning the cursor to a specific spot in text, or forcing menu selections.

NOTE

A note on the <expC>: While "character expression" means just that—a character string that can be put into the keyboard buffer—there are actually three major components used with KEYBOARD.

1. A string of text (characters) in quotes: `KEYBOARD "This is a string."`
2. Key equivalents, in quotes and braces: `KEYBOARD "{HOME}"`.
3. Functions that return character strings or keyboard equivalents in the string can also be used. Unlike ON KEY LABEL where functions are called like DO FuncName, here you must use the normal function format: `KEYBOARD FuncName()`.

Key Management

Once you start making use of ON KEY assignments, you need to be careful they don't overlap, recurs (calling the same routine over and over), or step on the environment. This isn't difficult, but has to be done faithfully. Your big allies are three simple commands: ON KEY, PUSH KEY, and POP KEY.

- `PUSH KEY [CLEAR]` This takes all currently active key label assignments and "pushes" them onto a stack. The stack is a last in, first out—LIFO—memory list that stores the key values and then replaces them if you issue POP KEY. Including the CLEAR clause removes all key assignments from memory, after they have been saved.
- `POP KEY [ALL]` In the above mentioned stack of saved key label assignments, you can restore them to active status with POP KEY. Adding the ALL, however, is drastic. It wipes out all current OKLs, and those stored in memory on the stack.
- `ON KEY` Used without any other clauses, this removes all currently active (but not stored) OKLs.

The typical approach to key management is to monitor the transition from one function or procedure to another and decide if key labels are being changed, or are not valid in a particular place. If so, you'd follow a procedure something like this:

```
FUNCTION GetSalary
PARAMETER cPosId

PUSH KEY CLEAR
ON KEY LABEL F3 DO AddSal
ON KEY LABEL F4 DO DelSal
ON KEY LABEL F5 BROWSE LAST
ON KEY LABEL F9 DO LookSal
...

POP KEY
RETURN .t.
*
```

In addition to the safety factor of controlling your OKL's, you may occasionally want to know during program execution what key assignments are active. FoxPro 2.0 introduced a new function to Xbase that returns the many values of **ON KEY LABEL, ON KEY ESCAPE** etc.

```
ON( (<expC1>[, <expC2>])
```

<expC1> This designates one of the six "Event Handling Commands" - ON ERROR use "ERROR", ON ESCAPE use "ESCAPE", ON KEY use "KEY", ON KEY LABEL use "LABEL", ON PAGE use "PAGE", ON READERROR use "READERROR". The function will return the current settings for the one specified.

[, <expC2>] For ON KEY LABEL only, using a "key label" will return the current setting for that key.

```
= ON("ERROR")
```

Return: DO worklist The current command, if any, otherwise a null string ("").

```
= ON("ESCAPE")
```

Return: DO NoExit The current command, if any, otherwise a null string ("").

```
= ON("LABEL","F2")
```

Return: CLEAR The currently assigned expression, if any.

Thinking About the User Interface

With the keyboard commands, this chapter has come to the end of a long—and yet partial—listing of user-interface elements. In the next several chapters, you'll be diving into the FoxPro Power Tools, where all user-interface issues are brought to bear on your application. Your skill in selecting and using the elements introduced here will probably be one of the decisive factors in the success of the application.

It's important to admit that much about creating a user interface is intuitive and even artistic. Few application developers have the time or inclination to assiduously study user-interface design. And it also takes a great deal of time to prepare and polish good user interface routines. Thus much UI goes by the seat of the pants. Insofar as the user interface is an aesthetic matter, this has some positive aspects.

But the temptation in the act of artistic creation is to forget who it's for—the user. The user interface also has a utilitarian commitment. At the least, it shouldn't get in the user's way and at best it should make their job easier.

Working with the user(s)—prototyping, experimenting, reacting to comment and observation of use—are extremely important in developing a good user interface. You, the developer, may have the brilliant first ideas, and you have control over the "look-and-feel" issues. But without refinement and modification under the harsh light of field testing, your user interface runs a risk—a risk of rejection.

Developing an application with a complex user interface can be a subtle business. There are so many possibilities, and all the possibilities have variations. Being systematic helps. Listening to users helps. Experience helps. Being creative helps.

Chapter 12
The Project Manager

The Project Manager is the core of the three programming Power Tools (Project Manager, Screen Builder, Menu Builder). Along with the Menu Builder, it is one of the most successful—and indispensable—components of the *evolving* FoxPro Integrated Development Environment (IDE). The word evolving is stressed, because the IDE is far from completed, or even integrated. That's the promise of version 3.0.

If you've been reading through the earlier chapters on building applications, you may have noticed there are a large number of components, and most of the components have files. There are data files (.DBF), program files (.PRG), report files (.FRX), query files (.QPR), bitmap files (.BMP), ...etc. All of these, and quite a few more, become the sum and substance of your applications. A small application may have dozens of files, a large one may have several hundred. Holding all of this together, and attempting to keep it organized, ranges in importance from a convenience to an absolute necessity. It is the Project Manager that performs this function. In this role, the Project Manager has two primary tasks:

- Maintain a listing of files used by the project.
- Build programs or applications.

In a sense the Project Manager is the File Manager for your application. Technically, you can list each and every file used (or even some that aren't). However, the Project Manager is coded to recognize certain file extensions. For these, it knows whether they can be edited, and whether than can be included in a "build" of a project (incorporated into your application). Table 12.1 contains a listing of these file extensions:

Table 12.1
Project manager supported files.

Extension	Type	Edit	Extension	Type	Edit
.DBF	Data files/tables	Yes	.QPX	Compiled queries	No
.CDX	Compound indexes	No	.FRT	Report files	Yes
.IDX	Index files	No	.FRM	Compiled reports	No
.PRG	Program files	Yes	.LBX	Label files	Yes
.FXP	Compiled programs	No	.LBL	Compiled labels	No
.SCX	Screen files	Yes	.FLL	Library files	No
.SPX	Compile screens	No	.FMT	Format files	Yes
.MPR	Menu files	Yes	.EXE	Executable file	No
.MPX	Compile menus	No	.APP	Application file	Yes
.QPR	Query files	Yes	.MEM	Memory file	No

You can list bitmap (.BMP) and icon files (.ICO) in the Project Manager, but it doesn't support them in any way and doesn't recognize their file extensions. This is an unfortunate omission, given the popularity of such items as picture buttons and wallpaper.

For files that are editable, (such as program files and tables), you can double click on the entries or select them with the **Enter** key, and the Project Manager places you into a Browse window, Edit window or other appropriate environment. This is called *launching* an edit session. Although you can accomplish the same thing through the system menu or by typing in commands, the Project Manager route is extremely convenient.

The second task of the Project Manager is to *build* your applications. The word build has special meaning here. In another context, like programming in C, this would be called a *make*. The Project Manager tracks all of the files needed by your project, checks to see if they have been updated, generates and compiles them, and where appropriate, puts them together into an application file (.APP) or an executable file (.EXE).

Using the Project Manager

The Project Manager has the hallmarks of a good programming tool: It does a lot for you, and it's easy to use. Figure 12.1 shows the Project Manager window.

Figure 12.1
The Project Manager window.

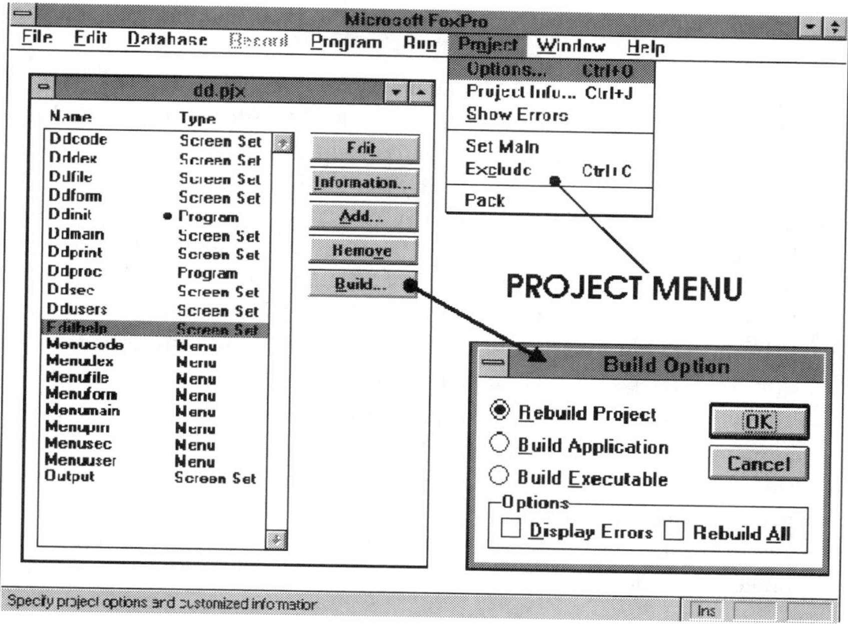

You can start and finish within this window. A new project is created by selecting File, New, Project, New or typing **CREATE PROJECT** in the

Command window. Then, using the Add button, begin creating the new files of your project, or adding existing files to the project.

One of the requirements of the Project Manager is that you identify a *main program*, the program that starts all other programs. In most applications, this is the initialization file. As a rule, this should be the first program created or added to the project. From here, the Project Manager can follow the execution trail—the function and procedure calls embedded in your files—until it tracks down everything that is apparently required by the current project. It doesn't matter whether you've listed them or not. The Project Manager automatically adds anything that's missing (unless it can't find the files at all).

If you're working with the Project Manager, it's desirable to keep it on the screen all the time. However, in FoxPro it takes up a considerable amount of screen space and can get in the way of observing other screens. You can close and save the project from the File option in the main menu, or type **CLOSE ALL** in the Command window, or double click on the Control Menu box (the easiest way). It can be restored to the screen by the File, Open (select file) options, or by typing **MODIFY PROJECT** <project name> in the Command window.

Fortunately, the Project Manager is very good at maintaining itself. About the only housekeeping matter that you need to attend to is the inclusion of files that are not directly called by your application, but you want to have included in the application file (if you a making an .APP or an .EXE). This might include report, labels, memory, and table files. You can add these to the Project Manager file list at any time. Be aware, however, that included files are by default *read-only*. They can't be modified by the user. This might be okay for memory files and tables with special codes, but when you want the files to be modifiable, you'll need to go to the Project Menu, and select the Exclude option (**Alt-P-C**) for each file. This places a Ø marker next to the file.

As a rule, only files you want explicitly included in the application, such as memory files are placed in the Project Manager list. Otherwise, you'll wind up with so many files it becomes difficult to find the ones you need for programming. It should be pointed out that the Project Manager is not a substitute for a Data Dictionary, and shouldn't be used to keep track of data tables and indexes.

Builds

Doing a build is as easy to do as it is to say. Press the **Build** button in the Project

Manager window, select **Re-build Project**, **Build Application**, or **Build Executable**, and away it goes. But this does not mean it's a trivial process. The Project Manager does a lot of work on your behalf:

- It tracks the location of all files listed in the Project Manager, and the location of all references in the programming. These include function and procedure calls, array declarations, API library calls, or calls for special files like memory (.MEM), report (.FRX) and RQBE (.QPR). If files are missing or there are references it can't find, the errors are logged to the project error file (.ERR).
- It compares the date and time (the time stamp) for each file on disk to the date and time stored in the Project Manager file. If the disk file has been updated or changed, it is generated or compiled, if appropriate, and incorporated into the project. Then the Project Manager dates and times are updated.
- Screens and menus are generated, then compiled. Program files are compiled. This produces an *object code*, which is stored in the memo file of the Project Manager (.FPT). The memo files tend to become enlarged. In fact you may notice from time to time that FoxPro does some housekeeping, "Checking Memo File" and "Packing Memo File." It tries to keep the size to a minimum and restore any damaged material. Occasionally the memo files will be trashed, although FoxPro is remarkably robust considering the use these files have. If you do not have a backup just create a new Project Manager file, tell it the main program, and let it rebuild the project.
- It scans the code for syntax or other generator and compiler errors, and creates a log file for your perusal.
- If you have specified either a Build App, or Build EXE, the Project Manager draws from the object files stored in its memo fields, and produces a composite file of object code. In the case of the App, this becomes the application file (.APP). To build the executable file (DOS/Windows), you must have the FoxPro for Windows Distribution Kit. The Project Manager hands-off the object code to the linker that comes with the Distribution Kit that produces the final executable file (.EXE).

The Project Manager is remarkably efficient and quick in doing these many tasks. Still, depending on your hardware (especially the disk drive arrangement), it takes time to do a build of a large project that has had changes in several files. As mentioned before, you need to reckon with the time it takes in your estimation of how fast you can churn out an application.

Debugging

One of the side benefits of using the Project Manager is the ready access it gives you to generator and compiler errors. All compiling and generating, whether started from the Command window, System menu, or the Project Manager produces an error log (a file with a .ERR extension). However, the first two don't automatically show you the log, or even provide a way of calling it up. The Project Manager can do both. The Build Option dialog box has a check box to automatically display errors. And if you'd rather do it yourself, there's the Show Errors option in the Project menu.

Either way, what you get is a listing of errors in an Edit window, showing the two major types—syntax errors, and reference errors. Most developers hate to have errors in the Project Manager build. Not necessarily because they seek perfection, but because FoxPro always halts the build and forces the programmer to press a key or two. Which means you can't go out for coffee.

Syntax errors are mostly the result of typing errors, memory lapses, or over-eager cutting and pasting. Most syntax errors can be dispatched quickly. Reference errors are also generally easy to fix. For the most part these are calls to files or procedures, which the Project Manager can't locate (and you chose not to locate during the build). Sometimes, you'll have these "unresolved references" on purpose, knowing full well that the missing routines are actually in a procedure file not being included in the build. But most of the time, you'll track down the references and locate the "missing" procedures.

Occasionally the Project Manager complains about references it thinks are program files, but are really arrays. The cure for this, and certain other reference errors, is to use the EXTERNAL directive.

Using EXTERNAL

The concept behind the EXTERNAL command is simple. You're telling the Project Manager not to bother looking for certain things. These are expressed in the clauses of the command:

```
EXTERNAL ARRAY  <array list>
EXTERNAL LABEL  <file list>
EXTERNAL LIBRARY  <file list>
EXTERNAL MENU  <file list>
```

```
EXTERNAL PROCEDURE  <file list>
EXTERNAL REPORT  <file list>
EXTERNAL SCREEN <file list>
```

There are two keys to using the command effectively: understanding when the Project Manager is likely to miss something, and putting the command in the right place.

The main candidates for using EXTERNAL are:

- The procedure or report is referenced via a macro or a name expression. For example:

  ```
  cProgName = "F:\PRG\HRPOS.PRG"
  DO (cProgName)
  ```

  The Project Manager has no way of knowing what to put into the macro expansion or name variable and so it thinks the file is missing. The solution is to put the EXTERNAL in the same procedure where the "hidden" call is being made:

  ```
  EXTERNAL PROCEDURE HRPOS
  cProgName = "F:\PRG\HRPOS.PRG"
  DO  (cProgName)
  ```

- The procedure (or function) is in a place where it is not listed in the Project Manager, and not available through a direct call. Most commonly this would be routines stored in a procedure file that isn't loaded with a particular project. In a large application, with many projects sharing a common initialization and procedure file, for example, leaving the procedure file out of the Project Manager list saves additional compilation time and storage space, but can be a nuisance, because of the missing references. The solution is to find each and every routine where a file, procedure, or array is missing and include the EXTERNAL in that procedure:

  ```
  FUNCTION ProcName
  EXTERNAL PROCEDURE NameChk
  EXTERNAL ARRAY aNames
  PARAMETER cLName
  IF NOT EMPTY( cLname )
    FOR i = 1 TO ALEN( aNames ,1)
      DO NameChk
    ENDFOR
  ENDIF
  ```

As illustrated above, the right place to put an EXTERNAL is immediately after the beginning of the function, procedure, screen or menu where the offending reference occurs. The command is ignored by the compiler and has no effect on your final code.

Project Information

The Project Manager provides several ways to augment your information about files and to include certain options in the Build process. All of this can be found in three dialog windows: Project Information, Files Information, and Options.

The Project Information dialog box, shown in Figure 12.2, is reached from the Project Menu (Project, Project Info..., or **Ctrl-J**).

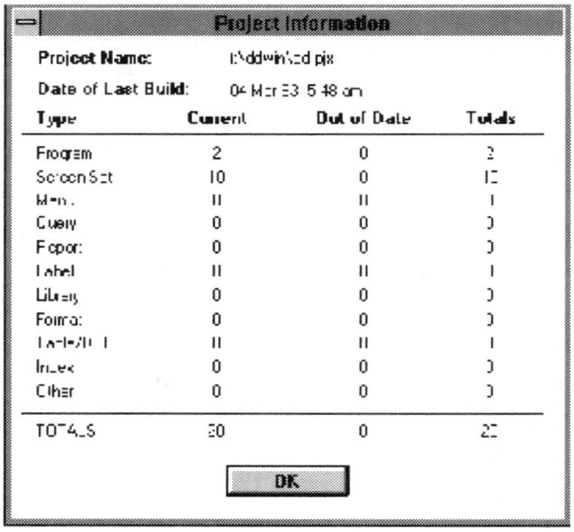

Figure 12.2
The Project Information dialog box.

Project Information

Project Name: [illegible]

Date of Last Build: [illegible]

Type	Current	Out of Date	Totals
Program	2	0	2
Screen Set	10	0	10
Menu	[illegible]	[illegible]	[illegible]
Query	0	0	[illegible]
Report	0	0	[illegible]
Label	[illegible]	[illegible]	[illegible]
Library	0	0	[illegible]
Format	0	0	[illegible]
Table/DBF	[illegible]	[illegible]	[illegible]
Index	0	0	[illegible]
Other	0	0	[illegible]
TOTALS	[illegible]	0	[illegible]

OK

This provides an overview of the files in your project by type and you can tell at a glance whether files are out-of-date or not. The File Information dialog box, shown in Figure 12.3, is reached by selecting a file in the Project Manager list, and selecting the **Information...** button. This provides some detail information about the status of the file, and the procedures and functions that are contained in it. Both of these screens are of little use unless you are having problems with a file or the Project Manager's handling of a build. Then it may be useful to check on updates, and other status information.

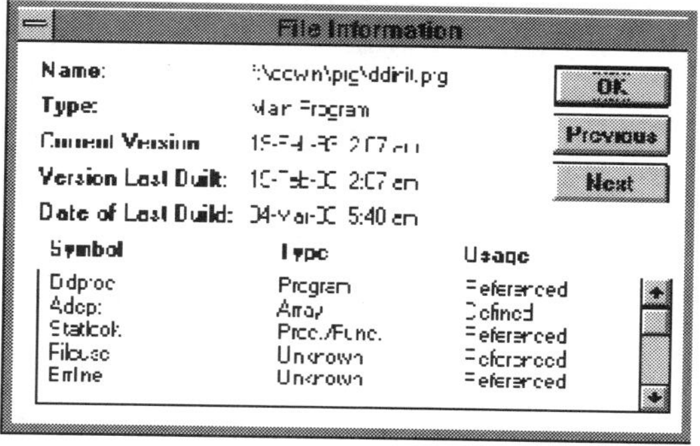

Figure 12.3
The File Information dialog box.

The third dialog box, Options, shown in Figure 12.4, is more important.

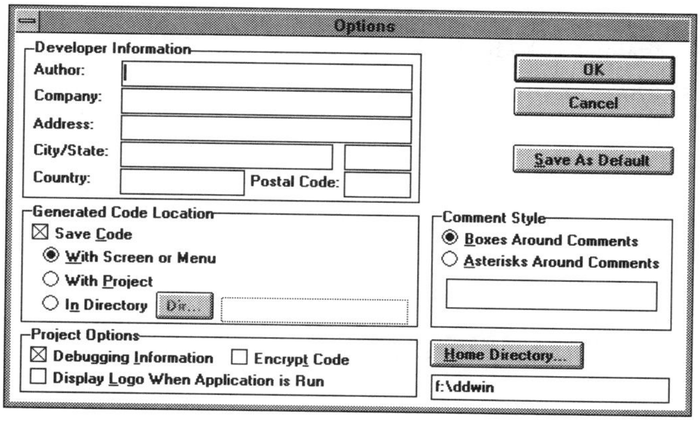

Figure 12.4
The Options dialog box.

It's reached from the Project menu. Interestingly, most of the options are actually related to code generated by the Screen Builder or the Menu Builder. In fact you can find virtually this same screen in Generating individual screens or menus. However, in the Project Manager, you can do it once for all screens and menus in your project. Sensible. This includes the named areas of the options screen: Developer Information, Generated Code Location, and Comment Style.

Developer Information stamps the header of every generated file with any of the information you choose to include here. This goes along with the Comment Style, which determines the border around the generated file headers and other comments. Generated Code Location has several options that might be exercised in controlling the output of code from the Screen and Menu Builders. The defaults are Save Code and With Screen or Menu. Saving is obvious. If you're keeping your project files in file type subdirectories, then saving output to those directories is desirable, at least during early project development. Later, however, when you are preparing projects for distribution, it might be desirable to shift output to the In Directory option. You can specify one directory to contain all the output files of both types, making it easier to package them.

Those options directly related to the Project Manager include:

- The choice of Home Directory..., which is usually handled automatically.
- Debugging Information, which should be on throughout the development process, but might be turned off to decrease the size of compiled files for distribution. (Debug information is mostly a matter of line numbers being compiled into the program so the FoxPro error reporting mechanisms can report.)
- Code encryption.
- Displaying the FoxPro for Windows Logo when running the application (.EXEs only).

Whenever you change any of these options, don't forget to Save as Default before leaving.

Setup for Applications

It should be pointed out that one project does not necessarily make an application. A complete "application" might consist of several projects and several "apps" (the generated kind). As mentioned earlier, a project file loaded with several hundred files is pretty unusable. So the logical solution is to split your application into a number of projects, and possibly a number of .APP files.

This is sort of application design on top of application design. You've already figured out what functions and elements your application should have, now you can use that knowledge to guide development of projects. For the most part they should follow "modules" or other functional groupings that make up your application.

However if you intend to create an executable file for your application (an .EXE), you need to be very careful that it will "find" all of the relevant files. In some situations it may be necessary to put all of your files into one very large project, so that the .EXE compiler/linker can do its job properly.

Multiuser/Network Considerations

One weakness of the current Project Manager is that it is not "multiuser friendly." There are two problems. Only one programmer at a time can open a specific Project Manager file. This can be a big problem, and is one of the leading motives for creating a number of smaller projects—to allow more programmers to work. The other problem is typical for network use. You can't complete a build on a project where somebody is using the .APP or .EXE file. This is normal network file-sharing protection, but it can present a logistical problem. The solution is fortunately easy—for programming, maintain a totally separate development area with a complete complement of files. You should do this as a matter of course, anyway. When it comes time to deliver a new .APP or .EXE to the production side, you simply have to pick your time, when nobody is using the old file.

Directory Mapping

One of the great benefits of the Project Manager, although it's a rather simple idea, is that it is *drive and home directory independent*. It doesn't store the disk drive or the name of the home directory with any of its file listings, although it does keep the currently designated home drive and subdirectory on record. If you move your project, or an application to a computer with a different drive letter or home subdirectory name, Project Manager asks—"The project has been moved, do you wish to make the current directory the home directory?"

The Project Manager is however, *subdirectory dependent*. It keeps the subdirectory path, under the current home directory, for all of its files. If you move the project to a place where the subdirectories are different, or remove some subdirectories, the Project Manager asks about missing files. This is easy to avoid: Stay with a standardized subdirectory pattern, and duplicate that pattern wherever the Project Manager goes. If you follow this it doesn't matter what the driver letter is. The builds will run without a hitch as long as the names of the subdirectories haven't changed.

Projects are under your control (theoretically anyway.) At least you should know about your own subdirectories, and the placement of files in them. If you follow the rule above, create a simple subdirectory pattern, and maintain an accurate CONFIG.FPW, the Project Manager treats you well. And you will praise its excellence. However, when the project is no longer under your control, when it has been delivered to the user, things may be different. You can no longer assume someone knows about subdirectories, much less which files are relevant. Which is to say, distribution of an application is another issue.

Backup for a Project

If you've been around computers for more than a week, much less become a programmer, you should already know that the only sure thing in computing is eventual disaster. And the only antidote is backup, backup, backup. The Project Manager and its related subdirectory structure can be very helpful in creating backup routines for all of your code and other files. There are a couple of shareware and freeware programs available on bulletin boards (Compuserve FoxForum in particular), that use the Project Manager file as the guide for doing a backup of a project. These generally work in conjunction with a file compression program (usually PKZIP), to preserve space, typically on a floppy disk. These are highly recommended.

If you want to go it on your own, a simple XCOPY *.* /S from DOS, starting in the home directory of the project and including the subdirectories will suffice, until your project becomes too big for one disk. (Assuming you're backing up to floppies.) Then you might graduate to PKZIP or another compression program, and feed it a batch file with the names of the files and subdirectories you want to backup. What matters is not the technique, but the unfailing execution. Remember, Mr. Murphy would have been a programmer, had he lived today.

Chapter 13
The Screen Builder

ost applications are built around user-interface screens. There are screens for data entry and edit, screens for information, screens for table maintenance, and so on. The FoxPro Screen Builder is *the* tool used to create most of those screens.

As you might have guessed, there is more to the Screen Builder than meets the eye. There are some aspects to it, so optimistically presented in the *Getting Started* tutorials, that are easy enough for a novice programmer to create useful screens almost immediately. There are also aspects that may require months to learn and master. How far you go with the Screen Builder may be driven by the type of applications you are creating, your own curiosity (and proclivity for hard-study), and your desire to master the language and techniques.

The issues involved, and the complexity of the techniques, are so broad that no book could hope to cover the diversity. Of necessity, this book makes some choices on how to approach building applications with the Screen Builder. These are not the only choices and certainly not the best choices for all circumstances. Hopefully they are a guide for your learning. However, your best bet is to build screens, experiment, read magazine articles, talk to other programmers, get information from bulletin boards, go to Fox User Group meetings, and build more screens. The pieces *will* fall together, and perhaps at times you'll come back to this book and find yourself saying, "Ah, *that's* what this means."

Some Preliminary Observations

On the most practical level, the Screen Builder can be viewed as three somewhat related parts:

- A screen designer.
- The location of input validation and control.
- The programmer's interface to READ code.

While there is no set pattern to creating a screen in the Screen Builder, it does usually have the components shown in Figure 13.1. After opening a new Screen Builder session, you decide on the type of window, its colors, and font. You place on it various screen objects like GETs, boxes, and text. For the data input elements (GETs) you may add various input controls (VALID, WHEN). Then you tie the screen (or screens) together with the READ controls. After saving the work to a Screen Builder file (.SCX or .SCT), you add the screen to a Project Manager project (if you didn't start there), and have the Project Manager do a build, which generates and compiles the screen. Finally you run the program or application.

FoxPro is a database-management system, so nothing is really more important than the data management. But FoxPro is also an application development system, and in that context the user interface is primary. The Screen Builder, being the number one Power Tool for the user interface, should play a large role in application development. So what does the Screen Builder really do for you?

- **Save a lot of time**. You save time because it handles all of the nasty decimal coordinates for locating objects on the screen. Because the Screen Builder is, mostly, WYSIWIG (What You See Is What You Get), it's a whole lot easier and quicker to put together a good looking screen. Then it generates the code automatically. That last part doesn't really save time. Make one small change and the whole screen will be regenerated. Over and over again. The process is quick, but it doesn't save time. The mechanics of the Screen Builder are also time consuming. A lot of clicks and keystrokes are required to navigate its windows.

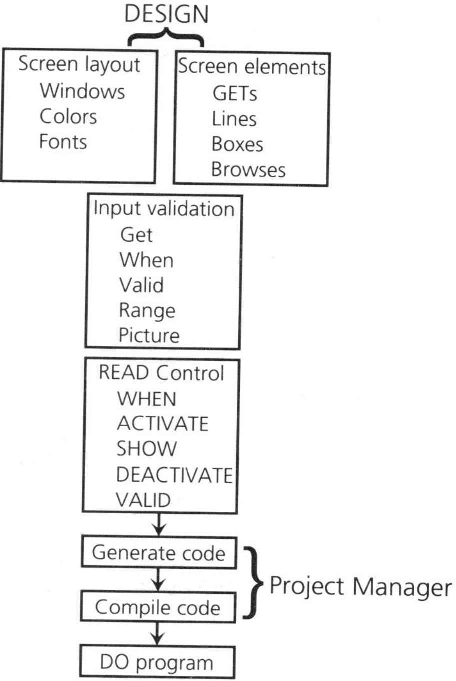

Figure 13.1 *The Screen Builder process.*

- **Provide organization and clarity.** The Screen Builder is a programming framework, and it provides a place to store your code. It has its own structure and terminology, which depending on how you use it, can organize and clarify the elements of a program. Ironically, the ability to make full use of the organizational aspects of the Screen Builder comes only after an arduous learning curve, and by the time you get done, you may have developed preferences for doing things outside of the Screen Builder.
- **Produce reusable code.** You can build various kinds of screen objects—lists, push button menus—according to your own style, then have them available as generic routines to be copied into any application. Of course, you could always do this with a library of other generic procedures and functions. The Screen Builder, however, enhances the visual aspects of your library building. The ability to freely copy screen objects from one Screen Builder screen to another can be very useful.

If you're getting the impression the Screen Builder may not be an unequivocal boon (or words to that effect), you'd be getting it right. For the most part, the

Screen Builder is a two-edged sword with nearly as many losses as gains. Yet it is indispensable, even central, to the task of building a FoxPro application. It's important to understand both its capabilities and its quirks.

The most obvious capability is that the Screen Builder helps you to produce screens. Working with fonts, and other elements of a graphical user interface (GUI) would be nearly impossible without the Screen Builder. In this respect it is a very strong tool, both intuitive to use, and efficient in handling the complexity of a Microsoft Windows screen.

NOTE

> Many people find the "screen" terminology used in conjunction with the Screen Builder to be confusing. Officially, the screen is the basic FoxPro for Windows window—the one that appears when you start the program. All other screens are either on that basic FoxPro window, or they are in other user defined windows. So from a Microsoft Windows perspective, the Screen Builder is mostly a "window builder." About 95 percent of the time, you will be putting your designs in user defined windows. However, in the fuzzy language of programming we still tend to say, "I'm building my screens," not,"I'm building my windows." So Fox's terminology is conventional for programming, but out of step with actual practice. You'll just have to get used to the wording "Screen Builder" and "Screen Sets."

The Screen Builder's other most obvious capability is that it generates code. You indicate where you want text, fields, and other screen elements, and then it generates the lines of code necessary to accomplish it. There are a jillion code generators of one kind or another. The vast majority of them are designed to create code, which can be incorporated with other code. The classic example, one that is most common with C and other languages, is the "Screen Painter" program. You place objects on a simulated screen, assign attributes, and then the screen painter generates code. This code is then added to your other programming. This is helpful, but if you need to change the screen code, then you have to regenerate and reincorporate the changes into the existing code. Then along came FoxPro 2.0 with a radically different tack: The Screen Builder files *are* the program.

The Screen Builder is most emphatically *not* just a design surface or a screen painter. When you create a screen with the Screen Builder, it stores everything you do, including code you write, in FoxPro database files with the extensions .SCX and .SCT. These files, and not the code generated from them, are the permanent housing for your code. In this way the coding structure of the Screen Builder is, to a very large extent, also the structure of your program. And significantly, the code generated by the Screen Builder is not intended to be changed or even be incorporated with other code. This generated code is put into a separate ASCII text file with a .SPR extension, after which it is compiled like any other program (.PRG) file. Throughout the *User's Guide* and *Developer's Guide*, Microsoft explains, warns, and cajoles that the output file from the Screen Builder should not be modified. Once more, here is the message:

Every time you generate code with the Screen Builder, the output file is overwritten. If you have made any changes in that file, they are gone. You have only three choices, make the changes to the output file again, or not generate again. Both are poor choices. The only real choice is to incorporate *all relevant code* in the Screen Builder.

The "almost" qualifier applies only to the occasional use of the output code (the .SPR) to track bugs or see how the code has been constructed. The FoxPro error-reporting system still uses line numbers, which relate to the .SPR file. It tells you nothing about what snippet or object they come from in the Screen Builder. As a result you sometimes need to refer to the .SPR to see where the bug locations really are. It's also of some instructional interest to see how the output files are constructed and coded. For more on this subject, the *Developer's Manual* has a more than adequate explanation of how the code is generated by the Screen Builder and how its structured.

The Screen Builder and the READ

The FoxPro manuals and the Screen Builder window give the impression that a READ is an inherent part of a screen. In fact, it seems to be a regular and subsidiary aspect of every screen. This is misleading. For one thing a screen does not require a READ. For another thing, the READ has a life of its own—with or without screens and the Screen Builder. This distinction is important, because the READ is really one of the most important control structures in FoxPro. In many programming techniques used with FoxPro, most especially event-driven programming, screens (windows) are clearly subordinate to the READ.

To fully understand the role of the READ and it's importance to FoxPro, it deserves an explanation of its own. This takes the discussion somewhat out of the range of the Screen Builder *per se*. But it all folds back together a bit later, hopefully making sense.

The READ

Since the days of Vulcan (the progenitor) and dBase II, the Xbase language has had the READ. Then, as now, the READ activates the GETs of your screen to allow user input. In the old days that's all it did. When the user moved off the last GET of a screen, the READ terminated. However, it was recognized that data input often needed more room than a single screen could provide. To solve this problem, the format file was introduced. The format file (.FRM) was a subspecies of a program file (.PRG) containing nothing but SAYs and GETs. It could contain several "pages" (screens) of data entry lines, and the program (in those days FoxBase+) would handle all the screen paging. It made it possible to create a crude but workable multipage entry screen.

However, if you needed to have the user make an entry not covered by the original GETs, for example to call up a subscreen for entry into another database, you were out of luck. That is, unless you got very creative and programmed your own *nested READ* (one READ calling another, calling another). This required very complex programming.

The nested READ capability, whether hand crafted or as later available through the VALID clause in Clipper and FoxPro, made it possible to call subroutines that issued another READ without losing your place in the original READ. This was a crucial feature—to allow the user to branch off into other subsystems. But there were still severe limitations. Only two READ commands could be used at a time. And control of the process of moving between READs was very complicated. Until FoxPro 2.0 (1990) this sort of subsystem to subsystem programming was very hard to do in the Xbase language.

Then came FoxPro 2.0 and all hell broke loose with the concept of a READ. First, there was the addition of the little clause, CYCLE, to the READ command. In one sense this has a simple interpretation: start at the top GET and go all the way to the last GET, keep going and you're back at the top GET. It's a cycle without automatic termination.

With the READ CYCLE you can allow the user to move around, more or less at will, through all the activated GETs, much like the setup for the old FORMAT command. But there's much, much more that comes with the READ CYCLE. In fact the people at Fox probably did programmers a disservice in calling it a CYCLE. A more familiar term, LOOP, might have abetted less confusion. The READ CYCLE is a READ LOOP, shown in Figure 13.2.

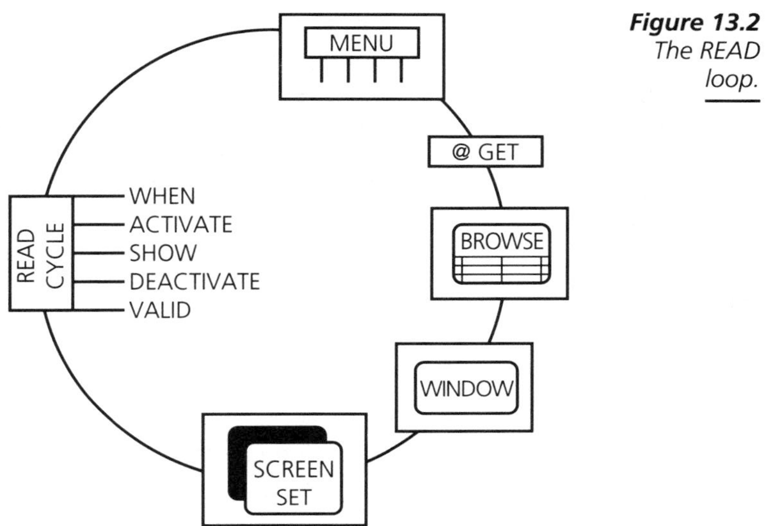

Figure 13.2 *The READ loop.*

Forget the GETs. This READ is no longer dependent on GETs, which is why some people refer to one of its manifestations as a "GETless READ." It is a loop in the classical sense of the DO WHILE...ENDDO and FOR...ENDFOR.

Like all programming loops, the READ loop has a beginning, middle, and end with stops for testing conditions at each point. The WHEN clause allows for testing conditions on whether to enter the READ loop or not. ACTIVATE, SHOW, and DEACTIVATE monitor window/screen set activity while the loop is active. And VALID tests for exit conditions at the "bottom" of the loop.

The only real difference from other loops is that the READ loop has no physical layout in your code. This is unlike a WHILE, which may start at the top of the page, have lots of code in the middle, and the ENDDO at the bottom of the page. All program code that affects this loop is "outside" rather than "inside" the loop. The READ loop is contained on a single command line, although it's visually helpful to space it out like this:

```
READ CYCLE ;
  WHEN StartOk();
  ACTIVATE WinCheck();
  SHOW GetPix();
  DEACTIVATE WinCheck();
  VALID EndOk()
```

This still doesn't look like a loop, which could be one reason why it has been illusive to visualize as a loop. (Another reason is that if you're using the Screen Builder, you don't even see how the READ is being used.) But for all practical and conceptual purposes, it is a loop, and if you consistently think about it that way, it should simplify much of the approach for how to use it. Take for example what Fox refers to as a "multi-window READ," shown in Figure 13.3.

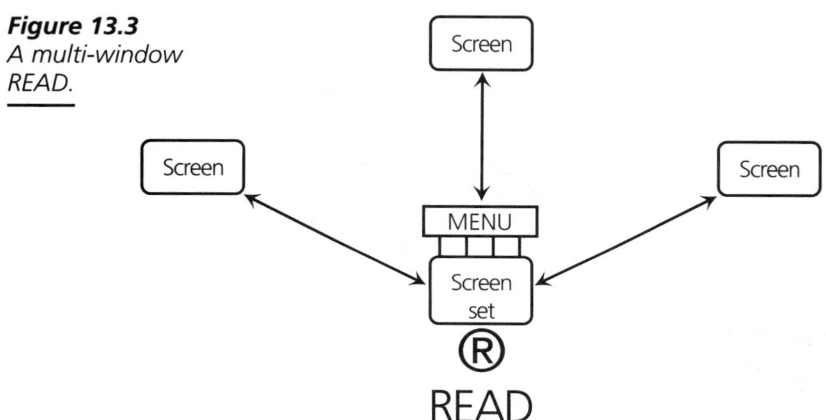

Figure 13.3
A multi-window READ.

In this version of the READ CYCLE one READ is issued for all the GETs in a number of screens. These screens (windows) can all be visible or hidden, as the application requires, but the GETs in them remain active. You can access any number of tables, have submenus, popups, and all kinds of user interface furbelows, but from the programmer's point of view all actions lead back to the clauses of this single READ CYCLE loop.

The WHEN, ACTIVATE, SHOW, DEACTIVATE, and VALID clauses of the READ can all take expressions or more commonly UDFs that monitor what the user is doing. All of the expressions or functions must return either .t. or .f. to the clauses. For example, the WHEN controls entry into the loop. If the WHEN is returned a false (.f.), then the user can not enter the READ or any of its subordinate windows, GETs, or menus.

The ACTIVATE and DEACTIVATE clauses are triggered every time the user leaves or enters a window (screen). Using all of the tools covered in Chapter 11, you can monitor what window the user was or is in, and act accordingly. If you return true (.t.) to either ACTIVATE or DEACTIVATE then the user will be allowed to continue in or out of a window. Otherwise not.

The SHOW clause is rather specialized. It is triggered only when the program issues a SHOW command (SHOW GET, SHOW GETS). It's primarily used to reissue @..SAY commands, called *refreshing* in the FoxPro manuals.

The most crucial of these clauses for the operation of the loop is the VALID. This performs the same function as the logical test at the top of a WHILE. If it is true, the READ terminates. If false, the READ continues. When a READ terminates, then all of its subordinate GETs are also terminated. In effect you drop out of the loop and close everything behind you.

As a rule, the multiwindow READ is created in the Screen Builder, where you would gather all the windows together in a single screen set, which in turn issues the single READ. The basic technique is simple, though there are plenty of complications. But before getting to complications there is one more example used by FoxPro for the READ CYCLE. In this case a READ is issued without any directly attached GETs. This uses the VALID clause to keep the READ open, until explicitly signaled to terminate. Then a number of subREADs (nested or otherwise) can be activated. Voila, the *foundation READ*.

Termination conditions in any of the subREADs puts the program back at the foundation READ, which in the VALID clause has the programming decide what to do next: Quit the program? Open another module?

In a "classic" foundation READ, the READ is part of an initialization file (or it could be a screen) and consists mainly of a WHEN clause that activates a main menu, and a VALID clause that monitors the termination of other READs, and windows. This can be a loop on a grand scale, although we are currently limited to four subordinate READs of any kind (nested, sub, or otherwise).

By now it may be more apparent what kind of animal this READ loop really is. If the DO WHILE ENDDO is primarily a processing loop, and the FOR ENDFOR is primarily an iterative loop, then the READ CYCLE is a loop for the user interface, sometimes called an *event loop*. It brackets the activity of people out there in userland as they wander about the windows/screens of the application, and it allows the programmer to master the demands of event-driven software.

All of the elements of a READ CYCLE loop can work together, more or less seamlessly, to give the user "freedom of the screen." At least as much as the programmer cares to give them. More or less seamlessly, because for all the conceptual strength of the READ CYCLE, FoxPro has hardly created the ideal user interface management system to support it. As you will soon discover, if you experiment with multiwindow READs and foundation READs, there are plenty of anomalies and quirks. The most troublesome being the confusing handling of a BROWSE.

However, event-driven programming aside, there are other practical uses of the READ CYCLE loop that are valuable. For example, The multiwindow READ technique, using a single READ for several windows, is one way to avoid the "too many READs" error, if you have a program with many levels of subroutines. In a similar fashion the foundation READ is one way of coordinating larger software applications that may require having two or more modules open at the same time.

This introduces the READ and some of the larger issues it may entail. Time to pull back a bit, get down, and get simple. You don't have to throw yourself into event-driven programming on day one. In fact, for much of the work done with a data-management system like FoxPro, "the basics" will do quite well, thank you.

Building a Basic Screen

The AED

There is one type of screen that is used so often in a data-management type of application that it ought to have its own name. It doesn't, however. In essence it has three tasks, all related directly to the data:

- **Add** records and data to a table.
- **Edit** data in the table.
- **Delete** records in the table.

There are usually other things going on, but these are the fundamental user activities in this type of screen. Call it an *AED* screen, for short.

In a database application, virtually every table has its own AED, if nothing else for maintenance purposes. There are usually other screens with data from multiple tables (often also AEDs), and then a raft of popup windows and other informational or decision making devices. Every application programmer builds hundreds of AEDs, literally, over a few years. So its worth spending some time to understand what's going on with such a basic and "simple" screen.

Here's an example drawn from a human resource system application that was also used frequently in Chapter 10. It's also a generic screen developed for maintaining a list of staff members, and their security information, which is a piece of the extended data dictionary system of Section IV.

In addition to all of the things said in previous chapters about designing a screen and the user interface, there are some specific things related to handling data which need to be taken into account for a basic screen (an AED), shown in Figure 13.4. In the beginning some of these might seem nit-picky. However, in the rough and tumble real world of users banging on your tables and screens, these "small points" turn into major issues (or major problems, if you let them).

Figure 13.4
Basic screen options.

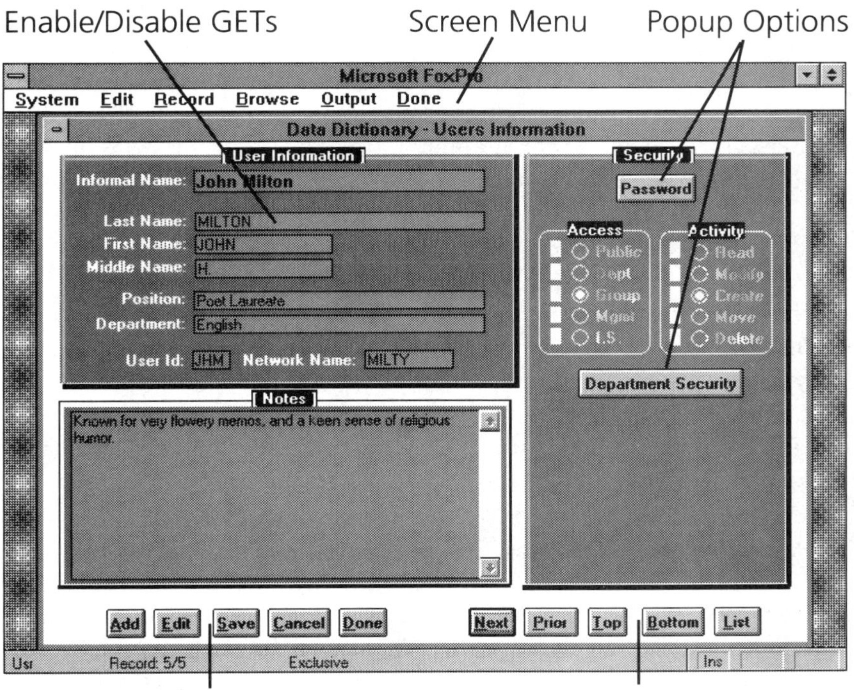

Most of these points are options you have concerning when and how data is presented to the user. They stem from some questions you need to ask yourself about the data and the type of screen you are building.

- On entering the screen, how should the user find the data? Not visible? Visible but not modifiable? Visible and modifiable?
- How does the user select records to view or modify?
- Can the user add new records?
- Can the user delete records?

These are pretty basic questions. There are umpteen different ways of answering them, both in the context of a particular screen, and the various programming techniques used. You should eventually be able to answer all of these questions in both contexts. Although screens are in some ways unique, you'll find that a great many of them have identical characteristics. This leads to the choice of certain programming approaches, which can be used repeatedly. And that, of course, can lead to reusable coding. One approach doesn't necessarily fit all, but if it covers 80 percent, it helps.

The approaches used here will be "justified," not because they are golden, but because it illustrates the type of thinking process that should be behind the selection of basic AED programming. You will have your own way of doing things, anyway. May they be the product of consideration and knowledge.

The actual Screen Builder coding for the options discussed here will be developed shortly with the example screen.

Table Based Elements

It's taken for granted that an AED screen is based on table information, as shown in Figure 13.5.

In the example screen, there are three tables involved: Users, user security, and departments. Users and user security have a relation based on the user ID. User security and departments share a relation on department ID. The user table contains basic information about people who use the application. It also contains some basic security information such as a password and access rights. Linked to this table is a more detailed listing of the user's specific security rights, the user security table. The user security table is based on assignment of rights to a department (a generic term here for any type of grouping). The departments are actually defined in the department table.

Based on this description of the tables involved, this screen is essentially a maintenance screen. It's not part of decision support, or of special processing, but intended for routine updating of tables—in short, a relatively typical

AED. The only slightly unusual aspect of this screen is the security elements—password, access rights, and departmental security. This is information that needs more protection than typical data. The special handling, however, doesn't change the basic character of the screen.

Figure 13.5
Tables and screens.

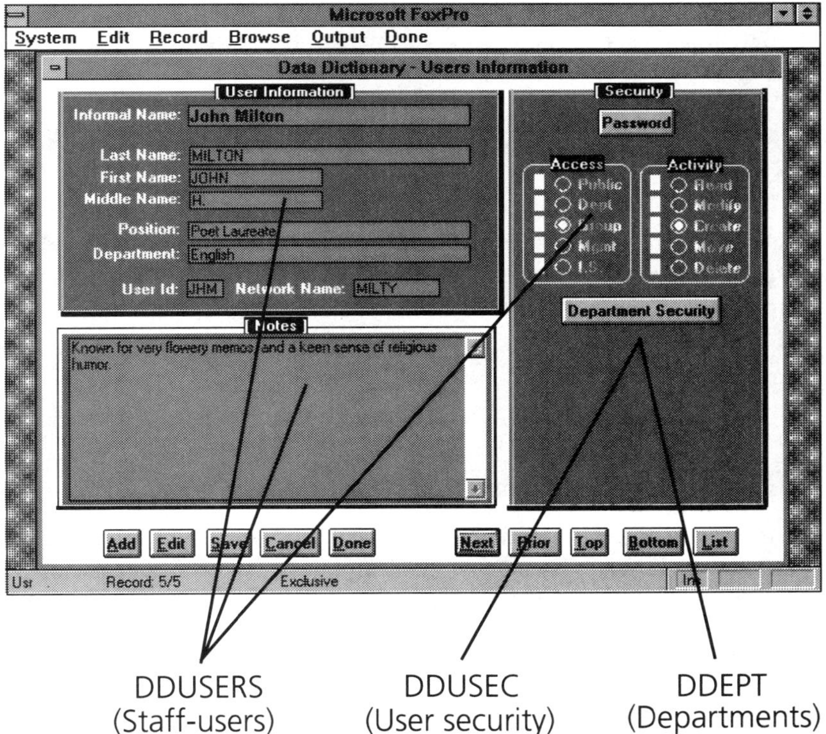

For almost any AED there are a series of questions you can ask yourself about the sequence of data presentation:

- **Should the user see information immediately upon entry to the screen?** This is a security screen. It contains data that is relatively private. Some of this information is deliberately hidden (such as password and departmental rights). However, in general the person who has gotten into the screen has already passed one or more security barriers to get there. Why not show them information? Most AED screens show information immediately.

- **Is the information editable?** This is a maintenance screen, which by definition is editable.
- **If the information is editable, is it immediately editable?** Since this is a security screen, you want any changes to be deliberate and controlled. So in this case the data is not immediately editable. The technique used is to DISABLE all of the GETs in the screen. When the user signals the intention to Add or Edit, the GETs are ENABLEd.

Direct or Indirect Entry?

One of the most important decisions for an AED, or any screen with data entry for that matter, is the method of entry. The Xbase language provides two basic methods, often called *direct entry* or *indirect entry.*

The @..GETs of your screen can do direct entry on the fields of a table, for example:

```
USE customer
@ 2,10 GET customer.lastname
READ
```

Any changes are immediate, and "destructive." The original data is not preserved. There's no going back if the user makes a mistake. This is the simplest entry scheme. It relies on the validation of GETs to screen the most egregious errors. Other data entry mistakes are up to the user to correct. If you trust the user or the data isn't that sensitive, then this method is the easiest.

Every other method tries to ameliorate the problem of the destructive element inherent in the direct entry. There are many variations, but the basic scheme is to save existing field values to memory variables, either to edit the variables, or to salvage a canceled entry.

The most common approach is indirect entry. The GETs provide entry into what are called *field variables*—memory variables named like the fields and loaded with the values from the fields. This is usually done with the SCATTER and GATHER commands.

```
USE customer
```

```
SCATTER MEMVAR
@ 2,10 GET m.lastname
READ
GATHER MEMVAR
```

The SCATTER MEMVAR command creates a variable for each field preceded by the *m-dot* (m.lastname). This provides indirect entry, because changes are made to variables and not to fields. Only when appropriate are the fields replaced by the values in the variables using GATHER MEMVAR.

The syntax for these two commands gives you a fair amount of control over the use of field variables:

```
SCATTER
 [FIELDS <field list>]
 [MEMO]
 TO <array>
 | TO <array> BLANK
 | MEMVAR
 | MEMVAR BLANK

GATHER
   [FIELDS <field list>]
   [MEMO]
    FROM <array>
   | MEMVAR
```

The FIELDS <field list> clause lets you specify which fields from a table to be copied to an array or field variables. Memo fields are included only if you also specify the MEMO clause.

Both commands support the creation of an array loaded with field values, or the field variables. Both approaches work in the Add/Edit context, but the m-dot variables are both distinctive and carry the same name as the field they contain, which makes them self-documenting. An array is far more anonymous—in fact arrays make it difficult to tell what contains what. For this reason most programmers use the field variable approach...

```
SCATTER MEMVAR MEMO           && For editing fields
SCATTER MEMVAR MEMO BLANK     && For new (blank) fields
```

and

```
GATHER MEMVAR MEMO            && To replace values in a table.
```

Because the data in the example screen is relatively sensitive, only indirect entry is used. Once the data has been changed, the user must explicitly signal to save the changes, or cancel the editing. This is a common pattern that can be applied without too much trouble to many, if not most, AED screens. The tendency is to pick one approach and then stick with it. This simplifies programming, but may not always reflect the data or the user's needs in a particular screen. However, consistency of user interface, is not an empty proposition. In an application, it's usually better to stick with the same basic approaches—screen to screen—than to confuse the user with changing the rules of entry.

All of these decisions are tempered by three data-oriented requirements: user support and convenience, data security, and data integrity. You want your screens to be as informative and open as possible. At the same time you don't want users doing things they shouldn't, and you don't want bad data (mistakes or otherwise) to get into the tables. The approach taken in this example screen is middle of the road—supportive of the user, but controlled.

Navigation Options

The term *navigation* is a holdover from mainframe database terminology. It really represents a basic activity of the user—finding the right data. In the case of this Users screen, it means finding a person to edit. There are many ways to select data for editing—SQL, Browse, and so on. For each screen you need to decide what methods are most appropriate. For the majority of basic AED screens, four navigation options are considered standard:

- **Next**, or any word that means move ahead one record in the table
- **Prior**, or any word that means move back one record in the table
- **Top**, first record of the table
- **Bottom**, last record of the table

By convention in FoxPro, these options are almost always available through push button controls.

These are simple options, but not very flexible. For bigger tables, or tables with more than one possible search criteria, some other form of navigation may be necessary. This could be as simple as a Browse picklist, or as complex as an RQBE window. In this sample screen a List button brings up a multifield Browse picklist so that selection can be made on Lastname, Firstname, or ID.

Record Options

The Record options are those that affect one record of a table at a time add, edit, delete. You may recall the discussion abut the stages of entering data in a GET from Chapter 8. This has some strong parallels for the record options:

- **Prior to Entry.** What options are open to a particular user? This may involve security rights or the nature of the data. In some cases deleting may not be allowed or appropriate. Some users may have edit clearance, but can't add or delete data. Whether certain options are visible or active in your screen depends on the rules you set up.
- **During Entry.** This is one of the major headaches of event-driven programming—what is allowed while the user is doing one of the three options (Add/Edit/Delete). In a highly controlled screen, the user isn't allowed to do anything else during these operations. In a truly event-driven scenario, the user is free to do anything, anytime. Which way a particular screen should go depends a lot on the nature of the data. In an accounting program, or other kinds of transaction entry, the user's options are usually tightly controlled. In a decision-support screen, where the user's own directions are important, the freedom of the event-driven model is appropriate. For a typical AED, usually a mixture of the two approaches are used. Perhaps the user is forced to complete an add, but may be allowed to do other things during an edit.
- **On Exit from Entry.** Somehow, sometime, a "during" stage needs to terminate. It can be by default, such as leaving the current window, or the completion of a process (like deletion). It can also be by intention, like pressing the Save or Cancel button. The point for the programmer is that you shouldn't leave any of the three record options in an indeterminate state forever. This is especially true if you are using indirect entry. Eventually the program has to know when to save or release the information in the memory variables.

The example screen makes distinctions between viewing, editing, and adding. The screen is always "viewable." Most of the data is visible all the time. However, adding new data or editing existing data must be initiated explicitly. Deleting is made even more explicit by "hiding" it in the Record screen menu.

Adding

Adding is virtually always an explicit action. A program has no way of knowing when the user may wish to add a new record to the table. In some programs, it's also important to test to see if the user is allowed to enter a new record. So somewhere, in the menu on a push button, or both the user needs to signal an "Add." The problems with an add isn't so much how to start it, but what goes on during the add and when to end it. When is the user done with entering data into a new record? When try to use a navigation button or push a Cancel key? Can they Delete the record while still adding? Can the user leave the current screen, or initiate a new program?

These are some of those minor questions that have major implications. When the user is "adding," what else are they permitted to do? If your program is restrictive, then it becomes *modal*. You are in "add mode," and other things may or may not be permitted. This can be quite contrary to the spirit of event-driven programming. On the other hand, there may be plenty of reasons why you don't want the user to leave a new record hanging. Maybe the information is needed by somebody else?

There is no one answer to the "Add" questions. A lot depends on the environment. If your application is multiuser, the impact of some of these questions can be much greater. And the programming becomes much more complex.

Editing

The editing capability has more options. In some screens it might make sense that any record that is visible, is by default available for editing. Then you don't need a push button or a menu option to signal for editing. In many cases completing an edit has far fewer implications than completing an add. If you're using direct entry, nothing is left hanging, should the user decide to go do something else. If you're using indirect entry, then you need to make decisions about what to do with those memory variables that contain the editing. Throw them away? Save them?

Testing to see whether something in fact has been edited is an important part of managing a data-entry screen. Most programmers develop (or appropriate) a routine to compare original table values with values in variables. (The software with this book has one too—ChkRead( ).)

Deleting

You're probably already familiar with the DELETE and RECALL procedures.

This is, of course, one of those basic maintenance chores that all tables need. When you build an AED screen, you should have made a couple of decisions about how to handle deletes.

First, are you using DELETE or are you creating blank records? The latter technique is a permanent and immediate change, the former gives you some breathing space between the DELETE and a PACK. The traditional route, DELETE, has the advantage of using RECALL. It has the disadvantage that you almost never do a PACK in the middle of the users work. PACKs almost always have to be done off-line, especially in multiuser situations, because they require locking the entire table. This makes them a maintenance job like reindexing.

The other option, blanking a record, is less of a maintenance hassle and is used in situations where a table is very dynamic (lots of records being added and removed). The blank records are reused (recycled) as "new" records, instead of using APPEND BLANK or INSERT.

This is usually faster than creating a new record. All the technique requires is a function that finds a blank record and uses it for new data (again one such function—ADDREC( )—is included with this book.)

Depending on how destructive a delete might be, and the type of delete you are using, you can decide where to put the delete option. If it's used a lot, and the individual deletions are not very significant, then you'd probably put it on a push button in the screen. Otherwise, the conventional wisdom is to put Delete in the screen menu, a move which forces a more deliberate selection. That's how the delete is handled in the example screen.

It's also considered part of good user-interface design to let the user know that a record has been deleted (if you are working with DELETE OFF so that deleted records can appear). A corollary move is to change the option (button or menu) to recall, if the record has already been deleted.

Screen Menu

In the days before the menu system of FoxPro 2.0, many screens did not have menus. With FoxPro for Windows, a menu-less screen is still possible, but considered very bad form. So virtually every screen has a menu, and usually the menu is customized for the screen. The best general advice for this kind of menu, which comes straight from the FoxPro manual, that it should contain options used only occasionally. To that could be added: it should contain menu equivalents for options also available on the screen.

In the case of the example screen, the menu carries two FoxPro "standard" menu options, System and Edit. The rest have been modified for a typical AED. The Record option provides access to the Save, Delete, and Navigational Options. Browse opens a Browse window of the same data as the screen, for quick overview and editing. Output provides access to a system Output Manager. And Done is an alternate to the Done push button at the bottom of the screen (a redundancy).

Chapter 13 covers the FoxPro Menu Builder and modifying menus on the fly.

Popup Options

As mentioned before, some screens just have too much information to be displayed all at once. You have several options: make a different screen, scroll "pages" through one screen, or provide a number of popup windows (or screens) that contain additional information. This last method is favored, mostly because it looks "modern," and FoxPro gives you such a wealth of tools to do it.

In an AED screen there are two kinds of popups that should be given special mention. The first type is the one that actually opens up a subscreen, probably from another table, in which the user can find support information or make a selection to bring back to the original screen. The second type are the various "list" devices available in FoxPro. Selection lists (picklists) are almost never displayed on a permanent basis, unless that's what the screen is all about. In an AED you typically have to use screen real estate wisely, and all listings are of the popup variety.

Starting the Screen Builder

Now comes the fun part, creating the screen in the Screen Builder.

Before you open the Screen Builder window, it's probably a good idea to first open all of the tables that will be needed, set index orders, and set any relations. The Screen Builder, like most of the other Power Tools can record the working table environment, and recreate it the next time you open a Screen Builder screen. Having the working files open, particularly with the aliases defined, is very handy when first building a screen with fields from the tables.

NOTE

While the Screen Builder will save the environment, meaning the setup for tables and relations, there are circumstances under which you might not want it to do so. A saved environment is in a sense hard coded into the Screen Builder files, and eventually into the code it produces. You may not want to have file paths of a specific directory structure included with your code, especially if your application is going to be distributed.

You can launch a new Screen Builder screen in any one of three ways:

1. **From the Project Manager.** For a new screen select **Add**, in the File Open dialog box select the file type as **Screen**, then select **New**. You'll be asked to give the screen a name. Be sure to enter (or select) the correct subdirectory (path) and then a file name.
2. **From the system menu**, select **File**, **New**, **Screen**, **New**. You will be reminded on the way out to give the new screen a name.
3. **In the Command window** type **CREATE SCREEN <path + screen name>**.

As you create a screen, your work is stored in Screen Builder files. These have the extensions .SCX (a .DBF by another name) and a .SCT (a .FPT memo file). The .SCX contains the basic parameters of the screen elements and coordinates. The .SCT memo file contains almost all the text and code—names, conditions, clauses. Because these are really standard FoxPro database files, you can open them for inspection or even modification (if you have the risk taker's mentality).

Modifying an existing screen file also has three routes:

1. **From the Project Manager**, select or double-click on the screen to be edited. This is by far the simplest method.
2. **From the System Menu**, select **File**, **Open**, and select the file name.
3. **In the Command window**, type **MODIFY SCREEN <path + screen name>**.

As suggested before, you'd need a darn good reason not to run all your screens through the Project Manager.

Compared to the original DOS version of the Screen Builder, the FoxPro for Windows version shows off the difference between a text oriented system and a GUI. The tool box (more usually called a toolbar) is probably the most obvious visual change. But underneath, this is a thoroughly graphic design surface that gives you control over color, fonts, windowing, sizing of elements, and other aspects of screen display. The Screen Builder dialog box is displayed in Figure 13.6.

Figure 13.6
The Screen Builder dialog box.

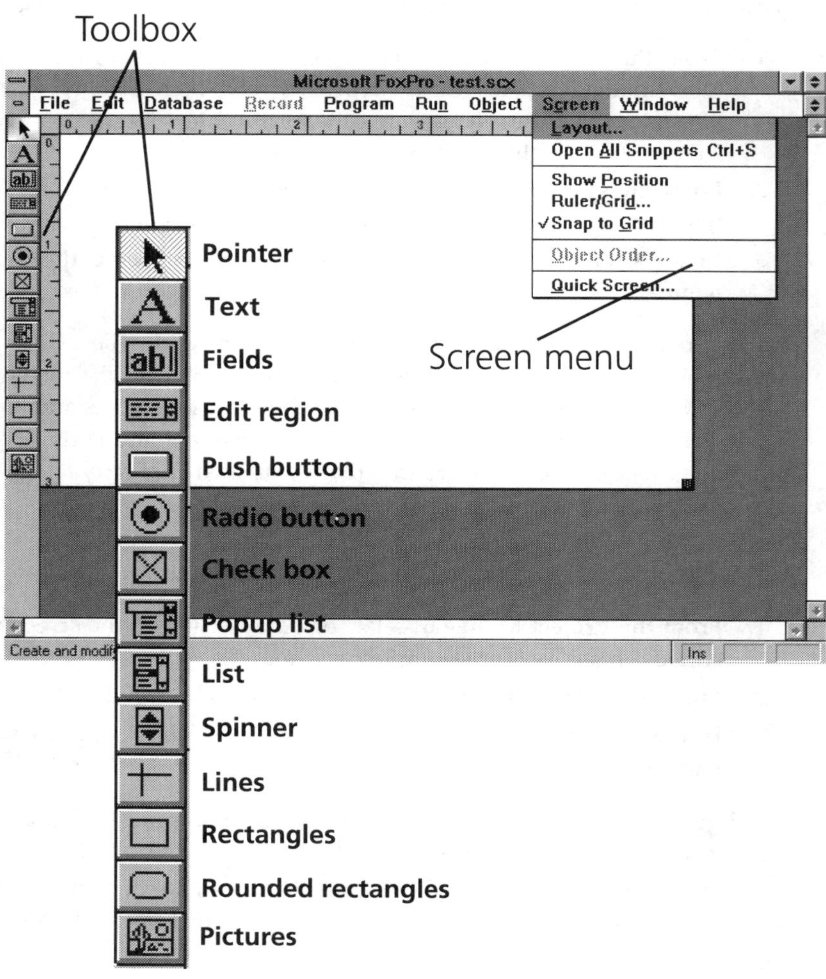

The "strategy" for building a screen, if you care to look at it that way, is usually to work from the surface down. That is, layout the basic screen and window conditions. Populate the screen with the various objects—fields, buttons, pictures. Then start adding the logic and programming "underneath." But this is a matter of personal preference. Some people like to work from the structural and programming aspects more than from screen design. It doesn't much matter.

What does matter is sticking to the original purpose of the screen, (data entry in the case of an AED), making it as easy and correct as possible.

Layout

The Screen Builder itself is in a window. In fact, it takes quite a bit of room. Enough so that you can't quite see a full screen window. In cases where you are working with a full screen or a full screen window, you'll find the Screen Layout window an absolute necessity.

Setting the Window

Like grabbing a piece of paper big enough for your drawing, or cutting the canvas for a painting, usually one of the first steps in building a screen is to choose the size of the window. You can do this in the main Screen Builder dialog box by grabbing the lower right corner of the default window size and dragging the area until you get it to the size you want. However, if you want a window to be full screen, or position a window in the full screen, it works better to use the Screen Layout dialog box, shown in Figure 13.7.

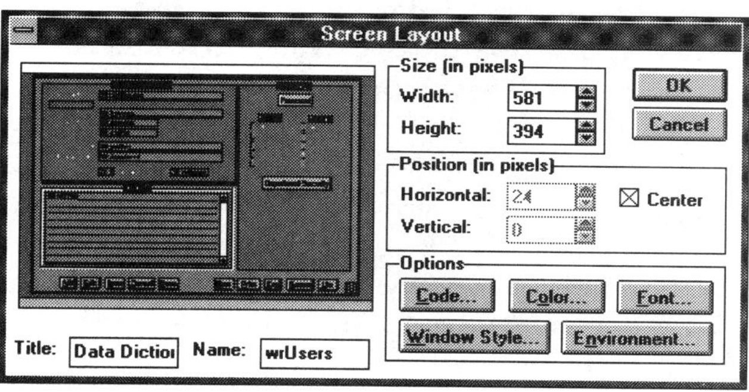

Figure 13.7 *The Screen Layout dialog box.*

This is reached through the Screen menu: Screen, Layout. The window area on the left is a scaled version of the full FoxPro screen area. You can move the window area around the screen or size it any way up to the full size of the screen. This is the best way to get a sense of proportion for how your screen elements are going to look, without actually generating code and running a program.

If you need more precision than the scaled window provides, there are the spinners on the right side of the Screen Layout dialog box that can be used for precisely setting size and location of a window on a pixel by pixel basis. These aren't needed very often.

Of much more importance are the five push buttons in the Options area. Of these, the Code button is the home of the READ clauses, and the other screen code areas. It's crucial not only to operating any particular screen, but also to the structure of your applications. We'll get back to it soon. However, for the moment, let's stick with things related to setting the screen.

Besides the size of the window, the other most basic choice is the window style, or type of window. Selecting the Window Style button brings up the Window Style dialog box, shown in Figure 13.8.

Figure 13.8
The Window Style dialog box.

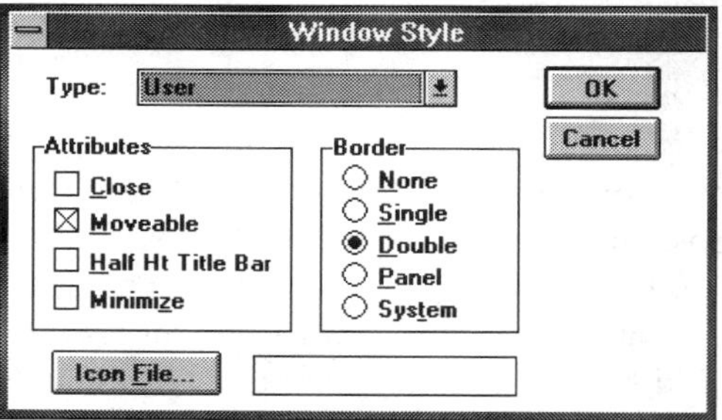

The popup list at the top lists five window styles: Desktop, System, Dialog, Alert, and User. The first four are FoxPro standard windows. Actually, one of these is *not* a FoxPro window—the Desktop. It's a Windows window. Desktop is the term used for the main FoxPro window, which when you get down to the code level becomes known as the SCREEN.

Interestingly, if you select the Desktop window style, FoxPro generates the command MODIFY WINDOW SCREEN, which is the only way you can modify the attributes of the main FoxPro window. While not exactly the same as the old DOS screen (the entire surface of your monitor's display area), this is the closest thing to it. For most applications, you treat the main FoxPro window as "ground zero"—the basic screen. As a rule you don't do much to modify it, or even put much into it. Most of the action in your applications resides in windows (the screens built by the Screen Builder), which sit on top of the Desktop.

The significance of the other three standard windows—System, Dialog, and Alert—is their border, and characteristics. If you choose to use one of these, instead of a user-defined window, you are accepting their given characteristics as described in Table 13.1.

Table 13.1
Characteristics of a user-defined window.

Type	Attributes	Border
System	Close Move (FLOAT) Minimize	System (PANE with system controls)
Dialog	Move (FLOAT)	Double
Alert	Move (FLOAT)	Double

Other than the System type, these are of dubious practical value (at least for now). The user-defined window type is more flexible.

NOTE

Be aware that the Window Style dialog box does not provide all of the available options for window definition. Missing are GROW and ZOOM. For this and several other reasons, some programmers prefer to define their own windows. While this presents some difficulties in coordinating with the Screen Builder, it is an option.

If you select one of the window styles that support the Minimize option (system or user-defined windows), you can use the Icon File push button to select a bitmap or icon file for an image to be placed on the Windows minimize icon (the icon your window is reduced to when minimized). This too is hard coded, which means the path and filename are coded directly into your program—a potential problem.

If you choose to accept one of the FoxPro window styles, then you need to consider naming and titling the window. For this you go back to the Screen Layout window.

Naming Windows

Naming windows and procedures in the Screen Builder is the subject of considerable debate. The official FoxPro stance is to let the Screen Builder do it. When you generate a program from the Screen Builder, it creates generic names for all of your windows and procedures. They look like this: _QEB0159GM. Microsoft maintains this prevents duplicate naming in your application and thus prevents clashes and conflicts. To which many programmers respond, "Balderdash. With names like these *we* can't figure out what procedure or window does what. That makes coding and debugging much harder. Besides if we can't keep a few dozen window and procedure names straight, we shouldn't be programming."

In recognition of this naming controversy, FoxPro has provided an alternate approach to both window and procedure names. These are the #WNAME and #NAME *generator directives*. These and the other pre-processor and generator directives are covered in their own section in this chapter.

The convention of this book is to specifically name all windows. Putting titles on windows is more a matter of design or "window dressing," with the exception of Browse windows, where as you will see, the title actually becomes the name of the window.

Screen Color and Fonts

Another of the push buttons in the Options section of the Screen Layout dialog box, is Color. This brings up the Screen Color dialog box, shown in Figure 13.9.

There are three things of note about this color selection:

1. **It is limited to sixteen colors.** This is the lowest common denominator, for running on standard VGA equipment. If you're playing it safe, then

use these colors and forget about it. If, however, you have an application that cries out for more subtlety in coloration—and you're sure the recipient hardware can handle it—then this sixteen-color palette isn't going to cut it. Unfortunately, you're going to have to manually define all your windows and add your own color schemes (probably in RGB format).

2. **This is the default window coloration for the background.** Other objects placed into the window will take on this default color, but you're free to define completely different colors for each and every object on the screen. This often happens, and it does take a lot of time playing with color combinations.
3. **Wallpaper, the MS Windows jargon for a background picture, is also a "color" option.** These can be a lot of fun to work with, but, from a design point of view, be careful. It may look great, but if the user can't see the text or entry areas on top of the wallpaper, you're not doing them any favors. In other words, most wallpaper is distracting. Use it with discretion.

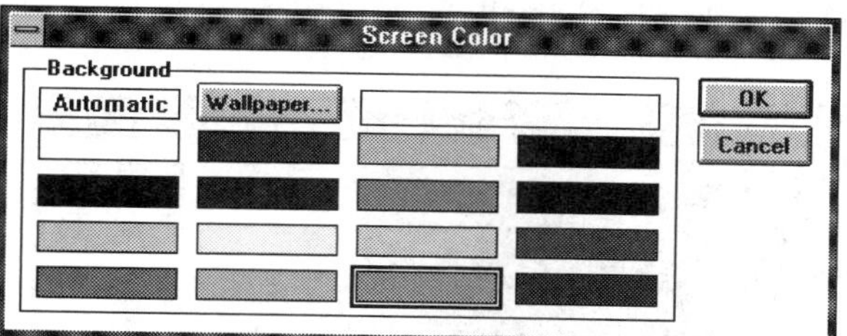

Figure 13.9 The Screen Color dialog box.

The final window layout push button is Font... This brings up the now familiar FoxPro font list, shown in Figure 13.10.

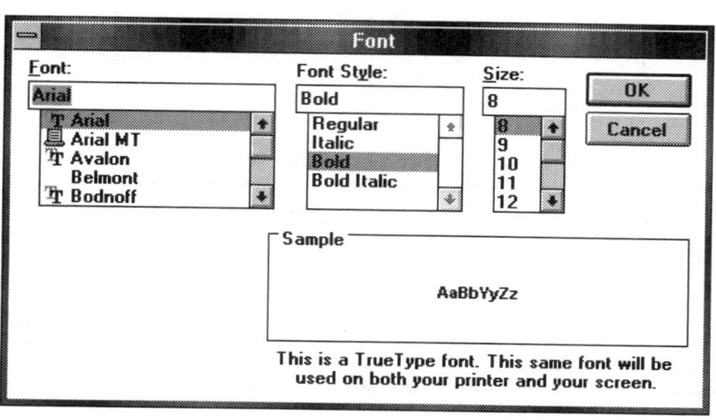

Figure 13.10 The Font dialog box.

Like the Screen Color dialog box, a selection made here is for the default text font. You can override the setting in any particular screen object. In designing some applications, it may be helpful to standardize on one to four fonts as "base" fonts, depending on the type of window. This can be another visual clue for the user. Just be sure that the fonts you choose are going to be available on all the target computers.

Arranging Screens

You might think that the Screen Layout dialog box, with its location and size coordinates, and the scaled layout window would be the place to determine how your window is to be arranged on the screen. Well, it is and it isn't. Most developers stumble on this one from time to time. There is another place where you can specify the location of windows and that's in the Arrange Screens dialog box of the screen generation process, shown in Figure 13.11.

Figure 13.11 The Arrange Screens dialog box.

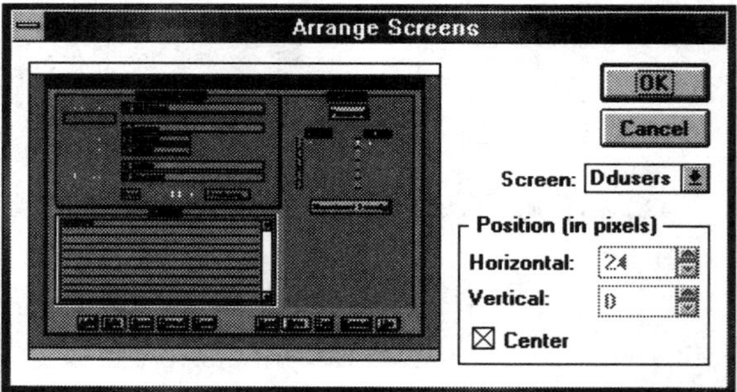

This can be reached via the system menu: Program, Generate, Arrange. But don't use this route.

WARNING

Using Arrange Screen, when coming from system menu, does not save the positioning. The next time you come back to generate, the settings will be gone. Only by going into Screen Generation through the Program Manager will your screen coordinates be saved.

While this window was designed to help you coordinate the placement of multiple windows on the screen—which is why it was attached to the generator and not the other screen windowing options—it can be used for any or the only window in the screen set. The window location values set here override any others. All you need to do is move the window around in the scale layout, until you get it in position, and then use the Save option in the menu.

The Basic Window

Figure 13.12 shows an example of a typical starting point for a screen. It is the basic layout for the users screen with some sectioning for design.

Figure 13.12
Basic layout for users screen.

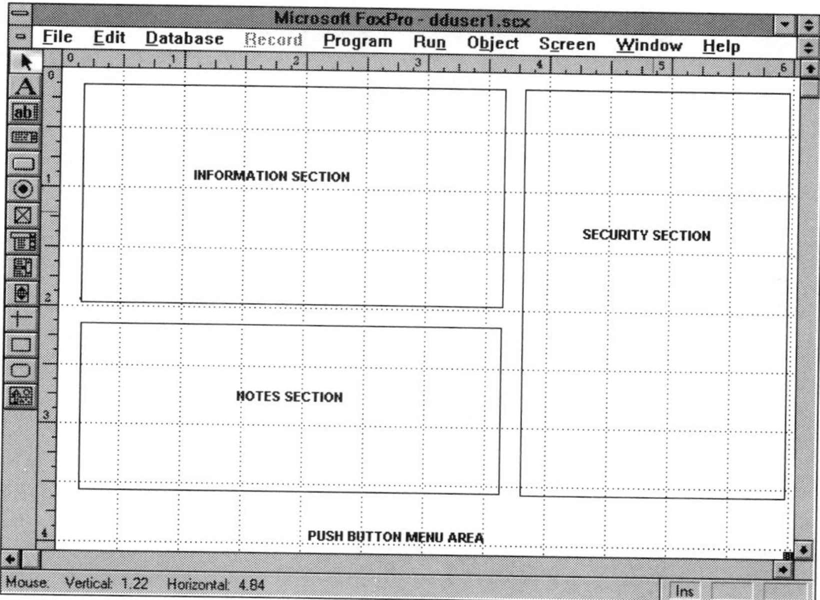

This is a user-defined window, named wrUsers, sized smaller than the main FoxPro window. It has a background color of cyan (W+/BG) and a default font of Arial. This was the easy part.

Screen Objects

Once the basic screen shape has been determined, you can set about putting the various screen objects into it. Hopefully you've had a look at the preceding chapters, particularly 8 and 11, that cover the screen objects in code level detail. That should leave the discussion here to concentrate on how these elements are orchestrated in the Screen Builder.

With a data entry (AED) screen, the logical place to start is with the fields from the underlying table(s). You need to look at the structure of these tables, or better, a printout from a data dictionary so you can make decisions about which fields are to be included in the screen, and what kind of screen objects should be used to present them. Of course, some experimentation is likely, but it is possible to make a list of fields and identify what FoxPro screen objects to use. For example in the Users screen, it looks like this:

Field	Field Name	Type	Width	Object	Validation
1	STAFFID	Character	3	GET	no dupes
2	NETNAME	Character	10	GET	
3	FIRSTNAME	Character	20	GET	
4	MIDINITS	Character	20	GET	
5	LASTNAME	Character	35	GET	no dupes
6	FULLNAME	Character	45	GET	
7	BIRTHDATE	Date	8	GET	valid date
8	DEPARTMENT	Character	30	GET	
9	POSITION	Character	40	GET	
10	PASSWORD	Character	8	DIALOG	encrypted
11	SECURITY1	Numeric	1	RADIO BUTTON	
12	SECURITY2	Numeric	1	RADIO BUTTON	
13	NOTES	Memo	10	EDIT REGION	
14	FLAG	Character	1	N/A	
15	STATUS	Character	1	N/A	
16	OPERATOR	Character	3	N/A	
17	SYSDATE	Date	8	N/A	

Using this sort of thing as a guide, you start putting the fields into the Screen Builder window with the Field tool.

Field Objects

In some cases it may be faster to use Quick Screen to dump all of the fields into the window, then rearrange them. You need to have already opened the Screen Builder before this option is available. Then select Screen, Quick Screen to open the dialog box shown in Figure 13.13.

Figure 13.13
The Quick Screen dialog box.

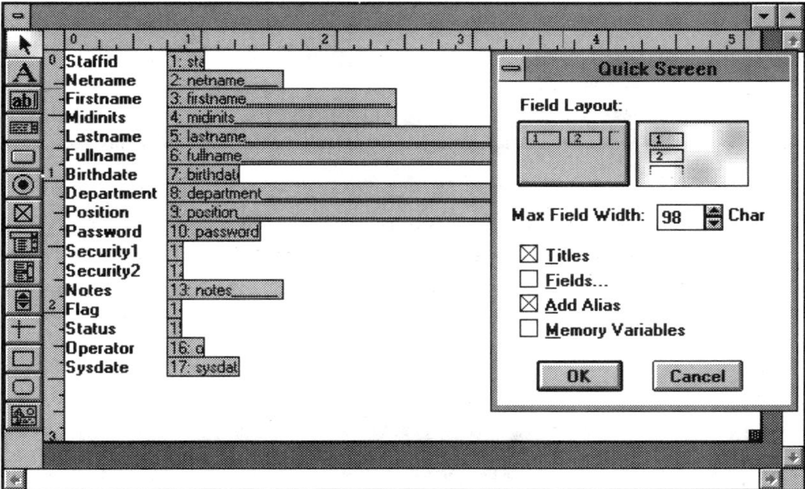

If you haven't opened the appropriate table, the File Open dialog box is displayed for you to select one. Although they're usually the default, be sure that Titles and Add Alias have been selected (and you've opened the table with the right alias, of course). You may also want to use the Fields option to select fields to be included, although its often quicker to simply delete the ones you don't want from the screen. Then the fields appear on the screen. Of course, you may need to spend considerable time moving the fields around and renaming the titles. Still, with a new screen and a modest number of fields, this is usually a good start.

Otherwise you can always use the single-field approach. You'll have to resort to this anyway as you define the attributes for individual fields. To define a new field object this way, select the Field tool from the tool box and click on the area where you want the field to be located. This automatically opens the Field dialog box, shown in Figure 13.14. (Double clicking or selecting an existing field has the same effect.)

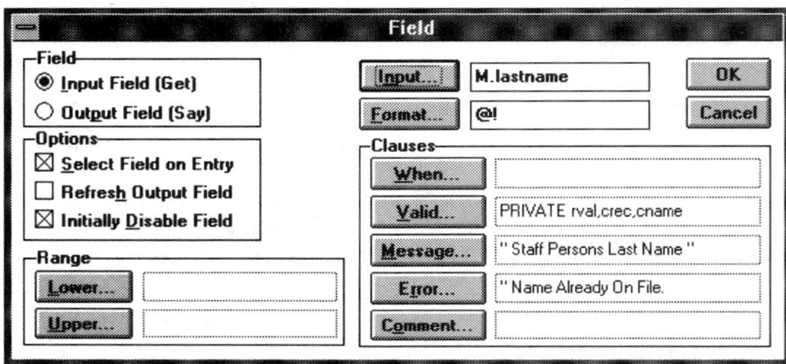

Figure 13.14 *The Field dialog box.*

By default, new fields are marked as Input Fields (GET). If you have any that are for display only, change the Field radio button to Output Field (SAY). If the field hasn't already been selected, then move to the Input... push button, and either enter the field name into the edit box, or use the button to summon the Choose Field/Variable dialog box, shown in Figure 13.15.

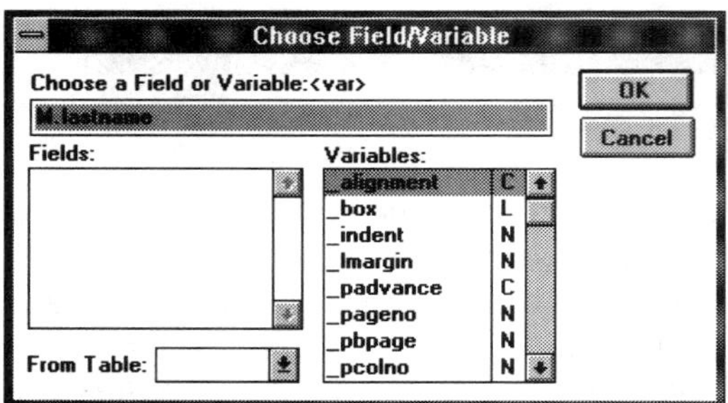

Figure 13.15 *The Choose Field/Variable dialog box.*

You've probably seen this dialog box before in other contexts. Select your field from one of the available tables, or choose one of the variables. One of the weaknesses of this dialog box is that it doesn't know anything about field memory variables (the m. variety), even though this may be the most common form for fields in the Screen Builder. If you're using the indirect entry method with SCATTER/GATHER, you'll have to edit each field and put the m. prefix in front of the field name, then scramble back to the Field dialog box. There's more work to do.

The Format button and edit region are there to specify any PICTURE or FUNCTION options for the field. Most developers learn the common options (@!, or @D) by heart, but need to use the Format lookup for the lesser options. The Format dialog box is displayed in Figure 13.16.

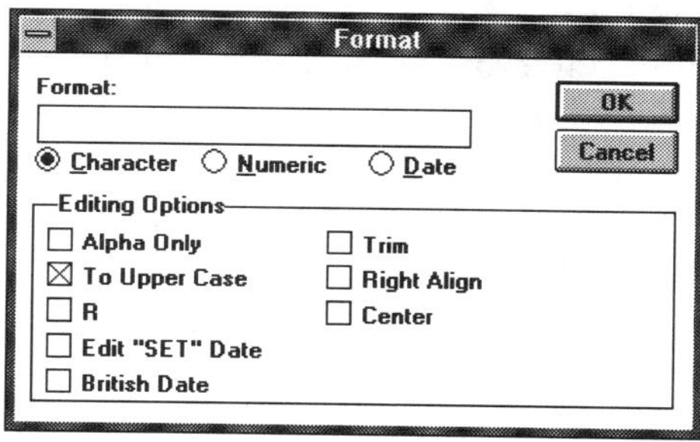

Figure 13.16 *The Format dialog box.*

There are three forms for this window, character, numeric, and date. These are all nearly identical to the format windows that appear for the Report Writer and other places in FoxPro. The Field dialog box also has one of the options in a check box over in the options area on the left—Select Field on Entry. This is equivalent to the PICTURE "@K" option.

Also in the options area are check boxes for Initially Disable Field and Refresh Output Field. The disable option, which puts the DISABLE clause on the GET, is used most frequently in screens where entry is not allowed until Edit is selected (as in the User Screen example). The refresh option is a curious little workaround.

The Screen Builder and FoxPro makes a big distinction between GETs and SAYs in terms of what they are in the screen. A GET is a GET, but a SAY is an object, at least as far as SHOW GET or SHOW GETS are concerned. These commands are designed to redisplay a GET field, or all fields. But they don't work with SAYs. In fact, the only way to refresh a SAY is to use good old-fashioned coding—reissue the SAY entirely. In its thoughtful way, FoxPro decided that rather than leave this loose end for the programmer, they'd automate the process of refreshing SAYs. If you check this box., the Screen

Builder puts the @..SAY code for the variable into the SHOW clause of the READ. Since this clause is executed every time the command SHOW GETS is issued, all the SAYs are redisplayed at the same time. This is nice, except a lot of programmers don't realize this code exists.

The other clauses of the GET—When... (WHEN), Valid...(VALID), Message... (MESSAGE), Error...(ERROR)—all look and behave like their normally coded counterparts. The RANGE clause is also present with its Lower and Upper expressions available as push buttons to the Expression Builder.

The Screen Builder doesn't bring anything new to the game of supporting and controlling the user at the GET level. You need to know what entry restrictions are needed for each field, and write VALID and WHEN expressions, UDFs, or procedures accordingly. What *is* different in the Screen Builder is the way these expressions are entered and stored—in the *code snippet*.

Snippets

When snippets were first introduced with FoxPro 2.0 for DOS, there was much collective scratching of heads among developers. Most had heard of *code fragments*, but not *snippets*. You see, Fox had a problem. The Screen Builder was designed to automate the process of coding GET clauses and other elements for the screen. Traditionally these had been handled by UDFs. But Fox didn't want to force users to write functions. So they made it possible in the Screen Builder to write code that worked with VALID or the other clauses, but that was neither an expression (something that could be included on the command line), nor a UDF. While the Screen Builder would eventually *generate* a function, it seemed to Fox these bits of code couldn't rightly be called a function or a procedure. So Fox decided to call them snippets. The Code Snippet dialog box is displayed in Figure 13.17.

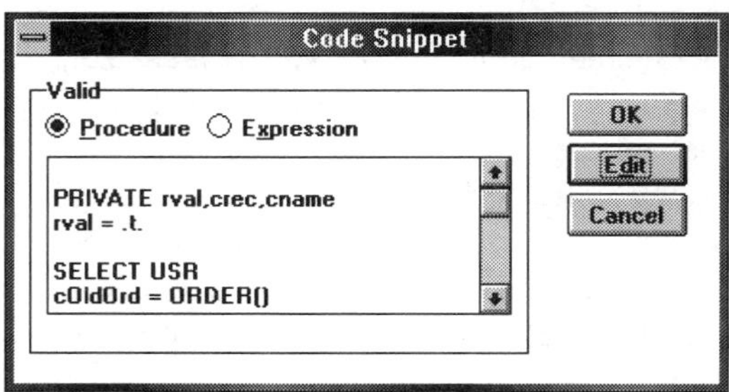

Figure 13.17 *The Code Snippet dialog box.*

A Snippet window shows up every time you select one of the Field Clause buttons (that goes for all forms of the GET). You'll notice the two radio buttons for Procedure and Expression. These are important. An Expression can be an expression or a function, but a Procedure can be an expression, a function, or a snippet. Now let's unravel the lingo.

The real object of a snippet is to return true or false (.t. or .f.) to its clause. For example, in the real code a VALID clause must either have an expression or a function that returns .t. or .f. The snippet may not look like real code, but it eventually has to come out that way. So whatever you choose, Procedure or Expression, the end result has to be the same.

If you choose Expression, then you need to construct a normal FoxPro logical expression (for example, `m.age > 50 AND m.startdate > CTOD("12/1/92")`. Or else you enter a function *without the = sign*, just like you would with a function after a clause:

```
IIF( m.age > 50 AND m.startdate > CTOD("12/1/92"),.t., .f.).
```

If you choose Procedure, then the rules change a bit because you have to keep in mind the Screen Builder is going to turn it into a function for you. That means you can't put the FUNCTION command into the snippet code, because the generator does the same thing and you get errors. You also can't use a PARAMETER statement, because you have no way to tell the generator to include arguments in the function call. However, for all practical purposes you are writing a function, and you have to think like it. For example, if you want to have a standalone function in your Procedure snippet code, it has to be prefixed with the equal sign (=), just like it would if you put it in any other type of code. You could even include a RETURN statement, if you're very careful about how it is used.

Nevertheless, when it comes to code snippets, think UDFs (minus the FUNCTION and PARAMETER), and you'll do well.

You also have the alternative of building real UDFs for the clauses, and putting only the function call (as an Expression) in the code snippet. These UDFs can then be stored anywhere—in a procedure file, in the Procedure section of the screen, or in another program file altogether. All that FoxPro cares is that it can find the function somewhere on its program path.

The Data Entry Fields

With the addition of the GET fields and color, the screen is beginning to take shape, as in Figure 13.18 on the next page.

Figure 13.18
The User screen.

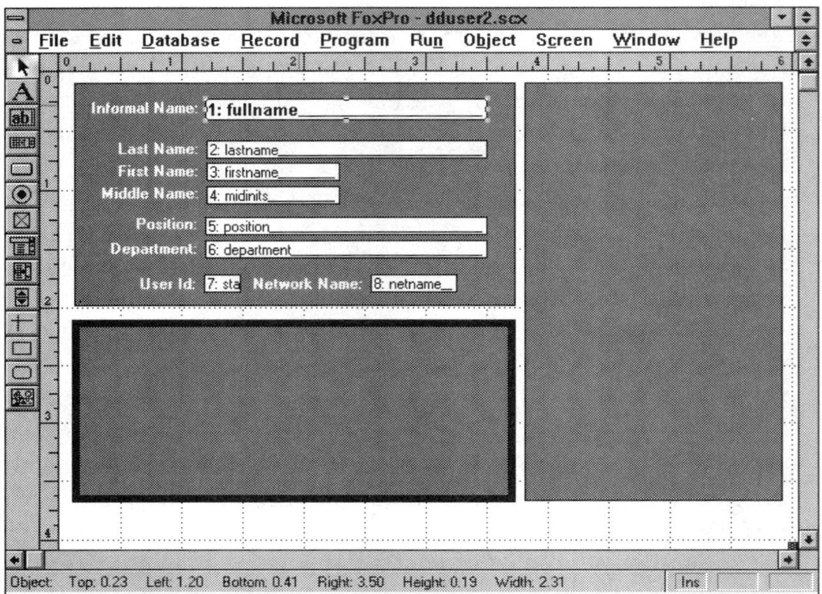

Next come the Controls. These serve the dual function of gathering more table information and operating as controls.

Edit Regions

Placing an Edit Region into your screen is usually making a link between a memo field and the FoxPro text editor. It doesn't have to be a memo field though. You can use an Edit Region to enter text into a standard character field or even a variable. The choice of an Edit Region should be based more on the need of the user to edit the text entry than on the size of the entry.

Like all of the options in the Toolbox, using the Edit Region tool is very simple: grab it with the mouse, and draw the outline of the area you want the Edit Region to inhabit. When you release the area, the Edit Region dialog box is displayed as in Figure 13.19.

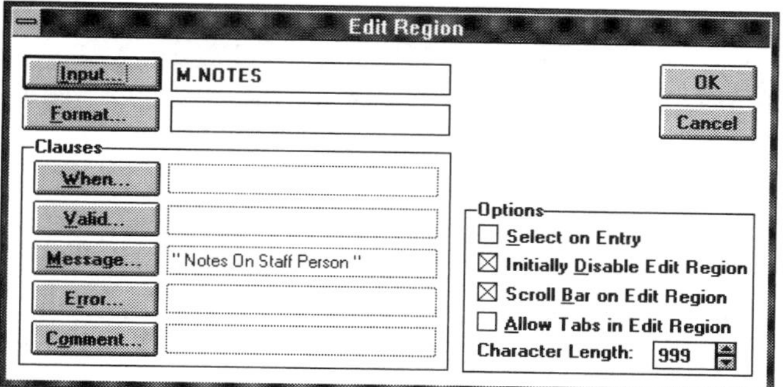

Figure 13.19
The Edit Region dialog box.

The Screen Builder's Edit Region is the @..EDIT command. You'll recognize the usual GET clauses, along with the Screen Builder's wording for the field or variable to be used—Input. The Format area let's you specify the two available FUNCTION options: I for centered text, and J for right-justified text. (Chapter 11 covers the use of the clauses and other options at the code level.) One edit region is used in the screen example. There's not much to it, except in most cases you'll find the region needs extra boxing or highlighting, in this case some simulated 3-D edging.

Controls

In some ways using the word Controls for the variety of specialized @..GET commands is a misnomer. Only a couple of them are regularly used for program control. Most of them are just what their names imply: They get information from the user. As a group, however, these are among the most interesting screen elements in the FoxPro Toolbox. With names like Spinners, Check Boxes, and Popups, you could expect no less.

NOTE

The value returned by many of the Controls (Push Buttons, Radio Buttons, Check Buttons) is either character or numeric, depending on the initialization value of the GET variable. Character returns the value of the prompt selected and numeric returns the order number of the prompt selected. The usual practice is to define these variables in the Setup area of the Screen Builder code, and assign them the data type you want to use. In most cases, it's clearer if the returned value is the prompt of the selection (character type variable).

The Screen Builder puts a friendly interface on the underlying syntax. In some cases the correspondence is quite clear. In other cases Microsoft has done some translating to make the rather cryptic GET options easier to understand. Following is a quick run through the highlights of these Controls.

Push Buttons

Push Buttons are mostly the "do something" controls. They are usually part of a Push Button menu, where a series of options are presented, or they are used like a gateway to underlying information or processing subroutines. They can also be just a simple multiple-choice type of screen element, but the evolving FoxPro conventions seem to have consigned them mostly to the first two uses. Again, while these kinds of design decisions are partly a matter of taste, the consistency of user interface issue is probably paramount.

Like all the other Toolbox items, you create a Push Button (or a series of them) by selecting the Push Button tool and outlining the area where you want the Push Button to go. This brings up the Push Button dialog box, shown in Figure 13.20.

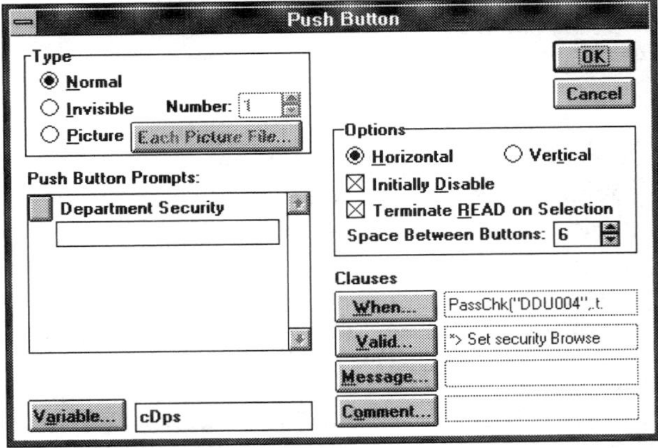

Figure 13.20
The Push Button dialog box.

You can actually create three kinds of buttons—a normal text button, an invisible button under an area, or a picture button with an icon or bitmap image on it. The buttons can be created one at a time or in a series by adding to the Push Button prompts list. Remember that you can use the hotkey "\<", termination "\?", and default "\!" symbols before a prompt (see Chapter 11 for details).

The VALID command has more significance here than in most other GETs. Other places, the VALID checks to see if any entry is correct or provide other kinds of support. With a Push Button, it usually is the clause that actually does something. If the clause is part of a Push Button menu, the VALID is usually an extended CASE statement to process the selection:

```
*> Push Button Menu VALID
DO CASE
CASE cTest = "Enter"
  DO TestEnter
CASE cTest = "Reject"
  DO TestDel
CASE cTest = "Hold"
  DO TestHold
CASE cTest = "Re-Process"
  DO TestProc
ENDCASE
```

If the Push Button is of the gateway type, then the code might look like this snippet, which summons a Browse window for data entry in a different table:

```
*> Set security Browse
DEFINE WINDOW wbUsec FROM 15,50 TO 30,68 SYSTEM COLOR SCHEME 10
;
  TITLE "Dept.Security" FLOAT CLOSE FONT "Arial",9

SELECT USC          && switch to user security table

BROWSE FIELDS ;
  DEPT:F:V=DepLook(),;
  SEC1:H="Acc",;
  SEC2:H="Act" ;
  KEY M.staffid ;
  WINDOW wbUsec

RELEASE WINDOW wbUsec
SELECT USR
```

As with all of the controls that can take a bitmap or icon image, you are required by the Screen Builder to select or enter a complete path and filename for the image (and the file has to currently exist). This path is then hard coded into the output like this:

```
LOCFILE("\ddwin\bmp\badguy.ico","BMP|ICO","Where is badguy?")
```

When your application is running, if this file doesn't exist, has been damaged, or moved to a subdirectory off the FoxPro search path, the user is dropped into the LOCFILE routine, which is the FoxPro File Open dialog box. In short, they'll be asked to go find your missing file. If they don't or can't, they'll get a syntax error. Of course this same potential problem exists with any of the files used by your application. But over the years, ways of dealing with it for database files and memory files have evolved. Now, you may put yourself in the position of using Picture Buttons throughout your application—potentially dozens of files—which increases the risk.

Radio Buttons

There a strong family resemblance in the way Radio Buttons and Push Buttons are constructed by the Screen Builder (not in how they look, of course). Radio Buttons are mostly used for "one of" selections. This could be as a permanent listing on the screen, or like a Push Button menu, or simply exclusionary choices where only one option can be active at a time. The Radio Button dialog box is displayed in Figure 13.21.

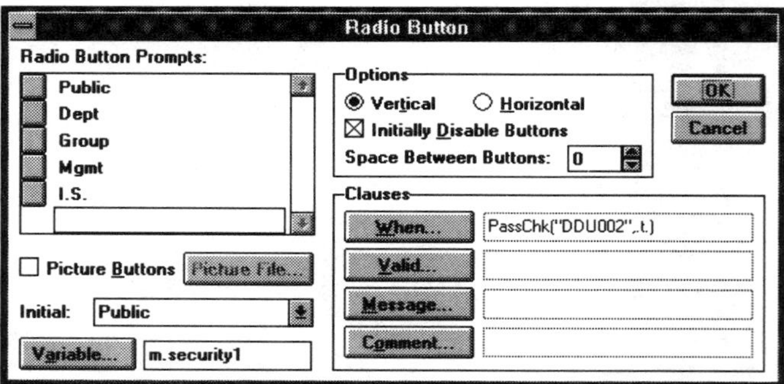

Figure 13.21 *The Radio Button dialog box.*

Check Boxes

Check Boxes are also closely related to Radio Buttons and Push Buttons in their construction, with the major exception that Check Boxes are built one at a time. As you can see in Figure 13.22, the Check Box dialog box is quite simple.

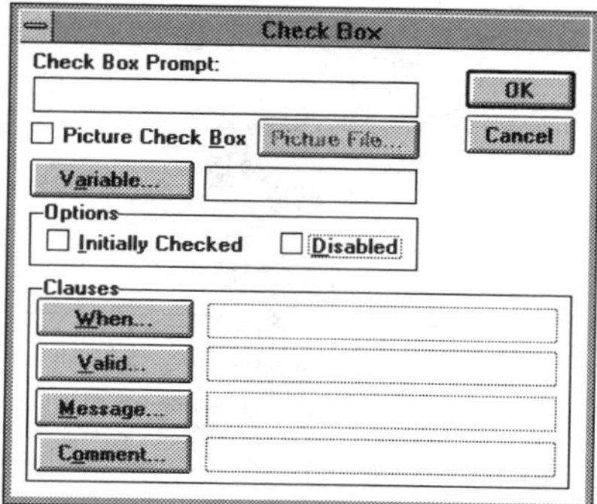

Figure 13.22
The Check Box dialog box.

Check Boxes are the equivalent of a yes/no GET, and are often used as part of a dialog box or screen presentation where the user needs to turn things on and off.

Popups and Lists

It's a bit of a stretch to call a Popup List, or a List a Control. These are screen elements to present lists for users to choose from. The List is a permanently visible object on the screen, whereas the Popup...pops-up. Otherwise the Screen Builder provides a very similar interface for creating each of them, shown in Figures 13.23 and 13.24.

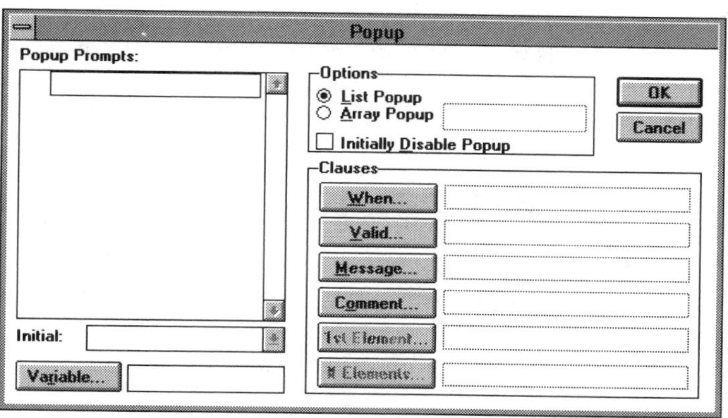

Figure 13.23
The Popup dialog box.

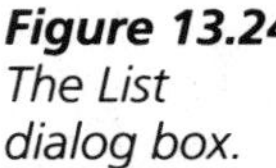

Figure 13.24 *The List dialog box.*

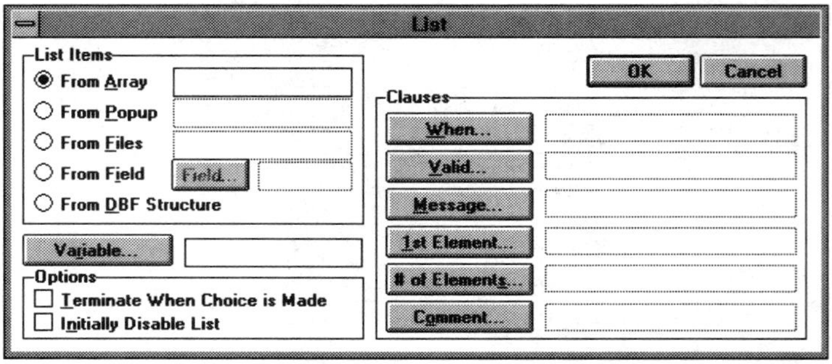

The major decision for both of these is how to load the items in the list. Using arrays, often in combination with an SQL-SELECT statement, is probably the simplest method. The Popup is handy for very short and static lists, since you can code them into the Popup Prompts section.

Spinners

Spinners are the newest member of the control family, being introduced with FoxPro for Windows. Spinners probably represent the high watermark of the mouse. In the quest for that totally mouseable interface, in which users need never sully fingers with touching a keyboard, the biggest stumbling block was numbers and their brethren, dates. The Spinner was the answer. (However, a piece of advice—keep Spinners away from data-entry people. They hate them.)

Like all of the controls in the Toolbox, adding a Spinner to the screen is nothing more than a stroke with the Spinner tool. The resulting Spinner dialog box, shown in Figure 13.25, looks quite familiar.

Figure 13.25 *The Spinner dialog box.*

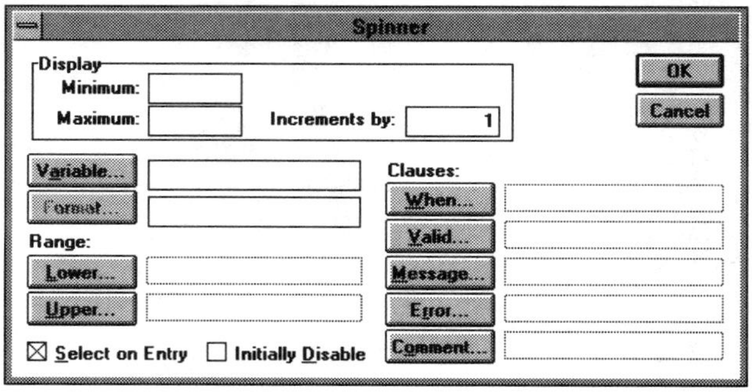

You'll notice that there are two named areas for Min/Max or Upper/Lower. The one for Display is just that. When moving the Spinner with a mouse, this sets the upper and lower limit of the spin mechanism. But if the user isn't using the mouse (!), that won't trap numbers out of a range, so you need to set the Range Upper/Lower values as well. But wait, even that might not quite do it, because neither of these trap a default value out of the range—you'd need to use the VALID to catch that.

The Spinner is a convenient point to do some explaining of how a GET of any kind fits into it's own little world within the confines of a Screen Builder dialog box, and within the slightly larger confines of a Screen Builder screen. It also shows just how much deliberation can go into even a "simple" screen element.

The work begins, more or less, with the notion that you need a way to get a date from a user, and the usual GET date field is too dull. Ah! You can use Spinners. Three of them, one each for month, day, and year. Quickly, you palm the mouse and whip the Spinner tool into service. The first Spinner is for the months. Up comes the Spinner dialog box, and you pause a moment.

Spinners can define numeric ranges. Months should be set for one to twelve. Days from one to thirty one, but not all months have thirty one days (something to work on there). Should the years have two or four digits (93 or 1993), which would determine the range? (You suddenly realize that you're re-inventing the wheel. The @D picture would take care of all of this date checking automatically. But nothing deters the creative programmer.) Pressing on, you define the Display Minimum as 1 and the Maximum as 12 for the month Spinner, and the same for the Range values.

Next you create the day Spinner. The Display and Range Min/Lower are easy, 1. The Display Max is 31, because there is no other way to qualify it. Range Upper is where you must trap entries that don't fit the month. Then you think, "What month?" If the user hasn't entered a month number, your routine has no idea what days for the month are appropriate. Another decision, do you force the user to enter a month before you'll let them enter a day? Okay. Even Spinners follow rules. So you decide to put something into the When... clause that won't allow day entry without the month already existing. You need to check the value of the month Spinner. Which makes you realize that so far you haven't defined any variables to hold the users input.

In the Screen Builder, defining variables is usually a two-part process. First, and most obvious, you have to define a variable for the Spinner dialog box. It won't let you exit without one (unless you cancel the whole thing). If you're content to let FoxPro define a default value for the variable, you're done after naming the variable in the Spinner dialog box. However, if you want to set your own defaults or manipulate the variable in other ways, you should go to the Setup area of the screen.

In the Setup code, you would define three variables (as in the example above) for month, day, year. All of them are numeric, and you can assign them values as you define them. The fourth variable may or may not be necessary in a particular application. However, it occurs to you that the numbers collected from the Spinners do not constitute a legitimate FoxPro date. They need to be converted, and that conversion should be stored in a specific variable.

The Setup variable definitions are very crude (they work, but crude). A more helpful and better defined variation would be:

```
REGIONAL nDay, nMonth, nYear, dDate
nMonth = MONTH(DATE())
nDay = DAY(DATE())
 nYear = VAL(SUBSTR(LTRIM(STR(YEAR(DATE()))),3,2))
dDate = {}
```

The date functions are guaranteed to send you scrounging through the *Language Reference* manual. They are used to assign default values from the current date. Also each variable is defined as REGIONAL, which takes care of any scoping problems for the Screen Builder. This is one of those places where your screen objects become linked to the larger activity of the Screen.

After this probably necessary diversion, you have three variables to use in the Spinner dialog boxes. You're also ready to create some code expressions for the day Spinner. The first expression goes into the When... clause: NOT EMPTY(nMonth). This prevents the user from entering a day without a number in the month. The second expression goes into the Range Maximum value:

```
IIF(INLIST(nMonth,1,3,5,7,8,10,12),31,IIF(nMonth=2,28,30))
```

This is the logic to check for the number of days in a given month number. Notifying the user of an out of range entry is taken care of by FoxPro, as long as you have left SET NOTIFY ON. This takes care of the day Spinner.

The year Spinner is similar. If you've chosen a two-digit year, then the Display and Range values are 0 and 99. After the user has entered the year, it's time for a little processing. If you want a real date out of the entry, for example to put into a date field in a table, then the VALID clause is used to code the example shown above. This checks to see if it has three numbers to work with, and then coverts them first into characters, and then into a date—loading the date variable in the process.

That takes care of the logic involved. All that's left is to dress up the screen visuals a bit.

Graphic Objects

Text is a graphic object. In many ways its a more malleable and expressive graphic object than most screen pictures. Using the Text tool, lay out the words. Select Object from the system menu to assign your text a font, a size, a color. The text takes on a personality and becomes a very potent graphic object. The Screen Builder makes it easy.

The same is true for most of the other graphic objects: lines, boxes, rounded rectangles (which includes circles).

"Sectioning" a screen can be very helpful. It guides the user's eye. It organizes and structures the often varied shapes of fields and other screen elements. If you have the time, you can strive to make your boxes and lines three-dimensional. The color palette in the Screen Builder isn't subtle, but there's enough to do a decent job of shading.

The Screen Picture dialog box, shown in Figure 13.26, makes the process of placing pictures into your screens almost painless.

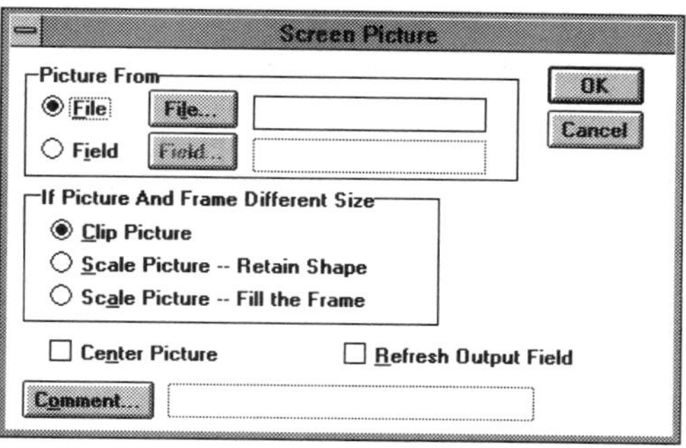

Figure 13.26
The Screen Picture dialog box.

You've got two sources, a bitmap file (.BMP) or an image stored in a General field. The former requires, as always, that you specify a complete path and filename to the graphic. The Picture dialog box, shown in Figure 13.27 on the next page, is a handy browsing feature of a specialized File Open dialog. You can bet developers will make their own versions. The General field requires only that the field named is loaded with an OLE compliant graphic.

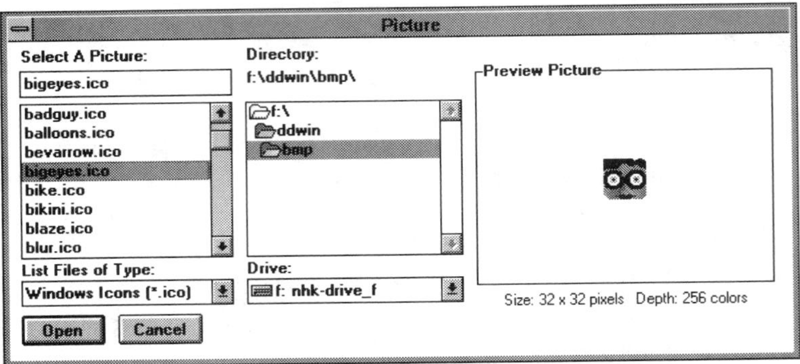

Figure 13.27 *The Picture dialog box.*

The only exception to the rule is getting pictures properly sized. Bitmap images, and especially icons, may not take kindly to being bent, stretched, or extruded. The picture and frame are options (Clip Picture, Scale Picture-Retain Shape, and Scale Picture-Fill the Frame) affect the behavior of an image. Clipping reduces the image to its "native" size. Scaling changes the shape of an image. Retain Shape keeps the image in proportion—it can get bigger or smaller, but the proportions remain the same. Fill the Frame stretches an image every which way, as long as you can stand the distortion.

The shaping options apply only to bitmap images, where the exact size of the image is a known quantity. Images from a General field can be almost anything. There, the Center Picture check box becomes useful to insure a degree of display uniformity. The other check box, Refresh Output Field does the same thing as for any other @..SAY (see Chapter 10), it refreshes all SAYS in the SHOW clause.

Object Order

Once you've completed the work of laying out the fields, controls, and pictures of your screen, it's time to put them in order—literally.

The order of objects on the screen is an important concept. *Every* object is numbered internally by FoxPro. As the user moves around the screen, FoxPro keeps tabs on which object is currently active via the current object number. This is reflected in an internal variable, _CUROBJ, which always contains the current object number.

The object order is significant in a couple of different ways. The first is simply the order of entry, as a user tabs through a data entry screen. For basic AED (Add/Edit/Delete) screens, this can be an important issue. Data entry people hate it when the cursor hops around fields. They want it to go in a nicely sequential pattern, either sideways or vertically. But predictably, in any case. That's what setting the object order does. To do this, open the Object Order dialog box, shown in Figure 13.28, from the Screen menu.

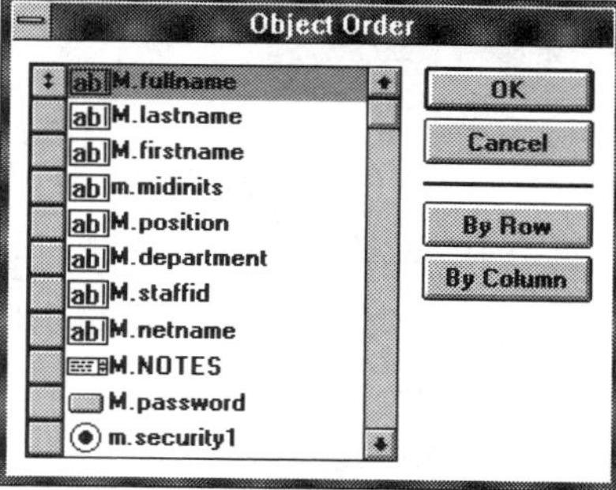

Figure 13.28
The Object Order dialog box.

You can adjust the order of objects in the screen simply by sliding them up and down with the mouse. The basic ordering, by row or by column can also be selected here.

The Finished Layout

At this point, the basic AED screen has been visually completed. All of the needed fields, text, boxes, and colors have been defined and put into place, as shown in Figure 13.29 on the next page.

Figure 13.29
Basic layout completed.

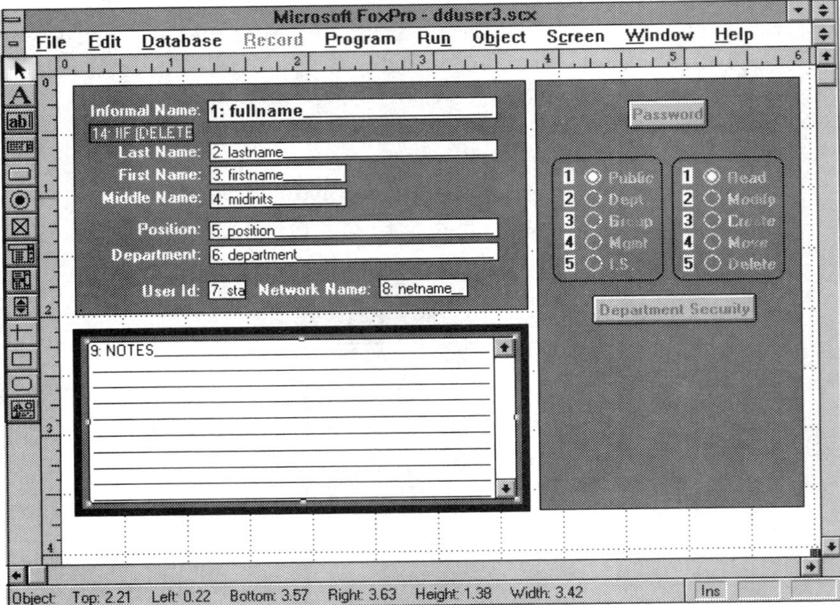

Screen Builder Programming

The Screen Builder generates a lot of code for you. Almost all of the visual elements have their code produced by the Screen Builder. But that doesn't let you off the hook, not by a long shot. You've already seen many cases where the GETs on the screen need you to provide various kinds of validation and processing code. There are even some major user interface elements, like BROWSE and the DEFINE POPUP, that can't be generated by the Screen Builder. These must be added through your own coding. Then there is the code that helps define the screen environment—the screen code. And finally the code that controls the screen (or screens)—the READ clauses.

It may be helpful to visualize the elements of Screen Builder programming as shown in Figure 13.30.

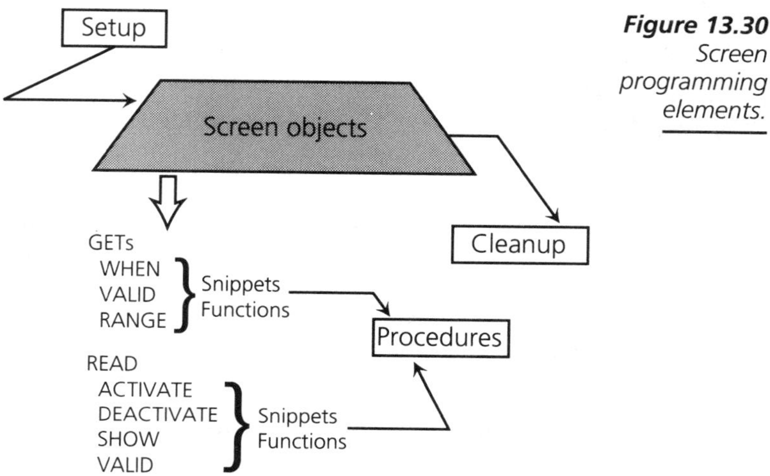

Figure 13.30 *Screen programming elements.*

These elements blend at various points, so you can't take this diagram to extremes, but in many ways these four—screen objects, GET clauses, screen code (setup and cleanup) and READ clauses—have different roles to perform, and require a certain amount of specialized programming. To put these roles in perspective, here's a brief review of each:

- **Screen objects.** By now these should be quite familiar. They are the "objects" you place on the screen with the Screen Builder Toolbox: fields, popups, lists, lines, and pictures . Many of these require variables and other values that you need to input, but don't require programming. If you can confine your screens to just these elements, then very little programming of any kind is necessary and the Screen Builder will crank out the code.
- **GET clauses.** For most screens, especially data entry screens like an AED, you'll want to validate user entry, provide information support, and do other things to control the order and manner of data entry. This is provided through the main clauses of individual GET objects, primarily WHEN and VALID. These are called the *GET level clauses* in the FoxPro manuals. For the most part, this *is* programming. You either build snippets or functions, some of which can become quite involved.
- **Screen code.** This has two sections: setup and cleanup. One sets the table, and the other cleans up. From the programming perspective, these are "bookends" code. What you do (or undo) in the setup, you undo (or do) in the cleanup. For example, if you close files in the setup,

you probably reopen them in the cleanup. These two sections can sometimes require a fair amount of programming.

- **READ clauses.** Although the Screen Builder doesn't even indicate these clauses belong to the READ, it's very important to separate this element from the rest. READ clauses are the controls for the screen, and perhaps several screens. The READ itself activates all of the GET screen elements. Every screen with GETs must be tied to a READ somewhere. The clauses of the READ are then used to monitor entrance and exit from the READ, and various other activities by the user, as they move about the screen. The FoxPro manuals refer to these as the *READ level clauses.* Some of the most difficult programming in FoxPro is associated with the READ clauses.

Table 13.2 lists the location and access for these programming elements.

Table 13.2
Programming element locations.

Programming element	Code location	Access
Setup	Screen code window Setup snippet	**Alt-C L C S**
Screen objects	Options and code snippets of each object.	Create with Toolbox Double-click on object Select, press **Enter**
GET CLAUSES	Clause Snippets of each object.	Double-click on object Select and press **Enter**
READ CLAUSES	Screen Code window Clauses section	**Alt-C L C or X or A or D or R**
CLEANUP	Screen Code window Cleanup and procedure snippet	**Alt-C L C C**
PROCEDURES	Screen Code window Cleanup and procedure snippet	**Alt-C L C C**

As you'll quickly discover, moving in and out of these various code locations takes time. Access is also difficult to automate, although you can use keyboard macros to a certain extent. There's also the "all or nothing" approach—the system menu Open All Snippets option, and its reverse (select the option holding down the **Shift** key) Close All Snippets. This is effective as long as the number of snippets is reasonable. For the most part, it's best to keep the Screen Code snippets open all the time, and judiciously add some of the READ clauses, or major GET clauses, as you work on them.

The FoxPro screen tends to become cluttered very easily. Expect to spend a fair amount of your programming time arranging things on the screen, either so you can work on them, or to get them out of the way so you can view your programs running.

Screen Code

Although it's possible to create screens without writing a line of code into either Setup or Cleanup, most of the time you will use these Screen Code locations extensively. They're both found in the Screen Code dialog box, which is accessed through the Layout option of the Screen menu. The Screen Code dialog box is displayed in Figure 13.31.

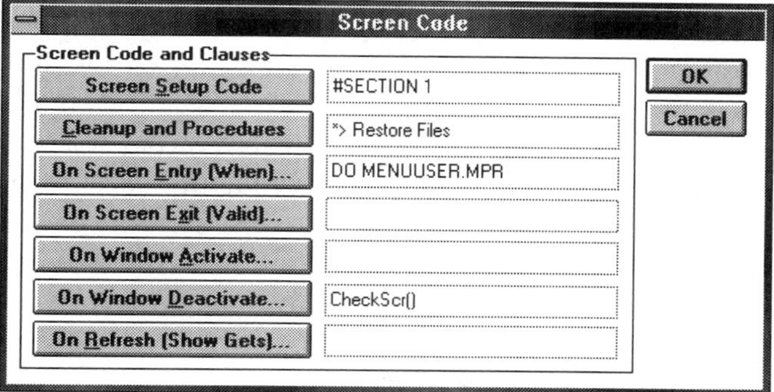

Figure 13.31
The Screen Code dialog box.

Cleanup shares a button with Procedures. This sometimes confuses people. Cleanup and Procedures are totally distinct code areas. Cleanup is really functionally paired with Setup. Procedures is an area where you can create procedures and functions that are used in various places throughout the screen.

For the most part, Setup and Cleanup are used to do exactly what their names imply: set the environment for a screen and then clean up and restore the environment before leaving. In Chapter 7 there was a discussion about the construction of functions and procedures, and how it is the "responsibility" of a properly constructed procedure to handle the preservation of an environment, when its called, and restore that environment on returning. This is exactly what Setup and Cleanup are about, and it underscores just how much a screen is a programming element just like any other program (.PRG), function, or procedure.

There are two major decisions facing the developer in Setup and Cleanup:

1. Let the Screen Builder create and release windows, or do it yourself.
2. Let the Screen Builder open and close tables, or do it yourself.

At first, it would seem that letting the Screen Builder do both is not only expedient, but probably the way Microsoft would prefer. This is essentially correct. However, there are many reasons—ranging from the requirements of an application to personal preference—for choosing not to let the Screen Builder do all the work. Unfortunately, it's not possible to catalog all of the decision factors, but here's a sampling:

- **Windows**. The Screen Builder does a good job of sizing and creating a window as the screen. If you only have one window, and you're not interested in special coloring or other window tricks, then the Screen Builder should do its thing. However, if you make use of more than one window in a screen, for example as popup frames, or if your application calls for more subtle use of color, then you would create your own windows in the Setup snippet.
- **Data tables.** The Screen Builder, like most of the Power Tools, can save your environment (in the Screen, Layout, Environment option). It preserves the tables, indexes, and relations active at the time the screen was saved, then reconstructs that table environment when you open the screen for work, or run your program. Under many circumstances, for example while you develop the program, or where the eventual user environment is stable and well known, this approach is both convenient and reliable.

  However, the Save Environment option saves both the filename and its current path (minus the drive letter and root subdirectory). If anything changes—a new filename, a different directory structure—then you need to reopen the Screen Builder, reset the environment, and recompile. This is a nuisance, but possible. But when the program is distributed, especially if it's out of your hands and into an environment where control of directories and other factors are uncertain, then the hard-coded directory references may be the undoing of your application.

For these, and other reasons involving control of tables in a multiuser environment, some developers choose not to let the Screen Builder open and close files. Instead, a system of indirect file referencing may be used, where the actual path to a file is assigned to a memory variable, so it can be changed on the fly without regeneration or recompiling. This is the basis of the data dictionary system explained later in this book.

Generator Directives

In recognition of some of the minor shortcomings of the Screen Builder, Microsoft has been adding to the stock of what are called *generator directives*. These are not extensions to the Xbase language, or even part of the FoxPro command structure. They are instructions to the generator program of the Screen Builder (GENSCRN.PRG) and the Menu Builder (GENMENU.PRG), and have relevance only in that context. Most of them are used in the Setup segment of the screen code, because they enhance or redefine parts of the screen environment.

- **#SECTION 1 | 2** Many developers use these two directives in all screens, as a matter of standardization. They provide a demarcation for the screen generator between code that goes first in the generated file—#SECTION 1—and comes after the definition of windows, but before the Screen layout code—#SECTION 2. In practice, most developers use the first section to contain environmental commands and other generator directives and the second section to declare REGIONAL variables and file openings.
- **#NAME <snippet name>** If you come to dislike the cryptic names assigned to snippet functions (such as _qrptzsz) by the screen generator, you can tell it to use a name of your own choosing with this generator directive. Just make sure that #NAME is the first entry in the snippet, such as #NAME WorkChk. This directive is also usable in the Menu Builder.
- **#READCLAUSES <clauses>** The Screen Builder interface does not provide for selection of all the READ clauses, specifically: [OBJECT <expN2>] [TIMEOUT <expN3>] [SAVE] [NOMOUSE] COLOR <color pair list> | COLOR SCHEME <expN4>]. This directive corrects that oversight, as in #READCLAUSES TIMEOUT 240. You can add clauses to the screen's READ by specifying them in #SECTION 1 of the Setup.

- **#WCLAUSES <clauses>** Just as the Screen Builder doesn't include all READ clauses, there are a few that it doesn't have for defining windows: [GROW | NOGROW] [ZOOM | NOZOOM] [MDI | NOMDI] COLOR <color pair list> | COLOR SCHEME <expN2>. These clauses are added to the end of the window defined for the screen, such as #WCLAUSES GROW ZOOM.
- **#WNAME <string>** Use this directive to have the generator substitute a cryptic name for the screen window. Put this directive in #SECTION 1. You can use any string for the argument of the directive, such as #WNAME winame.
- **#REDEFINE** This directive turns off the automatic code that tests for the existence of a window, then redefines it. If you are defining your own windows, you hardly need the Screen Builder to generate this additional code, so you would use #REDEFINE.
- **#INSERT <file>** This directive, opens the door for some very fancy generation techniques. This is very similar to procedures used in other programming languages, that let the programmer include certain standard files (and code). The file must be standard ASCII text, contain no other directives, and be available on the FoxPro search path. Otherwise, you can use this directive in any snippet, Setup, Cleanup, or in the Menu Builder snippets, such as #INSERT Update.prg.
- **#ITSEXPRESSION <char>** It seems to throw people, at first, but this is actually another kind of substitution command. This directive causes the generator to accept a variable as part of the Title definition of a window. Later, the variable can be loaded with an appropriate name, and the window will be defined at run-time with the value in the variable. This makes contextual titling possible. The procedure looks like this:

```
#SECTION 1
#ITSEXPRESSION ~
cWinTitle = "Staff Positions"
...
DEFINE WINDOW ~cWinTitle FROM 1,0 TO 22,79
```

- **#NOREAD** This directive turns off the READ for a screen, for example when the generator won't create a READ in the code. The variant of this, #NOREAD PLAIN, also prevents generation of the READ and allows only SAY, GET, EDIT, comments and other generator directives.

Setup Code

The following is the Setup snippet for the user's screen of the sample AED. You can see the typical sectioning and variable definition areas. However, there are a few things about this Setup which are definitely not standard, and should have a bit of explanation.

This screen allows the generator to define and release all windows. However, it does not use the Screen Builder to open and close files. Instead it uses a special function, FileUse(), to open files in a network environment, using a data dictionary system.

The PUSH MENU statement is included here in the Setup, so that it corresponds to the POP MENU used in the Cleanup. Some programmer's prefer to put it in the WHEN clause of the READ along with the menu program call. This screen does not use a SCATTER MEMVAR in the SHOW clause of the READ, and opts instead for loading data from the table only in very specific places in the menu and once here in the beginning of the screen.

```
#SECTION 1
#READCLAUSE TIMEOUT 240
#WCLAUSES GROW ZOOM
EXTERNAL ARRAY ASTFPBM

*> Save Environment
= PushEnv( )
= PushColor( )

#SECTION 2

*———————————————————[ DEFINE VARIABLES
*> Push Button Menu Vars
REGIONAL nSavRecno, is_bottom, is_top
is_add = .f.
is_edit = .f.
is_top = .f.
is_bottom = .f.
nSavRecno = 0
REGIONAL aStfPbm
DECLARE aStfPbm[10]
STORE "" TO aStfPbm

*> Field Vars
```

```
REGIONAL M.staffid, M.netname, M.department, M.password,
M.security1
REGIONAL M.security2, M.lastname, M.firstname, M.midinits, M.id
REGIONAL M.fullname, M.birthdate, M.position, M.notes
M.security1 = 0
M.security2 = 0

*────────────────────[ OPEN FILES
REGIONAL is_usr, is_usc
is_usr = .f.
is_usc = .f.
*> Save current open file information
REGIONAL cOldOrder, cOldAlias
cOldAlias = ALIAS()
cOldOrder = ORDER()

*> Department File
*#DOCCODE USE DDDEPT
IF NOT USED("DEP")
  IF NOT FileUse( DDDEPT ,"DEP",.t.,"DEPARTMENT","A",.f.,.t.)
    =ErrLine("Can't open Department file.",4)
    RETURN
  ENDIF
ELSE
    SELECT DEP
ENDIF

*> Put all departments/functions in an array
DECLARE aDeptFil[RECCOUNT(),1]
COPY ALL TO ARRAY aDeptFil FIELDS DEPARTMENT
USE

*> User security file
*#DOCCODE USE DDUSEC
IF NOT USED("USC")
  IF NOT FileUse( DDUSEC ,"USC",.t.,"STAFFID","A",.t.,.f.)
    =ErrLine("Can't open User Security file.",4)
    RETURN
  ENDIF
ELSE
  SELECT USC
  is_usc = .t.
ENDIF

*> User File
*#DOCCODE USE DDUSERS
IF NOT USED("USR")
```

```
  IF NOT FileUse( DDUSERS ,"USR",.t.,"STAFFID","A",.t.,.f.)
    =ErrLine("Can't open Users file.",4)
    RETURN
  ENDIF
ELSE
  SELECT USR
  is_usr = .t.
ENDIF
SET RELATION TO STAFFID INTO USC
GO TOP
nSavRecno = RECNO()

REGIONAL m.choice, m.toprec, m.bottomrec
m.choice = "Select"

*> Get vars for display
STORE 0 TO m.toprec, m.bottomrec
SCATTER MEMVAR MEMO
= StfDim("SAVE")

*> Help
cOldHelp = cHelpKey
cHelpKey = "_ Data Dictionary - User Information"

*> Change Screen Color
ACTIVATE SCREEN
@ 0,0 FILL TO 35,79.4 COLOR RGB(0,0,0,140,135,190)

*> Menu
PUSH MENU _MSYSMENU
```

Cleanup Code

There's not too much to say about the Cleanup, other than it reverses whatever the setup was in the Setup, and restores the original environment. The typical uses are to:

- Close files.
- Reopen, or reset previous files.
- Release windows.
- Restore previous SET commands.
- Reset the Help system.

- Releasing most variables (except global use PUBLICs).
- Reset security code values.
- Restore a previous menu.

Here's the Cleanup that matches the Setup from the user's screen example:

```
*==========================[ CLEANUP
]==================================
*> Close Files
IF NOT is_usc
  SELECT USC
  USE
ENDIF
IF NOT is_usr
  SELECT USR
  USE
ENDIF

*> Restore Previous File, if any.
IF NOT EMPTY( cOldAlias )
  SELECT ( cOldAlias )
  IF NOT EMPTY( cOldOrder )
    SET ORDER TO ( cOldOrder )
 ENDIF
ENDIF

*> Restore Screen Color
= PopColor()
ACTIVATE SCREEN
CLEAR

*> Restore Environment Settings
= PopEnv()

*> Restore Security
= PassOut()

*> Restore Help
cHelpKey = cOldHelp

*> Restore Menu
POP MENU _MSYSMENU
```

Procedures Section

Procedures is the space available in the Screen Builder to create your own procedures and functions that are used elsewhere in the screen. How much code is placed here depends on your inclination to create functions instead of letting the Screen Builder do it through snippets. (Remember that the Screen Builder turns all snippets into functions.) It's possible to define nearly every clause and snippet in a screen as an expression that uses a function. Some programmers feel that having them all together in the Procedure section makes them easier to find.

There is no special structure to the Procedure area, other than those required by defining functions and procedures. The Screen Generator always puts this area after the Cleanup code and before its own generated functions. The next section illustrates how screen elements and functions in the procedure area can be used.

A Push Button Menu

One of the most common aspects of an AED screen is the use of push buttons to perform repeated screen operations like navigation and record options. In fact, this use is so common, it's become known as a push putton menu (PBM). There's a utility window version, a picture (icon) button version, and just plain buttons. The sample screen used throughout this chapter takes yet another approach to the PBM.

The standard FoxPro Push Button (where the buttons are specified as the prompts of a single GET), sizes each button as large as the largest text string in the series. Outside of any aesthetic objection, this can chew up a considerable amount of screen space, especially with horizontal push buttons, shown in Figure 13.32.

Figure 13.32
PBM sizes.

There is a difference between a PBM created with a series of prompts under one variable, and one created using an individual GET and variable for each button. Obviously the individual button approach is more compact, but equally obvious, it's more work. However, because this kind of PBM is intended to be used in many screens, the design goal is to be as flexible as possible, while maintaining a consistent approach.

In one sense this is design decision minutiae. But from both the user's and the programmer's point of view, it's the pattern that counts. If the pattern makes sense in it's context, then it's a worthy contribution to the overall usability of an application. As a bonus, this approach is compact, efficient, and easy to control.

This approach to a Push Button Menu has several key aspects:

1. It is relatively easy to make a generic routine of a PBM, and even put it into a utility screen, as a floating window, ready for any application. This works well as long as you confine the options in the menu to purely generic operations. Put in other terms, the routines must not be "bound" to any particular screen.

   Including routines in the PBM options that are tightly bound to a particular screen makes it impossible to use a "generic" PBM. This is one of those more fundamental design decisions for a relatively important piece of the user interface, at least for a data entry (AED) screen. In this example, the choice has been made to include an option item (a Browse) that is customized for this particular screen, and there is code in some of the options that is also customized. This meant keeping all the PBM code with the screen, rather than as a generic function or screen.

2. All variables used in the PBM system are defined in the Setup Code of the screen.

```
*———[ SETUP CODE
*> Push Button Menu Vars
REGIONAL nSavRecno, is_bottom, is_top
is_add = .f.
is_edit = .f.
is_top = .f.
is_bottom = .f.
nSavRecno = 0
REGIONAL aStfPbm
DECLARE aStfPbm[10]
STORE "" TO aStfPbm
```

3. Each button is defined with its own variable. Each variable is an array element so that a marking of button order can be maintained, just as if it were a series of prompts using one variable. Normally the command SHOW GET aStfPbm ,3 would be used to designate the third push button. In this case, however, it comes out: SHOW GET aStfPbm[3].
4. Each button contains a reference in the VALID clause, which calls a common routine, StfValid(), to process the button selections.
5. Linked to the StfValid() routine is StfDim(), which handles all of the enabling and disabling of the push buttons in the menu (as appropriate). The screen colors were deliberately set so that disabled buttons and GETs are slightly visible.

```
*=====================[ PROCEDURES
]============================
*****************************************************************
*     FUNCTION: StfValid()
* Description: PUSH BUTTON MENU VALID
*  Created/By: 10/15/92, NK
*  Parameters: None
*   Called By: DDUSERS push button menu
*       Notes: Modified Standard PBM
*
* Change Log:
* 10/28/92 Added BrsMultKey() to staff <List> lookup, nk
*
*****************************************************************

#REGION 1
FUNCTION StfValid
* Process the "menu" selections from each button.
DO CASE
* ────────── RECORD OPTIONS ──────────────
*>─────────────────[ New Entry
CASE aStfPbm[1] = "Add"
  is_add = .t.                && set add/edit flags
  is_edit = .f.

  SCATTER MEMVAR BLANK MEMO   && load blank field
variables
  _CUROBJ = OBJNUM( m.fullname ) && set first entry field
  SHOW GETS WINDOW wrUsers ENABLED ONLY
  =StfDim("EDIT")             && disable buttons routine
 SET CURSOR ON
```

```
*>────────────────[ Edit Entry
CASE aStfPbm[2] = "Edit"
  is_add = .f. && set add/edit flags
  is_edit = .t.

  _CUROBJ = OBJNUM( M.fullname )
  SHOW GETS WINDOW wrUsers ENABLED ONLY
  =StfDim("EDIT")
  SET CURSOR ON

*>────────────────[ Save Current Information
CASE aStfPbm[3] = "Save"

 * Note the customized code appropriate only for this
screen.
 * Check for required name, and if name is duplicated.
 IF EMPTY(M.firstname) OR EMPTY(M.lastname)
   =TONE(1300,3)
   WAIT " Both First and Last Name Must Be Entered "
WINDOW NOWAIT
   _CUROBJ = OBJNUM( M.firstname )
   SHOW GET M.firstname
   RETURN (.t.)
 ELSE
   IF is_add
     SELECT USR
     IF NOT SEEK( UPPER(
TRIM(M.lastname)+TRIM(M.firstname)) )
     *> OK, add a new record
     IF AddRec( "A",5 )
       GATHER MEMVAR MEMO
       UNLOCK
     ENDIF
   ELSE
     = ErrLine("This person is already in the staff
file.",3)
     RETURN (.f.)
   ENDIF
 ENDIF

 IF is_edit
   IF RecLock(5)
     GATHER MEMVAR MEMO
     UNLOCK
   ENDIF
 ENDIF
```

```
 nSavrecno = RECNO()          && current record pointer
 is_add = .f.                 && reset add/edit flags
 is_edit = .f.
 SHOW GETS WINDOW wrUsers DISABLED ONLY
 =StfDim("SAVE")              && set buttons for a save.
 SET CURSOR OFF

 =TONE(400, 1)                && cue the user
 =TONE(800, 1)
 WAIT "SAVED" WINDOW NOWAIT TIMEOUT 5

 ENDIF

*>────────────────[ Cancel Current Action
CASE aStfPbm[4] = "Cancel"
  * Depending on whether user was adding a record or editing a
record
  * re-load variables.
      DO CASE
      CASE is_add
        IF nSavrecno > 0
          GOTO nSavrecno
          SCATTER MEMVAR MEMO
          is_add = .f.
        ENDIF
     CASE is_edit
       SCATTER MEMVAR MEMO
       is_edit = .f.
     ENDCASE

     SHOW GETS WINDOW wrUsers DISABLED ONLY
     =StfDim("SAVE")
     SET CURSOR OFF

     =TONE(1300,1)           && cue the user.
     =TONE(600 ,3)
     WAIT "Action Canceled" WINDOW NOWAIT TIMEOUT 5

    *>────────────────[ Return To Calling Menu
    CASE aStfPbm[5] = "Done"

      CLEAR READ
    * ──────────── NAVIGATION OPTIONS ────────────
    *>────────────────[ Next
    CASE aStfPbm[6] = "Next"
      IF NOT EOF()
        SKIP 1
```

```
    SCATTER MEMVAR MEMO
    =StfDim("NEXT")
    nSavrecno = RECNO()
  ELSE
    =StfDim("")
  ENDIF
*>————————————————[ Prior
CASE aStfPbm[7] = "Prior"
  IF NOT BOF()
    SKIP -1
    SCATTER MEMVAR MEMO
    =StfDim("PRIOR")
    nSavrecno = RECNO()
  ELSE
    =StfDim("")
   ENDIF

*>————————————————[ Top
CASE aStfPbm[8] = "Top"
  GO TOP
  is_top = .t.
  is_bottom = .f.
  nSavrecno = RECNO()
  SCATTER MEMVAR MEMO
  =StfDim("TOP")
*>————————————————[ Bottom
CASE aStfPbm[9] = "Bottom"
  GO BOTTOM
  is_top = .f.
  is_bottom = .t.
  nSavrecno = RECNO()
  SCATTER MEMVAR MEMO
  =StfDim("BOTTOM")
*>————————————————[ List/Browse
CASE aStfPbm[10] = "List"

  *Customized Multi-Browse for this screen.

  DEFINE WINDOW wbUsers FROM 3,0 TO 23,79 FLOAT TITLE
"Select Staff" ;
   COLOR SCHEME 10
 SELECT USR
 *> Multiple Field incremental search
 =BrsMultKey( "ON", "", "WBUSERS" )

 BROWSE FIELDS STAFFID:H="*ID",;
```

```
    NETNAME:H="*NetName",;
    FIRSTNAME:H="First Name",;
    LASTNAME:H="*Last Name",;
    POSITION ;
    NOMODIFY NOAPPEND NODELETE ;
    WINDOW wbUsers

  =BrsMultKey( "OFF", "" )

  RELEASE WINDOW wbUsers

  IF LASTKEY() = 27                && trap esc
    IF NOT is_add AND nSavrecno > 0
      GOTO nSavrecno
    ENDIF
  ELSE
    nSavrecno = RECNO()
    is_add = .F.
  ENDIF

  SCATTER MEMVAR MEMO
ENDCASE

STORE "" TO aStfPbm     && Important! Reset options.
SHOW GETS WINDOW wrUsers && Re-display the GETs.

RETURN (.t.)
*
***********************************************************************
*      FUNCTION: StfDim()
* Description: ENABLE/DISABLE PUSH BUTTON MENU
*  Created/By: 10/15/92, NK
*  Parameters: cDimTyp = Action type
*   Called By: StfValid()
*       Notes: Standard PBM format.
*
* Change Log:
*
***********************************************************************
FUNCTION StfDim
PARAMETER cDimTyp

IF RECCOUNT() > 0 && if nothing in table skip it.
  DO CASE
  CASE cDimtyp = "EDIT"
    SHOW GET aStfPbm[1] DISABLE && Add
    SHOW GET aStfPbm[2] DISABLE && Edit
```

```
    SHOW GET aStfPbm[3] ENABLE && Save
    SHOW GET aStfPbm[4] ENABLE && Cancel
    SHOW GET aStfPbm[5] DISABLE && Done

    SHOW GET aStfPbm[6] DISABLE && Next
    SHOW GET aStfPbm[7] DISABLE && Prior
    SHOW GET aStfPbm[8] DISABLE && Top
    SHOW GET aStfPbm[9] DISABLE && Bottom
    SHOW GET aStfPbm[10] DISABLE && List
  CASE cDimTyp = "SAVE"
    SHOW GET aStfPbm[1] ENABLE
    SHOW GET aStfPbm[2] ENABLE
    SHOW GET aStfPbm[3] DISABLE
    SHOW GET aStfPbm[4] DISABLE
    SHOW GET aStfPbm[5] ENABLE

    SHOW GET aStfPbm[6] ENABLE
    SHOW GET aStfPbm[7] ENABLE
    SHOW GET aStfPbm[8] ENABLE
    SHOW GET aStfPbm[9] ENABLE
    SHOW GET aStfPbm[10] ENABLE
  CASE cDimTyp = "TOP"
    SHOW GET aStfPbm[7] DISABLE
    SHOW GET aStfPbm[8] DISABLE
    SHOW GET aStfPbm[6] ENABLE
    SHOW GET aStfPbm[9] ENABLE
  CASE cDimTyp = "BOTTOM"
    SHOW GET aStfPbm[6] DISABLE
    SHOW GET aStfPbm[9] DISABLE
    SHOW GET aStfPbm[7] ENABLE
    SHOW GET aStfPbm[8] ENABLE
  CASE cDimTyp = "PRIOR"
    IF BOF()
      GO TOP
      is_top = .t.
      is_bottom = .f.
      SHOW GET aStfPbm[7] DISABLE
      SHOW GET aStfPbm[8] DISABLE
      SHOW GET aStfPbm[6] ENABLE
      SHOW GET aStfPbm[9] ENABLE
    ELSE
      is_top = .f.
      is_bottom = .f.
      SHOW GET aStfPbm[6] ENABLE
```

```
            SHOW GET aStfPbm[8] ENABLE
          ENDIF
        CASE cDimTyp = "NEXT"
          IF EOF()
            GO BOTTOM
       is_bottom = .t.
       is_top = .f.
       SHOW GET aStfPbm[6] DISABLE
       SHOW GET aStfPbm[9] DISABLE
       SHOW GET aStfPbm[7] ENABLE
       SHOW GET aStfPbm[8] ENABLE
     ELSE
       is_top = .f.
       is_bottom = .f.
       SHOW GET aStfPbm[7] ENABLE
       SHOW GET aStfPbm[8] ENABLE
       SHOW GET aStfPbm[10] ENABLE
     ENDIF
   ENDCASE

ELSE

  *> No records
  is_top = .f.
  is_bottom = .f.
  SHOW GET aStfPbm[2] DISABLE
  SHOW GET aStfPbm[3] DISABLE
  SHOW GET aStfPbm[4] DISABLE
  SHOW GET aStfPbm[6] DISABLE
  SHOW GET aStfPbm[7] DISABLE
  SHOW GET aStfPbm[8] DISABLE
  SHOW GET aStfPbm[9] DISABLE
  SHOW GET aStfPbm[10] DISABLE

ENDIF
RETURN (.t.)
*
```

Having added the final touches and the PBM, the user's screen is completed. If it's like most screens, you'll spend much more time adjusting things on and in the screen than you did to create it in the first place. This is especially true if the screen is being developed first as a "prototype" for users.The final screen is shown in Figure 13.33 on the next page.

Figure 13.33
The user's screen with PBM.

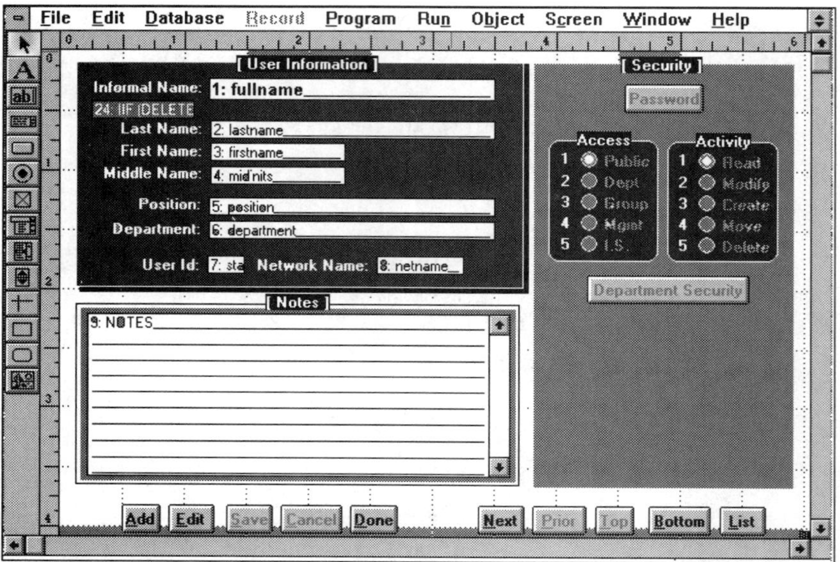

The READ: Clauses and Code

All screens that contain GETs must have a READ (somewhere) to activate the GETs. This is not the only function of the READ and its clauses. In FoxPro the READ is an event loop, which may have none, one, or many windows (screens) associated with it. Many of the clauses of the READ are designed to monitor the user as they roam around the screens of an application. Other clauses modify the behavior of objects under control of a READ. These are generalizations about the READ that sometimes become forgotten when working in the Screen Builder.

There are sixteen clauses of the READ, and several related commands and generator directives. In FoxPro, the access to all of this (unless you are writing your own code) is dispersed to several locations.

Some of the most important clauses (VALID and WHEN) are part of the Screen Builder in the Screen Code dialog box labeled Screen Code and Clauses. Four others are located in the Edit Screen Set dialog box of the Project Manager *and* in the Generate Screen dialog box. Six more can only be included using the #READCLAUSES generator directive. Although this is confusing, it underscores the use of the READ in more contexts than a single screen.

In the Screen Builder the majority of the available READ clauses are generated for you, depending on your selections. Outside of the Screen Code clauses, which we'll get to in a bit, Table 13.3 contains a rundown of the other clauses of the READ, what they do, and how to use them:

Table 13.3
Clauses of the READ.

Clause	Description and Usage
[CYCLE]	This is the clause that turns an ordinary READ into the READ loop. Virtually all screens with GETs use this clause. The only exceptions might be dialog boxes with only one or two GETs, or a screen that is terminated by leaving a specific GET. The default is READ CYCLE, but you can turn it off in a check box in the Generate Screen or Edit Screen Set dialog boxes.
[LOCK|NOLOCK]	In a multiuser application, this clause is used to turn off the automatic record locking of FoxPro. It is available as a checkbox in the Generate Screen or Edit Screen Set dialog boxes.
[MODAL]	This is a specific instance of turning a screen or menu into a "locked" situation, where the user cannot wander off into other areas of the program. Typically, this is used with dialog boxes, or screens that have critical information. It is available as a checkbox in the Generate Screen or Edit Screen Set dialog boxes.
WITH <window list>	Used in conjunction with the MODAL clause, this clause provides you with the option of listing other windows. It's reached through the Associated Windows... button in the Generate Screen or Edit Screen Set dialog boxes. Notice that you list windows by their title. This is an accommodation to the peculiar naming habits of the Browse windows.

(continued)

OBJECT <expN2>

As mentioned before, most objects in a screen are numbered. You can use this clause to initially select a particular object (a GET of some kind) by supplying its number in <expN2>. And how do you know its number? Good question. Since the number is liable to change if the screen is modified, you'd want a method that would adjust automatically. FoxPro fortunately provides the method: the OBJNUM( ) function returns the number of any object's variable. So if you know that the GET for a last name is cLastName you can make a READ like this:

```
READ CYCLE OBJECT OBJNUM( cLastName ).
```

Unfortunately, this clause is not directly available through the Screen Builder. You'll have to specify it with the generator directive #READCLAUSES, like this:

```
#READCLAUSES OBJECT OBJNUM( cLastName )
```

TIMEOUT <expN3>

It's typical for data entry screens to be "abandoned" by their users, perhaps to the peril of the security or integrity of the data. In situations where you don't want a screen to hang open forever, you can use this clause to specify when to terminate the record—in seconds for <expN3>. Note that you'd better have prepared code to handle a timeout termination—what does the program do next? You can test for a timeout with the READKEY( ) function, which returns 20, if terminated by a timeout without any changes having been made, and 276, if there have been changes. TIMEOUT is available only by using the #READCLAUSES directive, for example: `#READCLAUSES TIMEOUT 300.`

[SAVE]

This is a sneaky little clause. It preserves all object definitions, even when the READ has been terminated. It makes it possible to drop out of read temporarily, then resume at some point. Although it needs to be used with care because of the memory overhead and possible overlap of objects, this can be used to get around the five-read level maximum of FoxPro. This is another candidate for #READCLAUSES.

[NOMOUSE]

This clause prevents all mouse movement within a screen. In effect, it locks the user into doing data entry by using only the keyboard, and thus moving from GET to GET in a linear pattern. This is a #READCLAUSES option.

[COLOR]
[COLOR SCHEME]

Both of these clauses can be used to set the default color for the GET fields of a screen. This is color pair two of a color list, and looks like this:

```
COLOR ,GR+/B
```

This too is only available by using #READCLAUSES.

Screen Code

This is the portion of the READ clauses that are anonymously embedded in the Screen Builder. When the READ is joined by its CYCLE clause, it becomes an event loop. These five clauses—VALID, WHEN, ACTIVATE, DEACTIVATE, and SHOW—become the monitoring positions for user activity. Like their siblings for the GET, if you use them, these clauses all require either an expression that returns .t. or .f., or a function that also returns .t. or .f.

There's a specific order to which FoxPro fires these and related screen clauses, and it's useful to understand the implications. The order of execution on first issuing a READ is as follows:

1. The WHEN clause is executed. If it returns .t., the READ continues.
2. The GETs in the first window are activated. The "first window" implies that there may be more than one, which is true. The first window is the first window in the Screen Set list, the one in the Project Manager. This is the first window code generated, hence the first executed.
3. The ACTIVATE clause is executed.
4. The SHOW clause is executed. This is important because it's frequently used to load values into field variables (SCATTER MEMVAR), and display them on the screen.
5. The WHEN clause of the first GET in the first screen is executed. This gives you the opportunity to control access to the first entry.

NOTE

You should make mental note of how closely the READ level clauses are associated with GETs. Movement between windows, for example, does not invoke these clauses or this execution sequence unless of course, there is a READ, and there are some active GETs in the screen.

Most of the control implications of the READ clauses occur when the user switches between windows, which implies that these clauses are mostly of value when multiple screen sets are being used. This is largely but not exclusively true. Changing windows *includes* the FoxPro desktop, so that moving out of a current screen might just be an attempt to activate something in the desktop, or even a careless click of the mouse. The order of execution on activating a new window is as follows:

1. The VALID clause of the current GET field is executed, if the user is in a field. This means they can't actually change window venues, unless they pass the validation of the current GET, a needed precaution.
2. The window currently in use is deactivated (it becomes hidden).
3. The new window, usually triggered by selecting a GET field, is activated (made visible).
4. The DEACTIVATE clause is executed, but it still gives you an opportunity of examining conditions in the previous window.
5. The ACTIVATE clause is executed, but you can use the opportunity to check conditions in the current window.
6. The WHEN clause of the first field in the new window is executed.

You'll notice that none of the above mentions the VALID clause of the READ. In the sequence of events, it's a specialist—the terminator—of clauses. It's only invoked when the user attempts to exit a window (either because they've used **Esc** or **Ctrl-W**, or they've selected a button in the screen that automatically terminates a READ) or something in the GET level code has issued a CLEAR READ or the READ has timed-out.

The coding of these READ level clauses is one of the great challenges of FoxPro, if you choose to accept it. It's quite possible, however, to create an entire application without ever setting a line of code into these clauses. That's how *all* programming was done prior to FoxPro 2.0.

In working with basic data-entry type screens, these clauses are not as crucial as they are in more advanced and complex screen management, but they still have a role to play. They'll be introduced here, briefly. It will help you to separate these READ clauses from their berth in the Screen Code dialog box of the Screen Builder, and think of them as control clauses in a more generic sense.

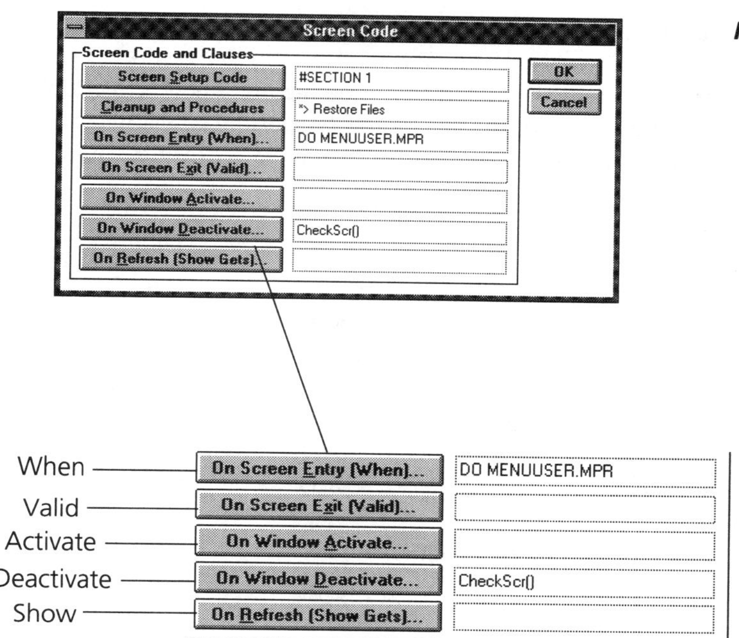

Figure 13.34 *Screen Builder Read*

When

As always, this is the entrance clause. Since it is the first READ clause executed on attempting to enter a new window (screen), you can use it to test for the appropriateness of access. For example in a security based system, you might use code like this in the snippet of the WHEN:

```
IF NOT PassWord( 3, 2)
  WAIT "You do not have clearance! Returning to previous
screen." ;
    WINDOW NOWAIT
ENDIF
```

However, by convention, the foremost use of the WHEN is to initiate a current screen menu. There's no particular necessity for doing this here, except this is the first clause to be executed when coming into a new screen, and you can take the opportunity to set the menu and make any adjustments to it. This is often very simple code, `DO ddusers.mpr`, which executes a new menu file.

Valid

In a foundation READ or a Multiscreen READ, the VALID clause plays a pivotal role. But for basic screen work, it's merely the exit clause. Mostly it's used to test whether the user can leave the current read, for example if all of the field entry conditions have been met. There are many times in a data entry screen where it might be necessary to compare a number of field entries before deciding if the entry as a whole was correct. This would be handled in the VALID.

For example the snippet code might be:

```
*> Test to see if any fields were updated.
IF CheckRead( )
   *No exit without a name being entered.
   IF EMPTY(m.lastname) AND EMPTY(m.firstname)
     =ErrLine("You must enter a name.",3)
     * Don't allow out of the READ
     RETURN .f.
 ENDIF
ENDIF
```

Activate and Deactivate

The ACTIVATE and DEACTIVATE clauses are the window-management clauses. Their primary mission in life is to give you the means of dealing with the window hopping of the user. As a result, their coding is usually hallmarked by the use of the many window functions, such as WONTOP( ), and WOUTPUT( ). These are part of routines to see where the user was, where they think they're going, and whether all of the window conditions you are monitoring are satisfied. You can think of these clauses as the WHEN and VALID of windows.

Theoretically, the DEACTIVATE clause is associated with leaving a window. Actually, you may have noticed that it doesn't execute until the user has already seen the activated new window (and the old window has already been hidden or closed). Don't worry. This clause has a logical role, as the place to test the conditions of the previous window. (Is it still open? Is it hidden? Should something be done?) For example:

```
* Test for positions window
IF UPPER( WLAST() ) = "POSITIONS"
  * close the file.
  SELECT positions
  USE
ENDIF
```

In a similar way, the ACTIVATE clause is logically related to accessing a new window. Presumably the window is already visible, although this isn't always necessary. For the most part, the code in this clause sees to it that all of the environmental conditions for being in the new window are correct. Are all the right tables open and set up? Are all the appropriate subordinate windows visible?) Typical code looks something like this:

```
*> Find out what window is open and act on it.
DO CASE
CASE WONTOP() = "POSITIONS"
   IF NOT USED("POS")
     USE positions ALIAS pos ORDER posid
   ENDIF
   IF NOT WEXIST("WBPOS")
     DEFINE WINDOW wbPos AT 2,0 SIZE 10,40 ;
       TITLE "Positions" COLOR SCHEME 10
  ENDIF
CASE WONTOP() = "EMPLOYEES"
    IF NOT USED("EMP")
      USE employees ALIAS emp ORDER empid
    ENDIF
ENDCASE
```

Show

The SHOW clause has only two triggers: SHOW GETS somewhere in the code of the screen, and execution in the startup sequence of entering a new READ. This latter is, of course, automatic. The former can be used anywhere in the screen code (but please not in the SHOW clause itself). It's important to note that the SHOW clause is invoked *before* the actual redisplay of GETs takes place. The purpose of this clause is really to get around a limitation of the SHOW GETS command (it operates only with GETs). Other objects like SAYs are not refreshed by SHOW GETS, and so a way was needed to handle these other objects at the same time as the GETs.

Whenever you check off the refresh option in an @..SAY field, the Screen Builder generates the code for that SAY in the SHOW clause. You can do much the same thing, by putting in any code relevant to redisplaying objects. There are typically three basic kinds of actions in the SHOW:

1. Load variables, typically from a table, using SCATTER MEMVAR or other method.
2. Set up any ENABLE or DISABLE controls over various GETs in the screen.
3. Execute any @..SAY command appropriate for the screen.

As a rule, these actions are conditioned by testing. (Is the user adding or editing? What table is currently active?) The general code looks something like this:

```
 *If positions is open refresh fields
IF USED("POS")
  IF is_add
    SCATTER MEMVAR MEMO BLANK
    SHOW GET m.newpos DISABLE
    SHOW GET m.inactive DISABLE
    * Display the position status again.
    cStatus = "NEW"
    @ 2,50 SAY cStatus
  ELSE
    SCATTER MEMVAR MEMO
    SHOW GET m.newpos ENABLE
    SHOW GET m.inactive ENABLE
    * Display the position status again.
    cStatus = "EDIT"
    @ 2,50 SAY cStatus
  ENDIF
ELSE        && positions is not open
  * Must be open employee browse, refresh it.
  SHOW WINDOW wbEmployee REFRESH
ENDIF
```

It's important for you to expand your knowledge of how these clauses work and interact, in a sense to prepare for the rigors of event-driven programming. While there is an almost unlimited number of variations for coding in these clauses, there are some types of coding that are used more often:

1. **Window control**—knowing how to get information about windows and how to manipulate them. This includes all of the window functions, DEFINE and MODIFY WINDOW, and the various aspects of window names and titles.
2. **Table status information and control of table pointers and indexes.** This is absolutely vital. The trickiest part of applications is often management of table environments. This gets even more tricky with multiple open windows and event driven programming.
3. **The use of SHOW GET and GETS, _CUROBJ, OBJNUM( ), ENABLE | DISABLE to manipulate the display and status of screen objects (mostly the GETs).** In a data-entry screen like an AED, the positioning of the entry cursor, field order, and options display can be crucial to the effectiveness of the screen.

The Screen Generator

The final step in the creation of a screen, or screen set, is to *generate* the code. You've heard the term many times already, but it will help a bit to explain what's happening when you generate a screen file (a .SPR).

A *screen set* is the term used for a Screen Builder list with more than one screen. FoxPro, and the Screen Generator in particular, behave differently if there is one or more than one screen in the list. The single screen is handled much like any other program you're familiar with in Xbase. A screen set produces code that is a combination of all of the participating screens under the control of a single READ. This is route to a multiwindow read.

The program that does the generation of code, the *screen generator*, is actually a FoxPro program—GENSCRN.PRG. It is usually located in the root directory where you keep the main FoxPro files, although you can move it anywhere on the FoxPro path (or use _GENSCRN=<Path> in the CONFIG.FPW). Because it's a normal .PRG, you can open the file and even modify it (at your own risk).

When you inaugurate a generate or generate/compile of a screen, the screen generator is invoked by FoxPro and given the name of your screen files

(.SCX or .SCT). The generator opens the two standard database files and proceeds to read the data in them as it generates the code. There is a specific order of generation for components of the output file. It may be helpful at times to understand this order, which is listed in Table 13.4.

Table 13.4
Order of generation for a screen file (.SPR).

Generation section	Content: Generated, User Coded
1. Setup code—1	#SECTION 1 Generator Directives PARAMETERS Environment settings
2. Environment code	SET <commands>
3. Open files	USE <file>, if generated.
4. Define windows	DEFINE WINDOW <name>, if generated.
5. Setup code—2	#SECTION 2 Define Regional variables Open files Define windows Browse/Memo/Popup elements Other Setup (help,security etc.)
6. Screen layout	@..GET, @..SAY
7. READ	READ and clauses
8. Release windows	RELEASE WINDOW <names>, if generated.
9. Close files	USE <file>, if generated.
10. Environment code	Reset environment
11. Cleanup	User reset of environment User close files User release windows
12. Procedures	User defined functions User defined procedures
13. READ snippets	Generated READ functions
14. GET snippets	Generated GET functions

The division of duties in the generation process is fairly clear. Depending on whether you've opted to have the screen generator handle file opening and window definition, you're adding the two sections of setup code, your piece of the cleanup code, and the UDFs or procedures for the GET and READ clauses (or other working functions).

The most important aspect of the generation process is what happens when there's more than one screen in the screen set. The process follows the same order as above, however, it performs each step by combining code from every screen in the set, in their order of appearance in the screen list. The only exception to the combining of code is for the READ clauses, where the screen generator uses only the *first* clauses it encounters. The screen generator is careful to label and use REGION statements to keep some of the sections separated, but the setup and cleanup code that you create is combined without any differentiation to the generated code from all screens in the set. This means it behooves you to be careful with the content of these sections in each screen. At best you can create redundancies, and at worst your code will step all over itself, and perhaps the generated code as well.

Generator Options

As mentioned before, there are two ways to generate a screen: using the Project Manager and through the system menu. Unless you are not using the Project Manager (for presumably a darn good reason), 99 percent of the time you should generate programs via the Project Manager. There are several reasons for this, not the least of which is convenience. However, the Project Manager is unique in capturing some of the screen arrangement information, and providing you with easy access to generation and compilation errors.

Either way, you'll pass through up to three very similar dialog boxes, shown in Figures 13.35, 13.36, and 13.37 on the next page.

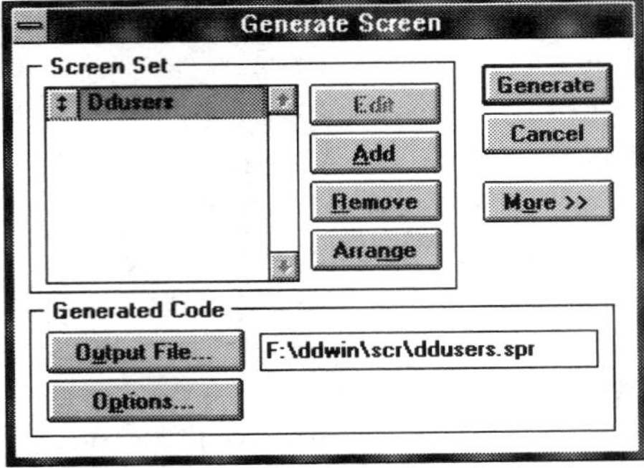

Figure 13.35 *The Generate Screen dialog box.*

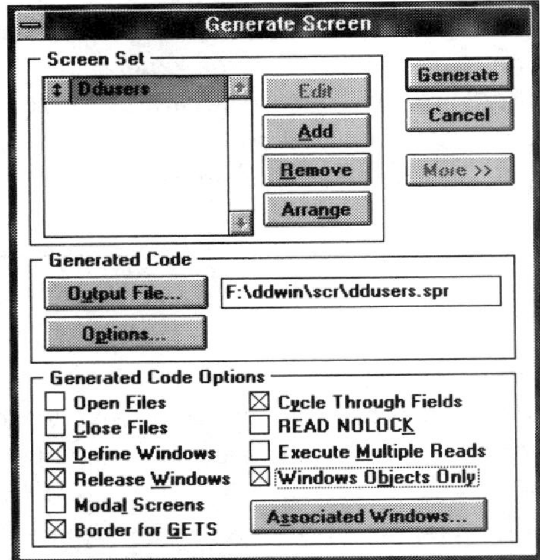

Figure 13.36 *The Generate Screen dialog box: Expanded.*

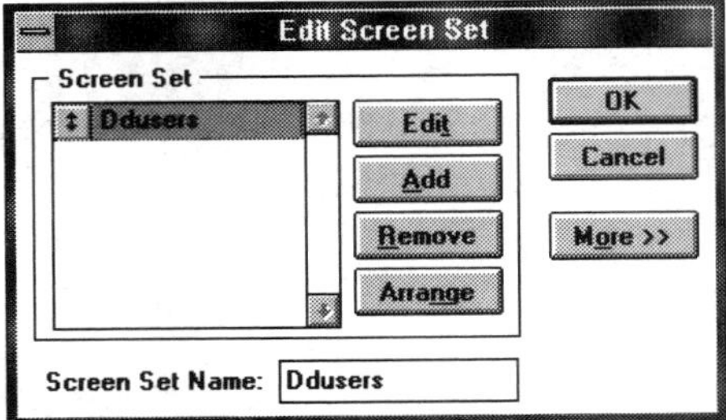

Figure 13.37 *The Edit Screen Set dialog box.*

In terms of generation, there are three types of options of most interest:

1. The Arrange option allows you to position one or more screens in the FoxPro main window. Remember that the Generate Screen dialog box does not retain any arrangements.
2. The READ-oriented options—Modal Screens, Associated Windows, Cycle Through Fields, Border for GETS, and READ NOLOCK—were covered previously in this chapter.
3. The Screen Set options—Open Files, Close Files, Define Windows, and Release Windows—are your most important choices (also discussed previously in this chapter). The defaults for these are for the screen generator to do the work. Note that the Generate Screen dialog box does not save alternate choices for these options.

Execute Multiple Reads is occasionally useful, because it allows you to specify a single READ be generated for each screen in a screen set.

The Windows Objects Only option is significant if you are *not* preparing code for another computer environment. By default, the screen generator creates code for your screen(s) for both DOS and Windows in the same file at the same time (using #IF,#ENDIF directives to keep the sections of different code from compiling together). This is very useful for cross-platform development. However, if you're a Windows purist turn this option off and save yourself generation time and a lot of useless code.

When generation is complete (and it does take quite a bit of time on files of any size), the Project Manager continues on to compile the program. With the Generate Screen dialog box, you'll have to go back to the system menu and select the Compile option. The end result of the whole process is two files: the .SPR, which contains the code, and the .SPX, which contains the compiled code ready to be run.

Run screens by calling them with the .SPR extension (so that FoxPro won't get them mixed up with regular .PRG files.), such as DO POSITION.SPR. For the record, Figure 13.38 on the next page shows how the HR System User's Screen looks, when it's fully operational.

Figure 13.37
The fully operational user's screen.

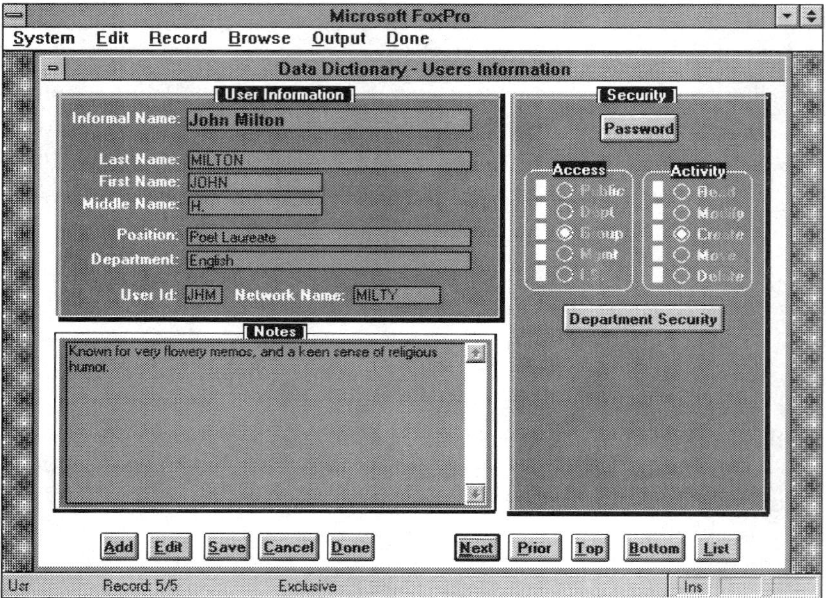

This completes the cycle for the creation of a basic Add/Edit/Delete screen using the Screen Builder.

Chapter 14
The Menu Builder

enu code is repetitive, nit-picky, and lengthy. If you use the Menu Builder, here's a sample of the programming you'll miss...

```
DEFINE POPUP record MARGIN RELATIVE SHADOW COLOR SCHEME 4
DEFINE BAR 1 OF record PROMPT "\<Add" ;
       KEY CTRL+INS, "CTRL+INS" ;
       SKIP FOR is_add OR is_edit
DEFINE BAR 2 OF record PROMPT "\<Edit" ;
       KEY CTRL+E, "CTRL+E" ;
       SKIP FOR is_add OR is_edit
DEFINE BAR 3 OF record PROMPT "\<Save" ;
       KEY CTRL+S, "CTRL+S" ;
       SKIP FOR NOT is_add AND NOT is_edit
ON SELECTION BAR 1 OF record ;
       DO _qdi03iv35 ;
       IN LOCFILE("\DDWIN\MNU\MENUUSER" ,"MPX;MPR|FXP;PRG"
,"Where is MENUUSER?")
```

```
ON SELECTION BAR 2 OF record ;
       DO _qdi03iv57 ;
       IN LOCFILE("\DDWIN\MNU\MENUUSER" ,"MPX;MPR|FXP;PRG";
,"Where is MENUUSER?")
ON SELECTION BAR 3 OF record ;
       DO _qdi03iv7m ;
       IN LOCFILE("\DDWIN\MNU\MENUUSER" ,"MPX;MPR|FXP;PRG";
,"Where is MENUUSER?")
```

Of course, if you do use it, you're buying into the FoxPro for Windows menu system, which itself is a piece of the Microsoft Windows menu system. As mentioned elsewhere, there are other ways of building menus in FoxPro for Windows. All of them are non standard in the Windows environment. Again, you'd have to be suffering from delusionary visions and a lack of sleep not to use the Menu Builder (not that this is so uncommon among programmers).

Basic Menu Components

There are a number of parallels between the Screen Builder and the Menu Builder. Both can be started (new or modify) through the system menu, the Command window, or the Project Manager. Both make use of code snippets, and have Setup and Cleanup sections. Both require a code generation phase, again through the system menu, the Command window, or the Project Manager. While you *can* create a menu without a screen, this is unusual—virtually all menus are associated with a screen.

However, not all screens have menus. Certainly dialog boxes don't usually have their own menus. And there's no programming rule that says all data entry screens must have their own menu, or any menu at all for that matter. But when you're working with the Menu Builder and the FoxPro menu system, *a* menu, whether tailored to a particular screen or not, is assumed to be omnipresent.

The question then becomes, How much do you want to modify the standard FoxPro menu? To answer that question, it helps to understand the components of a standard menu.

Elements of a Standard Menu

When you are in a Windows application, the second line (bar) of the window is the menu. With very few exceptions, every Windows menu begins with File. After that, however, there is little consistency. Menus are almost always modified to fit a specific application, your applications included.

There is one, and only one Menu bar. You cannot move or shape the system Menu bar. It's coloration and font can only be modified through the Windows Control Panel, which currently is not possible through programming. What you *can* modify is the content of the menu, first of all the pads. Pads are the options of the Menu bar. The Menu Builder calls them generically *prompts*.

The FoxPro *standard menu*, consists of the pads File, Edit, Database, Record, Program, Window, and Help. All of these can be modified, or even removed at your discretion. (You should note immediately that you do *not* have access of any kind to Browse, Report, Query, Object, Run, and all programming oriented pads like Screen, Project, and Menu.)

NOTE

When you are just starting a new menu, you can have the standard menu at your disposal simply by selecting Quick Menu from the Menu menu. This is handy because there is no way to copy menu Prompts, Results, and Options together as a unit from one menu to another. It's much easier to delete options and whole menu pads, than it is to copy or enter them.

All of the standard pads have an associated popup menu, which the Menu Builder calls a *submenu*. The popup, contains one or more menu options. You've probably noticed that menu pads are usually short, single-word prompts. Menu options are often fairly lengthy and more than one word. There is a reason for this configuration. Long or multi-word pads would quickly fill the visible Menu bar and push off on the right end. FoxPro can accommodate this eventuality, but this is poor user-interface design because if it's out of sight, it's out of mind. Menu popups, on the other hand are free to expand vertically as well as horizontally, which means you can have longer prompts (within reason).

While most Windows menu operations presumes the use of the mouse, it's long been a hallmark of good Windows design to have the menu system also totally available to keyboard users. This takes one of two forms (and sometimes both), a *hot key* or a *keyboard shortcut*.

By convention all menu pads, and most menu options have a hot-key, that is, a key that can be used in a sequence (usually beginning with **Alt**) to select menu items. This is created in the Menu Builder, just as it is with @..GET - Controls, by inserting the \< combination before the hotkey letter. This shows up in the menu pad or option as an underline of the letter—File.

The other keyboard method is the keyboard shortcut, a specific key combination that causes immediate execution of a pad or option, for example **Ctrl-X** to cut text. These are defined in the Options of the Menu Builder.

There are two other, even smaller details of a standard menu. You'll notice in the illustration above that one of the options of the Menu menu, Menu Bar Options..., contains an ellipsis (the three dots). This is a cue that selection of the option brings up a dialog box. The other visual cue is a pointer, > which indicates that another popup menu (submenu) will be displayed. The ellipses are not explicitly created by the Menu Builder. It's up to you to carry on the convention, as established by Windows, to put in the ellipses. The other symbol is automatically provided when you create a submenu to a Menu Option (called in the manual a *cascade menu*).

All of these components are part of the FoxPro menu system. They come "free" with the use of the Menu Builder, and you are encouraged to take full advantage of them. As you will see, the Menu System is very flexible—though standardized in form—and stands literally at your beck and call throughout the run of your application.

Menu Programming Options

Having established some common names for menu components, it's time to put menus first in a programming context, and then in the context of the Menu Builder.

It might help to think of the FoxPro menu system as a piece of software machinery that manages the menus, which can be turned on or off as needed. The system menu has a set of built-in subroutines, called the Menu Manager, that take the menu definitions you (or the Menu Builder) provide, stores them in a special memory area, and manages their presentation and operation. The system menu also has its own default definitions, which it uses if it gets no other instructions. The controls for this system begin with a SET command. The FoxPro Menu Manager is called in programs the SYSMENU, and there is a series of commands that invoke the manager in several guises:

- `SET SYSMENU ON` The system menu is on by default. In FoxPro this command puts the system menu into a state where it waits for user input (**F10**, or **Alt**) before it becomes activated.
- `SET SYSMENU OFF` Turns the system menu off and removes it from the screen.
- `SET SYSMENU AUTOMATIC` Officially invokes the system menu as both visible and active. When running in automatic (which it does by default), the Menu Manager—adds and removes, enables and disables pads, popups, and options, as appropriate. For example, the Database pad is disabled until a data file is opened, or the Browse pad is added only when a Browse window is opened. This saves you, the programmer, from an incredible amount of work, although there's still plenty for you to do with your own menu options.
- `SET SYSMENU TO DEFAULT` Restores the system menu to a default condition, usually the FoxPro startup definition. However, you can modify the default definition (see SET SYSMENU SAVE).
- `SET SYSMENU TO` Is very selective. It removes all pads from the screen except those immediately involved with the current action. If you're in the Command window, it removes all pads except Text, because that's what's needed in the Command window. This command is unusual, because it also works the same whether in interactive or in program mode.
- `SET SYSMENU SAVE` This form of the command saves the current menu configuration (however it was defined), as the default menu. If you modify this menu, and then later SET MENU TO DEFAULT, it returns to this saved definition. (You cannot, however, permanently modify the FoxPro default menu.)
- `SET SYSMENU NOSAVE` This is the true "reset" for the system menu. It always returns the menu definition back to the FoxPro startup configuration. SET SYSMENU TO DEFAULT only returns it back to the last defined default condition.

NOTE

Running the system menu doesn't necessarily involve using any of the above commands. SET SYSMENU ON and SET SYSMENU AUTOMATIC are the defaults, and should be enough for many applications. However, if you mess around with the default definitions, turn off the system menu, or create your own menus, you should at least close out your program with SET SYSMENU NOSAVE to restore FoxPro to the startup configuration. (Of course, if you're quitting FoxPro, it doesn't matter.)

System Menu Names

In addition to the name of the Menu Manager itself (SYSMENU), the pads and options of the system menu form a hierarchy (menu tree) of names starting with the name for the system menu bar:

```
_MSYSMENU
```

The the system menu pads, as listed in Table 14.1.

Table 14.1
System menu pad names.

Menu Pad	Name
Help	_MSM_SYSTEM
File	_MSM_FILE
Edit	_MSM_EDIT
Database	_MSM_DATA
Record	_MSM_RECRD
Program	_MSM_PROG
Text	_MSM_TEXT
Window	_MSM_WINDO

Next comes the names of the popups, listed in Table 14.2.

Table 14.2
Popup names.

Menu Popup	Name
Help	_MSYSTEM
File	_MFILE
Edit	_MEDIT
Database	_MDATA
Record	_MRECRD
Program	_MPROG
Text	_MTEXT
Window	_MWINDO

These are followed by the Options for the Popups of each pad, shown in Table 14.3 on the next page.

Table 14.3
Popup options names.

File Option	Name	Edit Option	Name	Database Option	Name	Record Option	Name
New...	_MFI_NEW	Undo	_MED_UNDO	Setup...	_MDA_SETUP	Append	_MRC_APPND
Open...	_MFI_OPEN	Redo	_MED_REDO	Browse	_MDA_BROW	Change	_MRC_CHNGE
Close	_MFI_CLOSE	Cut	_MED_CUT	Append From...	_MDA_APPND	Goto...	_MRC_GOTO
Close All	_MFI_CLALL	Copy	_MED_COPY	Copy To...	_MDA_COPY	Locate...	_MRC_LOCAT
Save	_MFI_SAVE	Paste	_MED_PASTE	Sort...	_MDA_SORT	Continue	_MRC_CONT
Save As	_MFI_SAVAS	Paste Special...	_MED_PSTLK	Total...	_MDA_TOTAL	Seek...	_MRC_SEEK
Revert	_MFI_REVERT	Clear	_MED_CLEAR	Average...	_MDA_AVG	Replace...	_MRC_REPL
Print Setup..	_MFI_SETUP	Insert Object...	_MED_INSOB	Count...	_MDA_COUNT	Delete...	_MRC_DELET
Print	_MFI_PRINT	Object...	_MED_OBJ	Sum...	_MDA_SUM	Recall...	_MRC_RECAL
Exit	_MFI_QUIT	Change Link...	_MED_LINK	Calculate...	_MDA_CALC		
		Convert to..	_MED_CYTST	Report...	_MDA_REPRT		
		Select All	_MED_SLCTA	Label...	_MDA_LABEL		
		Goto Line...	_MED_GOTO	Pack	_MDA_PACK		
		Find...	_MED_FIND	Reindex	_MDA_RINDX		
		Find Again	_MED_FINDA				
		Replace	_MED_REPL				
		Replace All	_MED_REPLA				
		Preferences...	_MED_PREF				

Program Option	Name	Window Option	Name	Help Option	Name
Do...	_MPR_DO	Hide	_MWI_HIDE	Contents	_MST_HELP
Cancel	_MPR_CANCL	Hide All	_MWI_HIDEA	Search for Help on...	_MST_HPSCH
Resume	_MPR_RESUM	Show All	_MWI_SHOWA	How to Use Help...	_MST_HPHOW
Debug	_MPR_DEBUG	Clear	_MWI_CLEAR	About FoxPro...	_MST_ABOUT
Trace	_MPR_TRACE	Cycle	_MWI_ROTAT	Calculator	_MST_CALCU

Compile...	_MPR_COMPL	Command	_MWI_CMD	Calendar/ Diary	_MST_DIARY
Generate...	_MPR_GENER	View	_MWI_VIEW	Filer	_MST_FILER
Macros...	_MPR_MACRO			Puzzle	_MST_PUZZL
Beautify...	_MPR_BEAUT				
FoxDoc...	_MPR_DOCUM				

The significance of these menu names is that they provide a way for you to configure your own system menu and menu options. These names can be used in *any* configuration, and always invoke their corresponding FoxPro function. In the Menu Builder, these are defined in the Result column as Bar#.

Maintaining the Menu Environment

When you start FoxPro, the system menu appears automatically. As a rule, right from the very first screen of your application, you'll be creating your own menus that redefine the system menu. As explained above, the system menu can always be restored using SET SYSMENU NOSAVE. But as you progress farther into your application, what happens to your menu definitions?

That's the role of PUSH MENU and POP MENU. These commands manipulate a "stack" of Menu bar definitions. As your application moves from one menu to another, it can "Push" one menu definition after another onto the menu stack, and as it returns, "Pop" the menus back. PUSH and POP both require the name of a specific Menu bar. Because the Menu Builder uses code that redefines the system Menu Bar with your menu, the "name" of your menu is always the name of the system menu bar - _MSYSMENU.

When you "Push" a menu definition on to the menu stack, the original menu is NOT cleared from the screen, and remains active. However, it's now "safe" for you to redefine and activate a new menu, using this syntax:

```
PUSH MENU < menu name >
PUSH MENU _MSYSMENU
```

The next variation returns the Menu bar to the first menu definition in the menu stack and then clears the stack. Its syntax is:

```
POP MENU < menu name > [ TO MASTER]
POP MENU _MSYSMENU
POP MENU _MSYSMENU TO MASTER
```

Integrating Menus and Screens

The FoxPro menu (system menu bar) is always around by default. You can also redefine it at any time. You can code your own menu definitions and activate them (the hard way), or create a menu with the Menu Builder and simply code:

```
DO <MENU NAME>.MPR
```

The extension is necessary, since the default file for the Menu Builder is an .MPR and not a .PRG. If you want to preserve menu definitions as you go, add the PUSH/POP commands discussed above:

```
PUSH MENU _MSYSMENU
DO <MENU NAME>.MPR
...
POP MENU _MSYSMENU
```

NOTE

It's important to keep in mind that a FoxPro system menu is not a "wait state." The program does not halt for a menu choice. This is part of the event-driven scenario being developed in FoxPro. Many a programmer has started a program with a menu (in the initialization file), thinking this will be the main menu screen only to have the program drop out immediately. Without a READ, other kind of loop, or some other command that can impose a wait state (like a BROWSE), a FoxPro program just keeps executing until it finishes.

Of course the majority of your applications are made up of screens, and most of the screens have a READ (somewhere). For the most part, a READ is just another wait state in which a menu can be active. However a READ MODAL does have a direct effect on the system menu—it disables it. Normally, when you want a modal state, it's probably a good idea to shut off the menu so the user can't go traipsing into uncontrolled territory. If you *do* want a menu active while in a READ MODAL, it's customary to include the call to a menu in the snippet of the WHEN clause of the READ.

Probably because it's convenient, many programmers always put their menu calls in the WHEN clause. This isn't necessary. You could put them into the setup code. (Both of these work because they're executed only once on entering a screen.) The point is to pick a location and stick with it, so you (and others) will always know where to look for menu calls.

To summarize the programming role of menus: The system menu is almost always available. It's one more user interface element that waits for some kind of input. You can redefine the system menu at any time, usually by calling a file generated with the Menu Builder. When combining a menu and a screen, it's conventional to put the menu call in the screen code (either the Setup or the When snippet). This sets the stage for using the Menu Builder.

Using the Menu Builder

The Menu Builder, shown in Figure 14.1 automates the creation of menu code, based on your definitions. It's designed to modify the standard FoxPro system menu. Like the Screen Builder, getting started with a new menu or modifying an existing menu is easiest from the Project Manager. Otherwise you can use CREATE or MODIFY MENU <menu name> from the Command window, or File, New, Menu, New and File, Open from the system menu.

The main Menu Builder is accompanied by its own menu pad, popup, and options. The process of building a menu is five easy pieces in any order:

1. Enter a menu **Prompt**. This will be a menu bar or a menu option.
2. Enter the type of **Result** that arises from a selection of a prompt.
3. Depending on the type of result, make entries in the Result Edit dialog box.
4. Add any desired **Options**.
5. Use **Try It**. You can always have a simulation of the menu in operation.

Your work in the Menu Builder is stored in two files with extensions .MNX and .MNT. Once you've created the menu, you can generate the menu code, just as you do with Screen Builder code, through the Project Manager or from the system menu. The menu generation program—GENMENU.PRG—creates a text program file with the extension .MPR, which is ready to be compiled like other program files, this time with the extension .MPX.

Figure 14.1
The Menu Builder.

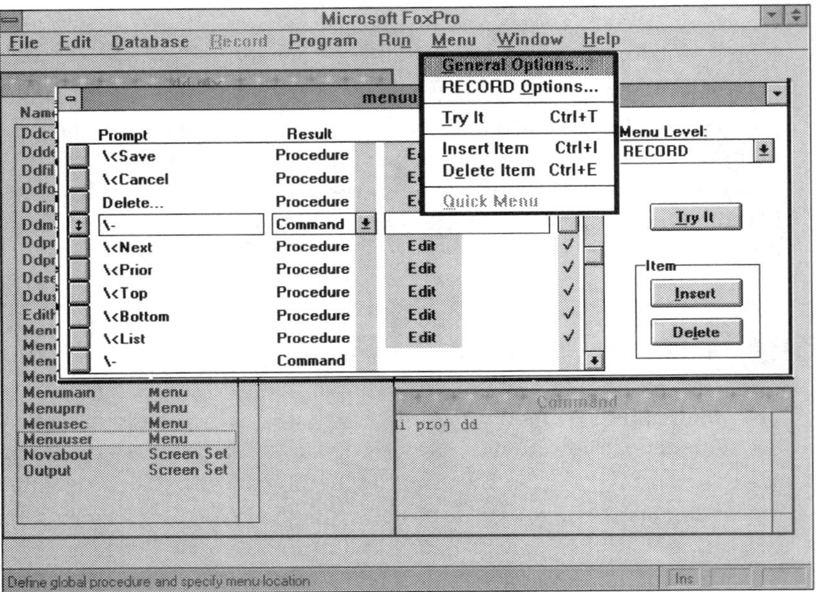

Menu Pads and Popup Options

The most logical approach to building a menu is to do it one "layer" at a time: menu pads then popup options, repeated for menu levels of popup options as needed. Starting with the Menu bar, define all of the pads in the prompt boxes. Some of these might be standard FoxPro pads, others will be your own creation. It helps to lay them all out and play with the order, if necessary. It's convention to maintain the order of standard FoxPro menu pads up to a point. If you think of it, this is also a good time to add the hot keys to the prompt, with the usual caveat that no two hot keys should be alike. Figure 14.2 shows a sample approach.

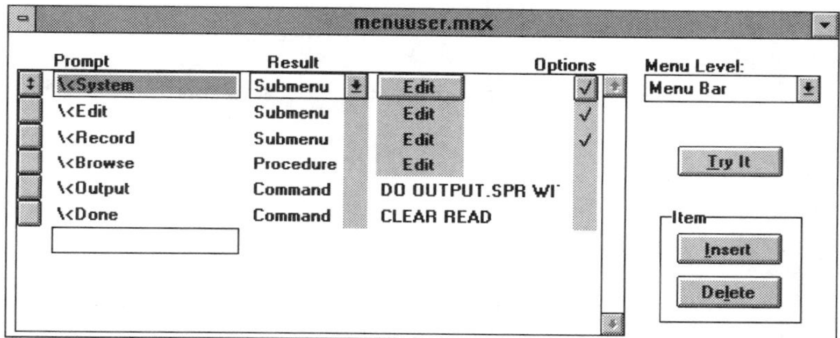

Figure 14.2
A Menu Builder example.

In the example above (taken from the menu for the users screen), the system menu has been modified by removing the Database, Program, Window, and Help pads. When building this kind of menu from scratch, it's usually faster to do a quick menu, and then delete the unwanted menu pads. User-defined Browse, Output, and Done pads were added, each with their own hot key.

Based on the intended action of the prompts, you then select the appropriate "result type:"

- **Command.** If the prompt calls for executing another program, screen, or some FoxPro command (single commands only), select this and enter the command desired. The syntax for the code generated is:

```
ON SELECTION BAR <option #> OF <menu namd> <Command>
```

- **Bar #.** If the prompt is a standard FoxPro menu pad or menu option, link it to the official "name" (see the tables above) by indicating the Bar # type, and entering the name of the pad or option, such as _MEDIT or _MFI_SAVAS. Typical code generated is:

```
DEFINE PAD _qdi03itul OF _MSYSMENU PROMPT "\<System" ;
 COLOR SCHEME 3 KEY ALT+S, ""
ON PAD _qdi03itul OF _MSYSMENU ACTIVATE POPUP _msystem
```

- **Submenu.** If the prompt should initialize a menu popup, then you select this type and go on to define the popup options. The syntax for the code generated is:

```
ON SELECTION BAR <option #> OF <menu name> ACTIVATE POPUP
<name>
```

- **Procedure.** In those cases where you want the Menu Builder file to contain the actual code required for a menu selection, choose this type and then enter the procedure code required. This is snippet coding just like the Screen Builder, and the procedure is generated with the rest of the menu code. The syntax for the code generated is:

```
ON SELECTION BAR <option #> OF <menu name> DO <procedure
name>
 IN <menu name>
```

Depending on the results type you selected, you may go on to create procedure snippets, or move to another menu tree level for additional popups and options. You've probably seen menu trees go to about three levels. Even that's a lot, because it forces people to use many keystrokes or clicks to get to something.

Procedures are created in the Menu Builder under the same guidelines as the Screen Builder. You should not use PROCEDURE, FUNCTION, or PARAMETER to start the snippet. Adding a return is not necessary.

Building procedures to be stored in the Menu Builder files also raises a structural issue about programming with the Menu Builder and the Screen Builder. It is functionally possible to have important processing and user interface code in both a Screen Builder screen and a Menu Builder menu, although they work together for the same Screen Set. Because these are two different tools, with different storage files, it can become confusing and time consuming to distribute important code to both places. For that reason, some developers advise that only code directly related to menu operation should be created in the Menu Builder, and that other operational code be created in the Screen Builder, as a more centralized and logical location for this kind of programming.

In practice this leaves only direct procedure and function calls, control of menu options, and menu modification commands in the Menu Builder files. This same approach applies to the Setup and Cleanup code of the Menu Builder, as well. There are times when this could become an exercise in hair-splitting. But the practice does save some time and can reduce overlaps in logic and processing, which cause errors.

The last piece of work on the prompt for each menu pad (or popup option) is to add prompt options, if any. There are four to choose from:

- **Shortcut...** Most of the menu pads and popup options of the system menu have keyboard shortcuts. When you create your own pads and options, decide which of them are used often enough for it to be convenient to also have a keyboard alternative. On menu pads, don't bother with a key text—there won't be any. Do bother to use a shortcut that includes the hot key letter of a menu pad, such as **Alt-P** for a **Process** pad.
- **Skip For...** is FoxPro's way to disable (and enable) menu pads and options. It gets used occasionally for context situations in a program. For example, a menu option Select Invoices is disabled when there are no invoices to be selected. It is also one of the most important elements in an application security system, since denying access to various menu options is one way of placing security control to various parts of a program. In using the Skip For it's important to keep reminding yourself that it disables a menu option when it is *true* to skip for a logical expression. For example, if you use the expression: M.security < 5 and it is true, then the option is disabled. If it is false, it is enabled. This is a case where the logic and the context always seem slightly askew.
- **Message...** is new with FoxPro and easy to overlook. The message you enter here is displayed in the status bar at the bottom of the screen, provided of course, that the status bar is enabled. This provides a helpful touch for people learning the application. Put messages in your menus!
- **Pad Name...** is for programmers who don't like the cryptic procedure names created automatically by the Menu Builder with SYS(2015). The usual code for pads comes out like this:

  ```
  DEFINE PAD _qdi03itu1 OF _MSYSMENU PROMPT "\<System".
  ```

  If you specify a name for a pad in this option, you get:

  ```
  DEFINE PAD msystem OF _MSYSMENU PROMPT "\<System"
  ```

  or some such thing.

General Options

When the menu file is called, the menu code executes from beginning to end. The Menu Manager loads and executes the entire menu code at once, from Setup to Cleanup in one fell swoop. After all of the code has executed, the newly defined menu sits in the Menu Manager memory, waiting for user input. This changes the way you should look at Setup, Procedure, and Cleanup code in the General Options dialog box, shown in Figure 14.3. This is the place to put code that affects the entire menu (rather than any particular bar, pad, or option).

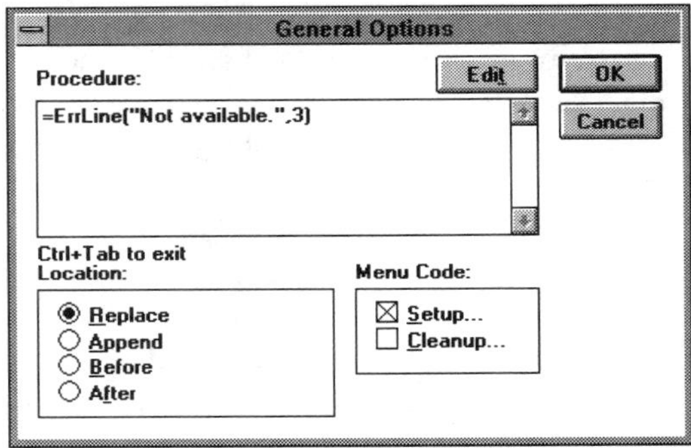

Figure 14.3 *The General Options dialog box.*

Again there are four options:

- **Procedure**, if you choose to create one, executes on every menu selection *if* there is no other procedure, command or bar# for that selection. This is the OTHERWISE of a CASE statement. Typically, this procedure is merely used to handle menu options that are not yet implemented and have nothing to execute. A simple WAIT "This option not yet available." WINDOW NOWAIT, or similar, suffices.
- **Setup...** handles definition of any variables used in the menu, and any other environmental settings that impact the way the menu operates. Although you can put almost anything in the menu Setup, including file openings, and variable processing, the best advice is don't. This also applies to using PUSH MENU in the Setup. You can't use POP MENU in the Cleanup, because it executes at the same time as the Setup code. This means your pushed menu gets popped—a nullifying effect. That, in turn, means the POP MENU usually must go in the cleanup of a

screen set. As a rule, what you cleanup in the screen, you should set up in the screen.

- **Cleanup...** in menu code is a misnomer. If you really programmed to cleanup what was done in the setup, you wind up with nothing, since the two segments execute consecutively. What really goes into the cleanup, by convention, is code that arranges any special "effects" in the menu, such as marking, enabling, and disabling.
- **Locations** are fairly obvious. You either insert your menu definition before some option, after some option, appended at the end of all options, or to replace all options. The tendency is to create an entire Menu Bar, and replace the existing one. This requires no mental bookkeeping. The other approaches are used mostly when the Menu Builder is creating Menu *stubs*, bits and pieces of menu code to be inserted in other parts of a program to modify a menu "on the fly."

Menu Options

Menu options perform the same role as the procedure and name options of the General Options window, only here they apply to a particular menu pad, or popup menu. The Menu Options dialog box, shown in Figure 14.4, is displayed in the Menu menu. If you're working with menu pads, then the Menu menu option reads Menu Bar Options..., otherwise it contains the name of the current popup menu, such as Record Options.

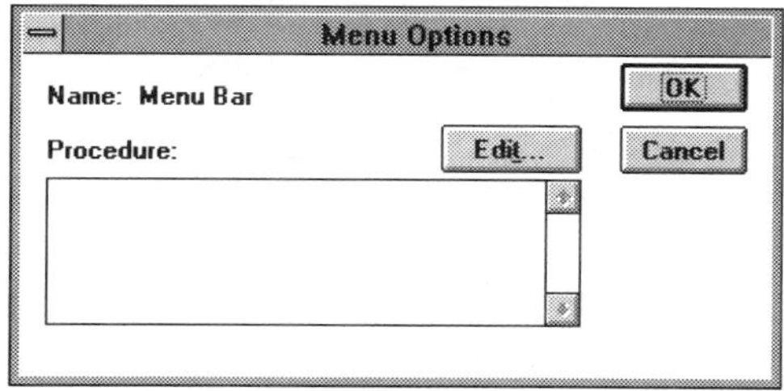

Figure 14.4 *The Menu Options dialog box.*

Code in the procedure snippet executes when any option in the bar or popup menu is selected, which makes it useful for programming that affects options in that popup. The example in the FoxPro *Developer's Guide* is a helpful illustration.

Chapter 15
Programming Elements

The FoxPro Power Tools are a step in the direction of automating the application development process. But they don't remove the necessity for programming. The Report Writer comes closest. Once the capabilities of the new FoxPro version of the Report Writer are mastered, there are very few reports (approaching none) that will require direct programming. The RQBE tool produces some powerful queries without needing programming. However, it doesn't cover the full capabilities of the FoxPro SQL - SELECT command. The Menu Builder removes most of the drudgery of producing menu code, especially for standard menus. But some of the Menu Builder options still need programming, and there are all kinds of subtle manipulations of menus that must be programmed. And then there is the Screen Builder.

Outside of its ability to generate screen code—principally the location and attributes of screen objects—the Screen Builder Power Tool is really a programming "shell," a framework on which to hang all sorts of programming. It's doubtful that without some programming knowledge, you could even produce a successful screen with the Screen Builder. And more advanced screen work, which is the subject of this chapter, can require programming skills of a high order.

It's also important to keep in perspective that not all of the FoxPro world revolves around the Power Tools. There are many programming elements either outside of, or peripheral to, the Power Tools. Data processing, program initialization, and specialized UDFs are just some of the items on a list of pure programming, which are also important parts of most applications.

The goal of this chapter is to put the Power Tools back into the overall context of building an application, and the general programming that is required. It covers many of the "hot topics" like event-driven programming and the foundation read, but the intent is not to provide a detailed way to do these things, but rather to focus on their purpose and general implementation.

This approach may seem abstract, but there is a rationale behind it. Many of the subjects covered in this chapter are in a state of flux. Event driven programming, multi-window screen sets, and Foundation READs are at the cutting edge of FoxPro programming. At the moment, it's a rather tortured and unpolished edge. There are gaps in the procedures, gaps in the tools, and gaps in the understanding of how best to use FoxPro for this kind of user interface programming. Charging into these gaps are dozens of ambitious and often very clever approaches developed by FoxPro programmers. The examples that come with FoxPro for Windows, numerous magazine articles, and bulletin board contributions are all testimony to the desire to explain and master these new techniques. And you are encouraged to absorb as much of this as you can, and even to incorporate the approaches into your applications.

However, the people at Microsoft/Fox are also aware of the strengths and shortcomings of FoxPro. And *they* will have the final word on approaches and techniques. It will be called FoxPro version 3.0.

As Microsoft Access and Visual Basic move toward the forefront of end-user database management, FoxPro seems destined to move even further into the realm of application development. This probably means a much more integrated and complete development environment is on the way. Many of the loose ends and unclear techniques we are now trying to overcome will no longer be issues.

Between now and the time FoxPro version 3.0 appears, you'll need to exercise judgement about adopting specialized techniques. Be wary of approaches that take you far from the standard use of the Power Tools, especially the Screen Builder and Menu Builder. You don't want to be in the position a year or two from now of not being able to make your approach square with Microsoft's. That's why the method in this book is to outline a general approach to these advanced topics, rather than promote a specific system.

Using a Foundation READ

Although it's been called the "mother of all READs," the basic use and coding of the foundation READ are very simple:

```
is_quit = .f.
READ VALID is_quit
```

This is all it takes to put the READ into its event-loop mode. Your program will not terminate until the VALID is triggered and is_quit is set to (.t.). Typically, this is done in a snippet of a menu option or a push button menu.

```
is_quit = .t.
CLEAR READ ALL
```

The CLEAR READ ALL sends the program execution into the READ VALID along with the changed value of is_quit. A return of true (.t.), causes the READ to terminate and program execution continues on the following line. This type of foundation READ loop is independent of screens, GETs, or any other element.

The most basic use of a foundation READ is to provide a "wait state" for a program. As you may recall, the FoxPro system menu resides in memory as part of the persistently active Menu Manager. When you execute a menu of your own, it doesn't stop the program. Without some other way to provide a wait state, a loop of some kind, your program would "fall through" a menu and terminate. The following code isn't enough:

```
* Set up your program
= ProgSet()
* Call the program menu.
DO ProgMenu.MPR
```

To make it work, just add a Foundation Read and clean up:

```
is_quit = .f.
READ VALID is_quit

*> Clean up the program.
= ProgClean()
```

Other loops could do the job, but as Microsoft points out, other kinds of loops force a constant activity in the processor of your computer. Presumably, the READ loop is truly passive and doesn't constantly hit the CPU.

The usual home for a foundation READ is in the initialization program of your application. You've seen examples of an init file elsewhere in this book. Typically, this is a standard program file (.PRG). It's just an expanded version of the skeleton code above: setup, menu call, foundation READ, cleanup.

There are many configurations for applications that can be built on a Foundation READ.

Your choice of configuration should be determined by the requirements of your application. The Foundation READ, in many respects, is just a simple way to take advantage of the FoxPro menu system at a main menu level, without going into a specific screen. But in a tightly controlled application, or where you choose to follow the more traditional programming techniques, you may skip the foundation READ and simply have a series of nested READs linked by menus. If your application is small, say two or three screens, you might choose to have all of them tied to the foundation READ in a multi-window READ. And so on. The combinations are endless.

One thing you need to pay attention to is the number of READs being executed simultaneously in your application. You are allowed to use five by FoxPro, although in cases where memory is short, only four might be available.These are often called *READ levels*. There's also a function, RDLEVEL( ), that returns the current number of READs in execution. You can use this to monitor how deeply your program is running into the READs.

Building upon a foundation READ is sort of the "grand architecture" point of view for an application. It's predicated on the acceptance of the FoxPro menu system, the use of READs as the controlling structure, and the screen/screen set approach of the Screen Builder. This is certainly not the only way to build an application. But it *is* the way Microsoft Fox seems to be going.

Coordinating the Elements

Working with a READ as the controlling structure of your programs entails the task of coordinating other elements within it. The task ranges from pretty darn simple to unbelievably complicated—from a basic READ all the way to full blown event-driven programming.

Basically, there are four categories of screen elements that can be coordinated with one or more READs.

1. Windows with GETs (READ windows)
2. Non-READ windows (BROWSE, Calculator)

3. System menus
4. Push button menus

In this context, *coordination* means getting all or most of these elements to coexist at the same time, and adjusting the elements as the user moves between them. The following example illustrates how this might be done.

A Scenario

The program starts with a foundation READ and a main menu. The user makes a program choice from the main menu, which opens another READ with three windows—two are windows with GETs and the other a BROWSE. At the same time a new menu is activated for the screen, as is a Push Button menu at the bottom of the windows with GETs. The user is allowed to move freely between the open windows. Data can be added or edited and reports run. At some point the user chooses to exit the program.

This example is just a variation of the basic Add/Edit/Delete screen from Chapter 13. Even things like foundation READs and multi-window screens don't have to be extraordinary.

The project (in the Project Manager, of course) has an initialization file (INIT.PRG). There is one screen set, comprised of three windows: There is a window for "users" (staff who use the application), a "user's security" window (a browse), and a "security" window with information about the various security checkpoints in the application. To stick to the main points, a lot of detail is omitted from these examples.

Start with a Foundation READ and the sections that go with it:

```
INIT.PRG
*———————————————————[ SETUP
* Set Environment
CLEAR ALL
SET TALK OFF

* Open Tables
USE ddsec ALIAS sec ORDER seclocid IN 0 && Security Table
USE ddusec ALIAS usc ORDER staffid IN 0 && User Security Table
USE ddusers ALIAS usr ORDER staffid IN 0 && Users Table
SET RELATION TO staffid INTO usc
SET SKIP TO usc

*Call the Menu
```

```
DO MainMenu.MPR

*> Set the Foundation READ.
is_Quit = .f.
READ VALID FrHandler()

*--------------------[ CLEANUP
SET SYSMENU TO DEFAULT
POP KEY
CLEAR ALL

*===================[ PROGRAM FUNCTIONS & PROCEDURES
]==================

* FOUNDATION READ VALID FUNCTION
FUNCTION FRHandler
* Test for exit conditions.

RETURN (is_Quit)
*
*END OF INIT.PRG
```

The main menu, built with the Menu Builder, is very simple and has only three pads: Users, Maintenance, and Quit. The Users pad, the one chosen, opens the screen set DDUSERS.SPR.

Windows and READs

In FoxPro the relationship between one or more windows and the READ is crucial for managing the user interface.

Screen Sets

When you create a screen in the Screen Builder, you are also creating the potential for a screen set. The Edit Screen Set dialog box is displayed in Figure 15.1.

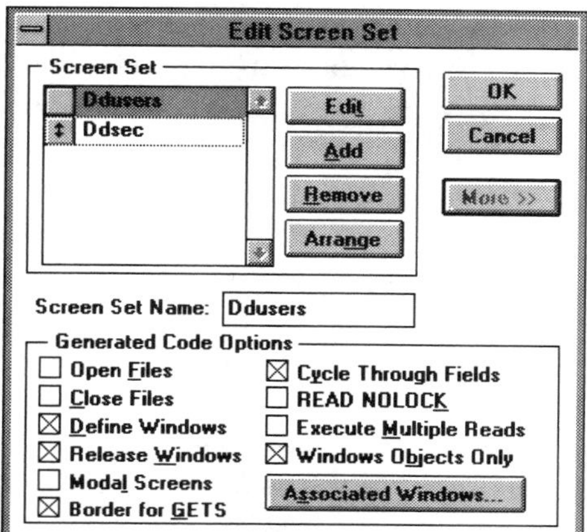

Figure 15.1 *The Edit Screen Set dialog box.*

To create a multi-window screen set, all you have to do is hit the Add button and find the other screen file (.SCX) you wish to include. When the Screen Builder generates these two screens, it concatenates their code into one .SPR file, and unless you check the Execute Multiple Reads option, both screens operate under one READ CYCLE. In this example the users and security screens have been combined into the users screen set.

Once the screens have been combined into a screen set, all of the GET objects (actually all of the objects) are ordered consecutively—from screen to screen. The READ CYCLE then allows the user to use **Tab** or **Enter** to get from one screen to the next, bringing each dialog box forward as they go. For each of the GETs, FoxPro assigns an object number, which if you recall, can be monitored with the OBJNUM( ), _CUROBJ combination. You have to pay attention to the fact that while you may ACTIVATE any READ window, the value of _CUROBJ remains the same (like back on the previous window). If you want to change the entry position in a multi-window screen set, you must not only ACTIVATE the new window, but also set _CUROBJ = OBJNUM(<some specific GET object>), then use SHOW GET <the specific GET object> to activate the entry point.

It's important to note that the order of screens in the screen set window list will be the order in which their code is generated. You need to be careful that the file opening (and closing) of each screen, along with other environment settings and variable definitions, don't step on each other. In this example, since all of the relevant tables are opened in the initialization file but overlap between the two screens, it's important that indexes, relations, and table pointers are kept in order.

The Screen Builder helps by segregating the variables from the different screens with a REGIONAL designation. You help your own cause by using the #SECTION 1, #SECTION 2 generator directives to keep these sections of each screen from getting mixed up. Likewise, when you set up a multi-window screen, it's a good idea to review the options in the More>> section of the Edit Screen Set dialog box. What might have been an appropriate setting for one dialog box, may not be true with two or more dialog boxes. For example one dialog box might have been set as a Modal Screen, which you may or may not want for the screen set.

If this is to be a Modal Screen (a READ MODAL), then you should also consider any other windows that you need to include as an associated window. If a window isn't included in this list, which you create by selecting the Associated Windows... button and entering the window titles, it won't be available to the user while they are in the screen. The most important to include are any Browse windows needed with the screen.

READ Windows

The way to start thinking about windows and READs is to emphasize a distinction: There are windows that contain GETs, which are activated by a READ. These are called *READ windows*. There are windows that contain no GETs, and though they may be part of a READ screen set, are called *nonREAD windows*. The typical Add/Edit/Delete screen (AED) is a READ window. A Browse is a nonREAD window. This distinction has some important ramifications within FoxPro, for example:

- **READ DEACTIVATE** triggers by moving *from* a READ window (or any user window).
- **READ ACTIVATE** is triggered only when moving *to* a READ window.

Many of the window functions have explicit behavior for READ windows.

One of the recurring themes of window management in FoxPro is the determination of whether a window is a READ or a nonREAD window. It's one reason behind the widely practiced convention of using window names that signal the type, such as WR = Read Window, WB = Browse Window (wbEmployee,wrInvoices). This makes checking for window type a simple matter of :

```
IF SUBSTR(UPPER(WONTOP( ), 1, 2)="WR" && READ Window
...
```

NOTE

The function WONTOP( ) returns the name of any kind of window, WOUTPUT( ) returns the name of the currently active READ window (any use-defined window), if any. Likewise WREAD( ) determines if the named window is a READ window.

The biggest responsibility when managing READ windows is to determine whether it's appropriate for the user to leave a window. This is especially true if records are being added or edited. Although there are different schools of thought on how far a user may go before "finishing" a new record or an edit, it's general practice to control the user to some degree—especially in a multiuser environment where other people may be waiting for the information.

Another important factor in this checking is that closing a window (**Ctrl-W**, **Esc**, or clicking on the close window handle) passes through the DEACTIVATE clause, and if you don't intervene, terminates the READ. The routine for this intervention is a function placed into the DEACTIVATE clause of the READ, for example:

```
IN SCREEN.SCX
  READ DEACTIVATE ChkRead()

IN INIT.PRG (Procedures Section - a Generic Routine)
FUNCTION ChkRead

IF SUBSTR(UPPER(WONTOP())1,2)="WR" && READ Window
  IF is_add OR is_edit
    WAIT "Please use Save or Cancel." WINDOW NOWAIT
    RETURN .f.
  ENDIF
ENDIF
RETURN .t.
*
```

Coordinating the Elements

There are some major screen elements that are not available as part of the Screen Builder Toolbox: most notably the BROWSE, but also including MODIFY MEMO, MODIFY FILE, DEFINE POPUP, calculator, diary, and filer windows. These all occur in nonREAD windows. They require a different approach to incorporate them into a screen set. Browses, because of their huge importance as both data entry and picklist objects, deserve special attention.

Coordinating the BROWSE

Adding one or more BROWSEs to a screen set is not particularly difficult. Keeping track of them can be. The most widely used approach for incorporation of a BROWSE in a screen follows this pattern:

1. Define a window for the BROWSE to occupy. Although it has its own window by default, the Browse window cannot be Zoomed, Minimized, and so on. Also, in many applications it's important to have the Browse show up in the same spot every time. You can't specify row and column locations for the standard Browse window. Some programmer's create a generic Browse window definition (keeping it in memory at all times), and simply move it around or resize it with MODIFY WINDOW.
2. Issue the BROWSE command, with all of the FIELD and other clauses as appropriate. Most importantly, you *must* add NOWAIT to the clause list. If you want FoxPro to keep the Browse window (and any memo field windows) open, also add the SAVE clause. The routine looks like this:

```
IN THE SETUP SECTION OF DDUSER.SCX:
 DEFINE WINDOW wbDepts AT 2,0 SIZE 20,77 FLOAT GROW ZOOM
MINIMIZE COLOR SCHEME 10
 BROWSE WINDOW wbDepts NOEDIT NOMODIFY NOAPPEND NODELETE
NOMENU TITLE "Department" NOWAIT SAVE
IN THE CLEANUP SECTION OF THE .SCX:
  RELEASE WINDOW wbDepts
```

This same approach can be used for MODIFY MEMO, DEFINE POPUP, and MODIFY FILE.

Because a Browse is always a nonREAD window, you have to take special steps to track any Browse windows in your screens. For one thing, because it's a nonREAD window, leaving or closing the Browse *does not* trigger the ACTIVATE or DEACTIVATE clauses. What do you do if you need to keep the Browse window permanently open, or need to make some special checks of its data?

If a Browse shares the screen with READ windows, as is the case of the current user screen example, then you can use the ACTIVATE clause as program control shifts to a new (presumably READ) window. A routine like the following can be used to test for the existence or visibility of the Browse:

IN THE READ ACTIVATE CLAUSE OF DDUSER.SCX:

```
READ ACTIVATE ActivSet()
```

IN INIT.PRG (FUNCTIONS & PROCEDURES):

```
FUNCTION ActivSet
IF NOT WVISIBLE( DEPARTMENT )
   IF WEXIST( DEPARTMENT )
    ACTIVATE WINDOW DEPARTMENT SAME
  ELSE
     IF NOT WEXIST( WBDEPTS )
       DEFINE WINDOW wbDepts AT 2,0 SIZE 20,77 FLOAT GROW ZOOM
MINIMIZE ;
     COLOR SCHEME 10
  ENDIF
  BROWSE WINDOW wbDepts NOEDIT NOMODIFY NOAPPEND NODELETE
NOMENU TITLE Department NOWAIT SAVE
 ENDIF
ENDIF
*
```

As you may have noticed in the example above, another peculiarity of the Browse (mentioned earlier in the book), is its chameleon-like assimilation of a name. If it's not part of a window with a title, and you give it no title, the Browse takes the alias of its primary file. If you title the window it's in, it takes that for a name. If you give the Browse a title, it takes that for a name. This all works something like the following...

```
DEFINE WINDOW wbTest FROM 1,0 TO 23,79.6 TITLE TEST1
BROWSE WINDOW wbTest TITLE TEST2

ACTIVATE WINDOW TEST2       && Activates the Browse
ACTIVATE WINDOW wbTest      && Activates the window not Browse
```

```
CLEAR WINDOWS                 && The Browse stays, window closes
RELEASE WINDOW TEST2          && The Browse closes
```

Based on this behavior, it's often best to test for a Browse window using the WTITLE() function, because much of the time, that's what the Browse is really using for a window name.

The Browse always selects its work area automatically. A READ window does not, so if a user can switch between a READ and a Browse window, you need to make sure that work areas, pointers, and indexes all follow appropriately. This can be done many ways, but a typical approach would be to put a function into the ACTIVATE clause of the screen READ.

IN DDUSER.SCX

```
READ ACTIVATE ActivSet()
```

IN INIT.PRG (FUNCTIONS & PROCEDURES):

```
FUNCTION ActivSet
IF NOT WREAD(WLAST()) && We are going from a Browse to a READ.
  IF WONTOP() = "WRSECURITY"
    SELECT SEC
  ELSE
    SELECT USR
  ENDIF
ENDIF
*
```

Menus and PBMs

Because menus are commonly used to launch new program modules (such as calling another screen), they usually require special treatment in a multi-window READ. This is especially true where a READ has been assigned to each window. You don't want the user hopping back and forth, executing READs willy-nilly. The program will quickly run out of READs and crash. The routine to handle this, also part of the suggested approach in the FoxPro sample programming, is to create a function in the menu of each READ screen. This has only a few things to do when a user selects a menu option to go to another window: First, determine if a READ window is currently active. If it is, save the name of the requested screen, CLEAR READ the current window to push control back to the next level of READ, presumably the foundation READ. However, if no READ window is active, go ahead and execute the request for a new screen. It's as simple as it looks:

IN THE MENU OPTIONS THAT CALL ANOTHER SCREEN (.SPR):

```
* Call the menu processing routine with name of new screen.
DO MENUCHK IN USERMENU.MPR WITH "ddsec.SPR"
```

IN THE MENU "PROCEDURES" SECTION (Menu Builder):

```
PROCEDURE MenuChk
PARAMETER cNewProg
* Check to see if any READ Window is active.
IF RDLEVEL()>1       && Presumes a Foundation READ.
  CLEAR READ
ELSE
  DO (cNewProg)
ENDIF
*
```

The CLEAR READ terminates the current screen's READ, and carries program execution back to the foundation READ's VALID clause, where it will be handled by another routine you'll see shortly. Although it's been terminated, the current screen doesn't *look* any different, which gives the user the impression of all of the windows being simultaneously active.

The management of a push button menu (a PBM) within a READ depends a lot on whether it's in a utility window, or a part of the screen. If it's in a window, then that window needs to be coordinated along with all the other windows of the screen set. In fact a control window, as this form of a push button menu is often called, is a rather special case, because the same window must be available whenever a READ window is activated. The responsibility for doing this might reside in two places: READ ACTIVATE at the screen level, and READ VALID at the foundation READ level. The calls and routine might look like this:

IN SCREEN.SCX:

```
READ ACTIVATE ContrlChk()
```

IN INIT.PRG:

```
READ VALID FRHandler()
```

IN INIT.PRG (Functions and Procedures):

```
FUNCTION FRHandler
= ContrlChk()
...
*
```

```
FUNCTION ContrlChk
PRIVATE cWin
* Check for open READ windows
cWin = UPPER(WCHILD("",0))    && Bottom Window
DO WHILE LEN(cWin) > 0        && There's a name to work with.
  IF SUBSTR(cWin,1,2) = "WR" && Using the window name.
    RETURN .t.
  ENDIF
  cWin = UPPER(WCHILD("",1)) && All other windows.
ENDDO
* The only remaining window is the control panel
* so release it.
IF NOT EMPTY(WONTOP())
  RELEASE WINDOW (WONTOP())
ENDIF
*
```

If the PBM isn't in a utility window, but "hard wired" into the window of the screen (as it is in the example screen), things are somewhat simpler. Coordination becomes a matter of synchronizing screen, push button menu, and system menu. This depends on what "philosophy" you've adopted concerning adding and editing records.

If you recall the discussion of Push Button Menus (PBMs) in chapter 13, there are two main aspects - navigation (Next, Prior, List etc.), and Record Operations (Add, Edit etc.). The navigation buttons are thoroughly standard for a database screen of almost any kind. The Record Operation buttons imply a control over data editing, which may or may not be necessary. If your screen(s) call for controlled adding and editing (with their corresponding "exit" options—Save and Cancel), then as the user attempts to move in and out of the edit window(s) you need to monitor the status of adding or editing as a prerequisite.

The coordination of menus and push button menus within a screen set (or from screen to screen), depends on the philosophy behind their use. (Or whether they are used at all.) Some programmers like to use both PBMs and menu options for the most common activities in a screen—again typically the navigation options and the record operations. The PBMs provide instant access for mouse users, and the menus provide a keystroke alternative, plus, making it possible to define keystroke shortcuts.

Another responsibility of both PBMs and menus is to make sure that only the appropriate options are available during certain operations. The FoxPro menu system meets you at least part of the way. It manages the pads and popups for File, Edit, and Window for you, or at least to the degree that you allow it. The most common situations that are your responsibility are during adding a new record or editing a record. This is one of those user control issues, about half way between utterly event-driven programming and a modal screen.

The method is quite simple, and makes extensive use of the SET SKIP OF aspect of a system menu. It also has a very common use of variables: status flags. These are almost always logical variables (containing either .t. or .f.), and by the convention adopted in this book begin with IS_ e.g. IS_ADD, IS_EDIT and attempt to be remindful of what status they flag. Occasionally status flags are PUBLIC, but more often than not they should be tightly bound to the routine (and usually screen or program) in which they are used. This is especially true in a multi-window READ, where IS_EDIT might be used two or more times. It's important that it be declared REGIONAL or modified to be unique for each screen, such as IS_USREDIT, IS_USCEDIT.

The rest of the technique is located in the Menu Builder. For each of the popup options involved, in this case under the Record pad: Add, Edit, Save, Cancel, Delete, Next, Prior, Top, Bottom, List, and Done. All but Save and Cancel have IS_ADD OR IS_EDIT in their Skip for option box. This means all of these options are disabled when an add record or edit record is in progress. This forces the user to either save or cancel to finish editing. Save and cancel have the reverse logic: NOT (IS_ADD) OR NOT (IS_EDIT), since they should both be active during an edit/add.

READs and Termination

Sooner or later the user will want to exit the program (as opposed to exiting a screen or Browse). That's the final piece of coordination between READs, or even between a READ and itself—terminating READs. This is important in several ways. For one thing, you need to know when the user wants out. You need to interpret the various ways this can be signaled in your program, and decide if it's appropriate for the user to leave a READ screen. These are *active exit events* typically menu selections like Done or Quit, or using the **Esc** key. There are also *passive exit events* that are triggered by certain actions within a program and without the user explicitly signaling an exit. These include the READ DEACTIVATE clause returning .t. when the user changes the window, or a READ TIMEOUT. In either the active of passive case, it's probably going to be necessary for your program to monitor the termination of a READ.

Structurally (remember in FoxPro you really can talk about the READ as a structural element), it becomes very important to distinguish between termination of a READ at the screen level, and termination of a READ (or all READs) at the foundation level. In some configurations, for example nested READs, or multi-window screens with individual READs, the termination of a single READ may not signal the end of work. As mentioned above in using menus with a READ, it's used only to move between windows (screens). In this approach, as one READ is terminated, another is called. This keeps the total number of READs under control (and under five).

In other configurations, specifically those with multiple windows under a single READ, the exit event is even more important, since an unwanted termination brings down all the screens at once. In these cases, you need to be very exact with monitoring READ termination events, and whether they affect a "local" level of the application, or perhaps the foundation READ itself.

Most commonly, in the READ DEACTIVATE and VALID clauses you can monitor for a termination event by using the READKEY( ) function in one or both of its formats: READKEY( ) and READKEY(1). Table 15.1 shows the values returned by the function for the specific terminating events:

Table 15.1
READ terminating events.

Terminating Event	READKEY( ) Value No Update/Update
<Esc>	12 / 268
<Ctrl>W	270
<Ctrl>Q	12 / 268
<Ctrl><Enter>	5 / 261
	READKEY(1)
CLEAR READ [ALL]	2
Terminating a GET - Control	3
READ Window Closed	4
READ DEACTIVATE clause returns .t.	5
READ TIMEOUT	6

How your routine interprets these events, and what it does about them is, to a certain extent, specific to your screens and application.

This example function was used previously to see if the user is coming from a READ window, and whether an edit or add is in progress.

IN THE READ DEACTIVATE:

```
ChkRead()
```

It returns .t. if nothing is happening, which causes the local READ to terminate. Here's a slightly expanded version, to illustrate how READKEY() can be used to qualify the user's intentions to exit:

IN INIT.PRG (Procedures Section - a Generic Routine)

```
FUNCTION ChkRead
IF SUBSTR(UPPER(WONTOP()),1,2)="WR" && READ Window
  DO CASE
  CASE is_add OR is_edit
    WAIT "Please use Save or Cancel." WINDOW NOWAIT
    RETURN .f.
 CASE READKEY() = 270 && Ctrl W (Save?)
    IF YesNo("Save changes and exit now?, 8, "Y")
      = SaveRec()
      CLEAR READ
    ELSE     && Stay in current window.
      RETURN .f.
    ENDIF
  ENDCASE
ENDIF
RETURN .t.
*
```

Once a local READ has been terminated, program execution falls back to the next level of READ. Since no window has been activated or deactivated at this level, but a CLEAR READ has been issued, the READ VALID kicks in. This is typically the foundation READ and the main handler in the VALID. There are many variations on what can be done in the Foundation READ's VALID. A simple case is used here, mostly to process termination conditions.

IN THE FOUNDATION READ VALID:

```
FUNCTION FRHandler

*————————————[ TERMINATION REQUEST
IF READKEY(1)=2             && Deliberate Termination
  IF is_Quit
    RETURN .t.              && Leave the program
```

```
    ELSE
      *Ask if the user wants to quit?
      IF YesNo("Leave the program now?", 8, "Y")
        RETURN .t.
      ENDIF
    ENDIF
  ENDIF

  * If not terminated, then check for a program call (from the
  menu).
  *————————————[ NEW PROGRAM REQUEST
  IF NOT EMPTY( cNewProg )
    cTmpProg = cNewProg       && clear newprog for next choice.
    cNewProg = ""
    DO (cTmpProg)
  ENDIF

  *————————————[ NO SPECIFIC REQUEST
  * The program will not be terminated. Find out what screen is
  on top
  * and re-activate it.
  cWindow = UPPER(CHILD("",0)
  DO WHILE NOT EMPTY(cWindow)
   IF SUBSTR(cWindow,1,2)="WR"
     cNewProg = TRIM(SUBSTR(cWindow,3,7))+".SPR"
     EXIT
   ENDIF
    cWindow = WCHILD("",1)
  ENDDO
  *IF a screen is available
  IF NOT EMPTY(cNewProg)
    DO (cNewProg)
    = ContrlChk() && Check to see if the control window is up.
  ENDIF
  *Valid does not terminate
  RETURN .f.
  *
```

In almost every application you should make a decision about how to provide termination events, at least from the user's point of view. Some programmers opt to assign termination values to keys, menus, and push buttons only. Typically this would be a CLEAR READ assigned to a function key, a Quit menu pad, and a Quit push button. All other means of termination—such as closing windows and pressing **Esc**—are in some way disabled or trapped, for example:

```
ON KEY LABEL ESC DO TermTrap
ON KEY LABEL CTRL+"W" DO TermTrap
ON KEY LABEL CTRL+"Q" DO TermTrap
IN THE READ DEACTIVATE SNIPPET: TermTrap()
```

This puts termination in the user's hands, but in a very controlled way. Other programmers prefer not to be quite so strict, and allow special keystrokes like **Esc** or **Ctrl-Q** to terminate a READ.

The first attempts at coordinating multiple screens, Browses, and other sundry events are almost bound to be frustrating. Depending on your preferred method of learning, you can borrow approaches lock stock and barrell, such as the EX1.PRG or EX2.PRG from the sample files, or you can take an outline like the one just presented and experiment until you get the feel of handling READs, windows, menus, and push buttons. An obvious piece of advice is not to be too ambitious in the beginning and, whatever you do, don't make any commitments about delivering an application (professional or otherwise) using these techniques, until you've done some thorough learning and testing.

A Test and Learn Setup

Because there are so many combinations of windows, GETs, and READs (clauses and all), it's very helpful to set up a testbed and try things for yourself. The following approach shown in Figure 15.2, keeps the setup as simple as possible.

Most of the action is in the Command window or the Debug window. This example uses table names from the Users window example. You should change these to any available tables of your own.

IN THE DEBUG WINDOW:

```
WONTOP()
WOUTPUT()
WREAD()
```

```
WTITLE()
WLAST()
WREAD(WLAST())
```

IN THE COMMAND WINDOW:

```
USE DDUSERS ALIAS USR ORDER STAFFID
DEFINE WINDOW wbUsers FROM 1,0 TO 10,40
BROWSE WINDOW wbUsers
DEFINE WINDOW wrUsers FROM 1,41 TO 10,79
ACTIVATE WINDOW wrUsers
cTest = SPACE(8)
@ 0,0 GET cTest
READ CYCLE
```

Once this is set up, you can test it by moving around with the mouse, keyboard, and menu selections, watching how the values in the Debug Window change. Edit the names of the windows and the titles and see how that affects the window functions.

Figure 15.2
Testing and learning.

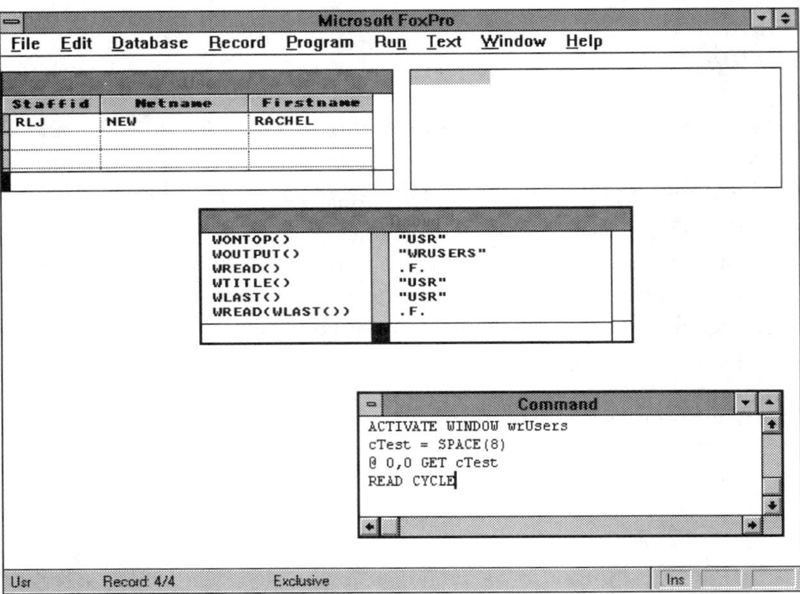

A simple extension, very useful for learning about the READ VALID clauses, is to create a small program file (.PRG) and use it in SET PROCEDURE TO. The setup is similar to the above with these additions and changes:

IN PROGRAM FILE TEST2.PRG:

```
FUNCTION TestWhen
  WAIT "In WHEN" WINDOW
RETURN .t.
*
FUNCTION TestAct
  WAIT "In ACTIVATE" WINDOW
RETURN .t.
*
FUNCTION TestDeac
  WAIT "In DEACTIVATE" WINDOW
RETURN .t.
*
FUNCTION TestShow
  WAIT "In SHOW" WINDOW
RETURN .t.
*
FUNCTION TestVal
  WAIT "In VALID" WINDOW
RETURN (.t.)
*
```

IN THE PROGRAM FILE TEST1.PRG (instead of the COMMAND WINDOW):

```
SET PROCEDURE TO TEST2
USE DDUSERS ALIAS USR ORDER STAFFID
DEFINE WINDOW wbUsers FROM 1,0 TO 10,40
BROWSE WINDOW wbUsers NOWAIT
DEFINE WINDOW wrUsers FROM 1,41 TO 10,79
ACTIVATE WINDOW wrUsers
cTest = SPACE(8)
@ 0,0 GET cTest
READ CYCLE ;
  WHEN TestWhen();
  ACTIVATE TestAct();
  DEACTIVATE TestDeac();
  SHOW TestShow();
  VALID TestVal();
```

The shift to a program file is necessary if you want to get the real behavior of both the Browse and the READ. From this point, you can try an almost infinite number of experiments involving the READ clauses. Shift windows, reshow the GET, and change files, orders. This simple structure is easy to modify and then monitor.

Event-Driven Programming

The approach in this section is not to prescribe *a way* to do event-driven programming, but to provide a foundation for considering the ways to do it in FoxPro—whether you create it yourself, or accept one of the many approaches being offered by professional developers.

First, to dispel a myth, event-driven programming does not mean the program exerts no control over the user. In fact, it implies a high degree of user monitoring, which may or may not be used to control or limit what the user can do. In even the most freedom granting software, an executive information system (EIS) for example, the programmer still has the responsibility of protecting the data, protecting the integrity of the program, and truth be known, protecting the users from themselves.

One of the things that event-driven programming definitely tends to be is passive. The person using the computer is the lead dancer, no matter what the tune. It is the user who triggers or creates the events, and your application responds to those events. This can be contrasted with the more traditional procedural programming, characterized by a sequence of options (like a hierarchy of menus), presented by the computer, that the user must, more or less, follow.

Don't be lulled by the word *passive*. Your programming task is anything but passive. It's well known that event-driven systems are the most difficult for programmers. This is especially true in FoxPro, since it does not *provide* an event-driven programming environment. It makes it possible for you to *create* one. And that means creating a lot of machinery to handle the user events, or in the jargon of the genre—you create event handlers, as shown in Figure 15.3.

As this diagram illustrates, user events have many forms and come at your program from all directions, often seemingly at once. If you don't get organized about managing events, your program will be like a baseball player trying to play the outfield solo. You'll have code all over the place, trying to handle the incoming user events, and most of the time you won't even know who's on first. And therein lies the first task of event-driven programming, answering these two questions:

1. What did the user just do?

2. What does it mean?

To answer these questions, you generally follow these steps:

1. **Trap** what the user just did.
2. **Identify** it.
3. **Interpret** what it means.
4. **Decide what to do**, if anything.
5. **Do it**.

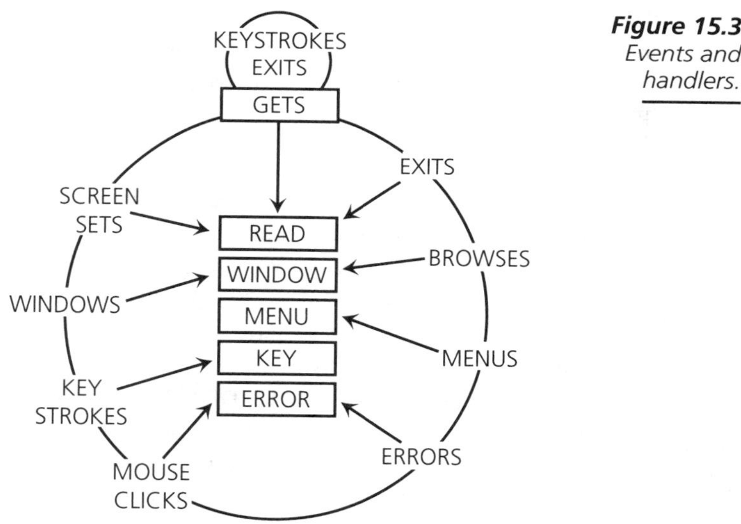

Figure 15.3 *Events and handlers.*

Event Traps

Programming for these steps has two components, *traps* and *handlers*. One component is provided by FoxPro—the event trap. There are eight of them:

- READ VALID
- READ ACTIVATE
- READ DEACTIVATE
- GET VALID
- ON KEY LABEL

- ON ERROR
- ON SELECTION MENU
- ON PAD

Each of these works in a specific way and responds to a particular event—such as exit events, errors, and menu choices.

The word *trap* may be a bit misleading, because in most cases program execution does not automatically stop at these commands. *Pass by* might be a better representation. A user-interface event, for example switching from one screen to another, triggers the window event traps in the READ—DEACTIVATE and ACTIVATE. If you haven't put any code of your own to respond to the trigger, then execution continues without the slightest pause.

Here's a brief description of how these traps work and their context within FoxPro.

- **READ VALID**—You've already encountered the READ VALID in several aspects including the foundation READ. It's function in an event-driven system can be anything from the primary location of user monitoring (such as windows, keys, and menus) to simply the "Exit" manager. At the very least, it plays a structural role by providing the most commonly used wait state, during which your program monitors for user interface events.
- **READ ACTIVATE** and **READ DEACTIVATE**—These are intended to be the window traps, although as explained above, they don't respond to nonREAD windows. The DEACTIVATE clause is also one route to exit a READ, so it often carries logic to trap events that close a window before exiting.
- **GET VALID**, **BROWSE VALID**, and **BROWSE <field>:V**—These are data-entry traps, primarily for keystrokes. In a database application, these traps play a very large role, not only in validating data, but also in relationship to many of the other event traps in FoxPro. It's quite characteristic for the data entry mode to change the meaning and effects of error trapping, keystrokes, and often for window management.
- **ON KEY LABEL**—Every key that has been assigned a command through the ON KEY LABEL command can be it's own trap. You could trap every key and key combination in the keyboard, if necessary. There are three other keystroke traps: ON ESCAPE, ON KEY, ON KEY =. These have largely been superseded by the "OKL"—ON KEY <label>—but can still be used. There is one limitation to the ON KEY

<label> trapping, which though usually not serious, needs to be considered. Microsoft Windows handles all mouse events in the Control menu, scroll bars, and other areas of window behavior. It may mean that ON KEY LABEL MOUSE, LEFTMOUSE, and RIGHTMOUSE may be unreliable at times.

- **ON ERROR**—This is the "official" error trap. FoxPro provides its own trapping for programming, hardware, and other errors. If you do nothing, the user gets the bad word directly from FoxPro, an unpleasant event in most cases. It's usual for all but the smallest applications to use the ON ERROR trap to provide a more user-friendly error reporting and recovery system. There is also an "unofficial" level of error trapping, often associated with data entry but potentially much broader, where an application intervenes in user activity to provide data and procedure validation.
- **ON SELECTION MENU | BAR** and **ON PAD**—These are the menu "traps" for the standard FoxPro system menu. They tend to be taken for granted, although they behave exactly like any of the other traps and are just as open to programming and modification.

Event Handlers

Each of the traps described above provides a "hook" (that is, a procedure call) to execute an event handler, which is a user defined function or procedure.

There are five basic handlers: read exit, window, error, menu, and keystroke. Each of these has a role to play in a fully event-driven system, although not every event-driven programming scheme takes all of them into account.

There are many advantages to consolidating the monitoring of user events, even if you're not pursuing a completely event-driven programming style. Logical consistency and ease of maintenance come with the territory. Rather than have, say, your keystrokes each with their own ON KEY LABEL definitions scattered throughout an application, they all refer to one keystroke handler, usually located in a strategic place (definitely not buried in some screen or snippet).

The more customization is necessary, the better it is to put the procedure close to the context for which it is designed. Centralized event handlers, those that are supposed to be generic and reside in a central location, can become

There are many ways to organize your event handlers. Here's one way that's relatively simple, since most of the code is confined to a single program file. In this case a project initialization file is used as the basic framework to control one or more screens with a Foundation READ.

First, an example of the placement of trap calls and handler functions in the file:

```
*> Initialize Error Handler
ON ERROR DO ErrHandler WITH ERROR(),MESSAGE(),MESSAGE(1),;
   SYS(16),LINENO(1)

*> Initialize Key Handler
ON KEY LABEL ESC  DO KeyHandler WITH "ESC"
ON KEY LABEL CTRL+"W" DO KeyHandler WITH "CTRL-W"

*> Call the main menu, menu trap is in MainMenu.SPR
DO MainMenu.MPR

*> Start Foundation READ with exit and window handlers
is_quit = .f.
READ CYCLE ;
     VALID      ValHandler(),;
     ACTIVATE   WinHandler(),;
     DEACTIVATE WinHandler()

*> In the procedures section of the Initialization File:

*> Foundation READ exit handler
FUNCTION ValHandler
...
RETURN
*
*> Window Handler
FUNCTION WinHandler
...
RETURN
*
*> Error Handler
FUNCTION ErrHandler
...
RETURN
*
*> Keystroke Handler
FUNCTION KeyHandler
...
RETURN
```

```
*
*> Menu Handler
PROCEDURE MnuHandler
```

When you are considering event-driven programming schemes, put the context of your application first. If you're writing an application of mostly generic data entry screens (AEDs), then a generic approach to event handlers will probably work. On the other hand, if your application is full of specialized screen work, local calculations and data processing, then you may find it better to adopt a more context oriented approach to event handlers.

All of the above implies that there are many ways to organize program event handlers. The following are code fragments that illustrate the event handlers, but are not intended to be a blueprint.

- **READ exit handler**—the VALID
  - The trap: READ VALID
  - The handler: VALID <function>
  - Example: `READ VALID ValHandler()`

    (Code for this is in the previous section of this chapter.)
- **Window handler**—A subset of the READ handler.
  - The trap: READ ACTIVATE or READ DEACTIVATE or READ VALID
  - The handler: ACTIVATE <function> and/or DEACTIVATE <function>
  - Example: `READ HANDLER WinHandler()`

    (Code examples are developed earlier in this chapter.)
- **Error handler**
  - The trap: ON ERROR <command>
  - The handler: <Error Procedure>
  - Example:

    ON ERROR DO ErrHandler WITH ERROR(), MESSAGE(), MESSAGE(1), SYS(16), LINENO(1)

```
...
PROCEDURE ErrHandler
PARAMETERS nErrNum, cErrMsg, cErrCode, cErrPrg, nErrLine

* Don't let printing mess up the error reporting.
*> Trap printer setup
IF SYS(100) <> "ON"
```

```
  SET CONSOLE ON
ENDIF
IF SYS(101) <> "SCREEN"
  SET DEVICE TO SCREEN
ENDIF
IF SYS(102) == "ON"
  SET PRINT OFF
ENDIF

*———————————[ ERROR NUMBER CASES
DO CASE
CASE INLIST(nErrNum,1,802,1162) && File Opening Problem
   *Use Retry Interface Option
   IF NOT UsrRetry("FILE")
   *Exit Routine
   DO ProgExit
 ENDIF
CASE ...
ENDCASE
*> Cleanup and return.
...
RETURN
*
```

Error handling has always been a part of Xbase programming. It is, however, an "event" with user inteface implications and programming options just like any of the other handlers.

- **Keystroke handler**
  - The trap: ON KEY <key name> <command>
  - The handler: <Key Handler Procedure>
  - Example: `ON KEY LABEL ESC DO KeyHandler WITH "ESC"`

```
PROCEDURE KeyHandler
PARAMETER cKey

* Make sure no intervening keystrokes mess things up.
PUSH KEY CLEAR
*————————————————[ KEYSTROKE CASES
DO CASE
CASE cKey = "ESC"              && Escape Key
   DO CASE
   CASE is_add OR is_edit      && no escape
```

```
         WAIT "Please Save or Cancel first." WINDOW NOWAIT
       CASE SUBSTR(WONTOP(),1,2)="WR"
          IF YesNo("Are you sure you want to exit?",8,"Y")
            CLEAR READ
          ENDIF
       CASE...
       ENDCASE
    CASE ...
    ENDCASE

    * Cleanup
    POP KEY
    RETURN
    *
```

- **Menu handler**
  - The trap: Menu Commands i.e. ON SELECTION <pad> etc.
  - The handler: <Menu Function>
  - Example: `ON SELECTION BAR 1 OF APPS DO MenuHandler WITH "DDUSERS.SPR"`

```
PROCEDURE MenuHandler
PARAMETER cProg

IF RDLEVEL() > 1
   *A screen is active, clear it and send control to READ
VALID.
   cNewProg = cProg
   CLEAR READ
ELSE
   *Ok to call new program
   DO (cProg)
ENDIF
...
RETURN
*
```

All of these handlers, one way or another, have to be part of a "wait state" - some mechanism that pauses the program to wait for user activity. Traditionally, the READ provides the wait state as an event loop. Other approaches usually involve DO WHILE loops in one of the other event handlers.

Given that the FoxPro environment can be event driven, does this mean you should rush out, master the techniques, and immediately begin programming all of your applications this way? Absolutely not. You can if you want to. But it's not necessary. In fact, in some cases, not even desirable.

Let your mind go back to basics for a moment. FoxPro, for all the user interface freedom and filigree it provides, is still a database-management system. In most database applications, the data is an ultimate responsibility, even if under the wing of producing a good user interface. Event-driven programming is primarily a user-interface issue. For those parts of your application with little or no user interface (such as data processing, data conversions, and maintenance), traditional programming techniques are far more germane. If this sort of thing makes up the bulk of your application, then event-driven programming may not be worth the trouble.

Integrating SQL

You've probably had some experience by now with the RQBE Power Tool. Because it puts so much under one roof, RQBE can be used for an extremely wide variety of query and reporting tasks. But, it's an interactive tool, literally and figuratively. It was designed primarily for interactive use and it's not available for distribution through compiled and linked (.EXE) programs. (It requires a full copy of FoxPro.) Which normally means you don't rely on RQBE for programming purposes, except perhaps to generate SQL code. After that, use the FoxPro SQL commands instead.

It was highly recommended in Section I that you use RQBE and see how it generates SQL code, and then do some SQL coding in the Command window. In this chapter, it's time to put some of that knowledge to work in an application, and perhaps extend it a bit with some SQL work you can't do from RQBE.

The most basic "skeleton" for SQL command (not the syntax) looks like this:

```
SELECT <field name(s)> ;
FROM <table name(s)> ;
WHERE <condition(s)>;
INTO <output option>
```

This gets translated into FoxPro code:

```
SELECT customerid, lastname, firstname, city ;
```

```
FROM customer ;
WHERE salestotal > 1000 ;
INTO CURSOR tmpfile
```

The next group of clauses can be seen as "post row selection" commands because they operate with sets of data that (usually) have come through the WHERE clause. These are GROUP BY, HAVING, and ORDER BY.

```
SELECT <field names> ;
    FROM <table names> ;
    WHERE <conditions>;
      GROUP BY <field names>;
      HAVING <conditions> ;
      ORDER BY <field names>;
    INTO <output option>
```

Typically the GROUP BY clause creates an intermediate table ordered so that the specified groupings can be available for the SQL functions (such as CNT and AVG). The HAVING clause then further qualifies this grouping, similar in effect to the WHERE clause, but at the group level instead of the record (row) level. Finally, the whole shooting match is handed off to the ORDER BY, which in effect, does a standard SORT on the resulting data, according to the specifications. The expanded query sample looks like this:

```
SELECT customerid, lastname, firstname, city ;
  FROM customer ;
  WHERE salestotal > 1000 ;
      GROUP BY state ;
      HAVING state = "M" ;
 ORDER BY city, lastname
 INTO CURSOR tmpfile
```

If you really want to see SQL crawl, use lots of these clauses. GROUP BY creates an intermediary file, loads, and then sorts it. HAVING works on this unindexed temporary table sequentially, and you know what that means. The bigger the tables, the longer the wait. Unless you are working with relatively small tables (under twenty-five thousand records), consider using standard FoxPro commands for post WHERE processing. However, the speed is no worse than doing the same things in the Report Writer.

Query output, in the command syntax, is the same as the options available from RQBE. However, in programming, you may put them to different uses, as in Table 15.2 on the next page.

Table 15.2
Options available in programming.

Output Clause	Usage
INTO ARRAY <array name>	Loading an array with SQL SELECT is a convenient way to build picklists. However, it is faster than a simple SEEK and SCAN only when the results of the query are indeterminate. If you know exactly what to load, then a query is hardly what you'd want to use.
INTO CURSOR <cursor name>	There are two kinds of SQL cursors (not to be confused with the editing cursor): the one created at the end of a query, and the one made by CREATE CURSOR. The former is a *phantom* file, and should never be used for post processing other than as a source of data. The cursor will be destroyed at the end of a work session.
INTO DBF|TABLE <table name>	Because output to a cursor isn't permanent, you can use this clause to create a standard .DBF.
TO FILE <file name> [ADDITIVE]	This option sends the results to a standard text file. The additive option makes it possible to load several queries into a single file.
TO PRINTER [PROMPT]	This directs output to a printer. With PROMPT option, the printer setup dialog is displayed.
TO SCREEN	By default screen display is sent to a Browse window. This causes output to be sent to the FoxPro main window.
(without TO clause) PREFERENCE NOWAIT	Output goes to a Browse window. This is the SQL default. By adding the two Browse clauses (PREFERENCE and NOWAIT) you can have a Browse window template, and have the Browse exit immediately back to program control—exactly as you would when integrating a Browse with the Screen Builder.

There are some query clauses to consider using every time you do a query...

- **NOT DELETED()**—If deleted is not set on.

- **NOT EMPTY(<field>)**—To exclude records (rows) containing no values.
- **EXISTS(SELECT * FROM <table> WHERE <condition>)**—To select each record of the query only against existing data.

These can be added to any WHERE clause to keep unwanted records out of the result. The last form, the so called "existence" test, is a subquery.

Sub-Queries

Nested queries, or subqueries as they are more properly called in FoxPro, can be very useful and are not supported by RQBE. They have many forms, but in general are easiest to use and understand as a tool to pluck information from a table not directly related to the main query tables, that will be tested against the main query. Here's an example:

```
SELECT customer, invtotal ;
  FROM customer cus, invoice inv ;
  WHERE cus.cno = inv.cno ;
  AND inv.ofcno = IN( SELECT ofcno ;
                        FROM office ;
                        WHERE ofctotal > 500000 );
INTO CURSOR tmpfile
```

The query asks: "Show all of the customers and their invoice totals where the sales office for the invoice is one of those that sells more than $500,000 a year." The information about the sales offices is a *subquery*, which provides a list of qualifying offices for the IN clause that is used by the main query. Notice that the subquery is framed by parentheses. This is required.

The use of the conditional clauses—EXIST, IN, ANY, SOME, ALL—in conjunction with a subquery is probably the most common. You should be careful using these in very large tables because SQL usually runs a row comparison of the main query against the column of results provided by the subquery. This can be very time consuming.

WARNING

You do not have the same freedom with subqueries as you do with the main SELECT query. These restrictions apply: Unless you use the "all fields" wildcard token (*) a subquery can only refer to one field. UNION and ORDER BY clauses can not be used. Only comparisons and EXIST, IN, ANY, SOME, and ALL can be used to connect a main query to a subquery. Finally, FoxPro does not support subqueries within subqueries (nested subqueries), although you can have more than one subquery at the same level (under the main WHERE).

In practice, all subqueries can be reworded to form just another WHERE expression. However, since there is no difference in performance, most programmers prefer the subquery format for its clarity (self documentation), when pulling data from a subsidiary table.

Self-Joins

This is neither technically or morally incorrect. It's actually a variant of the subquery format, only this time the subquery refers to the same table as the main query. It's used for the same purposes as any subquery—to provide a comparison list or result, against which the main query is tested. Here's an example:

```
SELECT cno, lastname, city ;
  FROM customer cus ;
  WHERE cus.salestotal > 1000 ;
    AND NOT EXIST( SELECT * ;
                      FROM customer cust ;
                      WHERE cust.crtype <> "X" ;
                        OR cust.status = "I" )
INTO ARRAY aCust
```

Notice the explicit declaration of a table alias, different than that used for the main query. This makes sense, since you're asking the query to give you the names of customers who have more than $1,000 in purchases while not being in the list of customers who have a bad credit rating or are inactive. All of which comes from the same table.

The Sequence of SQL

In descriptions of various SQL formulations, you'll see a lot of "appears to," "usually," and similar qualifiers. It's not that people don't know how FoxPro SQL works, it's just that they don't know how it works under every circumstance. The size of files, the type or lack of indexes, the number of fields included can all have major impact on the performance, and sometimes the results of a SQLSELECT. Which is another way of saying that the FoxPro SQL is very environmentally sensitive.

Another part of the performance uncertainty of FoxPro SQL stems from the rather mysterious inner workings. Processing SQL query is quite complicated, and with Rushmore optimization thrown in, there can be a lot of decisions made that affect performance. The rough order of processing appears to be:

1. The FoxPro for Windows command parser, the routine that breaks down every command into its constituent parts for processing, processes the SELECT statement. It also checks for syntax errors.
2. All references in the statement are validated: table names, field names, variables, and UDFs are checked for existence. In very complex queries, especially those with many table references, this alone can take quite a bit of time.
3. The components of the query are sent to the Rushmore optimizer. Its "black box" workings include things like checking for available indexes, examining current bitmaps, and a whole list of internal rules about how to process various types of queries. Ultimately, the optimizer actually maps out a strategy for the execution of the query.
4. The query is executed, piece-by-piece, and prepared for the chosen form of output. If you've specified many of the GROUP BY, ORDER BY, and HAVING clauses, these execution steps can become extremely lengthy.

When you see the steps laid out like this, and realize that the FoxPro SQL processor and Rushmore may do things like create temporary files and new indexes on the fly, you may understand why a SQL query isn't always the fastest way to retrieve data. It's just that Rushmore and FoxPro lightning-fast queries have been so hyped, people become disgusted if a query requires more than three seconds. That doesn't make SQL-SELECT one bit less valuable. It just isn't always faster than a speeding bullet.

Uses of SQL-SELECT

The variety of output options is the first suggestion of how and where to use a SQL-SELECT inside the programming of your applications. Use arrays for picklists, and other data manipulation routines. Use the default Browse options for an interactive screen. Use the .DBF or cursor output for further data management or reporting. Essentially, you should always consider SQL whenever you need to choose a method of extracting data. It's strength is when the result of a query are unknown. The query optimizer generally does a better job in working with multiple tables than you will. However, if you know already what you are looking for, and it can be readily defined as part of an index, then standard SEEK and SCAN are probably going to be quicker.

Because RQBE isn't available in the .EXE form of a FoxPro application, there have been many workarounds and third party products to fill the gap. These efforts are aimed primarily in replacing the interactive aspect of RQBE. In a much more modest fashion, you can insert some semi interactive SQL into your own applications using the following technique:

IN A SCREEN BUILDER WINDOW, or a .PRG:

```
cLast=SPACE(30)
cCity=SPACE(35)
@ 2,20 GET cLast PICTURE “@!”
@ 3,20 GET cCity PICTURE “@!”
READ
DO SELECTNM WITH cLast, cCity
```

IN A PROCEDURE:

```
PROCEDURE SelectNm
PARAMETER cLastName, cCityName
```

```
IF NOT EMPTY(cLastName)
  cWhere = "WHERE lastname = "+cLastName
ENDIF
IF NOT EMPTY( cCityName)
  IF NOT EMPTY( cWhere )
    cWhere = cWhere + "city = '"+cCityName+"'"
  ELSE
    cWhere = "WHERE city = '"+cCityName+"'"
  ENDIF
ENDIF

SELECT lastname, firstname, city, state, phone1 ;
  FROM customer ;
  &cWhere ;
INTO DBF MailLst

REPORT FORM MailLst TO PRINT PROMPT

RETURN
*
```

The macro substitution in this example has no effect on the performance of the query. The query parser has to pull apart and preprocess the whole query anyway—so a macro substitution has no impact.

SHORTCUT

Use the FoxPro SQL command CREATE CURSOR <name> to make temporary files for your applications. The big advantage, like all cursors, is that FoxPro removes the file for you, when the work area is closed. The SQL-CREATE command requires that you provide a file structure from an array, or you hard code it. The latter is obviously much simpler:

```
SELECT employees && template file
=AFIELDS(aEmp) && load array with field defs
CREATE CURSOR emptemp FROM ARRAY aEmp
```

Chapter 16
Special Data Elements

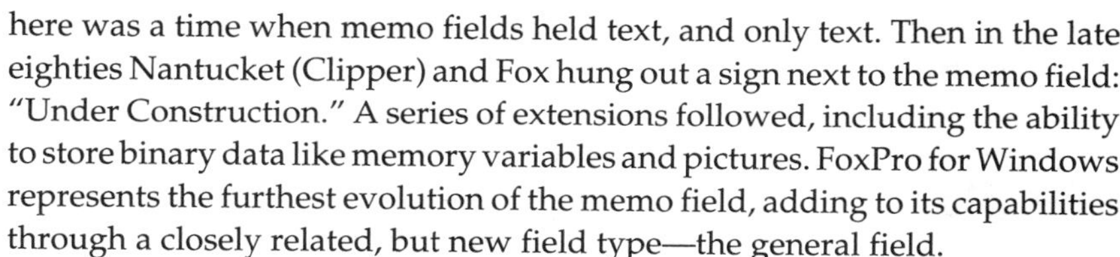

There was a time when memo fields held text, and only text. Then in the late eighties Nantucket (Clipper) and Fox hung out a sign next to the memo field: "Under Construction." A series of extensions followed, including the ability to store binary data like memory variables and pictures. FoxPro for Windows represents the furthest evolution of the memo field, adding to its capabilities through a closely related, but new field type—the general field.

The general field is a variant of the memo field, and is housed in the same file (the .FPT). Internally, FoxPro stores additional information about each entry into a general field that is not present in the standard memo field. That's what makes it possible to use it for such a wide variety of data elements, and maintain the links necessary for OLE. Together, the memo and general fields can now (officially) store the following data types:

- Text (ASCII)
- Graphics (.BMP format)
- Sound (.WAV format)
- Animation (.AVI format)
- Any OLE-compliant material

At a glance, you can see this is opening the door to Multimedia. However, this stage in the evolution of the general field presents far more possibilities than finished tools. FoxPro does provide ways to display, play, or run some of the data types. But that's it. There are no built-in data-management tools, similar to the Screen Builder, specifically for organizing or using multimedia data. Perhaps there never will be. After all, FoxPro is a data-management program and not a Multimedia authoring system.

However, FoxPro does give you enough tools to at least begin the process of turning capabilities into uses in your applications. Memo fields and general fields can be incorporated in a number of ways, some obvious, some not.

This chapter is an introduction to working with memo fields, object linking and embedding (OLE), and dynamic data exchange (DDE). For the latter two, especially DDE, the treatment is abbreviated. The FoxPro *Developer's Guide* does a good job of basic explanation, which hardly needs to be repeated, and a full treatment requires delving into the both the "client" and the "server"—not only FoxPro, but also the characteristics and programmability of software like Microsoft Word or Excel, which is beyond the scope of this book.

What will be modeled here, using memo fields, general fields (OLE), and DDE, is making an "object" out of a common business relationship, a *job*—the design, manufacture, and delivery of a customer's order for a customized product.

Example

The customer calls in an order, which is taken by a salesperson on a standard form. The form is scanned into the FoxPro table via OCR into a memo field. The order is processed and a design for the customization made (in a CAD program) and stored in the database. Meanwhile, a production budget is drawn up in Excel and the figures linked to the database. Finally, when the product is delivered, a visual record (photo) of the finished product is also stored in the database, along with financial details. This is, of course, a very rudimentary example, but enough to illustrate how many programs and how many kinds of data can be organized around an object in a FoxPro database.

The word object, as it is used here, shouldn't be confused with object-oriented programming or object-oriented databases. These are *methodologies* and special approaches. This object is simply a conglomeration from many kinds of data that can be pulled together in FoxPro as a single logical entity, an object that makes things easier to understand for the user.

Using the object (in this case a job) also provides a logical gateway into using other Windows programs. This points to one of the great strengths of the OLE concept—let the specialist programs do their work. FoxPro is a data manager, not a drawing program, a spreadsheet, or a word processor. It can do some of these things, but not well. However, FoxPro can store the results from all of these programs and provide a centralized clearinghouse for related information. In this way, you can form an information object, created from many parts but semantically linked (such as by subject matter).

For this example one file has been created with this structure:

```
MEMOSAMP.DBF/.FPT
  Field      Field Name     Type          Width     Dec
  1          CUSTOMERID     Character     8
  2          ORDER          Memo          10
  3          DESIGN         General       10
  4          FINISHED       General       10
  5          COSTEST        Numeric       10        2
  6          COSTACT        Numeric       10        2
** Total **                               59
```

IN SETUP OF MEMOSAMP.SCX:

```
#SECTION 1

nMmoWidth = SET("MEMOWIDTH")
SET MEMOWIDTH TO 72 && Important!

#SECTION 2

REGIONAL cSample, cProduct, cDate
cSample = "Order Form"
cProduct = SPACE(20)
cDate = SPACE(8)

*Open the test file
IF NOT USED("MS")
  USE MEMOSAMP ALIAS MS ORDER CUSTOMERID
ELSE
  SELECT MS
  GO TOP
ENDIF

DEFINE WINDOW wbJobs FROM 1,5 TO 15,75

BROWSE FIELDS ;
  customerid:H="ID",;
  order,;
```

```
     design,;
     finished,;
     costest:H="Est.Cost",;
     costact:H="Actual Cost" ;
   WINDOW wbJobs ;
   WHEN ShowRec() ;
   TITLE "Orders" ;
   NOWAIT

* END OF SETUP
```

Using Memo Fields

For the most part, memo fields tend to be taken for granted. That's probably because they are so easy to use. Create a memo field in your file, and then put it into an edit region (@..EDIT) in the Screen Builder. Done.

That's all there really is to it. But memo fields can be used for more than taking notes. For one thing, you can import and export text data for memo fields. You can scan entire manuals, sales forms, and so on into ASCII text files, then store the material in a memo field. On the output side, besides being instantly accessible through the Report Writer, memo fields can produce text (ASCII) files for word processing and other uses. The commands for these operations are very simple:

```
APPEND MEMO <memo field> FROM <file> [OVERWRITE]
COPY MEMO <memo field> TO <file> [ADDITIVE]
APPEND MEMO notes FROM F:\DOC\COMMENT.TXT
COPY MEMO notes TO F:\DOC\OUTPUT.TXT ADDITIVE
```

For most of the other memo field operations, the length of the field line is important:

```
SET MEMOWIDTH TO <lines>
```

This is a crucial value for many of the memo functions. Be sure you know what line length each memo field has been set to (if other than the default of 50). Be sure to reset the value when you're done working in a particular memo field.

There is an impression that memo fields are just big globs of text, which can't be sorted, searched, or manipulated except through the screen-editing methods. Memo fields can't be sorted by the usual FoxPro SORT command;

it would be pointless for most text anyway. But just to prove a point, here's how to sort a memo field, of a reasonable size:

```
*Sorting a memo field.
nM1 = MEMLINES( order )       && Get length of memo field
DECLARE aMemoSort[nM1]        && Create a holding array
FOR i = 1 TO nM1 && Load array with each line
   aMemoSort[i]=MLINE( order, i)
ENDFOR
=ASORT( aMemoSort )           && Sort the array
FOR i = 1 TO nM1              && Build a variable with sort
   * Variable is written "line by line" with carriage return.
   cSortVar = cSortVar + aMemoSort[i]+CHR(13)
ENDFOR
REPLACE order WITH cSortVar && replace the current memo field
```

This serves to introduce two of the useful functions provided by FoxPro for manipulating memo fields:

- `MEMLINES(<memo field>)`

  ```
  = MEMLINES( notes )
  ```

  Returns: 20.

  The number of lines in a memo field, as measured by the current setting of MEMOWIDTH. This drives the FOR..END FOR loop, a very common use for the function.

- `MLINE(<memo field>,<expN1>[,<expN2>] )`

  <expN1> is the number of the line to return.
  <expN2> is the offset from the beginning of memo field. It is typically set by using the _MLINE system memory variable.

  ```
  cLine = MLINE( notes, 1 )
  ```

  Returns: "Now is the time..." The text from the specified line, up to the length of the current setting of MEMOWIDTH. This function usually works in combinations. Another function determines what line to pull from the memo field, and MLINE( ) does the pulling.

Memo fields can also be searched, manipulated, and even edited while under program control. FoxPro gives you some very efficient functions that do most of the work. The first two (actually two pairs) are searching functions. One set returns the position number of the first letter of a string match. The other set returns the line number for the same thing. These numbers can then be used to extract lines or words from a memo field:

- `ATC(<expC1>,<expC2>,[<expN>])`
  <expC1> is the expression to search for.
  <expC2> is the expression to be searched.
  [<expN>] is the number of the occurrence to look for.

  ```
  ? ATC( "time" , cLine )
  ```

  Returns: 34, the position number in the memo field where the search string occurred, or 0 if none is found. This function is identical to the AT( ) function, except this one is *case insensitive.*

- `ATCLINE(<expC1>,<expC2>,[<expN>])`
  where <expC1> is the expression to search for, <expC2> is the expression to be searched.
  [<expN>] is the number of the occurrence to look for.

  ```
  ? ATCLINE( "time" , cLine, 1 )
  ```

  Returns: 3, the line number of the memo field where the search string occurred, or 0 if none is found. This function is identical to the ATLINE( ) function, except this one is *case insensitive.* Because it returns the line number, it's particularly suited for working with memo fields. The code fragment below get's the user's choice of word to find in a memo field, and uses ATC( ) to find its position. MODIFY MEMO has the unusual ability to highlight (select) a piece of text in a memo field based on its starting position and length. (This sets the editing selection on startup and does not require using the search option in the Edit menu.)

  ```
  * Get search string from user.
  cSearch = SPACE(10)
  @ 2,10 GET cSearch
  READ
  * Set up for memo edit
  nLen = LEN( cSearch )
  nStart = ATC( cSearch, notes )
  MODIFY MEMO notes RANGE nStart, nStart + nLen
  ```

Most of the time, when you want to change a memo field, you'll need to put the changed text into a variable (as in the sort example above), then do a

REPLACE. There is no way to STUFF( ) a memo field on a line-by-line basis. However, some other character string manipulation functions work in a memo field: STRTRAN( ), SUBSTR( ), EMPTY( ), RAT( ), and RATLINE( ).

In the example earlier in this chapter, a customer's order is taken by a salesperson and entered on an order form. The form is then scanned into a standard ASCII text file. The routine used here lets the user select the text file to be imported into the memo field, and then extracts some of the data from the field. In effect, this treats the memo field like another kind of database record.

IN PROCEDURES SECTION OF MEMOSAMP.SCX: (called by push button valid)

```
FUNCTION ProcSamp
DO CASE
...
CASE cSample = "Order Form"
  *——————————[ Load the ASCII format (memo)
  cFile = GETFILE(".TXT","Load the order form.")
  IF NOT EMPTY(cFile)
    APPEND MEMO ORDER FROM &cFile
    * parse some information out of it.
    = ShowOrder()
  ENDIF
CASE...
ENDCASE
```

IN PROCEDURES SECTION OF MEMOSAMP.SCX:

```
FUNCTION ShowOrder
PRIVATE nDateLine, nProdLine

*> Get the date
nDateLine = ATCLINE( "Date:", order )
cDate = RTRIM( MLINE( order, nDateLine ))

*> Get the basic product
nProdLine = ATCLINE( "Basic Product:", order )
cProduct = SUBSTR( MLINE( order, nProdline+1 ),1,20)

RETURN .t.
*
```

There are limitations to the FoxPro memo field tools. Searching, for example, becomes very slow on a record-by-record basis and large memo fields. There are however, a number of third-party utility programs that bring indexing, sorting, searching, and other capabilities to a memo field, if your application requires it.

OLE and GENERAL Fields

Object Linking and Embedding (OLE) provides the user with the ability to automatically link and move data from one Windows application to another. The OLE implementation in FoxPro is an *input only* capability, or in OLE terms, a *client only* capability. FoxPro is the client to various Windows applications (such as Microsoft Word, Lotus Ami, and Excel) that act as *servers*.

In this client capacity, the main advantage of FoxPro is its ability to store or reference OLE objects (files) produced by the server programs. The general field was created expressly to house the OLE material. In structure it's similar to the memo field. But it contains a header, of a sort, for each entry to keep a record of the source, type, and location of OLE data. Once the data, or the reference to the data is in the general fields, it becomes available to your applications through the Report Writer, Screen Builder and other programming.

Server to Client

OLE is yet another context for the terms client and server—where the information provider (server) communicates with the information consumer (client). You may be familiar with the terms in a data management context. The server is the database manager software (usually centralized) that receives and processes requests for data (usually in SQL) from client software. The OLE context is subtly but significantly different: In the database context the link between client and server, and the information provided, is transient. In the FoxPro OLE context, the link and the information are (usually) persistent.

The Three Forms of OLE

It's useful to think of OLE information in FoxPro as having three (not just two) forms of existence. As some waggish programmer said, "A *link* is a first date, *embedding* is... embedding, and *convert to static* is a marriage."

- **Linked.** When you establish an OLE *link*, FoxPro stores in a general field the *reference* to an OLE object (usually but not always a file). That reference contains information about the server, the type of object, and the location of the object. When you double click on a general field that contains a link, FoxPro goes out to the external file or program it has on reference, and displays, runs, or plays, depending on the type of data.
- **Embedded.** With an OLE embedded object the information itself is stored in the general field, along with information about the server and the type of data.
- **Static.** When you convert a general field to static, you are deliberately breaking all links between the client and server. Any embedded data remains, but it no longer is possible to access the server that created it. Essentially, the general field is no longer part of OLE, and the links cannot be reestablished.

When you embed an OLE object in a general field, it becomes "your" property—a part of the FoxPro application. At the user's request, it can be changed or updated by the server program, but it is not accessible from the server. This implies both security of access and the ability to customize an OLE object for a specific application. The same holds true for a static object, except it can no longer be modified. By contrast, a linked OLE object always has an external existence—it is tied to the server program and usually one of its files. In this form, the OLE object is available to other users and other programs: it's shared.

Whether to link, embed, or make static are decisions that need to be made by the application developer on a case-by-case basis. The general field makes no attempt to check for OLE type or data consistency. In practice you can mix and match as you see fit, even if that means breaking all the rules of relational structure.

The disadvantages, although they are a natural result of the OLE environment, are the most significant for linking and embedding.

The Role of the Environment

As you will quickly discover when you begin working with OLE, it's quite sensitive to it's environment. This means:

- **Memory.** It's typical of OLE applications, particularly those with interactive capabilities, to load and run three or more Windows applications.

This requires, at a minimum, 8 MB of RAM.

- **CPU.** Obviously, for running several major applications simultaneously, and maintaining links between them, the more power the better. Only the fastest 386 and 486 computers are sufficient for most OLE applications.
- **Disk Space.** Depending on the kind of data your application will be using for OLE, and the type of object—embedded, linked, or static—the amount of disk space required can be considerable. This is especially true of embedded graphics images. These tend to be large files in the first place, and embedding them usually means you've got *two* copies.
- **Directory Structure.** An active OLE application is *tightly bound* to its objects. A considerable amount of information about the server, the files and their locations, and other OLE information is stored with general field entries. For example:
  - A linked object needs to know where the file is, and where the server is.
  - An embedded object needs to know where the server is.
  - A static object needs to know only what kind of data it is.

  All of the location information translates simply into *directory locations*. FoxPro and OLE "hard code" directory locations, via the Windows OLE Register, into the information about the object. If anything changes the directory structure, or the location of the files—*zap*—your OLE links are gone. Of course, they can be rebuilt, using the Change Link option. But you have to ask yourself if there is something you want the application's users to do.
- **WIN.INI etc.** OLE requires that participating programs *register* with Windows to make their services available. This is normally an automatic part of installing any Windows software. But the system isn't infallible, and it is open to being changed by users. The same goes for various kinds of configuration and initialization parameters involving OLE servers, or the FoxPro environment itself. Differences in the fonts used by various programs on various machines will be a major thorn. Without doubt there are combinations out there that can trash your OLE connections.
- **Networks.** Running Windows on a network has it's own pitfalls, including specialized WIN.INI files and other Windows resources. Add in the requirements of OLE, and the network can be a hostile environment. Network security, drive mapping, and multiuser file

sharing all are factors, if you are working with OLE link objects, and to a lesser extent with embedded objects.

Despite the length of this list, none of this presents much of a problem on a single machine, or even a couple of machines on a LAN. But a FoxPro application that may run on dozens or even hundreds of machines? Under these circumstances, an OLE-intensive application (including DDE), is not easy to maintain.

Interactive OLE

From the end user's point of view, the interactive OLE of FoxPro is just like it is in other Windows programs, and just as easy. Perhaps the hardest decision is whether to use Paste or Insert Object... (embed), or Paste Special..., Paste Link (link).

First, have a table open that contains the general field you want to use. Then select the specific field and open it, usually in a Browse by double-clicking the field. After that, whether or not the OLE object to be put into the general field has been created plays a role. If not, then you'd start with Insert Object..., select the OLE application to use (such as Microsoft Word or Corel Draw), create the object (a document or a drawing). When you return, the new object is incorporated into the general field.

If the object (file) already exists, you have three options:

1. In the Insert Object... dialog box, select File and use the file open dialog to select the file you need.

Otherwise, with the other OLE application already running, you can place the object in the clipboard, and:

2. Use Paste, or
3. Paste Special...

Thereafter you can play or edit the general field simply by double-clicking on it in the Browse window. You can also use the Change Link... option of the Edit menu to reestablish or change links that have been lost.

And that's about it for the interactive use of OLE. It's already slick in this version of OLE, and with OLE 2.0 and FoxPro 3.0 in the future, it should be even better.

OLE in Programming

Turning to the programming aspects of OLE, it's not much more difficult than the interactive version. In fact, under program control you could probably make it clearer for the user which type of OLE they can choose—if they need to choose at all. However, you won't be able to simulate the opening of another OLE application, creating an OLE object, and returning to FoxPro. That's more like the role DDE plays, although it can't bring back OLE objects.

There are only three commands with specifics for OLE management: APPEND GENERAL, MODIFY GENERAL, and @..SAY. The latter is rarely used outside of the Screen Builder. The other two are more important from the standpoint of loading OLE objects into tables, and allowing the user access to them under program control.

APPEND GENERAL

The syntax for APPEND GENERAL is:

```
APPEND GENERAL <general field> FROM <file> [LINK] [CLASS <ole
class>]
```

FROM <file> requires that you provide (or at least locate) the file that will be used for the OLE object. A complete path and file name, including extension, are necessary.

[LINK] changes the command from the default *embedding* to *linking* of the OLE object.

[CLASS <ole class>] determines the origin of object, and is used to distinguish which OLE application you want to associate with an OLE file object. The extension of the file usually determines which application. For example, .DOC indicates a Microsoft Word file. However, more generic files such as .BMP (bitmap) might be associated with a number of programs. You would then use the CLASS clause to specify which of the available applications to use.

```
APPEND GENERAL notes FROM c:\word\doc\taxes.doc
APPEND GENERAL design FROM d:\corel\draw\horses.cdr LINK
```

This command looks and behaves exactly like the APPEND MEMO command with, of course, the appropriate additions for OLE specific information.

MODIFY GENERAL

The syntax for MODIFY GENERAL is:

```
MODIFY GENERAL <general field1>[,<general field2>...]
[NOMODIFY] [NOWAIT] [WINDOW <window name>] [IN [WINDOW] <window
name> | SCREEN ]
```

This should look suspiciously like the syntax for a MODIFY MEMO, a MODIFY FILE, or even a BROWSE. All of these are usually handled by defining a window for the WINDOW clause, and then a NOWAIT (when in the Screen Builder) to have the window stay open during a READ. With the OLE window, which this really is, it makes possible an interactive OLE session for the user, unless you specify NOMODIFY.

Lets put these two commands together. The example used for this chapter includes two buttons that add a record to the file and ask the user to select a CAD drawing to put into the general field.

```
IN PROCEDURES SECTION OF MEMOSAMP.SCX: (called by push button
valid)

FUNCTION ProcSamp
DO CASE
...
CASE cSample = "Design"
  *——————————[ LOAD THE DESIGNS (OLE)
  cFile = GETFILE("CDR", "Load the Design")
  IF NOT EMPTY( cFile )
     APPEND BLANK
     APPEND GENERAL design FROM &cFile LINK
  ENDIF
  * Have a look at it.
  DEFINE WINDOW wgDesign AT 2,0 SIZE 20,60 FLOAT GROW ZOOM
CLOSE TITLE cFile
  MODIFY GENERAL design NOMODIFY WINDOW wgDesign
  RELEASE WINDOW wgDesign
CASE...
ENDCASE
```

You'll probably find in working with OLE that distinctions are often made about OLE objects that are intended for user modification, and those that are not. The overhead of interactive objects, both in terms of programming in your application, and in the general Windows environment, tends to make programmers conservative with the number of active OLE links. Whereas, images and sounds that have been loaded into general fields (and usually made static) are simple to maintain and use.

DDE

Dynamic data exchange (DDE) is in many ways the older brother of OLE. It was Microsoft's first attempt at an interprocess communications API. (If you understand that last line, you're probably ready to deal with programming DDE.) If you scan through the DDE sections in *Developer's Guide* and the *Language Reference*, you may notice that the DDE functions don't look and work much like Xbase functions. In fact, they're not. They are more or less copies of C language routines, used throughout Windows software. Even the example code looks like it was written by a C programmer.

At one level, DDE programming can be quite straightforward. If you want to be creative or very useful, then it quickly becomes complicated. It isn't that the DDE functions themselves are difficult. It's that DDE is a two-way street. DDE establishes *connections* between two Windows applications that allows one or the other to make requests for data, and to execute commands or routines in the other application.

In this respect, the real advantage to DDE is that it can invoke the programming talents of Windows applications other than FoxPro. For instance you can access the macro programming language of Microsoft Word, and have it do all kinds of tasks. However, to make DDE work that way, you need to be fluent in the commands and operations of both sides—client *and* server. You also have to take into account all of the environmental factors involved, similar to those of OLE, and the relatively technical nature of DDE itself. Development of a full scale DDE application is not a trivial assignment.

For these and other lengthy reasons, this chapter can't cover the details of DDE programming. The *Developer's Guide* and sample programs do a reasonable job of introducing the subject. More than that would require a separate book. However, to put DDE into the context with the other special data elements, it's been included in the sample code for the customer order scenario. In this case DDE is used to collect data from Microsoft Excel, where the production budget and cost estimates are made for the customer's order.

IN PROCEDURES SECTION OF MEMOSAMP.SCX:
(called by push button valid)

```
FUNCTION ProcSamp

  DO CASE
  CASE...
  *——————————[ LOAD THE BUDGET FIGURES (DDE)
  CASE cSample = "DDE"
  * Get Excel running, load the production worksheet, get the
numbers
  * and come back to FPW.

  * Invoke Excel and load it with the worksheet.
 RUN /N d:\excel\excel.exe d:\excel\library\memosamp.xls
  * Open a DDE connection, and return to FoxPro.
  nChannel = DDEInitiate("Excel","System")
  = DDEExecute(nChannel, '[APP.ACTIVATE("FoxPro",1)]')
  = DDETerminate(nChannel)

  * Open a DDE connection, and request data.
  nChannel = DDEInitiate("Excel","System")
  IF nChannel <> -1
    * Set the spreadsheet "memosamp" as topic
    nChannel= DDEInitiate("Excel", "memosamp.xls" )

    * Request the data in specific row/col
    cBTotal = DDERequest( nChannel, "R10C4")
    cATotal = DDERequest( nChannel, "R10C6")

    * Update the database. Remember all DDE data is character.
    IF NOT EMPTY( cBtotal )
      REPLACE costest WITH VAL( cBtotal )
   ENDIF
   IF NOT EMPTY( cAtotal )
   REPLACE costact WITH VAL( cAtotal )
   ENDIF
  ENDIF

  * Close request channel
  =DDETerminate(nChannel)
  * Close Excel
  nChannel = DDEInitiate("Excel", "System")
  = DDEExecute(nChannel, '[ERROR(FALSE)]')
  = DDEExecute(nChannel, '[QUIT()]')
  = DDETerminate(nChannel)
```

```
    CASE...
    ENDCASE

*
```

This illustrates DDE with FoxPro in the role of a client. Unlike OLE, FoxPro 2.5 can be both a client and server for DDE.

A Few Observations about DDE

While DDE has been used successfully in some very sophisticated applications, it's important to remember that it has limitations. Like OLE, DDE is environmentally sensitive—even more so. It often relies on critical assumptions about the operating behavior and conditions for both the client and the server applications. Which is to say that DDE applications are generally not very robust in complex or changing environments.

DDE is also a "one data item at a time" system. Retrieving or sending large amounts of data through a DDE connection can become excruciatingly slow. Most successful DDE projects keep the data flow to a minimum, and instead use it to get critical data processing or operations executed from other Windows applications in the one piece at a time mode.

Finally, DDE is time consuming to develop, primarily because it has to be built and tested in two (or more) applications separately, then tested together as a DDE connection. Again, for simple uses, this doesn't provide much of hindrance. In larger projects, the back-and-forth testing and debugging can add considerably to the development time.

None of this means that programmers should shy away from DDE. It is however, a more basic and primitive form of linking applications. It can do things that OLE can't, like execute commands in another application. It also returns data in a more "traditional" format, such as character data, which makes it easier to incorporate in the data-oriented aspects of FoxPro. OLE can also work with "normal" data, but it's strengths lie in the storing of images, sound, and other nontraditional data elements. They both have their places in FoxPro applications.

Chapter 17
Multiuser Systems, Networks

nless you're building applications for personal use, it's quite likely your work is going to be running on a network or other multiuser system. If more than one person is going to be using the application at the same time, you have to take that into account. The first thing that comes to mind is probably the data files—how are people going to share them? But this isn't the only multiuser consideration. What about configuration (the FoxPro CONFIG.FPW)? Are all workstations going to have the same configuration? What about FoxPro's resource file, and other program work spaces? How are they allocated?

These and other questions are part of developing a multiuser application. Fortunately, once you have them answered you can do the same thing in nearly all of your applications. Unless you are absolutely certain that your application will *never* be multiuser, there's no reason *not* to design your application for multiuser operation. In fact, it can easily become an automatic part of application development.

The Multiuser Scene

In most people's minds, when it comes to PC database management, multiuser means local area network. About 95 percent of the time this is a correct assumption, though there are PC multiuser systems running on other operations systems such as Unix and OS/2. However, the principals of multiuser application development remain the same whether on a LAN, or running from a central processor with terminals. Sharing of resources, managing the integrity and security of the data, and optimizing operations are the main tasks. Your application should take these things into account, preferably from the beginning.

There are only a couple of ways to determine if your application is running on a network. Perhaps you've spotted the NETWORK( ) function. Unfortunately, this is useless. It returns .t. if the copy of FoxPro you are running is multiuser capable. *All* FoxPro copies are multiuser capable. There are third—party network functions that actually work, and even tell you what kind of network you're on. You can also use network login scripting to embed variables in your DOS environment, which FoxPro can read, to signal a network in use. On Novell networks, this is fairly simple:

```
IN THE USER'S LOGIN SCRIPT:
DOS SET USERNAME="%LOGIN_NAME"
```

In your program:

```
cUname = ALLTRIM(GETENV("USERNAME"))
is_network = IIF(NOT EMPTY(cUname),.t.,.f.)
```

Unfortunately, this isn't foolproof. A user could logout from the network, and the DOS variable remains in the environment to fool your program. Of course, if you've written a network application and the user isn't on a network, it's likely that file openings won't work (among other things).

Sharing Database Files

For obvious reasons, the biggest difference between a single-user program and a multiuser program is the sharing of data files, and usually other file types as well. However, FoxPro does not assume file sharing. Either in the

CONFIG.FPW, or the beginning of your application, you need to issue the command: SET EXCLUSIVE OFF. After that, FoxPro attempts to open all files in the shared mode. You should also use your network operating system's commands to set all of the appropriate application files (including .DBF, .CDX, and .FPT) as shared. If you are opening your own files, and want to have some of them non shareable, you need to issue the USE <filename> command with the EXCLUSIVE clause.

As any developer will tell you, opening files is the slowest operation in FoxPro for Windows. It's even slower on a network. As a solution, you can open all the files you need and leave them open but there is a risk of having them damaged by a power outage or user error.

However, the FoxPro file system is very robust. FoxPro itself keeps the resource and other files open throughout the run of a program. The only real damage to a file can occur with a sudden crash during a write operation. Only a fault-tolerant system can protect you from that. Also remember this is a multiuser environment. Somebody, somewhere, is using your application's files. Chances are the main files are always open, so why not in your program.

Locking Issues

When your application requests a lock, and FoxPro grants it, then your application has that file or record *exclusively*. *Locking* is the basic term for permitting only one program to access a file or a record. Notice, the word is program, not user. There are plenty of database-management operations done by programming, that don't require a user (except somewhere along the line to start the program). It should also be emphasized that locking isn't only the use of FLOCK() or RLOCK() (the specific locking functions). A file opened read-only, or EXCLUSIVE is equally as locked.

There is a tendency for developers to overthink—and consequently overuse—the instances of locking. For all practical purposes, there are only three basic reasons for locking:

- **When FoxPro requires it.** There are certain table operations for which FoxPro requires an exclusive use of the file. Most of these, INDEX, INSERT BLANK, MODIFY STRUCTURE, PACK, REINDEX, and ZAP are fairly obvious, because files must be completely rewritten during the process. Other operations require a complete lock of the file (either by exclusive use, or by file locking): APPEND, APPEND FROM, RE-

PLACE or DELETE or RECALL with <scope> greater than 1, and UPDATE.

- **To improve performance.** Because there is less checking and status management going on, files that are opened EXCLUSIVE or NOUPDATE (read only) process more rapidly. This becomes significant only in table operations on larger files (say 25,000 records or more). Most other table and record locking exact at least a small performance penalty.
- **To preserve data values for a period of time.** If you are running a report, and must have the most accurate data as of that moment, lock the relevant files *while the report is running*. You are preserving the stored data values during that period of time by not allowing other users to make changes or updates. Likewise, if a user is doing data entry, and must complete the entry before anyone else can make changes, then lock that record while they are editing.

Over and over again, as you consider the need for locking, ask yourself: Why does the data need to be preserved? And, if so, for how long? You might be surprised at the number of times your answer is, that it doesn't need to be preserved. The trickiest decisions are those involving record locking. Locking people out of files is not taboo, but it's poor form in a multiuser environment.

Don't be tempted to confuse data locking with data security. There's a big difference between whether a user is allowed to change a salary field value, and whether no one else should be allowed to change the field while the first user is making a change. The second case is a *sequencing issue.*

Most decisions to use locking, especially record locking, are based on the notion that each edit of a record is a distinct (one at a time) operation and that all the data in the record must be preserved from additional changes, during the time of the edit. Or put another way, simultaneous update is not allowed. Is this always necessary?

Look at this record, which is being simultaneously edited by three people:

```
FIELDS:  LASTNAME.  FIRSTNAME.  MIDINIT.  BIRTHDATE.  SSN.         SEX
ORIG.    Jones      John        J.        4/14/34     323-23-2443  M
DATA
USER 1:                                   4/15/34
USER 2:                                               313-23-2443
USER 3:             Joan                                           F
```

What fields may have *contention*? In some tables perhaps only one or two of the fields are important and probably subject to simultaneous update. The key words are *important* and *probably*. Theoretically, any field might possibly have simultaneous modification, but for which fields is it *likely*? A lot of tables contain fields that are seldom, if ever, updated. Still more tables have fields that are only occasionally modified, with a high probability they will never be updated simultaneously. *All* of the fields above fall into these first two categories. But still, it can happen.

Keep in mind that depending on the editing scheme you've implemented, FoxPro never updates the same field at exactly the same time. Even if two or more users finish editing the same field at exactly the same time, they will still have their entries processed to the file one at a time. The FoxPro and network locking systems guarantee this.

If there are fields with a reasonable probability for contention, how *important* is it for the person making the change to know that someone (or something) has changed the field or record in the meantime? In the example above, there are a couple of significant discrepancies. Which entry is correct? Who is to decide, and how? You might decide that in the case of this example table, the last entry is considered the best entry. The odds of a simultaneous update are so slim, and the relative importance so low, that a few sequencing mistakes are not worth the inconvenience to the users of installing record locking.

One last factor to think about is also a decision point: What editing method are you going to use? Table 17.1 lists your options.

Table 17.1
Editing methods.

Type of Edit	Description
Direct No backup	Direct editing of fields in a record. Every change is permanent. @..GET <field name>
Direct With backup	Direct editing of fields, but a backup copy is created with SCATTER MEMVAR, so that aborting the edit can restore original values.
Indirect No changes check	Editing on memory variables only. (Typically via SCATTER MEMVAR.) The record is not checked for changes before update. @..GET <memory variable>
Indirect With changes check	Editing on memory variables only. The record is checked for changes during editing and user is given save and cancel options.

Each method has it's own implications for record locking, as in Table 17.2.

Table 17.2
Editing methods and locking.

Type of Edit	Description of Locking
Direct No backup	Locking depends mostly on the number and importance of contention fields.
Direct With backup	Locking for the duration of the edit.
Indirect No changes check	Locking, if other factors indicate it, usually for the duration of the edit.
Indirect With changes check	Generally no locking, or locking only at the exact time of record update. Changes are allowed while users are editing the memory variables.

As you can see, locking decisions can be complex. Table 17.3 and 17.4 lay out the factors for each table to help you visualize the mix, and what an appropriate strategy might be.

Table 17.3
Locking decision factors: Example table.

Decision Factor	Entry Type	Value
Frequency of modification to table	Times a day.	20
Number of contention fields	#	3
Duration of average record modification	Seconds	30
Probability of simultaneous record modification	Low, medium, high	Low
Importance of changes	Low, medium, high	Low
Method of modification	Direct, indirect	Direct, with backup
Locking	None, auto, manual	None

Table 17.4
Locking decision factors: Airline reservation table.

Decision Factor	Entry Type	Value
Frequency of modification to table	Times a day.	22,000
Number of contention fields	#	6
Duration of average record modification	Seconds	5
Probability of simultaneous record modification	Low, medium, high	High
Importance of changes	Low, medium, high	High
Method of modification	Direct, indirect	Indirect, with checking
Locking	None, auto, manual	Manual, on update

In truth, what you're looking for are the extreme, or near extreme, table update conditions. Such tables (or screens if several tables are involved), may require something special—no locking on one end, and full record locking or even field locking on the other. Otherwise, some "middle-of-the-road" locking scheme might as well be applied all the time, such as the automatic locking FoxPro provides.

Automatic Locking

FoxPro, like most other multiuser database-management software, has built-in file and record locking capability for running on a multiuser system. This is a default condition. There is one other locking mechanism that is *not* on by default, SET LOCKS. This command controls the locking of table operations, like COUNT, and REPORT FORM, where you may not want to allow update while processing is in progress. When designing your locking strategies, it's important to understand what locking FoxPro automatically does and what it will or won't do if you SET LOCKS ON. Table 17.5 on the next page summarizes what FoxPro does.

Table 17.5
FoxPro Locking.

Command	What's Locked (Default)	With SET LOCKS ON
APPEND	Table	
APPEND BLANK	Table header	
APPEND FROM	Table	
APPEND FROM ARRAY	Table header	
APPEND MEMO	Current record	
AVERAGE	Not locked	Table
BROWSE,CHANGE,EDIT	Current records in all related tables	
CALCULATE	Not locked	Table
COPY TO	Not locked	Table
COPY TO ARRAY	Not locked	Table
COUNT	Not locked	Table
DELETE|RECALL	Current record	
DELETE|RECALL NEXT 1	Current record	
DELETE|RECALL RECORD <n>	Record n	
DELETE|RECALL SCOPE > 1	Table	
DELETE TAG	Table (EXCLUSIVE)	
DISPLAY SCOPE > 1	Not locked	Table
GATHER	Current record	
INDEX (new)	Table (EXCLUSIVE)	
INDEX (existing)	Not locked	Table
INSERT BLANK	Table (EXCLUSIVE)	
INSERT-SQL	Table header	
JOIN	Not locked	Table
LIST	Not locked	Table
LABEL	Not locked	Table
MODIFY MEMO	Current record	
MODIFY STRUCTURE	Table (EXCLUSIVE)	

PACK	Table (EXCLUSIVE)	
READ	Current record and records of all aliased fields.	
REINDEX	Table (EXCLUSIVE)	
REPLACE	Current record and records of all aliased fields	
REPLACE NEXT 1	Current record and records of all aliased fields.	
REPLACE RECORD <n>	Current record and records of all aliased fields.	
REPLACE SCOPE > 1	Table	
REPORT	Not locked	Table
SHOW GETS	Current record and records of all aliased fields.	
SORT	Not locked	Table
SUM	Not locked	Table
TOTAL	Not locked	Table
UPDATE	Table	
ZAP	Table (EXCLUSIVE)	

NOTE

You can also use this table as a guide for when locking is necessary, in general, whether automatic or manual.

Looking at this table, it would be an easy conclusion to say, "Great, let FoxPro do it." And perhaps you will, but you should also know the limitations of automatic locking:

1. **The automatic locks don't always do the locking at the right time, or sometimes at all.** This is particularly true in database processing, including updating and maintenance. The automatic locking can't follow a chain of relations during file processing and put locks on all related records. Occasionally FoxPro attempts to do a file lock, when it should only do a record lock. Or the sequence of your processing, moving from table to table, confuses the locking sequence. These aren't necessarily bugs in the automatic locking, it's just that there is an

implicit locking scheme and that may not coincide with the needs of your processing. This may also be true of how FoxPro handles locking of records in a READ.

2. **Many automatic locks are held too long.** For example, the automatic locking for a READ applies only to a READ direct. It starts the instant an edit begins on a record, and ends only when the user moves the pointer to another record. This could be a long time (it's even been called a *lunch lock*), perhaps too long for the good of your application. How bad it is depends on the importance of the data, and the probability of someone else needing it.
3. **Automatic locking can make it difficult to properly trap lock errors.** Assuming you have some sort of application error-trapping routine, any errors in locking—such as timeouts, too many retries, and unresolved contention—should be trapped, whether from automatic or manual locking. However, with automatic locking it may be difficult to know exactly where the lock failed, and that can make it hard to clean up or respond to the error. If you lock manually, then at each manual lock a specific ON ERROR response can be created, if necessary.
4. **You have no control over the sequence of locking and unlocking.** Of course, that's the whole point of an automatic function.

Actually it may all boil down to this: If your application has little or no complex table processing, and if you are using READ direct and don't mind the possibility of lengthy record locks, then the automatic locking may be a good fit. But automatic locking was designed to work with the interactive part of FoxPro—the menu system and the Command window—and is not nearly as robust or comprehensive for the program environment. Out of experience and necessity, most developers use a *mix* of automatic and manual locking.

Do-It-Yourself Locking

Drawing from previous discussion in the chapter, the issues of *when* to apply locks and for *how long*, spill over into the decisions about automatic versus manual locking. This section aims to show that doing it yourself is relatively easy, easy enough to become an automatic part of your programming.

There's one crucial setting for all multiuser locking:

```
SET REPROCESS TO <expN> [SECONDS] | [ TO AUTOMATIC]
```

This sets the number of times FoxPro attempts to complete a lock. It can do about three tries per second, depending on hardware, or you can use the optional SECONDS clause to have it do one per second (recommended). You can use numbers anywhere from minus two to thirty-two thousand. Minus two, minus one, and zero have special meanings. Minus 2 is equivalent to AUTOMATIC. Zero equals forever, an infinite number of retries (this is the default). If you ever use this setting, you should be prepared to trap for *Attempting to lock* errors, and let the user escape if necessary. The other version of zero, minus one, is much more draconian—the attempts continue indefinitely, there is no error generated, and **Esc** can't be used to cancel the attempt. Try this one in the lab, not on the users.

Use -2,-1, or 0 only when you know exactly why you're using them. Most of the time a reasonable number (one to ten) is better, and especially if using SECONDS. Make the number longer if the locking is an off-hours processing routine, make it shorter when interactive user activity is involved. Remember that functions like FLOCK( ) and LOCK( ) don't kick in and return .f. until SET REPROCESS has exhausted it's re-tries.

File Locking

Fortunately file locking is not required very often for user oriented activity. Locking an entire file in a multiuser environment can be very disruptive. Not to mention that it might be very difficult to get a file lock established on a busy network. Most applications avoid operations that require exclusive use of a file or file locks within the interactive user portions. The usual advice is to save the processing and maintenance routines, which usually do require full file locking, for times when there are no users on the system.

It pays to analyze your processing routines to optimize them for speed. This means using SET EXCLUSIVE ON or opening files EXCLUSIVE, for those files involved with updating, and using the NOUPDATE (read-only) clause for lookup files. For example:

```
USE hrpos           ALIAS pos ORDER posid EXCLUSIVE IN 0
USE hrassign ALIAS asn ORDER posid EXCLUSIVE IN 0
USE hrcode          ALIAS cod ORDER codtype NOUPDATE IN 0
```

If this isn't possible, then you need to fall back on the file locking function:

```
FLOCK( [<expN>|<expC>] )
```

<expN> is the number of the work area to lock.

<expC> is the alias of the work area to lock.

```
=FLOCK("POS")
```

Returns: .t. if the file is locked, and .f. if not.

Like all of the locking functions, FLOCK( ) attempts to set a file lock for the number of retries in SET REPROCESS TO. If it fails, and returns .f., you'll need to handle that eventuality in the program, for example cancel further processing or notify the operator.

This is a good point to mention the command that removes locks:

```
UNLOCK [IN <expN>|<expC>] | ALL
```

Although FoxPro automatically removes record locks when the table pointer is moved, and unlocks files when a command is complete, it's a very good habit to include an explicit UNLOCK with every manual lock. It guarantees the shortest amount of lock time, documents the duration of the lock, and is easy to do:

```
IF FLOCK( )
  DELETE ALL
  UNLOCK
ENDIF
```

A very simple UDF can be created to execute the file lock, and can set and reset the SET REPROCESS TO value to control how long the program should wait for a successful lock.

IN A PROCESSING PROGRAM:

```
IF FileLock(10)
  REPLACE ALL curryear WITH dNewYear
  UNLOCK
ELSE
  WAIT "Unable to update with new year!" WINDOW
ENDIF
```

IN THE STANDARD PROCEDURE FILE:

```
***************************************************************
* FUNCTION NAME.. FileLock()
* DESCRIPTION.... STANDARD FILE LOCKING PROCEDURE
* DATE........... Mon 12-30-1991 Fox2.5 Version
* PROGRAMMERS.... NK
* LAST CHANGE.... Mon 12-30-1991
```

```
* PARAMETERS..... nSetReproc = amount of time to wait before
quitting
* SYNTAX......... FileLock(<retries>)
* USAGE.......... = FileLock(5)
* RETURN......... .t./.f.
* NOTES.......... Standard file locking routine. Note that an
.f. return
* forces the abandonment of the calling action (REINDEX,PACK
etc.) and
* must be trapped in the routine. Assumes SET REPROCESS TO <n>
SECONDS.
* CALLED BY...... GUF
* CALLS.......... None
*******************************************************************
FUNCTION FileLock
PARAMETERS nSetReproc
IF PARAMETERS() < 1
  nSetReproc = 5
ENDIF
PRIVATE nOldReproc,is_ret
nOldReproc = SET("REPROCESS")
SET REPROCESS TO (nSetReproc) SECONDS

is_ret = FLOCK()

SET REPROCESS TO (nOldReproc) SECONDS
RETURN is_ret
*
```

Record Locking

The mix of automatic and manual locking for records is a bit more problematic than for file locking. There are three principal situations: Browses, Table Operations (such as DELETE and REPLACE), and READs.

Inside a BROWSE it's customary to let FoxPro do the locking. It locks the current record only when editing begins, and releases it as soon as the cursor moves from the record. This still doesn't defend against the lunch lock, but it's less likely in a Browse, where moving between records is the norm. If necessary, lunch locks can be broken with the use of the TIMEOUT clause.

If necessary, you can put explicit locking into a BROWSE through the WHEN (turn on locking) and VALID (turn off locking) clauses. This is used mostly to lock related records, rather than for the primary Browse file.

For table operations whose scope is a single record, typically REPLACE and APPEND, the manual approach involves record locks:

```
RLOCK( [<expN>|<expC>] | [<expC2>,<expN> | <expC1>] )
LOCK( )
```

<expN> is the number of the work area to lock the record.

<expC> is the alias of the work area to the lock record.

<expC2> is a list of record numbers to lock (it requires SET MULTILOCKS ON).

<expN> is the number of the work area for a list of records to lock.

<expC1> is the alias of the work area for a list of records to lock.

```
=RLOCK()
=RLOCK("POS")
=RLOCK(1,2,5,7,"Position")
```

Returns: .t. if the record is locked, .f. if the locking fails.

Just as with the FLOCK( ) function, it's common to create a simple UDF to add a bit more capability to the record locking function.

In a processing program:

```
IF RecLock(2)
  REPLACE curryear WITH dNewYear
  UNLOCK
ELSE
  WAIT "Unable to update with new year!" WINDOW
ENDIF
```

In the standard procedure file:

```
*****************************************************************************
* FUNCTION NAME.. RecLock()
* DESCRIPTION.... MANUAL LOCKING OF A RECORD
* DATE........... Mon 12-30-1991 22:16:34 Fox2 Version
* PROGRAMMERS.... NK
* LAST CHANGE.... Mon 12-30-1991
* PARAMETERS..... nSetReproc = Number of seconds to set
REPROCESS
* SYNTAX......... RecLock(<retries>)
* USAGE.......... = RecLock(5)

* RETURN......... .t./.f.
* NOTES.......... This is the standard network manual locking
```

```
procedure.
*                   Although FoxPro provides for record
locking,the manual
*                   use of RecLock() and UNLOCK makes for
quicker and more
*                   precise control.
* CALLED BY...... GUF
* CALLS.......... None
******************************************************************
FUNCTION RecLock
PARAMETERS nSetReproc
IF PARAMETERS() < 1
  nSetReproc = 5
ENDIF

PRIVATE nOldReproc, is_ret
is_err = .f.
nOldReproc = SET("REPROCESS")
SET REPROCESS TO (nSetReproc) SECONDS

*======================>> TRY THE LOCK
is_ret = RLOCK()

SET REPROCESS TO (nOldReproc) SECONDS
RETURN is_ret
*
```

In table operations where relations are involved, it's customary to always use manual locks. For the most part FoxPro can not follow a relational tree and lock all of the relevant records. Use of a manual lock and unlock for almost all of the commands requiring a record lock is the only way to guarantee the shortest possible duration for the lock.

There are many combinations to control record locking in a READ:

- **READ LOCK with direct entry into the GETs.** This is the only combination that can use automatic locking. It's also the default in the Screen Builder. Remember that in a READ FoxPro attempts to lock every record referenced by an alias in the screen. This is a shotgun approach that may lock too many for too long.
- **READ NOLOCK with direct entry.** By using NOLOCK (in the Screen Builder check box), you are disabling the automatic locking in the READ. If you choose to lock the record manually, the simplest method is to issue a SHOW GETS LOCK command at the start of editing, and an UNLOCK on exiting the edit.

- **READ NOLOCK with indirect entry into m.variables, full duration lock.** Usually handled just like a READ NOLOCK with direct entry with a SHOW GETS LOCK at the start of editing, and an UNLOCK at the end of editing, after a TIMEOUT, or in the VALID clause of the READ.
- **READ NOLOCK with indirect entry, lock only at update.** In this case the record is left open for editing (and the potential for being overwritten). A lock is performed only when the current field data is being saved to the table:

```
IF RecLock(5)
  GATHER MEMVAR MEMO
  UNLOCK
ENDIF
```

Creating ID Numbers

An important example of manual locking involves the creation of ID numbers. Most applications encounter the need to create IDs—*unique* numbers or other identification sequences. In fact, the classic advice for relational database systems is to make as many table relations based upon a pure ID key as possible.

Creating a sequence of IDs isn't hard at all. Especially if you're using a purely numeric ID. Just increment it by one for each new record. But in a multiuser environment, there's a complication. How can you be sure that an ID is absolutely unique, while multiple users might be creating them at the same time? Obviously you need a way to store the current ID, making it available to multiple users. But you also need a way to make sure that the ID each user gets is unique. There are several ways to do this, but here's a preferred method:

1. **Create a table to hold one or more sequence numbers** (bigger applications might need several). For example: HRSEQ.DBF -

   `SEQNAME C 10`—The name of the sequence (the ID type), such as EMPLOYEEID

   `SEQNUM N 6`—The sequence number or current ID stub.

   `SYSDATE D 8`—The date sequence incremented or updated.

   `SYSTIME C 5`—The time sequence incremented or updated.

   `OPERATOR C 3`—The initials of the operator making the change.

Whether the SEQNUM field is numeric or character, depends on you approach to the IDs. Some programmers use IDs that are mixes of lettering and numbers. Typically, these are intended to be "meaningful" IDs that carry information about the record, for example they might begin with the first four letters of a person's last name. These IDs must ultimately be character fields. Other programmers prefer pure numbers. Most experts on relational systems recommend "pure" IDs that have no meaning, which makes them immune to changes in the record. And still other programmers like numbers, but prefer to have them expressed as character strings, because these are easier to manipulate and use in programs. The classic approach to this is the familiar sequence numbers like 000325, which are padded left with zeros so they sort and index in proper order.

2. **Use code, or better a UDF, to access the file and update the ID.** The key to this procedure is to lock the sequence number while it is being updated. In practice this takes only a very short time, and presents no problem in the usual data entry environment. However, if your data entry is a computer process, which is many times faster - you'll need to check this routine to make sure it doesn't become a bottleneck for your application.

   In the program or screen:

```
IF AddRec("A",8)
  cSeq = IdMake("EMPLOYEEID")
  IF NOT EMPTY( cSeq )
    REPLACE EMPLOYEEID WITH cSeq
  ENDIF
ENDIF
```

   In procedures:

```
FUNCTION IDmake
PARAMETERS cSeqName

PRIVATE cId, cIdAlias
cId = ""
cIdAlias = ALIAS()

* Open the sequence file
IF NOT USED("SEQ")
  USE HRSEQ ALIAS SEQ ORDER SEQNAME
ELSE
```

```
  SELECT SEQ
ENDIF

* Lookup the sequence name
IF SEEK( cSeqName )
  * Lock and load
  IF RecLock(10)
    REPLACE seqnum WITH seqnum + 1
    cId = seqnum
    UNLOCK
  ENDIF
ENDIF

* If the sequence file is not left open.
USE
SELECT ( cIdAlias )

RETURN cId
*
```

Field Locking

Once in a while, except in financial or accounting applications where it's relatively common, it may be necessary to lock a *field* and not the whole record. For example, in some transaction-intensive applications where several data-entry people may be hitting on the same record at the same time, either because the record is very large (many fields), or because there aren't many records (or both).

FoxPro, and Xbase in general, has no built-in provision for field locking. Fortunately, the method is simple, although it adds overhead to the table and your program. For each field you wish to lock, you add a companion logical field. For example:

```
EMPSALARY N 9
EMPSALLOCK L 1
```

When the program goes to update the value in this field, you put some logic into the code snippet of the GET field's WHEN clause (as a procedure):

```
IF NOT empsallock
  IF RecLock(5)
    REPLACE empsallock WITH .t.
    UNLOCK
```

```
      RETURN .t.
    ELSE
      RETURN .f.
    ENDIF
  ELSE
    RETURN .f.
  ENDIF
```

This prevents entry into the field if it is already locked. If not, it puts a lock on the field. When the user is done editing the field, you reverse the lock with a few lines in the VALID clause:

```
IF RecLock(5)
  REPLACE empsallock WITH .f.
  UNLOCK
ENDIF
```

You'll notice, of course, that this approach requires a record lock (two of them). But they are very brief, compared to the lock for the duration set on the field.

Multilocks—Transaction Processing

MULTILOCKS is what FoxPro calls it. Most of the time, this is transaction processing. *Transactions* is a rubbery term, but generally means the updating of several tables with data from a single transaction (such as a sale, a contract, or a purchase). This is probably the most common type of business computerization, and is associated with high volume, high speed, high integrity, and high value requirements. FoxPro 2.5 does not support the common database methods for controlling transaction processing in a multiuser environment—COMMIT and ROLLBACK. This leaves the job to the programmer.

The role of SET MULTILOCKS ON is that it makes possible the simultaneous locking of multiple records *in the same table*. This is crucial for many kinds of updates with the typical parent-child configuration such as invoices/detail. To execute a complete transaction and guarantee that all of the appropriate updates have been made, it's necessary to lock all records associated with a transaction, then do the updating. If the locking or the updating fails at any point, then it must be possible to "roll back" or restore the original data (and usually make a notification that the transaction failed).

Setup for Networks

As you might expect, configurations for network applications are different from single-user applications. The sharing of files, the need for customization for users, the accommodation for different levels of hardware, and optimization for speed are all part of doing a setup for a multiuser application. Network administrators know what a task it is to install applications on dozens (or hundreds) of computers.

Directories

For the most part, the directory configuration on a LAN may be somewhat different than it would be on a single workstation. As pointed out before, the directory structure can use almost any format and nomenclature. Just keep it consistent from machine to machine so that the Project Manager can always find its files. However, the layout of directories is special for a network application:

- Workstation files directory

```
C:\<PROJECT> config.fpw, resource file
```

- FoxPro temporary work files directory

```
C:\FOXTEMP editwork, sortwork, progwork, tmpfiles
```

- FoxPro program directory

```
F:\APPS\FOXWIN (FoxPro for Windows program files)
```

- Development directory

```
F:\<PROJECT> resource files, project files, .app(s)
 __|____________________
 |   |   |   |   |
SCR PRG DBF MNU REP
```

- Production directory

```
F:\<PROJECT> resource files, .app(s), .mem files
 __|___
 |    |
```

```
        DBF REP
```

This layout distinguishes between *development* and *production* directories. It's usually necessary to separate the two after the initial version has been put into final testing. Some developers prefer to do the development on their own workstation, then move finished pieces to either a development directory on the network or directly to the production directory. There's no right or wrong way to do this. The goal is simply to avoid confusion over what is the most current version of the application, and to keep "real" data away from "test" data.

The workstation directory on the C: drive should have anything that customizes the application either to a particular person or to a workstation. In most cases, you'd start FoxPro so that it uses a local configuration file in this directory. (In some instances, such as a diskless workstation, you might use the person's home directory on the network for the same thing.) Using a Windows program item icon is the simplest way to accomplish the startup, as long as the C: drive is universally available on all workstations.

If workstation configurations are not standard, then another approach is available (in the AUTOEXEC.BAT file):

```
SET FOXPROCFG=<config.fpw path>
RESOURCE=<resource file path>
```

This method allows you to set the location of the FoxPro resource file.

Work Files

FoxPro *loves* to make .TMP (temporary) files. There is a program cache file, used to store segments of code, usually as a memory overflow. This is typically small (under 25 K), but it's critical that it be fast. Put it on the local drive if at all possible, and even better put it into a RAM disk.

During development, when you're editing files, there are text editor work files. These are the same size as the original document—usually not all that big—but there may be many of them. These should be on the workstation and not the server.

Sort and index work files may be crucial to the speed of maintenance routines and other tasks. They can also be extremely large, requiring up to three times the disk space as the original file. Sometimes these won't fit on a workstation and have to be located on the larger network drive.

CONFIG.FPW

The location of the work files, as well as several other network oriented settings are usually placed in the CONFIG.FPW.

```
EDITWORK = <path:directory>
SORTWORK = <path:directory>
PROGWORK = <path:directory>
TMPFILES = <path:directory>
```

Section IV

Building a *Complete* Application

ne of the biggest attractions of FoxPro is that it can handle so-called *industrial strength* applications. Read this to mean you can create database applications that at one time used to run only on minicomputers and mainframes. It's all part of the "downsizing" trend in which PC-based programs take on big data files and "mission critical" projects. There is, however, more to an industrial strength application than being able to handle big database files.

One of the reasons MIS people still look down their noses at PC database applications is their presumed lack of "systematic development." Not that mainframe systems are, in fact, all that perfectly developed. But at least conceptually, large-scale projects receive formal planning, testing, and documentation. PC projects are perceived to be much more seat-of-the-pants. And it must be confessed, they often are. The relative ease products like FoxPro bring to application development, has tended to maintain this 'ad hoc' tradition.

But as PC database applications aspire to bigger projects, even projects that run a company, the pressure mounts for at least some nod in the direction of the procedures and systems-oriented components developed for the "big iron." Among these are much more formalized security, data maintenance, and documentation. It's not that every application needs all these components, or to be overloaded with planning and procedures. But it's becoming more important to at least *think* about the relevance of a systems approach to your application.

This section is about applications that must stand the test of time, be maintained by other people, and probably be distributed (or even sold). For this kind of application, you need to take into account the full roster of application components:

- **Data tables**—the usual complement of data tables, indexes, and memo files that form the underlying database of the application.
- **Data dictionary**—a system for recording what tables and indexes are used in the application.
- **Configuration and initialization**—external and internal setup for starting the application, including the CONFIG.FPW and WIN.INI files, as well as specific startup routines for the application.
- **Login and security**—user login, with or without password and the application security. This usually includes access checking for menu options, and data entry and edit privileges.
- **Processing routines**—table updating and other purely processing elements of an application (that don't need user interfacing).
- **Screens**—data entry and edit, informational, and all other user-interface screens of the application.
- **Menus**—system- and screen-level menus for the entire application.
- **Reports**—printed reports.
- **Labels**—mailing list and label printing.
- **Queries**—queries (RQBE and SQL-SELECT) independent of printed reports. This might also include the Graphics Wizard.
- **Report management**—routines for selection of reports and various output methods.
- **OLE and DDE support**—connection to other Windows software via OLE or DDE.
- **Multiuser operation**—routines for multiple users (typically on a LAN).
- **Communications and fax**—ability of the application to use telephone services.
- **Data transfer**—transfer of data, usually via files, to and from other systems, either over LAN, direct cable, telephone connection, or sneaker net (floppies).
- **Peripheral input**—input from barcode devices, scanners, and analog equipment, though specialized, occurs in many applications.

- **Printer management**—control and access to multiple printers, and print forms. Fortunately this is not usually an issue in FoxPro for Windows.
- **System parameters**—operational parameters, such as system date, and the name of the owner, that are used to set up and operate the application.
- **System codes**—most applications have data that is stored in the form of codes. This is a data table and management system for handling all codes used in the application.
- **Help system**—on-line help system for the user. Either FoxPro for Windows or FoxPro for DOS style.
- **Maintenance routines**—user accessible routines for data integrity checking, reindexing and packing.
- **Maintenance**—version control and a system for defining and performing application maintenance over a period of time.
- **Programmer documentation**—documentation specifically for the programmer, including runs of FoxDoc, system diagrams, analytical notes, business rules, and other forms of system documentation.
- **Error trapping and recovery**—a system for replacing the FoxPro error messages with something more meaningful to users.
- **Data archiving**—the ability to archive and retrieve data (off line access).
- **Data backup and restoration**—routine (daily) data backup and restoration capability.
- **Distribution**—distribution of an application via compiling as an .EXE or through FoxPro .APP files. This has many issues concerning packaging, costs, and pricing.
- **Installation and setup procedures**—routines for first-time installation, and other application setup.
- **Data loading and conversion**—many applications require loading of databases, or conversion of existing data before they become useful. A system for identifying and managing conversion issues is important.
- **User documentation**—creation of manuals and procedure books to support the user.
- **User training**—user training in the operation and use of the application.
- **User support**—support of the user in case of emergencies, debug situations, and other assorted crises common to application implementation.

Most of what follows are suggestions about what you may need for a complete application, and what the end products might look like. It's taken for granted that every developer follows their own road, but hopefully some of the information gets you pointed in a useful direction.

The code included with the book can jump-start your efforts on building some of the more system oriented components. Most of it is relatively pedestrian—basic add, edit, and delete screens that provide access to various system files (with a few more complex routines). This is, after all, the "back end" of an application—maintenance oriented programming—parts of which only system administrators ever see. But it does comprise a fairly complete system, which you are free to dismember, appropriate, mutate, and incorporate.

Chapter 18
General Application Components

Startup and configuration, testing, error trapping, help systems, documentation, and distribution are all components common to most applications, although at widely different levels of implementation.

Application Startup

Few things in the life of a developer are more embarrassing than having an application fail to start at a demonstration. It happens mostly because applications are sensitive to their operating environment—files are missing or damaged, there are new network drive mappings, not enough memory is available—you name it. It's not that these problems can't show up any time during the run of an application, but the most obvious point is at startup.

Part of the startup process is in the arms of FoxPro (and before that, Windows itself). This too is of some concern to the application developer. You need to review all of the conditions that are required for your program, and step through the process of loading and running the application from the working environment of the computer, network (if any), and the settings of CONFIG.FPW. Your application itself, when it takes over from FoxPro, has two very important startup tasks to perform—to check that it has everything needed to operate, and to get all of those things set up. These tasks are usually performed in the initialization program (or screen).

Initializing an Application

A sample initialization file was presented, without much explanation, in Chapter 10. Now's the time to dig into its parts. It's a good framework for many of the topics that will be described in some detail (such as security and user parameters), as you go through Chapters 18 and 19.

General Environment

Presuming this is the place where your application starts and ends—that FoxPro calls this routine first and returns directly to Windows when the application is done—there is no "environment" to preserve. However, in the unusual case where your application normally starts and terminates with the Command window, you might need to pay more attention to re-establishing the Command window environment. Otherwise, your initialization program is free to immediately start configuration.

How much of this configuration is done in the CONFIG.FPW file, and how much in the initialization program depends on the nature of your working environment. You may find that changing settings in a configuration file is much more flexible than rebuilding and recompiling the initialization program. This tends to boil down to the old consistency versus flexibility debate. Instructions in the initialization file are standard, by nature, anywhere the application is run. The CONFIG.FPW is free to be different, (and potentially disruptive), on every computer. If there is a guideline for what goes where, it's along the lines that fixed settings (those that do not change from machine to machine) and settings that require testing and logic (such as programming like IF CURRDIR()<>"D") belong in the init file. Whereas machine-specific, or environment-specific settings like MEMLIMIT belong in the CONFIG.FPW file. (Actually MEMLIMIT must be in the CONFIG.FPW.)

The order of events at startup is not particularly critical with the exception of file opening and variable declaration. Depending on how long the startup takes, you might consider doing something for the users to let them know the program is running, such as:

```
*> Notify User of Startup
WAIT "Starting program, please wait." WINDOW NOWAIT
```

Preprocessor Directives

These new, and most welcome, additions to FoxPro—the *preprocessor directives*—are old standbys for other languages. When FoxPro compiles your code, it first makes a pass in which (among other things) it collects and evaluates all of the lines beginning with #DEFINE and possibly ending with #UNDEF. When you use

```
#DEFINE <constant name> <expr>
```

you're telling the compiler, "Take this word (the constant name) and everywhere you find it in the code, substitute the value (from the expression)." For example:

```
#DEFINE PI   3.14165
#DEFINE ESC   27
#DEFINE COMPANY "WIDGETWORKS INC. NA"
#DEFINE TRUE  .t.
```

This last one simply says, "For every occurrence of the word TRUE in the code (not in comments), substitute the value .t. Then out in the code of your program, you can use the word TRUE anywhere you might have used .t.

```
DO WHILE TRUE
...
ENDDO
is_Older = TRUE
```

This makes it possible for you to put readable, meaningful words, where before there had to be cryptic numbers, lengthy strings, or other cumbersome values. If you wish to turn off a definition, somewhere else in the code you can use the #UNDEF <constant name> directive.

This form of the preprocessor directives is a big help in making your code self documenting. It also has a marginal benefit in reducing memory storage space (fewer constant values to store), and in performance (values can be hard coded instead of evaluated). Finally, by putting all of your major #DEFINEs in one place, you'll make it very easy to change values or perform other maintenance, which are then automatically carried out throughout the rest of your code.

There are few limitations on the <constant name> and the <expr>clauses, except two: Don't use FoxPro key words for constant names or system variables in the expression. Obviously you might get some odd code if you do something like #DEFINE BROWSE "grazing". System variables, the ones beginning with an underscore, are not evaluated until runtime, so using them in preprocessor directives will have unpredictable results.

The other preprocessor directive construction, looks familiar yet strange:

```
#IF <expN1> | <expL1>
       <statements>
[#ELIF <expN2> | <expL2>
       <statements>
       ...
[#ELIF <expNn> | <expLn>
       <statements>]
#ELSE
       <statements>
#ENDIF
```

Essentially, it's a DO CASE..ENDCASE construction, although it looks like an IF..ENDIF. For comparison:

```
                          DO CASE
#IF nVersion = 2            CASE nVersion = 2
#ELIF nVersion = 1.5        CASE nVersion = 1.5
#ELIF nVersion = 1.0        CASE nVersion = 1.0
#ELSE                       OTHERWISE
#ENDIF                      ENDCASE
```

For the most part, this construction is used to segregate sections of code, using conditionals to tell the compiler, "compile this section, leave the rest." The Screen Builder uses this extensively when you specify building code for both DOS and Windows. In the example above, the directive could be used to separate code from different production versions of a program. In the intialization file example used here, the directive is used to distinguish code for development from production code.

```
*————————————————————[ PREPROCESSOR DIRECTIVES
#DEFINE TRUE      .t.
#DEFINE FALSE     .f.
#DEFINE ESC      27            && <Esc> exit value
#DEFINE CTRLW     23           && <Ctrl> W exit value
#DEFINE SHAREFILE .t.          && Open file shared
#DEFINE EXCLUFILE .f.          && Open file exclusive
#DEFINE READWRITE .t.          && Open file for update
#DEFINE READONLY  .f.          && Open file noupdate
#DEFINE OPENAGAIN .t.          && Open file again
#DEFINE PRODUCT   .t.          && Final product version
#DEFINE DEVELOP   .t.          && Development version

*————————————————————[ GENERAL ENVIRONMENT
* SET commands
SET TALK OFF                   && Applies only to program
SET SAFETY OFF                 && At your own risk, of course
SET BELL OFF                   && Make noise explicit
SET CONFIRM ON                 && GET exit on <Enter>
SET DELETE ON                  && Note: Troublemaker 1
SET EXACT OFF                  && Note: Troublemaker 2
SET MEMOWIDTH TO 50            && Default value
SET ESCAPE ON                  && Default
SET PROCEDURE TO HRPROC        && Procedure/Function Library
```

Use the SET commands to create the general operating environment. It's a good idea to make important default conditions explicit. For example, you might say SET EXACT OFF, even though that's the default, because you want to document the "policy" for the application. From this point on SET EXACT ON must be used explicitly and then returned to SET EXACT OFF. The SET commands also include SET PROCEDURE, which loads the .PRG file containing the library of routines. By convention, the procedure file has highly generic routines that could be used with almost any application. The init file itself contains less generic routines that are useful for the specific application.

```
*————————————————————[ NETWORK SETUP
*DOS variable USERNAME set by Novell System or User Login
Script
*DOS SET USERNAME="%LOGIN_NAME"
IF NOT EMPTY(GETENV("USERNAME"))
  SET EXCLUSIVE OFF            && Files are shared
  SET REFRESH TO 0,0           && Fastest refresh
  SET REPROCESS TO 3 SECONDS&& General timing for retries
ENDIF
```

The network setup, discussed in Chapter 17, is relatively simple, although you can use third-party software to beef-up the network awareness. This setup presumes a Novell network.

SET REFRESH can put a heavy load on a busy network, the fastest refresh, 0,0, means the most network traffic. Reduce this value accordingly.

```
*————————————————[ USER PARAMETERS
* Variables Defined:
* dFYEnd = Fiscal Year End
* cDDFile = Location of data dictionary
* cOrg   = Name of Organization
* cOrgSt1 = Address: Street 1
* cOrgSt2 = Address: Street 2
* cOrgCsz = Address: City,State ZIP
IF NOT FILE("SYS.MEM")
  DO SYSPARMS.SPR                    && Call system setup routine
ELSE
 RESTORE FROM SYS.MEM ADDITIVE       && Load user parameters
ENDIF
```

Most applications of any size make it possible for the users, or at least system administrators, to set some of the operating parameters. This routine in the init file checks to see if the user parameter file is available. If not, it calls the system setup routine so that anything critical can be entered. In some cases, it might be better if only a warning message is shown, and the program terminated. This all depends on the environment of the application and the complexity of the setup. Notice the documentation of the user variables.

```
*————————————————[ DEFINE VARIABLES
*> GENERAL VARIABLES
PUBLIC dDate1, dDate2, nColorCnt, nLastClk, cFullName,
cUserName
dDate1   = {}                && Generic date holders for
dDate2   = {}                && date comparison routines
nColorCnt = 0                && ColorSet Stack counter
nLastClk = 0                 && Mouse double-click counter
cFullName = ""               && User's full name
cUserName = ""               && User's network name
cOperator = ""               && User's Operator ID
*> APPLICATION VARIABLES
PUBLIC cEmployerId, cState, cRegion
cEmployerID = "03423"        && State required ID
cState    = "MT"             && Current reporting state
cRegion   = "NW"             && Current reporting region
```

The user parameters section loads the first variables used by the application. The variables not defined by users are declared next (being careful not to step on any of the user variables). For documentation and convenience, the variable definitions are often done in two parts—general variables used by almost all applications, and application-specific variables. The variables below are, of course, a mere sampling. It's a good idea to keep PUBLIC variables to a minimum, and be very explicit about where they are used.

```
*——————————————————————[ SCREEN SETUP
CLEAR
SET STATUS BAR ON            && Default
SET MESSAGE TO               && Default to statusbar
SET READBORDER ON            && Border the GETs

*> COLOR SCHEME DEFINITIONS
IF ISCOLOR()
  * #1 - User Defined Windows
  SET COLOR OF SCHEME 1 TO ;
     N/BG,N/W,W+/BG,W+/BG,BG+/BG,B/W*,GR+/BG,N+/N,W+/BG,W+/BG,+
  *Other Color Schemes...
ELSE
  *Monochrome Scheme Definitions
  * #1 - User Defined Windows
  SET COLOR OF SCHEME 1 TO ;
     N/W,N/W,W+/W,W+/W,W+/W,B/W*,GR+/W,N+/N,W+/W,W+/W,+
  *Other Color Schemes...
ENDIF
```

The screen setup section takes care of anything required by the basic FoxPro screen. You may want to clear any old images, set up the statusbar, and so forth.

The use of color scheme definitions in a FoxPro application is truly a mixed bag. While the FoxPro manuals seem to frown on anything but using the Windows Control Panel to set colors, in applications you have little choice but to do your own color schemes. Unfortunately, you don't have ultimate control in the FoxPro environment, because some colors are set by Windows (such as system window frames) and that's that. Although you can define color schemes using the full panoply of RGB colors, the Screen Builder has no way to take advantage of them, which leaves the developer to "hard code" colors beyond the basic VGA 16.

Depending on your approach to color, this section may be empty or very elaborate. If you have any suspicion that your application will be running on monochrome screens (such as most laptops), you should make provision here for alternate schemes that complement the ones you've defined for color operation.

File Opening

As mentioned in Chapter 17, it wasn't always customary to open all (or most) files and leave them open. For one thing there weren't enough work areas to go around, and there was always the danger that an open file could be trashed. Now FoxPro 2.5 can have 255 work areas (Note, however, your DOS or network file limits may affect the number.) The risk to open files is minimal. Go ahead and open your files.

Since opening files is about the slowest thing FoxPro does, program initialization is the place to take the performance "hit." People (usually) have more patience at the beginning of a program. However, if you've got more than a couple files to open, keep the user informed about the wait.

The file-management system described in the next chapter is based on a data dictionary. This section opens the main data dictionary file and loads the path to each of the application's files into a variable the same name as the file. A special file opening routine, FileUse(), is used to open files from the variables.

```
*———————————————————[ OPEN FILES
*> Data Dictionary Load
* The location of the data dictionary file is stored in the
user
* definable DDfile variable.
IF FileUse( DDfile, "fil", SHAREFILE, "", "", READWRITE )
  SCAN
    STORE TRIM(filename) TO cFile
    STORE TRIM(path)    TO &cFile
  ENDSCAN
ENDIF

*> Tracking File
#DOCCODE USE DDTRACK ALIAS DDT ORDER PRGUSER
IF NOT FileUse( ddtrack, "ddt", SHAREFILE,"prguser", "A",
READWRITE )
  = ErrLine("Unable to open user tracking file.",3)
ENDIF

*> Codes File
#DOCCODE USE DDCODES ALIAS DDT ORDER TYPECODE
IF NOT FileUse( ddcodes, SHAREFILE, "cod", "typcode", "A",
READWRITE )
  = ErrLine("Unable to open system codes file.",3)
ENDIF
```

The two files opened here are part of the data dictionary system used in Chapter 19. The lines with #DOCCODE are for the FoxPro code documentor, FoxDoc. It knows nothing about the FileUse() function, and consequently would miss the opening of files without the special #DOCCODE reference.

Support Systems

Once the files have been opened, you can go ahead and initialize various subsystems that may rely on some of the files. In this case there are three of them:

```
*———————————————————[ Error Trapping
#IF DEVELOP
  ON ERROR DO STATLOOK WITH ERROR(), MESSAGE(), MESSAGE(1),
SYS(16),;
    LINENO(1), SYS(102), SYS(100), SYS(101), WOUTPUT(),
LASTKEY()
#ELSE
  ON ERROR DO FPWERR WITH ERROR(), MESSAGE(), MESSAGE(1),
SYS(16),;
    LINENO(1), SYS(102), SYS(100), SYS(101)
#ENDIF

*———————————————————[ Security
*Initialize security system
PUBLIC nSec1,nSec2,aDept,cDept
nSec1 = 0                   && Access Level
nSec2 = 0                   && Activity Level
cDept = ""                  && Departmental Access
#DEFINE SECURITY .t.        && Turn security on/off
*==================>> LOG IN
= ChkLogin()
IF SECURITY
 *Open security file
 IF NOT USED("SEC")
   IF NOT FileUse( ddsec, "sec", SHAREFILE, "seclocid", "A",
READWRITE)
     =ErrLine("Unable to open security file.",3)
  ENDIF
 ELSE
   SELECT sec
 ENDIF
 PUBLIC aSecLoc             && array for security locations
```

```
  DECLARE aSecLoc(RECCOUNT(),4)     && declare and load array
  COPY TO ARRAY aSecLoc FIELDS SECLOCID,SEC1,SEC2,DEPT
  USE                 && this file not needed again
ENDIF

*———————————————[ Help System
PUBLIC cHelpKey
cHelpKey = "Welcome to the Application"
SET HELP TO (HRHELP)
SET HELP ON
```

All three of these subsystems, Error Trapping, Security, and Help, are discussed in this and the next chapter. They're typical for moderate to large size applications.

At this point, basic initialization is completed, and the first screen or module of an application is called. In FoxPro it's very common to install a foundation READ after this point, so that a main menu can be displayed along with an application screen (nonwindow).

User Defined Parameters

It's very common for applications to allow the users, or at least designated client administrators, to change some of the operating parameters. This can range from setting the date to complete configuration of directories, colors, and printers. The last two, color and printers, are now frequently the province of Windows rather than FoxPro or your application.

Some of the items that can be maintained in a parameters screen are:

- Organization name, addresses, and phone numbers.
- Important dates.
- The status of selected SET commands.
- Color scheme options.
- Sequence numbers.
- Constant or parametric values for calculations.
- Official titles and application nomenclature.
- An "About" screen that identifies the software version and developer's name.

Application Testing

You expect that a piece of commercial software, say FoxPro, has had extensive testing. You demand it, in fact. What about your own software? "Well, sure, I'd like to get it really tested. But there isn't enough time. And with the budget we've got..."

This is one of those "let's get real" points. For discussion's sake, let's say there are four levels of testing:

1. Commercial software, distributed to thousands or maybe millions of people with different computers and environments, has to be heavily tested. Not only reputation, but sheer practicality forces testing. If the product isn't close to bullet proof, then it winds up dead in the software marketplace, which can shoot holes in anything. Besides the volume of the market can (theoretically) subsidize the effort to test thoroughly.
2. It's a slightly different story for an application intended for limited distribution. Whether this is a "vertical market" application like a dental office package, or a piece of software developed within a corporation for use at branch offices, there is an implicit and sometimes contractual requirement for close support. Configuration, setup, and operation may all be part of the distribution. This means that while the software still needs as much testing as possible, it gets routinely fudged in lieu of on-site correction. There may or may not be any budget for formal testing.
3. Even further down the testing totem pole, are applications customized for a single or limited group of clients. Typically, these programs have little or no budget specifically for testing. So it's not surprising that testing is neither systematic nor extensive. Like the previous category, there is heavy reliance on the fix-it-as-you-go approach. It's also helped by the fact that the number of users is limited, or even controlled. Just as programmer's make lousy testers, because they instinctively know how to avoid bugs, a small group of users, especially those who have been involved in the development process, also manage to get themselves into patterns that don't cause problems. It's not that this system works all the time, but a very large percentage of applications survive on this basis.
4. Finally, there are applications that are essentially personal. Here testing is usually synonymous with debugging.

There are a couple of points to these categorizations:

- **Testing is *not* debugging.** Testing produces bugs, but even that doesn't go nearly far enough. Just *using* software produces bugs, especially early in the development cycle. Testing is intentional. You're *trying* to produce bugs, and more importantly record when and how they occurred. And remember, there are different kinds of bugs—those that crash the application, those that produce an error message but don't cause a crash, and then there are things that are wrong, but don't stop the program or even produce an error message. A bad calculation is just as much a bug as a syntax error. Testing has to catch them all, and in fact may concentrate on finding the things that don't produce an obvious message.
- **Real testing is expensive.** It's one thing for software theoreticians to wag their fingers and admonish "Thou shall test," and quite another to come up with the time and money to put software through a complete testing cycle. The more systematic and thorough, the more expensive it becomes. Yet there is no reliable table of cost and benefit ratios to help you determine how much testing is enough. Intuitively, more testing should make a better product, and it probably does. But there are so many exceptions (horror stories), nobody can guarantee a solid testing regime provides a solid product. Besides, as is well known, there is no such thing as a bug-free program.

While there are patterns for testing, and whole books written on the methodologies, it all boils down to what the application needs and what you can afford to do.

User Interface Testing versus Process Testing

It may be useful to consider your application's need for testing by examining how much of it is user interface, and how much is processing. While both aspects require testing, they don't need the same kind of testing, and generally not the same depth.

The user interface of your application, for the most part its screens, is composed of menus, push buttons, OKLs (ON KEY LABELs), GETs, and so on. Testing this requires people who will poke the keyboard in every which way, trample through any data entry, and attempt to make every wrong turn in the menu—in short the average user. There is no way a programmer, or a development team can do this. They know too much. Besides, this is mostly a numbers game. The more people in the most varied circumstances that can test an application the better. Of course, time, money, and management capability are limiting factors.

Process testing, on the other hand, is something that can be done in-house, even by programmers. In most database applications there are data processes of one kind or another: updating, transaction processing, calculations, and reporting. The name of the game here is to be systematic. A wide range of test data, simulations, and test reporting can all be organized to "exercise" your application's processing for accuracy and reliability. How much of this you do, once again depends on limiting factors like time and money. But this kind of testing is much more concrete, and even predictable.

Of the two kinds of testing, in general user-interface testing is much more expensive and time consuming. Even if you don't hire professional software testers, the management of a beta test, distribution of the program, and support and response can get very demanding very quickly. If your application has a lot of complex user interface elements, then you'll need to plan more extensive testing.

Configuration Testing

One aspect of testing, and certainly the nastiest from the perspective of commercial software development, is the necessity of running an application in a wide variety of computer environments. You may be lucky and are developing your application to run on a single type of computer with known specifications. You don't need configuration testing. Unfortunately, this is the exception rather than the rule. At worst, you may be sending your application out into the great unknown, where machines of every age, description, and condition may turn your robust programming into an inert lockup.

If your application will be distributed, and you don't know what computers it will run on, you may be forced to do at least a sampling of configuration tests—running the program on a certain number of machines. This can take the form of a public beta where test copies are distributed to a number of different people, or a professional testing house. Either way is very expensive.

In some corporate projects, you may have a better idea which computers will be used to run your application, in which case more limited configuration tests might be enough.

Configuration testing may also involve the problem of scale. Some applications will work like champs with small test databases. However, when suddenly confronted with monster files from the real world, performance goes to hell, and program components start producing mistakes. File sizes, real-time speed, communications, and network configurations all play a role in configuration testing.

The Testing Cycle

Full-scale professional testing is a very complex business. It starts with the adoption of one or more testing methodologies, the development of specific *test metrics* (measurement guidelines) for an application, and a complete plan and schedule for the *testing cycle*. That's way beyond the scope of this book, and probably beyond the budgets of most developers using FoxPro.

At a less rigorous level, there's still plenty you can do to effectively test your applications. But it still takes planning, effort, time, and money. As ever, it's a matter of judgment.

Planning for Testing

There are many programmers who will bridle at the mention of a testing plan. It sounds like something mainframers do. Which is true. It's also true on small projects or projects where very few people are involved that any kind of formal planning may be unnecessarily expensive. But somewhere between none and too much, there is a level of planning for testing that fits a more ambitious application. Probably, the most beneficial thing is to simply make sure testing is something that gets thought about.

- The best testing begins with quality control.
- Quality control begins with good programming habits.

Quality control comes before testing. If you, other project members, or even a company don't care about quality control, then expect your testing load to be that much greater. Good application design, coding conventions, documentation, and good project communications are all part of establishing a routine for application development that makes quality control possible, or even a natural outcome.

As for the testing itself, here are some suggestions:

- **Make testing fit the application.** Part of your planning for an application should be to review development procedures, and think about how *this* application should be tested as it develops. Not all applications are the same with respect to testing. Obviously a financial or accounting program requires a certain kind of testing, which is different from the testing for a parts list catalog.
- **Stick with the essentials.** Deciding what's important to test is the first job of planning. It hardly needs to be a ten page document, but you (and everybody else in the development) should understand what is unique about an application and, in that context, what types of testing need to be emphasized. If the database is very large, then performance tests become more important. If there are a large number of critical calculations, then reporting tests and formula checks are top priority. This is the key to making the best of limited testing resources.
- **Use documentation as part of the testing process.** Most programmers with experience know that certain kinds of problems are associated with certain kinds of programming. For example, in database applications shifting between program modules can cause problems with table pointers, indexes, and relations. This is extremely true of event-driven programming applied to database applications. Knowing this sort of thing, programmers should take extra steps to document those areas of the programs that contain context shifts from one database configuration to another. The same approach can be applied to locations in the program where complex calculations or table updating is taking place. The object of this documentation approach is not only to explain what's there, but to speed up the process of locating problems during testing.
- **Plan for development test databases.** For most database applications, there is nothing more critical to the success of testing than a good test database. No surprise. But often easier said than done. So plan for it. If necessary, assign the work and schedule it. Also plan the approach. Depending on the type of application, you may need to create a database from scratch, or perhaps you can make it part of a conversion process.

- **Plan for the end run.** This is hard. At the planning stage, it's difficult to visualize what the final period before delivery is going to be like. When you get there, nobody has the time or energy for planning. Yet this is typically when the most difficult testing takes place. And for what do you "plan?" Plan for something that goes counter to the chaos—if nothing else, a systematic check of critical testing elements: Have all modules been tested, and to what extent? Have all reports been tested? Have all data tables been checked for integrity and accuracy? Somebody, somewhere should be assigned to take a clear headed look at what's been done, and decide what further testing needs to be done.

All of this is common sense. But with some planning it's *organized* common sense.

Alpha Testing

By now the phrases *alpha* and *beta* testing are so common, that even nonprogrammers are quite familiar with them. Alpha is usually synonymous with in-house testing, and beta with using independent testers, whether professional or otherwise. While these terms have their use in general database application development, they are most relevant to commercial software where the product is either done and on the market, or it's still in development. Developing software for clients, either within a corporation or in a commercial sense, is somewhat different. From the day the application reaches some kind of prototype, to the day it is delivered, it's more or less in beta testing. Which is to say, very early in the testing cycle, many database applications are exposed to the users.

Even so, there is still a process of in-house testing, although it may overlap more or less constantly with beta testing. If you're the only programmer, in-house means programmer testing (which by the way, *is* testing). In larger shops, there may be people assigned to testing, or, in ideal situations, people whose job it is to test software.

Whatever the scale of alpha testing, the basic tasks remain the same:

- Catch and squash fatal error bugs.
- Do first testing of user interface elements.
- Develop a test database.
- Run processing simulations.

- Check processing and calculations for accuracy.

At the same time they write code, programmers generally wander about the pieces of the application that are working. In that sense they are also taking the first crack at testing the user interface. This is rarely, if ever, systematic. But for most applications, it's satisfactory for alpha testing.

The last three items on the list, however, don't work unless they are somewhat organized. It all starts with building a good test database. Hopefully data-table design has preceded the actual coding. Without that, it would be difficult to create a very useful test database. All applications have to have some kind of *sample* database, otherwise it would be impossible to even run the programs. The question is whether you choose to make the sample database into a *test* database.

If possible, the test database should be appropriately scaled for the application. Those tables that are expected to contain a large number of records should be equally as big for testing. This is especially true for applications that make heavy use of relations, SQL, and reporting. Performance issues can crop up in unexpected places, unless you are working with tables that can truly "exercise" the application.

Even more important than appropriately sized tables is the loading of data that tests the extremes of an application. Good test data should deliberately contain:

- "Garbage", such as nonASCII characters.
- Values that exceed maximum and minimum parameters for calculations and functions.
- Records with severe data-integrity problems (such as nulls and improper values).
- Tables with relational problems (such as missing keys, and widow and orphan records).

The trouble with introducing this kind of data into tables is that it becomes difficult to distinguish between artificial bad data, and bad data produced by the program. One way around the problem is solid documentation of what is test material and where it is located. However, you can also separate the time periods for each kind of testing, and use complete "test suites" of files in different subdirectories. (This is easy if you're using a data dictionary.) Early on, a sample database may be all that's needed. After the prototype(s) have been developed, you can introduce an aggressive test database for a controlled period of time.

Whatever pattern you adopt, the test database is used to run simulations of all of the table processes in the application. Table updating, data processing, reports and queries—anything that has a programmed sequence of events not directly tied to interactive user control. At the same time, it's convenient to carefully check calculations and processing in reports, printouts of the database, and other places where results appear.

The final aspect of the alpha phase is configuration testing. This is the most difficult for small operations. Access to a wide variety of configurations (computers, peripherals, etc.) may be limited. Access to client or target customer configurations may also be restricted. There is always the possibility of sending your applications to a professional testing lab, but this is very expensive. Do the best you can, then cross your fingers, and hope that nobody is running a vintage 1984 IBM AT, with 20 Mb of hard disk, 4 Mb of RAM, on a token ring network.

Beta Testing

There is an old axiom in many businesses that cater to the public: People don't know what they want, until you show them something. Software is no different. When you first put the application in the user's hands, that's when you find out (maybe), what people really want.

The sample group for a beta test can range anywhere from a spouse to several thousand people. (It's rumored that Microsoft had as many as seventy-five thousand people in the Windows NT beta test.) Only time, money, and management capability are required.

Once again, you are faced with decisions about the scale of the project, the time and resources available, and the target users for the application. If this is a commercial product, then you need a fairly large base of beta testers, at least fifty to one hundred people, to have a reasonable sample. If this is a corporate project of modest scale, or an application being customized for a specific client, then perhaps ten to twenty-five testers might be enough. Even smaller projects might get by with only a handful of people. Of course, the more people involved, the more difficult the management and the greater the expenses.

The expense of beta testing isn't really the cost of materials, or communications, but the time it takes to keep a beta running. Somebody has to plan, package, ship, monitor, and respond to a beta program. And this is just the mechanics. If you really want benefit from a beta program, you need to go beyond the basic bug reporting, and learn from the beta testers what they *think* about the program. Get their gut-level reactions.

This takes some skill, and even more time. In custom software development, it is a required step. In other kinds of development, it may seem like an elective task. It may be, but you're wasting half of the potential reward for doing a beta test.

Version Control

The beta test period is almost inevitably the first encounter with the problem of *version control*. Each time you ship all, or a portion, of your application to beta test sites, you've generated a version. In any case, it's not the same as the code you're working on two days later. In a one person project, this isn't much of a problem, although you still need to pay attention to what's new and what's not. But in a multiperson development effort, version control becomes a major issue.

There are many kinds of version control. At the most basic level, it's a cataloging of the components of an application (usually the files), and a running record of when these components are updated and then incorporated into a shipped version. In most cases, this record is extended to a logging system for developers, who approach the files as part of a library from which they can borrow. Version control keeps track of who has what, what they did, and when it was done.

Unfortunately, FoxPro has no built-in version control. In fact, because of the way FoxPro applications are built, most of the commercial version control software is of limited value. These programs are designed to work with standard ASCII text files, and can return meaningful line numbers and insert documentation for version changes. However, they don't know anything about the .DBF file structure used by FoxPro, and can only report that changes have occurred without being able to interpret the context.

For the time being, this leaves developers with creating their own version control system. Such as it may be. As usual, good documentation can go a long way toward helping with version control. It's a good idea to always name, date, and time stamp any significant changes to code, at least after it's gone past the prototype stage.

Various schemes have been devised around the FoxPro Project Manager, and these help with 'checking out' modules of the program. Since the Project Manager is not multiuser, that is a project file can only be opened by one programmer at a time, you can parcel out the application in several Project Manager files. These individualized Project Managers are then assigned or available on a controlled (sign out, sign in) basis.

Control of beta and final product versions is typically a matter of using different subdirectories. It's crude, but it works.

Error Trapping and Recovery

Except for the most bare bones of applications, it's customary for developers to provide an alternate error trapping facility. FoxPro still generates the first response to an error, but by using the ON ERROR command, your application can intervene with its own error handler. There you can not only inform the user of the error in something more approximating English, but you can also provide explanations and possible remedies, or at least how to make a graceful exit.

As you may recall from the initialization file, the error trap begins with a statement like:

```
ON ERROR DO STATLOOK WITH ERROR(), MESSAGE(), MESSAGE(1),
SYS(16),;
  LINENO(1), SYS(102), SYS(100), SYS(101), WOUTPUT(), LASTKEY()
```

The error trap routine itself receives the parameters and goes into a long CASE structure:

```
PARAMETER xErrNo, xMsg1, xMsg2,
DO CASE
CASE xErrNo = 3
CASE xErrNo = 43
CASE...
ENDCASE
```

It's traditional for books on programming to provide an example of error trapping routines. OK, that code fragment was it. What you should do is *not* re-invent the wheel. There are a couple of excellent error trapping systems in the public domain, most particularly Pat Adam's program FOXEROR2.PRG, which are available from Fox User Groups or on various bulletin board services. These routines have done the leg work of defining the error types, and building the basic responses. If you like, they can be modified to your own style and tastes in a few hours, as opposed to taking days to create the whole thing from scratch.

Application Documentation

Documentation of all kinds tends to fall naturally at the end of the development cycle. This often dooms documentation to a dry well for both time and resources. The fact that there are two very different kinds of documentation, *project documentation* and *user documentation*, complicates matters. It's difficult and usually not desirable to have the same people do both. The project developers (programmers, designers, analysts) are responsible for project documentation, of course. User documentation is more difficult, because all too frequently the developer(s) don't have the time, skill, or interest to do it. Large software companies get around this by hiring people whose sole job is to produce user documentation. This brings documentation into focus, at least for those people. But without the resources to hire professionals, user documentation can become a major problem.

For most applications neither kind of documentation comes easy. Software development is notorius for paying lip service to project documentation. That's because it requires disciplined work habits under pressure—a bad combination. And user documentation is expensive, by both time and money standards. This section tries to deal with the issues in both kinds of documentation within the context of tools and approaches available in FoxPro.

Project Documentation

All programmers know, in their heart of hearts, that good documentation is valuable. Yet, at one time or another, if not constantly, every programmer has faced the feeling that they don't have time for it.

Besides, who's to say what *good* documentation is? Some notes scratched on the back of a napkin? Probably not. Sixteen feet of three-ring binders, like mainframe OS docs? Also probably not. Nobody is asking you to spend more time documenting than you do programming, hopefully. But where does an application developer draw the line?

There *is* a kind of litmus test: *Good documentation allows for rapid comprehension of an application's purpose, design, and programming by someone not familiar with the project, but familiar with the context of development.* This is wordy, but necessary. It says, among other things, that if you're a FoxPro developer, that's your context and you hardly need to write documentation so a C programmer can understand it. But it also says *rapid comprehension*. That's really the goal. How fast can somebody who's not been working on the project (either never, or for a long time) pick up on the work?

There are at least five different categories of project documentation:

1. Analysis
2. Design: program and data
3. In-line code
4. Printed code
5. Code support such as cross references

All of these serve to communicate:

1. The nature and purpose of the application.
2. The important decisions that were made.
3. The specific programming choices.

To be complete the documentation covers the life cycle of the project. This includes any analysis and design that were done at the inception. It includes major project decisions to include (or not include) certain elements. In a database application it usually places emphasis on tables. Of course, there is the documentation in the code itself. This usually winds up being printed in a mountain of paper, and may be bolstered by additional mounds of printed support documentation. And when the application is delivered, maintenance documentation begins.

The scale of a project has a lot to do with the volume and kind of documentation. Small applications hardly need books of analysis and designs. But all FoxPro applications should have adequate data table and in-line code documentation. And since FoxPro gives you an excellent documentation tool, FoxDoc, it's easy enough to produce the mountains of printed paper.

In the end, the point of documentation is to do it. If you don't, then you should be taking a calculated risk that whatever time you save now, won't be lost ten-fold later.

Analysis and Design Documentation

Even the most cursory preparation for an application has some analysis and design. It's easy enough to put the primary documents in a binder. It's one small step further to label and index the information. But the biggest step is to extract from the chaff the kernels of information that might really help other people understand the purpose of the application and the design decisions that went into it.

Perhaps the two most useful types of analysis and design information are diagrams of the application, and documentation of the data tables. Nothing beats a good diagram for a quick presentation of module structure, table relations, and data flow. Unfortunately, not every project has people who can create diagrams. A written narrative may be the only substitute. However it's done, the point for this kind of documentation is *overview.*

Data table information can be as simple as the LIST STRUCTURE TO PRINT or the printout from FoxDoc, all the way to very complete data dictionary listings. Most projects keep a running record of table structure anyway. In the early stages of a project, this is the most helpful of all documentation. It's also vital for those who must do maintenance (or enhancement).

In-Line Code Documentation

The argument can be made, and is being made here, that along with overview documentation (especially. diagrams), and data table information, in-line code documentation is the cornerstone of modest but truly effective project documentation. It's not that programming has to read like a novel, or that verbosity is its own reward. But as stressed a couple of other times in this book, readable (consistently formatted) and intelligently explained code has no peer for communicating how an application was constructed, and documenting the crucial programming decisions.

Judge for yourself:

- **Code from programmer 1:**

```
* mark/clear a range of record selections from browse to
array
```

```
* okls rightmouse do mousemrk leftmouse do mousechk
* enter do enterchk spacebar do mousemrk
* put chk=markdisp() in browse
function mousemrk
cwontop = wontop()
if nstartptr = 0
       nmrow = mrow()
       na = ascan( amark, recno())
             if na = 0
                    dimension amark[ns]
                    amark[ns] = recno()
                          skip
                    nstartptr = recno()
                          ns=ns+1
             else
                    = adel(amark, na)
                          skip
                    nstartptr = recno()
                    ns=ns-1
             endif
                    show window (cwontop) refresh
                    wait "_ start" window nowait
else
      if nmrow > mrow()
             ntmpstart = nstartptr
             nstartptr = recno()
             go ntmpstart
             skip -1
             nendptr = recno()
      else
             skip
             nendptr = recno()
      endif
      go nstartptr
             scan while recno() <> nendptr
                   na = ascan( amark, recno())
                   if na = 0
                          dimension amark[ ns ]
                          amark[ns] = recno()
                          ns=ns+1
                   else
                              = adel( amark, na)
                              ns=ns-1
                              endif
                 endscan
```

```
                    nstartptr = 0
                    show window (cwontop) refresh
endif
return
```

- Code from programmer 2:

```
**************************************************************************
* FUNCTION NAME.. BrowseMrk()
* DESCRIPTION.... BROWSE: MARK SELECTED RECORDS INTO AN
ARRAY
* DATE........... Sat 08-22-1992 01:52:56
* PROGRAMMERS.... KMH, MHC
* LAST CHANGE.... Mon 08-31-1992 MHC, Reformatted and
Documented
* PARAMETERS..... None BUT assumes public variable
nLastClk and several
*                  other "local" variables (see below)
* SYNTAX......... BrowseMrk()
* USAGE.......... See setup below
* RETURN......... .t. : loads array aMark[] with record #
selections
* NOTES.......... Using a BROWSE, this function stores
selection of records
*                 in an array for further processing. It
is very fast and
*                 efficient but keep in mind that an array
like this can
*                 get BIG, meaning a memory hog..use
wisely. Note the
*                 relatively complex setup.
* CALLED BY...... GUF (General Use Function)
* CALLS.......... MouseMrk(), MouseChk(), EnterChk(),
MarkDisp()
*
*===================================[ SETUP
]=====================================*
*
* *--------------[ REQUIRED VARIABLES
* These are modified in the Browse and returned.
* DECLARE aMark[1]     && array to hold selections
* aMark[1] = 0 && initialize
* nStartPtr = 0        && pointer to first selection
* nS    = 1            && counter for current array
element
```

```
* nMrow   = 0          && screen position marker. This is
*                      && used to mark mouse position
* cOldHelp = cHelpKey
* cHelpKey = "_ Browse Select"
*
* *————————[ KEY ASSIGNMENTS
* PUSH KEY
* ON KEY LABEL RIGHTMOUSE DO MouseMrk
* ON KEY LABEL LEFTMOUSE DO MouseChk
* ON KEY LABEL ENTER   DO EnterChk
* ON KEY LABEL SPACEBAR  DO MouseMrk
*
* *————————[ BROWSE WINDOW
* DEFINE WINDOW wBrsMrk FROM 4,20 TO 20,60 SYSTEM FLOAT ;
* TITLE "Select" COLOR SCHEME 10
*
* *————————[ BROWSE
* BROWSE FIELD chk=MarkDisp():H="_", SSQ, INSP FREEZE CHK
;
*  NOMODIFY NODELETE NOMENU NOAPPEND WINDOW wBrsMrk
*
* *————————[ CLEAN UP
* ON KEY
* POP KEY
* RELEASE nStartPtr, n, nMrow
* RELEASE WINDOW wBrsMrk
* cHelpKey = cOldHelp
*

*****************************************************************************
FUNCTION MouseMrk

PRIVATE cWontop, nA, nTmpStart, nEndPtr

cWontop = WONTOP()             && get window name for
refresh
*——————[ Check selection position
IF nStartPtr = 0               && if first selection
  nMrow = MROW()               && mark mouse position
  nA = ASCAN( aMark, RECNO()) && see if this record
already chosen
  IF nA = 0                    && if not found, put in
array
    DIMENSION aMark[nS]        && redimension selection
array
    aMark[nS] = RECNO()        && store current record # in
```

```
array
    SKIP                        && skip to get "real" first
pointer
    nStartPtr = RECNO()         && store current record # in
pointer
    nS=nS+1                     && increment array counter
  ELSE                          && already selected record
    = ADEL(aMark, nA)           && delete from array
    SKIP                                && skip to get real
first pointer
    nStartPtr = RECNO()         && mark this as first
selection
    nS=nS-1                     && decrement array counter
 ENDIF
 SHOW WINDOW (cWontop) REFRESH
 WAIT "_ Start" WINDOW NOWAIT

ELSE // is an end selection

 *> trap an end pointer "above" the start pointer
 IF nMrow > MROW()
   nTmpStart = nStartPtr        && save the start pointer
   nStartPtr = RECNO()          && get the new start pointer
   GO nTmpStart                 && go to old start pointer
   SKIP -1                      && and get the new end
pointer
   nEndPtr = RECNO()            && reverse the pointers
 ELSE
   SKIP                         && one forward to get end
pointer
   nEndPtr = RECNO()
 ENDIF

 GO nStartPtr                   && go back to start for scan
 SCAN WHILE RECNO() <> nEndPtr     && loop from start to
end
   nA = ASCAN( aMark, RECNO())
   IF nA = 0                    && if not found, put in
array
     DIMENSION aMark[ nS ]
     aMark[nS] = RECNO()
     nS=nS+1                    && increment array counter
   ELSE                         && if found, remove from
array
     = ADEL( aMark, nA)
     nS=nS-1                    && decrement array counter
```

```
      ENDIF
    ENDSCAN

    nStartPtr = 0          && reset start pointer to new
    SHOW WINDOW (cWontop) REFRESH
  ENDIF // first selection

  RETURN
  *
```

This example was not made up. It's from two different programmers, with two styles of coding, but only one with documentation. The first programmer was at least aware of *clegic* (indented) display. It looks very much like a lot of C coding. But the lack of (any) documentation was a killer. When the second programmer took over (the first one transferred), she spent three hours trying to figure out what this and four related routines were doing. Properly documented, the whole thing would have been about a fifteen minute exercise.

The first programmer was aiming for speed, and the lean lower case style and big tabs accomplish that. He could even have skipped the tabs, and used a program called Beautify.

Beautify

FoxPro 2.5 has included this programmer's utility on the Program menu. It's main purpose in life is to provide some kind of formatted display for messy, quickly entered code. Just open the Beautify dialog box, make the settings you want, and Beautify formats your code. Or at least some of the formatting. It doesn't do any documentation, of course. Nor does it provide section dividers, or any other kind of visual documentation.

NOTE

The Beautify utility has an option, Action diagram symbols, that produces code with all of the loops, ifs, and cases connected by lines and other symbols. These can be very helpful in spot-checking your code for missing control structure elements (such as IF without ENDIF). You can't compile the code with an action diagram, but you can remove it by rerunning Beautify with Action diagram symbols unchecked, or simply use Edit, Undo, before doing any other editing.

Whether you use Beautify as the only formatting for your code, or you do all your own formatting and add documentation as you go, doesn't really matter very much as long as the end result is readable, comprehensible code.

Printed Code Documentation

It seems almost obligatory. You haven't done documentation until you've dumped a few hundred pages of code to the printer. Pound for pound and page for page, the utility of this practice is probably one of the bigger myths in programming. With experience comes the realization that it's much more efficient to go code hunting in the code on screen, in the file. However, there's no denying that in this paper-bound world some programmers feel more comfortable scanning a ream of printout. Besides, plunking a massive tome onto the project manager's (or client's) desk lends weight, literally, to your claims of a mighty effort.

At least these days, there's no excuse for the ugly, endless, printer dump of code. In fact FoxPro gives you a very useful way to cover a lot of printed documentation: FoxDoc.

FoxDoc

You should do at least one run with FoxDoc on a test application, and sample all of the options. In the long term, however, what you face are decisions about when (or whether) to use FoxDoc to make an impression, or to be useful project documentation. The difference is mostly a matter of customization.

FoxDoc is relatively easy to use, and once fed the basic information about your application, it can crank out the requisite ream of paper with little or no effort on your part. This can be very impressive, especially when neatly packaged. In all probability however, from the start it will be almost useless as a working document, and become increasingly so as time passes.

To cross the line from merely bulk documentation into working documentation is usually a matter of customizing FoxDoc. You need to make it truly appropriate to your application, your style of coding, and your needs for debugging and testing. Part of this customization is to make it easy to run FoxDoc with regularity (about once a week), so the output doesn't simply go out of date.

Customization of FoxDoc has a number of different angles:

1. **Application configuration.** FoxDoc let's you save most of your basic information, output selections, and options to a configuration file—FOXDOC.CFG. It's a good idea to plan for at least two config files: full documentation and working documentation. The first one attempts to run everything you consider relevant from an historical documentation point of view. The second is usually much slimmer, and aimed at providing documentation immediately useful in the programming process.

   You may actually need more than these two configuration files, if your application is very large. While the FoxPro environment gives FoxDoc a considerable amount of memory resources, it's not difficult for a large project to exceed the limits, especially if you are creating a cross reference. This leads to the necessity of *chunking* your application for FoxDoc. You need to break up the documentation into meaningful and useful modules, then create a number of configuration files with a Main File... set for the lead file of each module.

   Creating useful working documentation may be a process similar to chunking, as you single out areas of the application and restrict the number of reports and reported items. Be sure to save the various configuration files to the root directory of your project, and use the application information text to document what a particular configuration is supposed to do.

2. **Output selection.** There are about twenty FoxDoc output selections. They are not all equally valuable all the time. Table 18.1 lists the selections and attempts an evaluation of each. You'll find your own reasons for including or excluding selections, especially for working documentation.

Table 18.1
FoxDoc selections.

Output Selection	Full	Work	Description
Formatted source code	x	?	How much you allow FoxDoc to format your code depends on how much that's already been done. Good programmer formatting is often more sophisticated than FoxDoc can produce. But not every programmer has the time or patience. If you're relying heavily on FoxDoc to keep code clean, then run this selection every time.
Action diagrams	x	x	Action diagrams are one of the most useful things FoxDoc can do for you. Not only does it help with checking for control structure errors, but it can be an invaluable tool for simply reviewing the flow and structure of your application.
File headings	x	?	Most programmers find FoxDoc headings need customization. Not everybody wants all twelve heading options. (They can also take up a lot of space in the code files.) The programs called, and calling programs options are useful guides within your code for moving around an application.
Table/DBF summary	x	x	If you're not using a data dictionary system, this may be your best method of documenting file and field structure.
Index summary	x	x	Like the table summary, this is very useful in lieu of a more complete data dictionary listing.
Format file summary			Format files are seldom used these days. If you are using them, include this selection.

(continued)

Report form summary	x		At the end of a report building period, or for full documentation, run this selection.
Label file summary	x		As for reports, same for labels.
Screen file summary	x		For full reports.
Memory file summary	x		For full reports.
Library file summary			Use this only if you have to use any library calls (.FLL).
Procedure file summary	x		This can be lengthy and redundant in large applications.
Other File Summary			Only if you are using low level file operations, such as modify text files.
File listings	x		Like procedure listings, this can be lengthy.
System statistics	x	x	The bigger your application, the more satisfaction you'll get out of the statistics.
Cross reference		x	If your applications tend to have problems with variables or field definitions, this is a most useful tool. Otherwise, these reports can be huge, use a lot of RAM, and take time. Use, this only when its needed. Stick with local cross reference when ever possible to stay out of RAM trouble, and synchronize with any chunking you may be doing.
Tree diagram	x	?	These text-based tree diagrams can be useful, but do not have the clarity of graphical tree diagrams.

3. **Output options.** Fine tuning your selections is particularly important for header definitions, cross reference reports, tree diagram definitions, and formatted source code options. Much of this depends on your coding style, and the needs of your application.
4. **Code customization.** Code customization is something you may need to do if you are using a lot of macros, name references, and other indirect calling schemes in your application. FoxDoc attempts to identify macro substitutions and document the actual file calls. But it's not a mind

reader. You can help it's accuracy by adding this FoxDoc directive into your code:

```
*# DOCMACRO <macro name> value
```

For example:

```
*# DOCMACRO datatable hremploy.dbf
USE &datatable
```

The other approach to helping FoxDoc understand your code is to use...

```
*# DOCCODE <command statement>
```

For example:

```
*# DOCCODE USE hremploy ALIAS emp ORDER empid
=FileUse( hremploy, "EMP", .t., "EMPID","A",.t.)
```

Because the code in the example calls a function instead of the USE command, FoxDoc would miss all references to the file, alias, and indexes. The *# DOCCODE directive let's you tell FoxDoc what command is actually being executed. The same approach can be taken with calls that may have multiple values hidden by a macro substitution, for example:

```
cFile = DBF()
USE &cFile AGAIN
*# DOCCODE USE hrpos
*# DOCCODE USE hremp
*# DOCCODE USE hrassign
```

Along with *# DOCCODE and *# DOCMACRO, you can also use:

`*# FOXDOC PRGPATH <dos path>`
to change the path to application program files.
`*# FOXDOC DATAPATH <dos path>`
to change the path to application data files.
`*# FOXDOC XREF [ON | OFF | SUSPEND]`
to turn cross reference on or off or suspend it.
`*# FOXDOC FORMAT [ON | OFF | SUSPEND]`
to turn on or off or suspend code formatting.
`*# FOXDOC INDENT [ON | OFF | SUSPEND]`
to turn on or off or suspend code indenting.
`*# FOXDOC CAPITAL [ON | OFF | SUSPEND]`

to turn on or off or suspend code capitalization.
`*# FOXDOC EXPAND [ON | OFF | SUSPEND]`
to turn on or off or suspend keyword expansion.

All of these make it possible to block off sections of code, either to save on redundancy, or because you want to control the chunking of the application. This may be particularly true for using the cross reference on or off, or the resetting of data and program file paths.

5. **Keyword configuration.** Over time developers tend to create their own libraries of functions and procedures, which are used in many applications. If this is the case, or you are unhappy with the default FoxDoc selection or handling of keywords, then you can configure the FoxDoc keyword files: PROWORDS.FXD and FX2WORDS.FXD. These can be edited through the FoxPro editor (MODIFY COMMAND or from the menu). The first file, PROWORDS.FXD, contains the standard FoxPro commands and functions along with any instructions for their handling:
   - * comments out a keyword.
   - ! capitalizes, but does not cross reference. Use this for common commands like @..SAY or CLEAR.
   - @ capitalize and always cross references. Use this for important commands like SET DELETED, and SET EXACT.
   - % Do not capitalize, do not cross reference. Use this for often repeated variables.
   - **( )** Denotes a function if at the end of a keyword.

   You can use these same symbols when editing the FX2WORDS.FXD, which should contain all the user defined functions that you wish to have cross referenced in your application(s).
6. **Printing templates.** FoxDoc uses printing templates, generic instructions for output printing, in much the same sense as the Screen Builder and Menu Builder have a code generator. These templates make extensive use of the TEXTMERGE facilities of FoxPro. You can modify these templates to change format and content of the FoxDoc report, if needed. However you will need to learn the ins and outs of the template language approach of FoxPro. Printing Templates. This is not a simple task.

Customizing FoxDoc, like most specialized tailoring of the programming environment, takes a lot of time. However, once done, it's done. From then on, you should have documentation reports, both for full documentation and for working documentation, that may actually mean something in the context of your applications.

User Documentation

It would be a rare project indeed that had *no* user documentation. But the continuum of user documentation is very broad.

- **Minimal documentation** is screen oriented on-line help and one sheet of installation instructions.
- **Nominal documentation** is copied manual (often with the classic three-ring binder), an on-line help system, and basic installation instructions, usually with batch files.
- **Normal documentation** is a printed manual, frequently not typeset, context oriented on-line help, and integrated installation software and instructions.
- **Maximal documentation** is printed manual(s), with illustrations, and indexes, extensive context-oriented on-line help system, tutorial material (including computer based training), sample and supplementary material such as quick guides, integrated and automated installation software and instructions, and technical documentation for users.

Where your application falls on this continuum depends on a lot of factors—budget, time, complexity of the content, size or scope of the application, target users, life expectancy for use, availability of skilled people for documentation, and more. Depending on the type of application, some elements will be emphasized more than others. For example, an application for professionals in a specific field may require more technical documentation, and less tutorial material. If you're targeting the general public, however, you may emphasize the training and tutorial documentation.

As you can see, the line between user documentation and user training is very thin. Actually, the line is nonexistent. It's often said that good user documentation is one of the best ways to train. There is, however, a difference of intent between generic documentation, which describes and explains *what is*, and training documentation, which describes *how to*. As user documentation goes from minimal to maximal, it tends to shift from generic to training documentation.

On-Line Help System

On-Line help is typically available by pressing **F1**. This has become so standard that no application worthy of the name can be without it. It has several advantages in comparison with paper documentation:

- It's always available, unlike paper documentation which often has legs.
- To one degree or another is not only customizable, but changeable on the fly.
- You can build on-line help even as you program.
- Theoretically at least, on-line help should have faster lookup and searching.

This is one element of user documentation that should be answered with a definite "yes." Then, however, the issue becomes what kind and how much on-line help. This is a choice factor in FoxPro. There are *two* on-line help systems.

- **The Windows help system** is not a Fox product at all, but the standard Windows Help used by most commercial Windows applications. When FoxPro calls Windows Help, it's actually executing a separate program. This system has a built-in topic search mechanism, and also provides bookmarks and annotation to support user references. You can't create Windows Help within FoxPro. It's available as a Help compiler program, a stand-alone product normally acquired when you buy the FoxPro for Windows Distribution Kit.

  Its advantages are:

  - It's standard for all Windows applications.
  - It has all Help features built-in.
  - It is a complete help development environment for coordinating help content.
  - You can include graphics and special annotation markings.

  Its disadvantages are:

  - It cannot be created inside FoxPro (it requires a compiler).
  - It is not user/client modifiable.
  - The mechanics of the system are not programmable at any level.

  - This is a Windows-only system.

- The DBF help system is a carry-over from the DOS versions of FoxPro. It's based on a standard .DBF or .FPT file. FoxPro for Windows provides the necessary machinery to operate this system, including cross-reference links and topic management. With a little work, it can also have open-ended help searches and other amenities.

  Its advantages are:

  - It's user modifiable.
  - It's developer modifiable with FoxPro for Windows.
  - Some of the mechanics of the help system are programmable.
  - This system can be used in both DOS and Windows applications.

  Its disadvantages are:

  - It's not "Windows standard."
  - Enhancements, like user topic searching, must be programmed.

Under most circumstances, this boils down to two major considerations: Windows standard versus modifiability. The .DBF system is more malleable and transportable, even to the point of allowing users to participate in creating help screens. But it is not Windows standard.

Until you develop a system of your own, *any* help system is a lot of work. You need to master and configure the mechanics—the way the help is delivered. You need to create the content, text entry and screen design, and you need to load and test it within the application. This is not a project to be left until the eleventh hour of your first application.

NOTE

You should be aware that it is *illegal* to distribute either the Windows version help file (FOXHELP.HLP) or the .DBF-style help file (FOXHELP.DBF). In effect, if you distribute (not just sell) your application, you must create your own help file.

Unless you are building a very big (or very commercial) application that requires a very complete help system, you can probably get by with minimal planning for help. Some attention to the structure of topics might be in order. A topic list, even an outline is useful. Under ideal circumstances, programmers, project managers, and even clients can participate in building help screens (or text) as the project progresses. This is ideal. Unfortunately, the definition of help is usually somewhat fluid during development. Keystrokes change, even procedures and features change, which makes it necessary to change the help. This is one rationale for building the help system late in the development cycle. (And just one more thing to drive everybody nuts at the last minute.)

Creating a DBF Style System

While not quite as slick as the Windows help system, you can create a .DBF style help system that is very practical, and in many ways easier to manipulate. Given that a large number of FoxPro programs are custom database applications for specific clients or markets, the fact that a .DBF style Help permits user modification can be very attractive. The client likes it because they can "have it their way" and document their own procedures. *You* like it because *the client* can create some of the help for you.

However to make a system like this does take some preparation, both in the delivery mechanism and the content of the help. The software on disk with this book has all of the necessary ingredients. It provides customized, context sensitive help from the **F1** key and from the Help option of the system menu. The latter provides extensions to the help system including generic and specific topic searching, and user creation and editing of help. These routines replace all of the standard interface of the FoxPro .DBF style system.

The core of this (and any) help system is the content you load into the help file. In this case, a standard database file.

In the DBF Help System, FoxPro uses a standard .DBF (and a memo file) to store all of the help content. It's a very simple file with just three fields:

TOPIC	C	30	Stores the help topic, primary search item.
DETAILS	M	10	Stores the content of the help screen.
CLASS	C	20	Stores further classification of help, and secondary search items.

Actually, FoxPro does not require these exact fields. All it needs is the first field to be character and the second field be a memo field. So you can modify this structure in any way necessary. However, unless you're creating a very unique help system, it's easier to stick with the FoxPro structure.

Deciding on the help topics, then loading or creating the help screens are the biggest tasks in building a help system. As mentioned, it helps to make a listing of topics, at least as a starting point.

NOTE

You can not legally use the standard FOXHELP.DBF as the basis of your own help file. It contains a lot of specialized programming information, which Microsoft construes to be proprietary. The DDHELP.DBF provided with the book has already been chopped down and modified to a legal and normal application starter list.

The content of your help screens is normally heavily customized for the application. However there are several general kinds of screens (other than those provided by FoxPro for Windows), including:

- Welcome and introduction to the application.
- A map for visual guide to the modules and programs.
- A module-by-module description of what the application does.
- Procedural descriptions of processes and complicated entry screens.
- Rules and policies for certain kinds of entry and processing.
- Special "how to" instructions for screen elements.
- Field-level help, when necessary.
- An application specific glossary.
- Support information for the application, such as tables and diagrams.

When building the help system, there's always the need to balance the time it takes to create and load this information versus the belief that people will actually use the help system. Of course, if the on-line help is a substitute for a printed manual, your efforts take on special relevance.

If you've had a chance to look in the FOXHELP.DBF or DDHELP.DBF you may have noticed some topic entries with unusual markings: ▶ and ■. These have special meaning in the FoxPro .DBF help system. The first one is reserved for general topics, and the second for interface topics. All they really do is insure that a sorted help file puts topics with these markers at the beginning of the file. You may choose to keep some of the native FoxPro entries of this type, or add some of your own. If you add your own, when entering the topic be sure that your current working font is FoxFont, and type **Alt-16** for ▶ and **Alt-0254** for ■.

Loading the memo fields is the big job. Even with a relatively small number of screens (one memo field equals one help screen), hand typing help information is time consuming. The job can be jump-started by loading information created in other programs (like a word-processor) and stored in a standard .TXT (ASCII text) file. These can be imported directly into a memo field with:

```
APPEND MEMO <memo field> FROM <file name>
APPEND MEMO Notes FROM d:\doc\procs.txt
```

You can use line drawing and other ASCII symbols, however, these are not available in most Windows fonts. Be sure that your working font is Foxfont when using the help system.

The third field in the standard help .DBF, CLASS, is optional, but since the FoxPro searching routines use these for extended topic mapping, you might continue the same system. The meanings and codes for this field are in the *Developer's Guide*, and are built into the help edit screen included with the software disk. The help system on the disk uses this CLASS field for broad topic searches.

At some point during preparation of the help file, you'll probably want to sort the contents by topic. FoxPro does not use an index on the help file, so if you need to have it sorted, then you must use the SORT command directly. Be aware that sorting always puts the ▸ and ■ marked topics first. Any changes to the entries of the file, and you'll probably need to re-sort.

Once the help file has been created, and partially loaded for testing, you can proceed with the rest of the setup:

1. Insert the following in the intialization file:

   ```
   PUBLIC cHelpKey
   ```

   As a public variable, the current value is carried throughout the application. Whenever you need to reference a specific help topic, you change the value.

2. Wherever you want to have context-sensitive help available, you need to enter a value for cHelpKey. For those topics that are based on the FoxPro general or interface topics you need to include the ▸ (ASCII 16) or ■ symbol (ASCII 254), like this:

   ```
   cHelpKey = "■ Introducing The Application".
   ```

If the editor doesn't represent this character, just use the CHR( ) function in the code to make the conversion:

```
cHelpKey = CHR(254)+" Introducing The Application"
```

These can be placed in menu options (in a procedure), in the WHEN of screen READs and GETs, and in any other function or procedure. You should remember to save the value of cHelpKey as you enter a new module or screen, so that it can be restored on the way out.

3. Insert the following in the intialization file:

```
SET HELP TO DDHELP.DBF       && .DBF is required
SET HELP ON
cHelpKey = CHR(254)+" Introducing The Application"
ON KEY LABEL F1 DO HELPCALL WITH cHelpKey
```

These statements complete the setup for a help system. With the first statement, which opens the working help file, you must include the .DBF or else FoxPro assumes you are using the Windows help system. The OKL resets the procedure call of the **F1** key. This and several other procedures related to the help system are located in the application procedure file. (In this case they are in DDPROC.PRG with the software on disk.)

4. Insert the following in the procedure file:

```
PROCEDURE HELPCALL
```

This is called by **F1**, and uses the current value of cHelpKey to pass the topic to help: HELP &cHelpKey.

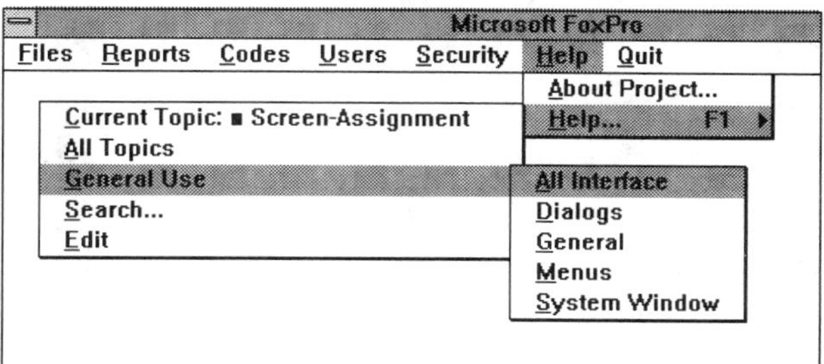

Figure 18.1 *Displays the Help Menu options.*

```
PROCEDURE HFILTER
```

This is called by Help, Help, All Topics or General in the modified system menu. The user has several generic ways to narrow the topic field.

```
PROCEDURE SEARCHHELP
```

This is called by HFILTER or by Help, Help, Search in the menu. It provides the user with a screen to make help topic searches.

```
PROCEDURE EDITHELP
```

This is called by Help, Help, Edit in the system menu. This is generally protected by security so that only authorized people may create or modify help screens. This procedure calls HELPEDIT.SPR, a screen set with MENUHELP.MPR menu. This is where the user does the actual help screen editing. Figure 18.2 displays the help edit screen.

Figure 18.2
The Help Edit screen.

All of these procedures are in the DDPROC.PRG file, part of the data dictionary system.

Manuals

The creation of professional-quality application manuals is a field unto itself. It's also very expensive. Whether your application requires this level of user documentation or not, you should consider using the content of the help file as part of building the manual. The redundancy is helpful, not to mention the time savings in not creating two sources of documentation. On the other hand, people generally expect the printed manuals to be more complete, and probably a bit more lavishly illustrated than on-line help.

On-line help can, in fact, be done by programmers, even while they're coding. This keeps the cost down. Preparation of a printed manual has a development track of its own, and in larger software houses, is always done by specialists or contract help. Doing it yourself requires a lot of time, access to a good laser printer (at the very least), and page layout software.

If your project calls for printed manual(s), be sure not to underestimate the time, people, and costs associated with it. It's not unheard of for the cost of commercial manuals to be a significant percentage of the cost for software development.

User Training and Support

The final piece of documentation for an application are the materials and approaches to training and support. Like so many other areas of documentation, scale means everything. If your application is intended for commercial sale, then you need to put greater emphasis on the training materials and support systems. If this is just a friendly application you're putting together for a work group, then training and support are nothing more than a chat over coffee.

One of the benefits of working on custom database applications is the close contact with the end users. (Also one of the main drawbacks, too.) Many developers manage to train the users at the same time the software is being prototyped and tested. While this has risks (users tend to become intolerant of buggy software), the rewards are a quicker and less expensive start up time.

Application Distribution

The word *distribution* is used loosely. Running a disk down the hall and handing it to a fellow worker is a form of distribution. So is shrink wrapped software with a price tag on it. The form of distribution probably isn't one of the make or break decisions for your application. But its also something you should give a little thought. It's all part of the development cycle, and it could take yet more of your time and resources.

Distribution Methods

FoxPro gives you three choices to package your application for distribution:

- **Interactive version.** This presumes the site receiving your application has a legal copy of FoxPro for each computer that will run the program. There are a few corporate situations where co-development or an open ended modification process might require the full interactive material (such as all screens and menus). But on the whole, this is the least practical way of shipping any program.
- **As an .APP file.** Sending an .APP (application) file is a little better than sending all the interactive development material, since most of the programming is in one file. But it still requires a full copy of FoxPro to run.
- **As an .EXE file.** This is by far the most convenient way to distribute an application is to compile it into a self executing program (an .EXE file). This requires that you purchase the Microsoft FoxPro for Windows Distribution Kit to get the .EXE compiler. However, your distribution sites do not need to purchase copies of FoxPro.

For all but the most controlled distributions, such as where the developer is on site to do the installation and configuration, it's definitely best to go with the Distribution Kit. By using your project files to specify exactly what is included in your application, you can be sure of a complete distribution package, while having the speed, convenience, and lower cost of a standalone program.

Installation and Setup

Because of the wide range in the forms of delivery for database application software, there are a corresponding number of conditions for its installation. These all revolve around who's available to do the work.

1. You (the developer) are there.
2. You are not there, but a surrogate (trained in the application) is.
3. A complete stranger, but computer literate is available.
4. A complete stranger and computer illiterate is the best it's going to be.

If the answer is ever Item 3 and especially Item 4, then you must consider formal ways for your application to be installed. Unfortunately, you are in for a rude shock, because installation into Windows is not what it used to be for DOS. First, you are installing *both* FoxPro for Windows and your application. As you may recall, installing FoxPro for Windows itself is a full scale Windows setup. Then your application, with all of its files and configuration needs must be added. Second, most users now expect a "real" Windows setup, not a Windows setup from DOS.

Fortunately, there is a much better way. If you are truly distributing your application, that is over some distance and to people who have no special knowledge of how to install it, then you should be using the FoxPro for Windows Distribution Kit to make an .EXE file, *and* with it comes a program called the SetupWizard. This program puts you through a question-and-answer session about your application, then generates one of those spiffy Windows setup routines that are so familiar with commercial Windows software. It takes care of registering your run-time version of FoxPro for Windows with WIN.INI, creates subdirectories, and decompresses your files. Given the difficulties of installing into Windows, the SetupWizard (itself a FoxPro for Windows application), is a true boon.

Data Conversion and Loading

For the vast majority of database applications you build with FoxPro, part of the setup process is to get the database loaded with start-up data. This might be nothing more than entering appropriate codes, user names, and other system data. Or it could be the entering of basic information to be used in the application's operation. The question then becomes, how does it get entered?

No coverage of application distribution and setup would be complete without mentioning the developer's worst nightmare—data conversion. True, there have been conversion projects that went smoothly, on time, and on budget. Somewhere. But so many of them have left a trail of broken schedules and frayed nerves.

Data conversion almost always is done at the last minute, for lots of legitimate timing requirements. However, at this point for the developer the application is basically finished, and the only impediment to getting up and running is the data conversion. For the user/client the program is just beginning, and the only impediment is data conversion. One is ready to be done with the project, and the other anticipates using it. And of course the data is valuable, otherwise why bother converting? This puts a big burden of expectations on getting the database loaded or converted.

With that as background to a data conversion, then comes the (inevitable) technical difficulties. If you're lucky, you're converting apples to oranges. Otherwise you might be going from EBCDIC to Xbase. In any case, you are converting from two different systems. If they are not the same file format, then you must first do some kind of file conversion, or perhaps several of them. That is, provided you can find the software tools to make the conversion. Most systems can create ASCII text files, but not all. Even if you are lucky and both sides are Xbase (.DBF files), there usually are major differences in field names, widths, and types. All of which becomes complicated by moving from one type of database structure to another. In all likelihood, your database schema (the fancy name for relational structure) bears no resemblance to the structure used in the old system. This requires splitting and piecing of data from various files to put them in various other files.

If you've ever done a major conversion, you know where this is leading. Conversions should have their time estimated on the basis of four times the estimate. If you think it will take eight hours, it will take thirty-two hours.

While no two conversion projects are identical, there are patterns. In fact your success at data conversions may well rest with how well you recognize the patterns and prepare accordingly. The following list covers the basic steps of most conversions. It's impossible to cover all of the wrinkles. Most of them simply require ingenuity, a mastery of FoxPro file manipulation programming, patience, good record keeping, and luck.

1. Identify the *final* file format involved in the source side of the conversion. It may start out as one thing in its native form, but you need to know if the source software can produce any file format more congenial for the transfer to Xbase. Of course a .DBF file is preferred, or any of the file formats supported by FoxPro. If the format turns out to be some kind of ASCII file, you need to examine it carefully as it may require complex programming to parse it.
2. Assuming the source system can't produce a .DBF file, figure out how the source file format gets converted into an Xbase file, not the final file mind you, but *an* Xbase file. It's much easier for you to work with .DBF files for final conversion routines. You need to come up with a third-party product that can make the transfer, or if necessary write your own low level routines (much work). The goal is to get all the relevant data into the .DBF format without losing its data definition.
3. Once the data has arrived in a .DBF format, by whatever means, you then need to *map* the field structures to the new database. If the project is big enough, actually draw a map showing how one field in the source data corresponds to a field in the new data. Indicate what, if any, conversion is necessary: renaming, data type conversion, width, and any other massaging of the data. Many conversions founder when the developer discovers that the source data contains things like compacted fields—fields where users jammed two or three fields worth of data into a single field and, being creative, used a variety of separators, a comma here a semi colon there. Untangling strange data constructions is one of the bogeymen in the conversion process.
4. Once the mapping has been done, then build the necessary routines and test them.
5. It's not unusual for a major conversion process to have four, five, or more steps. Sometimes many files are involved in a sequence of processing. At this point, accurate bookkeeping is not only desirable but paramount. Do keep records of every step, just as you keep backups of every file.
6. Rub your lucky rabbit's foot, cross your fingers, and run the conversion.

There are so many possible "gotchas" to even small conversions, that you never really know from one project to another exactly what to expect. Which is why the smart professional developer prefers billable hours for a data conversion. At the least, be honest with the user/client, tell them that data conversion will be difficult.

Chapter 19
Additional Application Components

his chapter covers application components that are optional, or at least application specific.

- Data dictionary
- Backup and archiving
- System codes
- Security system
- Output management

These are somewhat a matter of personal preference. To some developers a data dictionary is not an option, but a requirement. For others, a data dictionary is pure overkill. On the other hand, in one form or another most of them should be *considered* for most applications, especially if you're shooting for completeness. Besides, implementation is easy, most of them are also part of the software included with this book.

Software on Disk

The disk at the back of the book contains not only example code, functions, and procedures but a working data dictionary dystem, shown in Figure 19.1. This includes modules for file maintenance, system codes management, system security, and output management. It all comes in one project and has a main menu. But, you don't have to use the data dictionary system lock, stock, and barrel. The entire system was designed so that with very little grafting each module can be used as a stand-alone piece. However, if keeping it under one roof works for you, it could be a convenient platform to begin your own additions and modifications.

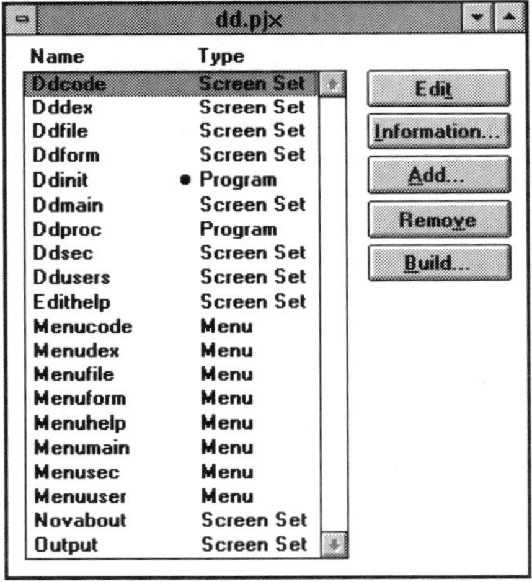

Figure 19.1 *A data dictionary project.*

The best way to become familiar with the system is to fire up the project file, DD.PRJ, build an app (DD.APP), run the program and take a look at the files. The most complex programming is part of the DDFILE.SPR screen, as well as in the procedure file DDPROC.PRG. This is by no means the endgame on an active data dictionary system, but it serves to illustrate that the "backend" of an application—especially a major application—has some important components, and presents it's own programming challenges.

Data Dictionary

In a database application keeping track of your data tables, field definitions, and indexes is an extremely important part of the project. You need this information for your programming and for system documentation, among other things. Most Xbase programmers quickly fall into the habit of doing the following:

```
USE <file name>
DISPLAY STRUCTURE TO PRINT
```

This produces the familiar:

```
Structure for table:        f:\dd\dbf\ddindex.dbf
Number of data records:     106
Date of last update:        04/18/93
Memo file block size:       64
 Field      Field Name     Type         Width    Dec      Index
 1          FILENAME       Character    8                 Asc
 2          ITYPE          Character    3
 3          INAME          Character    10
 4          IEXPR          Memo         10
 5          IFOREXPR       Memo         10
 6          I_OF           Character    8
 7          COMPACT        Numeric      1
 8          A_OR_D         Numeric      1
 9          UNIQUE         Numeric      1
 10         FLAG           Character    1
 11         STATUS         Character    1
 12         SYSDATE        Date         8
 13         OPERATOR       Character    3
** Total **                             66
```

While this is useful information, it leaves a lot out. What is the purpose of each field? What are the names of the index tags? What is the purpose of the file? These are the kinds of information that are part of a data dictionary. Some people call it *meta-data,* information about information. Whatever you call it, a data dictionary is the place to spell out the what's, why's, and wherefore's of an application's data—including information that is not part of the data tables, like system codes, and report forms.

In this approach, a data dictionary is a documentation tool, much like FoxDoc, only requiring manual input. If that were all, most programmers would rather stick with FoxDoc. But a data dictionary should also be an *active* part of an application. In most mainframe and minicomputer database systems, an active data dictionary is the source of information that regulates the data processing, system maintenance, and even the system programming. Partly from this background, and partly from the nature of a database application, a whole school of programming for personal computers, called *data-driven programming*, believes in using a data dictionary to directly guide and shape an application's development. The problem for Xbase developers has been that no commercial PC data dictionary system can be called a standard.

For years the Xbase community has been kicking around the idea of a "standard" data dictionary. It hasn't happened yet, and probably won't until one of the major Xbase vendors (Microsoft, Borland, or Computer Associates) creates one. That leaves developers who believe in data dictionaries to fashion their own, or buy one of the handful of third-party data dictionaries that are specifically designed for Xbase/FoxPro.

Why a Data Dictionary?

The problem with data dictionaries has always been not what they *could be*, but what they usually *are*. The list of what a data dictionary can do is impressive:

- Centralize an application's system information (meta-data).
- Provide on-line documentation of an application's most important elements.
- Feed information to various application sub-systems like file opening and security.
- Provide data for programming, especially the Screen Builder.
- Add flexibility to project development through "alternate" dictionary entries.
- Provide the basis for archiving data.
- Drive application maintenance routines.

The documentation aspect of a data dictionary has already been mentioned. Perhaps of greater importance is the role it can play in providing information to programming, application subsystems, and maintenance routines. Some of this active use of a data dictionary is being addressed by third-party products, but the road to complete integration with a development system is, and will continue to be, arduous.

Undeterred by the risks, many developers see even a partial implementation of a data dictionary as better than none. That's the position taken here. However, the position is taken with the understanding that not every application needs a data dictionary. Only projects that involve upwards of fifty or so files, and use components like security, and report form management are going to reap benefits beyond the work involved. Of course, the bigger the project, the more useful the data dictionary becomes. If you're embarking on a large scale, application, a data dictionary may be a necessity.

A Data Dictionary Implementation

Narrowly defined, a data dictionary contains information about data tables, such as field definitions, and indexes. Broadly defined, a data dictionary contains not only file information, but also information about any data used in an application. This can include system codes (ID definitions and data item codes), information about all kinds of files (memory files and report files), system parameters, security data and so on. This implementation of a data dictionary, while not comprehensive, leans far in the direction of a broad definition. Figure 19.2 charts a data dictionary system.

The centerpiece of this system is the data dictionary file manager. It becomes the repository of information about all types of data files used by the application. Next is the data dictionary security system, which provides a place to store information about users of the application, application security, and the security assigned to the users. Three smaller subsystems are the data dictionary codes manager, which is the storage location for all data codes used in the application, and the data dictionary of output forms that lists all of the reports, labels, and queries available to the system output manager.

Each of these subsystems is explained in detail in this chapter. As mentioned in the introduction, the software for the data dictionary system is on the accompanying disk. The starting point is the DD.PRJ project file, from which you can create a working .APP file. (See the README.DOC file on the disk for detailed installation and operation instructions.) Disk files include:

- **DD.PRJ**—The project file for the data dictionary system.
- **DDINIT.PRG**—The initialization file that starts the application.
- **DDPROC.PRG**—The procedures file containing many general use functions.
- **DDMAIN.SPX**—The main screen mostly to front for the main menu.
- **DDFILE.SPX**—File management module, main screen.
- **DDINDEX.SPX**—File management module, index screen.
- **DDCODE.SPX**—System codes management module, main screen.
- **DDUSERS.SPX**—Security system, system users screen.
- **DDSEC.SPX**—Security system, security locations screen.
- **DDFORM.SPX**—Report form management module, main screen.
- **OUTPUT.SPX**—Output management module, main screen.

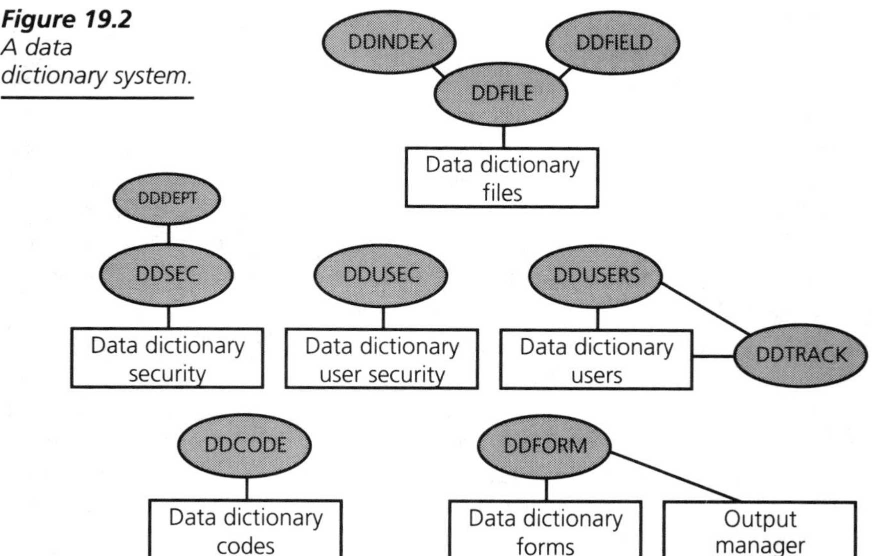

Figure 19.2
A data dictionary system.

Data Dictionary File Manager

This module of the data dictionary system controls three major pieces of system information: files, fields, and indexes. It's work begins when you define each of the data files used by your application. This should not be limited to data tables. Any kind of data file, such as memory (.MEM) files should be included. The file information includes details of the file, how it is used, its size, record count etc. Much of this can be automatically updated by the program. The File Manager is shown in Figure 19.3.

Figure 19.3
The data dictionary File Manager.

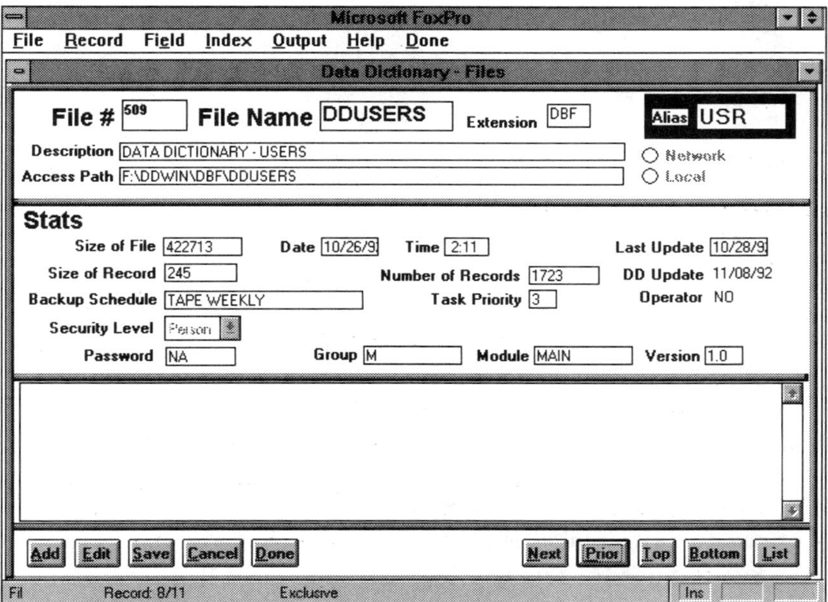

Built into the File Manager's repertoire is the ability to automatically update the list of fields and field information for each file (all, singly, or in groups). You then have the opportunity to enter detailed field definitions, including a rationale for the field, perhaps a history of its use, and any other information such as formulas and business rules. The same type of process is available for the indexes. The File Manager automatically updates the index list for each file. Your only task is to annotate the use of the indexes.

The detailed documentation of files, fields and indexes makes the data dictionary the place to explain how the data tables are related, how fields were expected to be used, and any other information that explains the relationships between tables, their fields, and the indexes available. It's also the place to put most of the "business rules" used by your application. You'll notice that space is allocated for definition of PICTURE and VALID clauses for each field. At the moment these can only be used for documentation purposes. With some complex programming they could be linked to the corresponding fields in the Screen Builder, but this is beyond the scope of the current system.

Application File Opening

One of the easiest and most useful applications of a data dictionary is to provide greater flexibility for opening files throughout an application. This should be contrasted with the usual methods of file opening:

```
USE HREMPLOY
```

or

```
USE F:\HR\DBF\HREMPLOY
```

The first method relies on the file being somewhere on the FoxPro path. The second has a path hard coded into the program. It's particularly vulnerable to changes in the disk environment. In fact, you could hardly use the second method for a distributed application. The first method, essentially the default approach, works as long as the subdirectory system remains the same as the FoxPro path established in the CONFIG.FPW file. This may be fairly stable, however during development, distribution to an unknown site, and particularly for operation on a network, subdirectories do change. Updating numerous copies of CONFIG.FPW can be a problem.

What a data dictionary system does is provide a place to list paths to all files, regardless of where they may be. As you move your files around (especially during development), you are free to change their paths and group them and isolate them. The actual paths of the files is transferred to the application by a relatively simple mechanism:

```
USE DDFILE ALIAS FIL
SCAN FOR fil.extension = "DBF"
   cFileName = fil.filename
   &cFileName = fil.path
ENDSCAN
```

This routine makes a variable out of the filename, then loads the path to the file into the variable. For example, the filename of ddfield becomes a variable ddfield, which is then loaded with the path to ddfield.dbf, "f:\hr\dbf\ddfield". Later in the application, when it becomes necessary to open the file ddfield, a special network file opening function FileUse( ) is called, which is passed the contents of ddfield, the correct path to the file. It looks like this:

```
 = FileUse( ddfield, "FLD", SHAREFILE, "FILENAME", "A",
READWRITE )
```

By centralizing the application file opening around the data dictionary, your program becomes free of all hard-coded paths, and the vagaries of maintaining multiple CONFIG.FPW files (as is typical on a network). All changes in filenames and paths are in one place.

During the course of development you may decide you want to maintain two copies of a particular file, one with correct data, and another with test data. In the data dictionary they are both given the same file name, but different paths. The active one is then assigned .DBF for an extension (the other left blank), which assures that the path to the active file is passed to the application.

Another even more dramatic example is to use the data dictionary for access to archived files. Say at some point the user signals they would like to see archived files. All that is necessary is a call to the data dictionary using the above routine, only this time a different file extension (or any other flagging system).

```
USE DDFILE ALIAS FIL
SCAN FOR fil.extension = "ARC"
   cFileName = fil.filename
   &cFileName = fil.path
ENDSCAN
```

The filename variables stay the same, but all of the paths have been redirected to the archive files. Your application continues to function as it always does, since it doesn't care where the files are located, only that it gets the right ones.

There are many variations possible on this approach. For example, it's not required to use memory variables to hold the paths. The data dictionary could be read directly. However, this adds time to the process of opening files, which is slow enough already, and the overhead for using the variables is minimum.

System Maintenance

Maintenance may not be a dirty word for developers, but it is generally an afterthought. It's yet another one of those nuisance details of an application, even a smallish application, that requires time and effort. In Xbase systems, there are in general three main tasks for system maintenance:

- Index maintenance
- File packing
- Data integrity checking

Each of these require programming individual routines, usually quite small but quite numerous, to be executed on a regular basis. Tied to these routines is usually some method for reporting results and problems, which means creating a battery of maintenance specific reports. These reports are especially important for data integrity checking, since human judgment is almost always required for evaluation and to clean up problems.

Indexes and Packing

These two are almost always mentioned in programming books, probably because a system that makes no provision to do them is in big trouble. While the FoxPro indexes are remarkably robust, no database system is immune to corrupted index files. On a regular basis, and on demand when necessary, an application must make it possible for users (or someone) to rebuild indexes.

Similarly, in the Xbase approach where the standard DELETE is being used to remove records, it's necessary to periodically PACK the tables, otherwise much disk space can be wasted.

In addition to being the repository of information about your applications files, fields, indexes, and supplier of paths to file opening, there are a number of system-maintenance routines that can use the data dictionary. Reindexing and packing tables are typical, and are built into the menu options of the File Manager.

Data Integrity Checking

Data integrity checking is unfortunately not regularly seen in FoxPro applications. However, if you're interested in maintaining a useful relational type database, this is a very important task. While there are many different data integrity checks, some of them quite specific to an application, here are four general types that should be a regular part of an application's maintenance:

1. **Checking key fields for nonunique values and nulls.** As one of the principal rules of a relational system (*entity integrity*), primary keys must be unique and contain no null (empty) values, which is a technical way of saying no two records should be identical. Nonunique keys in particular can be the bane of some systems. While well-designed data-entry screens make duplicates impossible, they happen anyway. Since duplicates can raise havoc with all kinds of system processes, this is one integrity check that pays for itself immediately. You may also wish to check secondary (foreign) keys for similar rules, although here they are sometimes relaxed.
2. **Checking fields for valid data.** As a rule (*domain integrity*), each field should contain data of only one data type, and of a consistent value for the definition of the field. For example, a zip code field should contain only zip codes. Not all fields are data-content sensitive. Big text fields are usually allowed much latitude. However, numeric fields in particular are subject to improper values, as are certain kinds of character fields. This varies from table to table, but it's relatively simple to create routines that check fields for appropriate values. Again, theoretically, good RANGE and VALID routines in the entry screens make bad data values impossible.

3. **Checking for widows and orphans in table relations.** *Widows* are primary keys that have no child records (no matching records in related data tables). This may or may not be a valid condition, depending on the relation between tables. Similarly, *orphans* are child records that no longer point to values in primary keys (foreign keys without a corresponding primary key). This is called *referential integrity*. These conditions can be caused by a number of problems, including bugs in the deletion routines, problems with aborted processes, and damaged index files. Most of them cause nasty errors in calculations, counts, and other updating routines. Again the checking routines are quite simple, just tedious to execute.
4. **Table-specific checking for business-rule violations.** Finally, it often occurs that a sequence of information is expected within a record. For example, if a social security number is entered, then a birthdate should also be entered. These are *business rules* embedded in the data table. For the most part, trapping for these mistakes is done in the entry screens or at processing time, but again no trapping is perfect. Maintenance routines should at least check for the most crucial violations of business rules.

For the most part, maintenance-checking routines are quite simple—not much more than this example:

```
 *Maintenance routine for employee file.
USE hremploy ALIAS emp ORDER empid
cEmpid = empid                  && store for comparison
SCAN
  DO CASE
  CASE EMPTY(empid)
      =WriteError("2001","Empty EMPID",RECNO())
  CASE cEmpid = empid
      =WriteError("2002","Duplicate EMPID",RECNO())
  CASE NOT EMPTY(socsecno) AND EMPTY(birthdate)
      =WriteError("2004", "Birthdate Required", RECNO())
  ENDCASE
  cEmpid = empid                && reload for comparison
ENDSCAN
USE
```

The only difficulty may be that there are so many maintenance routines—at least one for every file in the application, plus the requirement for reporting on the results, and making sure there are methods for correction. The data dictionary system is a convenient place to locate controls for maintenance checking, although it is not implemented in the current system. Better still some kind of task-processing mechanism (either something you write, or a commercial scheduling program) can use the information in the data dictionary to drive the maintenance routines and perform the tasks in the off-hours, usually late at night.

Backup and Archiving

Another off-hours task is running the backup and system archiving routines. This is one of those gray areas for applications. As a rule, network systems do the data backup, not the applications. However, data dictionary routines can be used to feed file lists and the like to a network backup system.

With single-machine applications, however, your program may be expected to include backup capability. If this is the case, there are a number of good backup routines for FoxPro applications available from bulletin boards or in publications. Like error-trapping routines, it's a lot more time and cost effective to use these (free) programs, than construct the wheel from scratch.

Archiving, however, is much more tied to the content of a specific application. That leaves less room for a generic system. If your application calls for archiving, be prepared to spend a considerable amount of time in planning and developing it. Although you can attempt to keep it simple, in most cases archiving becomes demanding—usually because the perceived need for it doesn't always match the reality of handling archived data.

Archiving systems usually have the following components:

- Special identification of records (or fields) to be archived. Often this is a flagging system of some kind, or uses date fields.
- A maintenance routine to do the archiving of data to specific archive files. These files may be normal .DBFs or possibly compressed files.
- A companion log routine to record what information went where, when.
- A deletion or blanking routine to remove archived records from the table.
- A method that allows users to select what archived information to retrieve. This is usually tied to the archive log.
- Routines that do the retrieval from the archive files. This may involve storage manipulation, decompression, and selection of specific records.
- A means for displaying the archived data, usually a clone of the original software or some other familiar system to allow user access.

- In some systems you may need a way to permit user updates (changes) to the archived data. This can be much more problematic, requiring special updating and logging routines.

Many of these elements are not easy to program, and need to be customized for an application. The type of storage device, the volume of archived material, the sensitivity of the data, and the kinds of retrieval required may play a big role in determining the scope of an archiving system. It's almost never a simple exercise.

System Codes

Database work, and especially relational database work, is littered with codes. These are the shorthand expressions for identification, or tagging of data items. A typical example is a set of codes for building locations, as in Table 19.1.

Table 19.1
A sample set of codes for building locations.

Building Code	Location
BH	Biggs Hall and Auditorium, 22 West Larpenteur
CP	Cherne Pool, West Sports Complex, 101 University
HH	Halvorsen Hall, 18 East Cooke
JH	Jurrens Hall, 19 West Cooke

Instead of loading a database with megabytes of redundant data, in this case the long form of each location, a two character code is used. The larger an application, and the larger its tables, the more likely you are to use coding like this to save disk space. Some codes, like the two letter abbreviations for states, or the postal service zip codes, have become so common we rarely think of them in their long form. However, in some applications even these common codes might need translating. That's the problem with codes—they're great for computers, but not always clear for people. Sure, you know in context that

GA stands for Georgia. But even in context would you know that UNIT11 is short for post operative recovery room, second floor?

When printing reports, or displaying information on the screen it's often important to include the translation of codes. In fact one of the rules of good interface design is that all but the most self-evident codes are accompanied by their description. This implies that somewhere you have stored the descriptions for the code.

Some codes are so numerous or so integral to an application, for example part numbers for an auto parts application, they are put into their own table with descriptions and entry values. However, almost every application has a number of miscellaneous codes with somewhere between three and several hundred items. Do you create a separate table for each of them? Do you hard code them into the program? One way leads to a proliferation of tiny files, which become a maintenance problem. The other leads to re-programming and rebuilding an application, if there are changes to the codes (and there will be).

There is a simple solution, create an application codes file.

The Codes File

By putting all of the miscellaneous codes used by your application in one file, you've reduced the total number of files and increased the maintainability of the system. As an example, the data dictionary system includes an access screen to a system codes file, DDCODE.DBF. The structure of this table provides fields to categorize the code, describe it, and attach secondary values.

Field	Field Name	Type	Width	Dec	Index
1	TYPE	Character	10		Asc
2	CODE	Character	10		Asc
3	MODULE	Character	8		
4	DESCRIPT	Character	40		
5	MISC	Character	40		
6	NUMERIC	Numeric	4		
7	STATUS	Character	1		
8	SYSDATE	Date	8		
9	OPERATOR	Character	3		

In a table like this, which may have codes of all kinds, it's likely that the code itself will not be unique. To have accurate lookups for the code (unique entities), all codes in this table are paired with a TYPE. For example, in a hospital application where there may be both UNITS that refer to areas of the hospital, and UNITS that refer to measurements, the codes might be entered like this:

```
TYPE         CODE        DESCRIPTION
LOCUNIT      ML          Middle Lobby
LOCUNIT      EOR         East Operating Room
MUNIT        ml          Milliliters
MUNIT        ppm         Parts per Million
```

The codes file can also be used as a lookup table for system values and parameters, for example:

```
TYPE       CODE       MODULE      DESCRIPTIONNUMERIC
SYSTEM     USERMAX    LAB         Maximum Number       Users12
                                  of Lab Users
```

One of the main benefits for using a system codes table is to make it relatively simple for users and clients to make their own changes to application codes. The access screen provided with the data dictionary system presumes the user will understand the rules for entering codes. This could be covered as part of the documentation. Or else, the access screen could be extended to provide specific on-line help, and entry control for different types of codes. Figure 19.4 shows a sample system codes dialog box.

Once the codes have been entered, you need to come up with the routines that use them in your application. These routines come in a number of flavors: SQL-SELECT, SCAN, and SEEK based programming. Sometimes the codes are loaded into arrays for use in list screen elements like @..LIST, @..GET - POPUP, and DEFINE POPUP. Other times, you may do simple lookups to provide data for a single field value.

Figure 19.4
A data dictionary system codes file.

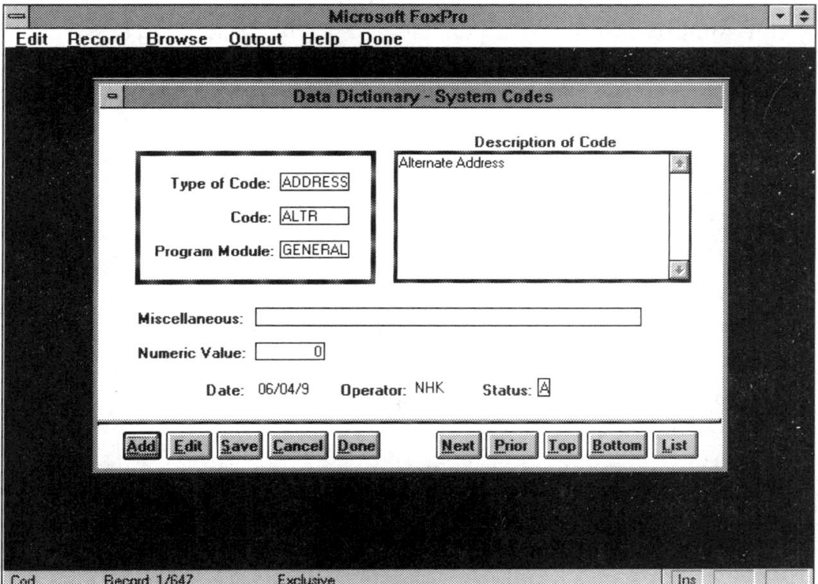

Code Fields

The majority use of codes in an application is for screens and reports. For the most part, lookup uses are typical indexed searches. These are easy. Entry of codes into application tables may be another matter. On the one hand, you can't assume the people doing the entry know the codes by heart, so you need to provide support. On the other hand, you shouldn't assume they *don't* know the codes, and may find it quicker to simply type them in.

This makes code-field entry and edit a somewhat unique proposition. Of course, you can take the easy way out and force the user to pick from code lists. In some kinds of data entry—no volume, low speed, occasional use—this is probably acceptable. In more demanding data-entry screens, you may find that forcing people to select all codes from lists (of any kind) will increase entry time by as much as 20 percent to 25 percent, compared to screens where users are allowed to enter codes by typing.

However, the ideal code-field entry is rather complex. It should do the following things:

1. Allow the user to enter a code by direct typing.
2. If they do enter a code directly, it must be validated.
3. If they don't know the code, the user must have a way to signal for support.
4. Once the user signals for support, an appropriate list of codes should be made available for selection.
5. The selection should be displayed on the screen and the code list disappears.
6. The description of the code should be displayed simultaneously with the code entry or selection.
7. The user needs to be able to cancel a code entry or selection at any time.

There are many ways to accomplish this. In fact you might find it a challenging exercise to work your way through coding the VALID routine for a code field. The procedure file that is part of the data dictionary system (DDPROC.PRG) contains three functions designed for code-field data entry. CodeLoad(), CodeValid(), and CodeSay(). You may find them a useful example.

Security

Does your application require protection against somebody accessing private information? Is your data secure, physically, on the disk as well as in your program? Can anybody use your application? These are all security questions.

Naturally the requirement for security varies widely. Some applications, like most commercial software, are meant to be used by everybody and therefore have no special provision for any kind of security. Other applications have *discretionary security*, meaning it can be turned on or off by the user to protect certain aspects of their work. Still other applications, for example accounting software, have at least password security and restrictions on access to certain sections of the program. You've probably seen examples of all these types.

But security doesn't end with passwords and access rights. This is yet another area where mainframe computer people look over at the PC side and shake their heads. Their notion of computer security is much broader and much more stringent. In fact, it's been codified. The National Computer Security Center (NCSC) guidelines, listed in Table 19.2, the so called "Orange Book," have become the widely accepted definition of the various levels of security.

Table 19.2
NCSC system security levels.

Level	Description
D	**Minimal protection:** No built-in security.
C1	**Discretionary security protection:** users are physically separated from the data, and access limitations can be enforced. The combination of network security and moderate security in an application can achieve this level.
C2	**Controlled access protection:** users can be made individually accountable for their actions through log-in procedures and audit trails. As a rule, these systems maintain a log of user activity and restrict access to many parts of an application. Only a handful of commercial PC applications have passed the requirements for this level.
B1	**Labeled security protection:** sections of the data (files) are labeled for their security sensitivity and user access is controlled accordingly. This level also controls the access and reuse of data by multiple users.
B2	**Structured protection:** the entire application system (hardware and software) are classified as "relatively resistant to penetration." Configuration and management controls are stringent. This is the beginning of "planned barriers" against security breach for all system resources—disk storage, keyboard, telecommunications, printing, and all software.
B3	**Security domains:** program areas requiring a high degree of security are excluded from other code and are designed for security protection from the outset. This includes measures to ensure both hardware and software are "highly resistant to penetration." In

(continued)

	addition to the tight controls of the B2 level, this level adds design requirements that minimize the risk of security breach through overlapping modules, overly complex code, or "backdoor" hardware configurations.
A1	**Verified protection:** functionally equivalent to B3 systems, but formally documented and tested. The system must be proven secure (sometimes by mathematical means), and consistent with the security goals. Often referred to as the "mother of all security systems."

Not that you're about to rush out and make your applications A1. But you ought to be aware that the range of security can be enormous. Of course, if you think in the context of Federal Government—the military, the CIA—then security and all it's trappings become more natural. In your applications, probably not under CIA contract, you need something less than A1. Would you settle for C2 or C1?

Security Issues

How much is enough, and how much is too much? After you've determined you need security at all, then you face the questions of "How much security?" and "What's it going to take to implement it?"

If you're working on a fairly large application, chances are that somewhere in the project analysis security came up as an issue, or perhaps it came up as one of its related forms—*data privacy*. Both security and data privacy reduce to the same concern: Who has access to what. Security tends to be from an organization's point of view, and data privacy from the individual user's viewpoint, but for the application developer it's all "what do I need to protect, and from what."

There are some basics to answer this question:

- Protect the data.
- Protect the application.
- Protect the system (hardware and software).

Protecting data is pretty obvious in a database application. You don't want people looking at data they don't have the right to see (both for security and privacy reasons), and you certainly don't want to give people the opportunity to change, tamper with, or trash your application's data.

Protecting the application may boil down to protecting data, but it's more at the level of what functions of an application may people use. For example, you may not want every user to have access to all of the maintenance routines, or the ability to run certain processes.

Protecting the system involves the various schemes for making sure your hardware and software can't be stolen, broken into, or destroyed without having backup and other security measures. For multiuser applications, those running on a LAN, this aspect of security is largely a matter of the network operating system (such as Novell Netware or Microsoft LAN Manager).

The protect "from what" part of security is usually "from people," although you could include protection from natural disasters like flood and fire. However, the physical aspect of protection is more a part of backup and archiving than it is of security. Security in most applications means protection from unwanted access (with or without malicious intent) by people.

To achieve the security you put "barriers" into your application. (This is the more security-oriented word for gateways.) These come in two forms: *active* and *passive*. PC users are not accustomed to a lot of active security—security barriers that are visible like password entry. Too many active barriers can turn your application into a kind of data prison, where users feel their every move is being monitored. Maybe it is, but they don't have to feel that way. This calls for more passive kinds of security, most of which occurs in the background and never interrupts the user except in cases of security violation.

Barriers come in many different forms, including password entry, data encryption, and access vetting. They cover all three areas of protection, but when it comes to implementation there are significant differences.

Security Implementations

Whether you think of security as a system of barriers, or a system of gateways, the point is to think of it as a system. Of course, if you determine your application needs only a single password barrier at startup time, you hardly need to be systematic about that. But if your application requires different kinds of security, at different locations in the program, then you'll be ahead of the game to treat security implementation as a whole.

Network Security

If you're thinking about security, chances are you're also building applications that run on a LAN. Any security system you devise for your application needs to work in concert with security measures taken on the network. For example, most networks allow supervisors to assign access rights to subdirectories. Obviously the subdirectories that contain your application must allow appropriate access to those who need it.

In this way, the network security is your applications' first level of security. It provides:

- Network login and password
- Network file access rights

Although FoxPro doesn't provide any tools to access network information, there are third-party products that can. You may find these invaluable, if you need to use the status of various network resources in your application.

Application and Data Security

Security inside of your application usually has two primary facets, control of access to modules and functions, and control of access to data. Your application contains various points where it checks the user for *access rights*, and then checks for *activity rights*. This is another way of saying "Can the user gain access to something, and once there, what can they do?" This applies across the board to application, data, and system security.

The most intrusive check for access rights is through login and password. This calls for the user to sign-in or identify themselves, which is often accompanied by password verification. This is usually applied in three general places:

- Application startup login or password
- Module login or password
- Screen login or password

As the user moves about your application, you can erect login and password barriers wherever *required*. And the emphasis must be on required. Loading up with these active barriers is a quick way to make any application unpopular. However, if people can easily understand why a module or screen is protected, they usually won't mind the inconvenience. Still, login and password security should be used sparingly, if at all.

Access and Activity Rights

Unlike password and login security, which is active, checking for access and activity rights is passive, unnoticed by the user, at least until a security violation occurs—and sometimes not even then. For that reason, you can sprinkle these "barriers" or "check points" liberally throughout an application. Other than a slight performance penalty, this is an invisible form of security.

Defining what is meant by access rights and activity rights usually varies from application to application. In a very broad sense, access rights are enforced by granting the user either general or specific access rights, then checking those rights as the user moves through the application. A simple example is to assign the user an access rights "level," say on a scale of one to ten. Out in the application, you have code in strategic spots like a menu, that is set to allow access only to people with level seven access rights.

Activity rights are usually defined by what the user is doing at a certain point in an application. Typically, this is in a data entry or edit screen. A user has gained access to a screen, but you may want to restrict some to looking at the data (read only). Others may have rights to change data, but not delete or add. These are activity rights in a data-entry screen. The rights might have a different set of definitions in a processing screen, or in choosing reports and queries.

Within an application, access and activity rights can be checked in a wide variety of places:

- Application module rights, usually in system and push button menus.
- Application procedure and function rights.
- Data rights: file level.
- Data rights: record level.
- Data rights: field level.

If you have an application that requires security checking all of the way down to the field level, you are going to need a fairly sophisticated system.

Implementing the barriers and checkpoints can be complex, not only for the development of the checking routines, but also because of the important choices you must make on how to handle security at the level of the individual.

The most fundamental choice in developing a security system is how closely you map an individual to security checkpoints, and as a related issue—how detailed is the security at each checkpoint. This needs a little explanation.

If you have twenty users for your application, which is running on a network, and you have determined there are twenty places where you need security checking, do you make a table that contains the rights for each user at each security location? And if you have two, three, or four items that are checked at each point, is every user assigned specific clearance for each item? A little math says the application would have to maintain a security matrix (a table of people and security items) with between eight hundred and sixteen hundred entries. This would present a significant maintenance problem, unless security is important enough to override the difficulty.

In certain government circles this tight individualized security is the norm. But in most database application software, it would certainly be excessive. Which means you need to devise an approach that's easier to maintain, without losing all the individualized aspects of security. As an example, one approach is developed in the data dictionary security system implemented below.

System Security

Most aspects of system security, especially physical control of equipment, is outside the responsibility of your applications. Which doesn't mean you can afford to ignore system security. This is especially true of custom software you may be developing, installing, and maintaining on an ongoing basis. If your application is security sensitive, then it may be part of your task to oversee or at least recommend appropriate security measures for workstations and servers of the network, tape backup equipment, procedures and archiving, and system access through telecommunications.

You may also need to consider using data encryption as part of the protection scheme. This has implications beyond your application, since encrypted data is protected even when people are not using your application. In fact, that might be the point. In a way it is a physical alteration of the data for security purposes. The security benefits are obvious, however the penalties and risks should not be overlooked. The process of encrypting and unencrypting data usually extracts some performance penalty, not a lot, but significant where the hardware is marginal. More importantly, there is always some risk to the data involved with encryption.

Data encryption routines are widely available. You can write your own, get routines from bulletin boards, or buy third-party products. They all can work. But few of them offer any kind of guarantee (perhaps none of them). Unlike the common data-compression products, such as the one that comes with MS-DOS 6.0, which only remove redundant data, encryption physically changes the data. For all practical purposes, a damaged and encrypted file can never be restored.

A Moderate Security System

The software on disk that comes with this book contains a module for handling application security. It's neither the simplest nor the most rigorous system around, but has worked in a number of applications where more than password security was needed, but elaborate user tracking and logging were not required.

The biggest advantage of this approach, shown in Figure 19.5 on the next page, is relative flexibility. It is more generalized than a one-to-one mapping of users and security points, yet it does provide considerable checking for users access and activity rights within the context of departments or functional areas within an application.

The security module is considered part of the data dictionary system, but can easily be disconnected and used alone. This approach to security divides the system into two parts: security locations within the application program, as controlled by the data dictionary (DDSEC.DBF), and the security assignments for individual users (DDUSEC.DBF).

Figure 19.5
A Data dictionary security system.

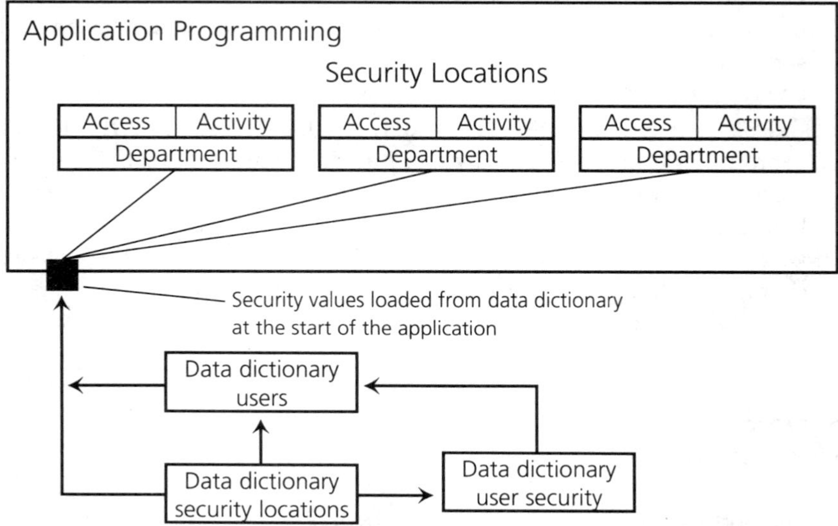

The Security Location Part

Anywhere in the application you need to install a security checkpoint, you would use the PassChk() and PassOut() functions (located in the DDPROC.PRG). Here's the function header:

```
**********************************************************************
* FUNCTION NAME.. PassChk()
* DESCRIPTION.... CHECKING FOR ACCESS/RIGHTS
* DATE.......... Thu 01-02-1992 21:40:33
* PROGRAMMERS.... NK
* LAST CHANGE.... Mon 10-12-1992 Major changes for new User
Security, NK
* Mon 07-13-1992 Major rewrite for DDSEC use
* Wed 02-19-1992 Major change to numeric sec codes and depts
* Wed 02-05-1992 Put _ALL into the routine
* PARAMETERS..... cSloc = Security Location ID, for lookup in
aSecLoc array
```

```
* is_msg = .t./.f. Give the user a failure message.
*
* SYNTAX......... PassChk(<SecLocId>,.t.)
* USAGE.......... IF NOT PassChk("0001",.t. )
* < Handle a failed pass >
* ENDIF
* RETURN......... .t./.f. pass/fail
* NOTES.......... This is an "in-line" access/rights checking
function. It is
* usually inserted into the code wherever the user needs to
* be vetted. By loading the arguments with the LOWEST LEVEL
* acceptable, only those people with >= levels will return
* TRUE (ok). In a sense, all arguments are optional. You
* can test for only RIGHTS, or ACCESS and DEPT or any
* combination that's appropriate. The DEPARTMENTS argument
* is used to cross check against the users 5 department
* access fields. [ Like all information in this routine, the
* relevant fields are in the DDUSEC.DBF. These fields are:
*
* DEPT, SEC1, SEC2
*
* If the user is in a "crossover department" this routine
* will reset nSec1 and nSec2 and save the original values
* to the last element of aDept. NOTE!! You must use the
* companion function PassOut() to replace the orginal
* security values to nSec1/nSec2, as the user leaves a
* a departmental program module.
*
* The (truly) optional message argument enables/disables
* a response to the user who has failed access/rights.
*
* nStep1 = Security Level 1: (ACCESS) << MUST ENTER
* 0=No check, 1=Public, 2=Departmental,
* 3=Work Group, 4=Supervisory, 5=IS Supervisor
* nStep2 = Security Level 2: (RIGHTS) << MUST ENTER
* 0=No check, 1=Read, 2=Add, 3=Modify,
* 4=Move, 5=Delete
* cDept = String containing permitted department.

* The string "_ALL" has special meaning in that it
* provides access to all departments. (_=CHR(254))
*
* CALLED BY...... GUF (General Use Function)
* CALLS.......... None
***************************************************************************
```

Because it's a function, PassChk() can be used in an almost unlimited number of places: in the Skip For snippets of menus and in the WHEN clauses of READS, Browses, and Gets. It contains only the ID number of the security location. The security location is defined in the DDSEC.DBF through the data dictionary security codes dialog box, shown in Figure 19.6.

Figure 19.6
The Data Dictionary Security Codes screen.

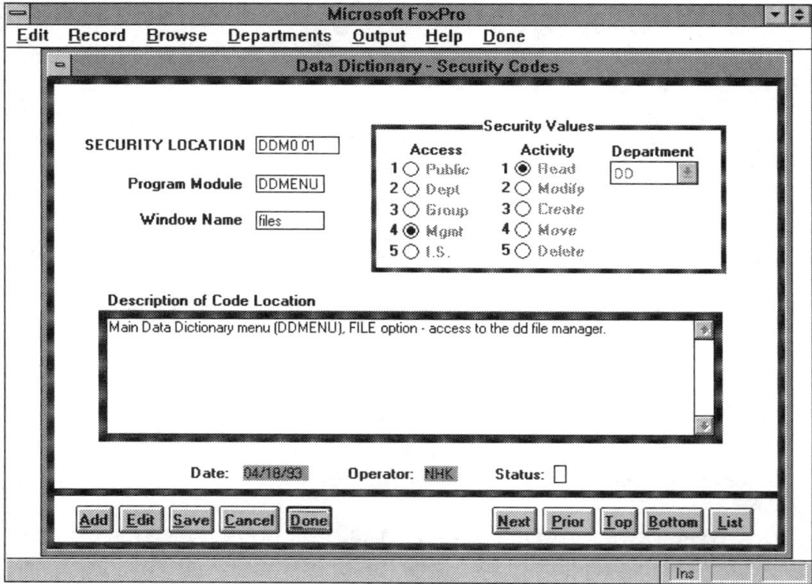

For every placement of the PassChk()function, you need to define a security location code (it's not important what, only that it be unique). For that location you then assign a department. For example, the accounting department. Actually, the word department is merely suggestive. You could call it a unit, or work group, functional area, anything that denotes working groups within an organization. The point for the department assignment is to designate areas of specific security. So, for example, the inventory department might have relatively low security requirements, but the payroll department are very high.

The security levels, assigned to each security location are for access and activity rights. The values run from one to five in ascending order of restriction and in general have the meanings in Table 19.3.

Table 19.3
Access and activity rights.

Level	Access	Activity
1	Public	Read
2	Departmental	Modify
3	Work group	Create
4	Management	Move
5	System supervisor	Delete

Like the departmental assignment, these are mostly suggestive. Any ranking of one to five would serve. At any security location, the user must meet *all* of the requirements, that is have clearance for the specific department, and rights greater than or equal to the specified rights for that location.

Although the developer must place the PassChk() function in the application, presumably in the most likely spots, this system makes it possible for the user or client to define all, any, or none of the checkpoints. Checkpoints may be deactivated by using zeros in the rights fields. Otherwise, the user can define and redefine what department a checkpoint belongs to and the relevant security levels. Some typical settings are shown in Table 19.4.

Table 19.4
Typical security settings.

Location	Access	Activity	Department
MM0001	2	1	RECEIVABLE
MM0002	3	4	PAYROLL
MM0003	3	2	PAYABLE

As the security locations are being programmed in the application, it's a good idea to enter their ID and description into the data dictionary.

The User's Part

The user's part of the security system begins with entering user information into the DDUSERS.DBF through the data dictionary Users Information screen, shown in Figure 19.7.

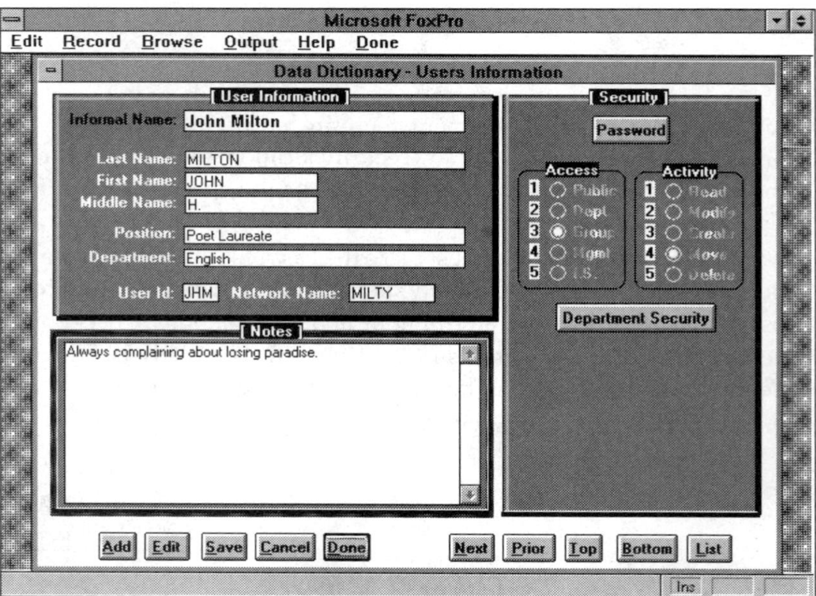

Figure 19.7
The Users Information screen.

The Users Information screen provides Browse access to the user security table (DDUSEC.DBF), shown in Table 19.5. This is one of the most important pieces of the security system.

Table 19.5
Table structure for DDUSEC.DBF.

Field	Type	Width	Key	Description
STAFFID	C	3	Y	Foreign key field from DDUSERS.DBF
DEPT	C	10		Department, unit, function area as defined in DDDEPT.DBF
SEC1	N	1		Access rights level: 1 - 5
SEC2	N	1		Activity rights level: 1 - 5

For each user listed in the users table DDUSERS.DBF, you can assign an affiliation with a specific "department" and the access and activity rights that go with it. For example, let's say that user X works in the marketing department, where he or she uses the marketing application with full rights. From time to time, however, user X is called over to the accounting department to fill in for an absent clerk. User X needs to have access to some of the accounting application, but only certain parts. And in those parts, user X should be able to modify but not add or delete information. The manager of the accounting department, in great wisdom, has created six function areas within the accounting application: payroll, general ledger, payables, receivables, purchase orders, and accounting general. The last one is access to the accounting application itself.

In the menu system of the application, where options for the accounting department are located, the developer has placed the PassChk() function in the Skip For snippets of the menu. These set minimal access rights to each option, for example the entry into the accounting submenu has a medium access restriction: department: ACCOUNTING, access level: 3, activity level: 1. To get past this barrier, user X would need a corresponding security entry in the User security table shown in Table 19.6 on the next page.

Table 19.6
The User security table.

Field	Value
STAFFID	XXX
DEPT	ACCOUNTING
SEC1	3
SEC2	2

The Users dialog box also is the place to enter the user's application password (if your program uses any). This password is encrypted, using encryption and decryption routines in the procedure file (DDPROC.PRG). There is also a function in the procedure file, PassWord(), that can be used to check a user's password in the application.

In addition to basic information about the people who use the application, stored in DDUSERS.DBF, this screen also provides access to the user tracking file, DDTRACK.DBF. This table is a kind of grab-bag for holding data about user selections for queries, reports, and last module entered. Its purpose is somewhat similar to the FoxPro resource file, only in this case customized to handle data for specific users. There are several routines in the procedures file (DDPROC.PRG) that rely on this file to store the environment, working files, and colors as a user moves between modules of an application (PushFiles()/PopFiles(), PushEnv()/PopEnv(), PushColor()/PopColor()). These are required functions for the data dictionary system.

Hooking up Security

To recap a bit, the steps for using the data dictionary security system are:

1. Define the checkpoints where security should be installed in the application (such as menus and push buttons) and assign a security location ID to each of them.
2. Install the PassChk() and PassOut() functions in the application at the checkpoints. Some checkpoints may also require the PassWord() function to confirm user identity.

3. Enter the security locations into the data dictionary, using the Security Codes dialog box describing their position in the application.
4. The developer, or preferrably the end user, defines the departments involved in the application and enter them through the Security Codes dialog box.
5. The end user defines for each security location the department, access rights, and activity rights.
6. The end user defines in the data dictionary Users Information dialog box the names, staff IDs, and so forth of all the people who will be given access to the application. The network name is critical for systems operating on a LAN.
7. The end user then defines for each user the departments to which they have access and the access and activity rights that go with them. The primary access and activity rights are also defined in the User Information dialog box, along with a password.

The final part of the security installation is for the developer to initialize the system. This has two pieces: a routine in the application initialization sequence, and a login function.

The main purpose of the initialization routine is to declare the security variables and arrays, load them, and call the login function to get the user's identity and security clearances. The two security arrays are key: aSecLoc[n,4] which contains all of the security locations in the application along with the department and rights values assigned to them; and aDept[n,3], which has all the user's department assignments and rights.

```
*——————————————————————[ Security
*Initialize security system
PUBLIC nSec1,nSec2,aDept,cDept
nSec1 = 0                          && Access Level
nSec2 = 0                          && Activity Level
cDept = ""                         && Departmental Access
#DEFINE SECURITY .t.               && Turn security on/off

*==================>> LOG IN
= ChkLogin()

IF SECURITY
  *Open security file
  IF NOT USED("SEC")
    IF NOT FileUse( ddsec, "sec", SHAREFILE, "seclocid", "A",
READWRITE)
```

```
      =ErrLine("Unable to open security file.",3)
    ENDIF
  ELSE
    SELECT sec
  ENDIF
  *> Load the Security Location Array
    PUBLIC aSecLoc                              && array for
security locations
    DECLARE aSecLoc(RECCOUNT(),4)   && declare and load array
    COPY TO ARRAY aSecLoc FIELDS SECLOCID,SEC1,SEC2,DEPT
    USE                                         && this file not
needed again
ENDIF
```

The login function, ChkLogin(), is also located in the intialization file. It gets the user's network name.

```
cUname = UPPER(TRIM(GETENV("USERNAME")))
```

The login function uses the name to do a lookup in the user files, DDUSERS.DBF and DDUSEC.DBF, and loads the security values assigned to the user.

As you may have noticed, setting up a security system is quite a lot of work—for both the developer and the user/client. It also takes some user training to show how the system works, and how to set up security locations that tie out with user security clearances. The reward for the effort, however, is a system that can be as stiff or relaxed as needed, and for the most part without intruding on the user. It can also be readily adjusted by the end user, as personnel changes along with organization policies. This feature alone is probably worth the setup effort.

Output Systems

Like all of the additional application components already covered in this chapter, output systems are a matter of scale. If your application has six reports and two queries, then what do you need an output system for? You don't. At the other extreme, if your application begins life with around two hundred reports, label forms, and queries, and because users are creating their own reports, is expected to have five hundred or more output forms in a couple of years, how can you *not* have an output system?

But what then, is an output system? For starters, the word *output* is intentional. FoxPro creates reports, labels, graphs, queries, lists, and files. So you can't really call it a "report" system, although report and output tend to be equated.

The system part is in recognition of the fact that managing a large number of *output formats* and specific *output forms* is not easy. There are complications at every turn: multiple types of output, sometimes for the same material; peripheral equipment like disk drives and printers (of all kinds); sometimes complex setup requirements for data tables and user input; multiuser requirements for concurrency and data integrity, network considerations like directories and printer queues, and in many cases issues of data security and privacy. In many cases only a systematic approach ensures that your application covers all of the output requirements without becoming a patchwork mess.

For the most part, FoxPro itself doesn't do much to help with output management. Except that it ties into the Windows facilities. Windows handles the choice of output formats, especially printers, and on a network Windows also handles some of the connections to network queues. This is a vast improvement over raw DOS for both the developer and the end user.

This still leaves a lot of loose ends in the management of output from an application. But before introducing one example of an output system, it's worthwhile to go into more detail on the elements that go into an output system, what can be called the "structure" of output.

The Structure of Output

With interactive FoxPro, output seems so direct. You go to the system menu, select a report and run it. It's the same in an application, right? Not quite.

1. When you select something for output in the interactive mode, FoxPro assumes the user knows about DOS files, directories, and the contents of certain .FRX files. The user has to navigate directories and select the correct report form, label form, and so on, often from dozens if not hundreds of entries.
2. Selecting an output form and then running it presumes that the complete table environment has been saved with the form (which it probably has) and that opening a bunch of files—and leaving them open—will not affect any other table configurations.
3. Running a report from the system menu presumes the user knows how to make their own filter expressions, and how to make other setup decisions.

4. It also assumes there is no other processing associated with running an output form.
5. It also assumes the user has the rights to run any output form they can find, and at any time.

You know what they say about assumptions. None of the conditions in this list is satisfactory for a general use application. In fact, some of the conditions are impossible in the environment of an application. Your program must be in control of the table setup, of multiuser operating conditions, and of related processing necessary for output. In short, the interactive mode violates the general structure of output in an application, shown in Figure 19.8.

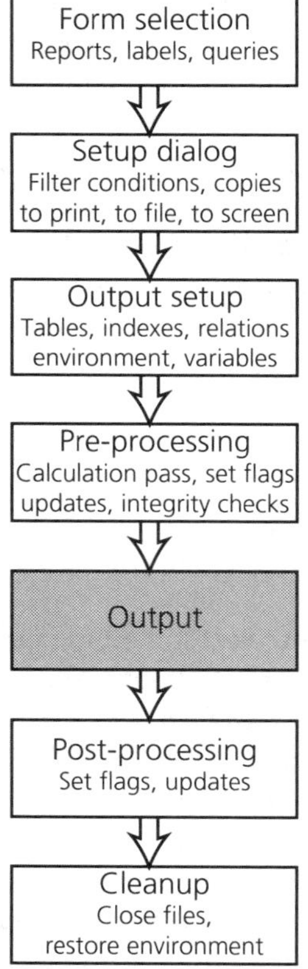

Figure 19.8
Output structure.

It's often surprising how many steps there can be in producing a report or making a label run. It's also somewhat surprising how many reports actually have all or most of this structure. Here's a description of each piece of the structure. See how many you've encountered either running reports in other applications, or in some work of your own.

1. **Form selection.** One way or another the user has to choose what they want to output. In FoxPro this could be one of several output forms: a Report Writer report, a Report Writer Label, a RQBE query, a program file, or a simple listing. If your application only has a couple of these types of output, and maybe ten or so items all together—no problem. But as mentioned above, when an application starts to have hundreds of output forms (and it's very easy to break the century mark even with relatively small applications), it's another ballgame. At some point, many applications need a "form selector," some way to narrow down the selections, make their content clear, and remove the necessity for the user to navigate subdirectories. It may also need to apply security restrictions to the selection process.
2. **Setup dialog.** It's a rare output form that doesn't need to have a dialog with the user before running. There are such standard items as number of copies and destination of output. There are also many kinds of conditions that users either must, or can specify—date ranges, selection criteria. Some of these are specific to the report being run, which means a large number of output dialogs are custom screens.
3. **Output setup.** Once the user has specified what output they want, and how they want to run it, your application then takes over and begins the setup process. In most cases developers do not save the environment with their reports, simply because FoxPro doesn't clean up (restore the original environment) after the run. You can't afford to have your application's table configuration trashed by a report, or run into a "too many files open" error.

   So output setup usually includes opening all of the files, indexes, and relations needed by the output form. It may also include changing some of the environment SET values, and defining variables that will be used in the output. Finally, before output begins, any necessary conditions for running on a network, especially file locking or selection of output queues, must be taken care of.

4. **Pre-processing.** Some output runs, especially reports, may require certain kinds of processing before the actual output run. For example you may need to do an SQL query to prepare one of the files for a report, or do a calculation pass. In some other situations, it may be necessary to set certain processing flags or do an integrity check of a table. If needed, this step has to be built into your output structure.
5. **Output.** Finally, you run the report, print the labels, or process the query. Of course, you've been able to handle any output destination (printer, screen, or file). And the user is kept informed of processing times, and report running length.
6. **Post-processing.** In a few cases, what was done needs to be undone, for instance if a report is aborted before it finishes. Or an audit trail may be created. This is called post-processing, and it usually involves situations where the output form itself triggers additional data updating or flagging.
7. **Cleanup.** Like any good application routine, the output process cleans up after itself: closing files, releasing windows and variables, then resetting the original environment.

Given the relative complexity and depth to the output structure, it's no wonder that developers make attempts to come up with a way to systematize the process. What makes it worth the effort is that once the system has been established, it is used over and over again. Reporting (and other forms of output) can be very repetitive. Often a basic report may have a half dozen "near clones," where only a field or two, or the format changes. What you need is an approach to organizing the output process that makes short work on such repetitive forms.

At the same time, you'd like an output system that makes the process easier for the user—without removing all of their options.

An Output System Implementation

The output system included with the software on disk for this book, addresses most of the structure of output, and most of the problems encountered with the interactive FoxPro. It includes a method for keeping track of all of the forms used by an application. It provides a mechanism for forms selection by the users. It takes care of some of the basic user output dialog, and it sets the stage for setup, pre-processing, and post-processing. It also is a good citizen of a network environment, and helps the user keep track of what they've run, and the preferences they've set. The system is shown in Figure 19.9.

Figure 19.9
An output system.

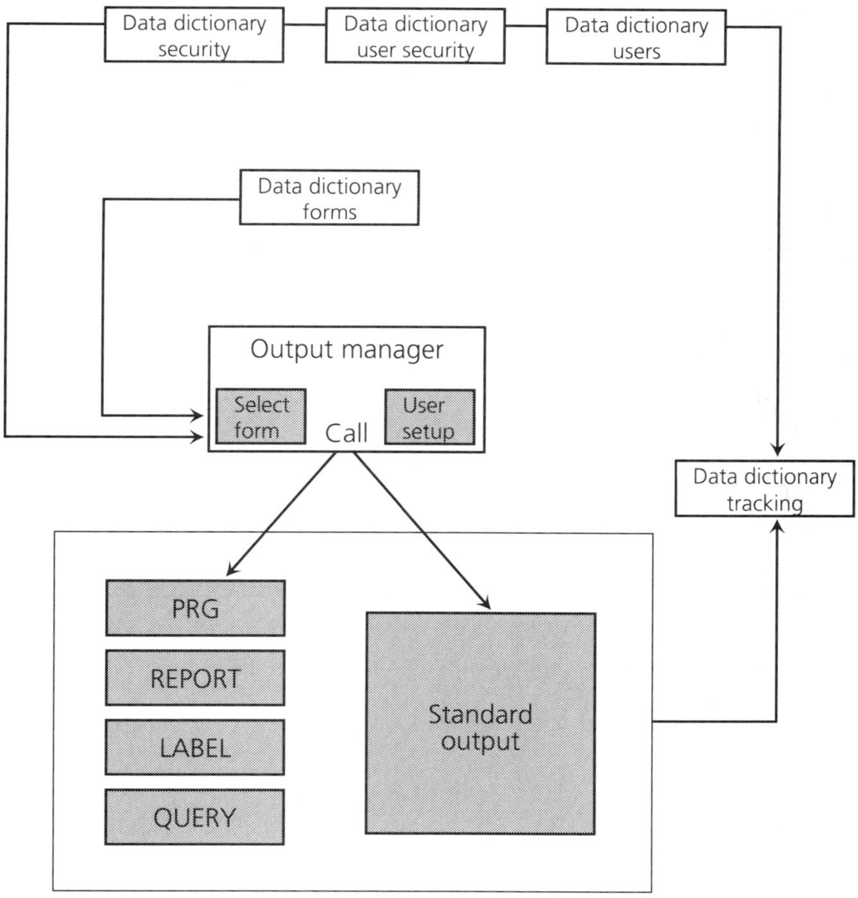

The system starts, as does everything else in this chapter, with the data dictionary system. Access to the forms file, DDFORMS.DBF, provides the means to catalog all of the various output forms: reports, queries, and labels. This is shown in Figure 19.10.

Figure 19.10
The Output Forms dialog box.

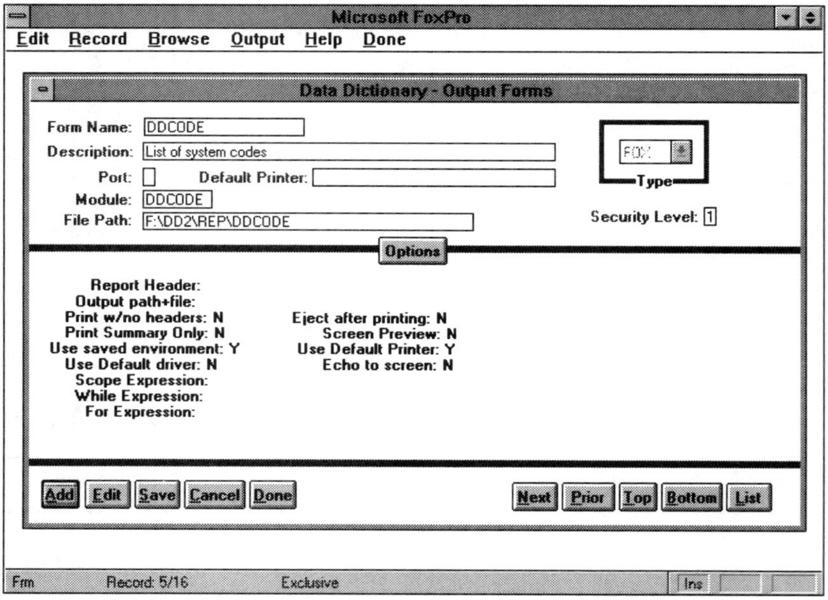

Table 19.7 lists the key fields in the table.

Table 19.7
Key fields.

Field	Type	Width	Description
FORM_NAME	C	8	DOS file name, or short name for the output form.
DESCRIPT	C	40	Descriptive name of the form—user friendly, please.
TYPE	C	3	The type of form: Report Writer, Label, RQBE.
MODULE	C	8	The program module associated with this form.
PATH	C	45	The path to the output file, if necessary.
SEC2	C	1	The security level (access rights) for this form.

With these fields you can establish a reasonable description of a form, categorize its type, and provide setup information. The MODULE field is used to filter the forms when the user pulls up a forms selection list. The module name can be passed to the output manager as a parameter, and only those forms with that name will be available for selection. Likewise the SEC2 field can be used to place a security requirement on the report. Only those people with an access level equal to or greater than the security level will even see the form in the selection list.

The information entered into the data dictionary forms table is then used by the Output Manager (OUTPUT.SCX), a Screen Builder program that contains all of the elements for coordinating the output system. The user interface is deliberately simple, as in Figure 19.11 on the next page.

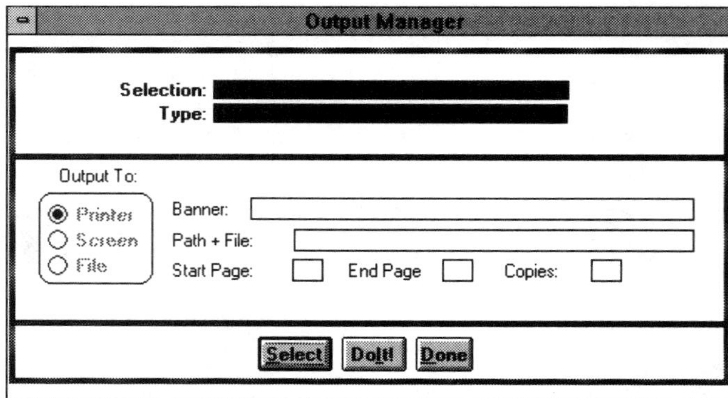

Figure 19.11 *The Output Manager dialog box.*

The Select button brings up a Browse window with the appropriate forms from the Forms file—already prescreened for the current program module, and by security level. The user selects a form, and information about how to run it is transferred to the Output Manager.

Depending on the type of form (report, query), various basic options appear in the Output Manager screen, and are available when the user selects an output destination (Printer, Screen, or File). Because this is a Windows system, the Output Manager makes no attempt to control selection of printer or network printer queues. This is usually handled by the user directly, prior to output, or by programming that uses the PROMPT clause (which brings up the FoxPro for Windows/Windows printer dialog box) with the output commands in the final output routines.

When the user is ready, they hit the DoIt! button and processing begins. Actually, what usually happens is that the Output Manager calls the appropriate subroutine to process the type of form. In some cases this may be a standard output, meaning that no user dialog box, special setup, or processing is required. These cases are handled by code in the Output Manager itself. More often than not, however, the Output Manager must call an external routine that handles the actual output procedures.

In this output system, these external procedures are a set of standard Screen Builder screens, one for each output form type, which are templates for user dialogs, setup, pre- and post-processing and cleanup. Although a large application may need many of these output routines, they are at least standardized and relatively simple to modify—especially by copying code from one template to another. Most of these routines contain code for interacting with a network operating system, doing the file setup chores, including file locking if necessary, and handling the more customized aspects of a user dialog. They also work with the data dictionary tracking file, to record the user's choice of forms, output expressions (including SCOPE, FOR, and WHILE), and other options.

Although the form of these output screen files is standardized, the approach here is to allow maximum latitude for the developer to either clone as many screens as needed, quickly and easily, or customize a screen to the max, including lengthy pre- and post-processing routines. Whatever it takes to run a particular output form.

Index

Symbols

A

B

C

D

E

F

G

H

I

K

L

M

N

O

P

Q

R

S

T

U

V

W

X

Y

Z

Miscellaneous

FoxPro 2.5 for Windows Supplementary Disk Instructions

The disk contains projects and code for a Data Dictionary System, and for code samples (functions and procedures) from the book. These are provided to supplement your own applications and your learning of FoxPro for Windows, and are not intended to be complete or standalone programs. Using them requires that you spend some time to set them up, learn how they operate, and hopefully modify them for your own purposes. Without getting into legal jargon, this means the code is not warranted in any way.

On the other hand, much of this code is being used in real applications (including my own), and is in a more or less constant state of upgrade, bug fixing, and refinement. Any comments, discoveries, or errors that you would like to have noted can be sent on to me through the E-mail at Compuserve: 72537,3006.

Thanks,
Nelson King

Installing the Disk

Although this disk accompanies a Windows book, the machinery for doing a true Windows Setup is very complex, and unecessary for example software like this. So this is a DOS installation.

You have two options:

1. Use the INSTALL.BAT program provided. This creates two project subdirectories, and a directory tree under each, just like those discussed in Chapter 12. It also copies about 2 MB of code material. Put the distribution disk in your 3.5-inch drive. Log to that drive (A: or B:), enter INSTALL, and then follow the instructions from there.
2. You can do your own configuration by creating the subdirectories, copying the self-extracting files (e.g. DDPRG.EXE) into the directories, and executing them. Note, however, that most of the routines and especially the project manager are expecting to find directories with specific names. You will need to 're-locate' the project manager references and make other changes as well.

Please refer to the file README.TXT on the accompanying disk for more complete instructions.